VHDL
Analysis and Modeling of Digital Systems

McGraw-Hill Series in Electrical and Computer Engineering

Senior Consulting Editor

Stephen W. Director, Carnegie Mellon University

Circuits and Systems
Communications and Signal Processing
Computer Engineering
Control Theory
Electromagnetics
Electronics and VLSI Circuits
Introductory
Power and Energy
Radar and Antennas

Previous Consulting Editors

Ronald N. Bracewell, Colin Cherry, James F. Gibbons, Willis W. Harman, Hubert Heffner, Edward W. Herold, John G. Linvill, Simon Ramo, Ronald A. Rohrer, Anthony E. Siegman, Charles Susskind, Frederick E. Terman, John G. Truxal, Ernest Weber, and John R. Whinnery

Computer Engineering

VHDL
Analysis and Modeling of Digital Systems

Zainalabedin Navabi

Northeastern University

McGraw-Hill, Inc.

New York   St. Louis   San Francisco   Auckland   Bogotá   Caracas
Lisbon   London   Madrid   Mexico   Milan   Montreal
New Delhi   Paris   San Juan   Singapore   Sydney   Tokyo   Toronto

VHDL
Analysis and Modeling of Digital Systems

International Editions 1993

Exclusive rights by McGraw-Hill Book Co.-Singapore for manufacture and export. This book cannot be re-exported from the country to which it is consigned by McGraw-Hill.

6 7 8 9 0 BJE 9 8 7

Library of Congress Cataloging-in-Publication Data

VHDL: analysis and modeling of digital systems / Zainalabedin Navabi
   p.   cm.—(McGraw-Hill series in electrical and computer engineering)
Includes bibliographical references and index.

ISBN 0-07-046472-3

1. VHDL (Computere hardware description language)   2. Digital integrated circuits—Design and construction—Data processing.
I. Title.   II. Series.
TK7874.N36   1993
621.39'2—dc20   92-24858

This book was set in Times Roman by Electronic Technical Publishing Services.
The editors were Anne T .Brown and John M. Morriss;
the production supervisor was Denise L. Puryear.
The cover was designed by Joseph Gillians.
Project supervision was done by Electronic Technical Publishing Services.

When ordering this title use ISBN 0-07-112732-1

Printed in Singapore

Zainalabedin Navabi is Associate Professor of Electrical and Computer Engineering at Northeastern University in Boston. Dr. Navabi is a senior member of IEEE, IEEE Computer Society, ACM, and Euromicro societies. He holds a BS degree in Electrical Engineering from the University of Texas at Austin, and MSEE and PhD from the University of Arizona. He has published many papers in the area of VLSI and CAD tools and environments, in journals and proceedings. Dr. Navabi has been involved in the design and definition of hardware description languages and tools since 1977, and has developed several HDL based simulators and hardware synthesis tools. He has held teaching and research positions at the University of Arizona in Tucson, Sharif University of Technology in Tehran, and Northeastern University in Boston. At the present time he teaches courses related to CAD, VLSI, and Digital System Design and Organization at Northeastern University. Dr. Navabi is involved in research focusing on utilization of hardware languages in digital system design environments. This research includes simulation, synthesis, modeling, and testing of hardware.

In the memory of my father,
Mohammad-Hussein Navabi,
who devoted his life to his family.

CONTENTS

PREFACE

This textbook introduces the Standard IEEE 1076 VHDL hardware description language. The intended audience includes students who have a basic knowledge of digital system design and engineers involved in various aspects of digital systems design and manufacturing. The emphasis in this book is on using VHDL for the design and modeling of digital systems and the material presented is suitable for an upper division undergraduate or a first year graduate course. For a one semester course on VHDL alone, the book can be used in its entirety. For a course on modeling or CPU design with VHDL, this book should be complemented by additional material in a related area.

Starting with introductory material on design automation and hardware description languages, this book presents a brief history of VHDL and its evolution into a standard hardware description language. Following this background material, the text presents a minimum set of VHDL elements necessary for generating basic designs, as well as timing concepts and concurrency related issues. This is followed by a presentation of the VHDL language from a low-level to a high-level fashion. The first concepts presented are more closely related to hardware which are easier for hardware designers to comprehend. Structural and gate list representations of hardware are described immediately after the basic concepts have been covered. This material is followed by descriptions of more advanced concepts for higher level hardware representations. Dataflow and behavioral level of hardware descriptions are the next topics. In the sections on dataflow description, clocking schemes and sequential circuit modeling are covered, while other sections describe behavioral descriptions and high level design representation. The book ends with a top-down design example that takes advantage of various levels of abstractions in VHDL.

VHDL examples are presented beginning in Chapter 3. The examples in Chapter 3 consist of partial code shown to illustrate certain language issues. These examples are not complete and cannot be simulated as presented in the book. The examples in the rest of the chapters, however, are complete and have been carefully chosen so that their execution and simulation depend on the content of the material covered prior to the presentation of the example. These examples therefore, can be executed without having to refer to the later parts of the book.

Each chapter includes problems related to the chapter material. Although the book can be used on its own to learn concepts of VHDL, it benefits the reader most if used with a simulation program. There are presently several low cost VHDL simulation software programs available and many vendors of more expensive software programs offer substantial discounts for educational use of their software.

OVERVIEW OF THE CHAPTERS

An outline of the contents in this text is given here. Chapters 1 and 2 are introductory and contain material with which many readers may already be familiar. It is, however, recommended that these chapters not be completely omitted, even by experienced readers. The language syntax and semantics are described in Chapters 3 through 8. The last chapter contains an example, but does not present any new language concepts or constructs. The chapters progressively develop the utility package which is included in its final form in Appendix A.

Chapter 1 gives an overview of the digital design process and the use of hardware description languages in this process. Levels of abstractions are defined here and then referred to in the rest of the text.

Chapter 2 describes the initiation and evolution of VHDL. It is important to become familiar with the terms and vocabulary used in this chapter.

Chapter 3 is a key chapter. The first part of this chapter shows the overall structure of VHDL. In the second part, important timing and concurrency issues are discussed. This chapter should be understood completely before continuing with the rest of the text.

Chapter 4 discusses wiring and component interconnections. Examples illustrate how components are instantiated, bound, and tested.

Chapter 5 presents design organization and parameterization. It discusses the use of subprograms and packages and shows how generic designs can be described and configured.

Chapter 6 offers a description of type declaration and usage in VHDL and discusses operations and operand types. The last part of the chapter contains information about attributes.

Chapter 7 discusses various signal assignments and dataflow descriptions. State machines, tri-state gates, and bussing structures are explained in detail. It also shows how complete designs can be described at the dataflow level of abstraction.

Chapter 8 covers the behavioral description of hardware. It discusses high level timing issues, handshaking, and behavioral representation for state machines. Text I/O is also discussed in this chapter. The last part of the chapter presents the VHDL description of several standard MSI parts and uses them in a complete design.

Chapter 9 ties it all together. All modeling techniques learned in the previous chapters are used to describe a CPU. The CPU is partitioned into registers, buses and logic units with each unit separately designed and described. The data section wires these components and a control section generates signals for control of data. The method used for partitioning and describing this CPU is also used to generate its VLSI layout.

Appendix A contains a package of utility functions and definitions. Appendix B provides sample sessions on four VHDL simulation environments software programs.

Appendix C offers VHDL descriptions for several standard MSI packages, while Appendix D presents complete behavioral and dataflow descriptions of the processor covered in Chapter 9. Appendix E contains VHDL language grammar syntax and Appendix F details the STANDARD and TEXT I/O packages.

INSTRUCTION MATERIAL

Instruction material to assist the educators teaching VHDL with this text is available from the publisher. This material includes a solutions manual, examples diskette, and a solutions diskette. The solutions manual contains solutions to the end-of-chapter problems along with a description and a simulation run for each. The examples diskette contains VHDL code, a test bench, simulation command file, and simulation report of all the examples presented in Chapters 4 to 9. The second diskette contains VHDL descriptions and simulation report files for the end-of-chapter problems of Chapters 3 to 9. Other teaching material for use in Digital Design or VLSI related courses is also available, and can be obtained by contacting McGraw-Hill or the author.

ACKNOWLEDGMENTS

Comments, reviews, and support of many people helped in the development of this book and the author wishes to thank them.

The idea for this book started from a set of course notes the author prepared for ECE 3401, a graduate course at Northeastern University. As this material evolved into a book, students in this course and my graduate students helped with reviewing the book and made useful suggestions.

Professor John G. Proakis, chairman of Electrical and Computer Engineering at Northeastern University, was very supportive and encouraged the development of this book. His leadership in the ECE Department has helped to create an ideal environment for research, teaching, and development of research and teaching material.

The following reviewers read many versions of this book and made suggestions that were very helpful in improving its contents: James H. Aylor, University of Virginia; Dong S. Ha, Virginia Polytechnic Institute and State University; Fred Hill, University of Arizona; John W. Hines, Wright-Patterson Air Force Base; and William Hudson, Kansas State University. The comments of Mr. Tedd Corman of View*logic* Systems Incorporated, who reviewed many chapters of the book, provided a helpful industrial perspective.

The editors and staff of McGraw-Hill, Inc. also were very helpful in providing timely feedback on reviewers' comments. For the selection of good reviewers, compilation of review responses, and making useful suggestions for improving the manuscript, I am particularly indebted to the ECE editor, Ms. Anne T. Brown.

Lastly, I want to express appreciation to my wife, Irma Navabi, and my sons Arash and Arvand, who have put up with my working habits for many years. This writing project was particularly intensive and they tolerated many late hours, missed vacations, and irregular eating and sleeping hours.

Zainalabedin Navabi

VHDL
Analysis and Modeling of Digital Systems

CHAPTER
1

HARDWARE
DESIGN
ENVIRONMENTS

As the size and complexity of digital systems increase, more computer aided design tools are introduced into the hardware design process. The early paper-and-pencil design methods have given way to sophisticated design entry, verification, and automatic hardware generation tools. The newest addition to this design methodology is the introduction of Hardware Description Languages (HDL). Although the concept of HDLs is not new, their widespread use in digital system design is no more than a decade old. Based on HDLs, new digital system CAD (Computer Aided Design) tools have been developed and are now being utilized by hardware designers. At the same time researchers are finding more ways in which HDLs can improve the process of digital system design.

This chapter discusses the concept of Hardware Description Languages and their use in a design environment. We will describe a design process, indicate where HDLs fit in this process, and describe simulation and synthesis, the two most frequent applications of HDLs.

1.1 DIGITAL SYSTEM DESIGN PROCESS

Figure 1.1 shows a typical process for the design of digital systems. An initial design idea goes through several transformations before its hardware implementation is obtained. At each step of transformation, the designer checks the result of the last transformation, adds more information to it and passes it through to the next step of transformation.

Initially, a hardware designer starts with a design idea. A more complete definition of the intended hardware must then be developed from the initial design idea.

1

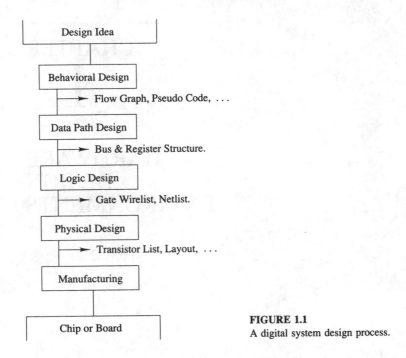

FIGURE 1.1
A digital system design process.

Therefore, it is necessary for the designer to generate a behavioral definition of the system under design. The product of this design stage may be a flow chart, a flow graph, or pseudo code.

The next phase in the design process is the design of the system data path. In this phase, the designer specifies the registers and logic units necessary for implementation of the system. These components may be interconnected using either bidirectional or unidirectional buses. Based on the intended behavior of the system, the procedure for controlling the movement of data between registers and logic units through buses is then developed. Figure 1.2 shows a possible result of the data path design phase. Data components in the data part of a circuit, communicate via system buses, and the control procedure controls flow of data between these components.

Logic design is the next step in the design process, and involves the use of primitive gates and flip-flops for the implementation of data registers, buses, logic units, and their controlling hardware. The result of this design stage is a netlist of gates and flip-flops.

The next design stage transforms the netlist of the previous stage into a transistor list or layout. This involves the replacement of gates and flip-flops with their transistor equivalents or library cells. This stage considers loading and timing requirements in its cell or transistor selection process.

The final step in the design is manufacturing, which uses the transistor list or layout specification to burn fuses of a field programmable device or to generate masks for IC fabrication.

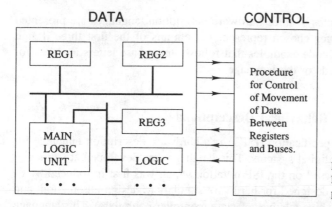

FIGURE 1.2
Result of the data path design phase.

1.1.1 Design Automation

In the design process, much of the work of transforming a design from one form to another is tedious and repetitive. These activities, as well as activities for verification of a design stage output, can be done at least in part by computers. This process is referred to as Design Automation (DA).

Design automation tools can help the designer with design entry, hardware generation, test sequence generation, documentation, verification, and design management. Such tools perform their specific tasks on the output of each of the design stages of Figure 1.1. For example, to verify the outcome of the data path design stage, the bussing and register structure is fed into a simulation program. Other DA tools include a synthesizer that can automatically generate a netlist from the register and bus structure of the system under design.

Hardware description languages provide formats for representing the outputs of various design stages. An HDL-based DA tool for the analysis of a circuit uses this format for its input description, and a synthesis tool transforms its HDL input into an HDL which contains more hardware information. In the sections that follow, we discuss hardware description languages, digital system simulation, and hardware synthesis.

1.2 HARDWARE DESCRIPTION LANGUAGES

Hardware description languages are used to describe hardware for the purpose of simulation, modeling, testing, design, and documentation of digital systems. These languages provide a convenient and compact format for the hierarchical representation of functional and wiring details of digital systems. Some HDLs consist of a simple set of symbols and notations which replace schematic diagrams of digital circuits, while others are more formally defined and may present the hardware at one or more levels of abstraction. Available software for HDLs include simulators and hardware synthesis programs. A simulation program can be used for design verification, while a synthesizer is used for automatic hardware generation.

In this section, examples of three hardware description languages are presented and discussed. The languages chosen represent the outputs of the first three design stages of Figure 1.1. In the code examples that follow, upper case letters are used for keywords and reserved words of the language.

1.2.1   A Language for Behavioral Descriptions

Instruction Set Processor Specification (ISPS) is a hardware description language for describing the behavior of digital systems. This language was developed at Carnegie-Mellon University and is based on the ISP notation which was first introduced by C. G. Bell in 1971. ISPS was designed for hardware simulation, design automation, and automatic generation of machine relative software (compiler-compilers). This language is a software-like programming language, but it includes constructs for specifying movement of data between registers and buses. CPU-like architectures can easily and efficiently be described in ISPS. The description of the Manchester University Mark-1 computer as it appeared in the ISPS reference manual is given in Figure 1.3.

The declarative part of this description indicates that the machine has an 8K, 32-bit memory (m), a 16-bit instruction register (pi), a 13-bit control register (cr), and

```
mark1 :=
  BEGIN
  ** memory.state **
  m[0:8191]<31:0>,
  ** processor.state **
  pi\present.instruction<15:0>'
     f\function<0:2> := pi<15:13>,
     s<0:12> := pi<12:0>,
  cr\control.register<12:0>,
  acc\accumulator<31:0>,
  ** instruction.execution ** {tc}
MAIN i.cycle :=
  BEGIN
  pi = m[cr]<15:0> NEXT
  DECODE f =>
    BEGIN
  0\jmp    := cr = m[s],
  1\jrp    := cr = cr + m[s],
  2\ldn    := acc = - m[s],
  3\sto    := m[s] = acc,
  4:5\sub  := acc = acc - m[s],
  6\cmp    := IF acc LSS 0 => cr = cr + 1,
  7\stp    := STOP(),
    END NEXT
  cr = cr + 1 NEXT
  RESTART i.cycle
  END
```

FIGURE 1.3
An ISPS example, a simple processor.
(Source: M. R. Barbacci, The ISPS Computer Description Language, Carnegie-Mellon University, 1981, p. 70.)

a 32-bit accumulator (*ac*). Also shown in this declarative part is the renaming of bits 15 to 13 of *pi* to *f*, and its bits 12:0 to *s*. The instruction execution of this machine begins by moving a word from the memory into the *pi* register. Following this fetch, a decode language construct decodes function bits of *pi* (*f* is equivalent to $pi\langle 15:13 \rangle$). Based on these bits, one of the seven instructions of *markl* is executed. For example, if *f* is 3, a store (*sto*) instruction will be executed which causes the accumulator to be stored at address *s* (bits 12 to 0 of *pi*) of the memory. When an instruction execution is complete, *cr* is incremented by 1, and the next instruction cycle begins.

This example shows that ISPS is easy to read and is close to the way a designer first thinks about the behavior of a hardware component. Referring to Figure 1.1, ISPS is most appropriate for representing the output of the behavior design stage of a design process. An ISPS simulator, therefore, can validate the initial plans of a designer for the design of a CPU-like architecture.

1.2.2 A Language for Describing Flow of Data

AHPL (A Hardware Programming Language) was developed at the University of Arizona, and has been used as a tool for teaching computer organization for over two decades. In fact, this language started as a set of notations for representation of hardware in an academic environment. These notations were used instead of spatially inefficient schematic diagrams. The evolution of the initial set of notations led to the development of the AHPL hardware language. The development of a compiler and a simulator established a place for this language in the family of hardware description languages.

Figure 1.4 shows an AHPL example description. This is a 4-bit sequential multiplier that uses the add-and-shift multiplication method. The circuit receives two operands from its *inputbus*, and produces the result on its 8-bit *result* output.

The description begins with the declaration of registers and buses. The circuit requires three 4-bit registers for the two operands and the intermediate results, a single flip-flop for the *done* indicator, and a 2-bit counter (*count*) for the number of bits shifted out of the first operand register. The external *dataready* and *inputbus* signals are declared as EXINPUTS and EXBUSES, respectively. The last of the declarations, CLUNITS, indicates the presence of combinational logic networks implementing a 2-bit incrementer and a 4-bit adder.

The circuit sequence part follows the declarations. Step 1 receives the operands and stores them in *ac1* and *ac2* registers. If there is a 1 on the *dataready* line, control proceeds to Step 2, otherwise Step 1 remains active. Step 2 sets the *busy* flip-flop to 1 and causes Step 3 to be skipped if *ac1[3]*, which is the least significant bit of the *ac1* register, is zero. In Step 3 the addition of the partial products is accomplished. Step 4 right shifts the catenation of the *extra* and *ac1* registers, increments the counter, and activates Step 2 if *count* has not reached (1,1). If the *count* register contains (1,1), control will proceed to Step 5 where the catenation of the *extra* and *ac1* registers is placed on the 8 *result* lines, a 1 is placed on line *done*, and the *busy* flip-flop is reset to zero. Step 5 returns control to step 1, waiting for another set of operands.

```
AHPLMODULE: multiplier.
    MEMORY: ac1[4]; ac2[4]; count[2]; extra[4]; busy.
    EXINPUTS: dataready.
    EXBUSES: inputbus[8].
    OUTPUTS: result[8]; done.
    CLUNITS: INC[2](count); ADD[5](extra; ac2);
1 ac1 <= inputbus[0:3];   ac2 <= inputbus[4:7];
    extra <= 4$0;
    => (~^dataready)/(1).
2 busy <= \1\;
    => (^ac1[3])/(4).
3 extra <= ADD[1:4](extra; ac2).
4 extra, ac1 <= \0\, extra, ac1[0:2];
    count <= INC(count);
    => (^(&/count))/(2).
5 result = extra, ac1;   done = \1\;   busy <= \0\;
    => (1).
    ENDSEQUENCE
    CONTROLRESET(1).
END.
```

FIGURE 1.4
An AHPL example, showing a
sequential multiplier.

1.2.3   A Language for Describing Netlists

Another way to describe a digital system is by its netlist, which specifies the interconnections of its components. A subset of the Genrad Hardware Description Language
(GHDL) can be used for this purpose. Figure 1.5 shows a logic diagram of a full-adder,
and its corresponding GHDL structural description.

The description specifies primitive gate types and their rise and fall delays.
Following a primitive specification, its instantiations that correspond to the gates of
the full-adder are listed. The description also shows inputs, outputs, and internal nodes
of the circuit.

The examples in this section present three very different ways of describing
hardware. The information contained in these descriptions varies in the detail of the
hardware that they present. Each description is suited for a Computer Aided Design
(CAD) tool at a different design stage. The ISPS description contains high level
behavioral information and can serve as a modeling tool for a hardware designer
as well as a CAD system user interface. The AHPL description, however, contains
more architectural information and is more appropriate for describing a circuit for
design and construction. The third description, GHDL, differs from both the ISPS and
AHPL descriptions in that it contains information that a CAD tool can use for detailed
analysis or manufacturing of a circuit.

1.3   HARDWARE SIMULATION

In a design automation environment, HDL descriptions of systems can be used for the
input of simulation programs. Simulators may be used to verify the results of any of the
design stages in Figure 1.1. In addition to the circuit description, a simulator needs a

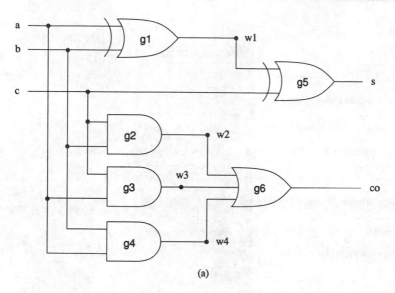

(a)

```
CCT full_adder (a, b, c, s, co)
XOR (RISE = 16, FALL = 12)
    g1 (w1, a, b),
    g5 (s, w1, c);
AND (RISE = 12, FALL = 10)
    g2 (w2, c , b),
    g3 (w3, c, a),
    g4 (w4, b, a);
OR (RISE = 12, FALL = 10)
    g6 (co, w2, w3, w4);
INPUT a, b, c;
WIRE w1, w2, w3, w4;
OUTPUT s, co;
ENDCIRCUIT full_adder
```

(b)

FIGURE 1.5
A Full-Adder, (a) logic diagram, (b) GHDL description.

set of simulation data or stimuli. The simulation program applies this data to the input description at the specified times and generates responses of the circuit. The results of a simulation program may be illustrated by waveforms, timing diagrams, or time-value tabular listings. These results are interpreted by the designer who determines whether to repeat a design stage if simulation results are not satisfactory.

As shown in Figure 1.6, simulators can be used at any design stage. At the upper levels of the design process, simulation provides information regarding the functionality of the system under design. Simulators for this purpose normally undergo a very quick run on their host computers. Simulation at a lower level of design process, for example, gate level or device simulation, runs much more slowly, but provides more detailed information about the timing and functionality of the circuit. To avoid

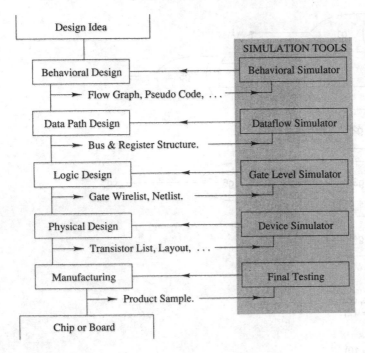

FIGURE 1.6
Verifying each design stage by simulating its output.

the high cost of low level simulation runs, simulators should be used to detect design flaws as early in the design process as possible.

Regardless of the level of design to which a simulation program is applied, digital system simulators have generally been classified into *oblivious* and *event driven* simulators. In oblivious simulation, each circuit component is evaluated at fixed time points, while in event driven simulation, a component is evaluated only when one of its inputs changes.

1.3.1 Oblivious Simulation

As an illustration of the oblivious simulation method, consider the gate network of Figure 1.7a. This is an exclusive-OR circuit that uses AND, OR, and NOT primitive gates, and is to be simulated with the data provided in Figure 1.7b.

The first phase of an oblivious simulation program converts the input circuit description to a machine readable tabular form. A simple example of such a table is shown in Figure 1.8. This table contains information regarding the circuit components and their interconnections, as well as the initial values for all nodes of the circuit.

After the initialization of the circuit, the simulation phase of an oblivious simulation method reads input values at fixed time intervals, applying them to the internal tabular representation of the circuit. At time t_i, input value of a and b are read from an input file. These values replace the old values of a and b in the value column

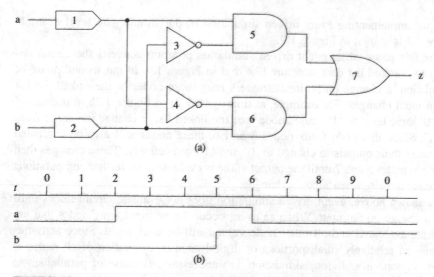

FIGURE 1.7
An exclusive-OR function in terms of AND, OR, and NOT gates, (a) logic diagram, (b) test data.

GATE	FUNCTION	INPUT 1	INPUT 2	VALUE
1	Input	a	—	0
2	Input	b	—	0
3	NOT	2	—	1
4	NOT	1	—	1
5	AND	1	3	0
6	AND	4	2	0
7	OR	5	6	0

FIGURE 1.8
Tabular representation of exclusive-OR circuit for oblivious simulation.

of the table of Figure 1.8. Using these new values, the output values of *all* circuit components will be reevaluated, and changes will be made to the value column of the affected components. A change in any value column indicates that the circuit has not stabilized, and more reevaluation of the table may be necessary. Sequential computation of all output values continues until a single pass through the table necessitates no new changes. At this time, all node values for time t_i will be reported, the time indicator will be incremented to t_{i+1}, and new data values will be read from the data file.

1.3.2 Event Driven Simulation

Event driven simulation, while more complex than oblivious simulation, is a more efficient method of digital system simulation. In event driven simulation, when an input is changed only those nodes that are affected are reevaluated. A data structure suitable for implementing event driven simulation of our simple gate level example of Figure 1.7 is shown in Figure 1.9.

The first phase of an event driven simulation program converts the circuit description to a linked list data structure like that in Figure 1.9. In the second phase of the simulation, a change on an input triggers only those nodes of the linked list for which an input changes. For example, at time t_2 ($t = 2$) in Figure 1.7b, transition of a from '0' logic level to '1' causes node 1 of the linked list to change its output from '0' to '1'. Since this node feeds nodes 3 and 6, these nodes will also be evaluated which causes their outputs to change to '0' and '1', respectively. These changes then propagate to nodes 5 and 7 until the output value is evaluated. No further computations will be done until t_5 when input b changes.

As shown above, event driven simulation does not evaluate circuit nodes until there is a change on an input. When an event occurs on an input, only nodes that are affected are evaluated and all other node values will be unchanged. Since activities occur only on relatively small portions of digital circuits, evaluation of all nodes at all times, as done in oblivious simulation, is unnecessary. Because of parallelism in hardware structures, event driven simulation is a more suitable simulation method for digital systems. The speed of this method justifies its more complex data structure and algorithm.

1.4   HARDWARE SYNTHESIS

A design aid that automatically transforms a design description from one form to another is called a synthesis tool. Hardware description languages are useful media for input and output of hardware synthesizers. Present synthesis tools replace the designer or provide design guidelines for performing one or more of the design stages in Figure 1.1. Application of various synthesis tools to the design stages of this figure is shown in Figure 1.10.

Many commercially available synthesis tools use the output of the data path design stage as input and produce a netlist for the circuit (tool category 2 in Figure 1.10). Tools that generate layout from netlists (tools 3 above) have been available and in use for over a decade. At the present time, development of synthesis programs is being concentrated on ways of producing efficient hardware from general behavioral descriptions of systems (tool categories 1, 4 or 6).

1.5   LEVELS OF ABSTRACTION

The design stages in Figure 1.1 use hardware descriptions at various levels of abstraction. The difference in the levels of abstraction becomes clear when we compare the three hardware description examples in Section 1.2.

The ISPS example presented a readable descriptionof the behavior of the Mark-1 computer. This description does not contain information on the bussing structure of the Mark-1 and does not provide any timing or delay information. The AHPL description of the multiplier described this system based on the flow of data through its registers and buses. This description provides clock level timing, but does not

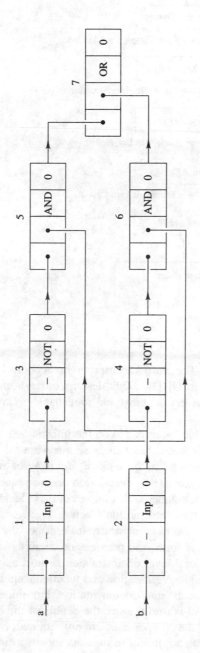

FIGURE 1.9
Linked list representation of exclusive-OR circuit for event driven simulation.

Legend:

In1	In2	Fnc	Out

In1: Input 1; In2: Input 2; Fnc: Function; Out: Output Value.

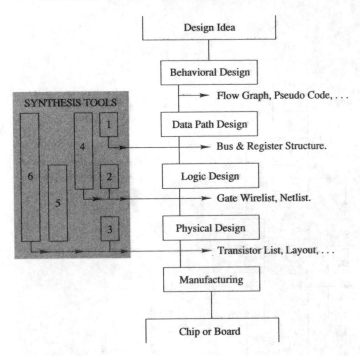

FIGURE 1.10
Categories of synthesis tools in a design process.

contain gate delay information. The third description in Section 1.2 is the structural description of a full-adder in GHDL. This description style provides detailed timing information, but becomes very lengthy and unreadable when used for large circuits.

Classifying descriptions of hardware based on the information they contain can be found in the literature. In this book, we take a simple view of this matter and consider abstraction levels of hardware at *behavioral*, *dataflow* or *structural* levels. The ISPS description of Mark-1, the AHPL description on the sequential multiplier, and the GHDL description of the full-adder are examples of these levels of abstraction. The following paragraphs define these abstraction levels.

A behavioral description is the most abstract. It describes the function of the design in a software-like procedural form, and provides no detail as to how the design is to be implemented. The behavioral level of abstraction is most appropriate for fast simulation of complex hardware units, verification and functional simulation of design ideas, modeling standard components, and documentation. For simulation and functional analysis, a behavioral model is useful since the details of the hardware, which may not be known to the user of the components, are not required. Such descriptions present an input-to-output mapping according to the data sheet specification provided by the component manufacturer. Descriptions at this level can be accessible to non-engineers as well as the end users of a hardware component, and can also serve as a good documentation media. The operation of large systems can also be modeled at this level for end users and manual writers.

A dataflow description is a concurrent representation of the flow of control and movement of data. Concurrent data components and carriers communicate through buses and interconnections, and a control hardware issues signals for the control of this communication. The level of hardware detail involved in dataflow descriptions is great enough that such descriptions cannot serve as an end user or nontechnical documentation media. This level of description, however, is abstract enough for a technically oriented designer to describe the components to be synthesized. Dataflow descriptions imply an architecture and a unique hardware. Simulation of these descriptions involves the movement of the data through registers and busses, and therefore is slower than the input-to-output mapping of behavioral descriptions. The function of the hardware is evident from dataflow descriptions.

A structural description is the lowest and most detailed level of description considered, and is the simplest to synthesize into hardware. Structural descriptions include a list of concurrently active components and their interconnections. The corresponding function of the hardware is not evident from such descriptions unless the components used are known. On the other hand, the hardware is clearly implied by these descriptions, and a simple wire router or printed circuit board layout generator can easily produce the described hardware. A structural description that describes wiring of logic gates is said to be the hardware description at gate-level. A gate level description provides input for detailed timing simulation.

1.6   SUMMARY

This chapter presented introductory material that relates to design of digital systems with hardware description languages. The intention was to give the reader an overall understanding of hardware description languages, the design process based on HDLs, design tools, and simulation and synthesis. The last part of the chapter discussed levels of abstraction that we will reference throughout the book.

REFERENCES

1. Wakerly, J. F., "Digital Design Principles and Practices," Prentice-Hall Inc., Englewood Cliffs, N.J., 1990.
2. Miczo, A., "Digital Logic Testing and Simulation," Harper & Row Publishers, New York, 1986.
3. Barbacci, M. R., et. al., "The ISPS Computer Description Language," Carnegie-Mellon University, 1981.
4. Hill, F. J., and G. R. Peterson, "Digital Systems: Hardware Organization and Design," 3rd ed., John Wiley, New York, 1987.
5. "System HILO GHDL Tutorial," Genrad Limited, Fareham, England, 1988.
6. Navabi, Z., and J. Spillane, "Templates For Synthesis From VHDL," *Proc. of the 1990 ASIC Seminar and Exposition*, September 1990.
7. Walker, R. A., and D. E. Thomas, "A Model of Design Representation and Synthesis," *Proc. of 22nd Design Automation Conference*, 1985.

PROBLEMS

1.1. Suggest a data path for the Mark-1 computer of Section 1.2.1.

1.2. Show the graphical representation of the data path of the four bit multiplier of Section 1.2.2.

1.3. Show a state diagram for the control part of the Multiplier circuit of Section 1.2.2.

1.4. Redesign the full-adder circuit of Section 1.2.3 using only two-input NAND gates. Show the GHDL description for this design.

1.5. Write pseudo code for implementing the oblivious simulation method of Section 1.3.1.

1.6. Write pseudo code for implementing the event driven simulation method of Section 1.3.2.

CHAPTER
2

VHDL
BACKGROUND

For the design of large digital systems, much engineering time is spent in changing formats for using various design aids and simulators. An integrated design environment is useful for better design efficiency in these systems. In an ideal design environment, the high level description of the system is understandable to the managers and to the designers, and it uniquely and unambiguously defines the hardware. This high level description can serve as the documentation for the part as well as an entry point into the design process. As the design process advances, additional details are added to the initial description of the part. These details enable the simulation and testing of the system at various levels of abstraction. By the last stage of design, the initial description has evolved into a detailed description which can be used by a program controlled machine for generation of final hardware in the form of layout, printed circuit board, or gate arrays.

This ideal design process can exist only if a language exists to describe hardware at various levels so that it can be understood by the managers, users, designers, testers, simulators, and machines. The IEEE standard VHDL hardware description language is such a language. VHDL was defined because a need existed for an integrated design and documentation language to communicate design data between various levels of abstractions. At the time, none of the existing hardware description languages fully satisfied these requirements, and the lack of precision in English made it too ambiguous for this purpose.

2.1 VHDL INITIATION

In the search for a standard design and documentation tool for the VHSIC (Very High Speed Integrated Circuits) program, the United States Department of Defense (DoD) in the summer of 1981 sponsored a workshop on hardware description languages at Woods Hole, Massachusetts. This workshop was arranged by the Institute for Defense Analysis (IDA) to study various hardware description methods, the need for a standard language, and the features that might be required by such a standard. Because the VHSIC program was under the restrictions of the United States International Traffic and Arms Regulations (ITAR), the VHDL component of this program was also initially subject to such restrictions.

In 1983, the DoD established requirements for a standard VHSIC Hardware Description Language (VHDL), based on the recommendations of the "Woods Hole" workshop. A contract for the development of the VHDL language, its environment, and its software was awarded to IBM, Texas Instruments, and Intermetrics corporations. Work on VHDL started in the summer of 1983. At that time language specifications were no longer under ITAR restrictions, but these restrictions still applied to government developed software.

VHDL 2.0 was released only 6 months after the project began. This version, however, allowed only concurrent statements, and lacked the capability to describe hardware in a sequential software-like fashion, a shortcoming that would seriously jeopardize the applicability of the language for high level behavioral descriptions. The language was significantly improved, as this and other shortcomings were corrected when VHDL 6.0 was released in December of 1984. Development of VHDL-based tools also began in 1984.

In 1985, ITAR restrictions were lifted from VHDL and its related software, and the VHDL 7.2 Language Reference Manual (LRM) copyright was transferred to IEEE for further development and standardization. This led to the development of the IEEE 1076/A VHDL Language Reference Manual (LRM), which was released in May of 1987. Later that year version B of the LRM was developed and approved by REVCOM (a committee of the IEEE Standards Board). VHDL 1076-1987 formally became the IEEE standard hardware description language in December of 1987.

2.2 EXISTING LANGUAGES

Early in the VHSIC program it was found that none of the existing hardware description languages could be used as a standard tool for the design, manufacturing, and documentation of digital circuits ranging from integrated circuits to complete systems. Part of the study for the development of the requirements of a VHSIC language, however, concentrated on the capabilities, shortcomings, and other characteristics of eight hardware description languages that were available at that time. These languages were AHPL, CDL, CONLAN, IDL, ISPS, TEGAS, TI-HDL, and ZEUS. We briefly describe the important features of these languages in order to provide a framework for understanding the VHDL requirements that are discussed in the next section.

2.2.1 AHPL

AHPL (A Hardware Programming Language) is an HDL for describing hardware at the dataflow level of abstraction. This language uses an implicit clock for synchronizing assignments of data to registers and flip-flops, but does not provide support for describing asynchronous circuits. The language descriptions consist of interacting concurrent modules, and hierarchy of modules is not supported. Data types in AHPL are fixed and restricted to bits, vectors of bits, and arrays of bits. Procedures or functions are only allowed in the context of combinational logic units. Delay and constraint specifications are not allowed in AHPL and assignment of values to buses and registers all occur at the same time without delay, since they are synchronized with an implicit clock.

2.2.2 CDL

CDL (Computer Design Language) is a hardware description language developed in an academic environment mainly for instruction in digital systems. This language is strictly a dataflow language, and does not support design hierarchy. In CDL, micro-statements are used for transfer of data into registers. Conditional micro-statements use if-then-else constructs and can be nested.

2.2.3 CONLAN

The CONLAN (CONsensus LANguage) project began as an attempt to establish a standard hardware description language. This platform consists of a family of languages for describing hardware at various levels of abstraction. Base CONLAN (*bcl*), for example, is the base language for all member languages. All operations in CONLAN are executed concurrently. CONLAN allows hierarchical description of hardware but has limited external use.

2.2.4 IDL

IDL (Interactive Design Language) is an internal IBM language with limited outside use. IDL was originally designed for automatic generation of PLA structures, but it was later extended to cover more general circuit descriptions. Hardware in IDL can be described in a hierarchy of structures. This language is primarily a concurrent hardware description language.

2.2.5 ISPS

ISPS (Instruction Set Processor Specification) is a very high level behavioral language and was mainly designed to create an environment for designing software based on a given hardware. Although the language is primarily targeted for CPU-like architectures, other digital systems can easily be described in it. Timing control in ISPS is limited. The "NEXT" construct allows timing control between statements of behavioral descriptions, but it is not possible to specify gate level timing and structural details.

2.2.6 TEGAS

TEGAS (TEst Generation And Simulation) is a system for test generation and simulation of digital circuits. Although several extended versions of this language have behavioral features, the main language (TEGAS Description Language or TDL) is only structural. Digital hardware can be described hierarchically in this language. Detailed timing specification can be specified in TDL.

2.2.7 TI-HDL

TI-HDL (Texas Instruments Hardware Description Language) is a multi-level language for the design and description of hardware. It allows hierarchical specification of hardware and supports description of synchronous, asynchronous, and combinatorial logic circuits. Behavioral descriptions in TI-HDL are sequential and software-like, and use if-then-else, case, for, and while constructs for program flow control. This language has fixed data types with no provision for adding user defined types.

2.2.8 ZEUS

The ZEUS hardware description language is a nonprocedural language that was created at General Electric Corporation. This language supports design hierarchy and allows definition of systems by their functionality or their structural arrangements. Timing in ZEUS is at the clock level and there are no provisions for gate delay specification or detailed timing constraints. Because of this timing arrangement, asynchronous circuits cannot be described in ZEUS. This language provides a close link to physical layout.

2.3 VHDL REQUIREMENTS

A DoD document entitled "Department of Defense Requirements for Hardware Description Languages," released in January of 1983, clearly stated the requirements for the VHSIC hardware description language. The present VHDL satisfies the requirements set forth in this detailed document. This section briefly describes the main features of VHDL requirements.

2.3.1 General Features

The DoD requirement document specifies that the VHSIC hardware description language should be a language for design and description of hardware. It indicates that VHDL should be usable for design documentation, high-level design, simulation, synthesis, and testing of hardware, as well as a driver for a physical design tool.

It emphasizes that VHDL is for the description of hardware from system to gate, and it clearly specifies that system software is not an issue and that physical design does not need to be addressed. Since in an actual digital system, all small or large elements of the system are active simultaneously and perform their tasks concurrently, the concurrency aspect of VHDL is heavily emphasized. In a hardware description language, concurrency means that transfer statements, descriptions of components, and instantiations of gates or logical units are all executed such that in the end they appear to have been executed simultaneously.

2.3.2   Support for Design Hierarchy

The DoD requirement document specified the need for hierarchical specification of hardware in VHDL. This feature is essential for a multi-level hardware language. A design consists of an interface description and a separate part for describing its operation. Several descriptions may exist for describing the operation of a design, all corresponding to the same interface description. The operation of a system can be specified based on its functionality, or it can be specified structurally in terms of its smaller subcomponents. Structural description of a component can be accomplished at all design levels. At the lowest levels, components are described by their functionality and use no subcomponents.

As an example of hierarchy in a digital system, consider the description for a processor shown in Figure 2.1. At the top level, the CPU may be described by the structural interconnection of registers, multiplexers, logic units such as the *alu* (Arithmetic Logic Unit), and perhaps sections of behavioral descriptions (shown by an array of small rectangles). The CPU can be simulated only when the operation of each of these components is specified. Components can either be specified behaviorally or they can be specified in terms of smaller subcomponents. For example, the *counter* may be specified by its behavior and the *alu* by interconnection of its individual components. Each of the *alu* components may be partitioned and described by interconnection of a multiplexer, an adder, and random logic. Figure 2.1 shows *logic* described by its behavior, while the *mux* component is described in terms of primitive gates. At the lowest level, the primitive gates should either be described by their behavior or exist in a design library which is accessible to the simulator.

2.3.3   Library Support

For design management, the need for libraries is specified for VHDL. User defined and system defined primitives and descriptions reside in the library system. The language should provide a mechanism for accessing various libraries. A library can contain only an interface description of a design, but several specifications of the operation of a system can reside in the same library.

Descriptions and models that are correct should be placed in the library after they have been compiled by the language compiler. In addition, libraries should be accessible to different designers.

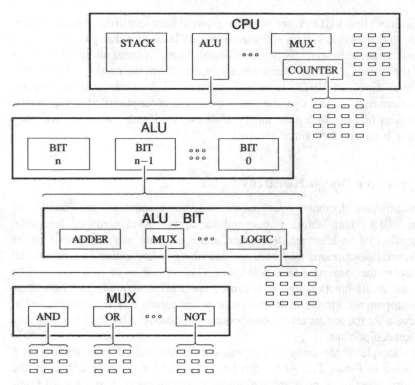

FIGURE 2.1
Example for hierarchical partitioning.

2.3.4   Sequential Statement

Although the strong features of a hardware description language should be its support for concurrent execution of processes and statements, the VHDL language requirements also specify the need for software-like sequential control. When a hardware designer partitions a system into concurrent components or subsections, the designer should then be able to describe the internal operational details by sequential programming language constructs such as case, if-then-else, and loop statements.

An example for the use of this feature is in the top-down design of a digital system such as the CPU shown in Figure 2.1. After an initial partitioning of the system into subcomponents, the designer concentrates on the hardware design of one of the subcomponents, for example, the *alu*. While this component is being designed, high level models for other components of this system will provide a simulation environment in which the component under design can be tested and simulated.

Sequential statements provide an easy method for modeling hardware components based on their functionality. Sequential or procedural capability is only for convenience—and the overall structure of the VHDL language remains highly concurrent.

2.3.5   Generic Design

In addition to inputs and outputs of a hardware component, other conditions may influence the way it operates. These include the environment where the hardware component is used, and the physical characteristics of the hardware component itself. It should not be necessary to generate a new hardware description for every specific condition. Furthermore, many hardware components in various logic families, for example, the *LS*, *F*, and *ALS* series of the 7400 logic family, are functionally equivalent, and differ only in their timing and loading characteristics.

A good hardware description language should allow the designer to configure the generic description of a component when it is used in a design. Generic descriptions should be configurable for size, physical characteristics, timing, loading, and environmental conditions. The ability to describe generic models of hardware was a DoD requirement for the VHDL language.

2.3.6   Type Declaration and Usage

A language for the description of hardware at various levels of abstractions should not be limited to Bit or Boolean types. VHDL requirements specify that the language ought to allow integer, floating point, and enumerate types, as well as user defined types. Types defined by the system or by the user should be placed in the library of the language environment and their use should be transparent to the user.

The language should provide the capability to redefine language operators for types that are defined by the user. For example, the language provides Boolean operators such as AND, OR, and NOT for the predefined logic values. A user needing a multi-level logic should be able to redefine these operators for the newly defined multi-level logic type.

In addition, a hardware description language should allow array type declarations and composite type definitions, such as statements or records in programming languages. The DoD document also specifies a strongly typed language and strong type checking.

2.3.7   Use of Subprograms

The ability to define and use functions and procedure was another VHDL requirement. Subprograms can be used for explicit type conversions, logic unit definitions, operator redefinitions, new operation definitions, and other applications commonly used in programming languages.

2.3.8   Timing Control

The ability to specify timing at all levels is another requirement for the VHDL language. VHDL should allow the designer to schedule values to signals and delay the actual assignment of values until a later time. For handshaking and gate or line delay modeling in the sequential descriptions, it should be possible to wait for the occurrence of an event or for a specific time duration.

The language should be general and it should allow any number of explicitly defined clock signals. The clocking scheme should be completely up to the user, since the language does not have an implicit clocking scheme or signal.

Constructs for edge detection, delay specification, setup and hold time specification, pulse width checking, and setting various time constraints should be provided.

2.3.9 Structural Specification

The DoD requirements for a standard hardware description language specified that the language should have constructs for specifying structural decomposition of hardware at all levels. It also should be possible to describe a generic one-bit design and use it when describing multi-bit regular structures in one or more dimensions. This requires constructs for iteration in the description of structures.

2.4 THE VHDL LANGUAGE

In its present form, VHDL satisfies all requirements of the 1983 DoD requirements document. The experience, researchers, software developers, and other users with VHDL since it became the IEEE standard in 1987 indicates this language is sufficiently rich for designing and describing today's digital systems.

As originally required, VHDL is a hardware description language with strong emphasis on concurrency. The language supports hierarchical description of hardware from system to gate or even switch level. VHDL has strong support at all levels for timing specification and violation detection. As expected, VHDL provides constructs for generic design specification and configuration.

A VHDL design entity is defined as an *entity declaration* and as an associated *architecture body*. The entity declaration specifies its interface and is used by architecture bodies of design entities at upper levels of hierarchy. The architecture body describes the operation of a design entity by specifying its interconnection with other design entities, by its behavior, or by a mixture of both. The VHDL language groups subprograms or design entities by use of *packages*. For customizing generic descriptions of design entities, *configurations* are used. VHDL also supports libraries and contains constructs for accessing packages, design entities, or configurations from various libraries.

A typical VHDL design environment is depicted in Figure 2.2. This figure shows that an analyzer program translates a VHDL description into an intermediate form and places it in a design library. The analyzer is responsible for lexical analysis and syntax check. Operations on the design library, such as creating new libraries, deleting the old, or deletion of packages or design entities from a library are done through the design environment. VHDL-based tools use the intermediate format from the design library. One well developed tool is the VHDL simulator, which simulates a design entity from the design library and produces a simulation report. A hardware synthesizer, test vector generator, or a physical design tool are examples of other VHDL-based tools.

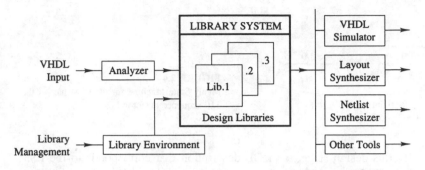

FIGURE 2.2
An example VHDL environment.

VHDL-based tools are widely available on platforms ranging from personal computers to multi-user Unix or Ultrix machines. Simulators for full VHDL IEEE 1076 are also available for a variety of platforms. In addition, several synthesis programs that take a subset of VHDL as input and generate a netlist are commercially available.

2.5   A VHDL-BASED DESIGN PROCESS

This section illustrates a way VHDL can facilitate the process of digital system design. For this purpose, we use a small sequence detector example and perform the design steps presented in Figure 1.1. At each step, we discuss how VHDL can be used to verify the result of that design stage.

In the field of digital system design, sequence detectors are representative of a large class of controller circuits. A CPU controller, for example, can be regarded as a generalization of such circuits. We will now consider the *sequence_detector* example shown in Figure 2.3. This circuit has *enable*, *x_in*, and *y_in* inputs. Once it has been enabled, it searches for a sequence of 110 on the *x_in* input. When the 110 sequence is found, it generates an output equal to the complement of the *y_in* input. The output of this system is on the *z_out* line.

As shown in Figure 1.1, the first step in the design of a digital system is to reproduce the system's behavioral design specification. Our system consists of a clocking circuit and a finite state machine (FSM) that detects the 110 sequence. The state machine shown in Figure 2.4 is the outcome of the "behavioral design" stage for the design of the FSM part.

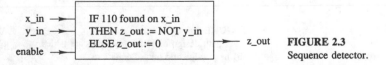

FIGURE 2.3
Sequence detector.

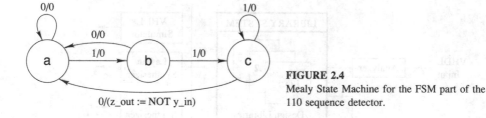

FIGURE 2.4
Mealy State Machine for the FSM part of the 110 sequence detector.

To verify this design stage, a VHDL description that corresponds to the FSM of Figure 2.4 should be developed and simulated. Such a description uses high level software-like language constructs and is at the behavioral level of abstraction, which is discussed in Chapter 8 of this book. The designer should perform the simulation with test data on the inputs of the circuit and verify the results. Errors at this level are mostly due to an incorrect interpretation of the problem and should be corrected before performing lower level design stages.

After satisfactory simulation of the behavioral description, the designer performs the next design stage, which is the data path design. For the FSM part of the circuit, the data path design involves the generation of next-state tables for the flip-flops of the circuit. Figure 2.5a shows the state assignment and transition tables for the FSM. These tables lead to the next-value equations for $V0$ and $V1$ state variables, and the output equation for z_out, as shown in Figure 2.5b.

The result of the data path design stage can be verified by developing a VHDL description based on the equations in Figure 2.5b. Such a description, at the dataflow level of abstraction, uses language constructs for specifying Boolean expressions and clock level timing which are covered in Chapter 7 of this book. Test data developed for verifying the behavioral design stage can also be used to test the dataflow description. Incorrect test results indicate errors in the development of the next-value and output equations. Since a dataflow simulation is faster than gate or transistor simulation and since a dataflow description is easier to debug than a description at a lower level,

STATE	V0	V1	x_in 0	x_in 1
a	0	0	00, 0	01, 0
b	0	1	00, 0	10, 0
c	1	0	00, y'	10, 0
-	1	1	-- -	-- -

$V0^+$, $V1^+$, z_out

(a)

$V0^+ = x\_in \cdot V1 + x\_in \cdot V0$
$V1^+ = x\_in \cdot V1' \cdot V0'$
$z\_out = x\_in' \cdot V0 \cdot y\_in'$

(b)

FIGURE 2.5
Data path design of FSM, (a) next-state tables, (b) next-value and output equations.

design errors should be found and corrected at this stage before performing the next design stage.

The last stage of the design process is performed after successful simulation of the dataflow VHDL model of the FSM. In this last stage, the designer uses logic gates and flip-flops to implement the equations of Figure 2.5b. Before actual implementation of the circuit, one more VHDL simulation should take place. For this phase, the simulation model is a structural description of the circuit which uses gates and flip-flops from a user design library. This simulation phase can be used for functional verification of the system, as well as for detailed timing analysis. An undesired response at this level is either due to timing problems or a structural design error. To correct this type of error, the designer needs to revise only the gate level implementation; upper level design stages need not be repeated.

The above discussion illustrates incremental design of a sequence detector, where every step of the design is checked by simulation. Synthesis tools ease this step-by-step design process by automatic translation of descriptions at higher levels of abstractions into lower levels. For example, several commercially available VHDL-based synthesis tools can use a FSM description as input and generate a netlist of gates and flip-flops.

2.6 SUMMARY

This chapter provided the reader with the history of the development of VHDL and some of the ideas behind this work. With this standard HDL, the efforts of tool developers, researchers, and software vendors have become more focused, resulting in better tools and more uniform environments. In the last part of the chapter we discussed some of the features of VHDL and its use in a design process. In addition to being an instrument for illustrating design process in VHDL, the example serves as a review of basic logic design techniques.

REFERENCES

1. Dewey, A., and A. Gadient, "VHDL Motivation," IEEE Design and Test of Computers, Vol. 3, April 1986.
2. Aylor, J. H., R. Waxman, and C. Scarratt, "VHDL—Feature Description and Analysis," IEEE Design and Test of Computers, Vol. 3, April 1986.
3. Nash, J. D., and L. F. Saunders, "VHDL Critique," IEEE Design and Test of Computers, Vol. 3, April 1986.
4. "IEEE Standard VHDL Language Reference Manual," IEEE Std. 1076-1987, The Institute of Electrical and Electronic Engineers, Inc., 1988.

PROBLEMS

2.1. Write pseudo code for the behavioral description of the state machine in Figure 2.4.

2.2. Complete the design of the Mealy machine in Figure 2.4.

CHAPTER
3

BASIC
CONCEPTS
IN VHDL

Various concepts of a language, be it a software or hardware language, are interdependent. A general knowledge of all of the language is therefore needed before advanced concepts are described in detail. The intent of this chapter is to give the reader this overall view of the VHDL language. For those who are interested only in gaining a basic knowledge of this language, this chapter can be useful and self-contained. In the first part of this chapter, a complete VHDL description is developed for the sequence detector of Chapter 2 to give the reader a general understanding of the structure of the language. The second part of this chapter is devoted to timing issues in VHDL. The examples presented in this chapter focus on specific areas of the language. In Chapters 4 through 8, further details of the language are described and presented with complete examples.

3.1 BASIC CONCEPTS

The VHDL language is used to describe hardware components and systems. Many language features in VHDL, therefore, are designed to facilitate this usage. In its simplest form, the description of a component in VHDL consists of an interface specification and an architectural specification. As shown in Figure 3.1, the interface description begins with the ENTITY keyword and contains the input-output ports of the component. Other external characteristics of a component, such as time and temperature dependencies, can also be included in the interface description of the component. The name of the component comes after the ENTITY keyword and is followed by IS, which is

```
ENTITY component_name IS
    input and output ports.
    physical and other parameters.
END component_name;
```

```
ARCHITECTURE   identifier   OF   component_name   IS
    declarations.
BEGIN
    specification of the functionality of the
    component in terms of its input lines and as
    influenced by physical and other parameters.
END   identifier;
```

FIGURE 3.1
Interface and architectural specifications.

also a VHDL keyword. An architectural specification begins with the ARCHITEC-TURE keyword, which describes the functionality of a component. This functionality depends on input-output signals and other parameters that are specified in the interface description. As shown in Figure 3.1, the heading of an architectural specification includes an identifier and the name of the component. A functional description of the component starts after the BEGIN keyword. Although VHDL is not case sensitive, for clarity we use uppercase letters here for its keywords and standard definitions.

Several architectural specifications with different identifiers can exist for one component with a given interface description. For example, a component can have one architectural specification at the behavioral level and another at the structural or gate interconnections level. For simulations in which the functionality of a system is under test, the behavioral architectural specification is used. In other simulations where the exact timing response of the component is to be verified, the architectural specification at the structural level is used. This situation is shown in Figure 3.2, where *component_i* has several architectural specifications, three of which are identified by their levels of abstractions as described in Chapter 1. These three descriptions of

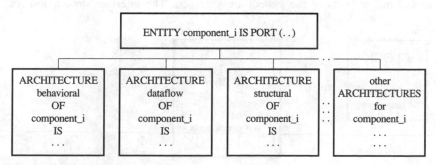

FIGURE 3.2
Multiple architectural specifications.

component_i are distinguished by referring to them as *component_i (behavioral), component_i (dataflow),* and *component_i (structural).* Although the *behavioral, dataflow,* and *structural* identifiers are not part of the language, we use them to specify levels of abstraction in VHDL descriptions.

In addition to multiple architectural specifications, VHDL allows an architecture to be configured for a specific technology or environment. For example, the *structural* description of *component_i* of Figure 3.2 can be designed such that it can be configured for CMOS or NMOS technology without a change in its functional description. This is a parametrization issue that is discussed in Chapter 5.

3.1.1   An Illustrative Example

An example in this section uses the *sequence_detector* of the previous chapter to illustrate interface and architectural specifications and various levels of abstraction in VHDL. We take a different point of view from that in Chapter 2 in developing a VHDL description for this example. This VHDL description is done in a top-down fashion. In this design strategy, the circuit is repeatedly partitioned into smaller components until the entire design is decomposed into low level components that exist in a certain design library. For our example, we also decompose parts of the circuit into primitive logic gates and flip-flops.

As shown in Figure 3.3, the example circuit is partitioned into a *clock_component* and an *fsm_component*. We assume that the *clock_component* is an off-the-shelf part and need not be described in detail. The *fsm_component*, on the other hand, is to be designed in terms of smaller components and is described in detail. The gate level implementation of the *fsm_component*, as shown in Figure 3.4, consists of AND gates, OR gates, Inverters, and rising edge flip-flops.

The following sections present descriptions corresponding to this design. Uppercase letters for the VHDL language keywords are used in all descriptions.

3.1.2   Interface Description

At the top level, a system can be described by its interface description. At this level, the input and output ports of the system are specified. The interface description for

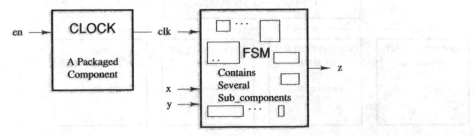

FIGURE 3.3
Sequence detector block diagram.

x

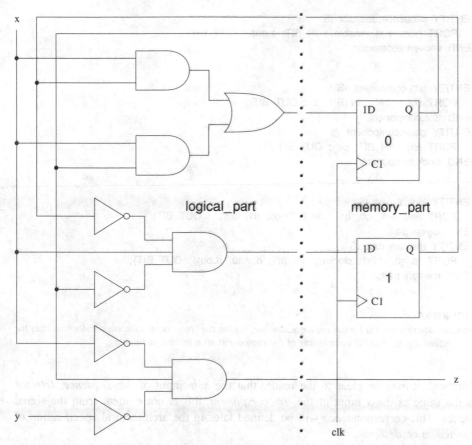

logical_part

memory_part

1D Q

0

C1

1D Q

1

C1

y

z

clk

FIGURE 3.4
Gate level implementation of the FSM component.

the *sequence_detector* in VHDL is shown in Figure 3.5a. The first line of this figure specifies the name of the component. This is followed by the PORT keyword with the name of the ports in parentheses ( ). The three inputs of the *sequence_detector* are named *x_in, y_in*, and *enable* and the single output of this circuit is named *z_out*. The keywords IN and OUT specify the mode of the port signals. A signal that is declared as mode IN cannot be assigned a value from within the component. Likewise, an OUT signal cannot be used on the right hand side of a signal assignment. The interface list of the *sequence_detector* also includes the types of the input-output signals. We are using type BIT which is part of the standard package in VHDL. Other types, for multi-value logic, can be defined and added to user libraries. This is discussed in Chapter 6.

As shown in Figure 3.3, the *sequence_detector* consists of a *clock_component* and an *fsm_component*. Figure 3.5b illustrates the interface descriptions of these components. The syntax used is similar to that of Figure 3.5a. The names of the input and output ports of these components are independent of those of the enclosing component.

```
ENTITY sequence_detector IS
    PORT (x_in, y_in, enable : IN BIT; z_out : OUT BIT);
END sequence_detector;
```
(a)

```
ENTITY fsm_component IS
    PORT (x, y, clk : IN BIT; z : OUT BIT);
END fsm_component;
ENTITY clock_component IS
    PORT (en : IN BIT; ck : OUT BIT);
END clock_component;
```
(b)

```
ENTITY logical_part IS
    PORT (in0, in1, q0, q1 : IN BIT; d0, d1, out1 : OUT BIT);
END logical_part;
ENTITY memory_part IS
    PORT (d_in0, d_in1, clocking: IN BIT; d_out0, d_out1: OUT BIT);
END memory_part;
```
(c)

FIGURE 3.5
Interface descriptions, (a) for the *sequence_detector*, (b) for the components of *sequence_detector* after the first partitioning, (c) For the components of *fsm_component* after its first partitioning.

Although it may be clear to the reader that the *x_in* input of the *sequence_detector* is the same as the *x* input of the *fsm_component,* this is not evident from the signal names. This correspondence will be defined later in the architectural specification of the *sequence_detector*.

Figure 3.4 demonstrates how the gate level implementation of the *fsm_component* partitions it into smaller components. A natural partitioning would be to separate the logic and the memory parts, as shown by the dotted line in Figure 3.4. The two flip-flops constitute what will be referred to as the *memory_part*, and the section of the circuit that consists of AND, OR and NOT gates constitutes the *logical_part*. Figure 3.5c shows the interface description for the *memory_part* and the *logical_part*. A block diagram corresponding to this partitioning is shown in Figure 3.6. This block diagram corresponds to the ENTITIES in Figure 3.5c. As noted before, various components can have their own independent port names. Naming conventions should depend on the component's function rather than on the environment in which it is used.

The interface description of all the major components are now complete. The following section addresses the architectural specifications of these components and the formation of a VHDL description for the *sequence_detector*.

3.1.3 Architectural Description

The functionality of a component is described in VHDL architectural bodies. This description can be in terms of other components, or in the form of a definition that

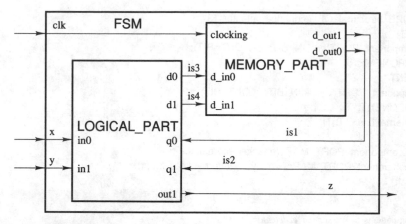

FIGURE 3.6
FSM internal block diagram. This unit is partitioned into a *memory_part* and a *logical_part*.

specifies the values of output signals in terms of the inputs (input/output mapping). It is also possible to mix these two forms of descriptions.

The description of the *sequence_detector* is done according to the tree structure shown in Figure 3.7. The description of the terminal nodes of this tree is self-contained, and that of the nonterminal nodes is in terms of the other components. For a complete description of the *sequence_detector*, all five components should be described in VHDL.

At the highest level, the *sequence_detector* is partitioned into the *clock_component* and the *fsm_component*. The VHDL description for this component, shown in Figure 3.8, specifies the wiring shown in Figure 3.3.

The VHDL description begins with the ARCHITECTURE keyword. Components that are needed within this architecture are then declared. A component declaration includes the name of the component and its ports. In the simple form we are using in this chapter, the port names in the component declarations are the same as those of the actual component. An *internal_line* for carrying the output of the *clock_component* into the clock input of the *fsm_component* has also been declared in the declarative part of the description in Figure 3.8.

The BEGIN keyword starts the body of the description in which the two components of the *sequence_detector* are instantiated. Instantiation refers to naming a

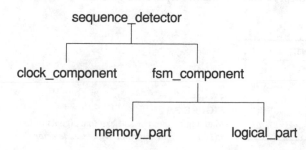

FIGURE 3.7
Tree structure of the *sequence_detector*. VHDL descriptions will correspond to branches shown here.

```
ARCHITECTURE structural OF sequence_detector IS
  COMPONENT
    clock_component PORT(en: IN BIT; ck: OUT BIT);
  END COMPONENT;
  COMPONENT
    fsm_component PORT(x,y,clk:IN BIT; z:OUT BIT);
  END COMPONENT;
  SIGNAL internal_line : BIT;
BEGIN
  c1 : clock_component PORT MAP (enable, internal_line);
  c2 : fsm_component PORT MAP (x_in, y_in, internal_line, z_out);
END structural;
```

FIGURE 3.8
Wiring major components of the *sequence_detector*.

component within another component for use as a subcomponent. Every instantiation begins with an arbitrary label, specifies the component name, and lists a mapping between the port names in the instantiation and the actual component. The signals that are the inputs or outputs of the *sequence_detector* or signals that have been declared in the declaration part can be used in the port map. The description specifies that the *clock_component* uses the *enable* input of the *sequence_detector* as its first input line, and it connects its output to the signal declared as *internal_line*. The *fsm_component* uses the *x_in* and *y_in* inputs of the *sequence_detector* as data inputs. It also uses the *internal_line* signal as the clock input, and it places its output in the *z_out* output of the *sequence_detector*.

Signals in the instantiations will be mapped to the ports of the instantiated component according to their ordering in the port map list. This is known as positional association of formal to actual elements. For example, ports of the *fsm_component* are mapped as shown in Figure 3.9.

Referring back to the tree structure in Figure 3.7, the description of the top node of this tree is now completed. Next, we move down one level and describe the *fsm_component* and the *clock_component*. The *fsm_component* is described at the structural level, and the *clock_component* at the behavioral level. Figure 3.10 shows the structural description of the *fsm_component*, specifying the wiring between the *logical_part* and the *memory_part* in accordance with the block diagram in Figure 3.6. In the declarative part, the *logical_part* and the *memory_part* components as well as

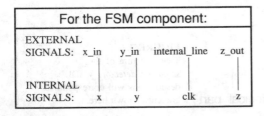

FIGURE 3.9
Mapping of internal and external signals of the *structural* architecture of *sequence_detector*.

four intermediate signals of type BIT are declared. In the body of the architecture of the *fsm_component*, component instantiations and port mappings take place. The signals *is1*, *is2*, *is3*, and *is4*, also shown in Figure 3.6, are used as carriers for connecting the input/output ports of the *logical_part* and the *memory_part*.

Figure 3.11 shows the behavioral description of the *clock_component*. The only input of this component is the *en* line and its output is *ck*. The description begins with the ARCHITECTURE keyword followed by an identifier that is in turn followed by the name of the component.

The PROCESS keyword begins the behavioral description of the *clock_compo-nent*. The process statement in VHDL is used for all behavioral descriptions. The syntax of language constructs in a VHDL process is similar to that of most high level software languages in that variables can be declared and used in processes. High level looping and branching constructs such as for-loop and if-then-else can also be used in a process. The process statement in Figure 3.11 declares the *periodic* local variable and initializes it to '1'. When the execution of the description of Figure 3.11 begins, if

```
ARCHITECTURE structural OF fsm_component IS
   COMPONENT logical_part
      PORT (in0, in1, q0, q1 : IN BIT; d0, d1, out1 : OUT BIT);
   END COMPONENT;
   COMPONENT memory_part
      PORT (d_in0, d_in1, clocking:IN BIT; d_out0, d_out1:OUT BIT);
   END COMPONENT;
   SIGNAL is1, is2, is3, is4 : BIT; -- intermediate signals
BEGIN
   c1 : logical_part PORT MAP (x, y, is1, is2, is3, is4, z);
   c2 : memory_part PORT MAP (is3, is4, clk, is1, is2);
END structural;
```

FIGURE 3.10
Structural architecture of FSM component.

```
ARCHITECTURE behavioral OF clock_component IS
BEGIN
   PROCESS
      VARIABLE periodic: BIT := '1';
   BEGIN
      IF en = '1' THEN
         periodic := NOT periodic;
      END IF;
      ck <= periodic;
      WAIT FOR 1 US;
   END PROCESS;
END behavioral;
```

FIGURE 3.11
Behavioral description of clock component.

the clock is enabled, i.e., *en* is '1', *periodic* will be complemented and assigned to the *ck* output signal of the *clock_component*. Following this assignment, a wait statement causes the execution of the process to be suspended for 1 microsecond. When this time expires, the process executes again, and complements *periodic* if *en* is '1', or holds the old value of *periodic* if *en* is '0'. Variables can be declared and used inside processes but they cannot be declared globally. Information can be transferred only between processes via signals. To use the value of a variable outside an architecture, it must be assigned to a declared signal. The := symbol is used for variable assignments, while <= is used for assignments into signals. Unlike signals, variables have no direct hardware significance and they do not have timing associated with them. These issues are discussed in the section on timing in this chapter, and also in Chapter 8. When execution of a process completes, it returns to the beginning and repeats the entire process. This causes the *ck* signal to be complemented every one microsecond, thus generating a periodic clock.

Moving down one more level to the lowest level of the tree in Figure 3.7, we now describe the *memory_part* and the *logical_part* in VHDL. The *logical_part* is described at the dataflow level of abstraction and is identified as such. Dataflow descriptions use various forms of VHDL signal assignment construct for describing the operation of hardware. The description, illustrated in Figure 3.12, consists of three* Boolean equations that are assigned to the three outputs of the *logical_part*. A signal assignment can have an AFTER clause which specifies the delay associated with the assignment. We use this delay to account for the gate delays. The three signal assignments in this description are concurrent and are always active. When a signal on the right hand side of any of the three assignments changes in value, the right hand side expression is evaluated and a value scheduled to be placed in the destination signal after the specified time. This behavior is similar to the way actual hardware components work. All components of a digital circuit are always active. As soon as a change occurs on an input of a gate, the gate starts propagating the effect of the new input value to its output.

At the dataflow level of abstraction, clocking schemes and register transfers can be precisely and conveniently specified. We have, therefore, used this level of abstraction for description of the *memory_part* also. The interface description of Figure 3.5c indicates the inputs and outputs of the *memory_part*, and Figure 3.13 shows the architectural specification of this part. As shown in this figure, the description of *memory_part (dataflow)* begins with the ARCHITECTURE keyword and includes a

```
ARCHITECTURE dataflow OF logical_part IS
BEGIN
    d0 <= ( in0 AND q0 ) OR ( in0 AND q1)   AFTER 12 NS;
    d1 <= ( NOT q0 ) AND ( NOT q1 ) AND in0   AFTER 14 NS;
    out1 <= ( NOT in0 ) AND ( NOT in1 ) AND q0   AFTER 14 NS;
END dataflow;
```

FIGURE 3.12
Dataflow description of the *logical_part*.

```
ARCHITECTURE dataflow OF memory_part IS
BEGIN
   BLOCK (clocking = '1' AND clocking' EVENT)
   BEGIN
      d_out0 <= GUARDED d_in0 AFTER 11 NS;
      d_out1 <= GUARDED d_in1 AFTER 11 NS;
   END BLOCK;
END dataflow;
```

FIGURE 3.13
Dataflow description of *memory_part*.

single block statement. This statement is used here to specify the clocking scheme. The expression in parentheses after the BLOCK keyword is the guard of the block. When the clock input (*clocking*) to the *memory_part* is '1', and there has been a change on this signal (an EVENT), then the guard expression of the block is TRUE. This situation arises when the *clocking* signal makes a low-to-high transition. The guard, therefore, represents the rising edge of the *clocking* signal. The keyword GUARDED on the right hand side of a signal assignment, enables the assignment only if the corresponding guard signal is true. In the body of the block, signal assignments to the two outputs of the *memory_part* are guarded by the rising edge of the *clocking* signal. The *d_in0* and *d_in1* inputs are assigned only to the *d_out0* and *d_out1* outputs on the rising edge of *clocking*. At all other times, these outputs hold their old values, regardless of the events on the *d_in* inputs.

Signal assignments in Figure 3.13 take place 11 nanoseconds after the rising edge of the *clocking*. This delay is to account for the internal delay of the flip-flops. Having defined all five components of the tree in Figure 3.7, the VHDL description of our *sequence_detector* is now complete. To run the descriptions and simulate the functionality of the circuit, component bindings have to be completed, and a test bench must be developed for the circuit. Chapters 4 and 5 deal with various forms of binding components of a design to actual components. Chapter 4 shows simple test benches, and the behavioral language constructs described in Chapters 6 and 8 provide more convenient methods of testing circuits.

3.1.4   Subprograms

As in most high level languages, VHDL allows the definition and use of functions and procedures generally referred to as subprograms. Most of the high level behavioral constructs in VHDL can be used in the body of functions and procedures. Subprograms can be declared, defined, and invoked much the same way as software languages. Values returned or altered by subprograms may or may not have a direct hardware significance. For example, we can use functions to represent Boolean equations, for type conversions, or for delay value calculations. While Boolean expressions may correspond to actual logic circuits, the other two applications do not represent hardware structures.

A procedure can be useful for type conversions, for description of counters, for analog to digital converters, or simply for outputting internal binary data in integer form. The *byte_to_integer* procedure for converting 8-bit binary data to integer is illustrated in Figure 3.14. A type declaration declares *byte* as an array of eight bits. Description of the *byte_to_integer* procedure uses this type (*byte*) to define its input vector. The procedure begins with the PROCEDURE keyword, followed by the identifier of the procedure and by its interface list. In the declarative part of this procedure, the *result* variable is declared as an integer and initialized to zero. In the body of the *byte_to_integer* procedure, a loop of eight iterations adds the weight of the bit positions, for the bits of the input that are '1', to the *result*. At the end of the loop the value in the *result* variable is assigned to the *oi* output.

As an example function, we replace part of the Boolean expressions in Figure 3.12 with a function. As shown in this figure, as well as in Figure 3.4, the logic at the *d* input of flip-flop 1 is the same as the logic for the *z* output. Instead of repeating the same expression for *d1* and *out1*, a function can be used for this purpose as shown in Figure 3.15.

In the declarative part of function *f* variable *x* is declared and in the body of *f* it is assigned to the appropriate Boolean expression. This expression is the return value of the function. The new description of the *logical_part* that takes advantage of function *f* is shown in Figure 3.16.

```
TYPE byte IS ARRAY ( 7 DOWNTO 0 ) OF BIT;
  ...
PROCEDURE byte_to_integer (ib : IN byte; oi : OUT INTEGER) IS
    VARIABLE result : INTEGER := 0;
BEGIN
    FOR i IN 0 TO 7 LOOP
      IF ib(i) = '1' THEN
        result := result + 2**i;
      END IF;
    END LOOP;
    oi := result;
END byte_to_integer;
```

FIGURE 3.14
Type conversion procedure: converting bytes to integers.

```
FUNCTION f (a, b, c : BIT) RETURN BIT IS
    VARIABLE x : BIT;
BEGIN
    x := ( (NOT a) AND (NOT b) AND c );
    RETURN x;
END f;
```

FIGURE 3.15
A simple Boolean function in a VHDL function definition.

```
┌─ARCHITECTURE  functional_dataflow  OF  logical_part  IS
├─BEGIN
│     d0  <=  ( in0  AND  q0 )  OR  ( in0  AND  q1)   AFTER  12  NS;
│     d1  <=  f (q0, q1, in0)   AFTER  14  NS;
│     out1  <=  f ( in0, in1, q0)   AFTER  14  NS;
└─END  functional_dataflow;
```

FIGURE 3.16
Description of *logical_part* of the *fsm_component* using functions.

3.1.5   VHDL Operators

Behavioral descriptions in VHDL can include most of the operations found in software languages. The text of behavioral descriptions resembles that of software programs except that constructs for control and time modeling are also included. Figure 3.17 shows the operations that can be used in VHDL.

Logical operators can be used for operands of the predefined BIT and BOOLEAN types and the result of the operation will be the same type as the operands. Relational operators always generate a Boolean result regardless of the type of operands. Operands of arithmetic operators must be of the same type and the result reflects the type of the operands. The concatenation operator is used for concatenating arrays of elements. For example, assuming *x_byte* and *y_byte* are two 8-bit arrays of BITs, the following concatenation forms a 16-bit array of BITs.

x_byte & y_byte

The type of the elements in concatenated arrays must be the same. This operator is particularly useful for merging buses or registers. In the chapters that follow, these operators are used and their application and usage becomes clear. In Chapter 6, types and issues related to types, such as type conversion and qualification, are discussed.

3.2   TIMING AND CONCURRENCY

In an electronic circuit, all components are always active and there is a timing associated with every event in the circuit. VHDL, being a language for describing such circuits, has constructs for accurate modeling of timing and concurrency in digital circuits. Concurrent constructs of the language are used in concurrent bodies and sequential statements are used in sequential bodies. An architecture is a concurrent body, while the body of a process statement is a sequential body. A sequential body within a concurrent body executes concurrently with concurrent constructs within the same body. Timing relationships between signals and various bodies in VHDL are complex and important. To illustrate these concepts, we start with the example in Figure 3.18.

Each gate in this circuit is assumed to have a delay of 12 nanoseconds. While all three inputs are high, the output at a stable '1' level, and nodes *w*, *x*, and *y* are at '0', '1', and '0', respectively. As illustrated in Figure 3.19, if input *a* switches from

PREDEFINED OPERATORS	
LOGICAL OPERATORS:	NOT AND OR NAND NOR XOR
OPERAND TYPE:	BIT BOOLEAN
RESULT TYPE:	BIT BOOLEAN
RESULT TYPE:	BIT BOOLEAN
RELATIONAL OPERATORS:	= /= < <= > >=
OPERAND TYPE:	any type
RESULT TYPE:	Boolean
ARITHMETIC OPERATORS:	+ − * / **
:	MOD REM ABS
OPERAND TYPE:	INTEGER REAL Physical
RESULT TYPE:	INTEGER REAL Physical
CONCATENATION OPERATOR:	&
OPERAND TYPE:	array of any type
RESULT TYPE:	array of any type

FIGURE 3.17
Basic VHDL predefined operators.

'1' to '0', gates *g1* and *g2* concurrently react to this change. As shown in the timing diagram in Figure 3.20, the *g1* gate causes node *w* to go to '1' after 12 ns, and *g2* causes node *x* to go to '0' after the same amount of time. At this time, gates *g3* and *g4* see a change at their inputs and they start reacting to their new input conditions. The change at the *x* input of *g4* turns the output off after 12 ns. At this same time, the change on *w* has caused node *y* to become '1'. The OR gate (*g4*) now has a '1'at its *y* input, which causes it to go back to '1' only 12 ns after it has gone to zero. As shown in Figure 3.20, this causes a 12 ns wide zero glitch on the output of the circuit which must be properly represented in a simulation model of this circuit.

This analysis would be more complex if the gates had unequal delay values, or if other inputs change when the circuit has not stabilized. From this analysis of

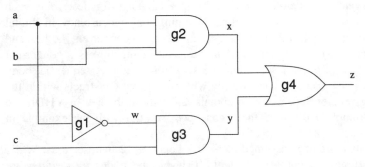

FIGURE 3.18
A gate circuit to illustrate timing and concurrency.

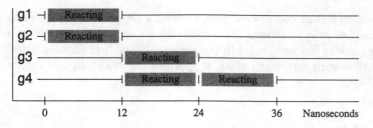

FIGURE 3.19
Gates of Figure 3.18 reacting to changes originated by *a* changing from '1' to '0'.

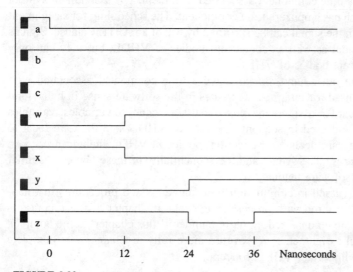

FIGURE 3.20
Timing diagram resulting from input *a* of circuit of Figure 3.18 changing from '1' to '0' at time zero.

a small example it is clear that treatment of timing and concurrency is especially important in a hardware language. For this reason, the VHDL language has a timing component associated with the signals and it provides constructs for concurrent signal assignments. Programming in VHDL requires a good understanding of these concepts, which are discussed here.

3.2.1   Objects and Classes

In a software language, a variable contains a value and can accept new values through assignment statements. Constants, on the other hand, have fixed values throughout a program run. Because it is necessary to model timing in a hardware language, VHDL, in addition to variables and constants, also supports signals. In the VHDL terminology, a signal, a variable, or a constant is called an object, and "signal," "variable," or "constant" are considered classes of objects. For example, a variable is an object whose class is variable.

As with variables, signals can receive values during a simulation run. We often use the term "carrier" to refer to objects that receive values and to objects that can be used for carrying values from one point in the program to another. Global carriers are carriers that can be used across architectural specifications. Only signals can be global carriers in VHDL.

3.2.2 Signals and Variables

A carrier in VHDL can be declared as a signal or as a variable. Signals have hardware significance and have a time component associated with them. The assignment symbol for signals is <= which has a nonzero time component. The scheduling for assignment of the right hand side to the signal can be specified by use of an AFTER clause. Signals can be used in sequential as well as concurrent bodies of VHDL, but they can only be declared in concurrent bodies of VHDL.

Variables, on the other hand, do not have a time component associated with them, and are mainly used for intermediate values in the software sense in behavioral descriptions. The standard := assignment is used to assign values to variables. Variables can only be declared and used in sequential bodies of VHDL, and they are local to the body in which they are declared. Sequential bodies in VHDL include *processes, functions,* and *procedures.* The syntax and the sequentiality of these bodies is similar to that found in most software languages.

Variables are discussed in conjunction with functions and procedures in Chapter 5 and again in conjunction with process statements in Chapter 8. Basic concepts of signal assignments are emphasized in the remainder of this chapter. Some complex issues related to signal assignments are covered more fully in Chapter 7 to complete our discussion of this important VHDL concept.

3.2.3 Signal Assignments

In its simplest form, a signal assignment consists of a target signal on the left hand side of a left arrow and an expression for defining a waveform on the right hand side (with no AFTER clause). Such an assignment specifies that the right hand side be assigned to the left hand side *delta* time later. Physically this time is zero seconds, but it has nonzero scheduling significance. For example, an assignment that is scheduled to occur two *delta* times later will be done after an assignment that is scheduled to occur after one *delta*, and the result of the later assignment will not be available for the earlier assignment. Both assignments, however, occur before the smallest physical time unit. This will become clearer when we discuss concurrency later in this section.

Optionally, a signal assignment can include an AFTER clause specifying that a physical time delay is to occur before the assignment to the left hand side takes place. If this time delay is zero, the simple form described above will apply.

Signal assignments can have *inertial* or *transport* delays. The *delay* architecture of the *example* entity in Figure 3.21 includes an assignment with inertial delay and an assignment with transport delay. Unless the TRANSPORT keyword is used in a signal assignment, the delay is considered to be the inertial type.

Inertial delays can be used to model delays through capacitive networks, such as the one shown in Figure 3.22 which corresponds to the first assignment of Figure 3.21. If a pulse whose width is less than five nanoseconds occurs on *waveform*, it will not appear on *target1*. On the other hand, the same pulse on *waveform* appears on *target2* exactly five nanoseconds later.

Figure 3.23 shows timing diagrams of *target1* and *target2* of Figure 3.21, when the same waveform (*waveform*) is used on the right hand side of both assignments. Also shown in this figure is the Exclusive-Or of *target1* and *target2* to illustrate their differences. Note that differences occur only when positive or negative pulses shorter than five nanoseconds appear on *waveform*.

Gate delays are caused by the internal resistance and capacitance of the gates and, therefore, are inertial. Carrier delays in electronic circuits that are caused by wire capacitance are also inertial. Since most hardware constructs can be represented by inertial delays, this is the default in signal assignments.

3.2.4   Concurrent and Sequential Assignments

In a software language, all assignments are sequential. This means that the order in which the statements appear is significant because they are executed from the top to the bottom. Sequential descriptions are the simplest to program and understand. As described earlier, events in hardware components are concurrent, and they need to be represented as such. Concurrent and sequential bodies of VHDL are discussed here.

```
ARCHITECTURE delay OF example IS
    SIGNAL target1, target2, waveform : BIT;
    -- this is a comment
BEGIN
    -- the following illustrates inertial delay
    target1 <= waveform AFTER 5 NS;
    -- the following illustrates transport delay
    target2 <= TRANSPORT waveform AFTER 5 NS;
    -- this architecture continues
END delay;
```

FIGURE 3.21
VHDL description for the demonstration of transport and inertial delays.

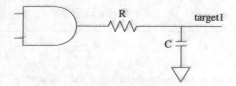

FIGURE 3.22
The RC delay is best represented by an inertial delay.

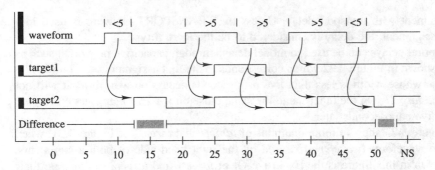

FIGURE 3.23
Illustrating the difference between inertial and transport delays.

3.2.4.1 CONCURRENCY. In an architectural body, all signal assignments are concurrent. When the value of a signal on the right hand side of an assignment changes, the entire right hand side waveform is evaluated and the result is assigned to the left hand side target. In Figure 3.21, for example, if the value of *waveform* changes, the new value will be scheduled for assignment to *target1* after five nanoseconds. Multiple assignments in the body of an architecture are simultaneously active, and the order in which they appear is not significant. Using concurrent assignments, an exact VHDL representation of the circuit in Figure 3.18 is shown in Figure 3.24.

This description consists of four concurrent assignments representing the four gates of Figure 3.18. When an input changes, the events in this description follow those of the actual circuit exactly. Since all the delays are caused by the gates, inertial delays are used for all of the assignments in Figure 3.24.

Multiple concurrent assignments can only be done to the same signal if a resolution function is provided to calculate a single value from several simultaneously driving values. Such signals are said to be resolved, and are be discussed in Chapter 7.

```
ENTITY figure_18_example IS
    PORT (a, b, c : IN BIT; z : OUT BIT);
END figure_18_example;

ARCHITECTURE   concurrent OF figure_18_example IS
    SIGNAL w, x, y : BIT;
BEGIN
    w <= NOT a AFTER 12 NS;
    x <= a AND b AFTER 12 NS;
    y <= c AND w AFTER 12 NS;
    z <= x OR y AFTER 12 NS;
END concurrent;
```

FIGURE 3.24
VHDL description for the gate level circuit in Figure 3.18 for the demonstration of timing and concurrency.

3.2.4.2 EVENTS AND TRANSACTIONS. Events and transactions are often referenced when discussing signal assignments. When a waveform causes the value of the target signal to change, an *event* is said to have occurred on the target signal. When a value is scheduled to be assigned to a target signal after a given time, a *transaction* is said to have been placed on the *driver* of the target signal. A transaction that does not change the value of a signal is still a transaction, but it does not cause an event on the signal. A transaction is represented by a value-time pair in parentheses. The value is the current value if the time element is zero; otherwise, the value is the future value for the driver of the signal.

As an example, consider the description in Figure 3.25. The declaration of signals *a*, *b*, and *c* causes the creation of these signals with '0' initial values. The initial value of each of these signals appears as though it has been the value of the signal for an infinitely long time prior to the start of simulation. Creation of the signals is referred to as *elaboration*, and assigning their initial values to them is called *initialization*.

After the initialization phase, values of *a*, *b*, and *c* signals are all zero. At the start of the simulation, at time 0 (this and other time values in the discussion of this example are in nanoseconds), the value of '0' on *a* causes a ('1',5NS) transaction to be scheduled for *b*, and a ('0',10NS) transaction for *c*. Also at this time, a '1' is scheduled for the *a* signal after 15 nanoseconds, causing a ('1',15NS) transaction on the driver of this signal. At time 5, the time element of the scheduled transaction for *b* becomes zero, and its value becomes current, which causes the value of this signal to change from '0' to '1'. This change of value is an event on *b*. Five nanoseconds later, at time 10, the scheduled transaction on *c* becomes current (its time element becomes zero), causing a driving value of '0' on this signal. Since at this time the value of *c* is already '0', this transaction does not cause an event on *c*.

Figure 3.26 shows events and transactions on signals in the description in Figure 3.25. Shaded areas signify transactions, and reverse modes signify initial values. Figure 3.26a shows the resulting timing diagram, with shaded areas indicating the transactions when they become current. Figure 3.26b shows the transactions that are placed on the *a*, *b* and *c* signals at the time this placement takes place. Figure 3.26c shows the transactions that exist on the signals before they become current. When a transaction is placed on the driver of a signal, it stays there and its time value decreases linearly with time until it becomes current. Figure 3.26c only shows transactions at five nanosecond intervals. A transaction is represented by a vertical box; the height of the box signifies the value of the time element in the transaction.

```
ARCHITECTURE demo OF example IS
   SIGNAL a, b, c : BIT := '0';
BEGIN
   a <= '1' AFTER 15 NS;
   b <= NOT a AFTER 5 NS;
   c <= a AFTER 10 NS;
END demo;
```

FIGURE 3.25
A simple description for illustrating events and transactions.

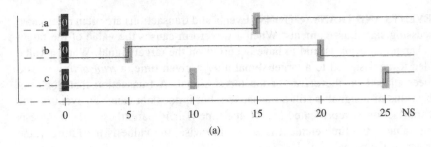

(a)

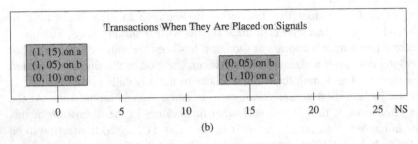

(b)

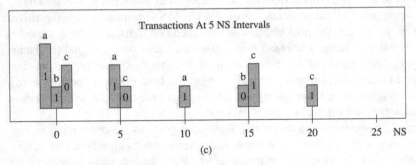

(c)

FIGURE 3.26
Events and transaction that occur on signals in Figure 3.25, (a) The resulting timing diagram showing transactions when they become current, (b) Transactions when they are placed on signals, (c) Transactions as their time values approach zero to become current.

No new transactions are placed on the signals in Figure 3.25 until time 15. At this time the transaction that was placed on the drive of *a* at time 0 becomes current, and changes the value of this signal to '1'. This event causes a ('0',5NS) transaction on *b* and a ('1',10NS) transaction on *c*. When these transactions become current; i.e., their time elements become 0 at time 15+5 NS and 15+10 NS, respectively, the values of *b* and *c* are the opposite of the values of their corresponding transaction. Therefore, both transactions cause events on these signals, at time 20 on *b*, and at time 25 on *c*.

3.2.4.3 DELTA DELAY. In the example presented in Figure 3.24, nonzero delays were used. For the purpose of demonstrating the concept of *delta* time delay, we consider another version of the circuit description shown in Figure 3.18. This description, shown in Figure 3.27, uses zero delay assignments for the internal nodes of the circuit

```
┌─ARCHITECTURE  not_properly_timed  OF  figure_18_example  IS
│     SIGNAL  w, x, y : BIT  :=  '0';
├─BEGIN
│     y  <=  c  AND  w;
│     w  <=  NOT  a;
│     x  <=  a  AND  b;
│     z  <=  x  OR  y  AFTER  36  NS;
└─END  not_properly_timed;
```

FIGURE 3.27
VHDL description for demonstrating the *delta* delay.

and a delayed assignment, with cumulative worst case delay of 36 nanoseconds for
the z output.

   In our analysis of this description we use the same input values used in the
analysis that led to the timing diagram in Figure 3.20. The new timing diagram,
showing the events and transactions (shaded areas), is shown in Figure 3.28. As
before, we assume that a, b, and c external signals are initialized to '1'; that is, their
values prior to time zero and at time zero are '1'. We also assume that, external to this
description, a '0' is assigned to the a signal at time zero. Since a is a signal, this new
value appears on it a *delta* time later at time *1δ*. One *delta* time after input a changes,
nodes w and x receive their new values; that is, w becomes '1' (value of NOT a) and
x becomes '0' (value of a AND b) at time *2δ*. The event on x causes a zero value
to be scheduled for output z after 36 nanoseconds, causing a ('0',36NS) transaction
of driver of z. The event on w causes the expression for y to be evaluated, and as a

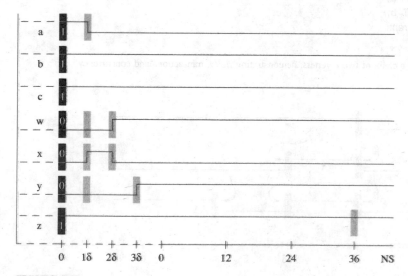

FIGURE 3.28
Timing diagram for the description of Figure 3.27, showing delta delays.

results the value at node y changes one *delta* time after w changes; it changes from '0' to '1' at time 3δ. The event on y then causes the output expression to be evaluated which again results in scheduling a new value on the output 36 nanoseconds after this event, placing a ('1',36NS) transaction on the driver of z.

The second transaction on the driver of the z output ('1',36NS) overwrites the first ('0',36NS), and since the value of z is already '1' the dominant transaction causes no event on this line. Although the steady state value on z is correct, the intermediate values on z are not modeled according to the actual circuit. Note that transactions on x and y at time zero do not translate to transactions on the z output 36 nanoseconds later. This is because the physical time delay absorbs all delta delays. Notice a glitch on x at zero time. Explanation of this glitch is left as an exercise.

Another example for illustrating *delta* time, transactions, and concurrency is shown in Figure 3.29. This description is for a chain of two zero-delay inverters, with a being the first input, c the output, and b the midpoint. Signals a, b, and c are initialized to '0'. A '1' is assigned to a causing a transaction on b, which in turn causes transaction on c.

The timing diagram in Figure 3.30 indicates that all transactions occur at zero time between $0 + 1\delta$ and $0 + 3\delta$. Every transaction in this analysis causes an event to occur. At time zero, a, b, and c signals have values that are specified in the declarations of the signals. At this time, a '1' is scheduled for a, and the comple-

```
ARCHITECTURE concurrent OF timing_demo IS
    SIGNAL   a, b, c : BIT := '0';
BEGIN
    a <= '1';
    b <= NOT a;
    c <= NOT b;
END concurrent;
```

FIGURE 3.29
Description for a chain of two inverters, demonstrating *delta*, transactions and concurrency.

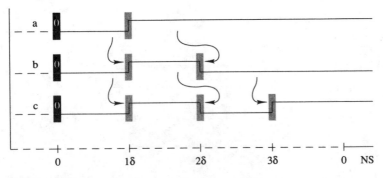

FIGURE 3.30
Timing diagram for *timing_demo* description of Figure 3.29.

ment of *a*, whose value is still '0' at time zero, is scheduled for *b*; therefore, both *a* and *b* will have ('1',0NS) transactions on their drivers. Also at time zero, the complement of signal *b*, whose value is '0' at this time, is scheduled for the *c* signal, causing the placement of a ('1',0NS) transaction on the driver of *c*. One *delta* time later at *1δ*, signals *a*, *b*, and *c* receive their new values which are all '1's. The new value on *a* causes a transaction on *b* one *delta* time later at *2δ*, which results in an event that changes *b* to '0'. Similarly, the value of *b* at *1δ* causes an event on *c* at *2δ*. The event on *b* at time *2δ* causes the right hand side of the assignment to *c* to be evaluated which causes another event on *c* one *delta* time later at *3δ*.

3.2.4.4 SEQUENTIAL ASSIGNMENTS. Assignments to signals in the sequential bodies of VHDL, for example, in the body of process statements, are done sequentially. This means that the order in which signal assignments appear is important, and it is legal to make multiple assignments to simple nonresolved signals. When a new transaction is to be placed on the driver of a signal, the transactions that are already scheduled for that signal will then be considered. The new transaction will either overwrite the previous transactions or be appended to them, depending on the timing of the new transaction and the type of the assignment.

A new transaction on the driver of a signal scheduled *before* an already existing transaction always overwrites the existing transaction. A new transaction on the driver of a signal scheduled *after* the already existing transaction is appended to the existing transaction if the delay is of transport type. For inertial delays, the new transaction scheduled after the existing transaction overwrites the existing transaction if it has a different value. Figure 3.31 summarizes this discussion on effective transactions on the driver of a signal. These issues will become clearer in the following examples.

When a sequential signal assignment statement is executed, a *(v1,t1)* transaction will be placed on the driver of the target signal. If an inertial assignment causes a second transaction *(v2,t2)* to be placed on the driver of the same signal, the first transaction will be overwritten by the second transaction if *t2* is less than *t1*. For example, in the description of Figure 3.32, the ('1',5NS) transaction is completely discarded, resulting in the timing diagram of Figure 3.33.

	TRANSPORT	INERTIAL
New Transaction is BEFORE Already Existing	Overwrite existing transaction.	Overwrite existing transaction.
New Transaction is AFTER Already Existing	Append the new transaction to the driver.	Overwrite existing if different values otherwise keep both.

FIGURE 3.31
Effective transactions on the driver of a signal when multiple sequential assignments are made to the signal.

```
┌ARCHITECTURE sequential OF overwriting_old IS
    SIGNAL   x : tit := 'Z';
├BEGIN
    PROCESS
    BEGIN
      x <= '1' AFTER 5 NS;
      x <= '0' AFTER 3 NS;
      WAIT;
    END PROCESS;
└END sequential;
```

FIGURE 3.32
Overwriting an old transaction. The new transaction is scheduled *before* the existing.

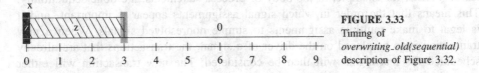

FIGURE 3.33
Timing of
overwriting_old(sequential)
description of Figure 3.32.

On the other hand, if *t2* of the most recent transaction *(v2,t2)* is greater than *t1* of the previous transaction *(v1,t1)*, the first transaction will be discarded if *v1* is not equal to *v2*, and both transactions will affect the target signal if *v1* is equal to *v2*. Figure 3.34 demonstrates the different value case, while Figure 3.35 demonstrates the case in which the values of the transactions are equal.

In the description of Figure 3.32, and the following descriptions that are used for illustration of the current topic (3.32, 3.34, 3.35, 3.36, and 3.37), signal *x* is declared as *tit*, which stands for trinary digit. We are assuming that this is a user defined type that takes on 'Z', '0', and '1' values, where 'Z' represents high impedance. Type definitions will be illustrated in Chapter 6. Another new feature used in this description which has not been discussed is the use of the wait statement without a time expression.

```
┌ARCHITECTURE sequential OF discarding_old IS
    SIGNAL x : tit := 'Z';
├BEGIN
    PROCESS
    BEGIN
      x <= '1' AFTER 5 NS;
      x <= '0' AFTER 8 NS;
      WAIT;
    END PROCESS;
└END sequential;
```

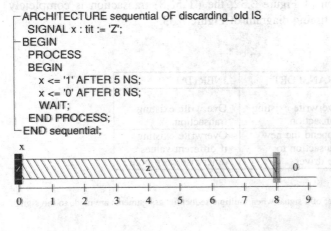

FIGURE 3.34
Discarding previous transactions of different value. The new transaction is scheduled *after* the existing, and has a different value.

This statement suspends the process forever, causing it to be executed only once. The wait statement will be discussed in detail in Chapter 8.

In Figure 3.34, a ('1',5NS) transaction is placed on the driver of the x signal by the first assignment. The second assignment generates the ('0',8NS) transaction which causes the ('1',5NS) transaction to be removed. Therefore, the only transaction on the driver of x is ('0',8NS). This transaction causes the 'Z' value on x to go to '0' at 8 ns.

In Figure 3.35, a ('0',5NS) transaction is placed on the driver of the x signal by the first assignment. The second assignment generates the ('0',8NS) transaction. Since the value of both transactions are '0', they will both remain on the driver of x. The x signal will, therefore, go to '0' at 5 ns and remain at this level.

Let us again assume that a *(v1,t1)* transaction is placed on the driver of the target signal. If a transport assignment causes a second transaction *(v2,t2)* to be placed on the driver of the same signal, the first transaction will be overwritten by the second transaction if *t2* is less than *t1*, just like an inertial assignment. If, however, *t2* is greater than *t1*, the second transaction will be appended to the first transaction. Figure 3.36 shows the case where a transport assignment causes a previous transaction to be overwritten, and Figure 3.37 includes an example in which the new transport assignment appends a new transaction to the existing transaction.

In Figure 3.36, a ('1',5NS) transaction is placed on the driver of the x signal by the first transport assignment. The second transport assignment generates the ('0',3NS) transaction which causes the ('1',5NS) transaction to be removed. As a result of the only remaining transaction on the driver of x, this signal will change value from 'Z' to '0' at 3 ns.

In Figure 3.37, a ('1',5NS) transaction is placed on the driver of the x signal by the first transport assignment. The second transport assignment generates the ('0',8NS) transaction which is appended to ('1',5NS). The two transactions cause x to go to '1' at 5 ns, and to '0' at 8 ns.

Figure 3.23 illustrates that glitches shorter than the inertial delay of a signal assignment do not appear on the output of the signal, while glitches of any size are delayed simply by the transport delay of a signal assignment. The difference in the

```
ARCHITECTURE sequential OF saving_all IS
  SIGNAL x : tit := 'Z';
BEGIN
  PROCESS
  BEGIN
    x <= '0' AFTER 5 NS;
    x <= '0' AFTER 8 NS;
    WAIT;
  END PROCESS;
END sequential;
```

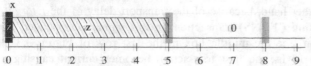

FIGURE 3.35
Saving previous transactions of same value. Transactions with the same value are both kept on the driver of x.

```
ARCHITECTURE sequential OF discarding_old IS
   SIGNAL x : tit := 'Z';
BEGIN
   PROCESS
   BEGIN
      x <= TRANSPORT '1' AFTER 5 NS;
      x <= TRANSPORT '0' AFTER 3 NS;
      WAIT;
   END PROCESS;
END sequential;
```

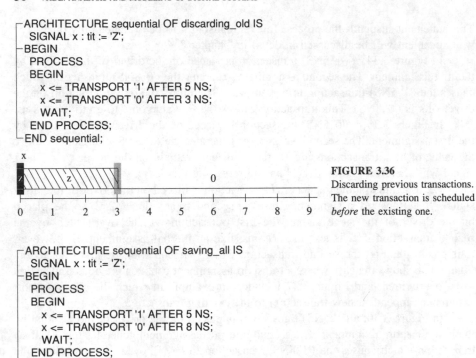

FIGURE 3.36
Discarding previous transactions.
The new transaction is scheduled
before the existing one.

```
ARCHITECTURE sequential OF saving_all IS
   SIGNAL x : tit := 'Z';
BEGIN
   PROCESS
   BEGIN
      x <= TRANSPORT '1' AFTER 5 NS;
      x <= TRANSPORT '0' AFTER 8 NS;
      WAIT;
   END PROCESS;
END sequential;
```

FIGURE 3.37
Appending transactions. Delay
type is transport, and the new
transaction is *after* the existing
one.

way glitches are handled by inertial and transport delays can be explained by the sequential placement of transactions on the driver of a signal. Consider, for example, the assignment of signal *a_glitch* to *i_target* and *t_target* signals in Figure 3.38.

Signals *a_glitch*, *i_target*, and *t_target* are initially zero. At time 10 NS, *a_glitch* changes from '0' to '1', which causes the placement of a ('1',5NS) transaction on *i_target*, and an equivalent transaction on the driver of the *t_target* signal. Two nanoseconds later, at 12 ns, the time element of these transactions is reduced by 2 ns, and the transactions become ('1',3NS). Also at time 12 ns, another event occurs on *a_glitch* which changes its value from '1' to '0'. This event causes placement of new ('0',5NS) transactions on the drivers of the two target signals. On the *i_target*, because of the inertial delay, the already existing ('1',3NS) transaction is overwritten by the new ('0',5NS) transaction as shown in the lower right box in Figure 3.31. This transaction becomes current five nanoseconds later, and appears just as a transaction on *i_target*. On the other hand, because of the transport delay of the *t_target*, at time 12 the already existing ('1',3NS) transaction on this signal is appended by the new ('0',5NS) transaction (see the middle box in the last row of Figure 3.31). Three nanoseconds later, at 15 ns, the first transaction becomes current causing a

```
┌─ARCHITECTURE glitch OF inertial_transport_demo IS
│   SIGNAL i_target, t_target, a_glitch : BIT := '0';
├─BEGIN
│   a_glitch <= '1' AFTER 10 NS, '0' AFTER 12 NS;
│   i_target <= a_glitch AFTER 5 NS;
│   t_target <= TRANSPORT a_glitch AFTER 5 NS;
└─END glitch;
```

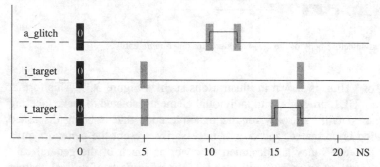

FIGURE 3.38
Glitches in inertial and transport delays.

'0' to '1' event on *t_target*. The other transaction on the driver of this signal becomes current at 17 ns which causes it to return to '0' at this time. The overall effect is that the 2 ns glitch on *a_glitch* appears just as a single transaction on *i_target*, but it fully appears on the *t_target* after the specified delay.

The two nanosecond pulse on the *a_glitch* signal can also be explained in terms of the sequential placement of transactions on the driver of the signal. The assignment to this signal in Figure 3.38 consists of two waveform elements, '1' after 10 ns and '0' after 12 ns. In an inertial assignment, the very first waveform element causes an inertial assignment, and all subsequent elements are treated as transport. In a transport assignment, all waveform elements are placed on the driver of a signal with transport delay. Because inertial delay is used in the assignment of values to *a_glitch*, this statement appears as a sequential assignment with inertial delay followed by a second sequential assignment with transport delay. The first assignment causes the (1,10NS) transaction to be placed on the driver of *a_glitch*, and the second assignment, being transport, appends the (0,12NS) transaction to the driver of this signal.

3.3 CONVENTIONS AND SYNTAX

In all the VHDL code in this book, we use vertical lines on the left hand side of the code to illustrate nesting levels. Indentation is also used, but the vertical bars make it easier to follow the beginning and end of a section of the code. In all VHDL code, we use uppercase letters for VHDL keywords, predefined entities, and standards. All other code, including names and labels, is in lowercase. When a VHDL keyword or predefined name is used in the text, it is also in uppercase. All other parts of code used in the text are in *italics*.

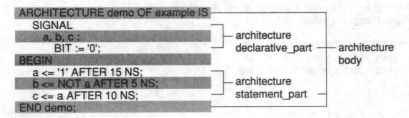

FIGURE 3.39
Syntax details of the architecture body of the *demo* architecture of *example* entity.

The syntax of VHDL is shown in illustrations such as Figure 3.39. This format is extracted from a VHDL program, with individual elements isolated to make labeling easy. These "syntax details" are only for the example code that is being discussed when the illustration is presented, and do not necessarily present the general syntax of the language. However, they are designed to cover as much of the general case as possible. For example, Figure 3.39 indicates that the main parts of an architecture body are the declarative part and the statement part but it obviously does not show all the variations of these language constructs. Where variations are important, we highlight them by showing syntax details in other examples. Appendix E shows the complete syntax of VHDL, from which all the "syntax details" illustrations of this book are drawn.

As stated earlier, VHDL is not case sensitive and has a is free format. In VHDL, long statements can continue over several lines. For comments, a pair of dashes (– –) is used. This pair, anywhere in a line, makes the rest of the line a comment. VHDL keywords are reserved words, and cannot be used for identifiers or as any other name. The complex syntax of the language can be overcome by developing templates of VHDL code for various applications.

3.4   SUMMARY

The first part of this chapter introduced the concept of design entity, and showed examples of VHDL descriptions at the three levels of abstractions that were introduced in Chapter 1. This introductory part is intended to provide the reader with a sample of the VDHL constructs and the general organization of the language. The second part of the chapter presented important issues regarding signals, delay types, transactions, delta delay, and other timing issues. We described signal assignments in concurrent and sequential bodies of VHDL, and showed how transactions appear on a signal in these bodies. An understanding of the timing issues presented in the second part of this chapter is essential to understanding VHDL.

REFERENCES

1. "IEEE Standard VHDL Language Reference Manual," IEEE Std. 1076-1987, The Institute of Electrical and Electronic Engineers, Inc., 1988.

2. Lipsett, L., C. Schaefer, and C. Ussery, "VHDL: Hardware Description and Design," Klewer Academic Publishing, Boston, 1988.

PROBLEMS

3.1. Write a dataflow description for an Exclusive OR gate.

3.2. Write a dataflow description for a Full Adder.

3.3. Wire four Full Adders to build a Nibble Adder.

3.4. Modify the Description of the Sequence Detector to detect the 101 sequence. Your circuit should detect overlapping sequences.

3.5. Write a behavioral description for a clock generator generating two nonoverlapping clock phases.

3.6. Write a procedure for converting integers between 0 and 255 to a byte.

3.7. List all the transactions in the following description:

```
ARCHITECTURE concurrent OF timing_demo IS
  SIGNAL  a, b, c : BIT := '0';
BEGIN
  b <= NOT a;
  c <= NOT b;
END concurrent;
```

3.8. List all the transactions in the following description:

```
ARCHITECTURE concurrent OF timing_demo IS
  SIGNAL  a, b, c : BIT := '0';
BEGIN
  a <= '1' AFTER 2 NS;
  b <= NOT a AFTER 3 NS;
  c <= NOT b AFTER 4 NS;
END concurrent;
```

3.9. List all the transactions in the following description:

```
ARCHITECTURE sequential OF timing_demo IS
  SIGNAL  a, b, c : BIT := '0';
BEGIN
  PROCESS
  BEGIN
    a <= '1';
    b <= NOT a;
    c <= NOT b;
    WAIT;
  END PROCESS;
END sequential;
```

3.10. Show the waveform on x:

```
┌ARCHITECTURE sequential   OF saving_all IS
│   SIGNAL  x : tit := 'Z';
├BEGIN
│   PROCESS
│   BEGIN
│     x <=   TRANSPORT '1' AFTER 5 NS;
│     x <=   TRANSPORT '0' AFTER 8 NS;
│     x <=   TRANSPORT '1' AFTER 6 NS;
│     WAIT;
│   END PROCESS;
└END sequential;
```

3.11. Show the waveform on x:

```
┌ARCHITECTURE sequential   OF saving_all IS
│   SIGNAL  x : tit := 'Z';
├BEGIN
│ · PROCESS
│   BEGIN
│     x <= TRANSPORT '0' AFTER 5 NS;
│     x <= '0' AFTER 3 NS;
│     x <= '1' AFTER 11 NS;
│     WAIT;
│   END PROCESS;
└END sequential;
```

3.12. For the architecture description shown below, show the list of all transactions on the signals. Include all initial transactions, final transactions, and those that are discarded. Each transaction should be specified as a parenthesized list of value and time (v,t). Show the resulting waveforms on all the signals. The WAIT UNTIL statement suspends the process until the condition becomes true. See Fig. P3.12.

3.13. Explain the glitch on signal x in Figure 3.28. *Hint*: the initial value of all signals are zero.

3.14. Explain the transactions on the w and y signals in Figure 3.28 at time 1δ.

3.15. The VHDL code shown below places a two nanosecond positive pulse on a. Assume that *toggle_when_transaction* returns the complemented value of its first argument when a transaction occurs on its second argument; otherwise, it returns the value of its first argument. Likewise, the *toggle_when_event* function returns the complemented value of its first argument when an event occurs on its second argument; otherwise, it returns the value of its first argument. Considering the assignments in this VHDL code, show all the transactions and events that occur on the t and e signals in a timing diagram. See Fig. P3.15.

3.16. Describe transactions on *i_target* and *t_target* signals in Figure 3.38, if the width of the glitch on *a_glitch* is seven nanoseconds.

3.17. We can use a signal assignment with inertial delay to remove pulses that are smaller than a certain width. Using only signal assignments, write a code fragment for removing positive pulses that are greater than a certain width.

```
ARCHITECTURE examining OF problem IS
   TYPE qit IS ('Z', '1', '0', 'X');
   SIGNAL w : qit := '0';
   SIGNAL x : qit;
   SIGNAL y : qit := 'Z';
   SIGNAL z : qit := '1';
   SIGNAL a, b : BIT;
BEGIN
   a <= '0', '1' AFTER 20 NS;
   b <= '0', '1' AFTER 40 NS;
   p1: PROCESS
   BEGIN
      w <= '1' AFTER 8 NS;
      w <= '1' AFTER 10 NS;
      WAIT UNTIL a = '1';
      w <= '0';
      y <= TRANSPORT '1' AFTER 5 NS;
      WAIT UNTIL b = '1';
      w <= '1' AFTER 10 NS;
      w <= '0' AFTER 13 NS;
      w <= 'Z' AFTER 08 NS;
      x <= '1';
      y <= TRANSPORT '0' AFTER 12 NS;
      y <= TRANSPORT 'Z' AFTER 15 NS;
      WAIT;
   END PROCESS p1;
   z <= x;
END examining;
```

FIGURE P3.12

```
ARCHITECTURE challenging   OF transaction_vs_event IS
   SIGNAL   a : BIT := '1';
   SIGNAL   t, e : BIT := '0';
BEGIN
   a <= '0', '1' AFTER 10 NS, '0' AFTER 12 NS, '0' AFTER 14 NS;
   t <= toggle_when_transaction (t, a);
   e <= toggle_when_event (e, a);
END challenging;
```

FIGURE P3.15

3.18. Using a single signal assignment, and using signal y as the source, generate signal x such that this new signal is a copy of y, except if there are pulses on y that are greater than width w. Pulses longer than w are trimmed when they appear on x.

CHAPTER
4

STRUCTURAL
SPECIFICATION
OF HARDWARE

To describe a system at the structural level, the components of that system are listed and the interconnections between them are specified. Because this level of abstraction closely corresponds to the actual hardware, it is easiest for hardware designers to understand and use. Software oriented readers, on the other hand, should pay attention to concurrency features in the language that is introduced in this chapter.

VHDL provides language constructs for concurrent instantiation of components, the primary constructs for structural specification of hardware. Other language constructs that support this level of abstraction include those for 1) the selection of a component from a certain package or parts library, 2) binding or associating the usage of a component to an available library, 3) wiring mechanisms, and 4) constructs for specification of repetitive hardware. This chapter describes all the constructs that are needed for the structural specification of digital systems.

The first part of this chapter presents a hierarchical description of a circuit and describes it in VHDL. This example illustrates the main language constructs for structural descriptions. A test bench in this part demonstrates a simple method for testing circuits. The second part of the chapter illustrates more advanced features of the language that can be used to associate components of a structural description with existing designs. An example in this part illustrates alternatives to using such language constructs.

Throughout the chapter, a set of notations and vocabulary is introduced for presenting and referencing VHDL descriptions. The vocabulary is consistent with that used in the IEEE VHDL 1076 Language Reference Manual (LRM). The development and enhancement of these notations continues throughout the book as new language constructs are introduced.

4.1 PARTS LIBRARY

This section presents VHDL descriptions for an inverter, a two-input NAND gate, and a three-input NAND gate. These primitive gates are used to form larger circuits in the later parts of this chapter and are regarded as off-the-shelf components or predefined cells of a library. The gate models are kept simple and use only VHDL simple signal assignments for the description of their operations.

4.1.1 Inverter Model

Figure 4.1 shows the logical symbol for an inverter, the VHDL description, and a graphical representation. The entity declaration of the inverter, shown in Figure 4.1b and further detailed in Figure 4.2, describes the inverter interface.

Figure 4.2 indicates that a port clause is bracketed between the beginning and end indications of an entity declaration. The port clause gives the declaration of all input and output ports of the entity. Two interface signal declarations are used to declare the *i1* input and the *o1* output ports of the inverter. The type of *i1* port is BIT and its mode is IN. The *o1* port is also of type BIT and its mode is OUT. The IN and OUT modes for *i1* and *o1* specify that these signals are the input and the output of the inverter. Ports can also have an INOUT mode which is mainly used for bidirectional lines. Type BIT is a predefined VHDL type. In addition to standard types, user defined types are also allowed. Type definition and usage are discussed in

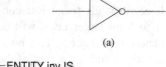

(a)

```
┌ENTITY inv IS
│   PORT (i1 : IN BIT; o1 : OUT BIT);
└END inv;
```

(b)

```
┌ARCHITECTURE single_delay OF inv IS
├BEGIN
│   o1 <= NOT i1 AFTER 4 NS;
└END single_delay;
```

(c)

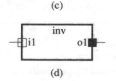

(d)

FIGURE 4.1
Inverter (a) symbol, (b) entity declaration, (c) architecture body, (d) notation.

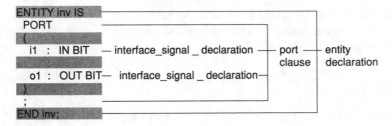

FIGURE 4.2
Details of the entity declaration of inverter.

Chapter 6. However, only predefined types are used in the design examples presented in this chapter and in Chapter 5.

Figure 4.1c shows the architecture body of *inv*, identified as *single_delay*. This architecture describes the internal operation of the inverter. A single signal assignment bracketed between the BEGIN and END keywords constitutes what is referred to as the statement part of the *single_delay* architecture of *inv*. This statement sets the complement of *i1* input to *o1* output, with a 4 nanosecond delay. The $<=$ symbol specifies the direction of assignment. When an event occurs on *i1* (i.e., *i1* changes value), the complement of the new value of *i1* is scheduled for the *o1* signal 4 ns later. TIME is a predefined type in VHDL and its units range from femtoseconds to hours. Other time units can also be defined.

Figure 4.1d shows a graphical representation for the interface description of the inverter. This symbol corresponds to the inverter entity declaration and is referred to as its *interface aspect*. A rectangular box represents the interface aspect of a hardware unit and includes its input/output ports as well as the entity name of its VHDL description. Input ports are shown by hollow boxes and output ports by black boxes. A half-filled box signifies the bidirectional port. The entity name is shown inside the rectangular box. Figure 4.3 shows the elements of aspect notation that we have introduced thus far.

Later in this chapter, *composition aspect*, which corresponds to an interconnection specification of smaller hardware units in order to form larger ones, will be presented. Presentation of aspect notation will be completed in Chapter 5. This notation provides a graphical correspondence to VHDL descriptions and is not part of the LRM.

4.1.2 NAND Gate Models

Logical symbols, entity declarations, architecture bodies, and interface aspects for a two-input and a three-input NAND gate are shown in Figures 4.4 and 4.6, respectively.

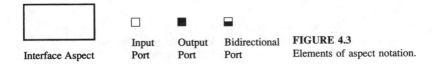

Interface Aspect   Input Port   Output Port   Bidirectional Port

FIGURE 4.3
Elements of aspect notation.

(a)

```
┌ENTITY nand2 IS
│    PORT (i1, i2 : IN BIT; o1 : OUT BIT);
└END nand2;
```

(b)

```
┌ARCHITECTURE single_delay OF nand2 IS
├BEGIN
│    o1 <= i1 NAND i2 AFTER 5 NS;
└END single_delay;
```

(c)

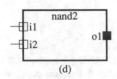

(d)

FIGURE 4.4
Two-input NAND (a) symbol, (b) entity declaration,
(c) architecture body, (d) notation.

As in the case of the inverter, the entity declaration of *nand2* has two interface signal declarations. The first interface declaration includes two signals, namely *i1* and *i2*. Since the type and mode of these two port signals are the same, they may be declared together by a single interface signal declaration so that mode and type need to be specified only once. Figure 4.5 shows the details of the *nand2* port clause. It indicates that *i1* and *i2* constitute an identifier list which, together with mode and type, form one of the interface signal declarations of the port clause of the two-input NAND gate. Declaration of all the interface signals forms the port interface list.

For the three-input NAND description in Figure 4.6b, the statement part consists of a single statement that assigns the NAND result of the *i1*, *i2* and *i3* signals to the output *o1* signal. An event on any of these input signals causes evaluation of the right hand side expression, and the new value will be assigned to *o1* after a delay of six nanoseconds. The part of the right hand side of a signal assignment, where values to be assigned to the left hand side target are specified, is referred to as the *waveform* in the VHDL syntax.

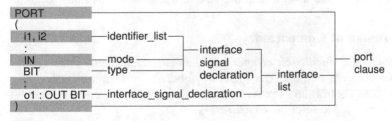

FIGURE 4.5
Port clause details for *nand2*.

(a)

```
ENTITY nand3 IS
   PORT (i1, i2, i3 : IN BIT; o1 : OUT BIT);
END nand3;
```

(b)

```
ARCHITECTURE single_delay OF nand3 IS
BEGIN
   o1 <= NOT (i1 AND i2 AND i3) AFTER 6 NS;
END single_delay;
```

(c)

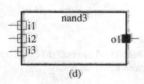

(d)

FIGURE 4.6
Three-input NAND (a) symbol, (b) entity declaration, (c) architecture body, (d) notation.

The primitive gates described in this section provide a sufficient set of parts for the description of larger components. Because of the few language tools that have been discussed and are available to us at this point in the book, the models that have been presented were limited in their capability to model timing and other physical characteristics of actual gates. More accurate gate models with better handling of timing and loading characteristics are developed in later chapters.

4.2 WIRING OF PRIMITIVES

Wiring of the primitive gates for generation of larger designs is demonstrated in this section. In VHDL, the operation of a design entity can be described in terms of its subcomponents. To completely specify this operation, we must indicate the component interconnections and link them to a set of available library cells. The main language constructs that support this style of hardware description are signal declarations, component declarations, configuration specifications, and component instantiations. These constructs are discussed here. For this purpose, a single bit comparator is designed and described in terms of the inverter and the NAND gates of the previous section.

4.2.1 Logic Design of Comparator

A single bit comparator circuit (*bit_comparator*) has two data inputs, three control inputs, and three compare outputs. The logical symbol for this circuit is shown in Figure 4.7. The three control inputs provide a mechanism for generation of multi-bit comparators by cascading several *bit_comparators*.

The $A>B$ output is 1 if the A input is greater than the B input (AB is 10) or if A is equal to B and the $>$ input is 1. The $A=B$ output is 1 if A is equal to B and the

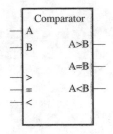

FIGURE 4.7
Logical symbol of a single bit comparator.

= input is 1. The $A<B$ output is the opposite of the $A>B$ output. This line becomes 1 if A input is less than B output (AB is 01) or if A is equal to B and the $<$ input is 1. Based on this functional description of the *bit_comparator*, Karnaugh maps for its three outputs are extracted as shown in Figure 4.8.

Boolean expressions for the three outputs of the *bit_comparator* resulting from applying minimization methods to the Karnaugh maps in Figure 4.8 are shown below. To avoid confusion, these expressions use *gt*, *eq* and *lt* instead of the $>$, $=$, and $<$ symbols used in the logical symbol in Figure 4.7. Other notational changes have been made for readability purposes.

Equation 4.1a $\qquad$ a_gt_b = a . gt + b'. gt + a . b'

Equation 4.1b $\qquad$ a_eq_b = a . b . eq + a'. b'. eq

Equation 4.1c $\qquad$ a_lt_b = a'. lt + b . lt + a'. b

Using DeMorgan's theorem, equations 4.1a to 4.1c can be transformed into equations 4.2a to 4.2c respectively. These equations have an appropriate form for all NAND and inverter implementations, which is of course what is available in our library of parts. The gate-level circuit diagram of the *bit_comparator*, resulting from these equations, is shown in Figure 4.9.

Equation 4.2a $\qquad$ a_gt_b = ((a . gt)'. (b'. gt)'. (a . b')')'

Equation 4.2b $\qquad$ a_eq_b = ((a . b . eq)'. (a'. b'. eq)')'

Equation 4.2c $\qquad$ a_lt_b = ((a'. lt)'. (b . lt)'. (a'. b)')'

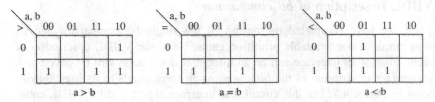

FIGURE 4.8
Karnaugh maps for the outputs of the single bit comparator.

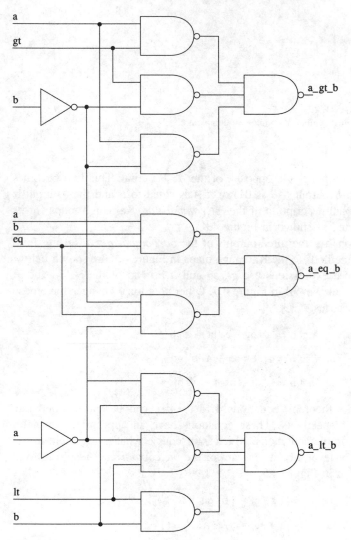

FIGURE 4.9
Logical diagram of *bit_comparator*.

4.2.2 VHDL Description of *bit_comparator*

At this point, we have completed the design of the single bit comparator and its definition in terms of our available primitive gates. Next, the VHDL description of this unit consisting of an interface and an architectural description will be developed.

The interface description of the *bit_comparator* corresponds to its logical symbol as shown in Figure 4.7. For this circuit, the interface aspect and its VHDL entity declaration (which is based on this aspect) are shown in Figure 4.10. Notations depicted in Figure 4.3 are used in the interface aspect of the *bit_comparator*. The entity

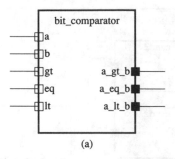

(a)

```
┌─ENTITY bit_comparator IS
│    PORT (a, b,                           -- data inputs
│        gt,                               -- previous greater than
│        eq,                               -- previous equal
│        lt : IN BIT;                      -- previous less than
│        a_gt_b,                           -- greater
│        a_eq_b,                           -- equal
│        a_lt_b : OUT BIT);                -- less than
└─END bit_comparator;
```

(b)

FIGURE 4.10
Interface description of *bit_comparator*, (a) interface aspect, (b) entity declaration.

declaration follows the same syntax used for the interface descriptions in Section 4.1 of this chapter. The two identifier lists in the port clause of this entity declaration contain five input ports and three output ports.

At the structural level the operation of the *bit_comparator* can be described in terms of its subcomponents and according to the gate level implementation in Figure 4.9. The description of this operation will be contained in a VHDL architecture body. The composition aspect of the *bit_comparator*, which corresponds to this body, is shown in Figure 4.11. This has been achieved by replacing the gates in Figure 4.9 with their interface aspects, as presented in Section 4.1. It consists of a graphical representation of interconnection specifications for the interface aspects of all its subcomponents. Names of input and output ports for components that constitute the *bit_comparator* are shown in their respective interface aspects. These names are local to the units they are used in and must not be confused with the same names used in other interface aspects. For example, several components in Figure 4.11 use $i2$ for their port name, but $i2$ is a different signal in each component. Signals immediately contained in the composition aspect of the *bit_comparator* are also unique. These signals are named either by the port names of the *bit_comparator*, such as a, b, eq, etc., or they are given arbitrary, but meaningful, names. Naming intermediate signals is necessary for the identification of each interconnection segment. Their names will be used in the VHDL description of the *bit_comparator*.

The architecture body that corresponds to the composition aspect in Figure 4.11 is shown in Figure 4.12. This body is the structural level description of the operation of the *bit_comparator* whose entity declaration is shown in Figure 4.10b. The first

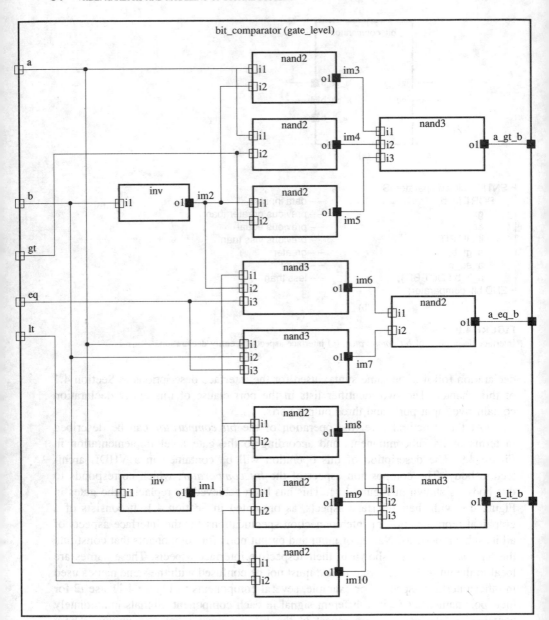

FIGURE 4.11
Composition Aspect of *bit_comparator*.

line of this VHDL description identifies the description as *gate_level* architecture for
the *bit_comparator* entity. The rest of the description, which consists of a declarative
part and a statement part, specifies the components and the way they are used in this
architecture.

```
ARCHITECTURE gate_level OF bit_comparator IS
    COMPONENT n1 PORT (i1: IN BIT; o1: OUT BIT); END COMPONENT;
    COMPONENT n2 PORT (i1, i2: IN BIT; o1: OUT BIT); END COMPONENT;
    COMPONENT n3 PORT (i1, i2, i3: IN BIT; o1: OUT BIT);
    END COMPONENT;
    FOR ALL : n1 USE ENTITY WORK.inv (single_delay);
    FOR ALL : n2 USE ENTITY WORK.nand2 (single_delay);
    FOR ALL : n3 USE ENTITY WORK.nand3 (single_delay);
    -- Intermediate signals
    SIGNAL im1,im2, im3, im4, im5, im6, im7, im8, im9, im10 : BIT;
BEGIN
    -- a_gt_b output
    g0 : n1 PORT MAP (a, im1);
    g1 : n1 PORT MAP (b, im2);
    g2 : n2 PORT MAP (a, im2, im3);
    g3 : n2 PORT MAP (a, gt, im4);
    g4 : n2 PORT MAP (im2, gt, im5);
    g5 : n3 PORT MAP (im3, im4, im5, a_gt_b);
    -- a_eq_b output
    g6 : n3 PORT MAP (im1, im2, eq, im6);
    g7 : n3 PORT MAP (a, b, eq, im7);
    g8 : n2 PORT MAP (im6, im7, a_eq_b);
    -- a_lt_b output
    g9 : n2 PORT MAP (im1, b, im8);
    g10 : n2 PORT MAP (im1, lt, im9);
    g11 : n2 PORT MAP (b, lt, im10);
    g12 : n3 PORT MAP (im8, im9, im10, a_lt_b);
END gate_level;
```

FIGURE 4.12
Architecture body of *bit_comparator* identified as *gate_level*.

Figure 4.13 shows the syntax details of the architecture body in Figure 4.12. Subcomponents in the *gate_level* description of the *bit_comparator* are *inv*, *nand2*, and *nand3*. The declarative part includes a component declaration and a configuration specification for each of these components. Component declarations define the interface to the component in an instantiation statement in the statement part of an architecture, and configuration specifications associate such an instance with an existing entity. For example, in the case of the *n3* component, a component declaration defines the ports of instantiations of *n3* (referred to as local ports) to be the same as those of the *nand3* entity, that is, (i1, i2, i3 : IN BIT; o1 : OUT BIT). The configuration of *n3* specifies that for all instantiations of this component (ALL : *n3*) the *single_delay* architecture of the *nand3* entity which exists in the WORK library should be used. In the configuration specification following the keyword FOR, the keyword ALL specifies that the association with the specified existing entity applies to *all* instances of that component. If different bindings are to be used for different instances of a component, the list of labels that binding applies to must be used instead of this keyword.

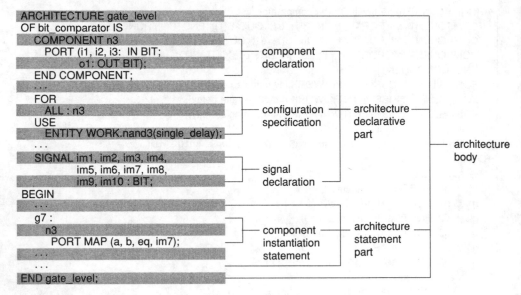

FIGURE 4.13
Syntax details of the architecture body of *bit_comparator*

Alternatives in the use of component declarations and configuration specifications are discussed later in this chapter. The word WORK in the configuration specification specifies the library where the *single_delay* architecture of the *nand3* entity resides. This is the default library and it refers to the current *work*ing library. Definition of new libraries are discussed in the section on design organization in Chapter 5. The default library is used in all the examples in this chapter.

In addition to the above constructs for defining components, the description in Figure 4.12 and the partial description in Figure 4.13 also include a signal declaration declaring several signals of type BIT. The keyword SIGNAL begins the declaration and is followed by a list of identifiers. BIT, the type indication for the signals, ends the declaration. Signals declared here are used as intermediate signals in the statement part of the *gate_level* architecture of *bit_comparator*, and are the same as those used in the composition aspect of the *bit_comparator*. Figure 4.13 indicates that the signal declarations are part of the architecture declarative part.

The architecture statement part describes what is shown graphically in the composition aspect of Figure 4.11. It consists of several instantiations of components that are declared and configured in the architecture declarative part. The wiring between these components is specified here. All component instantiations are concurrent and the order in which they appear is not important. An analogy exists between this ordering and the place of interface aspects of subcomponents of the *bit_comparator* within its composition aspect. It is clear that the operation of the *bit_comparator* does not depend on where interface aspects of its components are placed, it only depends on how they are interconnected.

Component instantiation statements include a label, component name, and association between the actual signals that are visible in the architecture body of the *bit_comparator* and the ports of the component being instantiated. Syntax details of the instantiation statement shown in Figure 4.13 are given in Figure 4.14. For this statement, *g7* is a label for instantiation of *n3* which is bound to the *nand3* entity. The mapping of ports specifies that the first three ports of this component are connected to the *a*, *b*, and *eq* inputs of the *bit_comparator*. These signal names are the primary ports of the *bit_comparator* entity and therefore are visible within its *gate_level* architecture body. The last port of *nand3*, which is its output, is connected to the *im7* intermediate signal. The next instantiation statement in the statement part of the architecture body of the *bit_comparator* (Figure 4.12) uses *im7* for the second input of a *nand2* component.

The last statement in Figure 4.12 ends the *gate_level* structural description of the single bit comparator. After a successful analysis of the gate_level architecture of the *bit_comparator* and all its subcomponents by a VHDL simulation system, this design entity becomes available in a design library and can be used in other designs. Designs that can use this unit include a test bench for it or a multi-bit comparator. The next section illustrates the latter.

4.3 WIRING ITERATIVE NETWORKS

In addition to language constructs for declaration, configuration, and instantiation of components, VHDL includes higher level constructs that can be used for definition of repetitive hardware at the structural level. Such constructs are discussed in this section. The example used is a 4-bit comparator and is referred to as a *nibble_comparator*. This circuit uses the *bit_comparator* circuit.

4.3.1 Design of a 4-Bit Comparator

A 4-bit comparator with two 4-bit data inputs, three control inputs, and three compare outputs is shown in Figure 4.15. The functionality of this circuit is similar to that of the *bit_comparator*. For the *nibble_comparator*, the discussion in Section 4.2.1 applies to 4-bit positive numbers instead of single bits of data. The $A>B$ output is 1 when data on the A input, treated as a 4-bit positive number, is greater than the 4-bit positive number on B, or when data on A and B are equal and the $>$ input is

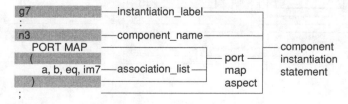

FIGURE 4.14
Component instantiation statement syntax details.

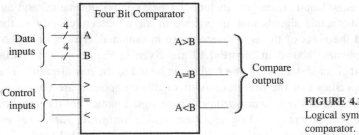

FIGURE 4.15
Logical symbol of a 4-bit comparator.

1. This arrangement makes it possible to wire together several *bit_comparator*s, or *nibble_comparator*s, or both for building comparators of any size.

The *nibble_comparator* can easily be built by cascading four *bit_comparator*s as shown in Figure 4.16. In this circuit, compare outputs of each of the *bit_comparator*s, for example, $A>B$, $A=B$, and $A<B$ of Bit 1, are connected to similarly named control inputs of a more significant bit, for example, $>$, $=$, and $<$ of Bit 2. The control inputs of the least significant bit, that is, $>$, $=$, and $<$ of Bit 0, are considered as the control inputs of the *nibble_comparator*, and the compare outputs of the most significant bit, that is, $A>B$, $A=B$, and $A<B$ of Bit 3, are the compare outputs of the 4-bit comparator circuit. When comparing two positive numbers with this arrangement, more significant comparator bits generate appropriate outputs if they can be determined by their corresponding data bits. A comparator bit only uses the outputs of a less significant bit if its own data bits are equal. With this scheme, the compare outputs of the *nibble_comparator* are generated faster by not having to depend on all *bit_comparator*s if the result can be determined by a few most significant bits. For example, when

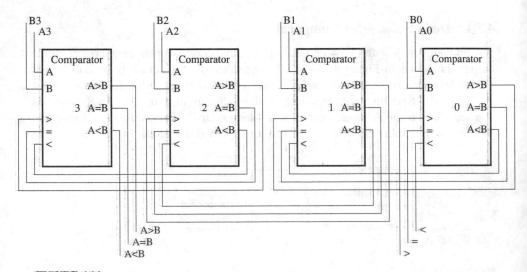

FIGURE 4.16
A 4-bit comparator using four single bit comparators.

comparing 0100 and 0011, the result is determined by bits 2 and 3 and there is no need for propagation of data through all four *bit_comparator*s.

4.3.2 VHDL Description of a 4-Bit Comparator

The interface aspect of the *nibble_comparator* and its entity declaration in accordance to this aspect are shown in Figures 4.17a and 4.17b respectively. The input and output ports of the interface aspect are the same as those of the logical symbol in Figure 4.15, which has a different naming convention. The entity declaration uses *nibble_comparator* as the entity name. The port clause of this declaration has three interface declarations for declaring data inputs, control inputs, and compare outputs. The *a* and *b* data inputs are 4-bit arrays of bits, and for their declaration the BIT_VECTOR type has been used. As with type BIT, BIT_VECTOR is a predefined type in VHDL and is available in the default standard package. Definition and usage of new packages and types are discussed in the section on design organization in Chapter 5.

The composition aspect of the *nibble_comparator*, shown in Figure 4.18, is derived from the schematic diagram in Figure 4.16. All signals in this aspect of the 4-bit comparator have names assigned to them. For those signals that are not primary ports of the *nibble_comparator*, intermediate names, *im(0)* through *im(8)*, are used. This figure indicates that four copies of the *gate_level* architecture of *bit_comparator*, shown in figure 4.12, are used for structural level implementation of the *nibble_comparator*.

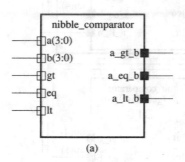

(a)

```
ENTITY nibble_comparator IS
    PORT (a, b, : IN BIT_VECTOR (3 DOWNTO );      -- a and b data
          gt,                                      -- previous greater than
          eq,                                      -- previous equal
          lt : IN BIT;                             -- previous less than
          a_gt_b,                                  -- a > b
          a_eq_b,                                  -- a = b
          a_lt_b : OUT BIT);                       -- a < b
END nibble_comparator;
```

(b)

FIGURE 4.17
Interface description of *nibble_comparator*, (a) interface aspect, (b) entity declaration.

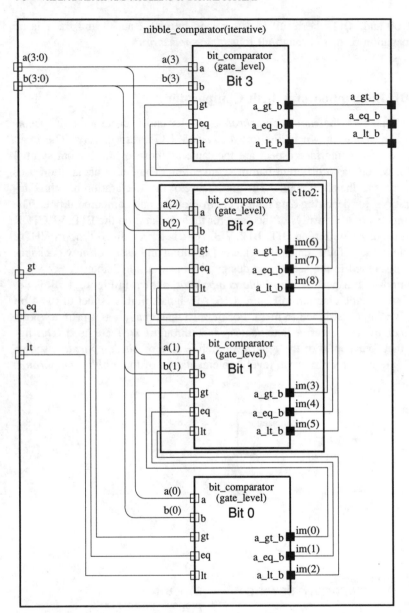

FIGURE 4.18
Composition aspect of *nibble_comparator*.

The VHDL description for the operation of this circuit directly corresponds to its composition aspect and is shown in Figure 4.19.

The name chosen for identifying this architecture is *iterative* and the reason for this selection will become evident shortly. In the declarative part, *comp1* is declared

```
┌ARCHITECTURE iterative OF nibble_comparator IS
│   COMPONENT comp1
│       PORT (a, b, gt, eq, lt : IN BIT; a_gt_b, a_eq_b, a_lt_b : OUT BIT);
│   END COMPONENT;
│   FOR ALL : comp1 USE ENTITY WORK.bit_comparator (gate_level);
│   SIGNAL im : BIT_VECTOR ( 0 TO 8);
├BEGIN
│   c0: comp1 PORT MAP (a(0), b(0), gt, eq, lt, im(0), im(1), im(2));
│   c1to2: FOR i IN 1 TO 2 GENERATE
│       c: comp1 PORT MAP (a(i), b(i), im(i*3-3), im(i*3-2), im(i*3-1),
│                   im(i*3+0), im(i*3+1), im(i*3+2) );
│   END GENERATE;
│   c3: comp1
│   PORT MAP (a(3), b(3), im(6), im(7), im(8), a_gt_b, a_eq_b, a_lt_b);
└END iterative;
```

FIGURE 4.19
Iterative architecture of *nibble_comparator*.

as a component with a port clause that is the same as that of the *bit_comparator* entity. Also in this part, by using a configuration specification, it is further specified that all instantiations of the *comp1* component are to be bound to the *gate_level* architecture of *bit_comparator*. In the statement part, four individual instances of *comp1* would complete the description of the *nibble_comparator*. In order to illustrate the use of higher level VHDL constructs, however, we have used two instances of *comp1* for the first and the last bits of the comparator, and the rest of the bits are instantiated in an iterative fashion, taking advantage of the VHDL generate statement.

In Figure 4.19, an instance of *comp1* that is labeled *c0* specifies wiring of a *bit_comparator* according to Bit 0 in Figure 4.18. Within the body of the *nibble_comparator*, the outputs of this bit are named *im(0)*, *im(1)*, and *im(2)*. Following the statement labeled *c0*, a generate statement labeled *c1to2* is used for wiring two *bit_comparators* for bits 1 and 2 of the 4-bit comparator. This statement uses a FOR loop with index *i* changing from 1 to 2. In the first iteration through the loop, the value of *i* is 1. Replacing *i* with this value in the port map of *comp1* results in the association list shown in Figure 4.20 for this instance of *comp1*. Therefore, it can be seen that the control inputs of the first instance of *comp1* generated by the generate statement are connected to *im(0)*, *im(1)*, and *im(2)* which are the output signals of the *c0* instance of *comp1*. The next and the final iteration through the FOR loop wires another *bit_comparator* according to Bit 2 of Figure 4.18. In Figure 4.19, the last instance of *comp1* is labeled *c3* and produces compare outputs of the most significant comparator bit. The outputs are named *a_gt_b*, *a_eq_b* and *a_lt_b* which are the same as the primary outputs of the *nibble_comparator*. This implies that the outputs of the last *bit_comparator* (Bit 3 in Figure 4.19) are directly connected to the outputs of the *nibble_comparator*.

If it were only for a 4-bit comparator, in which the first and last bits need to be treated individually, the use of generate statement would not be justified. For

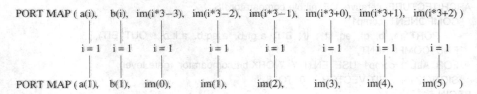

PORT MAP (a(i),   b(i),   im(i*3−3),   im(i*3−2),   im(i*3−1),   im(i*3+0),   im(i*3+1),   im(i*3+2))

i = 1   i = 1   i = 1   i = 1   i = 1   i = 1   i = 1   i = 1

PORT MAP (a(1),   b(1),   im(0),   im(1),   im(2),   im(3),   im(4),   im(5)   )

FIGURE 4.20
Association list of *c* instance of *comp1* within generate statement.

description of larger comparators, however, this method can substantially reduce the number of lines of code. Also, due to the use of generate statement, the description in Figure 4.19 can easily be changed to a description for any size comparator.

The syntax details of the generate statement in Figure 4.19 are shown in Figure 4.21. The statement begins with a label and, using a FOR loop for the generation scheme, it generates two instances of *comp1*. The *c1to2* label can optionally be placed at the end of the generate statement after the END GENERATE. A generate statement is considered to be like any other statement in the architecture statement part. It is a concurrent statement and several generate statements can be nested. Another form of the generate statement uses IF followed by a condition for the generation scheme instead of the FOR loop. Taking advantage of this form and using nested generate statements, a more flexible version of the architecture body of the *nibble_comparator* is developed and shown in Figure 4.22.

In the declarative part of this new description, a constant declaration is used for declaring the constant *n* as a predefined INTEGER type with a value of 4. This constant is used for declaring the size of *im* and for the range specification of the FOR loop generation scheme. The architecture body of Figure 4.22 can be used to describe the operation of any size comparator by declaring an appropriate value for constant *n*. VHDL also provides language constructs that allow declarations to be made based on the size of input vectors. To avoid presenting too many language issues at the same time, we have chosen not to take advantage of such constructs in this example. Such issues are addressed in Chapter 6.

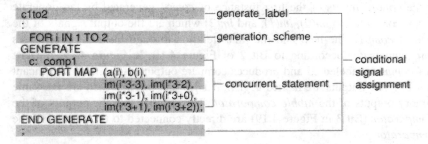

```
c1to2                                — generate_label
:
  FOR i IN 1 TO 2                    — generation_scheme
GENERATE
  c: comp1                                                    — conditional
    PORT MAP  (a(i), b(i),                                       signal
              im(i*3-3), im(i*3-2),    — concurrent_statement —  assignment
              im(i*3-1), im(i*3+0),
              im(i*3+1), im(i*3+2));
END GENERATE
;
```

FIGURE 4.21
Component instantiation statement syntax details.

```
ARCHITECTURE iterative OF nibble_comparator IS
   COMPONENT comp1
      PORT (a, b, gt, eq, lt : IN BIT; a_gt_b, a_eq_b, a_lt_b : OUT BIT);
   END COMPONENT;
   FOR ALL : comp1 USE ENTITY WORK.bit_comparator (gate_level);
   CONSTANT n : INTEGER := 4;
   SIGNAL im : BIT_VECTOR ( 0 TO (n-1)*3-1);
BEGIN
   c_all: FOR i IN 0 TO n-1 GENERATE
      l: IF i = 0 GENERATE
         least: comp1 PORT MAP (a(i), b(i), gt, eq, lt, im(0), im(1), im(2) );
      END GENERATE;
      m: IF i = n-1 GENERATE
         most: comp1 PORT MAP (a(i), b(i),
                              im(i*3-3), im(i*3-2), im(i*3-1), a_gt_b, a_eq_b, a_lt_b);
      END GENERATE;
      r: IF i > 0 AND i < n-1 GENERATE
         rest: comp1 PORT MAP (a(i), b(i), im(i*3-3), im(i*3-2), im(i*3-1),
                              im(i*3+0), im(i*3+1), im(i*3+2) );
      END GENERATE;
   END GENERATE;
END iterative;
```

FIGURE 4.22

A more flexible *iterative* architecture of *nibble_comparator*.

The architecture statement part in Figure 4.22 contains a generate statement which is labeled *c_all*, and which encloses three more generate statements labeled *l*, *m*, and *r*. Respectively, these three statements are used for port map specification of the *least* significant, *most* significant, and the *rest* of the bits of a comparator of size *n*. Since generate statements are concurrent statements, the order in which they appear inside the outer generate statement is unimportant. The comparator in this figure specifies the same wiring as that shown in Figure 4.19. Simulation results of these two versions of the *nibble_comparator* are identical.

4.4 MODELING A TEST BENCH

Testing the *nibble comparator* involves generating a test bench description and using it to provide stimuli to the input ports of the 4-bit comparator. A test bench must contain the circuit under test and should have sources for providing data to its inputs. Containment of the *nibble_comparator* as well as application of waveforms to its inputs can be modeled in VHDL. Development of a test bench for the comparator circuit requires the use of language constructs that are generally not considered to be at the structural level. In order to stay within the scope of this chapter, we develop only a simple test bench that only requires the use of signal assignments and component instantiations.

4.4.1 VHDL Description of A Simple Test Bench

The composition aspect of a test bench for the *nibble_comparator* is shown in Figure 4.23. The test bench does not have external ports. It provides waveforms for the *a* and *b* inputs, and connects the *gt*, *eq*, and *lt* control inputs to *gnd*, *vdd*, and *gnd*, respectively. This programs the comparator such that the *a_gt_b* (or *a_lt_b*) output becomes 1 only when *a* is greater than *b* (or *a* is less than *b*). Had the *gt* control input been connected to *vdd*, its corresponding output would become 1 when *a* is greater than or equal to *b*.

The VHDL description of the test bench is shown in Figure 4.24. The entity declaration specifies the entity name as *test_bench*. The absence of a port clause in this declaration indicates that there are no input or output ports for the test bench. The architecture of *test_bench* is identified as *input_output*, and the *comp4* component is declared in its declarative part. The local ports of this component are the same as the ports of the *nibble_comparator* entity. The configuration specification that follows the component declaration associates the *a1* instance of *comp4* to the *iterative* architecture of the *nibble_comparator*. Since only one instance of *comp4* is used, using *a1* or the ALL keyword in the configuration specification, are equivalent. Local signals *a*, *b*, *eql*, *lss*, *gtr*, *vdd*, and *gnd* are also declared in the declarative part. The *vdd* and *gnd* signals are initialized to '1' and '0', respectively. In VHDL, the := symbol is used for initialization of all objects and the default initial value for the standard BIT type is '0'. The statement part of Figure 4.24 contains three concurrent statements. The statement labeled *a1* is an instantiation of *comp4* and it specifies wiring to the ports of the *nibble_comparator* according to the composition aspect of Figure 4.23. The other two statements are signal assignments specifying waveforms to be applied to the *a* and *b* local signals. Each waveform consists of several elements each specifying a value and a time. After time 0, the four bits of signal *a* will have the "0000" value. The "1111" value is scheduled for these four bits at 500 nanoseconds, and other values follow at 500 ns or 1000 ns intervals. For readability of the test vectors on *a* and *b*, values are assigned to both inputs at each time interval. If the newly assigned values are the same as the values that an input already has, the new values do not cause

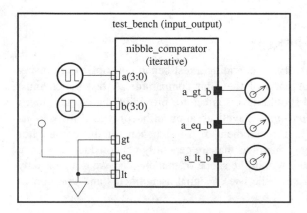

FIGURE 4.23
A test bench for *nibble_comparator*, the composition aspect.

```
ENTITY nibble_comparator_test_bench IS
END nibble_comparator_test_bench ;
--
ARCHITECTURE input_output OF nibble_comparator_test_bench IS
    COMPONENT comp4 PORT (a, b : IN bit_vector (3 DOWNTO 0);
                            gt, eq, lt : IN BIT; a_gt_b, a_eq_b, a_lt_b : OUT BIT);
    END COMPONENT;
    FOR a1 : comp4 USE ENTITY WORK.nibble_comparator(iterative);
    SIGNAL a, b : BIT_VECTOR (3 DOWNTO 0);
    SIGNAL eql, lss, gtr : BIT;
    SIGNAL vdd : BIT := '1';
    SIGNAL gnd : BIT := '0';
BEGIN
    a1: comp4 PORT MAP (a, b, gnd, vdd, gnd, gtr, eql, lss);
    a2:    a <= "0000",           ---- a = b (steady state)
                "1111" AFTER 0500 NS, -- a > b (worst case)
                "1110" AFTER 1500 NS, -- a < b (worst case)
                "1110" AFTER 2500 NS, -- a > b (need bit 1 info)
                "1010" AFTER 3500 NS, -- a < b (need bit 2 info)
                "0000" AFTER 4000 NS, -- a < b (steady state, prepare for next)
                "1111" AFTER 4500 NS, -- a = b (worst case)
                "0000" AFTER 5000 NS, -- a < b (need bit 3 only, best case)
                "0000" AFTER 5500 NS, -- a = b (worst case)
                "1111" AFTER 6000 NS; -- a > b (need bit 3 only, best case)
    a3 : b <= "0000",             ---- a = b (steady state)
                "1110" AFTER 0500 NS, -- a > b (worst case)
                "1111" AFTER 1500 NS, -- a < b (worst case)
                "1100" AFTER 2500 NS, -- a > b (need bit 1 info)
                "1100" AFTER 3500 NS, -- a < b (need bit 2 info)
                "1111" AFTER 4000 NS, -- a < b (steady state, prepare for next)
                "1111" AFTER 4500 NS, -- a = b (worst case)
                "1111" AFTER 5000 NS, -- a < b (need bit 3 only, best case)
                "0000" AFTER 5500 NS, -- a = b (worst case)
                "0000" AFTER 6000 NS; -- a > b (need bit 3 only, best case)
END input_output;
```

FIGURE 4.24
Test bench for *iterative* architecture of *nibble_comparator*.

events on this input. Values on *a* and *b* test the 4-bit comparator for most of its key operations.

The test bench used here is a simple one and we will continue using this style until more convenient data application methods are described in the later chapters. Chapter 6 describes several procedures that simplify development of test benches. Reading data from external files is discussed in Chapters 6 and 8.

Before analyzing simulation results, two points are worth mentioning. First, names used for local signals are *a* and *b* which are the same as those of the *nibble_comparator* input ports. This is done only for clarity, and any other name could be used for the local signals of the test bench. The port map determines the association between *a* of the *nibble_comparator* and the local *a* of the test bench. The second point has to do with the statement labels. While instantiation or generate statements require a label, labeling signal assignments is optional. The *a2* and *a3* labels, therefore, can be removed without violating the VHDL syntax. Where options exist, descriptions should generally be written for better readability.

4.4.2 Simulation

The result of the simulation run in which the *input_output* architecture of the *test_bench* is the top unit is shown in Figure 4.25. Simulation begins at 0 nanoseconds and ends at 6015 ns. This table shows only the times that an event occurs on one of the signals

TIME (NS)	SIGNALS				
	a(3:0)	b(3:0)	gtr	eql	lss
0000	"0000"	"0000"	'0'	'0'	'0'
0005	......	......	...	'1'	...
0500	"1111"	"1110"	...	...	...
0544	......	......	'1'	...	...
0548	......	......	...	'0'	...
1500	"1110"	"1111"	...	...	...
1544	......	......	'0'	...	...
0548	......	......	...	'0'	...
1500	"1110"	"1111"	...	...	...
1544	......	......	'0'	...	...
1548	......	......	...	...	'1'
2500	......	"1100"	...	...	...
2533	......	......	...	...	'0'
2537	......	......	'1'	...	...
3500	"1010"	......	...	...	...
3522	......	......	'0'	...	...
3526	......	......	...	...	'1'
4000	"0000"	"1111"	...	...	...
4500	"1111"	......	...	...	...
4544	......	......	...	'1'	...
4548	......	......	...	...	'0'
5000	"0000"	......	...	...	...
5011	......	......	...	'0'	...
5015	......	......	...	...	'1'
5500	......	"0000"	...	...	...
5544	......	......	...	...	'0'
5548	......	......	...	'1'	...
6000	"1111"	......	...	...	...
6011	......	......	'1'	...	...
6015	......	......	...	'0'	...

FIGURE 4.25
Simulation report for simulating the test bench in Figure 4.24. All events are observed.

being observed. New values of signals are shown when their values change. Dots indicate that the signals hold their previous value.

Five nanoseconds after the start of the simulation the "0000" values on a and b cause the eql output to become 1. For generating a 1 on the a_gt_b or a_lt_b outputs, the longest delay occurs when all but the least significant bits of a and b are the same. This situation occurs at times 500 ns and 1500 ns for the greater-than and less-than cases, respectively. For both cases, it takes 48 ns for the circuit to reach steady state. As seen from the simulation run at times 4500 and 5500 ns, the worst case delay for the a_eq_b output is also 48 ns. The fastest that this circuit can produce results is when its two operands are different only in their most significant bits. This occurs at times 5000 ns and 6000 ns, where the circuit produces appropriate outputs and reaches steady state only 15 ns later. Between the worst case of 48 ns and the best case of 15 ns, other delay values occur when bits 1 or 2 of the two operands are different. The event on the b input at 2500 ns, for example, causes the two operands to differ only in bit 1. The propagation of values, therefore, must occur through bits 1, 2, and 3 of the comparator, causing a 37 ns delay before the circuit reaches steady state at 2537 ns time. At 3500 ns, the event on the a input causes bits 2 of the two operands to be different. The result of this comparison becomes available at 3526 ns after propagating through bits 2 and 3.

The circuit we are simulating has several levels of hierarchical nesting. The *test_bench* contains the *nibble_comparator* which contains four instances of the *bit_comparator*, each of which contains several instances of inverters and NAND gates. Events that occur on the ports of the outermost components pass through the intermediate components, and reach the signal assignments that describe the operation of the innermost components. Evaluation of these assignments may result in generation of events on the output ports of the components that they are enclosed in. Such events will cause other components to evaluate their outputs or pass the events down to subcomponents within them. For an event in the architecture body of *test_bench*, evaluation of statements continues until the circuit reaches steady state. Outputs of a component are evaluated only if an event occurs on at least one of its inputs. Consider for example, the situation at 3500 ns, when bit 2 of a changes. This event causes events on input ports of *bit_comparator* number 2 (see Figure 4.18) which travel downward to eventually cause events on the right hand side of the signal assignments forming the Boolean expressions of the gates (see Figure 4.11) of this comparator bit. After these Boolean expressions are evaluated, they cause events upward to reach the output ports of comparator bit number 2. Since the outputs of this bit are connected to the input ports of bit 3, a similar downward and then upward propagation of events occurs inside this comparator bit. In the simulation of a VHDL description, such events occur, and at each stage only the affected statements are evaluated.

4.5 BINDING ALTERNATIVES

Configuration specifications in the architecture declarative part of a VHDL description associate an instance of a component with a design entity. So far in this chapter, we have used the combinations of *component declarations*, *configuration specifications*, and *component instantiation* in their simplest forms. VHDL, however, allows other forms of configuration specificationsthat make component instantiations significantly more flexible than previously presented.

For the purpose of illustration, consider the clocked, level-sensitive, set-reset latch of Figure 4.26. The structural level VHDL description of this circuit, using the *single_delay* architecture of the *nand2* entity in Section 4.1 for all its NAND gates, is depicted in Figure 4.27. This description uses four instances of *nand2* and generates the output of the latch on the *im3* signal. Since port signal *q* is an output (its mode is OUT), its value cannot be read. This implies that signal *q* cannot be used as input to any component, nor can it be used on the right hand side of a signal assignment. Therefore, we have used the *im3* intermediate signal for connecting the output of the *g3* instance of *nand2* to the input of the *g4* instance of this entity. A signal assignment statement is used to assign values of *im3* to *q*. The output of the latch, therefore, follows the output of the *g3* NAND gate. Because of the signal assignment,

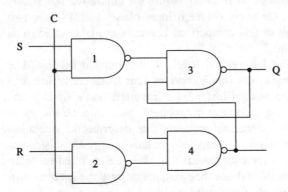

FIGURE 4.26
Logical diagram of a simple latch.

```
┌ENTITY sr_latch IS PORT (s, r, c : IN BIT; q : OUT BIT);
└END sr_latch;
--
┌ARCHITECTURE gate_level OF sr_latch IS
│    COMPONENT n2 PORT (i1, i2: IN BIT; o1: OUT BIT);
│    END COMPONENT;
│    FOR ALL : n2 USE ENTITY WORK.nand2 (single_delay);
│    SIGNAL im1, im2, im3, im4 : BIT;
├BEGIN
│    g1 : n2 PORT MAP (s, c, im1);
│    g2 : n2 PORT MAP (r, c, im2);
│    g3 : n2 PORT MAP (im1, im4, im3);
│    g4 : n2 PORT MAP (im3, im2, im4);
│    q <= im3;
└END gate_level;
```

FIGURE 4.27
VHDL description of set-reset latch.

q lags behind *im3* by one *delta*. Since the *delta* time is not real time, this does not add any additional delay to the output of the circuit.

The above implementation of the latch uses four identical gates with the same exact delays. Besides not representing a realistic design in which no two gates in the same package have exactly the same delay, the simulation of this circuit presents stability problems. Specifically, on initialization or for any other reason, if nodes *im3* and *im4* end up with the same value while the clock is zero, the circuit oscillates. However, this problem can be remedied easily by using a NAND gate with a different delay for the *g3* gate.

For the two-input NAND gate, a different architecture which has a smaller delay than the *single_delay* architecture of Figure 4.4c, is shown in Figure 4.28. The *single_delay* and *fast_single_delay* architectures of *nand2* have the same interface and are two different architecture bodies for the same entity declaration in Figure 4.4b.

The composition aspect and the architecture body of another version of *sr_latch* are shown in Figure 4.29. This design uses the *fast_single_delay* architecture of *nand2* for two of its NAND gates. All but the configuration specifications in the new *gate_level* architecture body of *sr_latch* are the same as the structural description of Figure 4.27. In the architecture body of Figure 4.29b, two configuration specifications are used. The first one binds instances of *n2* that are labeled *g1* and *g3* to the *fast_single_delay* architecture of the *nand2* entity, and the second configuration specification binds *g2* and *g4* instances of *n2* component to the *single_delay* architecture.

Since the *single_delay* architecture in *nand3* of Section 4.1 has a different delay than that of *nand2*, the problem of latch stability can also be solved by using *nand3* instead of the new fast two-input NAND gate. This usage demonstrates still another configuration mechanism in VHDL. A new composition aspect and architecture body for the *sr_latch* are shown in Figure 4.30. This version of the *gate_level* architecture of *sr_latch* uses the *single_delay* architecture of *nand3* for *g2* and *g4* instances of *n2*. The statement part of the architecture body of Figure 4.30b is the same as the original *gate_level* architecture of *sr_latch*. In the declarative part, however, component declarations and configuration specifications are done differently.

A component declaration is used to declare *n2* with *x*, *y*, and *z* local ports. This declaration presents a virtual design entity interface that is used in the component instantiation statements of the statement part. In their port maps, component instantiations specify an association between actual signals, for example, *s*, *c*, and *im2* for *g1*, and *x*, *y*, and *z* local ports.

The first configuration specification in Figure 4.30 binds the *single_delay* architecture of *nand2* to instances of *n2* that are labeled *g1* and *g3*. The port map aspect

```
┌ARCHITECTURE fast_single_delay OF nand2 IS
├BEGIN
│   o1  <= i1 NAND i2 AFTER 3 NS;
└END fast_single_delay;
```

FIGURE 4.28
A faster NAND gate.

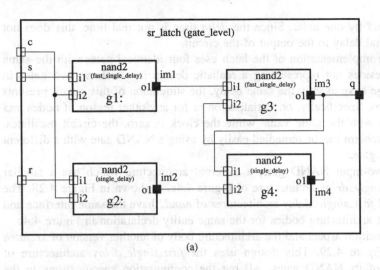

(a)

```
ARCHITECTURE gate_level OF sr_latch IS
   COMPONENT n2 PORT (i1, i2: IN BIT; o1: OUTBIT); END COMPONENT
   FOR g1, g3 : n2 USE ENTITY WORK.nand2 (fast_single_delay);
   FOR g2, g4: n2 USE ENTITY WORK.nand2 (single _delay);
   SIGNAL im1, im2, im3, im4 : BIT;
BEGIN
   g1 : n2 PORT MAP (s, c, im1);
   g2 : n2 PORT MAP (r, c, im2);
   g3 : n2 PORT MAP (im1, im4, im3);
   g4 : n2 PORT MAP (im3, im2, im4);
   q <= im3;
END gate_level;
```

(b)

FIGURE 4.29
SR-latch, using gates with different delays, (a) composition aspect, (b) architecture body.

associates *x*, *y*, and *z* local ports with the formals of the *nand2* entity, namely with *i1*, *i2*, and *o1*. The second configuration specification is used for configuring *g2* and *g4* instances of *n2*. These instances are associated with the *single_delay* architecture of *nand3*, which exists in the WORK library (the current working library). The optional port map associates local ports *x*, *x*, *y*, and *z* with *i1*, *i2*, *i3*, and *o1* of the *nand3* entity. Together, component instantiations, component declarations, and configuration specifications form a two-step association between signals of the statement part and the ports of *nand3*. For the *g2* instance of *n2*, this two-step association is illustrated in Figure 4.31. In the first step, actuals *r*, *c*, and *im2* are associated with *x*, *y*, and *z* local ports. In the second step, *x*, *y*, and *z* local ports are associated with formal ports of *nand3*. The net result is association of *r*, *r*, *c*, and *im2* with *in1*, *in2*, *in3*, and *o1*, respectively.

Configuration specification constructs in the previous section did not include port map specifications. With this language construct, specifying port maps is optional, and if missing, the association defaults to local port names declared within component

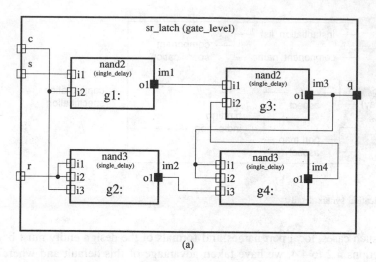

(a)

```
ARCHITECTURE gate_level OF sr_latch IS
    COMPONENT n2 PORT (x, y: IN BIT; z: OUT BIT); END COMPONENT;
    FOR g1, g3 : n2 USE
        ENTITY WORK.nand2 (single_delay) PORT MAP (x, y, z);
    FOR g2, g4: n2 USE
        ENTITY WORK.nand3 (single _delay) PORT MAP (x, x, y, z);
    SIGNAL im1, im2, im3, im4 : BIT;
BEGIN
    g1 : n2 PORT MAP (s, c, im1);
    g2 : n2 PORT MAP (r, c, im2);
    g3 : n2 PORT MAP (im1, im4, im3);
    g4 : n2 PORT MAP (im3, im2, im4);
    q <= im3;
END gate_level;
```

(b)

FIGURE 4.30
SR-latch, using *nand2* and *nand3* gates, (a) composition aspect, (b) architecture body.

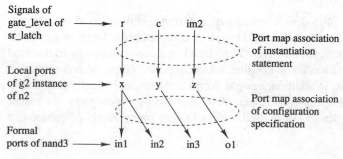

FIGURE 4.31
Two-step association.

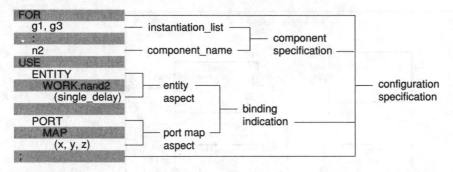

FIGURE 4.32
Configuration specification syntax details.

declarations. In such cases, local port names and formals of the design entity must be the same. In Sections 4.2 to 4.4, we have taken advantage of this default and where components are used, they are declared with the same port clause as that of their corresponding entity declarations.

To study other alternatives in configuration specifications, consider the syntax details of the construct for configuration in the *g1* and *g3* instances in *n2* of Figure 4.30, as shown in Figure 4.32. The instantiation list consists of the *g1* and *g3* labels. Other possibilities for this list are the keywords ALL or OTHERS. Configuration specifications that use OTHERS instead of a list of labels specify that the binding that follows applies to those labels of the component for which a binding has not been specified in the previous configuration specifications. For example, *g2, g4* in the instantiation list of the second configuration specification in Figure 4.30 can be replaced with OTHERS. The binding indication in Figure 4.32 has an entity aspect and a port map aspect. As previously discussed, when the port map aspect is absent, local port associations default to formal ports of the entity in the entity aspect that has the same name.

4.6   SUMMARY

A structural description for a design consists of a wiring specification of its subcomponents. In this chapter, the definition and usage of components in larger designs was illustrated. Generate statements also were introduced as a convenient way to describe repetitive hardware structures and a notation was defined for graphical representation of structural descriptions. In addition, various forms and options in component declarations and configuration specifications were discussed. Using simple gates, the reader should now be able to design larger digital circuits with many levels of component nesting.

REFERENCES

1. Wakerly, J. F., "Digital Design Principles and Practices," Prentice-Hall Inc., Englewood Cliffs, N.J., 1990.

2. "IEEE Standard VHDL Language Reference Manual," IEEE Std. 1076-1987, The Institute of Electrical and Electronic Engineers, Inc., 1988.
3. Lipsett, L., C. Schaefer, and C. Ussery, "VHDL: Hardware Description and Design," Klewer Academic Publishing, Boston, 1988.
4. Armstrong, J. R., "Chip-Level Modeling with VHDL," Prentice-Hall Inc., Englewood Cliffs, N.J., 1988.

PROBLEMS

4.1. Write VHDL descriptions for a two-input NOR gate and an XOR gate. Use single delay models similar to the ones used in Section 4.1. Use 4 ns and 7 ns delays for the NOR and XOR respectively. Use inertial delays.

4.2. The following description uses gates presented in Section 4.1 and the XOR gate in Problem 4.1. At time t_0 the values on the a and b inputs are '1', and the circuit is in steady state. At t_1 the value of a changes to '0'. Draw a detailed timing diagram and analyze the timing behavior of this circuit due to the event on a. Does a glitch appear on the output of the circuit? In any case, keeping the delay at 7 ns, how can you modify the XOR model of the previous problem to reverse the situation? The solution to this problem depends on code developed in Problem 4.1.

```
ENTITY problem_2 IS PORT (a, b : IN BIT; z : OUT BIT);
END problem_2;
    --
ARCHITECTURE glitch OF problem_2 IS
    COMPONENT n2 PORT (i1, i2: IN BIT; o1: OUT BIT); END COMPONENT;
    FOR ALL : n2 USE ENTITY WORK.nand2 (single_delay);
    COMPONENT n3 PORT (i1, i2, i3: IN BIT; o1: OUT BIT);
    END COMPONENT;
    FOR ALL : n3 USE ENTITY WORK.nand3 (single_delay);
    COMPONENT x2 PORT (i1, i2: IN BIT; o1: OUT BIT); END COMPONENT;
    FOR ALL : x2 USE ENTITY WORK.xor2 (single_delay);
    SIGNAL i1, i2 : BIT;
BEGIN
    g1 : n2 PORT MAP (a, b, i1);
    g2 : n3 PORT MAP (a, b, b, i2);
    g3 : x2 PORT MAP (i1, i2, z);
END glitch;
```

4.3. The following description uses gates presented in Section 4.1 and the XOR gate in Problem 4.1. If the a and b inputs are both '1' and a changes to '0', a glitch will appear on the z output of this circuit. Analyze the timing of this circuit showing all events that lead to the glitch on the output. Change the delay of the XOR model to transport delay. Does the behavior of the circuit change when a changes to '0'? After the '1' to '0' transition on input a, find when input b has to change so that the transport delay in the XOR model makes a glitch appear on the z output that would otherwise not be present. The solution to this problem depends on code developed in Problem 4.1.

```
ENTITY problem_3 IS PORT (a, b : IN BIT; z : OUT BIT);
END problem_3;

ARCHITECTURE glitch OF problem_3 IS
   COMPONENT n2 PORT (i1, i2: IN BIT; o1: OUT BIT); END COMPONENT;
   FOR ALL : n2 USE ENTITY WORK.nand2 (single_delay);
   COMPONENT n3 PORT (i1, i2, i3: IN BIT; o1: OUT BIT);
   END COMPONENT;
   FOR ALL : n3 USE ENTITY WORK.nand3 (single_delay);
   COMPONENT x2 PORT (i1, i2: IN BIT; o1: OUT BIT); END COMPONENT;
   FOR ALL : x2 USE ENTITY WORK.xor2 (single_delay);
   SIGNAL i1, i2 : BIT;
BEGIN
   g1 : n2 PORT MAP (a, b, i1);
   g2 : n3 PORT MAP (i1, b, b, i2);
   g3 : x2 PORT MAP (a, i2, z);
END glitch;
```

4.4. Write a test bench for the *bit_comparator* of Section 4.2. Find the worst case delay for this circuit. Why is this delay not equal to one-fourth of the worst case delay of the *nibble_comparator*? Analyze the timings of both circuits and answer this question.

4.5. Write a description of a Full Adder using the gates of Section 4.1 and XOR gate of Problem 4.1. What is the worst case delay for this circuit? The solution to this problem depends on code developed in Problem 4.1.

4.6. Write a VHDL description for a package of four NAND gates, using the *single_delay* model for each of the gates. Use the following entity declaration.

```
ENTITY four_nand2
   IS PORT (
               i1_a, i2_a, i1_b, i2_b,
               i1_c, i2_c, i1_d, i2_d : IN BIT;
               o1_a, o1_b, o1_c, o1_d : OUT BIT);
END four_nand2;
```

4.7. Use the *four_nand2* package of Problem 4.6 to describe a clocked SR latch. The solution to this problem depends on code developed in Problem 4.6.

4.8. The following description (Fig. P4.8) uses the *four_nand2* package of Problem 4.6. What Boolean function is this description implementing? The solution to this problem depends on code developed in Problem 4.6.

4.9. Use only two *four_nand2* packages of Problem 4.6 to describe a BCD prime number detector. The output is to be 1 when the input BCD number is a prime number. The number 1 is prime a number. The solution to this problem depends on code developed in Problem 4.6.

4.10. Using only XOR gate models of Problem 4.1, write a VHDL description for an 8-bit even/odd parity checker. The circuit has an 8-bit input vector and two outputs. The *odd* output is to become 1 when the number of 1s on the input in odd. The *even* output is the opposite of the *odd* output. Use generate statement(s). The solution to this problem depends on code developed in Problem 4.1.

```
ENTITY unknown IS PORT (a, b, c, d : IN BIT; z : OUT BIT);
END unknown;
--
ARCHITECTURE mystry OF unknown IS
    COMPONENT chip PORT (
            i1_a, i2_a, i1_b, i2_b,
            i1_c, i2_c, i1_d, i2_d : IN BIT;
            o1_a, o1_b, o1_c, o1_d : OUT BIT);
    END COMPONENT;
    FOR ALL : chip USE ENTITY WORK.four_nand2 (packing);
    SIGNAL i1, i2, i3 : BIT;
BEGIN
    g1 : chip PORT MAP (a, b, c, d, i1, i2, i3, i3, i1, i2, i3, z);
END mystry;
```

FIGURE P4.8

4.11. Describe an 8-bit adder using the Full Adder description in Problem 4.5. Take advantage of the generate statement. Write a test bench for this adder, and find the worst case delay. The solution to this problem depends on code developed in Problems 4.1 and 4.5.

4.12. If the inputs to the adder in Problem 4.11 are 2's complement numbers, an overflow may occur when adding two positive or two negative numbers. Use this adder in a design of an 8-bit adder with an overflow indication output. Do not modify the description of the original adder; rather, use it in a top level design that instantiates the adder of Problem 4.11 as well as gates of the overflow detection hardware. The solution to this problem depends on code developed in Problem 4.1, 4.5 and 4.11.

4.13. Using only *nand2* and *nand3* descriptions, write the VHDL description for a D-latch. Start with the description in Figure 4.30. Arrange the gates such that the circuit does not oscillate.

4.14. Use the generate statement to describe an 8-bit latch using the D-latch in Problem 4.13. Your *eight_latch* circuit should have a single clock, an 8-bit d input and an 8-bit q output. The solution to this problem depends on code developed in Problem 4.13.

4.15. Write VHDL description for a master-slave JK flip-flop. Use the *fast_single_delay* model of *nand2* to avoid oscillation. In addition to this gate, you can use all gates in Section 4.1.

4.16. Use the JK flip-flop in Problem 4.15 to design a 1-bit modular binary counter. Based on this module, build a 4-bit binary ripple up-counter. Design this counter such that it can easily be cascaded for building larger counters. The solution to this problem depends on code developed in Problem 4.15.

4.17. In the following description, the configuration specification is missing. Assume that the only component that you have available is the *nand3 (single_delay)* model. Write appropriate configurations such that this description implements function $f(a,b,c,d,e)$. See Fig. P4.17.

$$f (a, b, c, d, e) = a \cdot b + c \cdot d' + e$$

```
ENTITY function_f IS PORT (a, b, c, d, e : IN BIT; f : OUT BIT);
END function_f;
ARCHITECTURE configurable OF function_f IS
    COMPONENT n1 PORT (w: IN BIT; z: OUT BIT); END COMPONENT;
    COMPONENT n2 PORT (w, x: IN BIT; z: OUT BIT); END COMPONENT;
    COMPONENT n3 PORT (w, x, y: IN BIT; z: OUT BIT); END COMPONENT;
    ...
    SIGNAL i1, i2, i3, i4 : BIT;
BEGIN
    g0 : n1 PORT MAP (d, i1);
    g1 : n1 PORT MAP (e, i2);
    g2 : n2 PORT MAP (i1, c, i3);
    g3 : n2 PORT MAP (a, b, i4);
    g4 : n3 PORT MAP (i2, i3, i4, f);
END configurable;
```

FIGURE P4.17

# CHAPTER 5

DESIGN
ORGANIZATION
AND
PARAMETERIZATION

In a digital system design environment, functional design of a digital system is often done independently of the physical characteristics or the technology in which the design is being implemented. Hardware designers who use 74xx00 series components and designers who use pretested layouts of CMOS cells share many top level design stages. There is still more sharing when hardware designers use various series in the same logic family. Based on technology, power consumption, speed, and temperature range, components are categorized into various libraries from which designers choose specific components.

For supporting such design environments, VHDL provides language constructs for parametrizing and customizing designs, and for definition and usage of design libraries. These constructs enable a designer to generate a functional design independent of the specific technology and customize this generic design at a later stage. Specifically, *library*, *use clause*, *package*, and *configuration declarations* of VHDL are used for grouping or categorizing various components into design libraries and for customizing designs to use components in these libraries. By use of *generic* parameters, VHDL also allows a design to be parametrized such that the specific timing, number of bits, or even the wiring is determined when the design is configured.

Another language issue that can influence the organization of a design is the use of subprograms. As in any high level language, VHDL allows the definition and usage of *functions* and *procedures*. In addition to the important hardware implications of subprograms (which will be discussed in Chapters 6 and 7) these language constructs greatly improve readability and organization of a hardware description.

This chapter discusses subprograms, library packages, design paramterization, and design configuration. We demonstrate how utility functions, procedures, type definitions, or predesigned components can be grouped through utilization of the VHDL package construct. In addition, we will discuss the use of such packages in a design and the use of generic parameters. We also will explain post design specifications of physical characteristics, such as timing, and describe various methods that can be used to configure a design for a specific library of component or physical parameters.

5.1 DEFINITION AND USAGE OF SUBPROGRAMS

In many programming languages, subprograms are used to simplify coding, modularity, and readability of descriptions. VHDL uses subprograms for these applications as well as for those that are more specific to hardware descriptions. Regardless of the application, behavioral software-like constructs are allowed in subprograms. As stated earlier, VHDL allows two forms of subprograms, *functions* and *procedures*. Functions return value and cannot alter the values of their parameters. A procedure, on the other hand, is used as a statement, and can alter the values of its parameters.

5.1.1 A Functional Single Bit Comparator

The *bit_comparator* in Chapter 4 was designed at the gate level, to specify the interconnection of all its gates using component instantiations. A simpler description can be developed by using the Boolean equations (Equations 4.1a to 4.1c) of the three outputs of this circuit.

Equation 5.1a $\qquad$ a_gt_b = a . gt + b' . gt + a . b'

Equation 5.1b $\qquad$ a_eq_b = a . b . eq + a' . b' . eq

Equation 5.1c $\qquad$ a_lt_b = b . lt + a' . lt + b . a'

As evident from the equations of *a_gt_b* and *a_lt_b*, rearranged and repeated here for reference (and also from the schematic diagrams in Figure 4.9), one expression used with different signal names can be made to express both of these outputs. The *a_eq_b* output, however, requires a separate expression. Figure 5.1 shows a VHDL description that is based on these equations and one that takes advantage of the similarities between the *a_gt_b* and the *a_lt_b* outputs.

For the *bit_comparator* entity declaration in Figure 4.10b, the architecture body of Figure 5.1 is an alternative to the *gate_level* architecture in Figure 4.12. The declarative part of the *functional* architecture of the *bit_comparator* contains the body of two function subprograms. The first function returns a BIT value which is a function of *w*, *x*, and *gl* (greater or less). The *a_gt_b* and *a_lt_b* outputs use this function. The other function in the declarative part of the architecture of Figure 5.1 returns

```
ARCHITECTURE functional OF bit_comparator IS
    FUNCTION fgl (w, x, gl : BIT) RETURN BIT IS
    BEGIN
        RETURN  (w AND gl) OR (NOT x  AND  gl) OR (w  AND  NOT x);
    END fgl;
    FUNCTION feq (w, x, eq : BIT) RETURN BIT IS
    BEGIN
        RETURN  (w AND x AND eq) OR (NOT w  AND  NOT x  AND  eq);
    END feq;
BEGIN
    a_gt_b <= fgl (a, b, gt) AFTER 12 NS;
    a_eq_b <= feq (a, b, eq) AFTER 12 NS;
    a_lt_b <= fgl (b, a, lt) AFTER 12 NS;
END functional;
```

FIGURE 5.1
A functional *bit_comparator*, using the same function for two outputs.

the BIT value for the expression for the *a_eq_b* output. In the statement part of this architecture, three function calls are used for the three outputs of the *bit_comparator*. When a function is called, it returns its calculated value in zero time. Because of this, and in order for this description to better represent the actual circuit, the values returned by the functions are delayed 12 nanoseconds before they are assigned to the appropriate outputs of the circuit. This delay value is a rough estimate of the worst case propagation delay of each *bit_comparator*, and is based on the 48 ns worst case delay of the *nibble_comparator* discussed in Chapter 4.

The syntax details of the *fgl* function are shown in Figure 5.2. The subprogram specification includes the name of the function, its formal parameters, and the type of the value returned by the function. The subprogram statement part of this description contains a single sequential statement, namely, the return statement. This statement causes the value evaluated by the expression that follows it to be used as the return value of the *fgl* function.

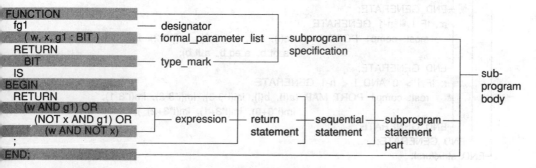

FIGURE 5.2
Syntax details of a subprogram body, a general view.

5.1.2   Using Procedures in a Test Bench

The main purpose of the test bench developed for the 4-bit comparator in Chapter 4 was to apply data to the 4-bit input of the *nibble_comparator*. We will discuss a procedure that can significantly simplify this process, and use another version of the *nibble_comparator* of Chapter 4 to demonstrate it. An architecture for a *nibble_comparator* that uses the *functional* architecture of the *bit_comparator* in Figure 5.1 is shown in Figure 5.3. This architecture is identified as *structural* and is an alternative to the *iterative* architecture of the *nibble_comparator* for the entity declaration of Figure 4.17. The configuration specification in the declarative part of this architecture associates all instances of the *bit_comparator* to the *functional* architecture of this unit.

The *procedural* version of the architecture of the *nibble_comparator_test_bench* shown in Figure 5.4 uses the *apply_data* procedure defined in the declarative part of this architecture to apply 4-bit data to the *a* and *b* inputs of the *structural* architecture in the *nibble_comparator*. The declarative part of this architectur begins with a type declaration declaring *integers* as a thirteen element array of INTEGER. This is a simple form of an array declaration which we use in our examples until the topic of type declaration is described in Chapter 6. The body of the *apply_data* subprogram follows the *integers* type declaration. The rest of the declarative part of the *procedural* architecture of the *nibble_comparator* contains a component declaration, configuration specification, and declaration of intermediate signals.

```
┌ARCHITECTURE structural OF nibble_comparator IS
│  ┌COMPONENT comp1
│  │   PORT (a, b, gt, eq, lt : IN BIT; a_gt_b, a_eq_b, a_lt_b : OUT BIT);
│  └END COMPONENT;
│   FOR ALL : comp1 USE ENTITY WORK.bit_comparator (functional);
│   CONSTANT n : INTEGER := 4;
│   SIGNAL im : BIT_VECTOR ( 0 TO (n-1)*3-1);
├BEGIN
│   ┌c_all: FOR i IN 0 TO n-1 GENERATE
│   │   ┌l: IF i = 0 GENERATE
│   │   │    least: comp1 PORT MAP (a(i), b(i), gt, eq, lt, im(0), im(1), im(2) );
│   │   └END GENERATE;
│   │   ┌m: IF i = n-1 GENERATE
│   │   │    most: comp1 PORT MAP (a(i), b(i), im(i*3-3), im(i*3-2), im(i*3-1),
│   │   │                            a_gt_b, a_eq_b, a_lt_b);
│   │   └END GENERATE;
│   │   ┌r: IF i > 0 AND i < n-1 GENERATE
│   │   │    rest: comp1 PORT MAP (a(i), b(i), im(i*3-3), im(i*3-2), im(i*3-1),
│   │   │                            im(i*3+0), im(i*3+1), im(i*3+2) );
│   │   └END GENERATE;
│   └END GENERATE;
└END structural;
```

FIGURE 5.3
Structural architecture of a *nibble_comparator*.

```
ARCHITECTURE procedural OF nibble_comparator_test_bench IS
    TYPE integers IS ARRAY (0 TO 12) OF INTEGER;
    PROCEDURE apply_data
        (SIGNAL target : OUT BIT_VECTOR (3 DOWNTO 0);
            CONSTANT values : IN integers;
                CONSTANT period : IN TIME)
        IS
        VARIABLE j : INTEGER;
        VARIABLE tmp : INTEGER := 0;
        VARIABLE buf : BIT_VECTOR (3 DOWNTO 0);
    BEGIN
        FOR i IN 0 TO 12 LOOP
            tmp := values (i);
            j := 0;
            WHILE j <= 3 LOOP
                IF (tmp MOD 2  =  1) THEN
                    buf (j) := '1';
                ELSE buf (j) := '0';
                END IF;
                tmp := tmp / 2;
                j := j + 1;
            END LOOP;
            target <= TRANSPORT buf AFTER i * period;
        END LOOP;
    END apply_data;
    COMPONENT comp4 PORT
        (a, b : IN BIT_VECTOR (3 DOWNTO 0);  gt, eq, lt : IN BIT;
        a_gt_b, a_eq_b, a_lt_b : OUT BIT);
    END COMPONENT;
    FOR a1 : comp4 USE ENTITY WORK.nibble_comparator(structural);
    SIGNAL a, b : BIT_VECTOR (3 DOWNTO 0);
    SIGNAL eql, lss, gtr : BIT;
    SIGNAL vdd : BIT := '1';
    SIGNAL gnd : BIT := '0';
BEGIN
    a1: comp4 PORT MAP (a, b, gnd, vdd, gnd, gtr, eql, lss);
    apply_data (a, 0&15&15&14&14&14&14&10&00&15&00&00&15, 500 NS);
    apply_data (b, 0&14&14&15&15&12&12&12&15&15&15&00&00, 500 NS);
END procedural;
```

FIGURE 5.4
Procedural architecture of *nibble_comparator*.

The *apply_data* procedure uses thirteen integers passed to it via an array of integers (*values*). After converting these integers to 4-bit binary numbers, they are assigned to the *target* signal. The values are applied at the time intervals passed to this procedure via the *period* parameter. The body of *apply_data* uses two loops; the outer loop reads one of the thirteen input integers and the inner loop converts that integer to a 4-bit binary number. This binary number is then assigned to the *target* output of the procedure. Transport delay is used for this assignment so that new transactions are appended to the existing ones. Each time through the loop a new transaction with a time value that is 500 ns more than the time value of the previous transaction is placed on the driver of *target*. The only way to insure that new transactions do not cause the removal of the older transactions when they have different values is to use transport delay. As shown in the table in Figure 3.31, new transactions with different values override the old ones if the delay is inertial.

In the procedural architecture of the *nibble_comparator_test_bench* the statement part consists of a component instantiation statement and two procedure calls to the *apply_data* subprogram. These two calls generate 4-bit data on the *a* and *b* signals every 500 ns. The formal parameters of the subprogram are the *target* signal, thirteen concatenated integers, and a time *period*. Concatenation of integers forms a thirteen element array of integers which is passed to the second formal parameter of the *apply_data* procedure (*values*). As demonstrated in this example, types and classes of formal and actual parameters must match. For example, the class and type of *target* are SIGNAL and BIT_VECTOR, respectively, which match with class and type declared for *a* or *b*. CONSTANT is the default class for a subprogram input and VARIABLE is the default for a subprogram output. A procedure call in the statement part of an architecture is a concurrent statement, and if it does not have any input signals, it is called only once at the beginning of the simulation run.

The simulation report of the *procedural* architecture of the *nibble_comparator_test_bench* (Figure 5.5) indicates that the data applied to the 4-bit inputs of the *nibble_comparator* by the use of the *apply_data* procedure are identical to the data assigned to the inputs of the comparator in the *input_output* architecture of the test bench in Figure 4.24, whose simulation report is shown in Figure 4.25.

Comparing the two simulation reports (Figures 5.5 and 4.25) indicates a difference in the timing of events occurring on the *grt*, *eql*, and *lss* outputs of the two versions of the *nibble_comparator*s. This is due to the cumulative rough delay estimate used with the Boolean functions in the *functional* architecture of the *bit_comparator* in contrast to the gate instantiations used in the *gate_level* architecture of this unit. It must be noted that in terms of the timing of events that occur in the actual hardware, the simulation report in Figure 4.25 is a more precise representation than that in Figure 5.5. The price paid for the convenient description of the *bit_comparator* in Figure 5.1 is the loss of precision in the simulation results.

5.1.3 Language Aspects of Subprograms

The general structure of subprograms was discussed in relation to the *fgl* function in Figure 5.2. The *apply_data* procedure is a larger example, and it contains other language features of subprograms. As shown in Figure 5.6, the procedure begins with a subprogram specification. This part specifies the formal parameter list, which is syntactically similar to an interface list. The first parameter in this list indicates that *target* is a 4-bit signal which can only be written into (its mode is OUT). The mode of the next two parameters is IN, and they are constants of *integers* and TIME types,

TIME (ns)	SIGNALS a(3:0)	b(3:0)	gtr	eql	lss
0000	"0000"	"0000"	'0'	'0'	'0'
0048	......	......	....	'1'	....
0500	"1111"	"1110"	....	......	...
0548	......	......	'1'	'0'	...
1500	"1110"	"1111"	....	...	...
1548	......	......	'0'	...	'1'
2500	......	"1100"	....	...	...
2536	......	......	'1'	...	'1'
3500	"1010"	......	....	...	...
3524	......	......	'0'	...	'1'
4000	"0000"	"1111"	...	...	...
4500	"1111"	......	...	...	...
4548	......	......	'1'	'0'	...
5000	"0000"	......	...	'0'	'1'
5012	......	......	...	'0'	'1'
5500	......	"0000"	...	...	...
5548	......	......	'1'	'0'	...
6000	"1111"	......	...	...	...
6012	......	......	'1'	'0'	...

FIGURE 5.5
Simulation report resulting from the *procedural* test bench. All events are observed.

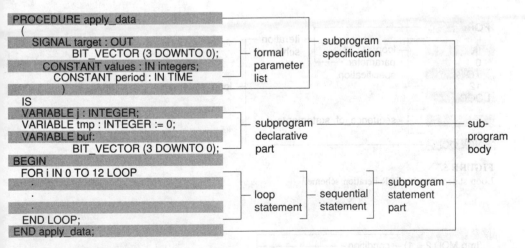

FIGURE 5.6
Details of a subprogram body.

respectively. If the class of an object, for example, SIGNAL or CONSTANT, for the parameters of *apply_data* is not specified, CONSTANT is assumed for the IN mode parameters and VARIABLE is assumed for the OUT mode parameters.

In the subprogram declaration in Figure 5.6, two INTEGER type variables and one BIT_VECTOR type are declared. Variables are initialized to their initial values each time a subprogram is called. If initial values are not specified, default initial values which depend on the type of an object are used. In this case *tmp* is initialized to 0, *j* is initialized to the smallest integer, and *buf* is initialized to the "0000" default. The body of the *apply_data* subprogram consists of a single loop statement. Details of this statement are shown in Figure 5.7.

The iteration scheme used with this loop statement causes the statements within the loop to be executed thirteen times, while *i* changes from 0 to 12. The value of this identifier can be used within the loop and it need not be declared. Referring to Figure 5.4, two variable assignments, a loop statement, and a signal assignment constitute the statement section of the outer loop statement. The inner loop statement uses the WHILE keyword and a condition for its iteration scheme. Within this loop, an if statement, which is detailed in Figure 5.8, assigns '0' or '1' to bits of *buf* according to the divisibility of *tmp* by 2. Each time through the loop, *tmp* is divided by 2 and *j* is incremented to keep the count of the evaluated bits of *buf*. As specified in the condition of the loop, the inner loop terminates when the variable *j* becomes greater than 3. At this time, the *buf* 4-bit vector contains the correct binary representation of the *i*th integer of the *values* array. This 4-bit binary is assigned to the *target* signal after a delay of $i * period$ (*i* times the *period*). The end of the *apply_data* procedure is indicated by the end statement which is followed by the procedure designator. Using this designator at the end of the procedure is optional.

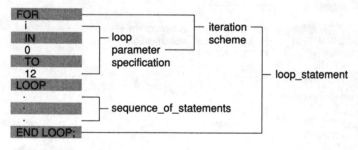

FIGURE 5.7
Loop statement with FOR iteration scheme.

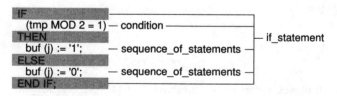

FIGURE 5.8
Details of the if statement of *apply_data* procedure.

The if statement in Figure 5.8, which is contained in the inner loop of *apply_data*, is itself a sequential statement. Sequential statements contained in this statement are simple assignment statements.

5.1.4 Utility Procedures

The *apply_data* procedure is a useful procedure for assigning binary data to multi-bit signals. Other useful procedures include those for converting binary data to integer data, and vice versa. Figure 5.9 shows one such procedure.

The *bin2int* procedure converts a binary vector of any length to its integer equivalent. The procedure assumes that the least significant bit of the input vector is bit number 0. Parameters *bin* and *int* contain the input binary and output integer, respectively. The iteration scheme in the main loop of this procedure indicates that the range of identifier *i* is in *bin*'RANGE. RANGE is an attribute and the value of *bin*'RANGE (read as *bin* **tick** RANGE) is the range of the actual array parameter that is passed to the *bin* formal parameter in the *bin2int* procedure. If this procedure is called to convert an 8-bit binary number whose right hand side least significant bit is bit 0, the range of *i* becomes 7 DOWNTO 0. Attributes and their applications are discussed in Chapter 6. For now, in addition to RANGE, the LENGTH attribute will also be used in this chapter. The result of the LENGTH attribute is the length of the array to which it is applied. For example, the range of *i* in the above procedure could alternatively be specified as (*bin*'LENGTH $-$ 1) DOWNTO 0.

Another utility procedure, this one for converting integers to binary, is shown in Figure 5.10. This subprogram performs the same function as that of the inner loop of the *apply_data* procedure, except that the *int2bin* procedure can be used for data of any size. The *int2bin* procedure places the least significant bit of the resulting binary number in position 0 of the *bin* output and it assumes that the actual parameter associated with *bin* contains bit 0. Since *int* is input, it cannot be written into. The *tmp* variable, therefore, is declared to save the input integer as it is successively divided by two.

```
PROCEDURE bin2int (bin : IN BIT_VECTOR; int : OUT INTEGER) IS
   VARIABLE result: INTEGER;
BEGIN
   result := 0;
   FOR i IN bin'RANGE LOOP
      IF bin(i) = '1' THEN
         result := result + 2**i;
      END IF;
   END LOOP;
   int := result;
END bin2int;
```

FIGURE 5.9
Procedure for binary to integer conversion.

```
PROCEDURE int2bin (int : IN INTEGER;  bin : OUT BIT_VECTOR) IS
    VARIABLE tmp : INTEGER;
BEGIN
    tmp := int;
    FOR i IN 0 TO (bin'LENGTH - 1) LOOP
        IF (tmp MOD 2  =  1) THEN
            bin (i) := '1';
        ELSE bin (i) := '0';
        END IF;
        tmp := tmp / 2;
    END LOOP;
END int2bin;
```

FIGURE 5.10
Procedure for integer to binary conversion.

```
PROCEDURE apply_data (
    SIGNAL target : OUT BIT_VECTOR (3 DOWNTO 0);
    CONSTANT values : IN integers;  CONSTANT period : IN TIME)
        IS
    VARIABLE buf : BIT_VECTOR (3 DOWNTO 0);
BEGIN
    FOR i IN 0 TO 12 LOOP
        int2bin (values(i), buf);
        target <= TRANSPORT buf AFTER i * period;
    END LOOP;
END apply_data;
```

FIGURE 5.11
Another version of *apply_data* procedure. This version takes advantage of the *int2bin* procedure.

Figure 5.11 shows another example for subprograms and their calling procedure. This is a version for the *apply_data* procedure which takes advantage of the *int2bin* utility procedure of Figure 5.10. This procedure could be written to take any number of integer inputs instead of the fixed thirteen. We defer adding this flexibility until type definitions and attributes are discussed in detail in Chapter 6.

5.2   PACKAGING PARTS AND UTILITIES

In the parts library of a hardware designer, gates or components are grouped according to their technology, physical characteristics, cost, complexity, or simply according to their availability. A designer chooses a certain group of components based on specific design requirements. In VHDL, packages can be used for this grouping of components. VHDL package constructs can also be used for packaging commonly used user defined types and subprograms.

5.2.1 Packaging Components

Gate level architectures of the *bit_comparator* and *sr_latch* in Chapter 4 (Figures 4.12 and 4.27, respectively) include declaration of the individual components that are used for their implementation. Alternatively, component declarations can be packaged and made available to all the architectures that use them. A package declaration containing declarations of *n1*, *n2*, and *n3* is shown in Figure 5.12. Bracketed between the heading of this statement and the END keyword, a package declaration includes components and other declarations as they would appear in the declarative part of an architecture.

Figure 5.13 shows a new version of the *gate_level* architecture of *bit_comparator* that takes advantage of the *simple_gates* package in Figure 5.12. This package has been made visible to the architecture of the *bit_comparator* by placing a use clause before its body.

The use clause specifies the name of the library, the name of the package, and the declarations that are to become visible. The ALL keyword makes all of the declarations in this package visible to the *gate_level* architecture of the *bit_comparator*. Instead of using this keyword, individual declarations can be listed, as depicted in the statement in Figure 5.14.

5.2.2 Packaging Subprograms

In order for various designs to share several subprograms, a package declaration must contain a declaration of the subprograms and the body of the subprograms must reside in a corresponding package body. A package declaration defines the interface of a package and includes the declarations that are to be visible from outside the package. A package body contains declarations that are local to it as well as bodies of locally or externally used subprograms. In the heading of a package body, the keyword BODY follows the PACKAGE keyword. Figures 5.15a and 5.15b show a package declaration and a package body (both named *basic_utilities*) in which the declaration and body of functions *fgl* and *feq* and the procedures *bin2int*, *int2bin*, and *apply_data* presented in Section 5.1, are included.

As discussed in the previous section, the *functional* architecture of the *bit_comparator* and the *procedural* architecture of the *nibble_comparator_test_bench* use these

```
PACKAGE simple_gates IS
    COMPONENT n1 PORT (i1: IN BIT; o1: OUT BIT); END COMPONENT;
    COMPONENT n2 PORT (i1, i2: IN BIT; o1: OUT BIT); END COMPONENT;
    COMPONENT
        n3 PORT (i1, i2, i3: IN BIT; o1: OUT BIT);
    END COMPONENT;
END simple_gates;
```

FIGURE 5.12
A package declaration containing component declarations of simple gates.

```
USE  WORK.simple_gates.ALL;
ARCHITECTURE  gate_level  OF  bit_comparator  IS
    FOR  ALL : n1  USE  ENTITY  WORK.inv  (single_delay);
    FOR  ALL : n2  USE  ENTITY  WORK.nand2  (single_delay);
    FOR  ALL : n3  USE  ENTITY  WORK.nand3  (single_delay);
    -- Intermediate  signals
    SIGNAL im1,im2, im3, im4, im5, im6, im7, im8, im9, im10 : BIT;
BEGIN
    -- a_gt_b  output
    g0 : n1  PORT  MAP  (a, im1);
    g1 : n1  PORT  MAP  (b, im2);
    g2 : n2  PORT  MAP  (a, im2, im3);
    g3 : n2  PORT  MAP  (a, gt, im4);
    g4 : n2  PORT  MAP  (im2, gt, im5);
    g5 : n3  PORT  MAP  (im3, im4, im5, a_gt_b);
    -- a_eq_b  output
    g6 : n3  PORT  MAP  (im1, im2, eq, im6);
    g7 : n3  PORT  MAP  (a, b, eq, im7);
    g8 : n2  PORT  MAP  (im6, im7, a_eq_b);
    -- a_lt_b  output
    g9 : n2  PORT  MAP  (im1, b, im8);
    g10 : n2  PORT  MAP  (im1, lt, im9);
    g11 : n2  PORT  MAP  (b, lt, im10);
    g12 : n3  PORT  MAP  (im8, im9, im10, a_lt_b);
END gate_level;
```

FIGURE 5.13
Using package of simple gates in *gate_level* of *bit_comparator*.

```
USE
  WORK.simple_gates.n1,
  WORK.simple_gates.n2,
  WORK.simple_gates.n3;
 .
-- n1, n2 and n3 component declarations are visible
 .
```

FIGURE 5.14
An alternative application of the use clause.

subprograms. New versions of these architectures, which take advantage of the *basic_utilities* package, are shown in Figures 5.16 and 5.17, respectively.

All declarations in the *basic_utilities* package declaration (Figure 5.15a) become visible to the architectures in Figures 5.16 and 5.17 through application of the use clause. Since the necessary subprogram bodies are included in the *basic_utilities* package body (Figure 5.15b), they need not be included in the declarative parts of the architectures where they are used.

```
┌─PACKAGE basic_utilities IS
│    TYPE integers IS ARRAY (0 TO 12) OF INTEGER;
│    FUNCTION fgl (w, x, gl : BIT) RETURN BIT;
│    FUNCTION feq (w, x, eq : BIT) RETURN BIT;
│    PROCEDURE bin2int (bin : IN BIT_VECTOR; int : OUT INTEGER);
│    PROCEDURE int2bin (int : IN INTEGER;  bin : OUT BIT_VECTOR);
│    PROCEDURE apply_data (
│        SIGNAL target : OUT BIT_VECTOR (3 DOWNTO 0);
│        CONSTANT values : IN integers;  CONSTANT period : IN TIME);
└─END basic_utilities;
```

FIGURE 5.15a
The *basic_utilities* package declaration.

A subprogram declaration only needs to be included in a package declaration if the subprogram, whose body is contained in the package body, is to be used from outside of the package. Functions and procedures that are used solely within the package containing their bodies do not have to be declared. This also applies to type declarations in that a type declared in the package declaration becomes visible to all descriptions that use that package, while a type declaration in a package body is only visible to that body.

5.3 DESIGN PARAMETRIZATION

Component models can be parametrized to better utilize gate or component models and to make general models usable in different design environments. The specific behavior of these models is dependent on the parameters that are determined by the design entities that use them. VHDL generic parameters can be used for this purpose. For example, a generic parameter can be used for timing and delay of a generic gate model. When this gate is used in a specific design environment, its generic parameters are determined. Usage of generic parameters and passing of values to these parameters is done in much the same way as it is with ports. The syntax of constructs related to ports and generics are similar, except that the generic clause and generic map aspect constructs use the keyword GENERIC instead of PORT. In general, generics are a means of communicating nonhardware and nonsignal information between designs.

In order to illustrate the usage of generics, we will revise the comparator example presented in the previous chapter, this time using gate models that have generic timing parameters, as shown in Figure 5.18.

An inverter, a two-input NAND gate, and a three-input NAND gate are shown in this figure. The entity declarations for these gates include a generic clause and a port clause, as shown in Figure 5.19. The generic clause in each of the gates in Figure 5.18 consists of a generic interface list which contains interface constant declarations for *tplh* and *tphl*. For the inverter, these generic parameters have default values of 5 ns and 3 ns, respectively.

Default values will be used for *tplh* and *tphl* if these generics are not specified by any other method. The port clause in Figure 5.19 contains an interface list which

```
PACKAGE BODY basic_utilities IS
    FUNCTION fgl (w, x, gl : BIT) RETURN BIT IS
    BEGIN
        RETURN  (w AND gl) OR (NOT x  AND  gl) OR (w  AND  NOT x);
    END fgl;
    FUNCTION feq (w, x, eq : BIT) RETURN BIT IS
    BEGIN
        RETURN  (w AND x AND eq) OR (NOT w  AND  NOT x  AND  eq);
    END feq;
    PROCEDURE bin2int (bin : IN BIT_VECTOR; int : OUT INTEGER) IS
        VARIABLE result: INTEGER;
    BEGIN
        result := 0;
        FOR i IN bin'RANGE LOOP
            IF bin(i) = '1' THEN
                result := result + 2**i;
            END IF;
        END LOOP;
        int := result;
    END bin2int;
    PROCEDURE int2bin (int : IN INTEGER;  bin : OUT BIT_VECTOR) IS
        VARIABLE tmp : INTEGER;
        VARIABLE buf : BIT_VECTOR (bin'RANGE);
    BEGIN
        tmp := int;
        FOR i IN 0 TO (bin'LENGTH - 1) LOOP
            IF (tmp MOD 2  =  1) THEN
                bin (i) := '1';
            ELSE bin (i) := '0';
            END IF;
            tmp := tmp / 2;
        END LOOP;
    END int2bin;
    PROCEDURE apply_data (
        SIGNAL target : OUT BIT_VECTOR (3 DOWNTO 0);
        CONSTANT values : IN integers;  CONSTANT period : IN TIME)
            IS
        VARIABLE buf : BIT_VECTOR (3 DOWNTO 0);
    BEGIN
        FOR i IN 0 TO 12 LOOP
            int2bin (values(i), buf);
            target <= TRANSPORT buf AFTER i * period;
        END LOOP;
    END apply_data;
END basic_utilities;
```

FIGURE 5.15b
The *basic_utilities* package body.

```
USE WORK.basic_utilities.ALL;
ARCHITECTURE functional OF bit_comparator IS
BEGIN
    a_gt_b <= fgl (a, b, gt) AFTER 12 NS;
    a_eq_b <= feq (a, b, eq) AFTER 12 NS;
    a_lt_b <= fgl (b, a, lt) AFTER 12 NS;
END functional;
```

FIGURE 5.16
Using functions of the *basic_utilities* package.

```
USE WORK.basic_utilities.ALL;
ARCHITECTURE procedural OF nibble_comparator_test_bench IS
    COMPONENT comp4 PORT (
        a, b : IN bit_vector (3 DOWNTO 0); gt, eq, lt : IN BIT;
        a_gt_b, a_eq_b, a_lt_b : OUT BIT);
    END COMPONENT;
    FOR a1 : comp4 USE ENTITY WORK.nibble_comparator(structural);
    SIGNAL a, b : BIT_VECTOR (3 DOWNTO 0);
    SIGNAL eql, lss, gtr : BIT;
    SIGNAL vdd : BIT := '1';
    SIGNAL gnd : BIT := '0';
BEGIN
    a1: comp4 PORT MAP (a, b, gnd, vdd, gnd, gtr, eql, lss);
    apply_data (a, 0&15&15&14&14&14&14&10&00&15&00&00&15, 500 NS);
    apply_data (b, 0&14&14&15&15&12&12&12&15&15&15&00&00, 500 NS);
END procedural;
```

FIGURE 5.17
Using procedures of the *basic_utilities* package.

consists of declarations for the input and the output of the inverter. Figures 4.2 and 4.5 illustrate the syntax structure of the port clause construct. Note that the port interface lists for *int_t*, *nand2_t*, and *nand3_t* in Figure 5.18 are identical to those for *inv*, *nand2*, and *nand3* in Chapter 4.

In the architecture bodies in Figure 5.18, appropriate logical expressions are assigned to the outputs of the gates after a delay value that is the average of low-to-high and high-to-low propagation delays. Note that for the default case, for example, *tplh* = 5 ns and *tphl* = 3 ns for the inverter, the time expression of the signal assignments evaluate delay values that are equal to those of similar gates in Chapter 4 (*inv* in Chapter 4 has a 4 ns delay).

Figure 5.20 shows interface aspects for the gates in Figure 5.18. As shown here, line arrows signify generics. This notation becomes part of the aspect notation that we introduced in Chapter 4. The composition aspects of the units using these gates must show how values are associated with these generics.

```
ENTITY inv_t IS
    GENERIC (tplh : TIME := 5 NS; tphl : TIME := 3 NS);
    PORT (i1 : IN BIT; o1 : OUT BIT);
END inv_t;
--
ARCHITECTURE average_delay OF inv_t IS
BEGIN
    o1 <= NOT i1 AFTER   (tplh + tphl) / 2;
END average_delay;


ENTITY nand2_t IS
    GENERIC (tplh : TIME := 6 NS; tphl : TIME := 4 NS);
    PORT (i1, i2 : IN BIT; o1 : OUT BIT);
END nand2_t;
--
ARCHITECTURE average_delay OF nand2_t IS
BEGIN
    o1 <= i1 NAND i2 AFTER   (tplh + tphl) / 2;
END average_delay;


ENTITY nand3_t IS
    GENERIC (tplh : TIME := 7 NS; tphl : TIME := 5 NS);
    PORT (i1, i2, i3 : IN BIT; o1 : OUT BIT);
END nand3_t;
--
ARCHITECTURE average_delay OF nand3_t IS
BEGIN
    o1 <= NOT ( i1 AND i2 AND i3 ) AFTER   (tplh + tphl) / 2;
END average_delay;
```

FIGURE 5.18
Parametrized gate models.

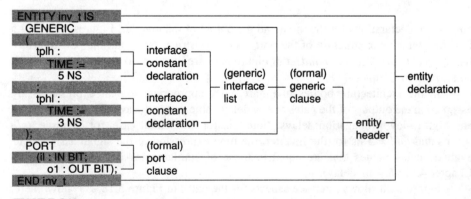

FIGURE 5.19
Details of the entity declaration of inverter with generics.

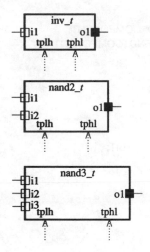

FIGURE 5.20
Interface aspects of *inv_t*, *nand2_t*, and *nand3_t*.

5.3.1 Using Default Values

Figure 5.21 shows an architecture for a *bit_comparator* that is identified as the *default_delay* and uses the gates shown in Figure 5.18. Except for the configuration specifications, this description is the same as the *gate_level* architecture of the *bit_comparator* in Chapter 4 (see Figure 4.12). Configuration specifications in Figure 5.21 associate instances of *n1*, *n2*, and *n3* components with the *average_delay* architectures for *inv_t*, *nand2_t*, and *nand3_t*.

Since no reference is made in the *default_delay* architecture of the *bit_comparator* to the generics of its components and no association is specified for the formal generic parameters of these components, the default values of generics determine the timing behavior of *average_delay* architecture for *inv_t*, *nand2_t*, and *nand3_t*. This can only be done because the entity declaration in these units includes default values for their generic parameters.

5.3.2 Using Fixed Values

Constants or other generics may be associated with the formal generic parameters of a component. This is done in much the same way that signals are associated with the formal ports of components. Figure 5.22 shows another architecture for the *bit_comparator*. In the declarative part of this architecture, declaration of *n1*, *n2*, and *n3* components includes local generic clauses as well as local port clauses. Each instantiation of any of these components in the statement part of the *fixed_delay* architecture of the *bit_comparator* contains a generic map aspect and a port map aspect.

The values used in the association list of the generic map aspects shown in Figure 5.23 are associated with the formal generics of *inv_t*, *nand2_t*, and *nand3_t*. These values are used in place of the default values in the generic interface list in the entity declaration for these entities. Since the component declarations do not include

```
ARCHITECTURE default_delay OF bit_comparator IS
    COMPONENT n1 PORT (i1: IN BIT; o1: OUT BIT); END COMPONENT;
    COMPONENT n2 PORT (i1, i2: IN BIT; o1: OUT BIT); END COMPONENT;
    COMPONENT n3 PORT (i1, i2, i3: IN BIT; o1: OUT BIT);
    END COMPONENT;
    FOR ALL : n1 USE ENTITY WORK.inv_t (average_delay);
    FOR ALL : n2 USE ENTITY WORK.nand2_t (average_delay);
    FOR ALL : n3 USE ENTITY WORK.nand3_t (average_delay);
-- Intermediate signals
    SIGNAL im1,im2, im3, im4, im5, im6, im7, im8, im9, im10 : BIT;
BEGIN
-- a_gt_b output
    g0 : n1 PORT MAP (a, im1);
    g1 : n1 PORT MAP (b, im2);
    g2 : n2 PORT MAP (a, im2, im3);
    g3 : n2 PORT MAP (a, gt, im4);
    g4 : n2 PORT MAP (im2, gt, im5);
    g5 : n3 PORT MAP (im3, im4, im5, a_gt_b);
-- a_eq_b output
    g6 : n3 PORT MAP (im1, im2, eq, im6);
    g7 : n3 PORT MAP (a, b, eq, im7);
    g8 : n2 PORT MAP (im6, im7, a_eq_b);
-- a_lt_b output
    g9 : n2 PORT MAP (im1, b, im8);
    g10 : n2 PORT MAP (im1, lt, im9);
    g11 : n2 PORT MAP (b, lt, im10);
    g12 : n3 PORT MAP (im8, im9, im10, a_lt_b);
END default_delay;
```

FIGURE 5.21
Using default values for the generics of logic gates.

default values to be associated with the formal generics of these components, inclusion of generic map aspects with instantiations of these components is required.

5.3.3   Passing Generic Parameters

Still another way to specify generic parameters is to pass values to them through other generics. In the more formal VHDL terminology, this can be stated: associating generics of components with the generic parameters of the architectures that instantiate those components. A version of the single bit comparator (*bit_comparator_t*) with generic parameters, whose entity declaration is shown in Figure 5.24a, illustrates this method.

This declaration contains a generic interface list that has six formal parameters of type TIME. As shown in Figure 5.24b, the *passed_delay* architecture of *bit_comparator_t*, uses generic map clauses to associate generic parameters in this entity with those in *inv_t*, *nand2_t*, and *nand3_t*. Six generics of the *bit_comparator_t*

```
ARCHITECTURE fixed_delay OF bit_comparator IS
    COMPONENT n1
        GENERIC (tplh, tphl : TIME);   PORT (i1: IN BIT; o1: OUT BIT);
    END COMPONENT;
    COMPONENT n2
        GENERIC (tplh, tphl : TIME);   PORT (i1, i2: IN BIT; o1: OUT BIT);
    END COMPONENT;
    COMPONENT n3
        GENERIC (tplh, tphl : TIME);   PORT (i1, i2, i3: IN BIT; o1: OUT BIT);
    END COMPONENT;
    FOR ALL : n1 USE ENTITY WORK.inv_t (average_delay);
    FOR ALL : n2 USE ENTITY WORK.nand2_t (average_delay);
    FOR ALL : n3 USE ENTITY WORK.nand3_t (average_delay);
-- Intermediate signals
    SIGNAL im1,im2, im3, im4, im5, im6, im7, im8, im9, im10 : BIT;
BEGIN
-- a_gt_b output
    g0 : n1 GENERIC MAP (2 NS, 4 NS) PORT MAP (a, im1);
    g1 : n1 GENERIC MAP (2 NS, 4 NS) PORT MAP (b, im2);
    g2 : n2 GENERIC MAP (3 NS, 5 NS) PORT MAP (a, im2, im3);
    g3 : n2 GENERIC MAP (3 NS, 5 NS) PORT MAP (a, gt, im4);
    g4 : n2 GENERIC MAP (3 NS, 5 NS) PORT MAP (im2, gt, im5);
    g5 : n3 GENERIC MAP (4 NS, 6 NS) PORT MAP (im3, im4, im5, a_gt_b);
-- a_eq_b output
    g6 : n3 GENERIC MAP (4 NS, 6 NS) PORT MAP (im1, im2, eq, im6);
    g7 : n3 GENERIC MAP (4 NS, 6 NS) PORT MAP (a, b, eq, im7);
    g8 : n2 GENERIC MAP (3 NS, 5 NS) PORT MAP (im6, im7, a_eq_b);
-- a_lt_b output
    g9 : n2 GENERIC MAP (3 NS, 5 NS) PORT MAP (im1, b, im8);
    g10 : n2 GENERIC MAP (3 NS, 5 NS) PORT MAP (im1, lt, im9);
    g11 : n2 GENERIC MAP (3 NS, 5 NS) PORT MAP (b, lt, im10);
    g12 : n3 GENERIC MAP (4 NS, 6 NS) PORT MAP (im8, im9, im10, a_lt_b);
END fixed_delay;
```

FIGURE 5.22
Associating fixed values with the generics of logic gates.

constitute three pairs of low-to-high and high-to-low propagation delay values that are used for calculating timing parameters of the three components in this entity. Unlike ports that can be read or written into, depending on their mode, generics can only be read.

To clarify the architectural description presented in Figure 5.24 and in order to keep up with our interface and composition aspect notations, we have shown the composition aspect of the *passed_delay* architecture of the *bit_comparator_t* in Figure 5.25. This figure shows graphically the passing of timing parameters for the *bit_comparator_t* to those of its individual components.

The entity declaration of the *bit_comparator* (Figure 5.24a) does not specify default values for its six generic parameters. This implies that the body using this entity

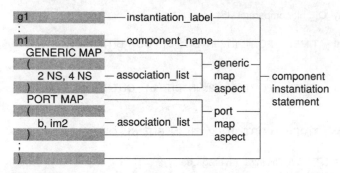

FIGURE 5.23
Component instantiation statement with generic map aspect.

must specify these parameters by declaration or by mapping. The *iterative* architecture of the *nibble_comparator* in Figure 4.19 is rewritten as shown in Figure 5.26 to use the latter version of the single bit comparator.

The *comp1* component is declared with default values for its timing parameters. Because of the absence of generic map aspects from the instantiations of *comp1* in the statement part of the *iterative* architecture of the *nibble_comparator*, the default generic values will be used by the *bit_comparator_t*. The *passed_delay* architecture of the *bit_comparator_t*, in turn, passes these values to *inv_t*, *nand2_t*, and *nand3_t*, which then overwrite the default values in the entity declaration of these units.

For a component whose declaration contains local generics (for example, declaration of *comp1* in the *iterative* architecture of the *nibble_comparator* in Figure 5.26), the absence of a generic map aspect from its instantiation (see, for example, *c0*, *c*, or *c3* instantiations of *comp1*) implies that all such generics are *open*. Instead of complete exclusion of the generic map aspect, it is possible to use it with component instantiations, using the OPEN keyword for the generics whose default values are to be used. For example, the *c0* instantiation of *comp1* can be written as shown in Figure 5.27.

Here, default values, as specified in the declaration of *comp1*, are associated with *tplh1*, *tplh2*, *tphl1*, and *tphl2*. For the *tplh3* and *tphl3* parameters, however, 8 ns and 10 ns will be used, respectively. Another method for associating OPEN with certain generics or ports is to use named association instead of positional association. In this case, values are specified only for the generics whose default values are not to be used. Figure 5.28 shows another possibility for *c0* instantiation of *comp1*. This instantiation, which is equivalent to that shown in Figure 5.27, uses named association for the *tplh3* and *tphl3* parameters. All other generic parameters are assumed OPEN.

As noted, OPEN and named association can be used in generic map aspects as well as port maps. Using OPEN in the association list of a port map aspect implies an open wire (signal) rather than a default value.

This section presented several alternatives for associating constants with generic parameters. The omission of both declaring and mapping of generics, as in the *default_delay* architecture of the *bit_comparator*, is best suited for cases where all in

```
ENTITY bit_comparator_t IS
    GENERIC (tplh1, tplh2, tplh3, tphl1, tphl2, tphl3 : TIME);
    PORT (a, b,                        -- data inputs
          gt,                          -- previous greater than
          eq,                          -- previous equal
          lt : IN BIT;                 -- previous less than
          a_gt_b,                      -- greater
          a_eq_b,                      -- equal
          a_lt_b : OUT BIT);           -- less than
END bit_comparator_t;
```
(a)

```
ARCHITECTURE passed_delay OF bit_comparator_t IS
    COMPONENT n1
        GENERIC (tplh, tphl : TIME);   PORT (i1: IN BIT; o1: OUT BIT);
    END COMPONENT;
    COMPONENT n2
        GENERIC (tplh, tphl : TIME);   PORT (i1, i2: IN BIT; o1: OUT BIT);
    END COMPONENT;
    COMPONENT n3
        GENERIC (tplh, tphl : TIME);   PORT (i1, i2, i3: IN BIT; o1: OUT BIT);
    END COMPONENT;
    FOR ALL : n1 USE ENTITY WORK.inv_t (average_delay);
    FOR ALL : n2 USE ENTITY WORK.nand2_t (average_delay);
    FOR ALL : n3 USE ENTITY WORK.nand3_t (average_delay);
-- Intermediate signals
    SIGNAL im1,im2, im3, im4, im5, im6, im7, im8, im9, im10 : BIT;
BEGIN
-- a_gt_b output
    g0 : n1 GENERIC MAP (tplh1, tphl1) PORT MAP (a, im1);
    g1 : n1 GENERIC MAP (tplh1, tphl1) PORT MAP (b, im2);
    g2 : n2 GENERIC MAP (tplh2, tphl2) PORT MAP (a, im2, im3);
    g3 : n2 GENERIC MAP (tplh2, tphl2) PORT MAP (a, gt, im4);
    g4 : n2 GENERIC MAP (tplh2, tphl2) PORT MAP (im2, gt, im5);
    g5 : n3 GENERIC MAP (tplh3, tphl3) PORT MAP (im3, im4, im5, a_gt_b);
-- a_eq_b output
    g6 : n3 GENERIC MAP (tplh3, tphl3) PORT MAP (im1, im2, eq, im6);
    g7 : n3 GENERIC MAP (tplh3, tphl3) PORT MAP (a, b, eq, im7);
    g8 : n2 GENERIC MAP (tplh2, tphl2) PORT MAP (im6, im7, a_eq_b);
-- a_lt_b output
    g9 : n2 GENERIC MAP (tplh2, tphl2) PORT MAP (im1, b, im8);
    g10 : n2 GENERIC MAP (tplh2, tphl2) PORT MAP (im1, lt, im9);
    g11 : n2 GENERIC MAP (tplh2, tphl2) PORT MAP (b, lt, im10);
    g12 : n3 GENERIC MAP (tplh3, tphl3) PORT MAP (im8, im9, im10, a_lt_b);
END passed_delay;
```
(b)

FIGURE 5.24

A bit comparator with timing parameters (a) entity declaration, (b) passing generics of bit comparator to its components.

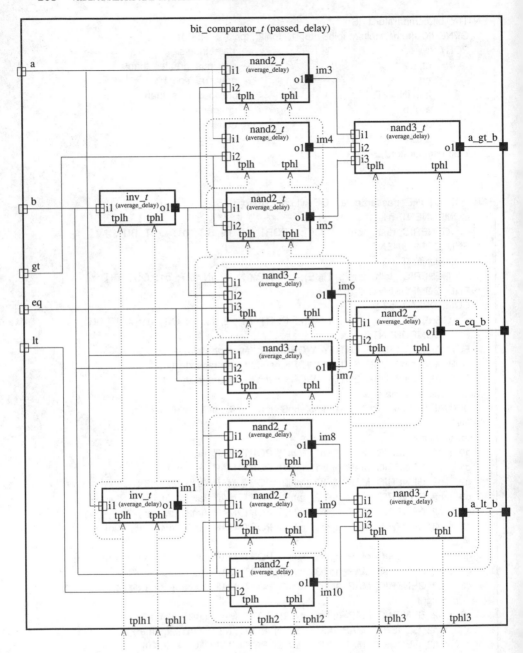

FIGURE 5.25
Composition aspect of *bit_comparator_t*. Dotted lines with arrows indicate generics.

```
┌ARCHITECTURE iterative OF nibble_comparator IS
│   COMPONENT comp1
│      GENERIC(tplh1 : TIME := 2 NS; tplh2 : TIME := 3 NS; tplh3 : TIME := 4 NS;
│               tphl1 : TIME := 4 NS; tphl2 : TIME := 5 NS; tphl3 : TIME := 6 NS);
│      PORT (a, b, gt, eq, lt : IN BIT; a_gt_b, a_eq_b, a_lt_b : OUT BIT);
│   END COMPONENT;
│   FOR ALL : comp1 USE ENTITY WORK.bit_comparator_t (passed_delay);
│   SIGNAL im : BIT_VECTOR ( 0 TO 8);
├BEGIN
│   c0: comp1 PORT MAP (a(0), b(0), gt, eq, lt, im(0), im(1), im(2));
│   c1to2: FOR i IN 1 TO 2 GENERATE
│      c: comp1 PORT MAP (a(i), b(i), im(i*3-3), im(i*3-2), im(i*3-1),
│                          im(i*3+0), im(i*3+1), im(i*3+2) );
│   END GENERATE;
│   c3: comp1 PORT MAP (a(3), b(3), im(6), im(7), im(8),
│                          a_gt_b, a_eq_b, a_lt_b);
└END iterative;
```

FIGURE 5.26
Passing default values of local generics to the generics of *bit_comparator_t*.

```
┌ARCHITECTURE iterative OF nibble_comparator IS
│   ...
├BEGIN
│   c0: comp1
│          GENERIC MAP (OPEN, OPEN, 8 NS, OPEN, OPEN, 10 NS)
│          PORT MAP (a(0), b(0), gt, eq, lt, im(0), im(1), im(2));
│   ...
└END iterative;
```

FIGURE 5.27
Associating constants with some of generics of *bit_comparator_t*, and using defaults for others.

```
┌ARCHITECTURE iterative OF nibble_comparator IS
│   ...
├BEGIN
│   c0: comp1
│          GENERIC MAP (tplh3 => 8 NS, tphl3 => 10 NS)
│          PORT MAP (a(0), b(0), gt, eq, lt, im(0), im(1), im(2));
│   ...
└END iterative;
```

FIGURE 5.28
Using named association in the generic association list of *comp1*.

stantiations of a component use the same delay values. The ability to associate values with individual instances of a component, as in the *fixed_delay* architecture of the *bit_comparator*, enables the modeler to account for loading and environmental effects. For example, if an inverter has a fan-out of 2, the values associated with its timing generics can be specified as twice that of an inverter that drives only one gate. In general, using default values in entity declarations or in component declarations is helpful and it alleviates the need to specify the same values for all instances of a component. If needed, these default values can easily be overwritten in the generic map aspects of component instantiations.

We have presented examples for specifying gate delay values in order to demonstrate the use of generics. Other uses of these parameters include passing fan-in and fan-outs, load resistance or capacitance, and even number of bits or size of a hardware structure. For example, size of a general model for a shift register or a memory array can be customized by using appropriate values for their generic parameters.

5.4 DESIGN CONFIGURATION

Binding a component instantiation to an actual component, as described in Section 5 of Chapter 4, does not have to be done in the architecture that uses this component. This binding can be deferred until later and accomplished by a configuration declaration. Therefore, it is possible to generate a generic design and specify the details of timing or a specific component library at a later stage. This way, a generic design can be tested for various logic families or a single test bench can be used to test various versions of the same component. By use of configurations, trying different descriptions of a component in an upper level design can easily be done even at the deepest level of nesting.

5.4.1   A General Purpose Test Bench

Several versions of the *bit_comparator* and *nibble_comparator* have been developed in this and the previous chapter. The *structural* architecture of the *nibble_comparator* in Figure 5.3 and the *iterative* architecture of the *nibble_comparator* in Figure 5.26 are two units that are very different in their underlaying structures. The former wires four *bit_comparator*s that are described by Boolean equations (shown in Figure 5.1), while the latter uses the *bit_comparator*s in Figure 5.24 that are made of gate level components. In spite of their differences, the *procedural* test bench in Figure 5.17 can be made to serve as a test bench for both units. This test bench takes advantage of the *basic_utilities* in Figure 5.15 for the generation of test vectors, and in its architecture body, the association of the *a1* instance of *comp4* with the *structural* architecture of the *nibble_comparator* is done by a configuration specification. Removing this specification converts our test bench to a fairly general purpose tester for different *nibble_comparator*s.

As shown in Figure 5.29, this general purpose test bench is identified as *customizable*. For testing different designs, modifying the test bench and replacing the old test bench with the modified version in the design library can be avoided by developing multiple configuration declarations for the same test bench.

The configuration declaration in Figure 5.30 configures the test bench in Figure 5.29 for testing the *structural* architecture of the *nibble_comparator*. This configuration declaration is identified as *functional*, and it associates the *a1* instance of

```
 | USE  WORK.basic_utilities.ALL;
┌─ARCHITECTURE  customizable  OF  nibble_comparator_test_bench  IS
 |   ┌─COMPONENT  comp4  PORT  (
 |   |     a, b : IN bit_vector (3 DOWNTO 0); gt, eq, lt : IN BIT;
 |   |     a_gt_b, a_eq_b, a_lt_b : OUT BIT);
 |   └─END COMPONENT;
 |     SIGNAL a, b : BIT_VECTOR (3 DOWNTO 0);
 |     SIGNAL eql, lss, gtr : BIT;
 |     SIGNAL vdd : BIT := '1';
 |     SIGNAL gnd : BIT := '0';
┌─BEGIN
 |     a1: comp4 PORT MAP (a, b, gnd, vdd, gnd, gtr, eql, lss);
 |     apply_data (a, 0&15&15&14&14&14&14&10&00&15&00&00&15, 500 NS);
 |     apply_data (b, 0&14&14&15&15&12&12&12&15&15&15&00&00, 500 NS);
└─END customizable;
```

FIGURE 5.29
A customizable test bench.

```
 | USE  WORK.ALL;
┌─CONFIGURATION  functional  OF  nibble_comparator_test_bench  IS
 |   ┌─FOR  customizable
 |   |    ┌─FOR  a1 : comp4
1   2   3     USE ENTITY WORK.nibble_comparator(structural);
 |   |    └─END FOR;
 |   └─END FOR;
└─END functional;
```

FIGURE 5.30
Configuring *customizable* for testing *structural* architecture of *nibble_comparator*.

comp4 with the *structural* architecture of the *nibble_comparator*. There are three levels of nestings in this description, and they are numbered accordingly. Note that these numbers are for illustration only and are not part of the code. The first level is the bracketing of the configuration declaration. The second level is for obtaining visibility into the *customizable* architecture of the *nibble_comparator_test_bench*, and the third level constitutes the binding of *a1* to an actual component. As indicated in the composition aspect of the *functional* configuration of *nibble_comparator_test_bench*, shown in Figure 5.31, a configuration declaration is placed on top of the entity for which component bindings need to be specified. As shown in our aspect notations, we use rounded rectangles to signify configuration declarations and the configuration name is placed in this rectangle. In Figure 5.31 the arrow with a triangular head that points to the *comp4* component illustrates that the binding for this component is specified by the configuration declaration from which the arrow originates.

In order to test the *iterative* architecture in Figure 5.26, the configuration declaration in Figure 5.32 must be used to configure our general purpose test bench

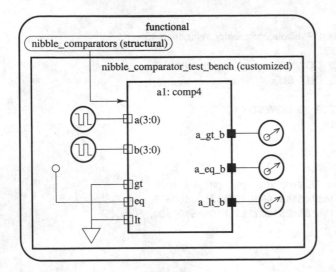

FIGURE 5.31
Composition aspect for *functional* configuration declaration, configuring *customizable* test bench.

```
USE  WORK.ALL;
CONFIGURATION  average_delay  OF  nibble_comparator_test_bench  IS
    FOR  customizable
        FOR  a1 :  comp4
            USE  ENTITY  WORK.nibble_comparator(iterative);
        END  FOR;
    END  FOR;
END  average_delay;
```

FIGURE 5.32
Configuring *customizable* for testing *iterative* architecture of *nibble_comparator*.

(*customizable*) to use this unit. This declaration is identified as *average_delay* and it binds the *a1* label of *comp4* to the *iterative* architecture of the *nibble_comparator*.

As in Figure 5.30, the configuration declaration in Figure 5.32 is preceded by a use statement, which makes the entity to be configured visible. The details in the rest of this figure are shown in Figure 5.33.

The heading in this statement specifies an identifier for the configuration declaration and the entity to be configured. This is followed by a block configuration within which the scope is limited to the statement part of the *customizable* architecture of the *nibble_comparator_test_bench*. In this block configuration, binding for all visible components can be specified by individual component configurations. Since our test bench contains only one component, namely the *nibble_comparator*, a single component configuration is needed. Component configurations begin with the FOR keyword followed by component specifications which were discussed in Chapter 4, and shown in Figure 4.32. Following the USE keyword, a binding indication is used to associate the *a1* instance of *comp4* to the *iterative* architecture of the *nibble_comparator*. As shown in this figure, there is only a minor difference between the syntax of component configurations and the configuration specifications discussed in Chapter 4. The former

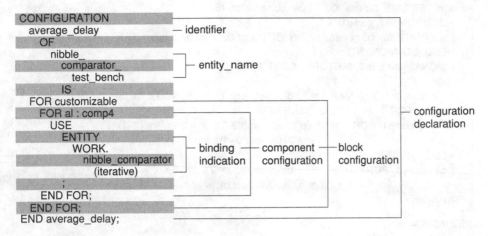

FIGURE 5.33
Details of configuration declaration.

requires END FOR, while the latter, which is used in declarative part of architectures, does not. Component configurations, however, offer more flexibility and many levels of component nestings can be specified within these constructs.

5.4.2   Configuring Nested Components

Initially, a designer may use components based on their functionality rather than timings or specific technology. These designs may be used in upper level designs, which may cause them to be buried under several levels of design hierarchy. Configuration declarations can be extended beyond configuring components of the immediate architectures and be used to configure several levels of component nestings.

Consider, for example, the three *bit_comparator*s that were developed in Section 5.3. These *bit_comparator*s (*default_delay*, *fixed_delay*, and *passed_delay* in Figures 5.21, 5.22, and 5.24, respectively) can be wired into a 4-bit comparator and tested using a single *nibble_comparator* description and a test bench.

The *flexible* architecture of the *nibble_comparator*, shown in Figure 5.34, wires four single bit comparators. Because of the absence of the configuration specification in the declarative part of this architecture, instances of *comp1* are not associated with actual components. Using this *nibble_comparator* and the *customizable* architecture of *nibble_comparator_test_bench* (Figure 5.29), three *bit_comparator*s presented in previous sections can be wired and tested. For this purpose, a configuration declaration must be placed on top of the customizable test bench to 1) associate instances of *comp4* with the *flexible* architecture of *nibble_comparator*, and 2) associate all *comp1* instances of the *flexible nibble_comparator* with the specific *bit_comparator* we are using to construct the 4-bit comparator.

Figure 5.35 shows the composition aspect for a configuration declaration for wiring and testing the *default_delay* architecture of the *bit_comparator*. As shown by the triangular arrows, binding for the *nibble_comparator* and for the instances of the

```
ARCHITECTURE flexible OF nibble_comparator IS
    COMPONENT comp1
        PORT (a, b, gt, eq, lt : IN BIT; a_gt_b, a_eq_b, a_lt_b : OUT BIT);
    END COMPONENT;
    SIGNAL im : BIT_VECTOR ( 0 TO 8);
BEGIN
    c0: comp1 PORT MAP (a(0), b(0), gt, eq, lt, im(0), im(1), im(2));
    c1to2: FOR i IN 1 TO 2 GENERATE
        c: comp1 PORT MAP (a(i), b(i), im(i*3-3), im(i*3-2), im(i*3-1),
                           im(i*3+0), im(i*3+1), im(i*3+2) );
    END GENERATE;
    c3: comp1 PORT MAP (a(3), b(3), im(6), im(7), im(8),
                        a_gt_b, a_eq_b, a_lt_b);
END flexible;
```

FIGURE 5.34
A general purpose *nibble_comparator*.

bit_comparator are specified by this configuration. The VHDL code in Figure 5.36 corresponds to this composition aspect. This description is the *default_bit_level* configuration for the *nibble_comparator_test_bench* and it can be read as follows:

>   The *default_bit_level* configuration declaration is for the *customizable* architecture of the *nibble_comparator_test_bench*. Inside this architecture, the *a1* instance of *comp4* is associated with the *flexible* architecture of the *nibble_comparator*. Within the *flexible* architecture of the *nibble_comparator*, the *c0* and *c3* instances of *comp1* are associated with the *default_delay* architecture of the *bit_comparator*. Also within this *flexible* block, inside the *c1to2* generate statement, *c* instances of *comp1* are associated with the *default_delay* architecture of the *bit_comparator*.

At each level of nesting, block configurations are needed to obtain the visibility of a component, and component configurations are needed to associate instances of components with actual components.

Figure 5.37 shows the configuration of the test bench for associating instances of *comp1* with the *fixed_delay* architecture of the *bit_comparator*. Except for the identifiers, this description is identical to that in Figure 5.36.

The third configuration declaration we will discuss is one for wiring and testing the *passed_delay* architecture of the *bit_comparator_t* entity. Since this entity includes generic parameters and the *flexible* architecture of the *nibble_comparator* does not provide default generic values in its declaration of *comp1*, any binding to this entity must include specification of its generic parameters. Figure 5.38 shows the composition aspect of a test bench for testing a *nibble_comparator* consisting of four such bit comparators.

This figure illustrates bindings of *comp4* and *comp1* to appropriate components, as well as association of values with the generics of the single bit comparators. The bit comparators used here use six generic parameters and are represented by the composition aspect in Figure 5.25. The VHDL description corresponding to the composition

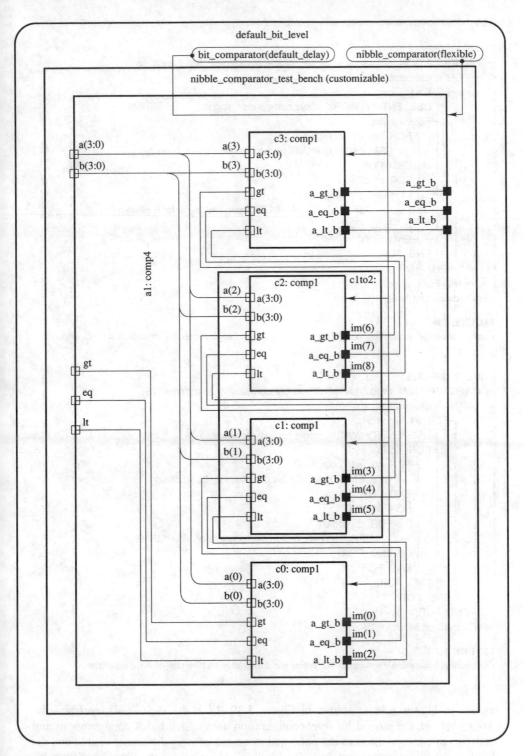

FIGURE 5.35
Composition aspect for configuring *customizable* test bench for testing *default_delay bit_comparator*.

115

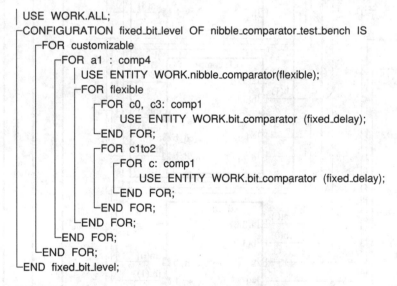

```
USE WORK.ALL;
CONFIGURATION default_bit_level OF nibble_comparator_test_bench IS
    FOR customizable
        FOR a1 : comp4
            USE ENTITY WORK.nibble_comparator(flexible);
            FOR flexible
                FOR c0, c3: comp1
                    USE ENTITY WORK.bit_comparator (default_delay);
                END FOR;
                FOR c1to2
                    FOR c: comp1
                        USE ENTITY WORK.bit_comparator (default_delay);
                    END FOR;
                END FOR;
            END FOR;
        END FOR;
    END FOR;
END default_bit_level;
```

FIGURE 5.36
Configuration declaration for configuring *customizable* test bench for testing *default_delay bit_comparator*.

```
USE WORK.ALL;
CONFIGURATION fixed_bit_level OF nibble_comparator_test_bench IS
    FOR customizable
        FOR a1 : comp4
            USE ENTITY WORK.nibble_comparator(flexible);
            FOR flexible
                FOR c0, c3: comp1
                    USE ENTITY WORK.bit_comparator (fixed_delay);
                END FOR;
                FOR c1to2
                    FOR c: comp1
                        USE ENTITY WORK.bit_comparator (fixed_delay);
                    END FOR;
                END FOR;
            END FOR;
        END FOR;
    END FOR;
END fixed_bit_level;
```

FIGURE 5.37
Configuring *customizable* test bench for testing the *fixed_delay* architecture of *bit_comparator*.

aspect in Figure 5.38 is shown in Figure 5.39. Like the *default_bit_level* and the *fixed_bit_level*, the *passed_bit_level* configuration uses nested block configurations and component configurations to the point that instances of *comp1* become visible and the binding for them can be specified. The binding indications of the latter configuration,

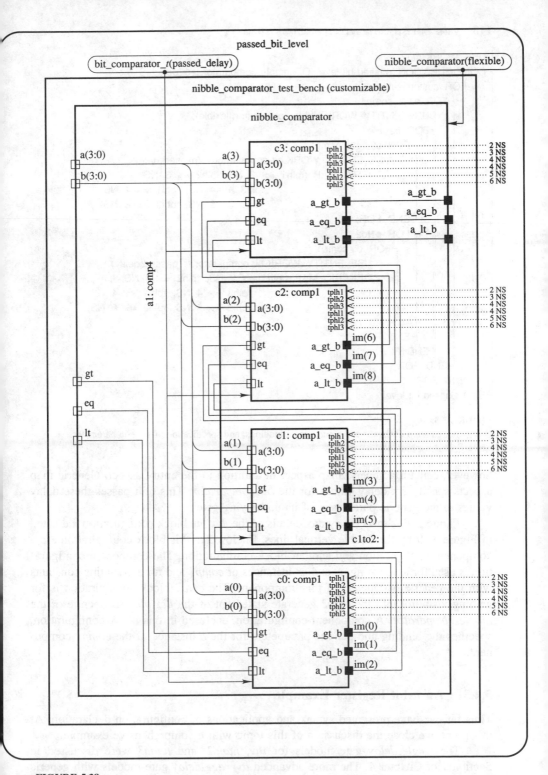

FIGURE 5.38
Composition aspect of the *passed_bit_level* configuration of the test bench
for testing *passed_delay* architecture of *bit_comparator_t*.

```
USE WORK.ALL;
CONFIGURATION passed_bit_level OF nibble_comparator_test_benchIS
  FOR customizable
    FOR a1 : comp4
      USE ENTITY WORK.nibble_comparator(flexible);
      FOR flexible
        FOR c0, c3: comp1
          USE ENTITY WORK.bit_comparator_t (passed_delay)
          GENERIC MAP (tplh1 => 2 NS, tplh2 => 3 NS,
                                  tplh3 => 4 NS, tphl1 => 4 NS,
                                  tphl2 => 5 NS, tphl3 => 6 NS);
        END FOR;
        FOR c1to2
          FOR c: comp1
            USE ENTITY WORK.bit_comparator_t (passed_delay)
            GENERIC MAP (tplh1 => 2 NS, tplh2 => 3 NS,
                                    tplh3 => 4 NS, tphl1 => 4 NS,
                                    tphl2 => 5 NS, tphl3 => 6 NS);
          END FOR;
        END FOR;
      END FOR;
    END FOR;
  END FOR;
END passed_bit_level;
```

FIGURE 5.39
Using configuration declarations for component bindings, and specification of generic parameters.

however, contain a generic map aspect in addition to the entity aspect. Generic map aspects specify six delay values for the *bit_comparator*. This unit passes these delay values to the generic parameters of its underlying gates.

Figure 5.40 shows the syntax details of the *flexible* block configuration indicated in Figure 5.39 by the double vertical lines. Enclosed in this block configuration are a component configuration and another block configuration. The component configuration is used for associating *c0* and *c3* instances of *comp1* and for associating constants with the generic parameters of this component. The *c1to2* block configuration is for gaining visibility into the *c1to2* generate statement of the *flexible* architecture of the *nibble_comparator*. A component configuration, enclosed in this block configuration, specifies the binding and generic parameters for the *c* instance of the *comp1* component.

5.4.3   An n-bit Register Example

Thus far, we have presented syntax and applications of configuration declaration. At this point, we close the discussion of this topic with a comprehensive example.

The *single_delay* gate models for *inv*, *nand2*, and *nand3* were discussed in Section 1 of Chapter 4. The more advanced *average_delay* gate models with generic

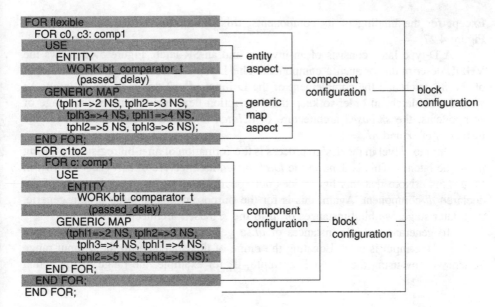

FIGURE 5.40
Details of a block configuration enclosing component configurations and other block configurations.

timing parameters were presented in Section 5.3. This section presents an n-bit register, using unspecified inverters and NAND gates. We will show how this unbound register can be configured to use specific gate models (*single_delay* or *average_delay*) for its underlying logical gates.

Figure 5.41 shows the *gate_level* architecture of a clocked SR-latch. This latch uses four instances of an *n2* component which are not bound to any specific structure.

```
ENTITY sr_latch IS PORT (s, r, c : IN BIT; q : OUT BIT);
END sr_latch;
--
ARCHITECTURE gate_level OF sr_latch IS
    COMPONENT n2 PORT (i1, i2: IN BIT; o1: OUT BIT); END COMPONENT;
    SIGNAL im1, im2, im3, im4 : BIT;
BEGIN
    g1 : n2 PORT MAP (s, c, im1);
    g2 : n2 PORT MAP (r, c, im2);
    g3 : n2 PORT MAP (im1, im4, im3);
    g4 : n2 PORT MAP (im3, im2, im4);
    q <= im3;
END gate_level;
```

FIGURE 5.41
Unbound VHDL description of set-reset latch.

Except for the binding of its components, this description is the same as that in Figure 4.27.

A D-type latch consists of an inverter and an SR-latch. Figure 5.42 shows the VHDL description for such a component. The D input is connected to the Set input of the SR-latch and the complement of the D input (*dbar*) drives its Reset input. As with the SR-latch, in order to keep the description flexible in terms of the usage of components, the *sr_based* architecture of *d_latch* does not specify bindings for the instances of *sr* and *n1*.

Our next level in the design process is the formation of an n-bit register by wiring n D-type latches. This is done in the *latch_based* architecture of *d_register*, shown in Figure 5.43. Note that this figure does not specify binding for the *di* instance of the declared *dl* component. Again, this is for the purpose of keeping the design generic. At a later stage, we bind instances of *dl* to the *sr_based* architecture of *d_latch*.

To generate multiple instances of *dl*, a generate statement with a range equal to that of the input is used. Equating the range of this statement to the *d* input range is achieved by using the RANGE attribute. If, for example, the range of the actual

```
ENTITY d_latch IS PORT (d, c : IN BIT; q : OUT BIT);
END d_latch;
--
ARCHITECTURE sr_based OF d_latch IS
    COMPONENT sr PORT (s, r, c : IN BIT; q : OUT BIT); END COMPONENT;
    COMPONENT n1 PORT (i1: IN BIT; o1: OUT BIT); END COMPONENT;
    SIGNAL dbar : BIT;
BEGIN
    c1 : sr PORT MAP (d, dbar, c, q);
    c2 : n1 PORT MAP (d, dbar);
END sr_based;
```

FIGURE 5.42
Unbound VHDL description of a D-latch.

```
ENTITY d_register IS
    PORT (d : IN BIT_VECTOR; c : IN BIT;   q : OUT BIT_VECTOR);
END d_register;
--
ARCHITECTURE latch_based OF d_register IS
    COMPONENT dl PORT (d, c : IN BIT; q : OUT BIT); END COMPONENT;
BEGIN
    dr : FOR i IN d'RANGE GENERATE
        di : dl PORT MAP (d(i), c, q(i));
    END GENERATE;
END latch_based;
```

FIGURE 5.43
Unbound VHDL description for an n-bit latch.

signal associated with *d* is 7 DOWNTO 0, then the generate statement generates eight instances of *dl*. This description completes the wiring of an n-bit register using basic gate level components.

In order to relate instances of the components used in the *latch_based* architecture of *d_register* to actual entities, a configuration declaration is needed. Figure 5.44 shows the composition aspect for such a configuration. The *average_gate_delay* configuration is placed on top of this architecture and is used to specify the bindings and generic parameters of its components at various nesting levels. All instances of *n1* and *n2* components are associated with the *average_delay* architectures of inverters and NAND gates presented in Figure 5.18.

Figure 5.45 shows the VHDL code that corresponds to this composition aspect. For visibility into an architecture or a block, block configurations are used. For binding a component label to an actual component, component configurations are used. A component configuration is possible only when an instance of that component has been made visible by the use of nested block configurations.

The numbers on the vertical lines in the *average_gate_delay* configuration of the *d_register* identify configuration constructs. The table in Figure 5.46 uses these numerical identifiers to describe the type and purpose of each construct. Column 2 shows whether a construct is block or component configuration. The next two columns indicate the purpose of the configuration, visibility into a block or binding to an entity. The last column shows other configurations that were used to gain visibility into a configuration.

Another configuration for the *d_register* is shown in Figure 5.47. Using this configuration declaration, the *n1* and *n2* components of the latch structures are bound to the *single_delay* architectures of *inv* and *nand2*, respectively. This description does not specify port map aspects for the *g1* and *g3* instances of *n2* or the *c2* instance of *n1*. Therefore, their local ports, from component declarations in the respective architectures (the architecture in Figure 5.41 for *g1* and *g3*, and the architecture in Figure 5.42 for *c2*) will be used for association with the formal ports of *n2* or *n1* components. For instance, the declaration of *n1* in the *sr_based* architecture of *d_latch* (shown in Figure 5.42) declares *i1* as the input and *o1* as output of this component. These local ports are associated with the formal ports of the *single_delay* architecture of *inv*. For the *g2* and *g4* instances of *n2*, however, the configuration declaration in Figure 5.47 specifies a port map aspect. Because of this, the local ports of the *n2* component are associated with *i1*, *i1*, *i2*, and *o1* before they are associated with the formal ports of the *single_delay* architecture of *nand3*. This causes the first two inputs of the three input NAND gate to be tied together and tied to the signal associated with *i1*. Referring to Figure 5.41, *r* is associated with *i1* in the *g2* instance of *n2*, and *im3* is associated with *i1* in the *g4* instance of this component. A similar association was described in Chapter 4. The description in Figure 4.30 uses a configuration specification to achieve what is done by the component configuration of Figure 5.47.

No design is considered complete until it is tested. We close the description of configuration declarations by presenting a test bench for the *single_gate_delay* config-

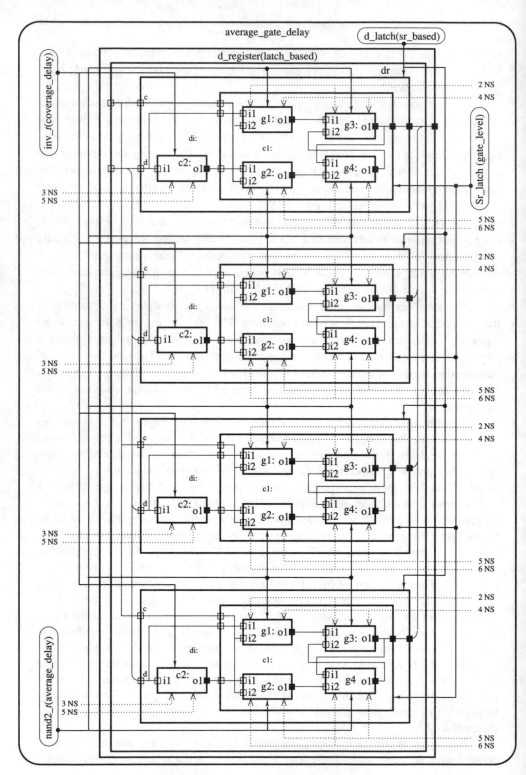

FIGURE 5.44
Composition aspect for configuring the *latch_based* architecture of *d_register*.

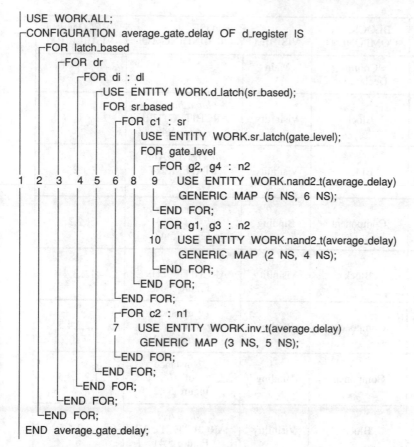

FIGURE 5.45
Configuring *d_register* for using *average_delay* gates.

uration of *d_register*, in Figure 5.48. In the statement part of the architecture shown in this figure, the *reg* component is instantiated. Using a configuration specification in the declarative part of this architecture, the *r8* instance of *reg* is associated with the *single_gate_delay* configuration which resides in the WORK library. 8-bit data is applied to the inputs of *reg*, and 100 ns wide pulses are applied to its clock input. Associating the 8-bit *data* signal with the n-bit *d* input of *d_register* causes this register to be used as an n-bit register.

The letter X preceding the string of values that are assigned to *data* is called a base specifier, and it specifies the base of the values that follow. This construct generates a binary bit string. Letter X is used for hexadecimal, letter O for octal, and letter B for binary base specification. For each base, in addition to the valid values of that base, an underline character can also be used. This character does not contribute to the value of the equivalent bit string and it is used merely for readability purposes.

CONFIG-URATION	BLOCK OR COMPONENT	PURPOSE VISIBILITY OR BINDING TO:		BECOMES VISIBLE BY
1	Config. Declaration	Main	–	–
2	Block	Visibility	*latch_based* ARCHITECTURE Figure 5.43	1
3	Block	Visibility	*dr* GENERATE STATEMENT Figure 5.43	1,2
4	Component	Binding	*di* instance of *dl* Figure 5.43	1,2,3
5	Block	Visibility	*sr_based* ARCHITECTURE Figure 5.42	1,2,3,4
6	Component	Binding	*c1* instance of *sr* Figure 5.42	1,2,3,4,5
7	Component	Binding	*c2* instance of *n1* Figure 5.42	1,2,3,4,5
8	Block	Visibility	*gate_level* ARCHITECTURE Figure 5.41	1,2,3,4,5, 6
9	Component	Binding	instances *g2, g4* of *n2* Figure 5.41	1,2,3,4,5 6,8
10	Component	Binding	instances *g1, g3* of *n2* Figure 5.41	1,2,3,4,5 6,8

FIGURE 5.46
Analyzing configuration constructs of the *average_gate_delay* configuration of d_register.

5.5 DESIGN LIBRARIES

As stated previously, logic families or groups of components can be categorized according to their physical characteristics, price, complexity, usage, or other properties. The VHDL language supports the use of design libraries for categorizing components or utilities. In general, libraries are used for design organization. Specific applications of libraries include sharing of components between designers, grouping components of

```
USE WORK.ALL;
CONFIGURATION single_gate_delay OF d_register IS
  FOR latch_based
    FOR dr
      FOR di : dl
        USE ENTITY WORK.d_latch(sr_based);
        FOR sr_based
          FOR c1 : sr
            USE ENTITY WORK.sr_latch(gate_level);
            FOR gate_level
              FOR g2, g4 : n2
                USE ENTITY WORK.nand3(single_delay)
                PORT MAP (i1, i1, i2, o1);
              END FOR;
              FOR g1, g3 : n2
                USE ENTITY WORK.nand2(single_delay);
              END FOR;
            END FOR;
          END FOR;
          FOR c2 : n1
            USE ENTITY WORK.inv(single_delay);
          END FOR;
        END FOR;
      END FOR;
    END FOR;
  END FOR;
END single_gate_delay;
```

FIGURE 5.47
Configuring *d_register* for using *single_delay* architectures of *inv* and *nand2*.

```
ARCHITECTURE single OF d_register_test_bench IS
  COMPONENT reg PORT (d : IN BIT_VECTOR (7 DOWNTO 0); c : IN BIT;
                      q : OUT BIT_VECTOR (7 DOWNTO 0) );
  END COMPONENT;
  FOR r8 : reg USE CONFIGURATION WORK.single_gate_delay;
  SIGNAL data, outdata : BIT_VECTOR (7 DOWNTO 0);
  SIGNAL clk : BIT;
BEGIN
  r8: reg PORT MAP (data, clk, outdata);
  data <= X"00", X"AA" AFTER 0500 NS, X"55" AFTER 1500 NS;
  clk <= '0', '1' AFTER 0200 NS, '0' AFTER 0300 NS,
             '1' AFTER 0700 NS, '0' AFTER 0800 NS,
             '1' AFTER 1700 NS, '0' AFTER 1800 NS;
END single;
```

FIGURE 5.48
Test bench for the *single_delay* architecture of *d_register*.

standard logic families, and categorizing special purpose utilities such as subprograms or types.

Predefined libraries in VHDL are the STD library and the WORK library. The STD library contains all the standard types and utilities. BIT, BIT_VECTOR, TIME and all other types that have been used up to this point in this book are defined in this library. Also included in this library are utility functions and procedures for reading and writing external ASCII files. The STD library is visible to all designs. The WORK library is simply a name that refers to the current working library. When a VHDL environment is created for a user, the keyword WORK refers to the root library of the user. As new libraries are created, the user can designate a new default library by equating one of the libraries to the WORK library.

Library management tasks, such as the creation or deletion of a library or aliasing it to WORK, are not part of the VHDL language. These tasks are done outside of VHDL and depend on the specific tool. Using a library, however, is supported by VHDL. The LIBRARY keyword followed by the name of a library makes it visible to a design. The following statement is assumed by all designs:

```
LIBRARY WORK;
```

To illustrate how to use and access libraries, we assume that a VHDL user has defined a library named *ls7400* as part of his design environment. We further assume that the *simple_gates* package declaration in Figure 5.12, the *inv*, *nand2*, and *nand3* entity declarations, and the *single_delay* architectures of these components have been compiled into the *ls7400* library. Figure 5.49 shows how a directory of this library might look.

In order to make the library visible and to make the component declarations in the *simple_gates* package declaration visible to a design, the statements shown in Figure 5.50 must appear in the description of the design.

The description that is shown in Figure 5.51 is another version of the *gate_level* architecture of *sr_latch* that uses the *simple_gates* package declaration in the *ls7400* library. In this description, the use clause is applied to make all component declarations of this package available.

LIBRARY "ls7400"	User:...	Date:...
simple_gates	PACKAGE DECLARATION	date
inv	ENTITY	...
inv(single_delay)	ARCHITECTURE	...
nand2	ENTITY	...
nand2(single_delay)	ARCHITECTURE	...
nand3	ENTITY	...
nand3(single_delay)	ARCHITECTURE	...

FIGURE 5.49
Directory of *ls7400* library containing package declarations, entities and architectures that have been compiled into it.

LIBRARY ls7400;
USE ls7400.simple_gates.ALL;

FIGURE 5.50
Making all declarations of *simple_gates* package of *ls7400* library available.

For associating g_1, g_2, g_3, and g_4 instances of *n2* in Figure 5.51 with components of the *ls7400* library, this library and its components must become visible to the VHDL description that makes this association. This requires the use of the statements in Figure 5.52 in the VHDL description that includes the corresponding binding indication construct(s).

A binding indication construct can appear in the declarative part of the architecture of Figure 5.51 as part of a configuration specification or it may appear in a configuration declaration as it did in Figure 5.47. In either case, the name of the library must be used before the entity name. Figure 5.53 shows a component config-

```
LIBRARY ls7400;
USE ls7400.simple_gates.ALL;
ARCHITECTURE gate_level OF sr_latch IS
  SIGNAL im1, im2, im3, im4 : BIT;
BEGIN
  g1 : n2 PORT MAP (s, c, im1);
  g2 : n2 PORT MAP (r, c, im2);
  g3 : n2 PORT MAP (im1, im4, im3);
  g4 : n2 PORT MAP (im3, im2, im4);
  q <= im3;
END gate_level;
```

FIGURE 5.51
Using component declarations of *simple_gates* package of *ls7400* library for description of set-reset latch.

```
LIBRARY ls7400;
USE ls7400.ALL;
```

FIGURE 5.52
Making all entities and architectures of the *ls7400* library available.

```
LIBRARY ls7400;
USE ls7400.ALL;
.
.
. . .  _FOR g1, g3 : n2
. . .  _   USE ENTITY ls7400.nand2(single_delay);
. . .  _END FOR;
```

FIGURE 5.53
Using a component configuration for associating *g1* and *g3* instances of *n2* of Figure 5.51 with *nand2* of *ls7400*.

uration that associates *g1* and *g3* instances of *n2* in Figure 5.51 with the *single_delay* architecture of the *nand2* entity in the *ls7400* library.

5.6   SUMMARY

This chapter provides tools for better hardware descriptions and design organization. This chapter began with the definition of subprograms and it emphasized the use of functions and procedures for simplifying descriptions. Two main issues were discussed: 1) using functions to describe Boolean expressions, and 2) using procedures to write better test bench models. Next, the subject of packaging utilities and components was addressed. As stated earlier, this topic is used mainly for the organization of a design. Design parametrization and configuration of designs were also discussed in great detail. Although simple examples and college level exercises can avoid some of these language issues, a large design environment with many logic families and technologies to choose from requires a great deal of library management and parameter specification. We believe VHDL is very strong in this area and that serious designers should learn to take advantage of such capabilities of the language. For small circuits and experimental models, design parametrization methods save many compilation runs.

REFERENCES

1. "IEEE Standard VHDL Language Reference Manual," IEEE Std. 1076-1987, The Institute of Electrical and Electronic Engineers, Inc., 1988.
2. Lipsett, L., C. Schaefer, and C. Ussery, "VHDL: Hardware Description and Design," Klewer Academic Publishing, Boston, 1988.

PROBLEMS

5.1. Write a function for the carry output of a full-adder.

5.2. Write a function for the sum output of a full-adder.

5.3. Write a function, *inc_bits*, that returns the 4-bit increment of its 4-bit input vector. Write Boolean expressions for the four bits of the output.

5.4. Using the carry and sum functions of Problems 5.1 and 5.2 write a functional description of a full-adder. Use an entity declaration with *a*, *b* and *ci* inputs and *s* and *co* outputs. In the *functional* architecture of this entity include the necessary functions. Use 21 ns and 18 ns delays for the sum and carry outputs, respectively. The solution to this problem depends on code developed in Problems 5.1 and 5.2.

5.5. The *apply_data* procedure in Figure 5.4 causes a transaction on its target every 500 ns even if the data on this line does not change from one time interval to another. Modify this procedure to remove unnecessary transactions.

5.6. Write a procedure, *apply_bit*, such that bits of a 24-bit wide string input to the procedure are applied to its target signal according to the specified time interval. Make sure no unnecessary transactions occur on the target of the procedure. A sample call to this procedure is shown here:

```
apply_bit (target, "110001000100001111001010", 300 NS);
```

5.7. Using *bin2int* and *int2bin*, write a function, *inc_bin*, that uses a binary input parameter and returns a binary value. The return value is the increment of the input parameter.

5.8. Write the package declaration and package body such that it includes the sum and carry of Problems 5.1 and 5.2, *inc_bits* of problem 5.3, *apply_bit* of problem 5.6, and *inc_bin* of problem 5.7. Use *additional_utilities* for the name of this package. The solution to this problem depends on code developed in Problems 5.1, 5.2, 5.3, 5.6 and 5.7.

5.9. Use the *apply_bit* procedure in the *additional_utilities* package in Problem 5.8 in a test bench for the full-adder in Problem 5.4. Use test vectors to test the full-adder for all eight input combinations. The solution to this problem depends on code developed in Problems 5.1, 5.2, 5.3, 5.6, 5.7 and 5.8.

5.10. Write an entity declaration and an *average_delay* architecture for an Exclusive-OR gate with a *tplh* of 9 ns and *tphl* of 7 ns. The entity declaration should contain generics for the timing parameters with the specified default values.

5.11. Use the XOR gate of Problem 5.10 and the basic gates of Figure 5.18 to write a gate level description for a full-adder. Use a configuration specification with generic map aspects to override the default values of the timing parameters of all gates with 11 ns. The solution to this problem depends on code developed in Problem 5.10.

5.12. Use the *apply_bit* procedure of the *additional_utilities* package in Problem 5.8 in a test bench for testing the full-adder in Problem 5.4 and the full-adder in Problem 5.11 in parallel. Declare two signals in this test bench to show the differences of the sum and carry outputs of the two versions of the full-adder. Use *difference_sum* and *difference_carry* for these signals, and use the XOR operation for subtracting the like signals. The solution to this problem depends on code developed in Problems 5.1, 5.2, 5.3, 5.6, 5.7, 5.8, 5.10 and 5.11.

5.13. Write a description for a full-adder using 2-input NAND and XOR gates. In this description, do not include the configuration specification.

5.14. Write a configuration declaration on top of the full-adder in Problem 5.13 to bind the components of this design with the XOR gate of Problem 5.10 and the gates of Figure 5.18. Specify 11 ns in this configuration declaration for timing generic parameters of all gates. The solution to this problem depends on code developed in Problems 5.10 and 5.13.

5.15. Develop a test bench for the full-adder of Problem 5.14. The solution to this problem depends on code developed in Problems 5.10, 5.13 and 5.14.

5.16. Use generate statements to describe an 8-bit adder using the full-adders in Problem 5.13. Write a configuration declaration on top of this adder for binding the underlaying gate components of the full-adder to the XOR gate of Problem 5.10 and the gates of Figure 5.18. Using this configuration declaration, specify the timing parameters as shown below:

Gate	tplh	tphl
NAND2	10 ns	11 ns
XOR	11 ns	13 ns

The solution to this problem depends on code developed in Problems 5.10 and 5.13.

5.17. Use the configured adder of Problem 5.16 in a test bench testing it for worst case delay. The solution to this problem depends on code developed in Problems 5.10, 5.13 and 5.16.

5.18. Write a procedure that assigns consecutive binary numbers to its OUT BIT_VECTOR lines. The parameters of the procedure are an 8-bit *target* output and a TIME *period*. When called, it will assign sequential binary numbers from 0 to 255 to its *target* signal output. These numbers are distanced by the amount of the constant associated with the *period* parameter. You can use the utilities of the *basic_utilities* package.

5.19. Design an 8-bit odd-parity checker using the XOR gate in Problem 5.10. Use generate statements and wire the gates for minimum delay. Use the default delay values of the XOR gate. Write a test bench for testing all the input combinations of this circuit. You may use the procedure developed in Problem 5.18. The solution to this problem depends on code developed in Problems 5.10 and 5.18.

5.20. Show the gate level implementation of a master-slave JK flip-flop. Use the gates in Figure 5.18, and write a configuration declaration on top of the flip-flop. Use reasonable delay values and avoid oscillation by using different delay values for the two cross-coupled gates.

CHAPTER
6

UTILITIES
FOR HIGH
LEVEL
DESCRIPTIONS

The previous two chapters discussed issues related to interconnecting, configuring, and testing hardware structures. In parallel with that, the VHDL constructs that support these tasks were also presented. For higher level hardware descriptions, however, more advanced utilities than those introduced thus far are needed. This chapter is devoted to the presentation of such issues. The two major topics covered in this chapter are types and attributes. Section 1 discusses type declaration and usage. This is followed by issues related to the type of subprogram parameters and operator operands. The last two sections discuss predefined and user-defined attributes.

Unlike the two previous chapters, this chapter does not develop complete and evolutionary examples. Instead, it presents isolated examples, some of which are improvements of the examples of Chapters 4 and 5. In order to develop more useful examples, VHDL constructs that are not necessarily related to types or attributes are also introduced as concepts are presented. In addition to making the examples in this chapter more interesting, this prepares the reader for the higher level descriptions presented in Chapters 7 and 8.

The development of the *basic_utilities* package begun in Chapter 5 continues in this chapter as we make improvements and add more utilities to the package. The examples in this chapter assume users have this package in their WORK design library.

6.1 TYPE DECLARATIONS AND USAGE

VHDL is a strongly typed language. Type declarations must be used for definition of objects and their types. Operations in VHDL are defined for specific types of operands. The STANDARD package in the STD library defines basic types such as BIT or INTEGER; other types also can be defined. Basic operators also can be defined to perform operations on operands of these new types. The general classes of types we will discuss in this chapter include the *scalar*, *composite*, and *file* types.

6.1.1 Enumeration Type for Multi-Value Logic

The basic scalar type is enumeration. This is defined as a set of all possible values that such a type can have. The BIT type of the STANDARD package is an enumeration of '0' and '1', and the BOOLEAN type of this package is an enumeration of FALSE and TRUE. CHARACTER, also in this package, is defined as the set of 128 ASCII characters. Other enumeration types can be defined by the use of the type declaration construct. For example, to define a four-value logic type which takes values '0', '1', 'Z', and 'X', the following declaration is needed:

```
TYPE qit IS ('0', '1', 'Z', 'X');
```

When this type is declared in the declarative part of an architecture, or if it is made visible to a design by inserting a use clause, then *qit* can be used to declare objects that can assume one of the four possible values, '0', '1', 'Z', or 'X'. The examples in this and the following chapters assume users have this type declaration included in the *basic_utilities* package in their WORK library. As BIT is used for *b*inary dig*it*s, we will use *qit* for the *q*uad-dig*it* system, and later *tit* for *t*rinary dig*it*s.

Figure 6.1 shows syntax details of the above type declaration. Enclosed in parentheses are four enumeration elements that are separated by commas. This forms the enumeration type definition which, together with the TYPE keyword, the *qit* identifier, and the IS keyword, forms a type declaration for declaring *qit*. Instead of using single characters enclosed in quotes, enumeration elements can be identifiers formed by a string of characters. For example, individual instruction mnemonics can be used as enumeration elements to declare an instruction set in a computing machine.

6.1.1.1 MODELING A FOUR-VALUE INVERTER. In the four-value logic system described above, '0' and '1' are for low and high logic values, respectively. The 'Z' value is for the high impedance or open value, and the 'X' value is unknown. Input to output mapping of an inverter in this value system is shown in Figure 6.2. As shown in the figure, inverting an unknown input 'X' results in an unknown, while a high impedance input is treated as a '1' and results in a '0' output. Figure 6.3 shows the entity declaration and the architecture body of an inverter that uses this logic value system.

The *qit* type is made visible to the description in Figure 6.3 when we specify the use of the package that contains it. This visibility enables us to use *qit* for the

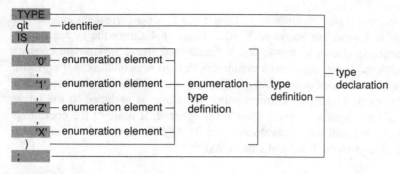

FIGURE 6.1
Syntax details of a type declaration.

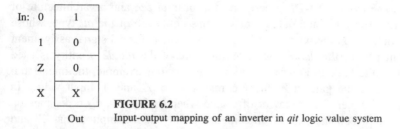

In: 0	1
1	0
Z	0
X	X

Out

FIGURE 6.2
Input-output mapping of an inverter in *qit* logic value system

```
USE WORK.basic_utilities.ALL;
-- FROM PACKAGE USE: qit
ENTITY inv_q IS
    GENERIC (tplh : TIME := 5 NS; tphl : TIME := 3 NS);
    PORT (i1 : IN qit; o1 : OUT qit);
END inv_q;
--
ARCHITECTURE double_delay OF inv_q IS
BEGIN
    o1 <= '1' AFTER tplh WHEN i1 = '0' ELSE
          '0' AFTER tphl WHEN i1 = '1' OR i1 = 'Z' ELSE
          'X' AFTER tplh;
END double_delay;
```

FIGURE 6.3
VHDL description of an inverter in *qit* logic value system.

type of the ports on the *inv_q* entity. The architectural description in Figure 6.3 uses a conditional signal assignment statement for implementing the table in Figure 6.2. This statement enables us to use different delay values for the rise and the fall propagation delays. The *tplh* generic parameter (the larger of the two delay parameters) is used for the gate delay value when the input is unknown. This gives the 'X' output the worst case propagation.

The conditional signal assignment in Figure 6.3 is a concurrent statement, and can only appear in concurrent bodies of VHDL. Figure 6.4 shows the syntax details for this statement. As shown in this figure, a conditional signal assignment consists of several conditional waveforms and a mandatory default nonconditional waveform. The conditions are evaluated sequentially in the order in which they are listed. If a condition evaluates to TRUE, its corresponding waveform is assigned to the target signal and all other assignments that follow it are ignored. If none of the conditions are satisfied, the nonconditional waveform, i.e., *'X' AFTER tplh* in the example in Figure 6.4 is assigned to the left hand side signal.

6.1.1.2 MODELING A FOUR-VALUE NAND GATE.
A two-input NAND gate in the *qit* logic values system can be modeled according to the input-output mapping shown in Figure 6.5.

Figure 6.6 shows the VHDL description for an interface and an architecture of a *nand2_q* entity. The input and output ports of this entity are of the *qit* type, whose declaration is included in the *basic_utilities* package. A conditional signal assignment in the statement part of the *double_delay* architecture of the *nand2_q* entity is used for implementing the table in Figure 6.4. As in the previous example, the open input is treated as '1', and the gate in Figure 6.6 responds to 'Z' and '1' input values in exactly the same manner. The behavior of a gate when its input is open depends on the technology in which the gate is implemented, and our assumption that 'Z' and

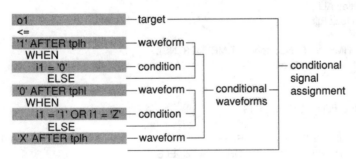

FIGURE 6.4
Syntax details of a conditional signal assignment.

In1:	0	1	Z	X
In2: 0	1	1	1	1
1	1	0	0	X
Z	1	0	0	X
X	1	X	X	X

Out

FIGURE 6.5
Input-output mapping of a NAND gate in *qit* logic value system.

```
USE  WORK.basic_utilities.ALL;
-- FROM PACKAGE USE: qit
ENTITY nand2_q IS
    GENERIC (tplh : TIME := 7 NS; tphl : TIME := 5 NS);
    PORT (i1, i2 : IN qit; o1 : OUT qit);
END nand2_q;
--
ARCHITECTURE double_delay OF nand2_q IS
BEGIN
    o1 <= '1' AFTER tplh WHEN i1 = '0' OR i2 = '0' ELSE
          '0' AFTER tphl WHEN (i1 = '1' AND i2 = '1') OR
                             (i1 = '1' AND i2 = 'Z') OR
                             (i1 = 'Z' AND i2 = '1') OR
                             (i1 = 'Z' AND i2 = 'Z') ELSE
          'X' AFTER tplh;
END double_delay;
```

FIGURE 6.6
VHDL description of a NAND gate in *qit* logic value system.

'1' are equivalent is not always true. For example, if an NMOS gate input becomes open, that input keeps its value for a few milliseconds before it becomes zero. This is due to the discharging of the input capacitance of such structures. This behavior can easily be modeled using RC circuit models connected to each of the inputs of a NAND description. The output of an RC circuit becomes '0' a few milliseconds after its input has become 'Z'. Modeling an NMOS NAND gate is left as an exercise.

6.1.1.3 INITIAL VALUES OF ENUMERATION TYPES. With declaration of objects, an initial value can optionally be specified using the initial value expression that follows the := symbol. If this symbol and its following expression are not present in the declaration of an object, a default initial value that depends on the type of the object is used. For the enumeration types, this value is the left-most enumeration element. For the gates in Figures 6.3 and 6.6, '0', which is the left-most element of the *qit* type, is the initial value for all the input and output ports. Had we used the 'Z', '0', '1', 'X' ordering for the definition of the *qit* type, default initial values of all the objects of this type would have been 'Z'.

6.1.2 Using Real Numbers for Timing Calculations

Besides the enumeration type, other types of the scalar classes are the INTEGER and REAL types. Both of these types are defined in the STANDARD package. The exact range of these types is implementation dependent, but they generally range from a small negative number to a large positive number depending on the word size of the host machine. For the INTEGER type, these numbers are restricted to integers.

We will use a load dependent model of a CMOS inverter in order to demonstrate the use of REAL and INTEGER numbers and their relationship to each other. The inverter contains its own pull-up and pull-down resistance values, and adjusts its delays according to the load capacitance at its output node. This capacitance value is passed to the inverter model by use of the generic parameters. A CMOS inverter with equivalent resistance

Corresponding to the composition aspect in Figure 6.7 are the *inv_rc* entity declaration and the *double_delay* architectural description for this entity, shown in Figure 6.8. The *inv_rc* entity contains a generic formal parameter of REAL type and two ports of *qit* type. The entity declaration part of this figure specifies the *rpu* and *rpd* constants and their values. Declaring these constants in the entity declaration causes them to be visible to all architectures that are written for this entity.

The declarative part of the *double_delay* architecture in Figure 6.8 defines the *tplh* and *tphl* constants in terms of the pull-up or the pull-down resistances and the load capacitance. The constructs used for these declarations are constant declarations that contain expressions for their values. Since all the generics and constants are defined at the initialization time, expressions based on these parameters can be used for the initial values of objects or for the values of other constants.

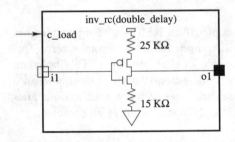

FIGURE 6.7
Composition aspect of an inverter with RC timing.

```
USE  WORK.basic_utilities.ALL;
-- FROM PACKAGE USE: qit
ENTITY inv_rc IS
    GENERIC (c_load : REAL := 0.066E-12);   -- Farads
    PORT (i1 : IN qit; o1 : OUT qit);
    CONSTANT rpu : REAL := 25000.0;   -- Ohms
    CONSTANT rpd : REAL := 15000.0;   -- Ohms
END inv_rc;
--
ARCHITECTURE double_delay OF inv_rc IS
    CONSTANT tplh : TIME := INTEGER ( rpu * c_load * 1.0E15) * 3 FS;
    CONSTANT tphl : TIME := INTEGER ( rpd * c_load * 1.0E15) * 3 FS;
BEGIN
    o1 <= '1' AFTER tplh WHEN i1 = '0' ELSE
          '0' AFTER tphl WHEN i1 = '1' OR i1 = 'Z' ELSE
          'X' AFTER tplh;
END double_delay;
```

FIGURE 6.8
An inverter model with RC timing parameters.

Because of the types of the *tplh* and *tphl* constants, the result of the evaluation of their constant value expressions must be of type TIME. A constant of type TIME can be formed by multiplying an integer number by a valid unit of this type. Since the resistance and capacitance values are of the REAL type, their multiplication result is a floating point number. A floating point number must be converted to an integer and it must be given a unit of TIME in order to be used for an object of type TIME. For this reason, in the constant value expressions of the *double_delay* architecture of *inv_rc*, we have used explicit REAL to INTEGER type conversion and have multiplied the resulting integer by an appropriate time unit. Explicit type conversions, such as those demonstrated here, can be done for closely related types.

Consider the constant expression for the *tplh* constant. This expression converts the multiplication of *rpu* and *c_load* to an integer by use of the explicit type conversion. Before this type conversion takes place, however, the RC product is multiplied by a factor of 1E15. This is done because normal pull resistance and load capacitance multiplications result in small fractions and converting these small floating point numbers to the INTEGER type results in zero. The 1E15 factor is compensated for by using the femtosecond (FS = 1E-15 s) time unit for the overall expression. Multiplication by a factor of 3 is also included in the constant expression of the *tplh* constant. This factor is used to account for the exponentiality of the waveforms. We are approximating the delay values that are based on exponential waveforms by linear RC equations. An exponential function takes about 3*RC to complete its transition from one value to another.

The *double_delay* architecture body of the *inv_rc* entity is similar to that in Figure 6.3. This architecture assumes resistance values in ohms and capacitance values in farads. In the next section we illustrate the use of units for such parameters.

6.1.3   Physical Types and RC Timing

Physical types in VHDL are another type in the scalar class. Values of a physical type are used with units defined in the type definition. Type TIME is a physical type that is defined in the STANDARD package and it is used for measuring time. The units of this type have been defined as FS, PS, NS, US, MS, SEC, MIN, and HR. Other physical types for measuring other quantities such as distance, temperature, resistance, and capacitance can also be defined.

Figure 6.9 shows the definition of *capacitance* as a type for measuring capacitance. This definition consists of the name of the physical type, a range constraint, a base unit declaration (declaration of *ffr*), and several secondary unit declarations (declarations of *pfr* to *kfr*). The units for this type range from *ffr* (*femto-*farads) to *kfr* (*kilo-*farads). The base unit is *ffr*, and all other units are defined in terms of this unit. Other units can be added to this type, provided they are multiples of the base unit. Only integer numbers can be used for the bounds of the range constraint of a physical type. Since we have specified 0 to 1E16 for the range constraint, negative capacitance values and values larger than 1E16 base units cannot be assigned to an object of type *capacitance*, although larger values of this type may be used in expressions. Another example of a physical type definition is that of *resistance*, as shown in Figure 6.10.

```
 ┌TYPE capacitance IS RANGE 0 TO 1E16
 ├UNITS
 │    ffr;   -- Femto Farads (base unit)
 │    pfr = 1000 ffr;
 │    nfr = 1000 pfr;
 │    ufr = 1000 nfr;
 │    mfr = 1000 ufr;
 │    far = 1000 mfr;
 │    kfr = 1000 far;
 └END UNITS;
```

FIGURE 6.9
Type definition for defining the *capacitance* physical type.

As defined by this type, an object of type *resistance* can have units ranging from l_o (milli-ohms = $10^{-3}\Omega$) to g_o (giga-ohms = $10^9\Omega$).

To illustrate the use of the *capacitance* and the *resistance* physical types, we show them in an alternative description for the *inv_rc* inverter. (The definitions for these types are assumed to be included in the *basic_utilities* package; if they are included, the definitions are available to designs that have a use clause specifying application of the *basic-utilities* package.)

Figure 6.11 shows an entity declaration and an architectural description for the *inv_rc* that takes advantage of the *resistance* and the *capacitance* physical types. Except for the types of the generics and the constants, this description is the same as that in Figure 6.8. The *inv_rc* entity declaration in Figure 6.11 has a generic parameter of type *capacitance*. This declaration also defines the pull-up and pull-down resistances in terms of the *resistance* type. The *double_delay* architecture of the *inv_rc* uses two constant declarations for declaring propagation delay parameters and assigning constant values to them. The expression evaluating the constant value for *tplh* uses *rpu* and *c_load* to evaluate the low-to-high propagation delay. In the first set of parentheses in the constant expression of this parameter, the *rpu* parameters are divided by the base unit for the *resistance* physical type. This results in an integer representing the value of *rpu* in terms of l_o ($10^{-3}\Omega$). Similarly, in the second set of parentheses, *c_load* is divided by the *capacitance* base unit. This converts any capacitance value that is

```
 ┌TYPE resistance IS RANGE 0 TO 1E16
 ├UNITS
 │    l_o;   -- Milli-Ohms (base unit)
 │    ohms = 1000 l_o;
 │    k_o = 1000 ohms;
 │    m_o = 1000 k_o;
 │    g_o = 1000 m_o;
 └END UNITS;
```

FIGURE 6.10
Type definition for defining the *resistance* physical type.

```
USE WORK.basic_utilities.ALL;
-- FROM PACKAGE USE: qit, resistance, capacitance
ENTITY inv_rc IS
    GENERIC (c_load : capacitance := 66 ffr);
    PORT (i1 : IN qit; o1 : OUT qit);
    CONSTANT rpu : resistance := 25000 ohms;
    CONSTANT rpd : resistance := 15000 ohms;
END inv_rc;
--
ARCHITECTURE double_delay OF inv_rc IS
    CONSTANT tplh : TIME := (rpu / 1 l_o) * (c_load / 1 ffr) * 3 FS 1000;
    CONSTANT tphl : TIME := (rpd / 1 l_o) * (c_load / 1 ffr) * 3 FS 1000;
BEGIN
    o1 <= '1' AFTER tplh WHEN i1 = '0' ELSE
          '0' AFTER tphl WHEN i1 = '1' OR i1 = 'Z' ELSE
          'X' AFTER tplh;
END double_delay;
```

FIGURE 6.11

Using *resistance* and *capacitance* physical types in the description of an inverter.

associated with the *c_load* generic parameter to an integer representing the amount of the capacitance in *ffr* (10^{-15} farads). Multiplying these two sets of parentheses results in an integer RC value which is scaled up by a factor of 10^{18}. Using FS (10^{-15} s) and dividing the *tplh* constant expression by 1000 compensates for the use of *l_o* and the *ffr* units. As shown in the description in Figure 6.8, a factor of 3 is used in order to account for the exponentiality of the waveforms. The constant expression for the *tphl* delay parameter is similar to that of the *tplh*. Dividing a physical type by one of its units removes the type from it and converts it to an integer. For best precision, the base unit should be used. Had we divided *rpu* by *k_o* instead of *l_o*, *rpu* values would have been rounded off to the smallest *k_o* values.

The VHDL multiplication operator is defined for multiplying integer and floating point numbers. It is also valid to multiply an integer or a floating point number by a physical type. Multiplication of two physical types, however, is not defined for the standard multiplication operator. Dividing the *resistance* and *capacitance* physical types by their base units enabled the use of the standard multiplication operator in the timing equations in Figure 6.11.

6.1.4 Array Declarations

The VHDL language includes constructs that can be used to declare multi-dimensional array types; these array types can then be used to declare objects. Array elements must all be of the same type. Arrays can be indexed with the normal integer indexing or indexed using the elements of an enumeration type. Arrays can be unconstrained, meaning that their range can be left unspecified.

A VHDL array type declaration begins with the keyword TYPE. The declaration specifies the name of the type that is being declared, the range of the array, and the type of each element in the array. Figure 6.12 shows the declarations of *qit_nibble*, *qit_byte*, *qit_word*, *qit_4by8*, and *qit_nibble_by_8*. The elements of *qit_nibble*, *qit_byte*, *qit_word*, and *qit_4by8* are of the previously defined *qit* type, and the type of the eight elements of *qit_nibble_by_8* is *qit_nibble* defined in the first line of the figure.

Once types declared in Figure 6.12 become visible to a design, they can be used to declare objects. For example, an 8-bit *qit* signal should be declared as:

```
SIGNAL sq8 : qit_byte := " ZZZZZZZZ";
```

The initial values of the eight lines of *sq8* signal are all 'Z'. For the individual bits of *sq8*, the 'Z' value overrides '0', which is the default initial value for the *qit* type. Recall that the left-most element is the default initial value in an enumeration type, which was '0' in the declaration of *qit*.

Figure 6.13 shows the syntax details of the type declaration used to define the *qit_byte* type in Figure 6.12. This declaration specifies the range of the arrays and the type of its elements. The range defines the upper and the lower bounds of the array. The DOWNTO descending range specification causes the left most bit and the right most bit of an object of type *qit_byte* to have indices of 7 and 0, respectively.

Figure 6.12 also shows the declaration of a two-dimensional array type, namely *qit_4by8*. This declaration uses two range specifications separated by commas. The first is a descending range and the second is an ascending range. The index (3,0), therefore, references the upper left bit of an object of type *qit_4by8*.

Referencing an element or groups of elements in an array can be achieved by indexing or by using slice specifications. To reference an array element by indexing, an

```
TYPE qit_nibble IS ARRAY ( 3 DOWNTO 0 ) OF qit;
TYPE qit_byte IS ARRAY ( 7 DOWNTO 0 ) OF qit;
TYPE qit_word IS ARRAY ( 15 DOWNTO 0 ) OF qit;
TYPE qit_4by8 IS ARRAY ( 3 DOWNTO 0, 0 TO 7 ) OF qit;
TYPE qit_nibble_by_8 IS ARRAY ( 0 TO 7 ) OF qit_nibble;
```

FIGURE 6.12
Declaring array types.

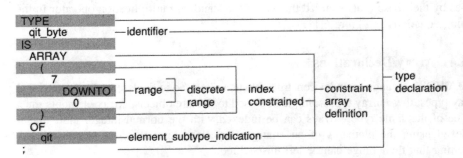

FIGURE 6.13
Syntax details of an array type declaration.

index for each of the ranges in the array must be specified. To reference an array slice, a discrete range should be specified. Figure 6.14 shows signal declaration and several valid assignments to signals of the types declared in Figure 6.12. The first declaration in Figure 6.14a declares *sq1* as a scalar of type *qit*. The next three declarations define *sq4*, *sq8*, and *sq16* as one-dimensional arrays of *qit*. The *sq_4_8* array is a 4-by-8 two-dimensional array of *qit*, and finally the *sq_nibble_8* signal is a one-dimensional array of size 8, whose elements are the *qit_nibble* type. The first signal assignment in Figure 6.14b assigns a slice of *sq16* to all of *sq8*. The second assignment assigns all of *sq4* to a slice of *sq16*. The next assignment indexes a bit of the *sq_4_8* two-dimensional *qit* array and it assigns this bit to the *sq1* signal. Multi-dimensional arrays such as *sq_4_8* can only be indexed and cannot be sliced. Therefore, it is more appropriate to use one-dimensional arrays of vectors such as those of *sq_nibble_8* type for declaring hardware memories. Figure 6.14b shows as assignment of nibble number two of the *sq_nibble_8* to the *sq4* signal. The next assignment, in Figure 6.14b shows an assignment for the right rotation of the *sq8* signal and the last assignment reverses the *sq8* bits and assigns them to the *sq4* signal. Reversing the order of bits is accomplished by concatenating the individual bits of *sq8* as is illustrated graphically in Figure 6.15.

Slicing an array with a range in the opposite direction of its declared range is considered to be a constraint error.

6.1.4.1 INITIALIZING MULTI-DIMENSIONAL ARRAYS.

Initial values for a one-dimensional array type signal must be placed in a set of parentheses and should follow the := symbol in the signal declaration. The initial values of individual array elements should be separated by commas. Nested sets of parentheses should be used

```
SIGNAL sq1 : qit;
SIGNAL sq4 : qit_nibble;
SIGNAL sq8 : qit_byte;
SIGNAL sq16 : qit_word;
SIGNAL sq_4_8 : qit_4by8;
SIGNAL sq_nibble_8 : qit_nibble_by_8;
```
                                (a)

```
sq8 <= sq16 (11 DOWNTO 4);              -- middle 8 bit slice of sq16 to sq8;
sq16 (15 DOWNTO 12) <= sq4;             -- sq4 into left 4 bit slice of sq16;
sq1 <= sq_4_8 (0, 7);                   -- lower right bit of sq_4_8 into sq1;
sq4 <= sq_nibble_8 (2);         -- third nibble (number 2) of sq_nibble_8 into sq4;
sq8 <= sq(0) & sq8 (7 DOWNTO 1);              -- right rotate sq8;
sq4 <= sq8(2) & sq8(3) & sq8(4) & sq8(5);      -- reversing sq8 into sq4;
```
                                (b)

FIGURE 6.14
Various forms of signal declarations and signal assignments based on signal declarations of Figure 6.12, (a) signal declarations, (b) valid signal assignments.

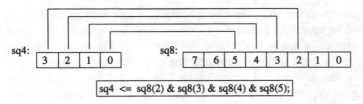

FIGURE 6.15
Referencing bits of a vector; reversing bits of *sq8* and assigning them to *sq4*.

for multi-dimensional arrays. In this case, the top level set of parentheses corresponds to the left-most range of the array.

Figure 6.16 shows initialization of the *sq_4_8* signal whose type is defined to be *qit_4by8* in Figure 6.12. The initial values of this array type signal are specified in a nesting of parenthesized sets of values. Shown in separate rows, the deepest level of nestings correspond to the 0 TO 7 range of *sq_4_8*. Since the left most range of the array is 3 DOWNTO 0, four such rows are needed to initialize all the elements in the array.

6.1.4.2   NON INTEGER INDEXING. In most languages, array indexing is done only with integers. VHDL allows the use of any type indication for index definition of arrays. Referring to Figure 6.13, the 7 DOWNTO 0 range was used for the definition of the array in this figure. Instead of using a range, a type indication can be used for the discrete range of an array. If an enumeration type is used for the discrete range specification of an array, the array must be indexed using the enumeration elements of this type. As an example, consider the following declaration of the *qit_2d* array:

    TYPE qit_2d IS ARRAY (qit, qit) OF qit;

This is a two-dimensional array, that has *qit* type elements. The *qit* type-marks also constitute the two discrete ranges of this array. Therefore, the enumeration elements of *qit* must be used to access elements in the *qit_2d* array. The two-input NAND gate description in Figure 6.17 uses this array for describing a NAND gate in the *qit* logic value system. For this and other examples in this chapter, we assume that the *qit_2d* type is included in the *basic_utilities* package, and can become visible by application of the use clause as shown in Figure 6.17.

```
SIGNAL sq_4_8 : qit_4by8 :=
            (
        ( '0', '0', '1', '1', 'Z', 'Z', 'X', 'X' ),
        ( 'X', 'X', '0', '0', '1', '1', 'Z', 'Z' ),
        ( 'Z', 'Z', 'X', 'X', '0', '0', '1', '1' ),
        ( '1', '1', 'Z', 'Z', 'X', ' X', '0', '0' )
            );
```

FIGURE 6.16
Initializing a two-dimensional array.

```
USE  WORK.basic_utilities.ALL;
-- FROM PACKAGE USE: qit, qit_2d
ENTITY nand2_q IS
    GENERIC (tplh : TIME := 7 NS; tphl : TIME := 5 NS);
    PORT (i1, i2 : IN qit; o1 : OUT qit);
END nand2_q;
--
ARCHITECTURE average_delay OF nand2_q IS
    CONSTANT qit_nand2_table : qit_2d := (
                                          ('1','1','1','1'),
                                          ('1','0','0','X'),
                                          ('1','0','0','X'),
                                          ('1','X','X','X'));
BEGIN
    o1 <= qit_nand2_table (i1, i2) AFTER (tplh + tphl) / 2;
END average_delay;
```

FIGURE 6.17
Using *qit* enumeration type for the discrete range of a two-dimensional array.

Figure 6.17 also shows the *nand2_q* entity and the *average_delay* architecture for this entity. Types *qit* and *qit_2d* are visible to this architecture. Since *qit* has four enumeration elements, the *qit_2d* is a 4-by-4 array with its rows and columns indexed as '0', '1', 'Z', and 'X'. In the declarative part of the *average_delay* architecture in *nand2_q*, the *qit_nand2_table* is declared as a constant array of type *qit_2d* and it is initialized according to the two-input NAND gate input-output mapping shown in Figure 6.5. The statement part of this architecture consists of a signal assignment whose right hand side is a look-up into the *qit_nand2_table*.

6.1.4.3 UNCONSTRAINED ARRAYS. VHDL allows the declaration of unconstrained arrays. This is particularly useful for developing generic descriptions or designs. The bounds of unconstrained arrays used for formal parameters are determined according to the actual parameters that are associated with them. The standard BIT_VECTOR is an unconstrained one-dimensional array of BITs. In the STANDARD package, this type is declared as shown here:

```
TYPE BIT_VECTOR IS ARRAY (NATURAL RANGE <>) OF BIT;
```

This declaration defines BIT_VECTOR as an array with type BIT elements, and specifies that it can be indexed by any range of natural numbers. NATURAL, also declared in the STANDARD package is a type for numbers ranging from 0 to the largest allowable integer. Another unconstrained array in the STANDARD package is the STRING type. This type is an unconstrained array of characters; when indexing it, positive numbers should be used.

Similar to the declaration we used to define BIT_VECTOR, we can define an unconstrained array of integers as shown here:

```
TYPE integer_vector IS ARRAY (NATURAL RANGE <>) OF INTEGER;
```

Figure 6.18 shows syntax details for this type declaration. The index definition of this array (which is read as "natural range box") indicates that for range specification of objects of this type or for other type declarations that are based on this type, any descending or ascending range of natural numbers can be used.

To illustrate the use of unconstrained arrays, a more general version of the *apply_data* procedure than that developed in Chapter 5 (Figure 5.15b) is shown in Figure 6.19. The *target* and the *values* formal parameters of this procedure are declared as unconstrained arrays of BITs and INTEGERs, respectively. The *target* parameter uses the predefined BIT_VECTOR type and the *values* parameter uses the *integer_vector* in Figure 6.18. To specify the range of the intermediate variable, *buf*, and the range of the for loop, we have used *target*'RANGE and *values*'RANGE, respectively. The *buf* variable stores the binary result of this procedure before assigning it to *target*. When an actual signal is associated with the *target* formal parameter, *target* becomes an array signal whose range is the same as that of the actual parameter. This range is then passed on to *buf*, making it a variable whose range is the same as the range of the actual parameter associated with *target*. The use of *values*'RANGE enables the *apply_data* procedure to loop for all the integers in the array associated with the

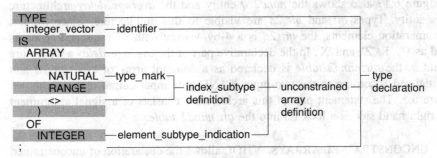

FIGURE 6.18
Syntax details of an unconstrained array declaration.

```
 PROCEDURE apply_data (
      SIGNAL target : OUT BIT_VECTOR;
      CONSTANT values : IN integer_vector; CONSTANT period : IN TIME)
 IS
      VARIABLE buf : BIT_VECTOR (target' RANGE);
 BEGIN
      FOR i IN values' RANGE LOOP
          int2bin (values(i), buf);
          target <= TRANSPORT buf AFTER i * period;
      END LOOP;
 END apply_data;
```

FIGURE 6.19
A generic version of the *apply_data* procedure.

values formal parameter. For example, in calling *apply_data*, if concatenation of 20 integers is associated with the *values* parameter, then the loop range becomes 0 TO 19. Each time through the loop, one of these integers is converted to its equivalent binary number and assigned to *values*. To make it possible to use this procedure in our designs, we first add the *integer_vector* type definition to the *basic_utilities* package declaration. Next, in the *basic_utilities* package body, we replace the *apply_data* procedure in Figure 5.15b with the new *apply_data* procedure in Figure 6.19. The declaration of the *apply_data* procedure in the *basic_utilities* package declaration (see Figure 5.15a) must be modified to conform to the new version of this procedure.

Another use of unconstrained arrays is in the design of generic hardware structures. Figure 6.20 shows an *n*-bit comparator that uses unconstrained arrays for its input signals. This comparator is based on the *bit_comparator* in Chapter 4 (see Figure 4.12). The entity declaration of the *n_bit_comparator* is similar to that of the *nibble_comparator* in Figure 4.17, except that the range of the input BIT_VECTORs is not specified. The *iterative* architecture of the *n_bit_comparator* is similar to that of

```
ENTITY n_bit_comparator IS
    PORT (a, b : IN BIT_VECTOR; gt, eq, lt : IN BIT;
           a_gt_b, a_eq_b, a_lt_b : OUT BIT);
END n_bit_comparator;
--
ARCHITECTURE structural OF n_bit_comparator IS
    COMPONENT comp1
        PORT (a, b, gt, eq, lt : IN BIT; a_gt_b, a_eq_b, a_lt_b OUT BIT);
    END COMPONENT;
    FOR ALL : comp1 USE ENTITY WORK.bit_comparator (gate_level);
    CONSTANT n : INTEGER := a' LENGTH;
    SIGNAL im : BIT_VECTOR ( 0 TO (n-1)*3-1);
BEGIN
    c_all: FOR i IN 0 TO n-1 GENERATE
      l: IF i = 0 GENERATE
          least: comp1 PORT MAP (a(i), b(i), gt, eq, lt,
                                        im(0), im(1), im(2) );
      END GENERATE;
      m: IF i = n-1 GENERATE
          most: comp1 PORT MAP (a(i), b(i), im(i*3-3), im(i*3-2), im(i*3-1),
                                        a_gt_b, a_eq_b, a_lt_b);
      END GENERATE;
      r: IF i > 0 AND i < n-1 GENERATE
          rest: comp1 PORT MAP (a(i), b(i), im(i*3-3), im(i*3-2), im(i*3-1),
                                        im(i*3+0), im(i*3+1), im(i*3+2) );
      END GENERATE;
    END GENERATE;
END structural;
```

FIGURE 6.20
An n-bit comparator, wiring *n* number of one-bit comparators.

the *nibble_comparator* in Figure 4.22, except that the value of constant *n* is defined as the length of the *a* operand, using the 'LENGTH attribute. Associating an instance of a component with the *n_bit_comparator* in Figure 6.20 causes association of fixed size signals with its *a* and *b* inputs. When this happens, the length and the range of the parameters in this entity are known, and constant *n* has a fixed integer value. The generate statement in the *structural* architecture of *n_bit_comparator* uses *n* to instantiate the appropriate number of *bit_comparators*. For the *n*-bit comparator to function properly, the *a* and *b* inputs must be of the same size. Furthermore, the range of these vectors must be descending and the indices of their right most bits must be zero.

The test bench in Figure 6.21 uses the generic *apply_data* procedure for testing a 6-bit comparator. The test bench associates 6-bit arrays with the input ports of the *n_bit_comparator* in Figure 6.20, which makes this variable-size comparator a 6-bit comparator. The *apply_data* procedure is called twice to assign values to the *a* and *b* inputs of the comparator under test. Since *a* and *b* are 6-bit signals, the *apply_data* procedure converts its input integers to 6-bit binary numbers. The two calls to this procedure use a different number of concatenated integers.

6.1.5 File Type and External File I/O

File declarations can be used to define a file type. A data type is associated with an identifier that is defined as a file type. This data type is the type of the data contained

```
ENTITY n_bit_comparator_test_bench IS
END n_bit_comparator_test_bench ;
   --
  USE WORK.basic_utilities.ALL;
  -- FROM PACKAGE USE: apply_data which uses integer_vector
ARCHITECTURE procedural OF n_bit_comparator_test_bench IS
     COMPONENT comp_n PORT (a, b : IN bit_vector;
                            gt, eq, lt : IN BIT;
                            a_gt_b, a_eq_b, a_lt_b : OUT BIT);
     END COMPONENT;
     FOR a1 : comp_n USE ENTITY WORK.n_bit_comparator(structural);
     SIGNAL a, b : BIT_VECTOR (5 DOWNTO 0);
     SIGNAL eql, lss, gtr : BIT;
     SIGNAL vdd : BIT := '1';
     SIGNAL gnd : BIT := '0';
BEGIN
     a1: comp_n PORT MAP (a, b, gnd, vdd, gnd, gtr, eql, lss);
     apply_data (a, 00&15&57&17, 500 NS);
     apply_data (b, 00&43&14&45&11&21&44&11, 500 NS);
END procedural;
```

FIGURE 6.21
Using generic *apply_data* procedure for testing *n_bit_comparator*.

in files of the specified type. The following statement declares *logic_data* as a file type whose contents are of the predefined CHARACTER type:

TYPE logic_data IS FILE OF CHARACTER;

This file type can be used in a file declaration to declare input and output files of this type. A file declaration uses an identifier for a file name, specifies its type as an existing file type, and associates it with a host system file name. Consider, for example, the following file declaration:

FILE input_logic_value_file : logic_data IS IN "input.dat";

This declaration specifies that *input_logic_value_file* is an input file object of type *logic_data*, as declared above, and it associates this file with the host system *input.dat* file. Data read from this file is in ASCII (elements of CHARACTER) form, and an object of the CHARACTER type must be associated with the operand that is used for reading from this file.

VHDL provides three operations, READ, WRITE, and ENDFILE for the file types. READ takes a file name and an object of the file data type as its argument. It reads the next data from the file and places it in its data argument. The arguments of the WRITE operation are similar to those of the READ operation. This operation writes data into the specified file. The ENDFILE operation takes a file name as its argument and returns TRUE if a subsequent READ cannot be done from the file. READ and WRITE operations are procedure calls, while ENDFILE is a function call.

As an example of file type declaration and external file I/O, consider the *assign_bits* procedure in Figure 6.22. This procedure reads CHARACTER type data from a specified host system input file, transforms this data into appropriate BIT type values, and assigns the bit values to its output signal. Each assignment is delayed from its previous assignment by the amount of time specified in the *period* TIME type parameter. In general, the function of this procedure is similar to that of the *apply_data* procedure in Chapter 5, or the modified version of it shown in Figure 6.19. Instead of converting integers and assigning them to a multi-bit *target* signal, the *target* parameter of the *assign_bits* procedure is a one-bit scalar, and its corresponding data is read from a file.

The declaration of *logic_data* file type must be visible to the procedure in Figure 6.22. The formal parameters of the *assign_bits* procedure consist of a BIT type output *target*, a STRING type input parameter for the host system file name, and a *period* of type TIME. In the declarative part of this procedure, the temporary variable, *char*, is declared for use as a buffer for characters read from the input file and the *input_value_file* is declared as the input file. The purpose of the *current* variable is to keep a record of timing. The *input_value_file* is associated with the host system file name that is passed to this procedure via the *file_name* formal parameter. In the statement part of the *assign_bits* procedure, a while loop uses the ENDFILE file operation to determine if more characters exist in the input file. In this case, the next character will be read from the file into the *char* buffer. If *char* is a '0' or a '1', *current* will be incremented by *period* and appropriate assignments, based on the value of *char*, will be made to the *target* signal. Note that *char* contains data of the CHARACTER type and cannot directly be assigned to *target* which is type BIT. The inner if statement of

```
-- File Type   logic_data is Visible
PROCEDURE assign_bits (
    SIGNAL target : OUT BIT; file_name : IN STRING; period : IN TIME)
IS
    VARIABLE char : CHARACTER;
    VARIABLE current : TIME := 0 NS;
    FILE input_value_file : logic_data IS IN file_name;
BEGIN
    WHILE NOT ENDFILE (input_value_file) LOOP
        READ (input_value_file, char);
        IF char = '0' OR char = '1' THEN
            current := current + period;
            IF char = '0' THEN
                target <= TRANSPORT '0' AFTER current;
            ELSIF char = '1' THEN
                target <= TRANSPORT '1' AFTER current;
            END IF;
        END IF;
    END LOOP;
END assign_bits;
```

FIGURE 6.22
A procedure for reading characters from a file and assigning them to a BIT type.

the *assign_bits* procedure converts '0' and '1' elements that belong to the CHARAC-
TER enumeration type to like elements for the BIT enumeration type. Literals like
'0' and '1' that are used in more than one enumeration type are said to be overloaded.

As with the *apply_data* procedure, the *assign_bits* procedure and its corresponding declarations become part of our design utilities when they are added to the *ba-
sic_utilities* package. Declaration of this procedure and the *logic_data* file declaration
will be placed in the *basic_utilities* package declaration. The subprogram body in
Figure 6.22 is also entered in the corresponding body of this package. When this has
been done a design can read binary data from a system file by making this procedure
call:

    assign_bits (a_signal, "unix_file.bit", 1500 NS);

A procedure call for the *assign_bits* procedure in a concurrent body of VHDL, for
example, the statement part of an architecture, is executed once at the beginning of
the simulation run. When *assign_bits* is called, it reads the entire *unix_file.bit* and
assigns '0's and '1's to the *a_signal* output of the procedure. If this procedure is called
a multiple number of times with the same file name, each time it is called reading
begins from the top of the file and the same data is re-read. This is because the file
declaration is contained in the declarative part of the procedure and a new file object
is declared each time it is called. This re-reading can be avoided if a file object is
declared outside of a procedure and then passed to the procedure that reads a file.

The next section shows an example for reading *qit* type data from an input
file. The VHDL standard TEXTIO package also provides several file types and their

corresponding read and write procedures. Chapter 8 illustrates the use of this standard VHDL package.

6.2   SUBPROGRAM PARAMETER TYPES AND OVERLOADING

In VHDL, subprograms with the same name and different types of parameters or results are distinguished from each other. A name used by more than one such subprogram is said to be overloaded. Overloading is a useful mechanism for using the same name for subprograms that perform the same operation on data of different types. VHDL allows overloading of user defined subprograms, standard functions, and operators.

Our first examples for overloading show how to define the essential logical operators for the *qit* type defined in the previous section. Figure 6.23 shows logic tables for AND, OR and inversion operations in the *qit* logic value system. As before, the high impedance 'Z' value is treated as a '1' by all three functions. If one input of the AND function is '0', the output is '0' even if the other input is unknown ('X'). Similarly, if at least one input of the OR function is '1', the output becomes '1'. The NOT table is a repetition of the logic value table for the inverter in Section 6.1, and is shown here for completeness. Figure 6.24 shows the declaration and definition of "AND", "OR", and "NOT" functions according to the tables in Figure 6.23. These definitions overload the corresponding VHDL operators that are defined for the BIT and the BOOLEAN types. In the declarations in Figure 6.24a, declarations of *qit*, *qit_2d*, and *qit_1d*, as well those for the "AND", "OR" and "NOT" functions are shown. The *qit_2d* and *qit_1d* arrays are used by the function definitions and must be visible to them. For the declarations and definitions of the functions that overload the operators, for example, the "AND" function overloading the AND operator, the operator symbol enclosed in double quotes must be used for the function name. Figure 6.24b shows the subprogram bodies for the functions declared in Figure 6.24a. The declarative part of each function consists of a constant declaration that sets a local array of type *qit* according to its corresponding table in Figure 6.23. A return statement constitutes the statement part of each of these functions. This statement returns the value of a table entry that is indexed by the input(s) of the function. The constant tables for the two input "AND" and "OR" functions are the *qit_2d* type, and the "NOT" function is the *qit_1d* type.

When a design uses AND, OR or NOT operators with BIT or BOOLEAN operands, the standard VHDL operators are used. If, however, the operand types of these operators are of the *qit* type, the functions in Figure 6.24 are used if they are visible to the design. For the examples that follow, we assume that the contents of Figure 6.24a are included in the *basic_utilities* package declaration and that the subprogram bodies in Figure 6.24b are included in the *basic_utilities* package body. Type declarations that are only used internally to a package do not have to be included in the package declaration; it is sufficient to declare them in the package body. Although types *qit_2d* and *qit_1d* fit this category, i.e., they are only used inside the *basic_utilities* package, we include them in the *basic_utilities* package declaration for possible future use, thus making them visible to all designs that use this package.

a:	0	1	Z	X
b: 0	0	0	0	0
1	0	1	1	X
Z	0	1	1	X
X	0	X	X	X

$z = a \cdot b$

(a)

a:	0	1	Z	X
b: 0	0	1	1	X
1	1	1	1	1
Z	1	1	1	1
X	X	1	1	X

$z = a + b$

(b)

a: 0	1
1	0
Z	0
X	X

$z = a'$

(c)

FIGURE 6.23
Tables for the basic logic functions in the *qit* four value logic system, (a) AND function, (b) OR function, (c) NOT function.

Figure 6.25 shows entity declaration and architecture bodies for a NOT, a two-input NAND, and a three-input NAND gate in the *qit* logic value system. These structures use the overloaded AND and NOT operators. The *inv_q*, *nand2_q*, and the *nand3_q* descriptions shown in this figure are similar to the parameterized gate models in Figure 5.18 in Chapter 5. The types of the input and output ports in the descriptions in Chapter 5 are of type BIT, and those in Figure 6.25 are of type *qit*. Because of this difference, the overloaded AND and NOT operators of Figure 6.24 are used by the *average_delay* architectures in the *inv_q*, *nand2_q*, and *nand3_q* entities instead of the standard VHDL operators. Unlike the *nand2* description in Chapter 5, the NAND function is not used by the *nand2_q* description because we have not provided an overloading function for the NAND operator. Using the NAND operator with operands of type *qit* is incorrect.

```
TYPE qit IS ('0', '1', 'Z', 'X');
TYPE qit_2d IS ARRAY (qit, qit) OF qit;
TYPE qit_1d IS ARRAY (qit) OF qit;
--
FUNCTION "AND" (a, b : qit) RETURN qit;
FUNCTION "OR" (a, b : qit) RETURN qit;
FUNCTION "NOT" (a : qit) RETURN qit;
```

(a)

```
FUNCTION "AND" (a, b : qit) RETURN qit IS
    CONSTANT qit_and_table : qit_2d := (
                                ('0','0','0','0'),
                                ('0','1','1','X'),
                                ('0','1','1','X'),
                                ('0','X','X','X'));
BEGIN
    RETURN qit_and_table (a, b);
END "AND";
--
FUNCTION "OR" (a, b : qit) RETURN qit IS
    CONSTANT qit_or_table : qit_2d := (
                                ('0','1','1',',X'),
                                ('1','1','1','1'),
                                ('1','1','1','1'),
                                (',X','1','1',',X'));
BEGIN
    RETURN qit_or_table (a, b);
END "OR";
--
FUNCTION "NOT" (a : qit) RETURN qit IS
    CONSTANT qit_not_table : qit_1d := ('1','0','0',' X');
BEGIN
    RETURN qit_not_table (a);
END "NOT";
```

(b)

FIGURE 6.24
Overloading basic logical functions for the *qit* four value logic system, (a) function declarations and other
necessary declarations, (b) definition of functions.

For the next example of overloading, consider the expressions used for calculating the *tplh* and *tphl* delay parameters in the *double_delay* architecture of the *inv_rc*
entity in Figure 6.11. Physical type to integer conversions, and integer to physical
type conversions were done in these expressions because the VHDL multiplication
operator is not defined for multiplying two physical types. By overloading this operator as shown in Figure 6.26, it can be made to accept *resistance* as the type of its first

```
USE WORK.basic_utilities.ALL;
-- FROM PACKAGE USE: qit, "NOT"
ENTITY inv_q IS
    GENERIC (tplh : TIME := 5 NS; tphl : TIME := 3 NS);
    PORT (i1 : IN qit; o1 : OUT qit);
END inv_q;
--
ARCHITECTURE average_delay OF inv_q IS
BEGIN
    o1 <= NOT i1 AFTER (tplh + tphl) / 2;
END average_delay;


USE WORK.basic_utilities.ALL;
-- FROM PACKAGE USE: qit, "AND"
ENTITY nand2_q IS
    GENERIC (tplh : TIME := 6 NS; tphl : TIME := 4 NS);
    PORT (i1, i2 : IN qit; o1 : OUT qit);
END nand2_q;
--
ARCHITECTURE average_delay OF nand2_q IS
BEGIN
    o1 <= NOT ( i1 AND i2 ) AFTER (tplh + tphl) / 2;
END average_delay;


USE WORK.basic_utilities.ALL;
-- FROM PACKAGE USE: qit, "AND"
ENTITY nand3_q IS
    GENERIC (tplh : TIME := 7 NS; tphl : TIME := 5 NS);
    PORT (i1, i2, i3 : IN qit; o1 : OUT qit);
END nand3_q;
--
ARCHITECTURE average_delay OF nand3_q IS
BEGIN
    o1 <= NOT ( i1 AND i2 AND i3) AFTER (tplh + tphl) / 2;
END average_delay;
```

FIGURE 6.25
Basic gates in the *qit* logic value system using overloaded AND and OR operators.

operand (left of the operator), *capacitance* as the type of its second operand (right of the operator), and produce results of type TIME.

The "*" overloading function uses the definition of *resistance* and *capacitance* physical types. In the statement part of this function, *resistance* and *capacitance* physical types are neutralized to equivalent integers and the result of multiplying these integers is multiplied by the appropriate unit of type TIME. This time expression is returned as the result of the function. By adding the declaration and the subprogram body in Figure 6.26 to the *basic_utilities* package, the "*" function can use *capaci-*

```
...
FUNCTION "*" (a : resistance; b : capacitance) RETURN TIME;
                    (a)

FUNCTION "*" (a : resistance; b : capacitance) RETURN TIME IS
BEGIN
    RETURN  ( ( a / 1 l_o) * ( b / 1 ffr ) * 1 FS ) / 1000;
END "*";
                    (b)
```

FIGURE 6.26
Overloading the multiplication operator for returning TIME when multiplying *resistance* and *capacitance* physical types, (a) function declaration, (b) the "*" subprogram body.

tance and *resistance* definitions from this package, and it becomes visible to designs that use this package. The *double_delay* architecture of *inv_rc* shown in Figure 6.27, uses the overloaded multiplication operator for calculating *tplh* and *tphl* propagation delays. The first multiplication operator in the constant value expressions of *tplh* and *tphl* is associated with the function in Figure 6.26. The other multiplication operator uses the standard VHDL operator. As shown, types *qit*, *resistance*, and *capacitance*, as well as the "*" function are visible to the description in Figure 6.27.

The final example in this section discusses overloading the *assign_bits* procedure in Figure 6.22. The overloading is done so that this procedure can accept data files containing *qit* type information and produce *qit* data on its output signal of type *qit*. In Figure 6.22, the name *assign_bits* is used to designate a procedure that reads ASCII data from a file, ignoring non '0' or '1' data, and then places the filtered data on a

```
USE  WORK.basic_utilities.ALL;
-- FROM PACKAGE USE: qit, capacitance, resistance, "*"
ENTITY inv_rc IS
    GENERIC (c_load : capacitance := 66 ffr);
    PORT (i1 : IN qit; o1 : OUT qit);
    CONSTANT rpu : resistance := 25 k_o;
    CONSTANT rpd : resistance := 15 k_o;
END inv_rc;
--
ARCHITECTURE double_delay OF inv_rc IS
    CONSTANT tplh : TIME := rpu * c_load * 3;
    CONSTANT tphl : TIME := rpd * c_load * 3;
BEGIN
    o1  <= '1' AFTER tplh WHEN i1 = '0' ELSE
           '0' AFTER tphl WHEN i1 = '1' OR i1 = 'Z' ELSE
           ',X' AFTER tplh;
END double_delay;
```

FIGURE 6.27
Using the overloaded multilplication operator in the *double_delay* architecture of *inv_rc*.

BIT type output signal. Figure 6.28 shows an *assign_bits* procedure that uses *qit* for the type of its first parameter and accepts the elements of the *qit* type from its input file. The *qit* version of the *assign_bits* procedure requires visibility of the enumeration type, *qit*, in addition to the file type, *logic_data*. The parameters of this procedure consist of an output signal of type *qit*, a STRING type input file name, and a *period* of type TIME. As in the description in Figure 6.22, this description uses *char* and *current* for temporary storage of input data and time of assignment, respectively.

When this procedure is called, a host system file is associated with the *file_name* parameter. As long as there are unread characters in this file, the procedure extracts a character from the file and increments the *current* variable by *period*. A case statement maps an extracted character to the appropriate *qit* element, and assigns this element to the output *target* signal. This mapping, which is implemented by choosing alternatives of a case statement, converts '0', '1' and uppercase or lowercase 'X' and 'Z' characters in the input file to the corresponding *qit* type enumeration elements. If the value of *char* does not match any of the case alternative

```
TYPE qit IS ('0', '1', 'Z', ',X');
TYPE logic_data IS FILE OF CHARACTER;
PROCEDURE assign_bits (SIGNAL target : OUT qit;
                          file_name : IN STRING; period : IN TIME);
```
(a)

```
PROCEDURE assign_bits (
    SIGNAL target : OUT qit; file_name : IN STRING; period : IN TIME)
IS
    VARIABLE char : CHARACTER;
    VARIABLE current : TIME := 0 NS;
    FILE input_value_file : logic_data IS IN file_name;
BEGIN
    WHILE NOT ENDFILE (input_value_file) LOOP
        READ (input_value_file, char);
        current := current + period;
        CASE char IS
            WHEN '0' => target <= TRANSPORT '0' AFTER current;
            WHEN '1' => target <= TRANSPORT '1' AFTER current;
            WHEN 'Z' | 'z' => target <= TRANSPORT 'Z' AFTER current;
            WHEN ',X' | 'x' => target <= TRANSPORT ',X' AFTER current;
            WHEN OTHERS => current := current - period;
        END CASE;
    END LOOP;
END assign_bits;
```
(b)

FIGURE 6.28
Overloading the *assign_bits* procedure for accepting and producing *qit* data, (a) procedure declaration and other necessary declarations, (b) the subprogram body.

choices, the last case statement alternative causes the *current* time tracking variable to decrement by *period*. Decrementing *current* and reading the next character from the file causes characters that cannot be mapped to the elements of *qit* to be ignored.

The two different *assign_bits* procedures shown in Figures 6.22 and 6.28 can coexist in the same library or even in the same package, for example, the *basic_utilities* package. In this case, the two procedures are said to be overloading each other. When the *assign_bits* procedure is called, the appropriate procedure is used based on the type of the first parameter in the association list of the procedure call statement.

This is the first time we have encountered a sequential case statement, so it is appropriate to elaborate on this construct. The syntax details of the case statement in Figure 6.28 are illustrated in Figure 6.29. The expression that follows the CASE keyword is checked against the choice(s) of all the case statement alternatives. When a match is found, the sequence of statements that follow the arrow is executed. If the value of the expression is not equal to any of the choices in the case statement alternatives, the case statement alternative with OTHERS as its choice is executed. Case statements must be complete, which means that all

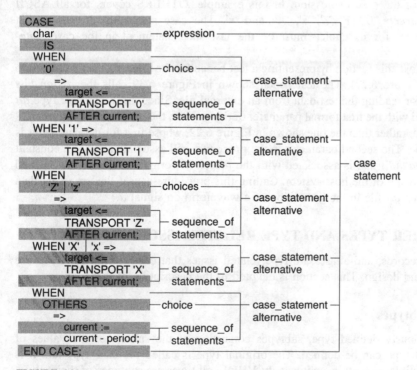

FIGURE 6.29
Syntax details of a sequential case statement.

```
USE  WORK.basic_utilities.ALL;
-- FROM PACKAGE USE: qit, capacitance, resistance, assign_bits (Fig 6.30)
ENTITY tester IS
END tester;
--
ARCHITECTURE input_output OF tester IS
    COMPONENT inv
        GENERIC (c_load : capacitance := 11 ffr);
        PORT (i1 : IN qit; o1 : OUT qit);
    END COMPONENT;
    FOR ALL : inv USE ENTITY WORK.inv_rc(double_delay);
    SIGNAL a, z : qit;
BEGIN
    assign_bits (a, "data.qit", 500 NS);
    i1 : inv PORT MAP (a, z);
END input_output;
```

FIGURE 6.30
Calling the overloaded *assign_bits* for testing an inverter.

possible choices of an expression must be accounted for. The use of OTHERS is necessary only if the prior case statement alternatives do not cover all possible values of the case expression. In this example, OTHERS covers for all ASCII characters except '0', '1', 'Z', 'z', 'X', and 'x'. The case statement alternative that uses OTHERS for its choice must be the last such statement in the case statement.

We close this section by presenting a test bench for the *double_delay* architecture of *inv_rc* (Figure 6.27). The test bench shown in Figure 6.30 calls the *assign_bits* procedure for reading the test data from an external file. Since the *a* signal of type *qit* is associated with the first formal parameter of *assign_bits*, the procedure in Figure 6.28 will be used, rather than the one shown in Figure 6.22, whose first formal parameter is the BIT type. The second parameter in the procedure call association list is a constant string ("*data.qit*") that is associated with the *file_name* formal parameter that is used for the file name of the host system. Calling this procedure causes the use of *qit* data from the *data.qit* file in the generation of a waveform on signal *a*.

6.3 OTHER TYPES AND TYPE RELATED ISSUES

Subtypes, records, and aliases are type related issues that can be used for hardware modeling and design. This section is devoted to the description of these topics.

6.3.1 Subtypes

For a previously defined type, subtypes consisting of the subsets of the values of the original type can be defined. The original type is called the base type and it is fully compatible with all its subtypes. In VHDL, all types are subtypes of themselves. Because of this, the word "subtype" is used to refer to all declared types and subtypes.

Subtypes are used when a subset of a previously defined type is to be utilized and when compatibility with the base type is to be preserved. For example, consider defining *compatible_nibble_bits* as:

```
SUBTYPE compatible_nibble_bits IS BIT_VECTOR ( 3 DOWNTO 0);
```

This declaration makes objects that are declared as *compatible_nibble_bits* compatible with other objects whose base types are BIT_VECTOR. As a counter example, consider the declaration of *nibble_bits* as:

```
TYPE nibble_bits IS ARRAY ( 3 DOWNTO 0 ) OF BIT;
```

If an object of type *nibble_bits* is to be assigned to a 4-bit BIT_VECTOR object, or if such objects are to be used in an expression, the use of explicit type conversions from *nibble_bits* to BIT_VECTOR or vice versa is required.

A subtype can be declared to have a range of enumeration elements of an enumeration type. For example, the following subtype declaration defines *ten_value_logic* as a subtype whose elements are integers between 0 and 9:

```
SUBTYPE ten_value_logic IS INTEGER RANGE 0 TO 9;
```

Objects of type *ten_value_logic* can be used in the same expressions with INTEGER type objects without requiring any form of a type conversion.

The definition of a general multi-level logic value system, that the definition of other logic value systems can be based on is an important application of this concept. For example, based on our *qit* type, subtypes such as *tit* and *bin* can be defined as shown here:

```
SUBTYPE tit IS qit RANGE '0' TO 'Z';
SUBTYPE bin IS qit RANGE '0' TO '1';
```

According to these declarations, the *tit* type is a three-value logic system that contains enumeration elements of '0', '1', and 'Z'and the *bin* type is a two-value logic which contains '0'and '1'. The base type for both of these subtypes is *qit*.

Assigning an object of a smaller subtype, e.g., *bin*, to an object of a larger subtype, e.g., *qit*, can be done directly and there is no need for any type conversion. The opposite is also possible, except that if an out of range value is assigned to the object of the smaller subtype, a simulation warning message will be issued.

In our example, the *bin* subtype contains all the enumeration elements of the predefined BIT type. These two types, however, are not compatible, so type conversion is required for assignments or operations that involve these two types.

6.3.2   Record Types

Arrays are composite types whose elements are all the same type. Records are also of the composite class, but they can consist of elements of different types. A record type definition consists of the declaration of the elements of the record that is bracketed between the RECORD keyword and the END RECORD keywords. Each record element declaration declares one or more identifiers and their types.

For example, consider an instruction format for a simple computer that has eight operations, four addressing modes, and an address space of 2^{11} words. Figure 6.31a shows the instruction format and the type declarations for these three fields. The opcode is an enumeration type whose elements are the instruction mnemonics, the addressing mode is an integer ranging from 0 to 3, and the address is an 11-bit BIT_VECTOR. In Figure 6.31b, the *instruction_format* type is declared as a record that contains three fields of *opc*, *mde*, and *adr* of types *opcode*, *mode*, and *address*, respectively. A signal of type *instruction_format*, shown in Figure 6.31c, is declared and the fields of this signal (*instr*) are initialized to *nop*, 0, and "00000000000". Figure 6.31d shows three signal assignments assigning values to the *instr* signal fields.

6.3.3 Alias Declaration

An object, an indexed part of it, or a slice of it can be given alternative names by using an alias declaration. This declaration can be used for signals, variables, or constants, and it can define new identifiers of the same class and type.

As an example, consider a flag register that is declared as a 4-bit BIT_VECTOR with a descending 3 DOWNTO 0 range. Starting with the most significant bit, the bits

```
| 15 14 13 | 12 11 |   10 09 08 07 06 05 04 03 02 01 00 |
 ---------------------------------------------------------
| opcode    | mode  |            address                  |
 ---------------------------------------------------------
|--------------------instruction_format--------------------|
```

```
TYPE opcode IS (sta, lda, add, sub, and, nop, jmp, jsr);
TYPE mode IS RANGE 0 TO 3;
TYPE address IS BIT_VECTOR (10 DOWNTO 0);
                    (a)
```

```
TYPE instruction_format IS RECORD
  opc : opcode;
  mde : mode;
  adr : address;
END RECORD;
                    (b)
```

```
SIGNAL instr : instruction_format := (nop, 0, "00000000000");
                    (c)
```

```
instr.opc <= lda;
instr.mde <= 2;
instr.adr <= "00011110000";
                    (d)
```

FIGURE 6.31
Record type, (a) three fields of an instruction, (b) declaration of instruction format, (c) a signal of record type, (d) referencing fields of a record type signal.

of this register are carry, overflow, negative, and zero flags. The declarations shown below specify aliases for each of the bits in the flag register:

```
ALIAS c_flag : BIT IS flag_register (3)
ALIAS v_flag : BIT IS flag_register (2)
ALIAS n_flag : BIT IS flag_register (1)
ALIAS z_flag : BIT IS flag_register (0)
```

With these declarations, the equivalent identifiers can be used instead of indexing the *flag_register*. An alias declaration specifies an identifier, its type, and the name of an object the identifier becomes an alias of.

For an example of using an alternative name for a slice of an array, consider the address field of the *instruction_format* in Figure 6.31. This 11-bit address can consist of a 3-bit page address and an 8-bit offset address as shown in Figure 6.32a. The alias declarations in Figure 6.32b equate *page* to the three most significant bits of the address field of an instruction and *offset* to its eight least significant bits. Figure 6.32c shows signal assignment to *page* and *offset* aliases. These assignments result in assigning an 11-bit address to the *adr* field of *instr*.

6.4 PREDEFINED ATTRIBUTES

Predefined attributes in VHDL provide functions for more efficient coding or mechanisms for modeling hardware characteristics. Attributes can be applied to arrays, types and signals and they have the following format:

```
array_or_type_or_signal_name' ATTRIBUTE_NAME
```

When reading this, the single quote (') is read as **tick**.

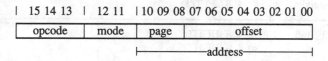

(a)

```
ALIAS page :
  BIT_VECTOR (2 DOWNTO 0) IS instr.adr (10 DOWNTO 8);
ALIAS offset :
  BIT_VECTOR (7 DOWNTO 0) IS instr.adr (7 DOWNTO 0);
```
(b)

```
page <= "001";
offset <= X"F1";
```
(c)

FIGURE 6.32
Alias declaration, (a) page and offset addresses, (b) alias declaration for the page and offset parts of the address, (c) assignments to page and offset parts of address.

This section discusses array, type, and signal attributes. All the predefined attributes are listed and categorically discussed. Examples are shown only for key attributes, however, other attributes are used in examples in the chapters that follow.

6.4.1   Array Attributes

Array attributes are used to find range, length, or boundaries of arrays. These attributes can only be used with array objects. Figure 6.33 shows all the predefined array attributes in VHDL and presents an example of each one. The examples are based on the *sq_4_8* signal declared in Figure 6.14a. The type of this signal is *qit_4by8*, as shown in Figure 6.12, which is a two-dimensional array with one range specified as 3 DOWNTO 0 and the other as 0 TO 7. A parenthesized number can follow array attributes. For multi-dimensional arrays, this number indicates the index range of the array, while for one-dimensional arrays it defaults to 1.

The examples in the previous chapters used 'RANGE and 'LENGTH attributes. More examples, based on *array_x* being an array object with ascending range, are shown here:

Condition *array_x*'LEFT < *array_x*'RIGHT is true.

Range *array_x*'LEFT TO *array_x*'RIGHT is equivalent to *array_x*'RANGE.

Expression *array_x*'HIGH - *array_x*'LOW + 1 is equivalent to *array_x*'LENGTH.

Result of *array_x* (*array_x*'LOW) is the value of *array_x* in its lowest index.

Attribute	Description	Example	Result
'LEFT	Left bound	sq_4_8'LEFT(1)	3
'RIGHT	Right bound	sq_4_8'RIGHT sq_4_8'RIGHT(2)	0 7
'HIGH	Upper bound	sq_4_8'HIGH(2)	7
'LOW	Lower bound	sq_4_8'LOWS(2)	0
'RANGE	Range	sq_4_8'RANGE(2) sq_4_8'RANGE(1)	0 TO 7 3 DOWNTO 0
'REVERSE_RANGE	Reverse Range	sq_4_8'REVERSE_RANGE(2) sq_4_8'REVERSE_RANGE(1)	7 DOWNTO 0 0 TO 3
'LENGTH	Length	sq_4_8'LENGTH	4

FIGURE 6.33
Predefined array attributes. The type of *sq_4_8* is *qit_4by8* in Figure 6.12.

6.4.2 Type Attributes

Type attributes are used for accessing elements of defined types and are only valid for nonarray types. Although several type and array attributes use the same names, it is important to realize that their meanings may be different. For example, when applied to an enumeration type, the 'RIGHT type attribute results in the right most enumeration element of that type. Attributes 'BASE, 'LEFT, 'RIGHT, 'HIGH, and 'LOW can be applied to any scalar type while attributes 'POS, 'VAL, 'SUCC, 'PRED, 'LEFTOF, and 'RIGHTOF can only be used with an integer type, an enumeration type, or a physical type. For example, using 'VAL(2) with an enumeration type results in the enumeration element in position 2 for this type. The positions of enumeration elements are numbered from left to right starting with 0.

Figure 6.34 shows a tabular list of all type attributes in VHDL and presents an example of each one. All examples refer to the *qit* and *tit* types that were defined in earlier sections of this chapter. The results of attributes 'LEFT, 'RIGHT, 'HIGH, and 'LOW correspond to the values of the types or subtypes that they are applied to, while the 'POS, 'VAL, 'SUCC, 'PRED, 'LEFTOF, and 'RIGHTOF attributes perform the specified functions on the base of the subtype. For example, *tit*'POS('X') results in 3, which is the position of 'X'in the *qit* type. Notice that 'X'is not even contained in the *tit* subtype.

6.4.3 Signal Attributes

Signal attributes are used for objects in the signal class of any type. Such attributes are used for finding events, transactions, or timing of events and transactions on signals. These attributes are most useful for modeling hardware properties.

Attributes 'STABLE, 'EVENT, 'LAST_EVENT, and 'LAST_VALUE deal with events occurring on a signal. For example, when 'EVENT is used with a signal, the result is true (BOOLEAN TRUE) when an event occurs on that signal, that is, the value of the signal changes. Attributes 'QUIET, 'ACTIVE, 'LAST_ACTIVE, and 'TRANSACTION have to do with the transactions that occur on a signal. For example, *s_signal*'ACTIVE is true when a transaction occurs on the *s_signal*, even if the transaction does not cause a change of value on this signal.

Results of the attributes 'DELAYED, 'STABLE, 'QUIET, and 'TRANSACTION are signals and can be used like signal objects. For example, *s_signal*'DELAYED' STABLE is only valid because *s_signal*'DELAYED results in a signal to which the 'STABLE signal attribute can be applied.

Figure 6.35 presents a list of the signal attributes and gives a simple example for each one, showing the kind and type of the result. Also shown in this figure is a box indicating whether the attribute deals with transactions or events on a signal.The *s1* signal used in the examples is assumed to be a scalar signal of type BIT. Signal attributes are time dependent, which means that their values may change continuously during simulation. Figure 6.36 shows an example waveform on *s1*, and the result of using various attributes with this BIT type signal. The waveform shown here includes transactions and events. Each transaction is indicated by a shaded area (■) of δ duration

Attribute	Description	Example	Result
'BASE	Base of type	tit'BASE	qit
'LEFT	Left bound of type or subtype.	tit'LEFT qit'LEFT	'0' '0'
'RIGHT	Right bound of type or subtype.	tit'RIGHT qit'RIGHT	'Z' 'X'
'HIGH	Upper bound of type or subtype.	INTEGER'HIGH tit'HIGH	Large 'Z'
'LOW	Lower bound of type or subtype.	POSITIVE'LOW qit'LOW	1 '0'
'POS(V)	Position of value *V* in *base* of type.	qit'POS('Z') tit'POS('X')	2 3
'VAl(P)	Value at Position *P* in *base* of type.	qit'VAL(3) tit'VAL(3)	'X' 'X'
'SUCC(V)	Value, after value *V* in *base* of type.	tit'SUCC('Z')	'X'
'PRED(V)	Value, before value *V* in *base* of type.	tit'PRED('1')	'0'
'LEFTOF(V)	Value, left of value *V* in *base* of type.	tit'LEFTOF('1') tit'LEFTOF('0')	'0' Error
'RIGHTOF(V)	Value, right of value *V* in *base* of type.	tit'RIGHTOF('1') tit'RIGHTOF('Z')	'Z' 'Z'

FIGURE 6.34
Predefined type attributes. *qit* and *tit* are enumeration types.

on the waveform. Events occur when a transaction causes the value of *s1* to change. Those attributes whose results are of the type of signal that they are applied to (type BIT for signal *s1*) are shown by logical waveforms and those with BOOLEAN or BIT results (independent of type of *s1*) are indicated with a block (■) for TRUE or '1' and a space (_) for FALSE or '0'. Attributes that result in a signal are shown in the **bold** font.

Common applications of signal attributes include edge detection, pulse width verification, glitch detection, and level mode analysis. For example, the 'STABLE

Attribute	T/E	Example	Kind	Type
Description				
'DELAYED	–	s1'DELAYED(5 NS)	SIGNAL	As *s1*
A copy of *s1*, but delayed by 5 NS. If no parameter or 0, delayed by δ. Equivalent to TRANSPORT delay of *s*1.				
'STABLE	EV	s1'STABLE(5 NS)	SIGNAL	BOOLEAN
A signal that is TRUE if *S1* has not changed in the last 5 NS. If used with no parameter or 0, the resulting signal is TRUE if *s1* has not changed in the current simulation time.				
'EVENT	EV	s1'EVENT	Value	BOOLEAN
If *s1* changes in the current simulation cycle, *s1*'EVENT will be TRUE for this cycle (δ time).				
'LAST_EVENT	EV	s1'LAST_EVENT	Value	Time
The amount of time since the last value change on *s1*. If *s1*'EVENT is TRUE, the value of *s1*'LAST_EVENT is 0.				
'LAST_VALUE	EV	s1'LAST_VALUE	VALUE	As *s1*
The value of *s1* before the most recent event occurs on it.				
'QUIET	TR	s1'QUIET(5 NS)	SIGNAL	BOOLEAN
A signal that is TRUE if no transaction has been placed on *s1* in the last 5 NS. If no parameter of 0, for current simulation cycle is assumed.				
'ACTIVE	TR	s1'ACTIVE	VALUE	BOOLEAN
If *s1* has had a transaction in the current simulation cycle, *s1*'ACTIVE will be TRUE for this simulation cycle, for δ time.				
'LAST_ACTIVE	TR	s1'LAST_ACTIVE	VALUE	TIME
The amount of time since the last transaction occurred on *s1*. If *s1*'ACTIVE is TRUE, *s1*'LAST_ACTIVE is 0.				
'TRANSACTION	TR	s1'TRANSACTION	SIGNAL	BIT
A signal that toggles each time a transaction occurs on *s1*.				

FIGURE 6.35
Predefined signal attributes. Signal *s* is assumed to be of type BIT.

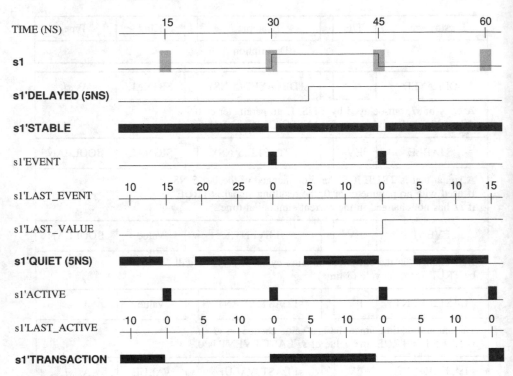

FIGURE 6.36
Results of signal attributes when applied to the BIT type signal, *s1*.

attribute in an edge trigger flip-flop can check for a change in the value of the clock, that is, an edge of a clock. Let us consider the description of the falling-edge D-type flip-flop in Figure 6.37. The statement part of this description consists of a conditional signal assignment which conditionally assigns the D-input to a temporary signal, *tmp*. If a new value is assigned to this signal, it will be assigned to the output after a delay of 8 NS. The condition of the conditional signal assignment becomes TRUE if 1) *c* is *zero*, and 2) *c* has *not* been *stable* during the current simulation cycle. In other words, the condition is TRUE if *c* changes, and this change causes it to be 0. Clearly, this condition detects the falling edge of *c* in the current simulation cycle. The *tmp* signal receives *d* on the falling edge of the clock; otherwise, *tmp* remains unchanged.

Although *c*'EVENT and NOT *c*'STABLE are equivalent in most cases, since the latter generates a signal, its use is recommended in concurrent statements.

As another example in the use of signal assignments, consider the *brief_t_flip_flop* in Figure 6.38. This is the description of a toggle flip-flop that toggles only when a positive pulse longer that 20 NS appears on its *t* input. As in the previous example, a conditional signal assignment assigns one of the two possible values to the *tmp* signal, which is then assigned to the output. The *tmp* signal, which stores the internal state

```
┌ENTITY brief_d_flip_flop IS
│    PORT (d, c : IN BIT; q : OUT BIT);
└END brief_d_flip_flop;
--
┌ARCHITECTURE falling_edge OF brief_d_flip_flop IS
│    SIGNAL tmp : BIT;
├BEGIN
│    tmp <= d WHEN (c = '0' AND NOT c' STABLE) ELSE tmp;
│    q <= tmp AFTER 8 NS;
└END falling_edge;
```

FIGURE 6.37
A simple falling edge flip-flop using signal attributes.

```
┌ENTITY brief_t_flip_flop IS
│    PORT (t : IN BIT; q : OUT BIT);
└END brief_t_flip_flop;
--
┌ARCHITECTURE toggle OF brief_t_flip_flop IS
│    SIGNAL tmp : BIT;
├BEGIN
│    tmp <= NOT tmp WHEN (
│            (t = '0' AND NOT t' STABLE) AND (t' DELAYED' STABLE(20 NS))
│                            ) ELSE tmp;
│    q <= tmp AFTER 8 NS;
└END toggle;
```

FIGURE 6.38
A simple toggle flip-flop using signal attributes.

of the flip-flop, is assigned to the complement of itself when the two conditions are TRUE. The first condition is the falling edge of t (t='0'AND NOT t'STABLE), which is the same as the condition in the example in Figure 6.37. The second condition is TRUE if t, before this last fall, has been stable for 20 NS. The operation t'DELAYED evaluates to a signal that is delayed from t by 0 NS and, therefore, it does not include the change that just occurred on it. If this delayed signal has been stable for at least 20 NS, then we can conclude that the width of the positive pulse on t has been at least 20 NS.

6.5 USER-DEFINED ATTRIBUTES

In addition to the predefined attributes, VHDL allows definition and use of user-defined attributes. Such attributes do not have simulation semantics, so it is up to the user to define them and use them in accordance with the way they are defined.

User-defined attributes may be applied to the elements of what is referred to as the entity class in VHDL. The entity class consists of entities, architectures, configurations, procedures, functions, packages, types, subtypes, constants, signals, variables, components, and labels. Before an attribute can be used, it has to be declared using an attribute declaration. An attribute declaration identifies a name as an attribute with a given type. For example, the following declaration declares *sub_dir* as an attribute that can take values of STRING type:

```
ATTRIBUTE sub_dir : STRING;
```

If the above declaration is made visible to a description, it can be associated with any of the elements of the entity class mentioned above, i.e., entity, architecture, configuration, etc. For example, in order to associate the *sub_dir* attribute with the *brief_d_flip_flop* entity in Figure 6.37, this attribute specification must appear in the declarative part of that entity:

```
ATTRIBUTE sub_dir OF brief_d_flip_flop : ENTITY IS "/user/vhdl";
```

The expression *brief_d_flip_flop'sub_dir*, anywhere in an architecture of the *brief_d_flip_flop* entity, evaluates to *"/user/vhdl"*.

Figure 6.39 shows two attribute definitions and usages. A package called *utility_attributes* declares attributes *sub_dir* and *delay*. The *sub_dir* attribute has a STRING

```
┌PACKAGE utility_attributes IS
│    TYPE timing IS RECORD
│        rise, fall : TIME;
│    END RECORD;
│    ATTRIBUTE delay : timing;
│    ATTRIBUTE sub_dir : STRING;
└END utility_attributes;
 --
│ USE WORK.utility_attributes.ALL;
│ -- FROM PACKAGE USE: delay, sub_dir
┌ENTITY brief_d_flip_flop IS
│    PORT (d, c : IN BIT; q : OUT BIT);
│    ATTRIBUTE sub_dir OF brief_d_flip_flop : ENTITY IS "/user/vhdl";
│    ATTRIBUTE delay OF q : SIGNAL IS (8 NS, 10 NS);
└END brief_d_flip_flop;
 --
┌ARCHITECTURE attributed_falling_edge OF brief_d_flip_flop IS
│    SIGNAL tmp : BIT;
├BEGIN
│    tmp <= d WHEN ( c= '0' AND NOT c' STABLE ) ELSE tmp;
│    q <= '1' AFTER q'delay.rise WHEN tmp = '1' ELSE
│        '0' AFTER q'delay.fall;
└END attributed_falling_edge;
```

FIGURE 6.39
Associating attributes to entities and signals.

type, and the type of the *delay* attribute is *timing* which is a record consisting of two fields of type TIME. The entity declaration of *brief_d_flip_flop*, also shown in Figure 6.39, makes use of both attributes defined in this package. In the declarative part of this entity, where both attributes have become visible by applying the use statement, the attributes are associated with the entity itself and with the output of this entity. In the statement part of the *attributed_falling_edge* architecture of the *brief_d_flip_flop* entity, the *rise* and *fall* fields of the *delay* attribute of the *q* output are used in calculating the delay values on this output.

An attribute specification for associating a user-defined attribute with an entity class can appear in any declarative part in which the attribute and the entity it is being applied to are visible. For example, in Figure 6.39, the attribute specification that associates *delay* with the *q* output could appear in the declarative part of the *attributed_falling_edge* architecture. In the same example, it is also worthwhile noting that if the *delay* attribute is to be applied to other signals, those signals should be listed along with *q*, separated by commas. If an attribute is to be applied to all visible signals, the keyword ALL can replace the list of individual signals. The keyword OTHERS can also be used to apply the attribute to all entity classes that have not been specified above it.

Values of user-defined attributes can be used in expressions or on the right hand side of assignments, but no assignments can be made to them.

6.6 PACKAGING BASIC UTILITIES

Chapter 5 introduced a package that we referred to as *basic_utilities*. This chapter added utility types, definitions, and subprograms to this package. We used this package in most of the examples in this chapter and we will continue using it and adding to it in the next two chapters. The present form of the *basic_utilities* package is shown for reference in Figure 6.40. In addition to items whose addition to this package were explicitly specified in the text of Chapters 5 and 6, the package also includes the *qit_vector*, *tit_vector*, and *tit* types and subtype. The *qit_vector* and *tit_vector* types are unconstrained arrays of *qit* and *tit*, respectively.

6.7 SUMMARY

This chapter presented tools for high level descriptions. Declaration of types and the usage of objects of various types were covered in the first part of the chapter. In the context of describing type related issues, we introduced the unconstrained array and file type. Unconstrained arrays are utilities in the language that not only make hardware descriptions very flexible; they are also very useful for software processes and programs. The basic I/O presented in this chapter showed a simple way to read or write from files. The overloading which is related to types was discussed next. This subject was discussed for user-defined subprograms as well as for the VHDL operators. Our emphasis on operator overloading was on the logic and hardware-

```
PACKAGE basic_utilities IS
    TYPE qit IS ('0', '1', 'Z', ',X');
    TYPE qit_2d IS ARRAY (qit, qit) OF qit;
    TYPE qit_1d IS ARRAY (qit) OF qit;
    TYPE qit_vector IS ARRAY (NATURAL RANGE <>) OF qit;
    SUBTYPE tit IS qit RANGE '0' TO 'Z';
    TYPE tit_vector IS ARRAY (NATURAL RANGE <>) OF tit;
    TYPE integer_vector IS ARRAY (NATURAL RANGE <>) OF INTEGER;
    TYPE logic_data IS FILE OF CHARACTER;
    TYPE capacitance IS RANGE 0 TO 1E16
    UNITS
        ffr;  -- Femto Farads (base unit)
        pfr = 1000 ffr;
        nfr = 1000 pfr;
        ufr = 1000 nfr;
        mfr = 1000 ufr;
        far = 1000 mfr;
        kfr = 1000 far;
    END UNITS;
    TYPE resistance IS RANGE 0 TO 1E16
    UNITS
        l_o;  -- Milli-Ohms (base unit)
        ohms = 1000 l_o;
        k_o = 1000 ohms;
        m_o = 1000 k_o;
        g_o = 1000 m_o;
    END UNITS;
    FUNCTION fgl (w, x, gl : BIT) RETURN BIT;
    FUNCTION feq (w, x, eq : BIT) RETURN BIT;
    PROCEDURE bin2int (bin : IN BIT_VECTOR; int : OUT INTEGER);
    PROCEDURE int2bin (int : IN INTEGER;  bin : OUT BIT_VECTOR);
    PROCEDURE apply_data ( SIGNAL target : OUT BIT_VECTOR;
        CONSTANT values : IN integer_vector;  CONSTANT period : IN TIME);
    PROCEDURE assign_bits ( SIGNAL s : OUT BIT; file_name : IN STRING; period : IN TIME
    PROCEDURE assign_bits ( SIGNAL s : OUT qit; file_name : IN STRING; period : IN TIME)
    FUNCTION "AND" (a, b : qit) RETURN qit;
    FUNCTION "OR" (a, b : qit) RETURN qit;
    FUNCTION "NOT" (a : qit) RETURN qit;
    FUNCTION "*" (a : resistance; b : capacitance) RETURN TIME;
END basic_utilities;
```

FIGURE 6.40
Present form of the *basic-utilities* package. (*continued*)

related operators, but by overloading the multiplication operator we indicated that any operator can be overloaded for any type of operand. Predefined attributes in VHDL can be looked upon as operators or predefined functions. The difference, however, is that such attributes apply to nonobjects as well as signal objects in the language. In

```
PACKAGE BODY basic_utilities IS
  FUNCTION "AND" (a, b : qit) RETURN qit IS
    CONSTANT qit_and_table : qit_2d := (
                              ('0','0','0','0'),
                              ('0','1','1','X'),
                              ('0','1','1','X'),
                              ('0','X','X','X'));
  BEGIN
    RETURN qit_and_table (a, b);
  END "AND";
  FUNCTION "OR" (a, b : qit) RETURN qit IS
    CONSTANT qit_or_table : qit_2d := (
                              ('0','1','1','X'),
                              ('1','1','1','1'),
                              ('1','1','1','1'),
                              ('X','1','1','X'));
  BEGIN
    RETURN qit_or_table (a, b);
  END "OR";
  FUNCTION "NOT" (a : qit) RETURN qit IS
    CONSTANT qit_not_table : qit_1d := ('1','0','0',' X');
  BEGIN
    RETURN qit_not_table (a);
  END "NOT";
  FUNCTION "*" (a : resistance; b : capacitance) RETURN TIME IS
  BEGIN
    RETURN ( ( a / 1 l_o) * ( b / 1 ffr ) * 1 FS ) / 1000;
  END "*";
  FUNCTION fgl (w, x, gl : BIT) RETURN BIT IS
  BEGIN
    RETURN  (w AND gl) OR (NOT x  AND  gl) OR (w  AND  NOT x);
  END fgl;
  FUNCTION feq (w, x, eq : BIT) RETURN BIT IS
  BEGIN
    RETURN  (w AND x AND eq) OR (NOT w  AND  NOT x  AND  eq);
  END feq;
  PROCEDURE bin2int (bin : IN BIT_VECTOR; int : OUT INTEGER) IS
    VARIABLE result: INTEGER;
  BEGIN
    result := 0;
    FOR i IN bin'RANGE LOOP
      IF bin(i) = '1'THEN   result := result + 2**i;
      END IF;
    END LOOP;
    int := result;
  END bin2int;
```

FIGURE 6.40

Present form of the *basic-utilities* package. (*continued*)

```
PROCEDURE int2bin (int : IN INTEGER;  bin : OUT BIT_VECTOR) IS
   VARIABLE tmp : INTEGER;
BEGIN
   tmp := int;
   FOR i IN 0 TO (bin'LENGTH - 1) LOOP
      IF (tmp MOD 2  =  1) THEN  bin (i) := '1';
      ELSE bin (i) := '0';
      END IF;
      tmp := tmp / 2;
   END LOOP;
END int2bin;
PROCEDURE apply_data ( SIGNAL target : OUT BIT_VECTOR;
   CONSTANT values : IN integer_vector; CONSTANT period : IN TIME)
IS
   VARIABLE buf : BIT_VECTOR (target'RANGE);
BEGIN
   FOR i IN values'RANGE LOOP
      int2bin (values(i), buf);
      target <= TRANSPORT buf AFTER i * period;
   END LOOP;
END apply_data;
PROCEDURE assign_bits (
   SIGNAL s : OUT BIT; file_name : IN STRING; period : IN TIME)
IS
   VARIABLE char : CHARACTER;
   VARIABLE current : TIME := 0 NS;
   FILE input_value_file : logic_data IS IN file_name;
BEGIN
   WHILE NOT ENDFILE (input_value_file) LOOP
      READ (input_value_file, char);
      IF char = '0' OR char = '1' THEN
         current := current + period;
         IF char = '0' THEN
            s <= TRANSPORT '0' AFTER current;
         ELSIF char = '1' THEN
            s <= TRANSPORT '1' AFTER current;
         END IF;
      END IF;
   END LOOP;
END assign_bits;
```

FIGURE 6.40
Present form of the *basic-utilities* package (*continued*).

modeling, hardware behavior attributes are very useful, as we will see in the following, chapters. Finally in this chapter, we presented the *basic_utilities* package. Elements of this package are useful for hardware modeling and the creation of the package demonstrates the importance of packaging capability in VHDL.

```
┌PROCEDURE assign_bits (
│   SIGNAL s : OUT qit; file_name : IN STRING; period : IN TIME)
├IS
│   VARIABLE char : CHARACTER;
│   VARIABLE current : TIME := 0 NS;
│   FILE input_value_file : logic_data IS IN file_name;
├BEGIN
│   WHILE NOT ENDFILE (input_value_file) LOOP
│     READ (input_value_file, char);
│     current := current + period;
│     CASE char IS
│       WHEN '0' => s <= TRANSPORT '0' AFTER current;
│       WHEN '1' => s <= TRANSPORT '1' AFTER current;
│       WHEN 'Z' | 'z' => s <= TRANSPORT 'Z' AFTER current;
│       WHEN 'X' | 'x' => s <= TRANSPORT 'X' AFTER current;
│       WHEN OTHERS => current := current - period;
│     END CASE;
│   END LOOP;
└END assign_bits;
END basic_utilities;
```

FIGURE 6.40
Present form of the *basic-utilities* package.

REFERENCES

1. "IEEE Standard VHDL Language Reference Manual," IEEE Std 1076-1987, The Institute of Electrical and Electronic Engineers, Inc., 1988.
2. Lipsett, L., C. Schaefer, and C. Ussery, "VHDL: Hardware Description and Design," Klewer Academic Publishing, Boston, 1988.

PROBLEMS

6.1. Write an entity declaration and a *double_delay* architecture for an XOR gate in the *qit* logic value system. Use a conditional signal assignment. Use a *tplh* of 9 ns and a *tphl* of 7 ns.

6.2. Write an entity declaration and an architecture for an RC circuit in the *qit* logic value system. The circuit has an input and an output. The output follows the input for '0', '1' or 'X' input values. If the input becomes 'Z', the output holds its old value for several milliseconds (use 8 ms).

6.3. Use the RC circuit in Problem 2 to describe an NMOS two-input NAND gate.
The solution to this problem depends on code developed in Problem 6.2.

6.4. Show type definition for the *distance* physical type, ranging from microns to meters.

6.5. Write a procedure, *apply_bit*, such that bits of an unconstrained string input to the procedure are applied to its target signal according to the specified time interval. Make sure no unnecessary transactions occur on the target of the procedure. A sample call to this procedure is shown here:

```
apply_bit (target, "110001000100001111001010", 300 NS);
```

6.6. Using *bin2int* and *int2bin*, write a function, *inc_qits*, that returns the increment of its *qit_vector* input parameter. The output of the function should be *qit_vector* type, and values 'X' and 'Z' should be treated as '1'. Use unconstrained arrays so that your function works regardless of the size of the input.

6.7. Use the concatenation operator to develop a complete VHDL description for an 8-bit logic shifter. The circuit has a 2-bit control input *c*. The value of $c=00$ is for no-operation, $c=01$ is for right rotate, $c=10$ is for left rotate, and $c=11$ is for arithmetic right shift. The data input and output of the circuit are of the *qit_vector* type, and their mapping is determined by the bits of *c*.

6.8. Write a procedure that assigns consecutive binary numbers to its OUT BIT_VECTOR lines. The procedure should have a *target* output that is an unconstrained array, and a TIME *period*. When called with an *n*-bit argument, it should assign sequential binary numbers from 0 to $2^n - 1$ to its *target* signal output. These numbers are distanced by the amount of the constant associated with the *period* parameter. For example, if called with a 2-bit vector and a *period* of 100 NS, then the target will receive this data:

"00", "01" AFTER 100 NS, "10" AFTER 200 NS, "11" AFTER 300 NS;

You can use all the procedures and utilities in the *basic_utilities* package.

6.9. Show the overloading function for the XOR operator for the *qit* logic value system.

6.10. Write an unconstrained odd parity checker function. The input is of *qit_vector* type and the output of *qit* type. Treat values 'Z' and 'X' as '1'. The function returns the XOR results of all its input bits.

6.11. Use the function in Problem 6.10 in an architecture for functional description of a parity checker circuit.

6.12. Speed is distance/time. Write the physical type for speed. Overload the division operator to evaluate speed when it is used for dividing distance by time (see Problem 6.4).

6.13. Rewrite the *int2bin* procedure such that it functions properly for any size output, declared with any range, and in any direction. Treat the left bit of the output as the most significant bit and the right-most bit as the least significant. Bit 3 is the MSB for a BIT_VECTOR ranging from 3 TO 10 associated with the output and the LSB is bit 10.

6.14. Rewrite the *bin2int* procedure such that it functions properly for any size output, declared with any range, and in any direction. Treat the left bit of the input as the most significant bit, and the right most bit as the least significant. Bit 3 is the MSB for a BIT_VECTOR ranging from 3 TO 10 associated with the input of this procedure and the LSB is bit 10.

6.15. Write an expression for detecting the falling edge on a clock that is the *qit* type. Falling edge occurs only when the clock makes a transition from '1' to '0'.

6.16. The 'TRANSACTION attribute toggles when a transaction occurs on its parameter. Write an expression such that it causes the value of signal *e* to toggle when an *event* occurs on *a*. Using this expression in the following VHDL code, show and justify all transactions and events that occur on the *a*, *t*, and *e* signals.

```
ARCHITECTURE challenging   OF transaction_vs_event IS
    SIGNAL   a : BIT := '1';
    SIGNAL   t, e : BIT := '0';
BEGIN
    a <= '0', '1' AFTER 10 NS, '0' AFTER 12 NS, '0' AFTER 14 NS;
    t <= a' TRANSACTION;
    e <= toggle_when_event_on_a__expression;
END challenging;
```

6.17. Use conditional signal assignments to describe a toggle flip-flop in *qit* logic value system. The output toggles when a complete positive pulse ('0' to '1' to '0') appears on the input.

6.18. Repeat Problem 6.7 for unconstrained input and output vectors. The output of the shifter should become all 'X' if the value of c is anything but "00", "01", "10", or "11". Take advantage of array attributes.

6.19. Use an array of BITS as shown below to model a master-slave *jk* flip-flop.

ARRAY(BIT, BIT, BIT) OF BIT

Use j, k and q values for the indices of this array, and let the array represent the next state of the flip-flop. In the declarative part of the architecture of the flip-flop declare a constant (for example, *jk-table*) of the type of the array shown above. Initialize this constant to appropriate next values of a *jk* flip-flop. In the statement part of the architecture of the flip-flop look up next q values by indexing the jk table using j, k and present q values.

CHAPTER

7

DATAFLOW
DESCRIPTIONS
IN VHDL

The middle ground between structural and behavioral descriptions is the dataflow or register transfer level of abstraction as we defined it in Chapter 1. Descriptions at this level specify flow of data through the registers and buses of a system. This flow is controlled by external signals that can be generated by other dataflow machines. Signal assignments constitute the primary VHDL constructs for description of hardware at the dataflow level. These constructs allow controlled movement of data through registers and buses. Various forms of controlled signal assignments, that is, *conditional*, *selected*, and *guarded* assignments, can be used for explicit clock control and handshaking specifications, and to make selections from among several sources.

This chapter discusses the forms of signal assignments not presented in the previous chapters. We also will demonstrate the use of signal assignments for data selection, clock control, and enabling registers and buses. The subject of concurrent assignment of values to signals is related to the various forms of signal assignments and is also dealt with in this chapter.

7.1 MULTIPLEXING AND DATA SELECTION

In a digital system, various forms of hardware structures are used for the selection and placement of data into buses or registers. The simplest form of data selection is the AND-OR logic shown in Figure 7.1.

174

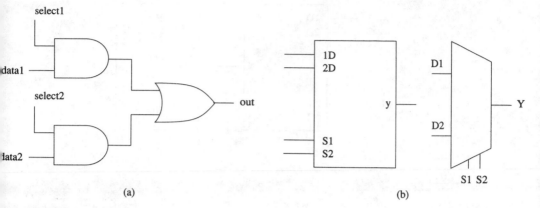

(a)   (b)

FIGURE 7.1
Basic data selection hardware, (a) logic diagram, (b) symbols.

This structure selects *data1* or *data2*, depending on the values of *select1* and *select2*. Other forms of hardware for the selection of data may consist of a wired connection of tri-state gate outputs, or a parallel connection of MOS transmission gates. Data selection is also referred to as multiplexing and the hardware that performs this task is called a multiplexer. Figure 7.1b shows two multiplexer symbols for the hardware of Figure 7.1a. In addition to the selection of data through a multiplexer, clocking is also often used to enable the acceptance of data by a register or memory structure. As shown in Figure 7.2, this scheme requires enabling of the *clock* signal by the use of an AND gate. On the rising edge of the clock, the data at the *d_input* of the flip-flop is loaded into the flip-flop, only when the *enable* input is active.

The two schemes for multiplexing and clock enabling can also be combined, as shown in Figure 7.3. In this case, data is loaded into the register on the edge of the clock when the clock is enabled and the data is selected by the input multiplexer.

Structures such as those described above can be described in VHDL using various forms of signal assignments.

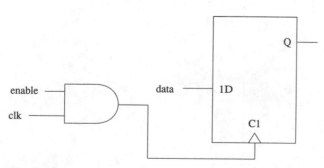

FIGURE 7.2
Selection of data by clock enabling.

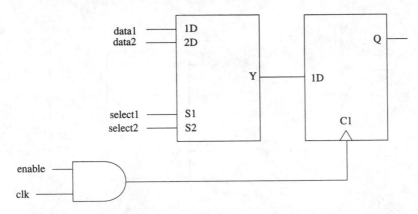

FIGURE 7.3
Multiplexing and clock enabling.

7.1.1 General Multiplexing

A 1-bit 8-to-1 multiplexer with eight select inputs is shown in Figure 7.4. The output of this structure becomes equal to one of the eight inputs when a corresponding select input is active. The symbol shown here does not specify what occurs if more than one select input is active, however, this usually depends on the hardware used for implementing the multiplexer.

The VHDL description that corresponds to this multiplexer is shown in Figure 7.5. This description uses the *qit* logic value system that is defined in the *basic_utilities* package. The ports of the system consist of eight data inputs, eight select inputs, and one output. Although an array of *qit* could be used for the ports, for a

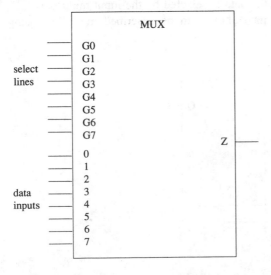

FIGURE 7.4
An eight-to-one multiplexer.

```
USE  WORK.basic_utilities.ALL;
-- FROM  PACKAGE  USE:  qit,  qit_vector
ENTITY  mux_8_to_1  IS
    PORT  (  i7,  i6,  i5,  i4,  i3,  i2,  i1,  i0  :  IN  qit;
             s7,  s6,  s5,  s4,  s3,  s2,  s1,  s0  :  IN  qit;  z  :  OUT  qit );
END  mux_8_to_1;
--
ARCHITECTURE  dataflow  OF  mux_8_to_1  IS
    SIGNAL  sel_lines  :  qit_vector  (  7  DOWNTO  0);
BEGIN
    sel_lines  <=  s7&s6&s5&s4&s3&s2&s1&s0;
    WITH  sel_lines  SELECT
        z <=  '0'  AFTER  3  NS  WHEN  "00000000",
              i7  AFTER  3  NS  WHEN  "10000000"  |  "Z0000000",
              i6  AFTER  3  NS  WHEN  "01000000"  |  "0Z000000",
              i5  AFTER  3  NS  WHEN  "00100000"  |  "00Z00000",
              i4  AFTER  3  NS  WHEN  "00010000"  |  "000Z0000",
              i3  AFTER  3  NS  WHEN  "00001000"  |  "0000Z000",
              i2  AFTER  3  NS  WHEN  "00000100"  |  "00000Z00",
              i1  AFTER  3  NS  WHEN  "00000010"  |  "000000Z0",
              i0  AFTER  3  NS  WHEN  "00000001"  |  "0000000Z",
              'X'  WHEN  OTHERS;
END  dataflow;
```

FIGURE 7.5
VHDL description for the eight-to-one multiplexer.

closer correspondence to the symbol in Figure 7.4, all inputs are declared as individual *qit* type lines.

In the *dataflow* architecture of the multiplexer, the *sel_lines* intermediate signal of the *qit_vector* type holds the concatenation of the eight select inputs. This 8-bit vector is then used in a selected signal assignment to select '0', 'X', or one of the eight data inputs to be assigned to the *z* output. If none of the select lines are active (*sel_lines* is "00000000"), a '0' will be scheduled for the *z* output after 3 nanoseconds. A data input, i.e., *i7, i6, i5, i5, i4, i3, i2, i1* or *i0*, will be assigned to the *z* output if its corresponding select line, i.e., *s7, s6, s5, s4, s3, s2, s1* or *s0*, is '1' or 'Z'. As in the gates discussing Chapter 6, we are treating open inputs as logic value '1'. Finally, the output of the multiplexer becomes 'X' or unknown if more than one select input is active, or if an 'X'appears on any of the select lines.

The syntax details of the selected signal assignment in Figure 7.5 are illustrated in Figure 7.6. The WITH keyword begins this language construct, and is followed by an expression. The possible values of this expression form the choices of the selected waveforms of the selected signal assignment. In our example, the expression is the 8-bit *sel_lines* signal. The next part of this construct consists of a left hand side target and the right hand side selected waveforms. For the target, ten waveforms are specified. Each of these waveforms is conditioned by one or more of the choices of the *sel_lines* expression. For the '0' AFTER 3 NS waveform, only one choice is specified, which

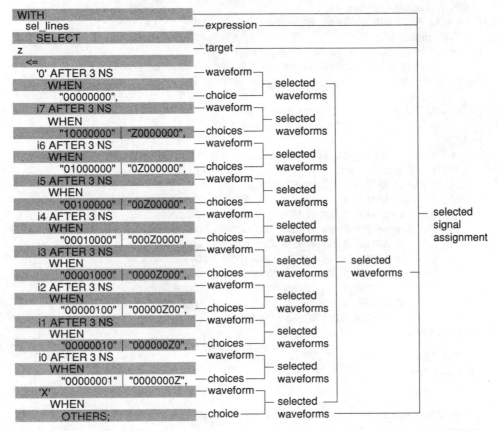

FIGURE 7.6
Syntax details of a selected signal assignment.

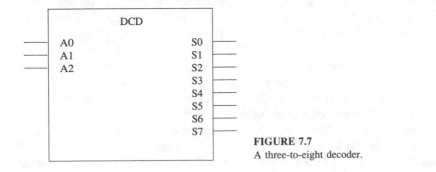

FIGURE 7.7
A three-to-eight decoder.

is the value of *sel_lines*, "00000000". For the waveforms that contain the data input signals (*i7* through *i0*), two choices separated by a vertical bar are specified. For the last waveform choice, i.e., 'X', OTHERS is used. This choice represents all possible values of the *sel_lines* signal that have not been explicitly specified. Choices used with the selected signal assignment must form a complete set of all possible values of the expression of this statement. The use of OTHERS eliminates the need to individually list all 65,536 ($= 4^8$) values of the *sel_lines* 8-bit *qit_vector*.

For another example of the use of the selected signal assignment construct, consider the 3-to-8 decoder in Figure 7.7. This decoder has a 3-bit address input and eight output lines. An output, *i*, becomes active (high) when the decimal equivalent of the input address is equal to *i*. As before, we treat 'Z' input value as logic '1'.

The VHDL description for this unit is shown in Figure 7.8. The elements of all inputs and outputs are of type *qit*. A single selected signal assignment, the target of which is the 8-bit output, *so* (selected output), is used for decoding the input. The right hand side of this assignment consists of selected waveforms that set the bits of the output according to the three bits of the input address. For the input bits, both '1' and 'Z' are taken as logic '1'. For each waveform, all possible combinations of 'Z's and '1's have been used as choices. The last waveform causes all bits of the output to become 'X' if any of the address bits is unknown. As in the previous example, the use of OTHERS with the last waveform reduces the amount of coding that would have been required if we were to list all possible values of the 3-bit long *qit* type address.

For a multiplexer with a decoded input, the decoder in Figure 7.8 can be used with the multiplexer in Figure 7.5. For large multiplexers and binary decoders which have regular input to output mappings, behavioral constructs can be used to simplify the descriptions. Specifying input-output values in a tabular form, such as in the

```
USE  WORK.basic_utilities.ALL;
-- FROM PACKAGE USE: qit_vector
ENTITY dcd_3_to_8 IS
    PORT ( adr : IN qit_vector (2 DOWNTO 0);
    so : OUT qit_vector (7 DOWNTO 0));
END dcd_3_to_8;
--
ARCHITECTURE dataflow OF dcd_3_to_8 IS
BEGIN
    WITH adr SELECT
        so <= "00000001" AFTER 2 NS WHEN "000",
              "00000010" AFTER 2 NS WHEN "00Z" | "001",
              "00000100" AFTER 2 NS WHEN "0Z0" | "010",
              "00001000" AFTER 2 NS WHEN "0ZZ" | "0Z1" | "01Z" | "011",
              "00010000" AFTER 2 NS WHEN "100" | "Z00",
              "00100000" AFTER 2 NS WHEN "Z0Z" | "Z01" | "10Z" | "101" ,
              "01000000" AFTER 2 NS WHEN "ZZ0" | "Z10" | "1Z0" | "110",
              "10000000" AFTER 2 NS WHEN "ZZZ" | "ZZ1" | "Z1Z" | "Z11" |
                                         "1ZZ" | "1Z1" | "11Z" | "111",
              "XXXXXXXX" WHEN OTHERS;
END dataflow;
```

FIGURE 7.8
VHDL description for the three-to-eight decoder.

descriptions in Figures 7.5 and 7.8, is most useful when describing circuits with random input to output mapping. For example, a seven-segment decoder can easily be described using a selected signal assignment.

7.1.2   Guarded Signal Assignments

Using conditional signal assignments for the description of edge trigger flip-flops was discussed in Chapter 6. Figure 7.9a provides a more complete example than the one in Figure 6.37. The corresponding circuit notation, illustrating the dependencies of the c and d inputs, is shown in Figure 7.9b. The *assigning* architecture of the *d_flipflop* entity specifies that the value of the d input is assigned to the *internal_state* signal on the rising edge of the clock. If this assignment causes the value of *internal_state* to change, the new value is assigned to q after *delay1*, and its complement to qb after *delay2*. The conditional assignment to the *internal_state* specifies that this signal receives its own value when an event other than the rising edge of the clock occurs on the d or c inputs. This feedback of information causes extra transactions on the internal state of the flip-flop, which may not be an accurate representation of the actual

```
ENTITY d_flipflop IS
  GENERIC (delay1 : TIME := 4 NS; delay2 : TIME :=5 NS);
  PORT (d, c : IN BIT; q, qb : OUT BIT);
END d_flipflop;
--
ARCHITECTURE assigning OF d_flipflop IS
  SIGNAL internal_state : BIT;
BEGIN
  internal_state <=d WHEN (c='1' AND NOT c'STABLE) ELSE internal_state;
  q <=internal_state AFTER delay1;
  qb <=NOT internal_state AFTER delay2;
END assigning;
```

(a)

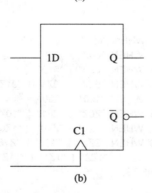

(b)

FIGURE 7.9
A basic flip-flop, that is, just a simple extension of the flip-flop in Figure 6.39, (a) VHDL description, (b) logic symbol.

hardware. This problem can be remedied by using what is referred to as a guarded signal assignment. A guarded signal assignment uses the keyword GUARDED on the right hand side of the assignment arrow, as shown here:

target <= GUARDED waveforms__or__conditional_waveforms__or__selected_waveforms;

Such an assignment executes only when a Boolean signal, GUARD, is TRUE. When GUARD is FALSE, the assignment does not execute even if events occur on the right hand side waveforms. In this case the right hand side is said to be disconnected from the left hand side target signal.

The GUARD signal can either be explicitly defined, or it can be provided implicitly by the use of a block statement with a guard expression. The *guarding* architecture of *d_flipflop*, shown in Figure 7.10, uses the latter method to define the GUARD signal. As in the *assigning* architecture in *d_flipflop* in Figure 7.9a, the architecture in Figure 7.10 describes the positive edge trigger flip-flop in Figure 7.9b. On the rising edge of the clock, the expression in the parentheses that follows the BLOCK keywords becomes TRUE. The value of this expression corresponds to that of the implicit GUARD signal, and it is used by the guarded signal assignments that assign values to the *q* and *qb* outputs. The value of the *d* input and its complement will be scheduled for *q* and *qb* when GUARD is TRUE. When GUARD is FALSE, *q* and *qb* are disconnected from their respective drivers, namely *d* and NOT *d*.

Figure 7.11 shows the syntax details of the block statement used in the *guarding* architecture of the *d_flipflop* entity. As shown, a block statement must begin with a label. This label may be used for gaining visibility into the block. The guard expression of the block is optional, and if used, defines an implicit GUARD signal that controls all the guarded assignments that appear in the statement part of the block. The statement part of the block may contain any number of concurrent statements and the entire block statement is considered a concurrent statement. Therefore, it is possible to nest block statements.

We have used the *assigning* and *guarding* architectures of the *d_flipflop* entity to demonstrate the use of conditional and guarded signal assignments when controlling assignment of values to signals. Parallel simulation of these two architectures is useful in understanding the timing details of the assignments used in them. A test bench for this purpose is shown in Figure 7.12.

```
ARCHITECTURE guarding OF d_flipflop IS
BEGIN
   ff: BLOCK ( c = '1' AND NOT c'STABLE )
   BEGIN
      q <= GUARDED d AFTER delay1;
      qb <= GUARDED NOT d AFTER delay2;
   END BLOCK ff;
END guarding;
```

FIGURE 7.10
The *guarding* architecture for the *d_flipflop* entity.

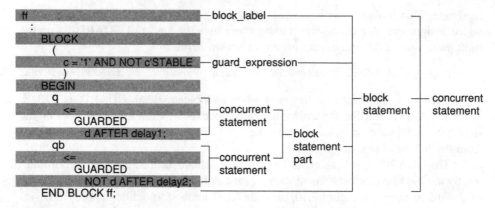

FIGURE 7.11
Syntax details of a guarded block statement with guarded signal assignments.

```
ENTITY flipflop_test IS END flipflop_test;
    --
ARCHITECTURE input_output OF flipflop_test IS
    COMPONENT
        flop PORT (d, c : IN BIT; q, qb : OUT BIT);
    END COMPONENT;
    FOR c1 : flop USE ENTITY WORK.d_flipflop (assigning);
    FOR c2 : flop USE ENTITY WORK.d_flipflop (guarding);
    SIGNAL dd, cc, q1, q2, qb1, qb2 : BIT;
BEGIN
    cc <= NOT cc AFTER 400 NS WHEN NOW < 2 US ELSE cc;
    dd <= NOT dd AFTER 1000 NS WHEN NOW < 2 US ELSE dd;
    c1: flop PORT MAP (dd, cc, q1, qb1);
    c2: flop PORT MAP (dd, cc, q2, qb2);
END input_output;
```

FIGURE 7.12
A test bench for testing *assigning* and *guarding* architectures of *d_flipflop*.

In this description, the *c1* instance of the declared *flop* component is associated with the *assigning* architecture of the *d_flipflop* entity, and the *c2* instance of *flop* is associated with the *guarding* architecture of this circuit. Periodic waveforms with different periods are generated for the clock (*cc*) and data (*dd*) inputs of both architectures. The outputs of the *assigning* architecture are *q1* and *qb1* and those of the *guarding* architecture are *q2* and *qb2*.

A conditional signal assignment generates a periodic waveform on *cc*. Every time *cc* changes, this assignment is executed, causing the complement of the new value of *cc* to be scheduled for *cc* after 400 ns. When the simulation time exceeds 2 us, the value of *cc* is assigned to itself, causing all future events to diminish on this signal. The predefined function, NOW, returns the simulation time and can be used like any other function. This method of generating a periodic signal is compact, and we will continue to use it in our sequential circuit examples.

Figure 7.13 shows simulation results in the test bench in Figure 7.12. In addition to the inputs and outputs of the *assigning* and *guarding* architectures of *d_flipflop* ($q1$, $qb1$ for *assigning* in Figure 7.9, and $q2$, $qb2$ for *guarding* in Figure 7.10), this report shows the *internal_state* signal of the *assigning* architecture (shown as $c1{:}state$) and the implied GUARD signal of the *ff* block of the *guarding* architecture (shown as $c2.ff{:}GUARD$). The report shows all transactions that occur on the displayed signals. Dots (.) indicate no transaction. In the time column, *delta* symbols (δ) following time values indicate simulation cycles at which events or transactions occur on any of the observed signals.

TIME (ns)	SIGNALS							
	cc	dd	q1	q2	qb1	qb2	c1: state	c2.ff: GUARD
0000	'0'	'0'	'0'	'0'	'0'	'0'	'0'	FALSE
$+\delta$	...	...	...	...	...	...	'0'	......
004	...	...	'0'	...	...	...	...	......
0005	...	...	...	...	'1'	...	...	......
0400	'1'	...	...	...	...	...	...	TRUE
$+\delta$	...	...	...	...	...	...	'0'	FALSE
$+\delta$	...	...	...	...	...	...	'0'	......
0404	...	...	...	'0'	...	...	...	......
0405	...	...	...	...	...	'1'	...	......
0800	'0'	...	...	...	...	...	...	FALSE
$+\delta$	...	...	...	...	...	...	'0'	FALSE
$+\delta$	...	...	...	...	...	...	'0'	......
1000	...	'1'	...	...	...	...	...	......
$+\delta$	...	...	...	...	...	...	'0'	......
1200	'1'	...	...	...	...	...	...	TRUE
$+\delta$	...	...	...	...	...	...	'1'	FALSE
$+\delta$	...	...	...	...	...	...	'1'	FALSE
1204	...	...	'1'	'1'	...	...	...	......
1205	...	...	...	...	'0'	'0'	...	......
1600	'0'	...	...	...	...	...	...	FALSE
$+\delta$	...	...	...	...	...	...	'1'	FALSE
$+\delta$	...	...	...	...	...	...	'1'	......
2000	'1'	'0'	...	...	...	...	...	TRUE
$+\delta$	'1'	'0'	...	...	...	...	'0'	FALSE
$+\delta$	...	...	...	...	...	...	'0'	......
2004	...	...	'0'	'0'	...	...	...	......
2005	...	...	...	...	'1'	'1'	...	......

FIGURE 7.13
Simulation results of the *input_output* architecture of the *flipflop_test* entity in Figure 7.12. All transactions are observed.

As expected, the *cc* and *dd* inputs toggle between '0'and '1' every 400 and 1000 ns, respectively. These inputs cause the same *events* on the outputs of the two architectures of the *d_flipflop* entity. There are, however, differences in the *transactions* that occur on the outputs, and in what occurs internally to these circuits. We discuss these differences and the justification for the events and transactions on various signals of architectures in Figure 7.9 and 7.10 in the following paragraphs.

The '0' transaction at 4 ns on the *q1* output of the *c1* instance of *flop* (associated with the *assigning* architecture of *d_flipflop*) is due to the initial execution of the statement that assigns *internal_state* of this circuit to its *q* output; this assignment is delayed and appears 4 ns later as a transaction on *q1*. Since the *guarding* architecture of *d_flipflop* does not use an intermediate signal, initializations occur directly on its outputs (*q2* and *qb2*) at time zero.

The transaction at 404 ns on *q2* is due to the fact that the guard expression of the *guarding* architecture is TRUE at 400 ns. This causes the value of input *d* to be assigned to *q2*, even if it does not cause a change in the value of this output. In the *assigning* architecture, the *internal_state* signal isolates such transactions from the outputs.

Internal to the *assigning* architecture of *d_flipflop*, every change in the clock results in two transactions on the *internal_state* signal. For the rising edge of the clock (at 400, 1200 and 2000 ns), one transaction occurs when condition *c='1' AND NOT c'STABLE* of the conditional signal assignment of Figure 7.9 becomes TRUE; at this time the value of *d* is assigned to the *internal_state* signal. The other transaction occurs when this condition becomes FALSE; at this time the value of *internal_state* is assigned to itself. On the falling edge of the clock (at 800 and 1600 ns), the change in *c* causes two events on *c'STABLE* which in turn cause the conditional signal assignment to be executed in two consecutive simulation cycles. In both these cycles, however, the *internal_signal* receives its own value.

The simulation report in Figure 7.13 indicates that the implied GUARD signal that is internal to the *guarding* architecture of *d_flipflop* (associated with the *c2* instance of *flop*) receives transactions on each edge of the clock. On the rising edge, this signal becomes TRUE for exactly one *delta* time. The guarded assignments of the *guarding* architecture execute only during this time; this causes *q* and *qb* to receive *d* and *NOT d*, respectively.

7.1.3   Nesting Guarded Blocks

The block statement in Figure 7.11 is a concurrent statement, as indicated in the syntax details. The statement part of the block statement can contain other concurrent statements. When nesting these statements, the implied GUARD signal within an inner block statement is defined by the guard expression of this statement only, and guard expressions do not automatically accumulate. For a GUARD signal to contain conditions of all its enclosing block statements, explicit ANDing of these expressions must be done.

For an example of nesting block statements, consider the *d_flipflop* in Figure 7.14. As indicated by the circuit notation, the *d* input will be clocked into the

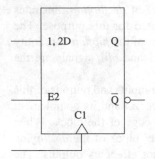

FIGURE 7.14
A positive edge trigger flip-flop with enable input.

flip-flop if the rising edge of the clock occurs while the enabling input is active. If either of these two conditions is not satisfied, the q and qb outputs remain unchanged. The VHDL description for this flip-flop is shown in Figure 7.15.

The entity declaration of *de_flipflop* uses the BIT type d, e, and c input ports for the data, enable, and clock inputs, respectively. The statement part of the *guarding* architecture of *de_flipflop* uses a block statement, labeled *edge*, for which the rising edge of the clock forms its guard expression. The *gate* block statement forms the statement part of the outer *edge* block statement. The *(e = '1' AND GUARD)* expression is the guard expression of the *gate* block. In this expression, GUARD refers to the implied GUARD signal outside the *gate* block and inside the *edge* block. Within the *gate* block, the GUARD signal is equivalent to:

$$(e = '1') \text{ AND } (c = '1' \text{ AND NOT } c'STABLE).$$

The guarded assignments to q and qb signals occur only when this signal is TRUE.

```
_ENTITY de_flipflop IS
    GENERIC (delay1 : TIME := 4 NS; delay2 : TIME := 5 NS);
    PORT (d, e, c : IN BIT; q, qb : OUT BIT);
_END de_flipflop;
--
_ARCHITECTURE guarding OF de_flipflop IS
_BEGIN
    _edge: BLOCK ( c = '1' AND NOT c'STABLE )
    _BEGIN
        _gate: BLOCK ( e = '1' AND GUARD )
        _BEGIN
            q <= GUARDED d AFTER delay1;
            qb <= GUARDED NOT d AFTER delay2;
        _END BLOCK gate;
    _END BLOCK edge;
_END guarding;
```

FIGURE 7.15
VHDL description for the positive edge trigger flip-flop with enable input in Figure 7.14.

A study of the simulation of the *guarding* architecture of *de_flipflop* illustrates important timing issues. The test bench in Figure 7.16 is used for this purpose. The *c1* label in the statement part of the *input_output* architecture of the *flipflop_test* entity is bound to the *guarding* architecture of *de_flipflop*. The *q1* and *qb1* signals are the outputs of this flip-flop.

Figure 7.17 shows all the transactions that occur on the inputs and outputs of this flip-flop between 0 and 3.2 microseconds. While *ee* is active, *dd* and its complement are assigned to the outputs of the *de_flipflop* on the rising edge of the clock. When *ee* becomes '0' at 2200 ns, the guard expression for the inner block of the *de_flipflop* becomes FALSE, and subsequent rising edges of *cc* do not effect its outputs. The drivers of the outputs are disconnected from them when the *ee* signal is zero.

Another event that deserves attention is the changing of clock at 2000 ns. This event occurs exactly at the same time that *dd* changes from '1' to '0'. At time 2000 ns, for a *delta* duration; the expression $c = '1'$ AND NOT $c'STABLE$ is TRUE. In this δ time duration, the data input of the flip-flop has a new value, '0'. Since at this time the implied GUARD signal that controls assignments into *q* and *qb* is TRUE, the values that are scheduled for these targets are based on this new value of the *dd* input. Therefore, the *q1* and *qb1* outputs will change to '0' and '1' at 2004 ns and 2005 ns, respectively.

7.1.4   Resolving Between Several Driving Values

Up to this point in the book, we have only discussed signals that correspond to simple circuit nodes. Multiple concurrent assignments cannot be made on such signals. This is analogous to driving a circuit node with more than one gate output. In hardware, this usually results in smoke or an unknown value; correspondingly, in VHDL it results in an error message. Figure 7.18 shows the *smoke_generator* architecture for an example entity.

```
ENTITY flipflop_test IS END flipflop_test;
--
ARCHITECTURE input_output OF flipflop_test IS
    COMPONENT
        ff1 PORT (d, e, c : IN BIT; q, qb : OUT BIT);
    END COMPONENT;
    FOR c1 : ff1 USE ENTITY WORK.de_flipflop (guarding);
    SIGNAL dd, ee, cc, q1, qb1 : BIT;
BEGIN
    cc <= NOT cc AFTER 400 NS WHEN NOW < 3 US ELSE cc;
    dd <= NOT dd AFTER 1000 NS WHEN NOW < 3 US ELSE dd;
    ee <= '1', '0' AFTER 2200 NS;
    c1: ff1 PORT MAP (dd, ee, cc, q1, qb1);
END input_output;
```

FIGURE 7.16
A test bench for testing the *guarding* architectures of *de_flipflop*.

TIME	SIGNALS				
(ns)	cc	ee	dd	q1	qb1
0000	'0'	'0'	'0'	'0'	'0'
δ	...	'1'	...	...	...
0400	'1'	...	...	...	...
0404	...	...	...	'0'	...
0405	...	...	...	...	'1'
0800	'0'	...	...	...	...
1000	...	...	'1'	...	...
1200	'1'	...	...	...	...
1204	...	...	...	'1'	...
1205	...	...	...	...	'0'
1600	'0'	...	...	...	...
2000	'1'	...	'0'	...	...
2004	...	...	...	'0'	...
2005	...	...	...	...	'1'
2200	...	'0'	...	...	...
2400	'0'	...	...	...	...
2800	'1'	...	...	...	...
3000	...	...	'1'	...	...
δ	...	...	'1'	...	...
3200	'0'	...	...	...	...
δ	'0'	...	...	...	...

FIGURE 7.17
Simulation results of the *input_output* architecture of the *flipflop_test* entity of Figure 7.16. All transactions are observed.

```
USE  WORK.basic_utilities.ALL;
-- FROM PACKAGE USE: qit
ENTITY  y_circuit IS
    PORT (a, b, c, d : IN qit; z : OUT qit);
END y_circuit;
--
ARCHITECTURE smoke_generator OF y_circuit IS
    SIGNAL circuit_node : qit;
BEGIN
    circuit_node <= a;
    circuit_node <= b;
    circuit_node <= c;
    circuit_node <= d;
    z <= circuit_node;
END smoke_generator;
```

FIGURE 7.18
Multiple sources for a simple signal. This results in an error message.

This description has an internal node to which the four inputs, *a*, *b*, *c*, and *d* are assigned. These assignments are concurrent, which causes four simultaneous driving values for the *circuit_node*; the description makes no provision for a resolution between these multiple values. For example, the *smoke_generator* architecture of *y_circuit* does not specify what the *circuit_node* value becomes if the value on the *a* input is '1' and the values of all other inputs are '0'.

This problem can be remedied by including a function name in the declaration of the *circuit_node* signal. This function gets called for the resolution of the multiple sources of this signal. An example for such a declaration is shown here:

    SIGNAL circuit_node : anding qit;

This declaration makes *circuit_node* a resolved signal, for which the name *anding* specifies a resolution function. The *anding* function is called each time an event occurs on any of the sources of the *circuit_node* signal. When called, this function returns a *qit* value that becomes the value for the *circuit_node*. As the name implies, the *anding* resolution function is expected to return the ANDing of all its sources. Figure 7.19 shows the *anding* resolution function.

This function uses *qit*, *qit_vector*, and the overloaded "AND" from the *basic_utilities* package. The parameter of a resolution function must be an array whose elements have the same type as the value that the function returns. The concatenation of all sources of a resolved signal are associated with the parameter of the resolution function of this signal. For the *anding* function, *qit* is the type of the value that it returns and *qit-vector* is the type of its parameter. This function can be used for resolving a *qit* type value for a *qit* type target signal from any number of *qit* type driving values.

In the declaration part of the *anding* function in Figure 7.19, the *accumulate* variable is declared and initialized to '1'. In the statement part of this function, a loop statement ANDs together all elements of the *drivers* parameter. The overloaded "AND" ANDs *accumulate* with each element of *drivers* according to the four value AND table in Chapter 6 (see Figure 6.23).

Figure 7.20 shows the *wired_and* architecture of the *y_circuit* entity. In its declaration part, this architecture defines the *anding* function and uses it for declaring

```
 --  USE qit, qit_vector, "AND" from basic_utilities
FUNCTION anding (drivers : qit_vector) RETURN qit IS
    VARIABLE accumulate : qit := '1';
BEGIN
    FOR i IN drivers'RANGE LOOP
        accumulate := accumulate AND drivers(i);
    END LOOP;
    RETURN accumulate;
END anding;
```

FIGURE 7.19
The *anding* resolution function ANDs all its drivers.

```
USE  WORK.basic_utilities.ALL;
-- FROM  PACKAGE  USE:  qit
ARCHITECTURE  wired_and  OF  y_circuit  IS
    FUNCTION  anding (drivers : qit_vector)  RETURN  qit  IS
        VARIABLE  accumulate : qit := '1';
    BEGIN
        FOR  i  IN  drivers'RANGE  LOOP
            accumulate := accumulate  AND  drivers(i);
        END LOOP;
        RETURN  accumulate;
    END  anding;
    SIGNAL  circuit_node : anding qit;
BEGIN
    circuit_node  <=  a;
    circuit_node  <=  b;
    circuit_node  <=  c;
    circuit_node  <=  d;
    z  <=  circuit_node;
END  wired_and;
```

FIGURE 7.20
Multiple sources for a simple signal. This results in ANDing all sources.

the *circuit_node* signal. Four assignments in the statement part of this architecture cause the concatenation of the values of a, b, c, and d signals to be associated with the *drivers* formal parameter of the *anding* function. An event on any of these inputs causes the *anding* function to be called for a new resolved value. The VHDL language does not specify the order in which multiple sources of a resolved signal are concatenated.

7.1.4.1 REVISITING MULTIPLEXER. Figure 7.21 shows an alternative description for the 8-to-1 multiplexer of Section 7.1.1. In the *multiple_assignments* architecture of *mux_8_to_1* in Figure 7.21, each data input is ANDed with its corresponding select line, and the result of this operation is assigned to the temporary signal t. Eight assignments to this signal generate eight concurrent drivers for it. Signal t is a resolved signal and it uses the *oring* subprogram for its resolution function. As indicated in the declaration part of the *multiple_assignments* architecture, the *oring* function ORs together the elements of its array input and returns the result. Since the concatenation of the drivers of signal t is associated with the array parameter of the *oring* function, the value this function returns is the OR result of these eight drivers. This value is assigned to the t signal which is then assigned to the z output of the multiplexer. The final result is that the z output is assigned to the OR combination of the data inputs ANDed with their respective select inputs. The OR operator of the resolution function and the AND operators in the statement part of the *multiple_assignments* architecture of the *mux_8_to_1* entity use OR and AND functions that are overloaded for *qit* operands.

```
USE  WORK.basic_utilities.ALL;
-- FROM PACKAGE USE: qit
ARCHITECTURE  multiple_assignments OF  mux_8_to_1  IS
    FUNCTION oring ( drivers : qit_vector) RETURN qit IS
       VARIABLE accumulate : qit := '0';
    BEGIN
       FOR i IN drivers'RANGE LOOP
          accumulate := accumulate OR drivers(i);
       END LOOP;
       RETURN accumulate;
    END oring;
    SIGNAL t : oring qit;
BEGIN
    t <= i7 AND s7;
    t <= i6 AND s6;
    t <= i5 AND s5;
    t <= i4 AND s4;
    t <= i3 AND s3;
    t <= i2 AND s2;
    t <= i1 AND s1;
    t <= i0 AND s0;
    z <= t;
END multiple_assignments;
```

FIGURE 7.21
Implementing the eight-to-one multiplexer using eight concurrent assignments.

The declaration of signal *t* specifies that the type of this signal is a subtype of *qit*, for which *oring* is the subtype indication. Instead of the syntax used in Figure 7.21, this *qit* subtype can be declared as a new subtype and used to declare resolved signals. The following statement shows how to define *ored_qit* as an *oring* subtype of *qit*:

```
SUBTYPE ored_qit IS oring qit;
```

Using *ored_qit*, any number of resolved signals that use *oring* for their resolution function may be declared. Declaring *t* is shown here as an example:

```
SIGNAL t : ored_qit;
```

For declaring a vector of *oring* resolved signals, the *ored_qit_vector* type definition shown here is needed:

```
TYPE ored_qit_vector IS ARRAY ( NATURAL RANGE <> ) OF ored_qit;
```

The following statement defines *t_byte* as an 8-bit signal; each element of this signal uses *oring* for resolving between the multiple values assigned to it.

```
SIGNAL t_byte : ored_qit_vector ( 7 DOWNTO 0 );
```

7.1.4.2 PACKAGING RESOLUTION FUNCTIONS. The *anding* and *oring* resolution functions are useful when an implicit or explicit AND or OR gate exists at a node where several drivers meet. Often, however, wiring several nodes of BIT or *qit* type does not result in either of these two functions. A third function, *wiring*, is useful for the representation of wiring several signals into a common node. For this purpose, we will use the two operand *wire* function shown in Figure 7.22.

This function describes the behavior of a node that has two *qit* type signals connected to it. Figure 7.23 shows the *wire* function table for *qit* type inputs. As shown in this table, if the two inputs are equal, the *wire* value will be the same as the inputs. Value 'Z' on either of the inputs is absorbed by a stronger value ('0', '1', or 'X'), and conflicting non 'Z' values on the inputs result in 'X' value for the *wire* value.

A resolution function that resolves a single value from multiple *qit* type values that drive a node is called *wiring*, and it is shown in Figure 7.24.

An architecture that uses this function must define it in its declarative part or else use a library that contains it. We can now add this and the other two functions described in this chapter to the body of the *basic_utilities* package. For the *wiring* function and its related types to be visible when the *basic_utilities* package is used, the declaration of this package must include the declarations shown in Figure 7.25. Similar declarations for the *anding* and *oring* functions are needed for the visibility of the functions and their related types.

Other useful resolution functions for our *basic_utilities* package are *anding* and *oring* for the BIT type. Such functions overload their similarly named functions of

```
FUNCTION wire (a, b : qit) RETURN qit IS
    CONSTANT qit_wire_table : qit_2d := (
                            ('0','X','0','X'),
                            ('X','1','1','X'),
                            ('0','1','Z','X'),
                            ('X','X','X','X'));
BEGIN
    RETURN qit_wire_table (a, b);
END wire;
```

FIGURE 7.22
The *wire* function for modeling wiring two *qit* type nodes.

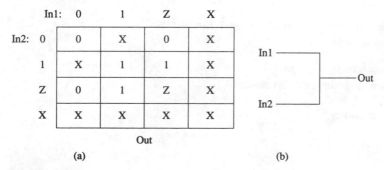

In1:	0	1	Z	X
In2: 0	0	X	0	X
1	X	1	1	X
Z	0	1	Z	X
X	X	X	X	X

Out

(a)   (b)

FIGURE 7.23
The *wire* function for *qit* type operands, (a) input-output mapping, (b) circuit notation.

```
FUNCTION wiring ( drivers : qit_vector) RETURN qit IS
    VARIABLE accumulate : qit := 'Z';
BEGIN
    FOR i IN drivers'RANGE LOOP
        accumulate := wire (accumulate, drivers(i));
    END LOOP;
    RETURN accumulate;
END wiring;
```

FIGURE 7.24
The *wiring* resolution function for *qit* type operands.

```
FUNCTION wiring ( drivers : qit_vector) RETURN qit;
SUBTYPE wired_qit IS wiring qit;
TYPE wired_qit_vector IS ARRAY (NATURAL RANGE <>) OF wired_qit;
```

FIGURE 7.25
Necessary declarations for visibility of the *wiring* resolution function and its related types and subtypes.

the *qit* type. Figure 7.26 shows an *oring* function with a BIT_VECTOR operand and a BIT type return value. Figure 7.26a presents the declarations for visibility of the *oring* function and its related types.

7.1.5 MOS Implementation of Multiplexer

Assigning multiple values to a resolved signal generates multiple drivers for such signals; these drivers then participate in the determination of a final value for the resolved signal. Guarded assignments can also be used for assigning values to a resolved signal. In this case, only those values that are on the right hand side of signal

```
FUNCTION oring ( drivers : BIT_VECTOR) RETURN BIT;
SUBTYPE ored_bit IS oring BIT;
TYPE ored_bit_vector IS ARRAY (NATURAL RANGE <>) OF ored_bit;
```
                    (a)

```
FUNCTION oring ( drivers : BIT_VECTOR) RETURN BIT IS
    VARIABLE accumulate : BIT := '0';
BEGIN
    FOR i IN drivers'RANGE LOOP
        accumulate := accumulate OR drivers(i);
    END LOOP;
    RETURN accumulate;
END oring;
```
                    (b)

FIGURE 7.26
The *oring* resolution function for the BIT type operands, (a) necessary type and subtype definitions for the *basic_utilities* package, (b) definition of function.

assignments with TRUE GUARD signal values participate in the determination of the final value of the target signal. A driver of a guarded signal assignment whose GUARD signal is FALSE is said to be "turned off." Description of an MOS multiplexer illustrates these issues.

A multiplexer can be efficiently implemented through the use of a MOS switch element. The behavior of a multiplexer implemented this way, however, is different from that of the AND-OR logic discussed in the previous section. Figure 7.27 shows an 8-bit NMOS multiplexer. A CMOS multiplexer uses transmission gates instead of the pass transistors shown in this figure, and it behaves in a similar fashion.

The multiplexer consists of eight pass transistors connected in parallel. The gates of the transistors constitute the eight multiplexer select lines ($s0$ through $s7$) and their sources are the data inputs ($i0$ through $i7$). The output of the multiplexer is taken from the common drain of the transistors. A '1' on the gate of a transistor turns the transistor on and causes the common drain to be driven by the value at the source of the transistor. If an si value is '1' and it becomes 'Z', the charge at the gate of the transistor keeps the transistor conducting (ON) for a few milliseconds. We therefore treat 'Z' at this input as '1'. When several transistors are conducting simultaneously, the common drain is driven by more than one source.

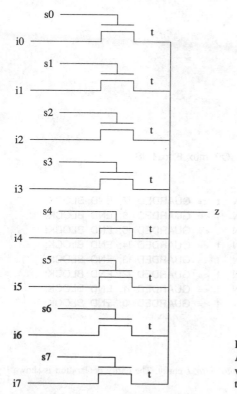

FIGURE 7.27
An NMOS eight-to-one multiplexer. The CMOS version uses transmission gates instead of pass transistors.

A block statement, like the one shown in Figure 7.28 properly describes the behavior of a transistor in the structure shown in Figure 7.27. An i_i input drives t only when s_i is '1'or 'Z'.

An NMOS version of the *mux_8_to_1* eight bit multiplexer uses eight block statements similar to those in Figure 7.28. The description of this multiplexer, shown in Figure 7.29, conditionally connects the i_i inputs to the internal t node. The inputs that are connected to node t are wired together at this node according to the *wire* logic detailed in Figure 7.23.

The *wired_qit* subtype of the *basic_utilities* package is used to declare the t signal. This declaration causes the multiple values assigned to this signal to be resolved according to the *wiring* function in Figure 7.24. The keyword BUS in the declaration of t specifies the kind of this signal—this will become clearer in the discussion that follows.

When an event occurs on any of the inputs in the description presented in Figure 7.29, or on any of the eight implied GUARD signals of the guarded block

```
b_i : BLOCK ( s_i = '1' OR s_i = 'Z')
BEGIN
    t <= GUARDED i_i;
END BLOCK;
```

FIGURE 7.28
A block statement modeling a transmission gate.

```
USE WORK.basic_utilities.ALL;
-- FROM PACKAGE USE: wired_qit
ARCHITECTURE multiple_guarded_assignments OF mux_8_to_1 IS
    SIGNAL t : wired_qit BUS;
BEGIN
    b7: BLOCK (s7 = '1' OR s7 = 'Z') BEGIN  t <= GUARDED i7; END BLOCK;
    b6: BLOCK (s6 = '1' OR s6 = 'Z') BEGIN  t <= GUARDED i6; END BLOCK;
    b5: BLOCK (s5 = '1' OR s5 = 'Z') BEGIN  t <= GUARDED i5; END BLOCK;
    b4: BLOCK (s4 = '1' OR s4 = 'Z') BEGIN  t <= GUARDED i4; END BLOCK;
    b3: BLOCK (s3 = '1' OR s3 = 'Z') BEGIN  t <= GUARDED i3; END BLOCK;
    b2: BLOCK (s2 = '1' OR s2 = 'Z') BEGIN  t <= GUARDED i2; END BLOCK;
    b1: BLOCK (s1 = '1' OR s1 = 'Z') BEGIN  t <= GUARDED i1; END BLOCK;
    b0: BLOCK (s0 = '1' OR s0 = 'Z') BEGIN  t <= GUARDED i0; END BLOCK;
    z <= t;
END multiple_guarded_assignments;
```

FIGURE 7.29
The *mutliple_guarded_assignments* architecture of the *mux_8_to_1* entity. The entity declaration is shown in Figure 7.5.

statements, the *wiring* resolution function is called. Concatenation of the i_i values whose corresponding GUARD signal is TRUE, i.e., the corresponding s_i's are either '1' or 'Z', is associated with the formal parameter in this function. The *wiring* function resolves a value based on these active i_i inputs. This value becomes the value of the output of the multiplexer.

An interesting situation arises when all the drivers of t are disconnected from it, and that is that all eight implied GUARD signals are FALSE. In this case, because of the BUS keyword is used in the declaration of t, the wiring resolution function is called with a NULL input parameter. The definition of the *wiring* function (see Figure 7.24) specifies that the initial value of the *accumulate* variable ('Z') is returned as the function value if the entire loop statement in the statement part of this function is skipped due to a NULL range. The end result is that the t signal receives a 'Z' value if all the s_i inputs of the multiplexer are '0'. Note that the pass transistor hardware we are modeling behaves in exactly the same way. If all the gate inputs in Figure 7.27 are '0', the common node, z, will be floating (i.e., high impedance).

The use of BUS in the declaration of t makes it a guarded signal. A resolved signal is guarded if its kind, i.e., BUS or REGISTER, is specified in its declaration. Events and transactions on the BUS and REGISTER kind of signals are exactly the same as long as at least one driver is turned on. If an event turns off the last active driver of a guarded signal, the resolution function is called for BUS signals with a NULL parameter; however, it will not be called if the kind of signal is REGISTER. After all the drivers are turned off, the latter kind of signals retain their last driven value.

As the name implies, the REGISTER signal kinds are useful for modeling register structures. Due to the charge at the gate input of MOS logic gates, connecting an inverter to the output of a transistor structure, such as the multiplexer, causes the data at this output to retain its value after all the transistors driving the node are turned off. This structure, shown in Figure 7.30, is a MOS half-register with multiplexed input.

Node t in Figure 7.30 can hold an undriven value for several milliseconds. Since the clock frequency and the rate of updating data is much higher than milliseconds, half-registers can be used for data storage in many applications.

Figure 7.31 shows a VHDL description for the *multiplexed_half_register* circuit. In the *guarded_assignments* architecture of this figure, the guarded signal t is declared with a *wired_qit* subtype and REGISTER kind. Since the *wired_qit* subtype is defined as a *wiring* subtype of *qit*, multiple *qit* type values driving node t are resolved by the *wiring* function. If all drivers are turned off, node t and node z retain their values indefinitely.

7.1.5.1 DELAYING DISCONNECTIONS.
VHDL allows the time delay specification to be used in the disconnection of drivers of a guarded signal. As with other signals, the placement of values on guarded signals can be done by using an AFTER clause in the signal assignment statement. For example, in order to delay the assignment of the $i5$ input of the multiplexer in Figure 7.29 to signal t, the following statement should replace the block statement labeled $b5$:

```
b5: BLOCK (s5 = '1' OR s5 = 'Z')
        BEGIN  t <= GUARDED i5 AFTER 4 NS; END BLOCK;
```

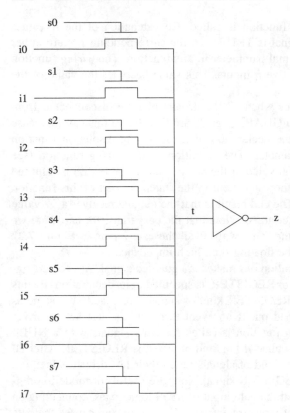

FIGURE 7.30
An NMOS half-register with multiplexed input.

With this replacement, if *i5* changes value while the guard expression of the *b5* block is TRUE, the new value of *i5* will be assigned to *t* after 4 ns. Similarly, if the guard expression changes from FALSE to TRUE, after a 4 ns delay, the value of *i5* will be assigned to *t* at the time of guard expression turning to TRUE. It should be evident from this discussion that the 4 nanosecond delay only applies when a driver is connected, or is being connected, and does not apply when a driver is disconnected from a guarded signal.

A disconnection specification statement can be used to specify the disconnection delay for a guarded signal within a guarded signal assignment. Such a statement contains the name of the signal, its type, and a time expression that specifies the disconnection delay value. To demonstrate the application of this statement, consider the *multiple_guarded_assignments* architecture of *mux_8_to_1* in Figure 7.29. To delay disconnection of the *t* drivers, the following statement should be added to the declarative part of this architecture:

```
DISCONNECT t : wired_qit AFTER 6 NS;
```

With the inclusion of this statement, if a *t* driver, e.g., *i6*, *i5* or *i4*, is turned off because its guard expression becomes FALSE, the effect of this driver remains on *t* for 6 nanoseconds after it has been turned off. The overall effect of this is that the

```
USE  WORK.basic_utilities.ALL;
-- FROM  PACKAGE  USE:  qit, wired_qit
ENTITY  multiplexed_half_register  IS
    PORT  (i7, i6, i5, i4, i3, i2, i1, i0 : IN qit;
            s7, s6, s5, s4, s3, s2, s1, s0 : IN qit; z : OUT qit );
END  multiplexed_half_register;
--
ARCHITECTURE  guarded_assignments  OF  multiplexed_half_register  IS
    SIGNAL  t : wired_qit  REGISTER;
BEGIN
    b7: BLOCK (s7 = '1' OR s7 = 'Z') BEGIN   t <= GUARDED i7; END BLOCK;
    b6: BLOCK (s6 = '1' OR s6 = 'Z') BEGIN   t <= GUARDED i6; END BLOCK;
    b5: BLOCK (s5 = '1' OR s5 = 'Z') BEGIN   t <= GUARDED i5; END BLOCK;
    b4: BLOCK (s4 = '1' OR s4 = 'Z') BEGIN   t <= GUARDED i4; END BLOCK;
    b3: BLOCK (s3 = '1' OR s3 = 'Z') BEGIN   t <= GUARDED i3; END BLOCK;
    b2: BLOCK (s2 = '1' OR s2 = 'Z') BEGIN   t <= GUARDED i2; END BLOCK;
    b1: BLOCK (s1 = '1' OR s1 = 'Z') BEGIN   t <= GUARDED i1; END BLOCK;
    b0: BLOCK (s0 = '1' OR s0 = 'Z') BEGIN   t <= GUARDED i0; END BLOCK;
    z <= NOT t AFTER 8 NS;
END  guarded_assignments;
```

FIGURE 7.31

The *multiple_guarded_assignments* architecture of the *multiplexed_half_register* entity. The entity declaration is shown in Figure 7.5.

output of the multiplexer changes to 'Z' 6 nanoseconds after the last source has been turned off.

The declarative part of an architecture can contain disconnection statements for any number of guarded signals that the designer declares within that architecture. If a disconnection is specified for several signals of the same type, the signal names should appear in a list separated by commas (this is referred to as a guarded signal list) following the DISCONNECT keyword. The ALL keyword used for the signal list implies that the disconnection specification applies to all signals of the type specified. If OTHERS is used in place of the signal list, the disconnection specification applies to signals of the specified type for which disconnection has not been specified in the statements above this statement.

7.1.5.2   A RECOMMENDATION. If resolved nonguarded signals (with no kind specified) are used on the left hand side of guarded assignments, the implied GUARD signals controlling these assignments that become FALSE do not turn off the corresponding drivers. Instead, the value of the driver when it was active continues to be used as a driving value, even when the driver is turned off. The author recommends the use of a guarded signal on the left hand side of guarded assignments if there are multiple such assignments to the signal. In most cases, the drivers that are left on the output of resolved nonguarded signals at the time that their corresponding guard has become false, complicates the analysis of a circuit.

7.1.6 A General Multiplexer

While the multiplexers developed to this point in the chapter demonstrate many language concepts, they do not necessarily use the most efficient coding techniques offered by VHDL. A code-efficient multi-bit multiplexer that uses guarded blocks is shown in Figure 7.32. The iterative description of the *mux_n_to_1* entity in this figure declares data inputs and select lines as unconstrained arrays of *qit*. The port clause specifies the type and kind of the output *z* as *wired_qit* and BUS, respectively. As before, the *wired_qit* of the *basic_utilities* package, defined as a *wiring* subtype of *qit*, is used to specify the resolution of the multiplexer output node.

The architecture in Figure 7.32 uses a generate statement to generate as many guarded block statements as there are elements in the parameter associated with the *i* input of the *mux_n_to_1* entity. The b_j block encloses a guarded assignment of input i_j to the guarded output, *z*. The description expects the ranges of *i* and *s* inputs to be the same.

A simple test bench is presented in Figure 7.33 for the multi-bit multiplexer to illustrate how a *qit* type can be associated with the *z* formal parameter of the *mux_n_to_1* entity. This is, of course, possible because *wired_qit* is a subtype of *qit*—as stated earlier, types and subtypes are completely compatible. This compatibility, however, does not exist between *qit_vector* and *wired_qit_vector*, since the latter is defined as a new type. These types are closely related and the designer can convert them from one type to the other, using the type conversion methods discussed in Chapter 6 (Section 6.1.2).

The simulation run of the *mux_tester* shown in Figure 7.34 verifies the correctness of the description of *mux_n_to_1*. At time 0, the output is 'Z', since none of the four select lines are active. At 15000 ns, the output becomes 'X' because a

```
USE  WORK.basic_utilities.ALL;
-- FROM PACKAGE USE: qit, qit_vector, wired_qit
ENTITY mux_n_to_1 IS
    PORT (i, s : IN qit_vector; z : OUT wired_qit BUS);
END mux_n_to_1;
--
ARCHITECTURE multiple_guarded_assignments OF mux_n_to_1 IS
BEGIN
    bi: FOR j IN i'RANGE GENERATE
        bj: BLOCK (s(j) = '1' OR s(j) = 'Z')
        BEGIN
            z <= GUARDED i(j);
        END BLOCK;
    END GENERATE;
END multiple_guarded_assignments;
```

FIGURE 7.32
The *mutiple_guarded_assignments* architecture of the *mux_n_to_1* entity. The circuit is a general n-bit multiplexer.

```
 USE  WORK.basic_utilities.ALL;
 ENTITY  mux_tester  IS
 END  mux_tester;
 --
 ARCHITECTURE  input_output  OF  mux_tester  IS
     COMPONENT  mux  PORT (i, s : IN  qit_vector; z : OUT  wired_qit  BUS);
     END  COMPONENT;
     FOR  ALL : mux  USE
         ENTITY  WORK.mux_n_to_1  (multiple_guarded_assignments);
     SIGNAL  ii, ss : qit_vector (3 DOWNTO 0) := "0000";
     SIGNAL  zz : qit;
 BEGIN
     ii <= "1010" AFTER  10 US, "Z100" AFTER  20 US, "0011" AFTER  30 US;
     ss <= "0010" AFTER  05 US, "1100" AFTER  15 US, "000Z" AFTER  25 US;
     mm : mux  PORT  MAP (ii, ss, zz);
 END  input_output;
```

FIGURE 7.33
A test bench for the *guarded_assignments* architecture of *mux_n_to_1* entity. This entity is used as a 4-bit multiplexer.

TIME	SIGNALS		
(ns)	ii(3:0)	ss(3:0)	zz
00000	"0000"	"0000"	'0'
δ	......	......	'Z'
05000	......	"0010"	...
δ	......	......	'0'
10000	"1010"	......	...
δ	......	......	'1'
15000	......	"1100"	...
δ	......	......	'X'
20000	"Z100"	......	...
δ	......	......	'1'
25000	......	"000Z"	...
δ	......	......	'0'
30000	"0011"	......	...
δ	......	......	'1'

FIGURE 7.34
Simulation results of the *input_output* architecture of the *mux_tester* entity in Figure 7.33, testing the *mux_n_to_1* circuit. All events are observed.

'1' and a '0' (bits 3 and 2) are simultaneously driving the output node. Events on the zz output of the multiplexer occur δ time after events on its inputs. This is due to the signal assignment to the z output in the statement part of the *guarded_assignments* architecture of the *mux_n_to_1* entity in Figure 7.32. Had we not declared the z port of this entity as a guarded signal, an intermediate guarded signal, such as t in the description of *mux_8_to_1* multiplexer, would have been required. This signal would delay assignments to the output by 2δ. An interested reader can verify by simulation that the output of the *mux_8_to_1* circuit in Figure 7.29 is 2δ behind its input.

7.2 STATE MACHINE DESCRIPTION

State diagrams are used to graphically represent state machines. An important part of digital systems, state machines can appear explicitly in a digital system for the control and sequencing of events, or they can be embedded in sequential components, such as counters and shift-registers. At the dataflow level, where we separate control and data of a hardware system, the design and description of state machines for implementing the control unit become important. VHDL provides convenient constructs to describe various forms of state machines at various levels of abstraction. At the dataflow level, description of a state machine has a close correspondence to the state diagram of the machine. We will use block statements, signal assignments, and guarded assignments in this section to accurately describe state machines in VHDL.

7.2.1 A Sequence Detector

A sequence detector is a classical example of an application of state machines in hardware. Figure 7.35 shows the state diagram for a sequence detector that continuously searches for the 1011 sequence on its *x* input. This diagram is a Mealy machine, which means that the output is a function of the input while the machine is in a stable state.

    The states of this machine are labeled according to the significant input sequences they detect. For example, in the reset state, if a '1' followed by a '0' appears on the *x* input, the machine moves to the *10* state.

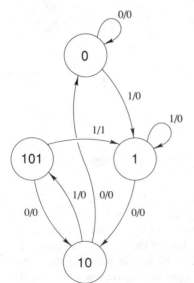

FIGURE 7.35
A 1011 mealy sequence detector. State names indicate detected sequences.

The VHDL description in Figure 7.36 corresponds to the state diagram of the 1011 detector. The entity declaration of this circuit has two BIT type inputs, x and clk, and an output, z. The architectural description of the *detector* is called *singular_state_machine*, indicating that it can only have one active state at any given time.

The declarative part of the *singular_state_machine* architecture of *detector* contains the *state* enumeration type definition, the enumeration elements of which are the state designators of the state machine in Figure 7.35. This is followed by the *state_vector* type definition that defines an unconstrained array of *state*, which is then followed by the *one_of* resolution function. The last declaration in this declarative part indicates that *current* is a guarded resolved signal of type *state*. The kind of this sig-

```
ENTITY detector IS
    PORT (x, clk : IN BIT; z : OUT BIT);
END detector;
ARCHITECTURE singular_state_machine OF detector IS
    TYPE state IS (reset, got1, got10, got101);
    TYPE state_vector IS ARRAY (NATURAL RANGE <>) OF state;
    FUNCTION one_of (sources : state_vector) RETURN state IS
    BEGIN
        RETURN sources(sources'LEFT);
    END one_of;
    SIGNAL current : one_of state REGISTER := reset;
BEGIN
    clocking : BLOCK (clk = '1' AND NOT clk'STABLE)
    BEGIN
        s1: BLOCK ( current = reset AND GUARD )
        BEGIN
            current <= GUARDED got1 WHEN x = '1' ELSE reset;
        END BLOCK s1;
        s2: BLOCK ( current = got1 AND GUARD )
        BEGIN
            current <= GUARDED got10 WHEN x = '0' ELSE got1;
        END BLOCK s2;
        s3: BLOCK ( current = got10 AND GUARD )
        BEGIN
            current <= GUARDED got101 WHEN x = '1' ELSE reset;
        END BLOCK s3;
        s4: BLOCK ( current = got101 AND GUARD)
        BEGIN
            current <= GUARDED got1 WHEN x = '1' ELSE got10;
            z <= '1' WHEN ( current = got101 AND x = '1') ELSE '0';
        END BLOCK s4;
    END BLOCK clocking;
END singular_state_machine;
```

FIGURE 7.36
VHDL description of 1011 detector. Only one simultaneous active state.

nal is REGISTER and it uses the *one_of* resolution function. This resolution function chooses one of the driving values of *current* for assignment to this signal. Shortly it becomes clear that *current* has only one driving value at any one time; the use of 'LEFT in the statement part of the *one_of* function, therefore, returns just that one value.

The statement part of the architecture in Figure 7.36 consists of the *clocking* block statement that uses the rising edge of *clk* for its guard expression. Nested in this block statement are four block statements that correspond to the states of the state machine. We refer to these blocks (labeled *s1*, *s2*, *s3* and *s4*) as state blocks. The implied GUARD signal within each of these inner state blocks is TRUE if *current* equals the state designator, i.e., *reset*, *got1*, *got10*, or *got101* of that state; and if the guard expression of the outer *clocking* block statement is also TRUE. The *current* signal represents the current active state of the state machine. Initially, this signal is equal to *reset*. In this initial state on the rising edge of the clock, the implied GUARD signal in the *s1* block becomes TRUE. Depending on the value of *x*, the guarded signal assignment within this block assigns *got1* or *reset* to the *current* signal. If *current* becomes *got1*, the next rising edge of the clock sets *current* to *got10* or *got1* depending on the value of *x*. The edges of the clock cause assignment of values to *current* according to the state diagram in Figure 7.35. When *current* is equal to *got101*, the signal assignment in the *s4* block assigns a '1' to the *z* output if *x* is '1'. This statement does not use the guard expression of the *s4* block; therefore, it can be placed anywhere in the statement part of the *detector* architecture. In our description, the place of this statement corresponds to its activating state.

Since there are four concurrent signal assignments that use *current* for their targets, this signal is declared as a resolved signal. The logic that we used to describe the *singular_state_machine* architecture of the *detector* entity does not allow any more than one driver for this signal at any one time. As soon as a new value is assigned to *current*, the guard expression that allows this assignment to take place becomes FALSE, causing the removal of the previous driving value from it. This leaves the *current* signal with only one active driver at any one time, and the 'LEFT in the *one_of* function returns that one driver.

7.2.2 Allowing Multiple Active States

Although a standard finite state machine is defined for one active state at any given time, the ability to handle multiple active states enables us to describe pipeline and multiple state machines. An alternative description for the state machine in Figure 7.35 is shown in Figure 7.37. The states of the machine are represented by the elements of the declared *s* signal. As shown in Figure 7.26, declaration of *s* as an *ored_bit_vector* makes *s(1)*, *s(2)*, *s(3)*, and *s(4)* resolved signals of type BIT and the *oring* resolution function. This declaration also specifies that *s* is a guarded signal of REGISTER kind, *s(1)* is initialized to '1', and *s(2)* through *s(4)* are initially '0'.

The statement part of the *multiple_state_machine* architecture of *detector* contains the *clocking* block statement for the clock edge detection. Nested in this block statement are four block statements that use the elements of *s* in their guard expressions and they correspond to the states of the state machine in Figure 7.35. In a state

```
USE WORK.basic_utilities.ALL;
-- FROM PACKAGE USE: ored_bit_vector
ARCHITECTURE multiple_state_machine OF detector IS
    SIGNAL s : ored_bit_vector (1 TO 4) REGISTER := "1000";
BEGIN
    clocking : BLOCK (clk = '1' AND NOT clk'STABLE)
    BEGIN
        s1: BLOCK (s(1) = '1' AND GUARD)
        BEGIN
            s(1) <= GUARDED '1' WHEN x = '0' ELSE '0';
            s(2) <= GUARDED '1' WHEN x = '1' ELSE '0';
        END BLOCK s1;
        s2: BLOCK (s(2) = '1' AND GUARD)
        BEGIN
            s(3) <= GUARDED '1' WHEN x = '0' ELSE '0';
            s(2) <= GUARDED '1' WHEN x = '1' ELSE '0';
        END BLOCK s2;
        s3: BLOCK (s(3) = '1' AND GUARD)
        BEGIN
            s(1) <= GUARDED '1' WHEN x = '0' ELSE '0';
            s(4) <= GUARDED '1' WHEN x = '1' ELSE '0';
        END BLOCK s3;
        s4: BLOCK (s(4) = '1' AND GUARD)
        BEGIN
            s(3) <= GUARDED '1' WHEN x = '0' ELSE '0';
            s(2) <= GUARDED '1' WHEN x = '1' ELSE '0';
            z <= '1' WHEN (s(4) = '1' AND x = '1') ELSE '0';
        END BLOCK s4;
        s <= GUARDED "0000";
    END BLOCK clocking;
END multiple_state_machine;
```

FIGURE 7.37
VHDL description of 1011 detector. More than one state can simultaneously be active.

block, other states become active based on the input conditions. Since four separate signals (elements of s) are used to specify current active states, any number of these states can be active simultaneously. Because the *oring* resolution function is associated with the elements of s, one or more assignments to an element of s are able to activate that state.

The expected behavior of a state machine description is that each state dies out after it conditionally activates its next states(s). Since our state signals are of the REGISTER kind, this does not happen automatically. If all the drivers of an element of s are turned off, the *oring* resolution function is not called and the signal retains its previous value. In order to keep at least one driver active and cause all elements of s to become '0' after they cause activation of other states, we drive all elements of s with '0's on the edge of each clock. This is achieved by the last guarded signal assignment in the statement part of the architecture in Figure 7.37. On the rising edge of each clock, the '0' on an element of s is ORed with all other values that drive this signal. If this '0' is the only driver for that element, it causes the value to become '0'. On the other hand, if this element is activated by other '1's, the '0' will have no effect on the value that is assigned to the s element.

7.2.3 Outputs of Mealy and Moore Machines

Mealy and Moore machines make their state transitions in exactly the same way. The state transitions portion of the description styles presented in Figures 7.36 and 7.37 apply to Moore machines as well as Mealy machines. The main difference between these machines is the way they assign values to the outputs.

In a Mealy machine, inputs and states of the machine participate in the formation of conditions for assigning values to the outputs. In a Moore machine, the states alone are used in conditional signal assignments to the output signals. In either machine, several states can provide values for the output signals. This requires either resolved output signals using a resolution function such as *oring*, or it requires a single conditional or selected signal assignment to assign value to each unresolved output. The advantage of using resolved outputs is that assignments to the outputs can be placed in the description next to the state making the assignment, instead of combining all conditions into a condition for a single signal assignment.

7.3 OPEN COLLECTOR GATES

The concept of resolution functions and resolved signals is very useful for modeling various bus forms. A bussing structure formed by connecting the outputs of open collector gates is very common. Figure 7.38a shows an open collector NAND gate, and Figure 7.38b shows a 74LS03 package that consists of four such gates.

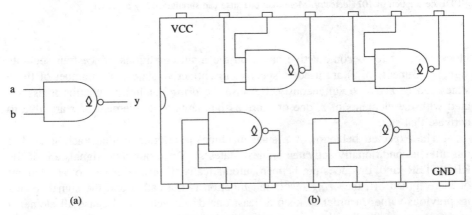

(a) (b)

FIGURE 7.38
Open collector NAND gate, (a) A two-input NAND gate, (b) TTL 74LS03 SSI package.

Figure 7.39 shows the VHDL description of an open collector two-input NAND gate. This description uses the *qit* type and the overloaded AND operator from the *basic_utilities* package. The simple test bench in Figure 7.40a and the simulation report in Figure 7.40b indicate that the *open_output* architecture of *nand2* operates as expected. The output node is 'Z' if any of the inputs is '0'; otherwise it is '0'.

Figure 7.41 shows the VHDL description for the TTL 74LS03 package. The *structural* architecture of the *sn7403* entity instantiates four *open_output* architectures of *nand2*. As shown in the simulation of an individual NAND gate, if an output is used without a pull-up resistor, its value is either '0' or 'Z'. We now demonstrate how resolution functions can be used to model pull-up resistors.

In general, the function of a pull-up resistor is to produce a '1' if none of its drivers is '0', and to produce a '0' if at least one driver is '0'. For the *qit* type, this function is the same as the *anding* function that we described earlier in Section 7.1.4.2 of this chapter. Therefore, we can use the following declaration for modeling a circuit node that is connected to a five-volt supply through a pull-up resistor:

```
SIGNAL pull_up : anded_qit;
```

Associating this signal with an output port of an open collector gate is equivalent to connecting that output to a pull-up resistor in hardware.

The gate level design in Figure 7.42 illustrates the use of pull-up resistors. This circuit uses four NAND gates of a 74LS03 package for implementing an Exclusive-NOR function. Gates *g1* and *g2* serve as inverters for inverting the *aa* and the *bb* inputs. In order to be able to use these outputs for the inputs of other gates, they have been pulled up by *pull_up_1* and *pull_up_2* resistors. These outputs are used for the inputs of *g3* and *g4* gates; the outputs of these gates are tied together to the *pull_up_3* resistor. The resulting Boolean expression on the *yy* output is:

$$yy = (aa' . bb)' . (bb' . aa)' = (aa \oplus bb)'$$

```
USE WORK.basic_utilities.ALL;
-- FROM PACKAGE USE: qit, "AND"
ENTITY nand2 IS
    PORT (a, b : IN qit; y : OUT qit);
    CONSTANT tplh : TIME := 10 NS;
    CONSTANT tphl : TIME := 12 NS;
END nand2;
--
ARCHITECTURE open_output OF nand2 IS
BEGIN
    y <= '0' AFTER tphl WHEN (a AND b) = '1' ELSE
         'Z' AFTER tplh WHEN (a AND b) = '0' ELSE
         'X' AFTER tphl;
END open_output;
```

FIGURE 7.39
VHDL description of a NAND gate with open collector output.

```
ENTITY test_nand2 IS END test_nand2;
    --
USE WORK.basic_utilities.ALL;
-- FROM PACKAGE USE: qit, assign_bits
ARCHITECTURE input_output OF test_nand2 IS
    COMPONENT nand2 PORT (a, b : IN qit; y : OUT qit); END COMPONENT;
    FOR ALL : nand2 USE ENTITY WORK.nand2 (open_output);
    SIGNAL aa, bb, yy : qit;
BEGIN
    assign_bits (aa, "qit_data", 500 NS);
    assign_bits (bb, "qit_data", 750 NS);
    c1: nand2 PORT MAP (aa, bb, yy);
END input_output;
```

(a)

TIME	SIGNALS		
(ns)	aa	bb	yy
0000	'0'	'0'	'0'
0010	...	...	'Z'
1000	'1'	...	...
1500	...	'1'	...
1512	...	...	'0'
2500	'0'	...	...
2510	...	...	'Z'
3000	'Z'	...	...
3012	...	...	'0'
3750	...	'0'	...
3760	...	...	'Z'
4000	'0'	...	...
4500	'1'	'Z'	...
4512	...	...	'0'
5000	'0'	...	...
5010	...	...	'Z'
5500	'Z'	...	...
5512	...	...	'0'
6000	...	'0'	...
6010	...	...	'Z'
6750	...	'1'	...
6762	...	...	'0'
7500	...	'0'	...
7510	...	...	'Z'
8250	...	'Z'	...
8262	...	...	'0'

(b)

FIGURE 7.40
Testing the open-collector NAND gate of Figure 7.39, (a) test bench using external file data, (b) simulation report. All events are observed.

```
USE WORK.basic_utilities.ALL;
-- FROM PACKAGE USE: qit
ENTITY sn7403 IS
   PORT (a1, a2, a3, a4, b1, b2, b3, b4 : IN qit; y1, y2, y3, y4 : OUT qit);
END sn7403;
--
ARCHITECTURE structural OF sn7403 IS
    COMPONENT nand2 PORT (a, b : IN qit; y : OUT qit); END COMPONENT;
    FOR ALL : nand2 USE ENTITY WORK.nand2 (open_output);
BEGIN
    g1: nand2 PORT MAP ( a1, b1, y1 );
    g2: nand2 PORT MAP ( a2, b2, y2 );
    g3: nand2 PORT MAP ( a3, b3, y3 );
    g4: nand2 PORT MAP ( a4, b4, y4 );
END structural;
```

FIGURE 7.41
VHDL description of TTL 74LS03 which contains four open collector NAND gates.

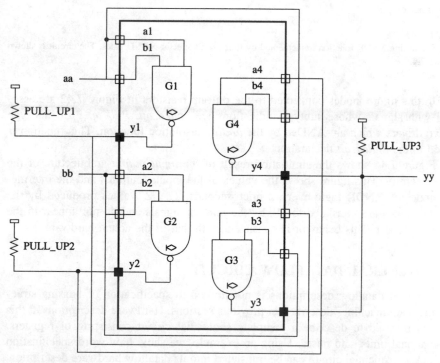

FIGURE 7.42
Implementing XNOR logic using open collector NAND gates.

The VHDL description in Figure 7.43 specifies the wiring in Figure 7.42 and it provides test data to the *aa* and the *bb* inputs.

```
USE  WORK.basic_utilities.ALL;
-- FROM PACKAGE USE: qit, anded_qit
ENTITY test_xnor IS END test_xnor;
    --
ARCHITECTURE input_output OF test_xnor IS
    COMPONENT sn7403
        PORT (a1, a2, a3, a4, b1, b2, b3, b4 : IN qit; y1, y2, y3, y4 OUT qit);
    END COMPONENT;
    FOR ALL : sn7403 USE ENTITY WORK.sn7403 (structural);
    SIGNAL aa, bb : qit;
    SIGNAL pull_up_1, pull_up_2, pull_up_3 : anded_qit := 'Z';
BEGIN
    aa <=
        '1', '0' AFTER 10US, '1' AFTER 30US, '0' AFTER 50US, 'Z' AFTER 60US;
    bb <= '0', '1' AFTER 20US, '0' AFTER 40US, 'Z' AFTER 70US;
    c1: sn7403 PORT MAP (
        aa,            bb,             pull_up_1,      pull_up_2,
        aa,            bb,             bb,             aa,
        pull_up_1,     pull_up_2,      pull_up_3,      pull_up_3);
END input_output;
```

FIGURE 7.43
Wiring and testing XNOR function implemented by four open collector NAND gates. The circuit is shown
in Figure 7.42.

In this figure, nodes connected to the pull-up resistors in Figure 7.42 are associated with signals whose subtype indications are *anded_qit*. *Pull_up_3* of this type
has two drivers which are ANDed by the *anding* resolution function. This function is
implied in the *anded_qit* declaration.

Figure 7.44 shows the simulation result of the *input_output* architecture of the
test_xnor entity. This figure shows the values of the inputs, outputs, and the intermediate nodes of XNOR logic every 2 microseconds. The 'Z' values produced by the
individual gates are translated to ',1', by the *pull_up* signals and do not appear in the
simulation report. This behavior is consistent with that of the actual hardware.

7.4   A GENERAL DATAFLOW CIRCUIT

Application of dataflow descriptions is not limited to specification of bussing structures and state machines described in previous sections. Hardware descriptions at this
level can be used to describe a complete sequential circuit consisting of registers,
combinational units, and buses. Using an example, we show how word specification
of a clocked sequential circuit can be translated into its dataflow hardware description.

The circuit to design is a sequential comparator that keeps a modulo-16 count
of matching consecutive data set pairs. The circuit uses an 8-bit *data*, a *clk*, and a
reset input. The 4-bit output is called *matches*. If on any two consecutive rising edges
of the clock, the same data appears on *data*, then the output will be incremented by
1. The synchronous reset of the circuit resets the output count to zero.

TIME	SIGNALS				
(us)	aa	bb	pull_up_1	pull_up_2	pull_up_3
00	'1'	'0'	'0'	'0'	'0'
02	'1'	'0'	'0'	'1'	'0'
04	'1'	'0'	'0'	'1'	'0'
06	'1'	'0'	'0'	'1'	'0'
08	'1'	'0'	'0'	'1'	'0'
10	'0'	'0'	'0'	'1'	'0'
12	'0'	'0'	'1'	'1'	'1'
14	'0'	'0'	'1'	'1'	'1'
16	'0'	'0'	'1'	'1'	'1'
18	'0'	'0'	'1'	'1'	'1'
20	'0'	'1'	'1'	'1'	'1'
22	'0'	'1'	'1'	'0'	'0'
24	'0'	'1'	'1'	'0'	'0'
26	'0'	'1'	'1'	'0'	'0'
28	'0'	'1'	'1'	'0'	'0'
30	'1'	'1'	'1'	'0'	'0'
32	'1'	'1'	'0'	'0'	'1'
34	'1'	'1'	'0'	'0'	'1'
36	'1'	'1'	'0'	'0'	'1'
38	'1'	'1'	'0'	'0'	'1'
40	'1'	'0'	'0'	'0'	'1'
42	'1'	'0'	'0'	'1'	'0'
44	'1'	'0'	'0'	'1'	'0'
46	'1'	'0'	'0'	'1'	'0'
48	'1'	'0'	'0'	'1'	'0'
50	'0'	'0'	'0'	'1'	'0'
52	'0'	'0'	'1'	'1'	'1'
54	'0'	'0'	'1'	'1'	'1'
56	'0'	'0'	'1'	'1'	'1'
58	'0'	'0'	'1'	'1'	'1'
60	'Z'	'0'	'1'	'1'	'1'
62	'Z'	'0'	'0'	'1'	'0'
64	'Z'	'0'	'0'	'1'	'0'
66	'Z'	'0'	'0'	'1'	'0'
68	'Z'	'0'	'0'	'1'	'0'
70	'Z'	'Z'	'0'	'1'	'0'

FIGURE 7.44
Simulation results for testing XNOR implementation using open collector NAND gates. Results are observed at 2 us intervals.

The hardware implementation of this circuit, using standard parts, requires a register for holding the old data, a comparator for comparing new and old data, a counter for keeping the count, and perhaps a few logic gates used as "glue logic." At the dataflow level, however, there is no need to be concerned with the component level details of this circuit; rather, flow of data between registers and buses can be captured directly in a VHDL description of this unit.

```
USE  WORK.basic_utilities.ALL;
-- FROM  PACKAGE  USE: bin2int, int2bin
ENTITY  sequential_comparator  IS
    PORT (data : IN BIT_VECTOR (7 DOWNTO 0); clk, reset : IN BIT;
               matches : OUT BIT_VECTOR (3 DOWNTO 0));
END sequential_comparator;
--
ARCHITECTURE  dataflow  OF  sequential_comparator  IS
    FUNCTION inc (x : BIT_VECTOR) RETURN BIT_VECTOR IS
        VARIABLE i : INTEGER;
        VARIABLE t : BIT_VECTOR (x'RANGE);
    BEGIN
        bin2int (x, i);
        i := i + 1; IF i >= 2**x'LENGTH THEN i := 0; END IF;
        int2bin (i, t);
        RETURN t;
    END inc;
    SIGNAL buff : BIT_VECTOR (7 DOWNTO 0);
    SIGNAL count : BIT_VECTOR (3 DOWNTO 0);
BEGIN
    edge: BLOCK (clk = '0' AND NOT clk'STABLE)
    BEGIN
        buff <= GUARDED data;
        count <= GUARDED "0000" WHEN reset = '1' ELSE
                          inc (count) WHEN data = buff ELSE count;
    END BLOCK;
    matches <= count;
END dataflow;
```

FIGURE 7.45
Dataflow description of the sequential comparator circuit.

The VHDL description for the *sequential_comparator* is shown in Figure 7.45. The *dataflow* architecture of this circuit uses the *inc* function for incrementing the 4-bit output counter. This function takes advantage of the *bin2int* and *int2bin* procedures in the *basic_utilities* package. In the statement part of the architecture in Figure 7.45, a guarded block statement detects the falling edge of the clock. On this edge, the new data on the *data* input lines is clocked into the 8-bit buffer. Also on the same edge of the clock, the count signal is incremented if the new data and the previous data are equal. Loading *buff* and incrementing *count* are done by concurrent signal assignments and take place simultaneously. A careful study of timing, however, reveals that the condition for incrementing *count* uses the old data in *buff*. The following paragraph elaborates on this timing issue.

If in a simulation cycle at time t, clock makes a 1 to 0 transition, data on the *data* input lines is assigned to *buff*. The new data in *buff* will not be available until $t+\delta$. At time t, the old data in *buff* is compared with what appears on *data* at time t. If these data sets are equal, the *count* signal is incremented. The result of this incrementing becomes available on *count* at $t+\delta$, which is the same time that the new data appears on *buff*. The assignment of *count* to the *matches* output causes this output to lag behind the internal count by another *delta*.

Figure 7.46 shows the sequence of events in the *sequential_comparator*. Understanding timing and clocking is essential in the understanding of dataflow, to be able to use this level of abstraction for the description of systems.

| TIME | SIGNALS | | | | | |
(ns)	reset	clk	data(7:0)	buff(7:0)	count(3:0)	matches
0000	'0'	'0'	"00000000"	"00000000"	"0000"	"0000"
δ	...	...	....	....	......	"0000"
0200	...	...	"11110101"	....	......	......
0500	...	'1'	....	....	......	......
1000	...	'0'	....	....	......	......
δ	...	...	....	"11110101"	"0000"	......
1200	...	...	"01010110"	....	......	......
1500	...	'1'	....	....	......	......
1700	...	...	"11111110"	....	......	......
2000	...	'0'	....	....	......	......
δ	...	...	....	"11111110"	"0000"	......
2500	...	'1'	....	....	......	......
3000	...	'0'	....	....	......	......
δ	...	...	....	"11111110"	"0001"	......
δ	...	...	....	....	......	"0001"
3200	...	...	"01010100"	....	......	......
3500	...	'1'	....	....	......	......
3700	...	...	"00010001"	....	......	......
4000	...	'0'	....	....	......	......
δ	...	...	....	"00010001"	"0001"	......
4200	...	...	"10010110"	....	......	......
4500	...	'1'	....	....	......	......
5000	...	'0'	....	....	......	......
δ	...	...	....	"10010110"	"0001"	......
5500	...	'1'	....	....	......	......
6000	...	'0'	....	....	......	......
δ	...	...	....	"10010110"	"0010"	......
δ	...	...	....	....	......	"0010"
6500	...	'1'	....	....	......	......
7000	...	'0'	....	....	......	......
δ	...	...	....	"10010110"	"0011"	......
δ	...	...	....	....	......	"0011"
7500	...	'1'	....	....	......	......
8000	...	'0'	....	....	......	......
δ	...	...	....	"10010110"	"0100"	......
δ	...	...	....	....	......	"0100"
8500	...	'1'	....	....	......	......

FIGURE 7.46
Simulation results for testing dataflow architecture of *sequential_comparator*. All transactions are observed.

7.5 UPDATING BASIC UTILITIES

The *basic_utilities* package was used extensively in the examples in this chapter. We specified the addition of several resolution functions and their related type definitions to this package. Another useful function to have in this package is the *inc* function from the *sequential_comparator* example. For reference, the contributions added to the *basic_utilities* package in this chapter are shown in Figure 7.47.

7.6 SUMMARY

This chapter presented signal assignments, guarded assignments, and resolution functions, which are considered to be among the most important hardware related constructs in the VHDL language. We focused on resolution functions and how they can be used to model various bussing structures and registers. Various forms of sig-

```
PACKAGE basic_utilities IS
    .
    .
    .
    FUNCTION wire (a, b : qit) RETURN qit;
    --
    FUNCTION oring ( drivers : qit_vector) RETURN qit;
    SUBTYPE ored_qit IS oring qit;
    TYPE ored_qit_vector IS ARRAY (NATURAL RANGE <>) OF ored_qit;
    --
    FUNCTION anding ( drivers : qit_vector) RETURN qit;
    SUBTYPE anded_qit IS anding qit;
    TYPE anded_qit_vector IS ARRAY (NATURAL RANGE <>) OF anded_qit;
    --
    FUNCTION wiring ( drivers : qit_vector) RETURN qit;
    SUBTYPE wired_qit IS wiring qit;
    TYPE wired_qit_vector IS ARRAY (NATURAL RANGE <>) OF wired_qit;
    --
    FUNCTION oring ( drivers : BIT_VECTOR) RETURN BIT;
    SUBTYPE ored_bit IS oring BIT;
    TYPE ored_bit_vector IS ARRAY (NATURAL RANGE <>) OF ored_bit;
    --
    FUNCTION anding ( drivers : BIT_VECTOR) RETURN BIT;
    SUBTYPE anded_bit IS anding bit;
    TYPE anded_bit_vector IS ARRAY (NATURAL RANGE <>) OF anded_bit;
    --
    FUNCTION inc (x : BIT_VECTOR) RETURN BIT_VECTOR;
END basic_utilities;
```

FIGURE 7.47
Resolution functions and *inc* function added to the *basic_utilities* package in Chapter 7. (*continued*)

```
PACKAGE BODY basic_utilities IS
    .
    .
    .

    FUNCTION wire (a, b : qit) RETURN qit IS
        CONSTANT qit_and_table : qit_2d := (
                                    ('0','X','0','X'),
                                    ('X','1','1','X'),
                                    ('0','1','Z','X'),
                                    ('X','X','X','X'));
    BEGIN
        RETURN qit_and_table (a, b);
    END wire;
    FUNCTION oring ( drivers : qit_vector) RETURN qit IS
        VARIABLE accumulate : qit := '0';
    BEGIN
        FOR i IN drivers'RANGE LOOP
            accumulate := accumulate OR drivers(i);
        END LOOP;
        RETURN accumulate;
    END oring;
    FUNCTION anding ( drivers : qit_vector) RETURN qit IS
        VARIABLE accumulate : qit := '1';
    BEGIN
        FOR i IN drivers'RANGE LOOP
            accumulate := accumulate AND drivers(i);
        END LOOP;
        RETURN accumulate;
    END anding;
    FUNCTION wiring ( drivers : qit_vector) RETURN qit IS
        VARIABLE accumulate : qit := 'Z';
    BEGIN
        FOR i IN drivers'RANGE LOOP
            accumulate := wire (accumulate, drivers(i));
        END LOOP;
        RETURN accumulate;
    END wiring;
```

FIGURE 7.47

Resolution functions and *inc* function added to the *basic_utilities* package in Chapter 7. (*continued*)

nal assignments in VHDL provide tools for describing complex bussing structures in register transfer level descriptions.

The first part of this chapter presented forms of signal assignments that had not been encountered in the examples in previous chapters. Guarded signal assignment and the concept of disconnection, or turning off a source, were presented next. This prepared the way for describing resolution functions, multiple drivers of signals, and guarded signals. Although VHDL only requires resolution of signals with multiple

```
FUNCTION oring ( drivers : BIT_VECTOR) RETURN BIT IS
    VARIABLE accumulate : BIT := '0';
BEGIN
    FOR i IN drivers'RANGE LOOP
        accumulate := accumulate OR drivers(i);
    END LOOP;
    RETURN accumulate;
END oring;
FUNCTION anding ( drivers : BIT_VECTOR) RETURN BIT IS
    VARIABLE accumulate : BIT := '1';
BEGIN
    FOR i IN drivers'RANGE LOOP
        accumulate := accumulate AND drivers(i);
    END LOOP;
    RETURN accumulate;
END anding;
FUNCTION inc (x : BIT_VECTOR) RETURN BIT_VECTOR IS
    VARIABLE i : INTEGER;
    VARIABLE t : BIT_VECTOR (x'RANGE);
BEGIN
    bin2int (x, i);
    i := i + 1; IF i >= 2**x'LENGTH THEN i := 0; END IF;
    int2bin (i, t);
    RETURN t;
END inc;
END basic_utilities;
```

FIGURE 7.47
Resolution functions and *inc* function added to the *basic_utilities* package in Chapter 7.

concurrent sources, in general a resolved signal is a better representation of a circuit node. In VHDL, a regular signal retains its value indefinitely—this behavior is different from a hardware node that loses its value as soon as its driver is removed. A resolved signal, on the other hand, can be made to act in exactly the same way as a hardware circuit node. A resolution function for such a node can be written to match its technology-dependent behavior. The resolution functions developed in this chapter are typical of the way buses function in a digital system. Hardware designers develop their own libraries of resolution functions, based on the design styles and the technologies they are working with. The last part of this chapter presented a dataflow description for an entire system. This demonstrated that signal assignments, resolution functions, and guarded block statements are applicable to high level designs as well as to low level buses or flip-flops.

REFERENCES

1. Wakerly, J. F., "Digital Design Principles and Practices," Prentice-Hall Inc., Englewood Cliffs, N.J., 1990.

2. Hill, F. J., and G. R. Peterson, "Digital Systems: Hardware Organization and Design," 3rd ed., John Wiley and Sons, New York, 1987.
3. "IEEE Standard VHDL Language Reference Manual," IEEE Std 1076-1987, The Institute of Electrical and Electronic Engineers, Inc., 1988.
4. Lipsett, L., C. Schaefer, and C. Ussery, "VHDL: Hardware Description and Design," Klewer Academic Publishing, Boston, 1988.
5. Armstrong, J. R., "Chip-Level Modeling with VHDL," Prentice-Hall Inc., Englewood Cliffs, N.J., 1988.

PROBLEMS

7.1. Write functions *qit2bit* and *bit2qit* for converting an unconstrained *qit_vector* to a BIT_ VECTOR, and an unconstrained BIT_VECTOR to a *qit_vector*, respectively. Take advantage of arrays with noninteger indices for converting from one base type to another.

7.2. Use a selected signal assignment to describe a BCD to seven-segment decoder. Use *qit* as the base type of all elements of inputs and outputs. You may use the functions you created in Problem 7.1.

7.3. Write a description for an 8-to-1 multiplexer with a 3-bit decoded input in the *qit* logic value system. Take advantage of the functions you prepared in Problem 7.1.

7.4. Wire the multiplexer in Figure 7.5 and the decoder of Figure 7.8 to generate a multiplexer with decoded input.

7.5. A decoder with an enable input is easily cascadable. Write a VHDL description for a 3-to-8 decoder with an active low enable input and an active high enable input. When disabled, all outputs have to be 0. Use the *qit* logic value system.

7.6. Write a VHDL description for wiring two of the decoders in Problem 7.5 to implement a 4-to-16 decoder.

7.7. Use guarded signal assignments to describe a simple latch with *q* and NOT *q* outputs that functions the same as a latch formed by cross-coupled NOR gates with clocked inputs. Use reasonable delay values.

7.8. Use two of the latches in Problem 7.7 and necessary logic operations to describe a master-slave JK flip-flop.

7.9. Use guarded block statements to describe an 8-bit shift register. The structure has a serial input for right shifting the data and a single serial output. All activities are synchronized with the leading edge of the clock.

7.10. Write a description for a universal 8-bit shift register with a 2-bit mode select input, an 8-bit parallel data input, and an 8-bit data output. The unit performs a right shift if the mode is 01, left shift if the mode is 10, and a parallel load of the eight bit input if the mode is 11. All activities are synchronized with the leading edge of the clock.

7.11. Write a description for a clocked T-type flip-flop. If T is '1' on the rising edge of the clock, the outputs of the flip-flop toggle. Use the *qit* logic value system.

7.12. Write a VHDL description for a rising edge trigger D-type flip-flop with asynchronous set and reset inputs and two outputs. Label the data, clock, set and reset inputs *d*, *c*, *s* and *r*, respectively. Active *s* or *r* inputs override the clocked values on the *d* input; *s* and *r* cannot simultaneously be active. Changes on *d* without the rising edge of *c* have no effect on the *q* and *qb* outputs of the flip-flop. Use delay parameters *sq_delay*, *rq_delay*, and *cq_delay* for setting, resetting, and clocking the flip-flop, respectively. Develop a test bench for testing this flip-flop. Generate a simple periodic clock using a conditional signal assignment.

7.13. Given the following description, show waveforms on *x1*, *x2* and *diff* in a timing diagram. Explain the reason for different waveforms on *x1* and *x2*.

```
ENTITY find_out IS END find_out;
--
ARCHITECTURE comparing OF find_out IS
    SIGNAL c, x1, x2, diff : BIT := '0';
BEGIN
    c <= '0', '1' AFTER 60 NS, '0' AFTER 120 NS;
    x1 <= '1' AFTER 6 NS WHEN c'EVENT ELSE x1;
    x2 <= '1' AFTER 6 NS WHEN NOT c'STABLE ELSE x2;
    diff <= x1 XOR x2;
END comparing;
```

7.14. A resolution function, named *majority*, resolves to the majority of '1's or '0's on its inputs. If there are more ones ('1's) than zeros, the function generates a '1' output. If there are more zeros ('0's) than ones, the function generates a '0' output. If the number of '1's and '0's are equal the output will be 'E'. A) Declare all necessary types, and write the description of the *majority* function. B) Declare types and subtypes that can be used for declaring signals that can take advantage of this resolution function. C) Package all of the above, and show how a single-bit signal *candidate* and a 16-bit signal *candidate_16* should be declared such that placement of multiple values on these signals will resolve according to the *majority* function.

7.15. A resolution function, named *all_same*, resolves all '1's on its sources to '1' and all '0's to zero. This function generates 'E', indicating an error condition if conflicting values are placed at its sources. A) Declare all necessary types, and write the description of the *all_same* function. B) Declare types and subtypes that can be used for declaring signals that can take advantage of this resolution function. C) Package all of the above, and show how a single-bit signal *x* and a 16-bit signal *x16* should be declared such that placement of multiple values on these signals will resolve according to the *all_same* function. D) What actual hardware construct behaves like the *all_same* function?

7.16. Ten controlled sources (*s(i)* where *i* is 1 to 10) that range between −25 and +25 volts are connected to the sources of 10 parallel MOS transistors. The common drain of these transistors is node *n*. Each source, *s(i)*, is controlled by a control line, *c(i)*, that is connected to the gate of the MOS transistors. Control line voltages also range between −25 to +25. A control line, *c(i)*, turns its corresponding transistor on, i.e., causes it to conduct which in turn causes node *n* be driven by source *s(i)* when *c(i)* is greater than or equal to +5 volts. The on-resistance of the parallel transistors is 10 KΩ. Node *n* is also connected to a 25 V supply through a 10 KΩ pull-up resistor. At any time, any number of controlled sources may be active. A) Write a resolution function that returns the voltage at node *n* depending on the value and number of active sources. B) In a test architecture, declare a resolved guarded signal (node *n*) whose resolution function is that in Part A. Use guarded block statements to conditionally drive this signal (node *n*) with up to 10 sources, each of which can take a value between −25 and +25. This is analogous to connecting 10 parallel MOS transistors to node *n* and applying various voltages to the sources of these transistors. Use a generate statement instead of 10 individual block statements.

7.17. Use a block statement, a resolution function, a conditional signal assignment, and a disconnection specification to model a tri-state noninverting buffer. The gate has data and enable inputs x and e, and output z. When e is '1', the z output is driven by x; otherwise, the output is in the high impedance state. The inputs and outputs are of type qit and output is a guarded signal. Use the three delay values *tp_e_z_float*, *tp_x_z_high*, and *tp_x_z_low* where: *tp_e_z_float* is for e changing to '0' and causing the output to disconnect from the input; *tp_x_z_high* is for e equal to '1'and x changing to '1' causing the output to become '1', or when x is '1' and e changes to '1'; and *tp_x_z_low* is for e equal to '1' and x changing to '0' causing the output to become '0', or when x is '0' and e changes to '1'. Use '0' and '1' values for the inputs, and map 'X' and 'Z' into '0' and '1', respectively. Use two such buffers for implementing a 2-to-1 multiplexer.

7.18. Design a Mealy sequence detector and develop a tester for this circuit. The circuit monitors its x input for the 10110 sequence. When this sequence is found, the z output becomes '1'. A valid data bit is one that coincides with the rising edge of the clock, c. Make sure that you understand the behavior of a Mealy machine output. A) Write a VHDL dataflow description for this sequence detector. B) Show a test bench that tests this circuit for the 10110110101 sequence on the x input. Use a periodic clock.

7.19. Accurately model the circuit shown below in VHDL at the dataflow level. This circuit uses positive edge triggered D flip-flop. Flip-flop 1 has an asynchronous reset in addition to the synchronous D input. The reset input has priority over the clock input. Write a complete VHDL description at the dataflow level for modeling this circuit. Your description should include an ENTITY and an ARCHITECTURE.

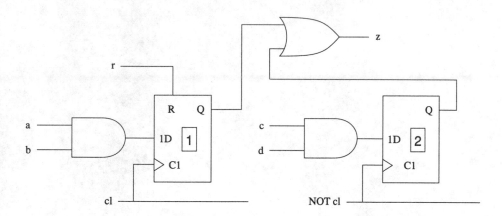

7.20. Write the complete VHDL description for a Moore machine detecting 10111 or 11001. The circuit continuously monitors its x input. When in five consecutive clock pulses either sequence is found, the z output becomes '1' and stays at this level for a complete clock pulse. Write a VHDL dataflow description for this sequence detector. Show a test bench that tests this circuit for the 1011001011100110100 sequence on the x input. Use a periodic clock.

7.21. Write the complete VHDL description for a circuit with an input x and two outputs, $z1$ and $z2$. The circuit consists of two concurrent Mealy machines. The $z1$ output becomes '1' when a 1011 sequence is found on the input, and the $z2$ output becomes '1' when a 110 sequence is found x. Your description should be capable of having multiple active states.

7.22. Write a VHDL description for a Moore state machine with resetting capability. While continuously searching for 1011 on the data input x, if the reset input, r, becomes '1', the circuit returns to a reset state. In this state, all previously received data will be ignored and a complete 1011 is required before the output becomes '1'. While not reset, circuit responds to overlapping valid sequences.

7.23. Describe a synchronous shifter circuit with a left serial input, *lsi*, and an 8-bit shift register. The circuit synchronously resets when a '1' appears on its reset input. After a reset, for every five clock pulses, a data bit from the *lsi* input is shifted into the 8-bit register. You may use utilities of the *basic_utilities* package.

BEHAVIORAL DESCRIPTION OF HARDWARE

Most hardware characteristics can be described by the methods and techniques presented in the previous chapters. Although the emphasis has been on the structural and dataflow descriptions, we have also shown how subprograms can be used to represent hardware modules at the behavioral level. The use of such constructs, however, has mainly been for nonhardware processes.

In this chapter, the emphasis is on behavioral descriptions of hardware components. We show how a hardware unit can be described by its input/output mapping without specifying its technology, netlist, or even its data path.

The chapter begins by presenting key VHDL constructs for behavioral descriptions of concurrent bodies. This is followed by a description of high level constructs for handshaking, timing, and formatted I/O. Next, we present a complete design using standard MSI parts. The behavioral description of these parts will be described in detail. A configuration declaration and a test bench complete the design and testing of this MSI-based design.

8.1 PROCESS STATEMENT

A simple signal assignment in the statement part of an architecture is a *process* which is always active and executing concurrent with other processes within the same architecture. This process has a single target, and executes when an event occurs on one

219

of the signals on its right hand side. Therefore, it is said to be sensitive to signals on the right hand side of the signal assignment. A different kind of a process is a process statement which is also active at all times, executing concurrently with other processes, but can be made sensitive to selected signals.

A process statement can assign values to more than one signal and can contain sequential statements. This statement begins with the PROCESS keyword and ends with END PROCESS. As shown in Figure 8.1, a process statement has a declarative part and a statement part. All constructs allowed in the declarative and statement parts of subprograms can be used in process statements. The semantics of subprograms and the sequential statements used within them, however, are different from those in the process statements.

8.1.1 Declarative Part of a Process

Variable, file, or constant objects can be declared in the declarative part of a process. Such objects are only visible to the process within which they are declared. Signals and constants declared in the declarative part of an architecture that encloses a process statement can be used inside a process. Such signals are the only means of communication between different processes.

Initialization of objects declared in a process is done only once at the beginning of a simulation run. These objects stay alive for the entire simulation run. This way a variable declared in a process can be used to hold memory status or the internal state of a hardware system. Note that initializations in a subprogram are performed each time the subprogram is called.

8.1.2 Statement Part of a Process

The statement part of a process is sequential, always active, and it executes in zero time. The following paragraphs and examples will elaborate on these concepts.

Only sequential statements are allowed in the statement part of a process. These statements provide high level program flow control for assignment of values to signals and variables. For selection and assignment of values to signals, if, loop or case statements can be used. Although the syntax of many concurrent and sequential statements is the same, in general, concurrent statements are not allowed in the statement

PROCESS

declarative_part
...

BEGIN

statement_part
...

END   PROCESS;

FIGURE 8.1
A process statement block diagram.

part of a process statement. Conditional and selected signal assignments are strictly concurrent, and they cannot be used in a process statement.

Program flow inside a process starts at the beginning of its statement part and proceeds toward the end of this part. Statements reached by the program flow are executed sequentially in zero time. Consider, for example, the partial code in Figure 8.2. In this example, the assignment of *a* to *x* is executed before assigning *b* to *y*. Both assignments schedule values to their left hand side targets, which will appear one *delta* time later.

Figure 8.3 shows another partial code in which assignment of values to *x* and *y* use 10 ns and 6 ns delays, respectively. When the flow of program reaches the first assignment, the value of *a* is scheduled for *x* after 10 ns. Following the execution of this statement, the signal assignment assigning *b* to *y* is executed. As the result of this execution, the value of *b* is scheduled for the *y* target after 6 ns. The end result is that the *y* signal receives the value of *b* 4 ns sooner than *x* receives *a*, even though the scheduling of the former was done after that of the latter.

Another partial code, demonstrating the availability of data assigned to signals, is shown in Figure 8.4. In this figure, we assume that the value of *x* is '0' be-

```
┌ARCHITECTURE sequentiality_demo OF partial_process IS
├BEGIN
│      ┌PROCESS
│      ├BEGIN
│      │  ...
│      │  x <= a;
│      │  y <= b;
│      │  ...
│      └END PROCESS;
└END sequentiality_demo;
```

FIGURE 8.2
Sequentiality in process statements. The amount of real time between the execution of one statement and the next is zero. Both statements occur in one simulation cycle.

```
┌ARCHITECTURE execution_time_demo OF partial_process IS
├BEGIN
│    ┌PROCESS
│    ├BEGIN
│    │  ...
│    │  x <= a AFTER 10 NS;
│    │  y <= b AFTER 6 NS;
│    │  ...
│    └END PROCESS;
└END execution_time_demo;
```

FIGURE 8.3
Partial code for demonstration of zero execution time of a process statement.

```
ARCHITECTURE data_availability_demo OF partial_process IS
BEGIN
    PROCESS
    BEGIN
        ...
        x <= '1';
        IF x = '1' THEN
            perform  action_1
        ELSE
            perform  action_2
        END IF;
        ...
    END PROCESS;
END data_availability_demo;
```

FIGURE 8.4
Partial code for demonstrating delay in assignment of values to signals.

fore the flow of the program reaches the signal assignment that uses x on the left hand side. Execution of this statement causes '1' to be scheduled for the x target after a δ delay. The if statement in this figure is executed immediately after the execution of the signal assignment. Since these two statements are executed during the same simulation cycle (in zero time), the new value of x is not available when the if statement is executed. The condition of this statement, therefore, will not be satisfied and *action_2* is performed. Had x been a variable, the symbol := would have to be used to assign a value to it, and its new value, '1', would be available when the if statement is executed. In that case, *action_1* would have been performed.

The statement part of a process is always active. When the program flow reaches the last sequential statement of this part the execution returns to the first statement in the statement part and continues. This behavior is different from that of subprograms; in subprogram execution, the subprogram terminates when the flow of the program reaches the last statement in its statement part. In fact, a procedure with an infinite loop in its statement parts behaves the same as a process statement.

8.1.3 Sensitivity List

A process statement is always active and executes at all times if not suspended. A mechanism for suspending and subsequently conditionally activating a process is the use of sensitivity list. Following a PROCESS keyword, a list of signals in parentheses can be specified; this list is called the sensitivity list, and the process is activated when an event occurs on any of these signals. When the program flow reaches the last sequential statement, the process becomes suspended, although alive, until another event occurs on a signal that it is sensitive to. Regardless of the events on the sensitivity list signals, processes are executed once at the beginning of the simulation run.

The signal assignment of Figure 8.5a is considered to be a process and it is equivalent to the process statement in Figure 8.5b. These two processes are only activated when an event occurs on *b*, and they become suspended after the new value of *b* is scheduled for *a*.

8.1.4 A First Process Example

Figure 8.6 shows the logic symbol for a D-type flip-flop with asynchronous active-high set and reset inputs. The VHDL description in Figure 8.7 corresponds to this D-type flip-flop. The description demonstrates concurrency of processes, sensitivity lists, and several process related timing issues.

The behavioral architecture of the *d_sr_flipflop* in Figure 8.7 uses an internal state to record the status of the current memory. The statement part of this architecture includes three concurrent processes, one of which is a process statement sensitive to inputs *rst*, *set* and *clk*. When an event occurs on any of these signals, the *dff* process becomes active. This process uses an if statement to schedule a value for *state*. When the value of *state* changes, the signal assignments to *q* and *qb* become active, causing these outputs to receive their values after one δ delay. From the time that values are scheduled for the *state* signal to the time that *state* changes, all three processes are suspended.

The if statement in the statement part of the *dff* process gives a higher priority to the asynchronous inputs than to the clock. If, for example, the clock edge appears while the *set* input is high, value of '1' on the *state* signal will be reinstated. This description makes no provisions for the illegal case of *set* and *rst* both being '1' simultaneously.

```
...                PROCESS
...                BEGIN
a <= b;              a <= b;
...                END PROCESS;
    (a)                (b)
```

FIGURE 8.5
A simple process with sensitivity list, (a) signal assignment, (b) equivalent process statement.

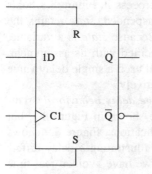

FIGURE 8.6
A positive edge trigger D-Type flip-flop with asynchronous set and reset inputs.

```
ENTITY d_sr_flipflop IS
    GENERIC (sq_delay, rq_delay, cq_delay : TIME := 6 NS);
    PORT (d, set, rst, clk : IN BIT; q, qb : OUT BIT);
END d_sr_flipflop;
--
ARCHITECTURE behavioral OF d_sr_flipflop IS
    SIGNAL state : BIT := '0';
BEGIN
    dff: PROCESS (rst, set, clk)
    BEGIN
    IF set = '1' THEN
        state <= '1' AFTER sq_delay;
    ELSIF rst = '1' THEN
        state <= '0' AFTER rq_delay;
    ELSIF clk = '1' AND clk'EVENT THEN
        state <= d AFTER cq_delay;
    END IF;
    END PROCESS dff;
    q <= state;
    qb <= NOT state;
END behavioral;
```

FIGURE 8.7
VHDL description for the flip-flop of Figure 8.6.

Since the internal state of the flip-flop is realized by use of a signal, there are always two simulation cycles between input and output changes; one for assignment of values to *state*, and one for assigning *state* or its complement to the outputs. If the delay values, i.e., *sq_delay*, *rq_delay*, and *cq_delay* are nonzero, the first δ delay (the delay for the assignment of values to *state*) will be absorbed in the nonzero delay values, and only the second δ delay appears on the output.

Another architecture for the *d_sr_flipflop* entity is shown in Figure 8.8. For zero delay parameter values, this architecture reduces the δ delays between inputs and outputs to only one *delta*. For nonzero delay parameters, no δ delay will appear on the outputs. Comparison of the two models of *d_sr_flipflop* is useful in understanding signals and variables in process statements.

The variable declared in the declarative part of *dff* process in Figure 8.8 holds the internal state of the flip-flop. When this process is suspended, *state* retains the value assigned to it in the last activation of the process. Because *state* is a variable, no delays are associated with it and no delays can be specified with its assignment. Therefore, we have averaged the three delay parameters and used a single delay value for assigning *state* and its complement to *q* and *qb*, respectively.

It is probably obvious to the reader that the *average_delay_behavioral* architecture for a D-type flip-flop is less accurate than the one shown in Figure 8.7, but avoiding the extra δ delay may be important in some applications. Figure 8.9 shows the results of simultaneous simulation of the two models, illustrating δ delay differences between them. For a better illustration of δ delays, we have avoided real time

```
┌ARCHITECTURE  average_delay_behavioral  OF  d_sr_flipflop  IS
├BEGIN
   ┌dff: PROCESS (rst, set, clk)
   │ VARIABLE state : BIT := '0';
   ├BEGIN
   │ IF set = '1' THEN
   │    state := '1';
   │ ELSIF rst = '1' THEN
   │    state := '0';
   │ ELSIF clk = '1' AND clk'EVENT THEN
   │    state := d;
   │ END IF;
   │ q <= state AFTER (sq_delay + rq_delay + cq_delay)/3;
   │ qb <= NOT state AFTER (sq_delay + rq_delay + cq_delay)/3;
   └END PROCESS dff;
└END average_delay_behavioral;
```

FIGURE 8.8
Alternative architecture for *d_sr_flipflop* entity; reducing δ delay by one.

differences between the two models by using equal values for the three timing parameters. This way, average values for the *average_delay_behavioral* and the individual values for the *behavioral* architectures are equal.

The simulation report in this figure shows the two architectures tested for asynchronous setting (*ss*='1' at 200 ns), asynchronous resetting (*rr* = '1' at 1400 ns), and clocking them with *dd*='1' and *dd*='0' (at 2500 ns and 3500 ns, respectively). In all these cases, *q* and *qb* of the *behavioral* architecture (*q1* and *qb1*) receive their values one delta time after their corresponding physical delay values. However, for the *average_delay_behavioral*, the only delays seen on the outputs (*q2* and *qb2*) are the physical delays that are equal to the average of the three delay parameters.

8.1.5 Syntax Details of Process Statements

Figure 8.10 shows the syntax details for the process statement used in the description of Figure 8.8. The label of a process, which precedes this statement, is optional, but, if used, it should also be placed at the end of the process statement. The sensitivity list is also optional and it can contain any number of signals that are visible outside of the process. Objects declared inside a process cannot be used in its sensitivity list for that process.

As shown in Figure 8.10, only sequential statements are allowed in the statement part of a process, whereas, the process statements themselves are considered concurrent statements. This implies that processes cannot be nested. Where nesting of behavioral sequential bodies is necessary, procedures can be called from processes. It is, of course, possible to nest procedures since procedure calls are both concurrent and sequential statements.

TIME (ns)	SIGNALS							
	ss	rr	cc	dd	q1	q2	qb1	qb2
0000	'0'	'0'	'0'	'0'	'0'	'0'	'0'	'0'
δ	...	...	...	...	...	...	'1'	...
0006	...	...	...	...	...	...	...	'1'
0200	'1'	...	...	...	...	...	...	...
0206	...	...	...	...	...	'1'	...	'0'
δ	...	...	...	...	'1'	...	'0'	...
0500	...	...	'1'	...	...	...	...	...
1000	...	...	'0'	...	...	...	...	...
1200	'0'	...	...	...	...	...	...	...
1400	...	'1'	...	...	...	...	...	...
1406	...	...	...	...	...	'0'	...	'1'
δ	...	...	...	...	'0'	...	'1'	...
1500	...	...	'1'	...	...	...	...	...
2000	...	...	'0'	...	...	...	...	...
2200	...	'0'	...	...	...	...	...	...
2400	...	...	...	'1'	...	...	...	...
2500	...	...	'1'	...	...	...	...	...
2506	...	...	...	...	...	'1'	...	'0'
δ	...	...	...	...	'1'	...	'0'	...
3000	...	...	'0'	...	...	...	...	...
3300	...	...	...	'0'	...	...	...	...
3500	...	...	'1'	...	...	...	...	...
3506	...	...	...	...	...	'0'	...	'1'
δ	...	...	...	...	'0'	...	'1'	...
4000	...	...	'0'	...	...	...	...	...

FIGURE 8.9
Simultaneous simulation of *behavioral* and *average_delay_behavioral* architectures of *d_sr_flipflop*. All events are observed.

8.1.6 Behavioral Flow Control Constructs

As stated previously, software-like program flow control constructs such as if, loop, and case statements are considered sequential statements, and can appear only in sub-programs and processes. Although the semantics of a process statement as a whole are different from those in a subprogram, the semantics of individual sequential statements (among them, program flow control statements) are equivalent. Most such constructs have been described in relation to subprograms in the previous chapters. Statements related to flow control that we have not encountered in the examples in previous chapters are the loop statement without iteration scheme, exit statement, and the next statement.

The loop statement without an iteration scheme, i.e., without FOR or WHILE, is an infinite loop. The only way to exit from this loop is to use an exit statement. For example, the loop shown in Figure 8.11 terminates only when x is equal to 25. If this condition does not occur, the looping continues indefinitely.

Next and exit statements can be used within loop statements. A next statement reached by the program flow within a loop causes the rest of the loop to be skipped

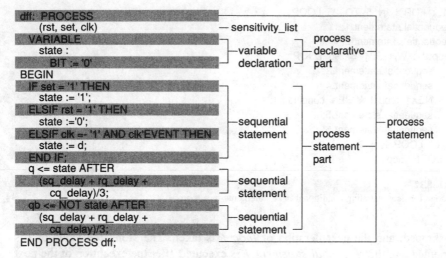

FIGURE 8.10
Syntax details of a process statement with sensitivity list, declarative part, and statement part.

```
long_running : LOOP
    ...
    IF  x = 25  THEN  EXIT;
    END  IF;
    ...
END  LOOP  long_running;
```

FIGURE 8.11
Partial code for demonstrating exiting from a potentially infinite loop.

and the next iteration to be taken. An exit statement causes the termination of the loop that it applies to. Both statements can be used optionally with a loop label and a condition, as presented here:

    NEXT loop_label WHEN condition;

The if statement of Figure 8.11 can be replaced with the exit statement shown here:

    EXIT WHEN x = 25;

If the optional loop label of the next or the exit statements is not included, the next or exit statements apply to their innermost enclosing loop. Inclusion of this label, however, enables the application of these statements to selected outer loops. Consider the partial code in Figure 8.12.

While in the *loop_2* loop, if after the execution of *sequential_ statement_4 condition_1* is TRUE, the next statement causes the remainder of *loop_2* and *loop_1* loops

```
loop_1 : FOR i IN 5 TO 25 LOOP
    sequential_statement_1;
    sequential_statement_2;
    loop_2 : WHILE j <= 90 LOOP
        sequential_statement_3;
        sequential_statement_4;
        NEXT loop_1 WHEN condition_1;
        sequential_statement_5;
        sequential_statement_6;
    END LOOP loop_2;
END LOOP loop_1;
```

FIGURE 8.12
Partial code for demonstrating conditional next statements in a loop.

to be skipped, and the next iteration of *loop_1* is taken. Therefore, the value of i is incremented and the *sequential_statement_1* is executed after the execution of the next statement.

8.2   ASSERTION STATEMENT

The assertion statement is a useful statement for observing activity in a circuit or defining constraints or conditions in the way a circuit operates. The general format of this statement is:

ASSERT assertion_condition REPORT "reporting_message" SEVERITY severity_level;

The statement is said to "occur" when the Boolean *assertion_condition* expression becomes FALSE. At this point, the *reporting_message* is issued, and the simulator takes the action specified by the *severity_level* parameter. The latter parameter can be NOTE, WARNING, ERROR or FAILURE. The ERROR or FAILURE severity levels cause the simulation to stop after issuing the *reporting_message* and a simulation error or failure message. The other two *severity_levels* cause appropriate messages to be issued and the simulation to continue. The REPORT keyword and its following *reporting_message*, as well as the SEVERITY keyword and *severity_level*, are optional parts of the assertion statement. If the REPORT is not present, only the system messages are issued, and the absence of the SEVERITY keyword and its accompanying *severity_level* defaults to the ERROR severity level. The exact series of actions taken by different severity level parameters is simulation-dependent.

8.2.1   Sequential Use of Assertion Statements

Sequential and concurrent VHDL bodies can use assertion statements. A sequential assertion statement issues the *reporting_message* if its *assertion_condition* is FALSE when the program flow reaches the statement. Figure 8.13 shows an example illustrating this use of the assertion statement.

```
┌ARCHITECTURE behavioral OF d_sr_flipflop IS
│   SIGNAL state : BIT := '0';
├BEGIN
│   ┌dff: PROCESS (rst, set, clk)
│   ├BEGIN
│   │   ┌ASSERT
│   │   │      (NOT (set = '1' AND rst = '1'))
│   │   ├REPORT
│   │   │      "set and rst are both 1"
│   │   └SEVERITY NOTE;
│   │   ┌IF set = '1' THEN
│   │   │      state <= '1' AFTER sq_delay;
│   │   ├ELSIF rst = '1' THEN
│   │   │      state <= '0' AFTER rq_delay;
│   │   ├ELSIF clk = '1' AND clk'EVENT THEN
│   │   │      state <= d AFTER cq_delay;
│   │   └END IF;
│   └END PROCESS dff;
│   q <= state;
│   qb <= NOT state;
└END behavioral;
```

FIGURE 8.13
A modified *behavioral* architecture of *d_sr_flipflop*, checking for simultaneous assertion of *set* and *rst*.

In the modified *behavioral* architecture of the *d_sr_flipflop* in this figure, the assertion statement checks to see if the *set* and *rst* inputs are simultaneously active. Obviously, this case is undesirable, and a good model should be able to detect it. When simulating this *behavioral* architecture of *d_sr_flipflop*, if *set* and *rst* are both 1 at the same time, the message "set and rst are both 1" is issued and the simulation continues execution with the if statement that follows the assertion statement. The condition in this statement specifies that the statement issues the message when *NOT (set='1' AND rst='1')* becomes FALSE. In other words, the assertion statement occurs when the expression *(set='1' AND rst='1')* becomes TRUE.

Because of the negation associated with the condition of assertion statements, they can be somewhat confusing, so care must be taken when writing this condition. The expression "ASSERT condition ..." reads as "make sure that this condition is satisfied; otherwise, ...". Therefore, it is clear that a good case must be used as the condition of the statement. The problem arises, however, in the many situations where the good cases are too many to list, and it is easier to write the complement of the unwanted case. For checking errors, then, we will always use *ASSERT(NOT(unwanted_cases))*. After cancelling the two negations, this is equivalent to *ASSERT(wanted_cases)*. For cases in which grouping good cases is as easy as grouping unwanted cases, this negation is not necessary. For example, this statement stops the simulation when *numb* becomes negative:

```
ASSERT numb >= 0;
```

8.2.2 Concurrent Assertion Statements

For cases where violation of constraints must be continuously checked and reported, concurrent assertion statements should be used. These cases include checking of timing constraints such as pulse width, setup time, and hold time. A concurrent assertion statement can be placed in the statement part of an architecture or in the statement part of an entity declaration; we will show the latter shortly. In either case, it is observed at all times and it occurs when an event causes its condition to become FALSE.

Figure 8.14 shows setup and hold times for a positive edge trigger clocked D-type flip-flop. The setup time is the minimum required time between changes on the data input and the triggering edge of the clock. An expression for checking this timing constraint can be based on this statement:

> When (clock changes from zero to 1)$^{--1}$, if the (data input has not been stable at least for the amount of the setup time)$^{--2}$, then a setup time violation has occurred.

The VHDL expression corresponding to this statement is:

```
(clock = '1' AND   NOT clock'STABLE)--1
AND
(NOT data'STABLE (setup_time))--2
```

The numbered parentheses sets around the above statements indicate the corresponding VHDL code in the expression. The setup time is violated when the expression becomes TRUE or when its complement becomes FALSE. Thus, the assertion statement for checking and reporting a setup time violation should use the *assertion_condition* shown here:

```
NOT ((clock = '1' AND   NOT clock'STABLE) AND (NOT data'STABLE (setup_time)))
```

The hold time, also shown in Figure 8.14, is the minimum time that data input of a flip-flop should stay stable after the effective edge of the clock. The following statement describes the circumstances that violate this timing constraint:

> When (there is a change on the data input)$^{--1}$, if the (logic value on the clock is '1')$^{--2}$ and the (clock has got a new value more recent than the amount of hold time)$^{--3}$, then a hold time violation has occurred.

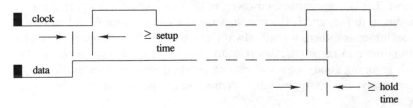

FIGURE 8.14
Setup and hold times for a positive edge trigger D-Type flip-flop.

The VHDL expression based on this statement is:

```
(data'EVENT)--1
AND
(clock = '1')--2
AND
(NOT clock'STABLE (hold_time))--3
```

The condition for the assertion statement that would issue a message when hold time is violated should be as shown here:

```
NOT ((data'EVENT) AND (clock = '1') AND (NOT clock'STABLE (hold_time)))
```

Figure 8.15 shows a new entity declaration for the *d_sr_flipflop* that was first described in Figure 8.7. This entity declaration uses *setup* and *hold* generic timing parameters. In the statement part of this entity declaration, two assertion statements check for setup and hold time violations. Each statement issues an appropriate message if a violation occurs, and also causes the issuance of a system warning message.

The effect of placing these statements in the statement part of the entity declaration is exactly the same as using them in the statement part of an architecture for this entity. The difference is that the statements in the entity statement part apply to all architectures, rather than the one that contains them. For completeness, the *behavioral* architecture of Figure 8.13 is also included in Figure 8.15. This description is a fairly complete model for a rising edge D-type flip-flop with asynchronous set and reset inputs.

We have shown that assertion statements can be used in concurrent and sequential bodies of VHDL. It must be noted, however, that sequential assertion statements execute only when program flow reaches them. For example, if an assertion statement for checking the minimum pulse width on the *d* input is placed in the *dff* process statement in Figure 8.15, in most cases it fails to report violations of this kind. This is because the *dff* process is not sensitive to this input and glitches on *d* do not activate this process. This will not be seen by the assertion statement, so the glitches go undetected.

8.3 SEQUENTIAL WAIT STATEMENTS

The wait statement is a highly behavioral construct for modeling delays, handshaking, and hardware dependencies. This statement comes in four different forms and can be used only in procedures and processes that do not have the optional sensitivity list. When a program flow reaches a wait statement, the process or procedure that encloses it is suspended. The sequential body resumes after the conditions specified by the wait statement are met.

Four forms of the wait statement are shown here:

```
WAIT FOR    waiting_time;
WAIT ON     waiting_sensitivity_list;
WAIT UNTIL  waiting_condition;
WAIT;
```

```
ENTITY d_sr_flipflop IS
    GENERIC (sq_delay, rq_delay, cq_delay : TIME := 6 NS;
                setup, hold : TIME := 4 NS);
    PORT (d, set, rst, clk : IN BIT; q, qb : OUT BIT);
BEGIN
    ASSERT
        (NOT (clk = '1' AND clk'EVENT AND NOT d'STABLE(setup) ))
    REPORT
        "setup time violation"
    SEVERITY WARNING;
    ASSERT
        (NOT (d'EVENT AND clk = '1' AND NOT clk'STABLE(hold) ))
    REPORT
        "Hold time violation"
    SEVERITY WARNING;
END d_sr_flipflop;
--
ARCHITECTURE behavioral OF d_sr_flipflop IS
    SIGNAL state : BIT := '0';
BEGIN
    dff: PROCESS (rst, set, clk)
    BEGIN
        ASSERT
            (NOT (set = '1' AND rst = '1'))
        REPORT
            "set and rst are both 1"
        SEVERITY NOTE;
        IF set = '1' THEN
            state <= '1' AFTER sq_delay;
        ELSIF rst = '1' THEN
            state <= '0' AFTER rq_delay;
        ELSIF clk = '1' AND clk'EVENT THEN
            state <= d AFTER cq_delay;
        END IF;
    END PROCESS dff;
    q <= state;
    qb <= NOT state;
END behavioral;
```

FIGURE 8.15
A complete D-flip-flop description, using assertion statements for illegal set-reset combinations, and setup and hold time violations.

WAIT FOR causes suspension of a sequential body until the *waiting_time* elapses. The suspension caused by WAIT ON is resumed when an event occurs on any of the signals in the *waiting_sensitivity_list*. If a sequential body is suspended by a WAIT UNTIL, that body is resumed when the Boolean *waiting_condition* turns from FALSE to TRUE. If the flow of program reaches a WAIT UNTIL when the *waiting_condition* is TRUE, suspension occurs, and resumption does not occur until condition turns from TRUE to FALSE and then from FALSE to TRUE. The fourth form of wait statement, WAIT, suspends a process forever.

The sensitivity list of a process statement is equivalent to a WAIT ON statement placed at the end of the statement part of the process. The *waiting_sensitivity_list* in this statement is the list of signals that would appear in the process sensitivity list. Therefore, the sensitivity list provides a simple, yet limited way of suspending and activating a process; the more general method is the use of wait statements. The two methods cannot be combined.

8.3.1   A Behavioral State Machine

Chapter 7 presented two methods for describing state machines. A more behavioral method that uses process statements and wait constructs is shown here. The example we use is the Moore implementation of the 1011 detector discussed in the previous chapter, whose state diagram is shown in Figure 8.16. As shown in this diagram, the output becomes '1' and stays '1' for a complete clock cycle when the 1011 sequence appears on the x input on four consecutive clock edges.

Figure 8.17 shows the VHDL description for this sequence detector. The enumeration literals of the *state* type, declared in the declarative part of the *behavioral_state_machine* architecture of *moore_detector*, correspond to the state designators of the state machine. The *current* signal of *state* type is initialized to *reset* and it is used in the statement part of this architecture for containing the present active state of the machine. A process statement forms the statement part and a case statement in

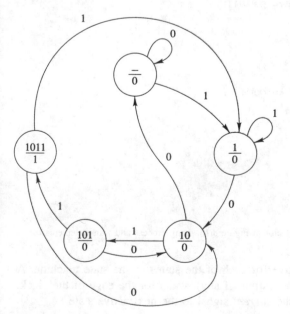

FIGURE 8.16
A Moore machine state diagram for detecting 1011 sequence.

```
ENTITY moore_detector IS
    PORT (x, clk : IN BIT; z : OUT BIT);
END moore_detector;
    --
ARCHITECTURE behavioral_state_machine OF moore_detector IS
    TYPE state IS (reset, got1, got10, got101, got1011);
    SIGNAL current : state := reset;
BEGIN
    PROCESS
    BEGIN
        CASE current IS
        WHEN reset =>
            WAIT UNTIL clk = '1';
            IF x = '1' THEN current <= got1;
            ELSE current <= reset;
            END IF;
        WHEN got1 =>
            WAIT UNTIL clk = '1';
            IF x = '0' THEN current <= got10;
            ELSE current <= got1;
            END IF;
        WHEN got10 =>
            WAIT UNTIL clk = '1';
            IF x = '1' THEN current <= got101;
            ELSE current <= reset;
            END IF;
        WHEN got101 =>
            WAIT UNTIL clk = '1';
            IF x = '1' THEN current <= got1011;
            ELSE current <= got10;
            END IF;
        WHEN got1011 =>
            z <= '1';
            WAIT UNTIL clk = '1';
            IF x = '1' THEN current <= got1;
            ELSE current <= got10;
            END IF;
        END CASE;
        WAIT FOR 1 NS;
        z <= '0';
    END PROCESS;
END behavioral_state_machine;
```

FIGURE 8.17
VHDL description of the 1011 sequence detector in Figure 8.16, using process and wait statements.

this part contains one case alternative for each of the states of the state machine. A case alternative sets the value of the output (if any), waits for the edge of the clock, and depending on the inputs, sets the *current* signal to the next active state.

Following the case statement, a wait statement suspends the enclosing process statement for 1 ns, and after resumption of this process the z output is set to zero and the case statement is executed again. The reason for this 1 ns wait is to create a delay between setting *current* and using it in the case expression. Since *current* is a signal, the new value assigned to it will be available in the next simulation cycle (δ time later), and the 1 ns delay gives enough time for the new value to settle and be used by the case expression. If this wait statement were not present, assigning a new value to *current* and re-execution of the case statement would take place during the same simulation cycle, causing the old value of *current* to be reused by the case expression. The following statement instead of the "WAIT FOR 1 NS;" statement would also serve this purpose:

WAIT ON   *current* 'TRANSACTION ;

The former, however, provides a realistic time delay between state and output changes. Following the wait statement, the assignment of '0' to the output signal, z, is necessary to reset this signal so that it can conditionally be assigned a '1' depending on the next state of the machine. Individual states had to have specific assignment of values to the output if the statement assigning '0' to z was to be removed.

The above description style is an accurate representation for state machines. It is easy to read, can be used for Mealy and Moore machine representations, and uses convenient behavioral constructs for state transitions. However, due to the use of a case statement and a single signal for active state representation, only one state can be active simultaneously. We use the style with concurrent block statements, presented in Chapter 7, when multiple active states are needed.

The above discussion illustrates the use of wait statements for describing state machines, and demonstrates several complex timing issues of VHDL. Because the individual states of the style presented here are controlled by separate wait statements, this description offers flexibility in the control of timing beyond standard state machine requirements. Alternatively, a state machine can be more easily described by a process statement that is sensitive to the events on the clock. In the statement part of such a process, an if statement detects the correct edge of the clock, and a case statement similar to the one in Figure 8.17 implements the branching of the states. Assignment of values to the output should be done outside of the process statement using a conditional signal assignment. In such a description, detection of the clock edge is done only once outside of the case statement, instead of within each state as it was done in Figure 8.17. This issue is dealt with in Problem 8.4 at the end of this chapter. Problem 8.5 deals with adding reset capability to a state machine. For this purpose, an if statement, following the case statement can be used to set the current state of the machine to a reset state if a resetting condition is satisfied.

8.3.2   Two Phase Clocking

A very common clocking scheme in MOS circuits is two-phase nonoverlapping clocking. This scheme insures input to output isolation in master-slave registers, and eliminates many charge sharing problems. Figure 8.18 shows generation of a second clock phase, $c2$, from a periodic first phase, $c1$. We are assuming the period of $c1$ is 1 us with a 500 ns duty cycle.

The *phase2* process in this figure stays suspended while $c1$ is '1'. Ten nanoseconds after $c1$ changes from '1' to '0', $c2$ becomes '1', and the process goes into suspension again for 480 ns. While suspended, $c2$ stays at '1'. When *phase2* resumes, it assigns a zero to $c2$, and becomes suspended again, waiting for $c1$ to change from '1' to '0'. This process continues until it is suspended indefinitely due to lack of events on $c1$. Figure 8.19 shows a timing diagram that results from a periodic waveform on $c1$.

8.3.3 Implementing Handshaking

Asynchronous communication between systems is done by handshaking. Handshaking refers to the signaling that occurs between two systems as one transfers data to the other. When a system prepares data for transfer to another system, the sending system informs the receiving system that the data is ready. When the receiving system accepts the data, it informs the sending system it has received it.

Handshaking can be fully responsive or partially responsive. In a fully responsive process, all events on the handshaking signals of one system occur in response

```
...
phase2: PROCESS
BEGIN
    WAIT UNTIL c1 = '0';
    WAIT FOR 10 NS;
    c2 <= '1';
    WAIT FOR 480 NS;
    c2 <= '0';
END PROCESS phase2;
...
```

FIGURE 8.18
Partial code for generation of second phase of a two phase nonoverlapping clocking.

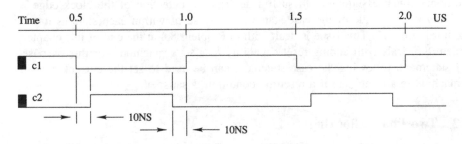

FIGURE 8.19
Two nonoverlapping phases of clock, $c2$ generated by the *phase2* process in Figure 8.18.

to events on the signals of the other system as they communicate. Handshaking requires at least one signal for this specific purpose and can use as many as six for a two-way, fully responsive communication. Exchanging data without handshaking is called nonresponsive communication. Figure 8.20 shows a fully responsive two-line handshaking process for transfering data on *data_lines* from system A to system B.

System A places valid data on *data_lines* and informs system B of this new data by raising the *data_ready* line. When system B is ready to accept data, it does so, and it informs system A that it has accepted data by raising *accepted*. When system A sees that data on *data_lines* are no longer needed by system B, it removes valid data from *data_lines*, and lowers the *data_ready* line. System B acknowledges this, and informs system A that it can accept new data by lowering its *accepted* signal.

A variation of this system can include a third handshaking line used by system B to inform system A that it is ready to accept new data. Fully responsive handshaking is performed when no assumptions are possible as to the relative speed of the communicating systems. Other less responsive handshakings can be done in which the *data_ready* line returns to zero after a fixed amount of time, instead of waiting for *accepted* to become '1'.

Figure 8.21 shows the corresponding VHDL code for the handshaking process in Figure 8.20. Partial code sections in this figure are sequentially executed by system A and B when they need to talk to each other. In all forms of handshaking, various forms of wait statements are very useful and descriptive.

For a comprehensive example of modeling handshaking in VHDL, consider *system_i* that works as an interface between *system_a* and *system_b*, as depicted in Figure 8.22. *System_a* uses handshaking to provide 4-bit data, and *system_b* uses handshaking to receive 16-bit data. The interface *system_i* accumulates four data nibbles that it receives from *system_a* and it makes a 16-bit data available to system *system_b*. The first nibble received from *system_a* forms the least significant four bits of the data that becomes available for *system_b*. *System_i* is capable of talking to *system_a* and *system_b* simultaneously. It should be possible for *system_i* to be involved in transmitting the previously accumulated data to *system_b*, while accumulating a new 16-bit data from *system_a*.

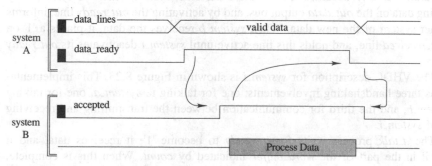

FIGURE 8.20
Signals of a fully responsive two-line handshaking.

```
              -- start the following when ready to send data
              data_lines  <= newly_prepared_data;
  System      data_ready  <= '1';
    A         WAIT  UNTIL  accepted = '1';
              data_ready  <= '0';
              --can use data_lines for other purposes


              -- start the following when ready to accept data
              WAIT UNTIL data_ready = '1';
  System      accepted  <= '1';
    B         -- start processing the newly received data
              WAIT UNTIL data_ready = '0';
              accepted  <= '0';
```

FIGURE 8.21
VHDL code for fully responsive two line handshaking.

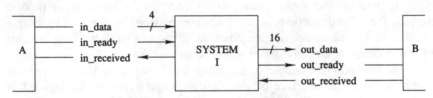

FIGURE 8.22
Interfacing *system_a* and *system_b*. *System_i* uses handshaking to talk to both systems.

When *system_a* has a nibble ready on the *in_data* lines, it places a '1' on the *in_ready* line. The data and the *in_ready* line stay valid until this system sees a '1' on its *in_received* input. The interface *system_i* waits in an idle state looking for *in_ready* to become '1'. When this happens, it receives data from *in_data* and acknowledges that it has received the data by placing a '1' on *in_received*. The interface holds *in_received* active until *in_ready* becomes '0'. On the other side, *system_i* talks to *system_b* by providing data on the *out_data* output bus, and by activating the *out_ready* line, informs the other system of the new data. When *system_b* receives the data, it places a '1' on the *out_received* line, and holds this line active until *system_i* deactivates its *out_ready* output.

The VHDL description for *system_i* is shown in Figure 8.23. This implementation has three handshaking involvements; one for talking to *system_a*, one for talking to *system_b*, and the third for communication between the transmitting and receiving parts of *system_i*.

The *a_talk* process waits for *in_ready* to become '1', it receives data, and it places it in the part of the *word_buffer* indicated by *count*. When this is complete, it indicates that data has been accepted by placing a '1' on *in_received* (statement following END CASE). This line stays active until *system_a* deactivates the *in_ready*

```
┌ENTITY system_i IS
│   PORT (in_data : IN BIT_VECTOR (3 DOWNTO 0);
│       out_data : OUT BIT_VECTOR (15 DOWNTO 0);
│       in_ready, out_received : IN BIT; in_received, out_ready : OUT BIT);
└END system_i;
--
┌ARCHITECTURE waiting OF system_i IS
│   SIGNAL buffer_full, buffer_picked : BIT := '0';
│   SIGNAL word_buffer : BIT_VECTOR (15 DOWNTO 0);
├BEGIN
│   ┌a_talk: PROCESS
│   │   VARIABLE count : INTEGER RANGE 0 TO 4 := 0;
│   ├BEGIN
│   │   WAIT UNTIL in_ready = '1';
│   │   count := count + 1;
│   │   CASE count IS
│   │       WHEN 0 => NULL;
│   │       WHEN 1 => word_buffer (03 DOWNTO 00) <= in_data;
│   │       WHEN 2 => word_buffer (07 DOWNTO 04) <= in_data;
│   │       WHEN 3 => word_buffer (11 DOWNTO 08) <= in_data;
│   │       WHEN 4 => word_buffer (15 DOWNTO 12) <= in_data;
│   │               buffer_full <= '1';
│   │               WAIT UNTIL buffer_picked = '1';
│   │               buffer_full <= '0';
│   │               count := 0;
│   │   END CASE;
│   │   in_received <= '1';
│   │   WAIT UNTIL in_ready = '0';
│   │   in_received <= '0';
│   └END PROCESS a_talk;
│   ┌b_talk: PROCESS
│   ├BEGIN
│   │   IF buffer_full = '0' THEN WAIT UNTIL buffer_full = '1'; END IF;
│   │   out_data <= word_buffer;
│   │   buffer_picked <= '1';
│   │   WAIT UNTIL buffer_full = '0';
│   │   buffer_picked <= '0';
│   │   out_ready <= '1';
│   │   WAIT UNTIL out_received = '1';
│   │   out_ready <= '0';
│   └END PROCESS b_talk;
└END waiting;
```

FIGURE 8.23
VHDL model for the interface between systems A and B in Figure 8.22.

line. In accumulating data in the *word_buffer*, if the data received is the forth nibble (choice 4 of the case alternative), the *a_talk* process asserts the *buffer_full* internal handshaking signal to indicate that data is ready to be transmitted to *system_b*. This line stays active until the buffer has been received by the *b_talk* process as indicated by the *buffer_picked* signal issued by *b_talk*. When the buffer is picked, the nibble count is set to zero and *word_buffer* starts being refilled. While waiting for the buffer to be picked, *system_i* keeps *system_a* waiting by not issuing the *in_received* signal.

The *b_talk* process waits for a full buffer. This waiting is implemented by the first if statement in this process which causes the process to continue if *buffer_full* is '1'. The if statement is used so that the WAIT UNTIL does not hold the process, if *buffer_full* is already '1' when this statement is reached. Remember that the "WAIT UNTIL buffer_full = '1'" statement resumes the process only when *buffer_full* changes from '0' to '1'. When this process finds a full buffer, it assigns it to the *out_data* output lines, and causes the resumption of *a_talk* by setting *buffer_picked* to '1'. This line returns to zero only when *a_talk* acknowledges that it knows a buffer has been received. At this time, *b_talk* communicates with *system_b* for sending the 16-bit data on *out_data* to this system. When *system_b* acknowledges the reception of data by raising its *out_received* line, the *b_talk* process deactivates *out_ready* and returns to the beginning of its statement part.

In the *a_talk* process, the *count* variable keeps a count of the number of nibbles received. Since *count* is not needed across processes, it is declared as a variable in *a_talk*. According to the declaration of this variable, the only values it can take are integers between 0 and 4. The program flow never reaches the case statement when *count* is zero and considering this alternative is unnecessary. However, the case statement requires coverage of all choices or OTHERS to be used; therefore, we have covered the *count* value of zero by a NULL case alternative.

8.4   FORMATTED ASCII I/O OPERATIONS

Basic unformatted input/output to external files was described in Chapter 6. The methods described used primitive VHDL file operations and can be used with any data type. VHDL also supports a TEXTIO package which includes types and procedures for ASCII line oriented input or output. This package is in the STD Library, and is shown in Appendix F.

The TEXTIO package defines a LINE type which is used for all file readings and writings. The file type provided by this package is TEXT and it defines files of ASCII strings. Procedures defined in this package for handling input/output are READ, READLINE, WRITE, and WRITELINE. In addition, function ENDFILE provides a mechanism for checking the status of a file.

The READLINE(f,l) procedure reads a line of file *f* and places it in buffer *l*. The READ(l,v,...) reads a value *v* of its type from *l*. The WRITE(l,v,...) writes the value *v* to LINE *l* and WRITELINE(f,l) writes *l* to file *f*. Function ENDFILE(f) returns TRUE if the end of FILE is reached. READ and WRITE procedures are valid for values of types BIT, BIT_VECTOR, BOOLEAN, CHARACTER, INTEGER, REAL,

STRING, and TIME. Other parameters of these procedures include orientation, size, and unit if *v* is of type TIME.

For reading from a file, after READLINE reads a line, data can be extracted from the line (or buffer) using READ. This can continue until the entire buffer is consumed. For writing to a file, a LINE type variable is filled with data using WRITE and the line is written to the file using WRITELINE.

8.4.1 Basic Screen Output

In our first ASCII I/O example, we develop a debugging mechanism for resolution functions and apply this mechanism to one of the resolution functions in Chapter 7. Knowing the driving values of a resolved signal's drivers gives an insight into a resolution function for debugging and learning purposes.

Figure 8.24 shows the *one_of* resolution function we used to implement a Mealy state machine in Chapter 7 (*singular_state_machine* of Figure 7.36). The double vertical lines in this figure indicate the new code being added to observe the active drivers of the signals that are resolved by this resolution function.

The *one_of* function uses types and procedures from the TEXTIO package in the standard STD library and these utilities are made visible to it by the application of the use statement in the description in Figure 8.24. In the declarative part of this function, variable *l* of type LINE is declared to act as a buffer for outputting strings.

```
USE STD.TEXTIO.ALL;
...
TYPE state IS (reset, got1, got10, got101);
TYPE state_vector IS ARRAY (NATURAL RANGE <>) OF state;
FUNCTION one_of (sources : state_vector) RETURN state IS
    VARIABLE l : LINE;
    FILE flush : TEXT IS OUT "/dev/tty";
    VARIABLE state_string : STRING (1 TO 7);
BEGIN
    FOR i IN sources'RANGE LOOP
        CASE sources(i) IS
            WHEN reset  => state_string := "reset  ";
            WHEN got1   => state_string := "got1   ";
            WHEN got10  => state_string := "got10  ";
            WHEN got101 => state_string := "got101 ";
        END CASE;
        WRITE (l, state_string, LEFT, 7);
    END LOOP;
    WRITELINE (flush, l);
    RETURN sources(sources'LEFT);
END one_of;
```

FIGURE 8.24
A resolution function that writes its active drivers each time it is called.

The *flush* file is declared as an output text file with the logical file name of */dev/tty*. In the Unix operating system, this logical name refers to the standard output or screen. A for loop in the statement part of the *one_of* function translates all the active states to their corresponding strings. These strings are appended to the end of the *l* buffer by the WRITE procedure call. The keyword LEFT specifies the left justification of this string when it is appended to *l* and the number 7 specifies its length in characters. When strings corresponding to all active states have been appended to *l*, this buffer is displayed by the WRITELINE procedure call.

When the *one_of* resolution function is called, the file declaration in its declarative part is initialized, and the list of active states is displayed. A time stamp can also be generated by writing the value returned by the NOW function to *l*. This provides additional information as to when the function is called and is also a useful debugging feature. The example that follows illustrates this.

8.4.2 A Display Procedure

The procedure shown in Figure 8.25 has two signal parameters. When called, it displays the current simulation time and the new value of its signal parameter that has just changed.

The declarative part of this procedure is the same as that in Figure 8.24. The file declaration initializes *flush* every time the procedure is called. In its statement part, a call to the WRITE procedure writes the current simulation time, sized to eight characters and using nanosecond units, to *l*. The if statement following this procedure call appends the new value of the signal that has had an event and a *filler* string to *l*. The filler string is used in place of the value of the signal that has been stable. At the end, the WRITELINE procedure call writes this assembled buffer (*l*) to the screen.

```
PROCEDURE display (SIGNAL value1, value2 : BIT) IS
    FILE flush : TEXT IS OUT "/dev/tty";
    VARIABLE filler : STRING (1 TO 3) := " ..";
    VARIABLE I : LINE;
BEGIN
    WRITE (I, NOW, RIGHT, 8, NS);
    IF value1'EVENT THEN
        WRITE (I, value1, RIGHT, 3);
        WRITE (I, filler, LEFT, 0);
    ELSE
        WRITE (I, filler, LEFT, 0);
        WRITE (I, value2, RIGHT, 3);
    END IF;
    WRITELINE (flush, I);
END display;
```

FIGURE 8.25
A display procedure for displaying time and value of a signal that has just changed.

Using 0 for the size parameter in the procedure call that writes *filler* to *l* results in a minimum use of space for this string.

Figure 8.26 shows a two-phase clock generator that uses the *phase2* process of Section 8.3.2 for generating a second clock phase, *c2*, from *c1*, and uses the *display* procedure for displaying these nonoverlapping clock phases. The use statement at the beginning of this description provides the *display* procedure with its needed visibility into the standard TEXTIO package. A concurrent procedure call in the statement part of the *input_output* architecture of *two_phase_clock* entity calls the *display* procedure when an event occurs on *c1* or *c2*.

8.4.3 Simulation Report

In order to have the ability to to generate a simulation report in which new output lines are appended to the end of a file, we must insure that the file initialization, unlike the previous two examples, is done only once at the beginning of the report generation. This implies that for this purpose, a file declaration must be placed in a process statement or in the statement part of an architecture, or if declared in a subprogram, the entire report must be generated in one subprogram call. The same thing applies to an input file. Reinitialization of an input file causes the next READLINE to be done from its beginning.

For the procedure in Figure 8.25 to write into a file, it either has to be called from a process statement with a declared file passed to it, or else the task this procedure

```
USE  STD.TEXTIO.ALL;
ENTITY two_phase_clock IS END two_phase_clock;
--
ARCHITECTURE input_output OF two_phase_clock IS
    -- procedure of Figure 8.25 goes here
    SIGNAL c1 : BIT := '1';
    SIGNAL c2 : BIT := '0';
BEGIN
    phase1: c1 <= NOT c1 AFTER 500 NS WHEN NOW < 4 US ELSE c1;
    phase2: PROCESS
    BEGIN
        WAIT UNTIL c1 = '0';
        WAIT FOR 10 NS;
        c2 <= '1';
        WAIT FOR 480 NS;
        c2 <= '0';
    END PROCESS phase2;
    display (c1, c2);
END input_output;
```

FIGURE 8.26
Using *display* procedure for displaying two nonoverlapping clock phases.

performs should be placed in a process statement. We have used the latter alternative for generating a simulation report for the *two_phase_clock* circuit.

The description in Figure 8.27 repeats the clock description and adds to it the *writing* process for writing BIT values of *c1* and *c2* to the logical *clock.out* file. This new section of code is made to stand out by the double vertical lines. The *flush* file is initialized at the beginning of the simulation and stays open for the entire simulation run. For every event on *c1* or *c2*, a new line is appended to the *clock.out* file. The complete run of the *input_output* architecture of *two_phase_clock* in Figure 8.27 generates the report shown in Figure 8.28 in the *clock.out* file.

Figure 8.29 shows another example for using TEXTIO to generate a simulation report. The example we are using is the familiar *two_phase_clock* circuit, and in the

```
USE  STD.TEXTIO.ALL;
ENTITY two_phase_clock IS  END  two_phase_clock;
--
ARCHITECTURE input_output OF two_phase_clock IS
    SIGNAL c1 : BIT := '1';
    SIGNAL c2 : BIT := '0';
BEGIN
    phase1: c1 <= NOT c1 AFTER 500 NS WHEN NOW < 4 US ELSE c1;
    phase2: PROCESS
    BEGIN
        WAIT UNTIL c1 = '0';
        WAIT FOR 10 NS;
        c2 <= '1';
        WAIT FOR 480 NS;
        c2 <= '0';
    END PROCESS phase2;
    writing: PROCESS (c1, c2)
        FILE flush : TEXT IS OUT "clock.out";
        VARIABLE filler : STRING (1 TO 3) := " ..";
        VARIABLE I : LINE;
    BEGIN
        WRITE (I, NOW, RIGHT, 8, NS);
        IF c1'EVENT THEN
            WRITE (I, c1, RIGHT, 3);
            WRITE (I, filler, LEFT, 0);
        ELSE
            WRITE (I, filler, LEFT, 0);
            WRITE (I, c2, RIGHT, 3);
        END IF;
        WRITELINE (flush, I);
    END PROCESS writing;
END input_output;
```

FIGURE 8.27
The *input_output* architecture of *two_phase_clock* circuit with a process statement for generating a simulation report.

0	ns	..	0
500	ns	0	..
510	ns	..	1
990	ns	..	0
1000	ns	1	..
1500	ns	0	..
1510	ns	..	1
1990	ns	..	0
2000	ns	1	..
2500	ns	0	..
2510	ns	..	1
2990	ns	..	0
3000	ns	1	..
3500	ns	0	..
3510	ns	..	1
3990	ns	..	0
4000	ns	1	..

FIGURE 8.28
File generated by running the *input_output* architecture in Figure 8.27.

figure, double vertical lines indicate new code. The *input_output* architecture of this figure generates an ASCII time plot with 5 ns time resolution.

A *print_tick* signal activates the *plotting* process every 5 ns. The output file (*clock4.out*), a header (*header*), *l*, and the *append_wave_slice* procedure are declared in the declarative part of the process. In its statement part, at the start of simulation when NOW equals zero, the header line is written to the beginning of the output file. After this line, every 5 nanoseconds a new line is written to the output file containing the simulation time and string representation for the values and transitions of *c1* and *c2*. String representations are appended to *l* by the *append_wave_slice* procedure. The "| " and " |" strings represent low and high, respectively; they are low and high wave slices if turned 90° in the counterclockwise direction. The transition strings are used when the last event on the signal associated with the *s* parameter of the *append_wave_slice* procedure is more recent than the print resolution. This is done by the first if statement in the statement part of this procedure. The "s'LAST_VALUE /= s" expression in the condition part of the if statement causes "| " and " |" strings to be used at the beginning of simulation, while s'LAST_EVENT continues to be zero and less than the print resolution.

Figure 8.30 shows a portion of the file generated by running the description of Figure 8.29. This file can easily be turned into a continuous waveform by simple editing on a personal computer. VHDL allows the first 128 ASCII characters, but does not support ASCII extensions, which include line and edge segments (| └ ┐ ┌ ┘). Such characters are needed for a continuous waveform.

Figure 8.29 illustrates a method by which a subprogram can be used to input or output to an already declared open file (file *flush* in that figure). Alternatively, a file object can be passed to a function or procedure as a subprogram parameter. The following statements illustrate subprogram declarations for passing file objects to

```
ARCHITECTURE input_output OF two_phase_clock IS
    ...
    SIGNAL print_tick : BIT := '0';
    CONSTANT print_resolution : TIME := 5 NS;
BEGIN
    --phase1: and phase2: processes remain the same as
                those shown in Figure~8.27.
    print_tick <= NOT print_tick AFTER print_resolution WHEN NOW <= 2 US
                ELSE print_tick;
    plotting: PROCESS (print_tick, c1, c2)
        FILE flush : TEXT IS OUT "clock4.out";
        VARIABLE header : STRING (1 TO 18) := "          c1   c2   ";
        VARIABLE I : LINE;
        PROCEDURE append_wave_slice (SIGNAL s : BIT) IS
            CONSTANT lo_value : STRING (1 TO 3) := "|  ";
            CONSTANT hi_value : STRING (1 TO 3) := "  |";
            CONSTANT lo_to_hi : STRING (1 TO 3) := ".-+";
            CONSTANT hi_to_lo : STRING (1 TO 3) := "+-.";
        BEGIN
            IF s'LAST_EVENT < print_resolution AND s'LAST_VALUE /= s
            THEN          .
                IF s = '1' THEN
                    WRITE (I, lo_to_hi, RIGHT, 5);
                ELSE
                    WRITE (I, hi_to_lo, RIGHT, 5);
                END IF;
            ELSE
                IF s = '1' THEN
                    WRITE (I, hi_value, RIGHT, 5);
                ELSE
                    WRITE (I, lo_value, RIGHT, 5);
                END IF;
            END IF;
        END append_wave_slice;
    BEGIN
        IF NOW = 0 US THEN
            WRITE (I, header, LEFT, 0);
            WRITELINE (flush, I);
        END IF;
        WRITE (I, NOW, RIGHT, 8, NS);
        append_wave_slice (c1);
        append_wave_slice (c2);
        WRITELINE (flush, I);
    END PROCESS plotting;
END input_output;
```

FIGURE 8.29
Generating an ASCII plot file with five ns time resolution.

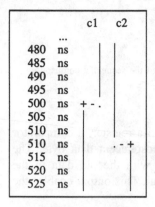

FIGURE 8.30
Partial plot generated by the *plotting* process of Figure 8.29.

procedures for reading or writing from open files:

```
PROCEDURE reading_from_file (VARIABLE in_file : IN TEXT;
                        ... other parameters ...);

PROCEDURE writing_to_file (VARIABLE out_file : OUT TEXT;
                       ... other parameters ...);
```

This method offers a more modular description for subprograms using external files. Note that in this case, the variable of type LINE can be declared in the subprogram and calls to READLINE or WRITELINE should be done in the corresponding subprograms.

8.5   MSI BASED DESIGN

This section shows the design of an overall system using standard parts. The parts we use are from the 74LS00 logic family while the example circuit is a variation of the sequential comparator in Chapter 7.

The design strategy is as follows: after an initial understanding of the functionality of the circuit we are to design, we partition it into several functional components and the components are mapped into standard parts. If such a mapping is not possible, more partitioning is done. Once the standard parts are chosen, they are assembled to perform the necessary functions and wired together to form the implementation of the system.

8.5.1   Top Level Partitioning

The circuit shown in the block diagram in Figure 8.31 keeps a modulo-16 count of consecutive equal data bytes on *data_in*. It has synchronous active low clear and load inputs, *clear_bar* and *load_bar*. The *clear_bar* input clears the output count and the *load_bar* loads the *count_in* into the counter.

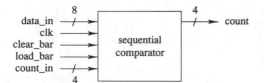

FIGURE 8.31
Block diagram of the sequential comparator
circuit.

Figure 8.32 shows the partitioning of this circuit into a register, a comparator pair, and a counter. The register component keeps the most recent data byte. The comparator pair compares the incoming data on *data_in* with the old data in the register and asserts its output if the two data bytes are equal. This output enables the synchronous counting of the counter.

The MSI components that most closely correspond to this partitioning are the 74LS85 4-bit magnitude comparator, the 74LS377 8-bit register, and the 74LS163 4-bit binary counter, all shown in Figure 8.33.

The 74LS85 has three outputs that indicate the relation of values of the 4-bit inputs. The $P<Q$ outputs become '1' when input P is less than input Q, likewise the $P>Q$ output becomes '1' when input P is greater than Q. When the two inputs are equal, the values on $<$, $=$, and $>$ inputs appear on their corresponding output lines.

The 74LS377 is a positive edge trigger 8-bit register with an active low enable input. If this input is low on the edge of the clock, data is clocked into the register.

The 74LS163 is a 4-bit binary counter with a synchronous active low parallel load and reset inputs. The counting is enabled when loading is disabled and count enable inputs $G3$ and $G4$ are high. When the count reaches 15, the $5CT=15$ output becomes '1' and the next clock starts the count from 0.

8.5.2 Description of Components

For describing the necessary components of the sequential comparator circuit, and in general for describing any of the 74LS parts, we use the *qit* type of the *basic_utilities* package for the logic value system. The 'Z' value of this system is needed to describe components with three-state outputs, and the 'X' value can be used to show illegal, unknown, or uninitialized logic values. We have extended the *basic_utilities* package

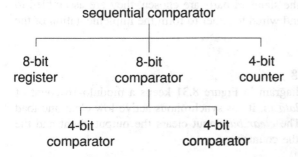

FIGURE 8.32
Partitioning sequential comparator
circuit into smaller functional
components.

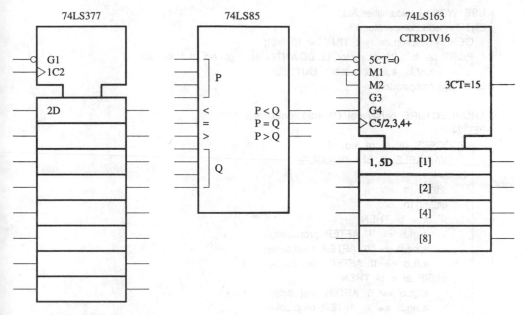

FIGURE 8.33
Standard MSI parts for the implementation of sequential comparator according to the partitioning of Figure 8.32.

to include *qit* conversion procedures and other necessary utilities. The final form of this package is shown in Appendix A.

The VHDL description for the 74LS85 4-bit magnitude comparator is shown in Figure 8.34. Unlike the comparator descriptions in Chapter 4, this description is purely behavioral and its functionality rather than its hardware details is evident from its model. The *qit2int* procedure in *basic_utilities* package converts *qit* type inputs to integers so that the relational operators of VHDL ($=$ $<$ $>$ $>=$ $<=$ $\neq$) can be used for their comparison. Since the outputs are nonresolved and non-guarded signals, they retain their values and only change these values when new values are assigned to them. Therefore, we have assigned new values to all output signals any time an input changes.

Figure 8.35 shows the VHDL description for the 74LS377 register. This description is at the dataflow level and uses a guarded signal assignment for assigning the 8-bit input vector to the *q8* output. An explicit GUARD signal is used instead of the standard practice of using implicit GUARD signal of a block statement. This is done to demonstrate the equivalency of these two methods. GUARD is TRUE on the edge of the clock when *q_bar* (enable input of register) is low. We are assuming the clock is never 'Z', and we have not worked this situation in the edge detection.

A description for the 4-bit binary counter is presented in Figure 8.36. The *counting* process statement in the behavioral description of the *ls163_counter* uses a variable for the internal storage of the count value. When an event occurs on *clk* (any edge), this process becomes active. If this event causes *clk* to be '1' *(rising edge*

```
USE WORK.basic_utilities.ALL;
ENTITY ls85_comparator IS
   GENERIC (prop_delay : TIME := 10 NS);
   PORT (a, b : IN qit_vector (3 DOWNTO 0);  gt, eq, lt : IN qit;
         a_gt_b, a_eq_b, a_lt_b : OUT qit);
END ls85_comparator;
--
ARCHITECTURE behavioral OF ls85_comparator IS
BEGIN
   PROCESS (a, b, gt, eq, lt)
      VARIABLE ai, bi : INTEGER;
   BEGIN
      qit2int (a, ai);
      qit2int (b, bi);
      IF ai > bi THEN
         a_gt_b <= '1' AFTER prop_delay;
         a_eq_b <= '0' AFTER prop_delay;
         a_lt_b <= '0' AFTER prop_delay;
      ELSIF ai < bi THEN
         a_gt_b <= '0' AFTER prop_delay;
         a_eq_b <= '0' AFTER prop_delay;
         a_lt_b <= '1' AFTER prop_delay;
      ELSIF ai = bi THEN
         a_gt_b <= gt AFTER prop_delay;
         a_eq_b <= eq AFTER prop_delay;
         a_lt_b <= lt AFTER prop_delay;
      END IF;
   END PROCESS;
END behavioral;
```

FIGURE 8.34
Behavioral description of the 74LS85 4-Bit magnitude comparator.

```
USE WORK.basic_utilities.ALL;
ENTITY ls377_register IS
   GENERIC (prop_delay : TIME := 7 NS);
   PORT (clk, g_bar : IN qit; d8 : IN qit_vector (7 DOWNTO 0);
         q8 : OUT qit_vector (7 DOWNTO 0));
END ls377_register;
--
ARCHITECTURE dataflow OF ls377_register IS
   SIGNAL GUARD : BOOLEAN;
BEGIN
   GUARD <= NOT clk'STABLE AND clk = '1' AND (g_bar = '0');
   q8 <= GUARDED d8 AFTER prop_delay;
END dataflow;
```

FIGURE 8.35
Dataflow description of the 74LS377 8-bit clocked register.

```
USE  WORK.basic_utilities.ALL;
ENTITY ls163_counter IS
   GENERIC (prop_delay : TIME := 12 NS);
   PORT (clk, clr_bar, ld_bar, enp, ent : IN qit;
         abcd : IN qit_vector (3 DOWNTO 0);
         q_abcd : OUT qit_vector (3 DOWNTO 0); rco : OUT qit);
END ls163_counter;
--
ARCHITECTURE behavioral OF ls163_counter IS
BEGIN
   counting : PROCESS (clk)
      VARIABLE internal_count : qit_vector (3 DOWNTO 0) := "0000";
   BEGIN
      IF (clk = '1') THEN
          IF (clr_bar = '0') THEN
              internal_count := "0000";
          ELSIF (ld_bar = '0') THEN
              internal_count := abcd;
          ELSIF (enp = '1' AND ent = '1') THEN
              internal_count := inc (internal_count);
              IF (internal_count = "1111") THEN
                  rco <= '1' AFTER prop_delay;
              ELSE
                  rco <= '0';
              END IF;
          END IF;
          q_abcd <= internal_count AFTER prop_delay;
      END IF;
   END PROCESS counting;
END behavioral;
```

FIGURE 8.36
Behavioral description of the 74LS163 4-bit synchronous counter.

detection), the internal count is either loaded with the input value, set to zero, or incremented depending on load, clear, and enable control lines. The carry out (*rco*) output becomes '1' when the count reaches "1111". The *internal_count* variable is assigned to the *q_abcd* output in the statement part of the *counting* process.

8.5.3 Design Implementation

Figure 8.37 shows the composition aspect of the sequential comparator. This implementation is accomplished according to the partitioning shown in Figure 8.32, which uses two 74LS85 packages for realizing an 8-bit comparator, a 74LS377 for the register, and a 74LS163 for the counter. The figure shows an entity declaration to specify the wiring of components, and a configuration declaration (rounded rectangle) for bindings and generic parameter specifications.

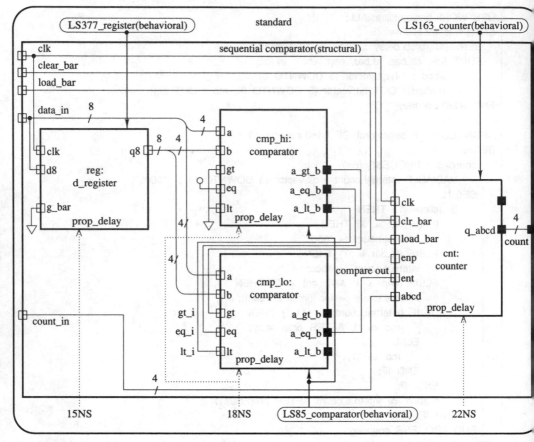

FIGURE 8.37
Composition aspect of the sequential comparator.

The VHDL description for the sequential comparator circuit is shown in Figure 8.38. In the statement part of the entity declaration of *sequential_comparator*, an assertion statement issues warning messages whenever short glitches are observed on the clock input of the circuit. The declarative part of the *structural* architecture of *sequential_comparator* declares the necessary components and the statement part of this architecture specifies their wirings.

The *standard* configuration in Figure 8.39 associates the components of this design with the 74LS parts and specifies timing parameters of these parts. The configured *structural* architecture of the *sequential_comparator* should be referenced by CONFIGURATION *library.standard* where *library* is the name of the library that this configuration is compiled in.

Figure 8.40 shows a simple test bench for verifying the basic operations of *sequential_comparator*. The configuration specification in this figure indicates that the *mfi* instance of *seq_comp* is associated with the configuration declaration in Figure 8.39.

```
USE  WORK.basic_utilities.ALL;
ENTITY sequential_comparator IS
    PORT (data_in : IN qit_vector (7 DOWNTO 0);
            clk, clear_bar, load_bar : IN qit;
            count_in : IN qit_vector (3 DOWNTO 0);
            count : OUT qit_vector (3 DOWNTO 0) );
BEGIN
    ASSERT NOT
        ((clk='0' AND NOT clk'STABLE) AND NOT clk'DELAYED'STABLE (1 US))
    REPORT "Minimum Clock Width Violation" SEVERITY WARNING;
END sequential_comparator;
--
ARCHITECTURE structural OF sequential_comparator IS
    COMPONENT d_register
        PORT (clk, g_bar : IN qit; d8 : IN qit_vector (7 DOWNTO 0);
            q8 : OUT qit_vector (7 DOWNTO 0));
    END COMPONENT;
    COMPONENT comparator
        PORT (a, b : IN qit_vector (3 DOWNTO 0);   gt, eq, lt : IN qit;
            a_gt_b, a_eq_b, a_lt_b : OUT qit);
    END COMPONENT;
    COMPONENT counter
        PORT (clk, clr_bar, ld_bar, enp, ent : IN qit;
            abcd : IN qit_vector (3 DOWNTO 0);
            q_abcd : OUT qit_vector (3 DOWNTO 0); rco : OUT qit);
    END COMPONENT;
    SIGNAL gnd : qit := '0'; SIGNAL vdd : qit := '1';
    SIGNAL old_data : qit_vector (7 DOWNTO 0);
    SIGNAL compare_out : qit;
    SIGNAL gt_i, eq_i, lt_i : qit;
BEGIN
    reg: d_register PORT MAP (clk, gnd, data_in, old_data);
    cmp_lo: comparator PORT MAP (data_in (3 DOWNTO 0),
            old_data (3 DOWNTO 0), gnd, vdd, gnd, gt_i, eq_i, lt_i);
    cmp_hi: comparator PORT MAP (data_in (7 DOWNTO 4),
            old_data (7 DOWNTO 4), gt_i, eq_i, lt_i, OPEN, compare_out, OPEN);
    cnt: counter PORT MAP (clk, clear_bar, load_bar, vdd, compare_out,
            count_in, count, OPEN);
END structural;
```

FIGURE 8.38
Structural implementation of the sequential comparator.

8.6 SUMMARY

This chapter presented descriptions of hardware at the behavioral level and discussed how a process statement can be used to describe the main functionality of a module. In the early part of the chapter, syntax and semantics for various forms of this construct were described. We then showed how process statements are used to describe control-

```
USE WORK.ALL;
CONFIGURATION standard OF sequential_comparator IS
    FOR structural
        FOR reg : d_register
            USE ENTITY WORK.ls377_register (dataflow)
            GENERIC MAP (prop_delay => 15 NS);
        END FOR;
        FOR ALL : comparator
            USE ENTITY WORK.ls85_comparator (behavioral)
            GENERIC MAP (prop_delay => 18 NS);
        END FOR;
        FOR cnt : counter
            USE ENTITY WORK.ls163_counter (behavioral)
            GENERIC MAP (prop_delay => 22 NS);
        END FOR;
    END FOR;
END standard;
```

FIGURE 8.39
Configuring the *structural* architecture of the *sequential_comparator* entity.

```
USE WORK.basic_utilities.ALL;
ENTITY test_sequential_comparator IS END test_sequential_comparator;
--
ARCHITECTURE input_output OF test_sequential_comparator IS
    COMPONENT seq_comp
    PORT (data_in : IN qit_vector (7 DOWNTO 0);
            clk, clear_bar, load_bar : IN qit;
            count_in : IN qit_vector (3 DOWNTO 0);
            count : OUT qit_vector (3 DOWNTO 0) );
    END COMPONENT;
    FOR mfi : seq_comp USE CONFIGURATION WORK.standard;
    SIGNAL data : qit_vector (7 DOWNTO 0);
    SIGNAL ck, cl_bar, ld_bar : qit;
    SIGNAL cnt : qit_vector (3 DOWNTO 0);
    SIGNAL cnt_out : qit_vector (3 DOWNTO 0);
BEGIN
    ck <= NOT ck AFTER 2 US WHEN NOW <= 70 US ELSE ck;
    cl_bar <= '1', '0' AFTER 60 US;
    ld_bar <= '1', '0' AFTER 50 US, '1' AFTER 55 US;
    cnt <= "1111", "1011" AFTER 40 US, "0111" AFTER 55 US;
    data <= "00000000", "01110111" AFTER 3 US, "10101100" AFTER 5 US,
            "01010100" AFTER 25 US;
    mfi : seq_comp PORT MAP (data, ck, cl_bar, ld_bar, cnt, cnt_out);
END input_output;
```

FIGURE 8.40
Test bench for testing the *standard* configuration of *sequential_comparator*.

ling hardware, handshaking, and file I/O. Various forms of wait statements were extensively used in these descriptions.

Although behavioral level constructs of VHDL provide a convenient method for describing very complex hardware, a hardware designer can completely describe a digital circuit without having to use these constructs. Behavioral descriptions can be read and understood by nontechnical managers and others who are not very familiar with VHDL.

REFERENCES

1. "IEEE Standard VHDL Language Reference Manual," IEEE Std 1076-1987, The Institute of Electrical and Electronic Engineers, Inc., 1988.
2. Lipsett, L., C. Schaefer, and C. Ussery, "VHDL: Hardware Description and Design," Klewer Academic Publishing, Boston, 1988.
3. Armstrong, J. R., "Chip-Level Modeling with VHDL," Prentice-Hall Inc., Englewood Cliffs, N.J., 1988.

PROBLEMS

8.1. Write a VHDL description for a D-type flip-flop with a d input, asynchronous set and reset inputs, with q and qb outputs. Use three delay parameters for set-input to q, reset-input to q, and d-input to q (as in Figure 8.7). Your description should have only one *delta* delay between the input and output changes and for the nonzero delay values the delta delay should not appear on the output.

8.2. Write an assertion statement to issue a warning message if a negative pulse shorter than 1 us appears on the input clock.

8.3. Write an assertion statement to issue a warning message if the frequency of the observing clock is lower that 100 KHz. If the clock is too slow in some MOS circuits, the circuit loses information. Assume symmetrical clock pulses.

8.4. An equivalent description for the Moore state machine in Figure 8.17 is shown here in Figure 8.41. Modify this description to one for a Mealy machine detecting the same sequence. Write a test bench and compare the Mealy and Moore machine outputs.

8.5. Write a behavioral description for a Mealy machine that continuously monitors its x input for the 11010 sequence. When the sequence is found, the output becomes '1', and it returns to '0' with the clock. The circuit has a synchronous reset input that resets the circuit to its initial state when it becomes '1'. Use the style presented in Problem 8.4.

8.6. Write a description for an asynchronous circuit that generates one positive pulse for every two complete positive pulses that appear on its input. Use wait statements and processes.

8.7. Write a behavioral description for a divide-by-n circuit in which n is passed to it via a generic parameter. The circuit has an x input and a z output. For every n positive pulse on x, one positive pulse should appear on z.

8.8. Generate two phases of a clock using a single triggering signal as its input as shown below. Width of the short pulses on the triggering signal determine the time that both phases are zero. Use wait and process statements.

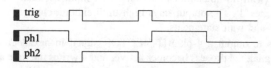

```
ENTITY moore_detector IS
    PORT (x, clk : IN BIT; z : OUT BIT);
END moore_detector;
--
ARCHITECTURE behavioral_state_machine OF moore_detector IS
    TYPE state IS (reset, got1, got10, got101, got1011);
    SIGNAL current : state := reset;
BEGIN
    PROCESS (clk)
    BEGIN
        IF clk = '1' THEN
            CASE current IS
            WHEN reset =>
                IF x = '1' THEN current <= got1;
                ELSE current <= reset;
                END IF;
            WHEN got1 =>
                IF x = '0' THEN current <= got10;
                ELSE current <= got1;
                END IF;
            WHEN got10 =>
                IF x = '1' THEN current <= got101;
                ELSE current <= reset;
                END IF;
            WHEN got101 =>
                IF x = '1' THEN current <= got1011;
                ELSE current <= got10;
                END IF;
            WHEN got1011 =>
                IF x = '1' THEN current <= got1;
                ELSE current <= got10;
                END IF;
            END CASE;
        END IF;
    END PROCESS;
    z <= '1' WHEN current = got1011 ELSE '0';
END behavioral_state_machine;
```

FIGURE 8.41
Moore state machine; equivalent to description given in Figure 8.17.

8.9. Write a behavioral description for modeling an asynchronous circuit. The circuit has inputs x and y, and output z. If a 0-to-1 transition on x is immediately followed by a 1-to-0 transition on y (with no other transitions on either input between these two transitions), the output becomes '1'. The output stays high until either x changes to '0' or y changes to '1'. Use process and wait statements.

8.10. Write a process to output a 4-bit BIT_VECTOR signal in hexadecimal. When an event occurs on the signal, the process becomes active, and it writes the time and the hexadecimal representation of the signal to an output file. To test this process, use it in a description of a synchronous binary up-counter, and output the counter output to a file named *hex.out*. You may use the utilities in the *basic_utilities* package. The statement shows a simple implementation of the binary counter:

count <= inc (count) WHEN clk = '1' AND clk'EVENT ELSE count;

8.11. Write a procedure (*print_hex*) to convert an unconstrained BIT_VECTOR to a string of hexadecimal digits and print it to a declared file. The subprogram declaration should be specified this way:

PROCEDURE print_hex (VARIABLE hex : OUT TEXT; bin : BIT_VECTOR);

In this declaration, *hex* is the open text file object to which writing is to be done, and *bin* is the binary data to be printed. Use this procedure in a description of a synchronous binary up-counter to verify its functioning. Use the method suggested in Problem 8.10 to implement the counter.

8.12. Write a procedure for reading hexadecimal data from a text file. When the procedure is called, it reads a new line from the file. Each line consists of time and hex data separated by a space. The hex data needs to be converted to binary data and then assigned to a target signal parameter in the procedure at the specified time. The subprogram declaration should be stated this way:

PROCEDURE assign_hex (SIGNAL bin : OUT BIT_VECTOR;
VARIABLE success : OUT BOOLEAN; VARIABLE hex_data : IN TEXT);

When the procedure is called, it reads a line of a file object passed to it via the *hex_data* parameter and assigns the data read from the file to the *bin* signal. If an end-of-file is reached and the reading is not successful, the *success* output of the procedure becomes FALSE. To verify the behavior of this procedure, use it in a process statement and assign the values read from a test file to a signal output in your test description.

8.13. A 4-bit shift register has a *mode*, a *serial_input*, and *clock* inputs as well as four *parallel_input* lines. The four lines of outputs are *parallel_output*. When *mode* is high, the shift register is in the right-shift mode and on the falling edge of the *clock*, the *serial_input* is clocked into the shift register. When *mode* is low, on the falling edge of the *clock*, the *parallel_input* is loaded into the shift register. A) For this shift register, write an *entity* with a *generic* delay. With this delay proper output appears on the *parallel_output* the falling edge of the clock. B) Write the pure *behavioral* architectural body for this shift register. Be sure to use the *generic* delay for the final output.

8.14. Use a process statement to develop a behavioral description for a Toggle flip-flop. The flip-flop has a single *t* input and two *q* and *nq* outputs. After the rising edge of the *t* input, the two outputs will be complemented. The *q* output has a low-to-high propagation delay of *q_tplh* and a high-to-low propagation delay of *q_tphl*. The *nq* output has a low-to-high propagation delay of *nq_tplh* and a high-to-low propagation delay of *nq_tphl*. Pass the propagation delays as generic parameters and use them in your behavioral description. Write the complete description using the entity declaration shown here:

```
ENTITY t_ff IS
    GENERIC( q_tplh, q_tphl, nq_tplh, nq_tphl : TIME);
    PORT (t : IN BIT; q, nq OUT BIT);
END t_ff;
```

8.15. In this problem you will configure and use the T flip-flop of the previous problem. Write a description of an *n*-bit *t_register* using *t_ff*s of Problem 8.14. For the *t_register*, write a configuration declaration that uses the behavioral *t_ff* with *q_tplh, q_tphl, nq_tplh, nq_tphl* delay values of 2 ns, 4 ns, 3 ns, and 5 ns, respectively. The output of a T flip-flop has a frequency half of that of its input. Two cascaded T flip-flops can be used as a divide by four circuit. Use two configured *t_registers* to build a parallel 8-bit divide-by-4 circuit.

8.16. In this problem you will use a 10 value logic system of integers ranging between 0 and 9. When an input reaches value 0, it is considered low and when it reaches 9, it is considered high. A) Define the ten value type using the integer base type. B) Write a description of an inverter using this value system. When the input reaches the low level (0), the output starts switching to high, and linearly changes from 0 to 9 in 30 ns. When the input reaches the high level (9), the output starts switching to low and linearly changes from 9 to 0 in 20 ns. You need not be concerned about the input changing too fast for the output to respond. Model linear changes on the output only, considering only extreme low and high values at the input of the inverter.

8.17. Use the 10 value logic system in the previous problem to model waveform dependencies in logic gates. Model an inverter with an input threshold value of 5, so that the inverter starts switching to its high state when the input state crosses 5 in the downward direction and starts switching to its low state when its input crosses the threshold (5) in the upward direction. Complete transitions of the output of the inverter from high state (9) to low state (0) take 20 ns (2 ns each state), while the transitions from low to high takes 30 ns (3 ns each state). The output should respond to changes on the input while making a transition, i.e., if the input switches from state 5 to 6 while the output is making a low-to-high transition, the direction of the output should change. This is not an easy problem. Also, you can easily modify this problem to make the speed of the output depend on the speed of the input.

8.18. Develop a behavioral model of an 8-bit sequential multiplier. The 4-bit version of this multiplier was discussed in Chapter 1 (Section 1.2.2). Use the same interface and signaling as the multiplier in Chapter 1, i.e., use *dataready, busy* and *done*. The circuit receives two 8-bit operands when the input *dataready* becomes '1'. This causes the multiplication process to begin and the *busy* flag to become active. Using the add-shift method, the multiplier takes one or two clock pulses for each bit of the multiplicand. When the process is completed, *done* becomes '1' for one clock period and *busy* returns to zero. The circuit receives two operands from its *inputbus*, and produces the result on its 8-bit *result* output. Your behavioral description of this circuit should model it at the clock level. That is, the number of clock pulses that the behavioral model takes for multiplication of two numbers should be the same as that of an actual circuit using the add-shift method.

CPU
MODELING
AND
DESIGN

Concepts of VHDL, the syntax and semantics of its constructs, and various ways that a hardware component can be described in VHDL were discussed in the previous chapters. No additional VHDL constructs are presented in this chapter; instead we will use the constructs of earlier chapters to describe a simple 8-bit processor. A CPU structure represents a large class of digital systems and its description involves the use of many important constructs of VHDL.

This chapter begins by introducing and describing a CPU example at a high level of abstraction, then capturing this high level information in a behavioral VHDL description. Following that, the data path of this machine and its structural details is designed and the information is then used to develop the dataflow description for our example CPU. The last part of this chapter develops a test bench for testing the behavioral or dataflow models. Various descriptions of this CPU are presented in Appendix D. The end-of-chapter problems suggest ways for enhancing the capabilities of this processor as well as improving its test bench.

9.1 DEFINING A COMPREHENSIVE EXAMPLE

The CPU that we use in this chapter is *a r*educed *p*rocessor, which we refer to as PAR-1 (pronounced and written as "Parwan"). Parwan, first developed to teach computer hardware to novice logic design students, employs a reduced hardware requirement and a simple instruction set. The implementation of the machine in terms of MSI and SSI parts was illustrated for this purpose. Later, a senior design project for students in a VLSI design course capitalized on this processor. Using standard public-domain CAD tools, Parwan was designed as a full custom VLSI chip (see Figure 9.1) and fabricated at the Massachusetts Microelectronics Center (M^2C). Because of its reduced architecture and simple instruction set, it is easier to explore the hardware details of Parwan and students are able to see the inner workings of a CPU down to its transistors and gates.

We will use Parwan to illustrate the use of VHDL as a language for modeling and design of CPU-like architectures. The use of this simple architecture enables us to show modeling styles and applications of hardware description languages without overshadowing these concepts with the complexity of an architecture.

The behavioral description of Parwan, presented later in this chapter, is written according to the functionality of this CPU as it is first described to a user, or in our case to a student. Its dataflow description considers register transfer level hardware details and utilizes the same partitioning previously employed when generating the layout shown in Figure 9.1. The actual chip, its dataflow description, and its behavioral description all have the same functionality and input/output ports.

9.2 PARWAN CPU

Because of the size of its data registers and buses, Parwan is generally considered to be an 8-bit processor. This machine has an 8-bit external data bus and a 12-bit address bus. It has the basic arithmetic and logical operations and several jump and branch instructions, along with direct and indirect addressing modes. Parwan also has a simple subroutine call instruction and an input interrupt that resets the machine.

9.2.1 Memory Organization of Parwan

Parwan is capable of addressing 4096 bytes of memory through its 12-bit address bus (*adbus*). This memory is partitioned into sixteen pages of 256 bytes each. As shown in Figure 9.2, the four most significant bits of *adbus* constitute the page address and its eight least significant bits are the offset. In this figure, and in the future examples of this chapter, we use hexadecimal numbers for the addresses. We separate page and offset parts of the address by a colon. In spite of the 16 pages of memory partitioning the Parwan's memory is treated as a contiguous 4K memory and page crossing is done automatically. This memory is also used for communication with input and output devices. Due to its memory mapped I/O, Parwan does not have separate I/O instructions.

9.2.2 Instruction Set

With two addressing modes, Parwan has a total of 23 instructions, as summarized in Figure 9.3. The main and only CPU data register is the accumulator, which is

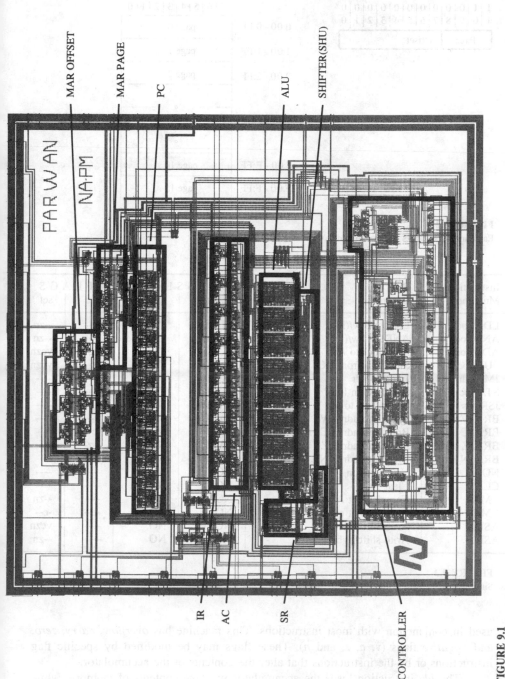

MAR OFFSET

MAR PAGE

PC

ALU

SHIFTER(SHU)

IR

AC

SR

CONTROLLER

FIGURE 9.1
VLSI Implementation of Parwan, fabricated at Massachusetts Microelectronics Center.

ADDRESS:

1	1	0	0	0	0	0	0	0	0	0	0
1	0	9	8	7	6	5	4	3	2	1	0

Page	Offset

MEMORY:

7 | 6 | 5 | 4 | 3 | 2 | 1 | 0

0:00 - 0:FF	page 0 ..
1:00 - 1:FF	page 1 ..
2:00 - 2:FF	page 2 ..
∘	∘
∘	∘
∘	∘
E:00 - E:FF	page 14 ..
F:00 - F:FF	page 15 ..

FIGURE 9.2
Page and offset Parts of Parwan addresses.

Instruction Mnemonic	Brief Description	ADDRESSING			FLAGS	
		Bits	Scheme	Indirect	use	set
LDA loc	Load AC w/(loc)	12	FULL	YES	----	--zn
AND loc	AND AC w/(loc)	12	FULL	YES	----	--zn
ADD loc	Add (loc) to AC	12	FULL	YES	-c--	vczn
SUB loc	Sub (loc) from AC	12	FULL	YES	-c--	vczn
JMP adr	Jump to adr	12	FULL	YES	----	----
STA loc	Store AC in loc	12	FULL	YES	----	----
JSR tos	Subroutine to tos	8	PAGE	NO	----	----
BRA_V adr	Branch to adr if V	8	PAGE	NO	v---	----
BRA_C adr	Branch to adr if C	8	PAGE	NO	-c--	----
BRA_Z adr	Branch to adr if Z	8	PAGE	NO	--z-	----
BRA_N adr	Branch to adr if N	8	PAGE	NO	---n	----
NOP	No operation	-	NONE	NO	----	----
CLA	Clear AC	-	NONE	NO	----	----
CMA	Complement AC	-	NONE	NO	----	--zn
CMC	Complement carry	-	NONE	NO	-c--	-c--
ASL	Arith shift left	-	NONE	NO	----	vczn
ASR	Arith shift right	-	NONE	NO	----	--zn

FIGURE 9.3
Summary of Parwan instructions.

used in conjunction with most instructions. This machine has *overflow*, *carry*, *zero*, and *negative* flags (v, c, z, and n). These flags may be modified by specific flag instructions or by the instructions that alter the contents of the accumulator.

The *lda* instruction loads the accumulator with the contents of memory, while the *and*, *add*, and *sub* instructions access memory for an operand, perform the specified operation (ANDing, adding, and subtracting), and load the results in the accumulator.

Flags z and n are set or reset based on the results of *lda*, *and*, *add*, and *sub*. Instructions *add* and *sub* also influence v and c flags (overflow and carry), depending on the outcome of the corresponding operations. The *sta* instruction stores the contents of accumulator into the specified memory location. Execution of the *jmp* instruction causes the next instruction to be received from the address specified by the instruction. Instructions *lda*, *and*, *add*, *sub*, *jmp*, and *sta* use 12-bit addresses, and can be used with the indirect addressing mode. We refer to these instructions as having a full-addressing scheme.

The addressing scheme of *jsr* and branch instructions is page-addressing. These instructions can only point to the page that they appear in. The *jsr* instruction with an 8-bit *tos* (top of subroutine) address causes the next instruction to be received from memory location *tos+1* of the current page. At the end of a subroutine, a return from subroutine can be accomplished by an indirect jump to *tos*. Four branch instructions, *bra_v*, *bra_c*, *bra_z*, and *bra_n* cause the next instruction to be received from the specified location of the current page if the respective flags v, c, z, or n are set.

Instructions *nop*, *cla*, *cma*, *cmc*, *asl*, and *asr* are nonaddress instructions and perform operations on the internal registers of the CPU flags. The *nop* instruction performs no operation, *cla* clears the accumulator, *cma* complements the accumulator, *cmc* complements the c flag, and *asl* and *asr* cause arithmetic left or right shift of the contents of accumulator. When shifting left, the most significant bit of the accumulator is shifted into the carry flag, and the overflow flag is set if the sign of accumulator changes. The *asr* instruction extends the sign of accumulator and shifts out its least significant bit. Both shift instructions affect the zero and negative flags.

9.2.3 Instruction Format

As shown in Figure 9.3, there are three groups of Parwan instructions. Full-address instructions requiring two bytes can access all of Parwan's memory and be used with indirect addressing. Page-address instructions requiring two bytes can access the current page, but cannot use indirect addressing. The third group, which are nonaddress instructions, do not use the memory for their operands. Figure 9.4 shows the opcodes and format of these instructions.

9.2.3.1 FULL ADDRESS INSTRUCTIONS. The opcode specifying the operation of a full-address instruction is formed by the three most significant bits of the first byte. The next bit (bit number 4) specifies direct or indirect addressing modes (0 for direct, 1 for indirect), and the other four bits (the least significant four) contain the page number of the operand of the instruction. The second byte of a full-address instruction specifies the offset address, which together with the page address, completes a 12-bit address for the operand. Figure 9.5 shows the formation of a complete 12-bit address for this group of Parwan instructions.

9.2.3.2 PAGE ADDRESS INSTRUCTIONS. Figure 9.6 shows the format for *jsr* and branch instructions. These instructions reference memory within the page where they appear. The opcode of *jsr* is 110 and the other five bits of the first instruction byte

Instruction Mnemonic	Fields and Bits		
	Opcode 7 6 5	D/I 4	3 2 1 0
LDA loc	0 0 0	0/1	page adr
AND loc	0 0 1	0/1	page adr
ADD loc	0 1 0	0/1	page adr
SUB loc	0 1 1	0/1	page adr
JMP adr	1 0 0	0/1	page adr
STA loc	1 0 1	0/1	page adr
JSR tos	1 1 0	-	- - - -
BRA_V adr	1 1 1	1	1 0 0 0
BRA_C adr	1 1 1	1	0 1 0 0
BRA_Z adr	1 1 1	1	0 0 1 0
BRA_N adr	1 1 1	1	0 0 0 1
NOP	1 1 1	0	0 0 0 0
CLA	1 1 1	0	0 0 0 1
CMA	1 1 1	0	0 0 1 0
CMC	1 1 1	0	0 1 0 0
ASL	1 1 1	0	1 0 0 0
ASR	1 1 1	0	1 0 0 1

FIGURE 9.4
Parwan instruction opcodes.

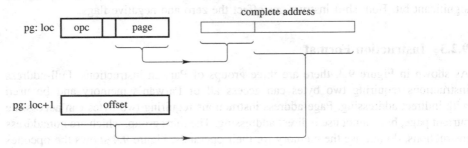

FIGURE 9.5
Addressing in full-address instructions.

are ignored. The opcode field of a branch instruction contains 111. Bit 4 is always 1 and its least significant bits specify the condition for a branch. The second byte of *jsr* and branch instructions specify the jump address within the current page.

For a branch example, consider the instruction shown in Figure 9.7. At location 0D on page 5, a *bra_c* causes the next instruction to be received from location 6A of page 5 if the carry flag is set, or from location 0F of page 5 if the carry flag is zero. Figure 9.8 shows the execution of a *jsr* instruction at location 5:11. The byte at location 5:12 specifies that the subroutine begins at location 33 of the current page (5:33). The first location of a subroutine is reserved for the return address, and the programmer is not allowed to use it for program information, i.e., code or data. The

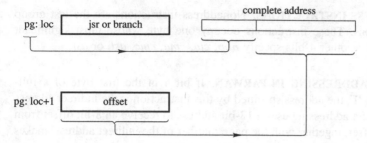

FIGURE 9.6
Addressing in page-address instructions.

programmer is required to use an indirect jump instruction at the end of a subroutine to return from it. Figure 9.8 shows a *jmp-indirect* instruction at locations 5:55 and 5:56. After the execution of *jsr*, the return address (the address of the instruction that follows *jsr* in memory, which in this example is location 5:13) is placed in the first location of the subroutine (location 5:33). The indirect jump at location 5:55 causes the program flow to return to location 5:13 after the subroutine completes.

```
            MEMORY
          ┌──────────────┐
          │     ...      │
5:0D      │ 1 1 1 1 0 1 0 0 │
5:0E      │     6 A      │
5:0F      │     ...      │
          └──────────────┘
```

FIGURE 9.7
A branch instruction.

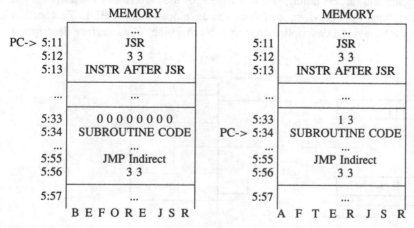

FIGURE 9.8
An example for the execution of *jsr*. Memory and *pc*, before and after *jsr*.

9.2.3.3 NONADDRESS INSTRUCTIONS. Nonaddress instructions are the last group of Parwan instructions. These instructions occupy one byte whose most significant four bits are 1110. The other 4-bits specify *nop*, *cla*, *cma*, *cmc*, *asl*, or *asr*.

9.2.3.4 INDIRECT ADDRESSING IN PARWAN. If bit 4 of the first byte of a full-address instruction is '1', the address specified by this instruction is the indirect address of the operand. Indirect addressing uses a 12-bit address to receive an 8-bit offset from the memory. This offset, together with the page number of the indirect address, makes a complete address for the actual operand of the instruction.

Figure 9.9 shows an example of indirect addressing in Parwan. It is assumed that a full-address instruction with indirect addressing is in locations 0:25 and 0:26. The 12-bit address of this instruction (6:35) points to 1F in the memory which is used with page number 6 to form 6:1F as the actual address of the operand.

9.2.4 Programming in Parwan Assembly

For a better understanding of Parwan instructions, consider the program shown in Figure 9.10. The assembly code of this figure adds ten data bytes which are stored in memory starting from location 4:25, and stores the result at 4:03. The code begins at location 0:15 and assumes constants 25, 10, and 1 are stored in 4:00, 4:01, and 4:02, respectively. Although Parwan does not have an immediate addressing mode, series of shifts and adds can generate any necessary constant. Modifying this processor to handle immediate addressing mode is dealt with in a series of problem at the end of the chapter.

9.3 BEHAVIORAL DESCRIPTION OF PARWAN

A more compact and far less ambiguous description of the behavior of Parwan than the "word" description of the previous section can be developed using VHDL. This section presents such a behavioral description for our 8-bit machine. The interface description

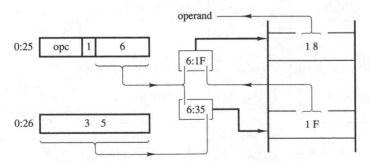

FIGURE 9.9
An example for indirect addressing in Parwan.

```
                          -- load 25 in 4:00
                          -- load 10 in 4:01
                          -- load 01 in 4:02
0:15   cla                -- clear accumulator
0:16   asl                -- clears carry
0:17   add, i   4:00      -- add bytes
0:19   sta      4:03      -- store partial sum
0:1B   lda      4:00      -- load pointer
0:1D   add      4:02      -- increment pointer
0:1F   sta      4:00      -- store pointer back
0:21   lda      4:01      -- load count
0:23   sub      4:02      -- decrement count
0:25   bra_z    :2D       -- end if zero count
0:27   sta      4:01      -- store count back
0:29   lda      4:03      -- get partial sum
0:2B   jmp      0:17      -- go for next byte
0:2D   nop                -- adding completed
```

FIGURE 9.10
An example program for Parwan CPU.

of this machine is kept at the hardware level, using bits for external control signals and memory and data buses.

9.3.1 Timing and Clocking

The interface of our behavioral description includes a clock signal which is not used. This signal is included for compatibility with the actual chip and with the dataflow model that we develop later in this chapter. The timing of the behavioral model is independent of the clock and may not necessarily match those of the actual chip and the more realistic models.

Timing is introduced in a behavioral model when reading or writing from or to the memory. This timing is only for synchronization with the memory in order that the same memory model can be used for the behavioral as well as other more detailed models. Parwan uses a static memory with an active high read and write lines.

9.3.2 Packages

When describing Parwan at the behavioral level, we use the *basic_utilities* package presented in the previous chapters. This package is compiled and placed in a design library named *cmos*. Another library called *par_library* contains packages that include utilities which are needed to describe Parwan and do not appear in the *basic_utilities* package.

9.3.2.1 PAR_UTILITIES PACKAGE. The first of two packages appearing in *par_library* is *par_utilities*, whose package declaration is shown in Figure 9.11. This package

```
LIBRARY cmos;
USE cmos.basic_utilities.ALL;
--
PACKAGE par_utilities IS
    FUNCTION "XOR" (a, b : qit) RETURN qit ;
    FUNCTION "AND" (a, b : qit_vector) RETURN qit_vector;
    FUNCTION "OR" (a, b : qit_vector) RETURN qit_vector;
    FUNCTION "NOT" (a : qit_vector) RETURN qit_vector;
    SUBTYPE nibble IS qit_vector (3 DOWNTO 0);
    SUBTYPE byte IS qit_vector (7 DOWNTO 0);
    SUBTYPE twelve IS qit_vector (11 DOWNTO 0);
    SUBTYPE wired_nibble IS wired_qit_vector (3 DOWNTO 0);
    SUBTYPE wired_byte IS wired_qit_vector (7 DOWNTO 0);
    SUBTYPE wired_twelve IS wired_qit_vector (11 DOWNTO 0);
    SUBTYPE ored_nibble IS ored_qit_vector (3 DOWNTO 0);
    SUBTYPE ored_byte IS ored_qit_vector (7 DOWNTO 0);
    SUBTYPE ored_twelve IS ored_qit_vector (11 DOWNTO 0);
    CONSTANT zero_4 : nibble := "0000";
    CONSTANT zero_8 : byte := "00000000";
    CONSTANT zero_12 : twelve := "000000000000";
    FUNCTION add_cv (a, b : qit_vector; cin : qit) RETURN qit_vector;
    FUNCTION sub_cv (a, b : qit_vector; cin : qit) RETURN qit_vector;
    FUNCTION set_if_zero (a : qit_vector) RETURN qit;
END par_utilities;
```

FIGURE 9.11
Declarations of *par_utilities* package of *par_library*.

uses the *basic_utilities* package of the *cmos* library and includes several type and function declarations.

Subtypes *nibble*, *byte*, and *twelve* are *qit_vectors* of 4, 8, and 12 *qit*s long. Types *wired_nibble* (*ored_nibble*), *wired_byte* (*ored_byte*), and *wired_twelve* (*ored_twelve*) are resolved *qit_vectors* using the *wiring* (*oring*) resolution functions of the *basic_utilities* package. Function "XOR" of the *par_utilities* package overloads the XOR operator for *qit* operands. Functions "AND", "OR" and "NOT" overload their corresponding functions in the *basic_utilities* package for *qit_vector* operands. Recall that the *basic_utilities* package overloads basic logical operators with functions for *qit* type operands.

The *par_utilities* package also includes *add_cv* and *sub_cv* functions. These functions perform the respective addition or subtraction on their *n qit* long *qit_vector* operands and return a *qit_vector* of length *n+2*. The two most significant *qit*s of the result (positions *n+1* and *n*) are the overflow and carry indicators. The last function in the package in Figure 9.11 is *set_if_zero*, which returns a '1' if its unconstrained *qit_vector* parameter contains all zeros. Figure 9.12 shows the body of the *par_utilities* package.

9.3.2.2 PAR_PARAMETERS PACKAGE. Another package in the *par_library* is *par_parameters*. This package, shown in Figure 9.13, defines bit patterns for opcodes

```
┌─PACKAGE BODY par_utilities IS
│  ┌─FUNCTION "XOR" (a, b : qit) RETURN qit IS
│  │     CONSTANT qit_or_table : qit_2d := (
│  │       ('0','1','1','X'), ('1','0','0','X'), ('1','0','0','X'), ('X','X','X','X'));
│  ├─BEGIN   RETURN qit_or_table (a, b);
│  └─END "XOR";
│  ┌─FUNCTION "AND" (a,b : qit_vector) RETURN qit_vector IS
│  │     VARIABLE r : qit_vector (a'RANGE);
│  ├─BEGIN
│  │     loop1: FOR i IN a'RANGE LOOP
│  │        r(i) := a(i) AND b(i);
│  │     END LOOP loop1;   RETURN r;
│  └─END "AND";
│  ┌─FUNCTION "OR" (a,b: qit_vector) RETURN qit_vector IS
│  │     VARIABLE r: qit_vector (a'RANGE);
│  ├─BEGIN
│  │     loop1: FOR i IN a'RANGE LOOP
│  │        r(i) := a(i) OR b(i);
│  │     END LOOP loop1;   RETURN r;
│  └─END "OR";
│  ┌─FUNCTION "NOT" (a: qit_vector) RETURN qit_vector IS
│  │     VARIABLE r: qit_vector (a'RANGE);
│  ├─BEGIN
│  │     loop1: FOR i IN a'RANGE LOOP
│  │        r(i) := NOT a(i);
│  │     END LOOP loop1;   RETURN r;
│  └─END "NOT";
```

FIGURE 9.12

Body of the *par_utilities* package of *par_library* library. (*continued on following page*)

and groups of instructions. In naming opcodes, we avoid VHDL reserved words and use names that are similar to Parwan mnemonics. The *par_parameters* package is primarily used for the readability of behavioral descriptions of Parwan components. In all cases, bit patterns equivalent to the defined constants could be used as well.

9.3.3 Interface Description of Parwan

The interface of the Parwan behavioral description, described according to the fabricated chip in Figure 9.1, is pin-compatible with its dataflow description. The declarative part of the entity in this CPU uses signals whose types are *qit*, *qit_vector*, or their resolved subtypes. Although using string type for the inputs and outputs of Parwan would simplify instruction representation and decoding at the behavioral level, it would also require different types of input and output signals for different Parwan models. For consistency between various models and the actual hardware this feature has been avoided.

Figure 9.14 shows the interface description of Parwan. This description uses the *basic_utilities* package from the *cmos* library, and *par_utilities* and *par_parameters*

```
FUNCTION add_cv (a, b : qit_vector; cin : qit) RETURN qit_vector IS
   VARIABLE r, c: qit_vector (a'LEFT + 2 DOWNTO 0);  -- extra r bits: msb overflow,
                                                                   next carry
   VARIABLE a_sign, b_sign: qit;
BEGIN
   a_sign := a(a'LEFT);    b_sign := b(b'LEFT);
   r(0) := a(0) XOR b(0) XOR cin;
   c(0) := ((a(0) XOR b(0)) AND cin) OR (a(0) AND b(0));
   FOR i IN 1 TO (a'LEFT) LOOP
      r(i) := a(i) XOR b(i) XOR c(i-1);
      c(i) := ((a(i) XOR b(i)) AND c(i-1)) OR (a(i) AND b(i));
   END LOOP;
   r(a'LEFT+1) := c(a'LEFT);
   IF a_sign = b_sign AND r(a'LEFT) /= a_sign
      THEN r(a'LEFT+2) := '1'; --overflow
   ELSE r(a'LEFT+2) := '0'; END IF;
   RETURN r;
END add_cv;
FUNCTION sub_cv (a, b : qit_vector; cin : qit) RETURN qit_vector IS
   VARIABLE not_b : qit_vector (b'LEFT DOWNTO 0);
   VARIABLE not_c : qit;
   VARIABLE r : qit_vector (a'LEFT + 2 DOWNTO 0);
BEGIN
   not_b := NOT b;    not_c := NOT cin;
   r := add_cv (a, not_b, not_c);
   RETURN r;
END sub_cv;
FUNCTION set_if_zero (a : qit_vector) RETURN qit IS
   VARIABLE zero : qit := '1';
BEGIN
   FOR i IN a'RANGE LOOP
      IF a(i) /= '0' THEN
         zero := '0'; EXIT;
      END IF;
   END LOOP;
   RETURN zero;
END set_if_zero;
END par_utilities;
```

FIGURE 9.12
Body of the *par_utilities* package of *par_library* library. (*continued from previous page*)

from the *par_library* package. The generic clause specifies memory read and write timing parameters, as well as a cycle time and a simulation run time. The cycle time is equivalent to a complete read or write cycle. The port clause in Figure 9.14 contains inputs and outputs of Parwan. The *databus* bidirectional bus is a resolved signal that uses the wiring resolution function of the *basic_utilities* package. This declaration allows multiple sources to drive the bus. For example, in reading from the

```
LIBRARY cmos;
USE cmos.basic_utilities.ALL;
---
PACKAGE par_parameters IS
    CONSTANT single_byte_instructions : qit_vector (3 DOWNTO 0) := "1110";
    CONSTANT cla : qit_vector (3 DOWNTO 0) := "0001";
    CONSTANT cma : qit_vector (3 DOWNTO 0) := "0010";
    CONSTANT cmc : qit_vector (3 DOWNTO 0) := "0100";
    CONSTANT asl : qit_vector (3 DOWNTO 0) := "1000";
    CONSTANT asr : qit_vector (3 DOWNTO 0) := "1001";
    CONSTANT jsr : qit_vector (2 DOWNTO 0) := "110";
    CONSTANT bra : qit_vector (3 DOWNTO 0) := "1111";
    CONSTANT indirect : qit := '1';
    CONSTANT jmp : qit_vector (2 DOWNTO 0) := "100";
    CONSTANT sta : qit_vector (2 DOWNTO 0) := "101";
    CONSTANT lda : qit_vector (2 DOWNTO 0) := "000";
    CONSTANT ann : qit_vector (2 DOWNTO 0) := "001";
    CONSTANT add : qit_vector (2 DOWNTO 0) := "010";
    CONSTANT sbb : qit_vector (2 DOWNTO 0) := "011";
END par_parameters;
```

FIGURE 9.13
Declaration of the *par_parameters* package of *par_library*.

```
LIBRARY cmos;
USE cmos.basic_utilities.ALL;
LIBRARY par_library;
USE par_library.par_utilities.ALL;
USE par_library.par_parameters.ALL;
--
ENTITY par_central_processing_unit IS
    GENERIC (read_high_time, read_low_time,
             write_high_time, write_low_time : TIME := 2 US;
             cycle_time : TIME := 4 US; run_time : TIME := 140 US);
    PORT (clk : IN qit;
          interrupt : IN qit;
          read_mem, write_mem : OUT qit;
          databus : INOUT wired_byte BUS := "ZZZZZZZZ"; adbus : OUT twelve
          );
END par_central_processing_unit;
```

FIGURE 9.14
Interface description of Parwan.

memory, the CPU drives the bus with 'Z's, while the memory drives it with the data from the memory. For writing into the memory, the role of the CPU and the memory are reversed. The *databus* declaration also allows multiple peripherals to connect to the CPU.

9.3.4 Parwan Behavioral Architecture

The high level behavioral description of Parwan presented here models this machine from an instruction execution point of view. The functionality of this model is identical to lower level models, e.g., dataflow and gate level, and to the actual hardware. However, this model is by no means perfect. At this stage of design, when the bussing structure of the machine is not known, it is not possible to generate a model that complies with the clock level timing of the actual hardware. Furthermore, we are only modeling the good behavior of Parwan. Unanticipated data inputs, unusually long delays, or faulty inputs can cause the behavioral model to generate responses that are very different from the response of the actual hardware or the lower level models.

Figure 9.15 outlines the *behavioral* architecture of the *par_central_processing_unit*. The description contains a process statement in which the if statements separate various instructions or groups of instructions. The declarative part of the process, shown in Figure 9.16, contains the declarations of temporary variables and buffers.

In the statement part of the process statement in Figure 9.15, an if statement halts the simulation when the *run_time* is reached. Following this statement, a check is made for the interrupt input. Figure 9.17 shows the code that is executed if the interrupt input is '1'. After setting the program counter to zero, the processor waits for one *cycle_time* before checking *interrupt* again.

When the *interrupt* input becomes '0', the first instruction byte is read from the memory. Figure 9.18 shows how the *byte1* variable stores this byte. The wait statement that follows the assignment of '1' to *read_mem*, allows sufficient time for the memory unit to respond to a read request. The wait statement which appears after the signal assignment that resets *read_mem* to zero, stops subsequent '1' values from overwriting the zero value on this signal. The last statement in Figure 9.18 increments the program counter in order to make it ready for reading the next byte.

After reading the first byte of an instruction, the behavioral description in Figure 9.15 checks for those instructions that use only one memory byte. For these instructions, the code of Figure 9.19 is executed. This code checks bits 3 to 0 of the instruction byte for *cla*, *cma*, *cmc*, *asl*, or *asr*, and performs appropriate operations.

For instructions that use two memory bytes, another byte is read from the memory and placed in the *byte2* variable, shown in Figure 9.20. This is followed by the if statements that check for various types of two-byte instructions.

The outline in Figure 9.15 handles the execution of *jsr* as the first two-byte instruction. The code for the execution of this instruction, presented in Figure 9.21, shows that the offset part of the program counter is first written to the top of subroutine. The top of subroutine is a memory location whose page number is the page number that already exists on *adbus* (the current page), and whose offset is taken from the second instruction byte (*byte2*). Transferring the contents of *pc* to this location forms the subroutine return address. In order to prepare the program counter for fetching the next instruction from the subroutine, *pc* is set to the increment of *byte2*. The execution of subroutine instructions continues until the indirect jump at the end of subroutine (which must be put there by the programmer) is reached.

```
┌ARCHITECTURE behavioral OF par_central_processing_unit IS
├BEGIN
│   ┌PROCESS
│   │   ‖   Declare necessary variables; Figure 9.16.
│   ├BEGIN
│   │   _IF NOW > run_time THEN WAIT; END IF;
│   │   ┌IF interrupt = '1' THEN
│   │   │   ‖   Handle interrupt; Figure 9.17.
│   │   ├ELSE   -- no interrupt
│   │   │   ‖   Read first byte into byte1, increment pc; Figure 9.18.
│   │   │   ┌IF byte1 (7 DOWNTO 4) = single_byte_instructions THEN
│   │   │   │   ‖   Execute single-byte instructions; Figure 9.19.
│   │   │   ├ELSE   -- two-byte instructions
│   │   │   │   ‖   Read second byte into byte2, increment pc; Figure 9.20.
│   │   │   │   ┌IF byte1 (7 DOWNTO 5) = jsr THEN
│   │   │   │   │   ‖   Execute jsr instruction, byte2 has address; Figure 9.21.
│   │   │   │   ├ELSIF byte1 (7 DOWNTO 4) = bra THEN
│   │   │   │   │   ‖   Execute bra instructions, address in byte2; Figure 9.22.
│   │   │   │   ├ELSE -- all other two-byte instructions
│   │   │   │   │   ┌IF byte1 (4) = indirect THEN
│   │   │   │   │   │   ‖   Use byte1 and byte2 to get address; Figure 9.23.
│   │   │   │   │   └END IF; -- ends indirect
│   │   │   │   │   ┌IF byte1 (7 DOWNTO 5) = jmp THEN
│   │   │   │   │   │   ‖   Execute jmp instruction; Figure 9.24;
│   │   │   │   │   ├ELSIF byte1 (7 DOWNTO 5) = sta THEN
│   │   │   │   │   │   ‖   Execute sta instruction, write ac; Figure 9.25.
│   │   │   │   │   ├ELSE -- read operand for lda, and, add, sub
│   │   │   │   │   │   ‖   Read memory onto databus; Figure 9.26, top.
│   │   │   │   │   │   ‖   Execute lda, and, add, and sub;  Figure 9.26, middle.
│   │   │   │   │   │   ‖   Remove memory from databus; Figure 9.26, bottom.
│   │   │   │   │   └END IF; -- jmp / sta / lda, and, add, sub
│   │   │   │   └END IF; -- jsr / bra / other double-byte instructions
│   │   │   └END IF; -- single-byte / double-byte
│   │   └END IF; -- interrupt / otherwise
│   └END PROCESS;
└END behavioral;
```

FIGURE 9.15
Outline of the Parwan behavioral description.

```
┌ VARIABLE pc : twelve;
│ VARIABLE ac, byte1, byte2 : byte;
│ VARIABLE v, c, z, n : qit;
└ VARIABLE temp : qit_vector (9 DOWNTO 0);
```

FIGURE 9.16
Variable declarations of the Parwan behavioral model.

```
pc := zero_12;
WAIT FOR cycle_time;
```

FIGURE 9.17
Interrupt handling of the Parwan behavioral model.

```
adbus <= pc;
read_mem <= '1';   WAIT FOR read_high_time;
byte1 := byte (databus);
read_mem <= '0';   WAIT FOR read_low_time;
pc := inc (pc);
```

FIGURE 9.18
Reading the first byte from the memory (part of the Parwan behavioral model).

```
CASE byte1 (3 DOWNTO 0) IS
  WHEN cla =>
    ac := zero_8;
  WHEN cma =>
    ac := NOT ac;
    IF ac = zero_8 THEN z := '1'; END IF;
    n := ac (7);
  WHEN cmc =>
    c := NOT c;
  WHEN asl =>
    c := ac (7);
    ac := ac (6 DOWNTO 0) & '0';
    IF ac = zero_8 THEN z := '1'; END IF;
    n := ac (7);
    IF c /= n THEN v := '1'; END IF;
  WHEN asr =>
    ac := ac (7) & ac (7 DOWNTO 1);
    IF ac = zero_8 THEN z := '1'; END IF;
    n := ac (7);
  WHEN OTHERS => NULL;
END CASE;
```

FIGURE 9.19
Executing single-byte instructions in the behavioral model of Parwan.

The code for the branch instructions follows that of *jsr* in the outline in Figure 9.15. The execution of branch code shown in Figure 9.22 causes the conditional loading of the offset part of the program counter with the contents of *byte2*. Therefore, branching is to the current page only.

```
adbus <= pc;
read_mem <= '1';   WAIT FOR read_high_time;
byte2 := byte (databus);
read_mem <= '0';   WAIT FOR read_low_time;
pc := inc (pc);
```

FIGURE 9.20
Reading the second byte from the memory (part of Parwan behavioral model).

```
databus <= wired_byte (pc (7 DOWNTO 0) );
adbus (7 DOWNTO 0) <= byte2;
write_mem <= '1';   WAIT FOR write_high_time;
write_mem <= '0';   WAIT FOR write_low_time;
databus <= "ZZZZZZZZ";
pc (7 DOWNTO 0) := inc (byte2);
```

FIGURE 9.21
Execution of the *jsr* instruction in the behavioral model of Parwan.

```
IF
   ( byte1 (3) = '1' AND v = '1' ) OR
   ( byte1 (2) = '1' AND c = '1' ) OR
   ( byte1 (1) = '1' AND z = '1' ) OR
   ( byte1 (0) = '1' AND n = '1' )
THEN
   pc (7 DOWNTO 0) := byte2;
END IF;
```

FIGURE 9.22
Execution of branch instructions in the Parwan behavioral model.

If a two-byte instruction is not *jsr* or any of the branch instructions, the *behavioral* architecture of the *par_central_processing_unit* checks for indirect addressing. For indirect addressing (see Figure 9.23), a 12-bit address whose page number comes from the least significant nibble of *byte1* and whose offset is *byte2* is used for addressing the memory and reading the actual offset. This newly read byte replaces the old contents of *byte2*. After execution of the code in Figure 9.23, the least significant nibble of *byte1* contains the page while *byte2* has the offset of the actual address of the operand.

The code for the full-address instructions follows that of indirect addressing shown in Figure 9.15. The first such instruction is *jmp*, which loads the program counter with the 12-bit address that is available from *byte1* and *byte2* variables.

The next full-address instruction is *sta* which writes the accumulator into the memory location specified by the least significant nibble of *byte1* and by *byte2*. Figure 9.25 shows the code for this instruction.

```
adbus (11 DOWNTO 8) <= byte1 (3 DOWNTO 0);
adbus (7 DOWNTO 0) <= byte2;
read_mem <= '1';   WAIT FOR read_high_time;
byte2 := byte (databus);
read_mem <= '0';   WAIT FOR read_low_time;
```

FIGURE 9.23
Handling indirect addressing by the Parwan behavioral model.

```
pc := byte1 (3 DOWNTO 0) & byte2;
```

FIGURE 9.24
Execution of *jmp* instruction in the Parwan behavioral model.

```
adbus <= byte1 (3 DOWNTO 0) & byte2;
databus <= wired_byte (ac);
write_mem <= '1';   WAIT FOR write_high_time;
write_mem <= '0';   WAIT FOR write_low_time;
databus <= "ZZZZZZZZ";
```

FIGURE 9.25
Execution of *sta* instruction in the Parwan behavioral model.

The last group of full-address instructions are *lda*, *and*, *add*, and *sub*. As shown in Figure 9.26, the actual operand is read from the memory and is kept on the *databus* by keeping the *read_mem* signal active for execution of these instructions. A case statement separates these four instructions and performs their corresponding operations. The *read_mem* signal is disabled at the end to indicate to the memory that the *databus* is no longer needed. This causes the memory unit to release the bus by setting it to high impedance.

The process statement in the Parwan behavioral description uses at least one cycle time for the execution of each Parwan instruction. Each time through the process statement, one complete instruction is executed and this may take up to three cycles. Execution of a new instruction begins when the program reaches the beginning of the process statement. A complete behavioral description of Parwan consists of Figures 9.16 to 9.26 which are inserted in their specified places in Figure 9.15. This description is shown in Appendix D.

9.4 PARWAN BUSSING STRUCTURE

The bussing structure of a CPU describes the way its registers and logic units are connected. The first step in the hardware design process of a CPU is the design of this structure. Figure 9.27 shows the bussing structure of Parwan. This diagram is useful

```
adbus (11 DOWNTO 8) <= byte1 (3 DOWNTO 0);
adbus (7 DOWNTO 0) <= byte2;
read_mem <= '1';   WAIT FOR read_high_time;
CASE byte1 (7 DOWNTO 5) IS
  WHEN lda =>
    ac := byte (databus);
  WHEN ann =>
    ac := ac AND byte (databus);
  WHEN add =>
    temp := add_cv (ac, byte (databus), c);
    ac := temp (7 DOWNTO 0);
    c := temp (8);
    v := temp (9);
  WHEN sbb =>
    temp := sub_cv (ac, byte (databus), c);
    ac := temp (7 DOWNTO 0);
    c := temp (8);
    v := temp (9);
  WHEN OTHERS => NULL;
END CASE;
IF ac = zero_8 THEN z := '1'; END IF;
n := ac (7);
read_mem <= '0';   WAIT FOR read_low_time;
```

FIGURE 9.26
Execution of *lda*, *and*, *add*, and *sub* instructions in the Parwan behavioral model.

when performing a detailed study of timing for the individual machine instructions and will be used when developing a dataflow description of Parwan in the next section. In this diagram, names of major buses and registers appear in capital letters, and all other signal names are in lowercase letters. Only signal names to be referenced in this section are shown.

9.4.1 Interconnection of Components

The major components of Parwan are *ac*, *ir*, *pc*, *mar*, *sr*, *alu*, and *shu*. Data flows between these components through buses and hard-wired interconnections. Figure 9.27 uses a hollow triangle to show controlled interconnection of a register or logic unit output to a bus, and uses an arrow for permanent wired connections. For example, the output of *shu*, labeled *obus*, connects to *dbus* only when a signal named *obus_on_dbus* is active. On the other hand, connection of the accumulator output (*ac_out*) to the input of *alu* is hard-wired. In general, connections to buses with multiple sources must be controlled. VLSI implementation of Parwan uses transmission gates for implementing the selection of data on to multi-source buses.

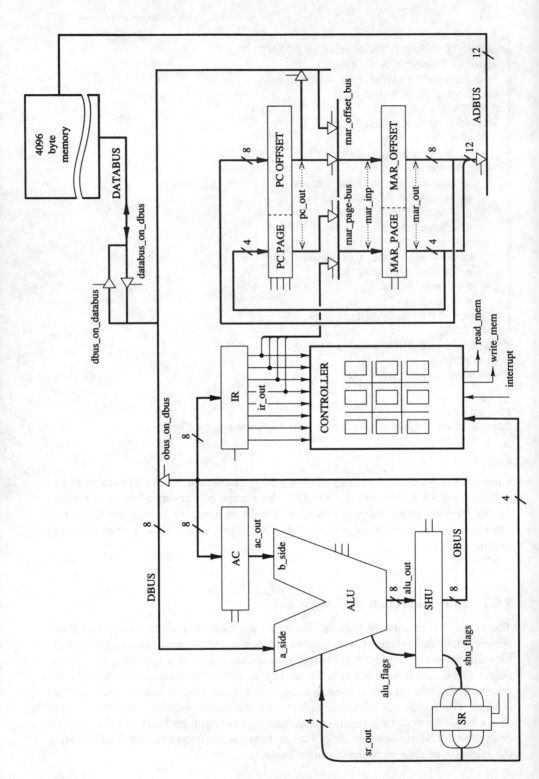

9.4.2 Global View of Parwan Components

Of the seven Parwan components, *ac*, *ir*, *pc*, *mar*, and *sr* are registers, and *alu* and *shu* are combinatorial logic units. Each component has a set of inputs and outputs and several control lines. In addition, register structures have clock inputs that are all connected to the main system clock.

The accumulator, *ac*, is an 8-bit register that provides one operand of *alu*. The instruction register, *ir*, connects to *dbus* through *alu*, and provides instruction bits to the controller, and page address to the address bus (*adbus*). The 12-bit program counter register, *pc*, is a binary up-counter that provides instruction addresses to *adbus* through the memory address register (*mar*). This register is an address buffer. The *mar* and *pc* registers have page and offset parts that are identified by *mar_page*, *pc_page*, *mar_offset*, and *pc_offset*. Page numbers are stored in their four most significant bits.

The arithmetic logic unit, *alu*, is a combinatorial logic unit with two sets of 8-bit inputs, four flag inputs, and three control inputs. The outputs of this unit are connected to the inputs of the *shu* unit. The shifter (*shu*) is also a combinatorial logic unit, and performs right and left shiftings of its 8-bit operand. The status register, *sr*, has four inputs and four outputs. Outputs of this register pass through *alu* and *shu* and circle back to its own inputs. This allows flags to be modified by either one of these logical units.

Figure 9.27 also shows a controller; a unit that generates control signals for the data components and buses. These signals cause the movement of data through system buses, and storage of this data into registers. The controller makes its decisions based on its state, external interrupt, and bits of *ir* and *sr*.

9.4.3 Instruction Execution

The bussing structure in Figure 9.27 provides the necessary registers and the data path for executing the Parwan instructions. Based on an instruction in *ir*, the controller generates control signals in an appropriate order for the proper execution of the instruction. For an illustration of this mechanism, we describe the sequence of events for execution of a *lda* instruction.

Initially, the program counter contains the address of instruction to be fetched. Fetching begins by moving the address from *pc* to *mar* and incrementing *pc*. For this move to take place, the address in *pc* must be placed on *mar_bus* and *mar* must be enabled and clocked. When this is completed, the controller activates the signal that places *mar* on *adbus* and at the same time it asserts *read_mem*. This causes the byte from the memory to appear on *databus*, which must now pass through *dbus*, *alu*, *shu*, and *obus* to reach *ir*. For this purpose, the controller activates the *databus_on_dbus* control signal, instructs *alu* to place its *a_side* on its output, and instructs the shifter

---

FIGURE 9.27
Parwan bussing structure.

unit to place its data input on its output without shifting it. The data on the output of *shu* becomes available for loading into *ir*.

Following an instruction fetch, the controller makes appropriate decisions based on the bits of *ir*. In our example, the most significant bits of *ir* are 0000, indicating a direct address *lda* instruction. To complete the address for the full-address *lda* instruction, the controller causes the current contents of *pc* to be clocked into *mar* and then be placed on *adbus* while it asserts *read_mem*. The byte read from the memory will pass through *dbus* and *mar_bus* to reach the input of *mar_offset* register. At the same time controller activates a signal which will place *ir* on *mar_page* register. Clocking *mar* while its load input is enabled causes the full address of the operand of *lda* to be clocked into this register.

The next read from the memory places the operand of the *lda* instruction on *databus*. This 8-bit data passes through *dbus* and becomes available on the *a_side* of *alu*. The controller instructs *alu* to place its *a_side* input on its output, and it causes *shu* to pass its input to its output without shifting. The *lda* operand now appears on *obus*, the controller enables the loading of *ac*, and on the edge of the clock, the operand of *lda* is clocked into the accumulator.

Execution of other instructions is done in a manner similar to the procedure described for *lda*. For the *and*, *add*, and *sub* instructions, when the operand of instruction becomes available on the *a_side* of *alu*, the controller signals *alu* to perform *and*, *add*, or *sub* operations instead of passing the operand through to the output of *alu*. For indirect addressing, the controller causes an extra read from the memory before performing the operation.

9.5 DATAFLOW DESCRIPTION OF PARWAN

The behavioral description in Section 9.2 presented an unambiguous description of the correct operation of Parwan. Hardware implementation of this machine, or even its bussing structure, is not apparent from the description in Figure 9.15. This section presents a description of Parwan which is closer to its actual hardware. This description consists of the structural interconnection of the data registers and logic units and it uses a dataflow description for the controller. Since the overall description deals with controlling the flow of data through registers and buses, we refer to it as the dataflow description of Parwan.

9.5.1 Data and Control Partitioning

Figure 9.28 shows data and control partitioning that we use for the dataflow description of Parwan. The data section contains the interconnection specification of CPU components. This includes instantiation of individual components and conditional placement of their outputs on appropriate buses. The control section uses external control signals and signals from the data section, and generates signals to control conditional assignments of data into registers or buses of the data section.

Figure 9.29 shows a list of control signals generated by the control section to control data movement in the data section. The names are chosen according to the

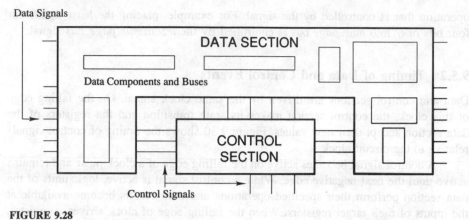

FIGURE 9.28
Data and control sections of Parwan CPU.

RELATED TO:	SIGNAL CATEGORY AND NAME
Register control signals	
AC	load_ac, zero_ac
IR	load_ir
PC	increment_pc, load_page_pc, load_offset_pc, reset_pc
MAR	load_page_mar, load_offset_mar
SR	load_sr, cm_carry_sr
Bus connection control signals	
MAR_BUS	pc_on_mar_page_bus, ir_on_mar_page_bus
	pc_on_mar_offset_bus, dbus_on_mar_offset_bus
DBUS	pc_offset_on_dbus, obus_on_dbus, databus_on_dbus
ADBUS	mar_on_adbus
DATABUS	dbus_on_databus
Logic unit function control signals	
SHU	arith_shift_left, arith_shift_right
ALU	alu_code
Memory control and other external signals	
Etc.	read_mem, write_mem, interrupt

FIGURE 9.29
Inputs and outputs of Parwan control section.

operation that is controlled by the signal. For example, placing the least significant four bits of *ir* into *mar_page* bus is controlled by the *ir_on_mar_page_bus* signal.

9.5.2 Timing of Data and Control Events

Data and control sections are driven by the same clock signal. On the falling edge of this clock, the control section makes its state transition and the registers of the data section accept their new values. Figure 9.30 shows the timing of control signals relative to the circuit clock.

A control signal becomes active on the falling edge of a clock pulse and remains active until the next negative edge. While a control signal is active, logic units of the data section perform their specified operations and their results become available at the inputs of their target registers. When the falling edge of clock arrives, a register, whose load input is enabled, accepts its input. The width of control signals allow for all logic unit and bus propagation delays.

The control section consists of master-slave D-type flip-flops that accept their inputs when the clock becomes '1' and change their outputs when clock returns to '0'. Control flip-flops and data registers are synchronized with the falling edge of the clock.

9.5.3 General Description Methodology

The Parwan description is based on the partitioning in Figure 9.28. The individual components of the data section, shown in Figure 9.27, are independently described at the behavioral or dataflow level. We describe the data section by wiring its components, and bussing component outputs according to the bus structure in Figure 9.27. After the completion of the data section, a state machine description style is used for the description of the control section of Parwan. An overall description wires the data and the control sections.

9.5.4 Description of Components

Components of the data section are *alu*, *shu*, *sr*, *ac*, *ir*, *pc*, and *mar*, and are described in this order. The *basic_utilities* package in the *cmos* library and the *par_utilities* in the *par_library* are used for describing these components. We assume that these components are compiled into the *par_dataflow* VHDL design library.

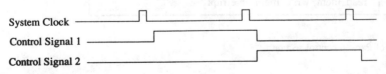

FIGURE 9.30
Timing of control signals.

9.5.4.1 ARITHMETIC LOGIC UNIT. The *alu* has two 8-bit operands, three select lines, four flag inputs, eight data outputs, and four flag outputs. The three select lines select the operation of *alu* according to the table in Figure 9.31. This figure also shows the flags that may be affected by *alu* operations.

Figure 9.32 shows the logic symbol for Parwan *alu*. This symbol follows the IEEE standard notation. To implement this *alu*, the *alu_operations* package in Figure 9.33 is used in addition to *basic_utilities* and *par_utilities*. This package defines a

S2	S1	S0	OPERATION	FLAGS
0	0	0	a AND b	zn
0	0	1	NOT b	zn
1	0	0	a	zn
1	0	1	b PLUS a	vczn
1	1	0	b	zn
1	1	1	b MINUS a	vczn

FIGURE 9.31
Operations and flags of *alu*.

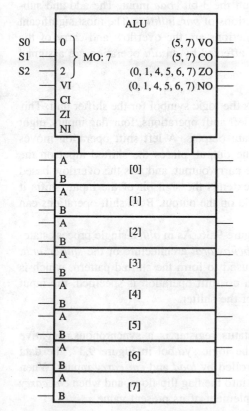

FIGURE 9.32
Logic symbol for Parwan *alu*.

```
LIBRARY cmos;
USE cmos.basic_utilities.ALL;
PACKAGE alu_operations IS
    CONSTANT a_and_b  : qit_vector (2 DOWNTO 0) := "000";
    CONSTANT b_compl  : qit_vector (2 DOWNTO 0) := "001";
    CONSTANT a_input  : qit_vector (2 DOWNTO 0) := "100";
    CONSTANT a_add_b  : qit_vector (2 DOWNTO 0) := "101";
    CONSTANT b_input  : qit_vector (2 DOWNTO 0) := "110";
    CONSTANT a_sub_b  : qit_vector (2 DOWNTO 0) := "111";
END alu_operations;
```

FIGURE 9.33
Package declaration for the *alu_operations* package.

name equivalent for the operation codes of *alu* and is merely used for readability of *alu* code.

Figure 9.34 shows the VHDL description for the Parwan *alu*. The type of the elements of all inputs and outputs is *qit* of the *basic_utilities* package. Types *nibble* and *byte* are defined in *par_utilities* and are used in the entity declaration of the *arithmatic_logic_unit*. In the *behavioral* architecture of *arithmatic_logic_unit*, a case statement selects the *alu* operations based on the 3-bit *code* input. The add and subtract operations use *add_cv* and *sub_cv* functions of *par_utilities*. The most significant bits of the *qit_vector* returned by these functions are the overflow and carry of the corresponding operations. Flag outputs not affected by an *alu* operation are assigned to the values of the input flags.

9.5.4.2 SHIFTER UNIT. Figure 9.35 shows the logic symbol for the shifter unit. This unit has two mode lines that select right or left shift operations, four flag inputs, eight data inputs, four flag outputs, and eight data outputs. A left shift operation moves a '0' into the least significant position of the output, places the shifted input on the output, moves the most significant bit to the carry output, and sets the overflow based on a sign change. A right shift operation extends the sign bit of the input, shifts it one place to the right, and makes it available on the output. Both shift operations can affect negative and zero flag.

The description of *shu* is shown in Figure 9.36. As in *alu*, a single process statement constitutes the statement part of the *behavioral* architecture of the *shifter_unit*. For shifting, the concatenation operator is used to form the shifted pattern, which is assigned to the temporary variable *t*. When no shift operation is specified, the input data and flags are assigned to the outputs of the shifter.

9.5.4.3 STATUS REGISTER UNIT. The status register is a synchronous, negative edge-trigger, 4-bit register. As shown in the logic symbol in Figure 9.37, the data loaded into the flags is synchronously controlled by *load* and *cm_carry* inputs. When *load* is active, all four input flags are loaded into the flag flip-flops, and when *cm_carry* is active, the *c* flag is loaded with the complement of its present value.

```
ENTITY arithmatic_logic_unit IS
    PORT (a_side, b_side : IN byte; code : IN qit_vector (2 DOWNTO 0);
          in_flags : IN nibble; z_out : OUT byte;  out_flags : OUT nibble);
END arithmatic_logic_unit;
--
ARCHITECTURE behavioral OF arithmatic_logic_unit IS
BEGIN
    coding: PROCESS (a_side, b_side, code)
        VARIABLE t : qit_vector (9 DOWNTO 0);
        VARIABLE v, c, z, n : qit;
        ALIAS n_flag_in : qit IS in_flags(0);
        ALIAS z_flag_in : qit IS in_flags(1);
        ALIAS c_flag_in : qit IS in_flags(2);
        ALIAS v_flag_in : qit IS in_flags(3);
    BEGIN
        CASE code IS
            WHEN a_add_b =>
                t := add_cv (b_side, a_side, c_flag_in);
                c := t(8);  v := t(9);  -- other flags are set at the end
            WHEN a_sub_b =>
                t := sub_cv (b_side, a_side, c_flag_in);
                c := t(8);  v := t(9);
            WHEN a_and_b =>
                t (7 DOWNTO 0) := a_side AND b_side;
                c := c_flag_in;  v := v_flag_in;
            WHEN a_input  =>
                t (7 DOWNTO 0) := a_side;
                c := c_flag_in;  v := v_flag_in;
            WHEN b_input  =>
                t (7 DOWNTO 0) := b_side;
                c := c_flag_in;  v := v_flag_in;
            WHEN b_compl =>
                t (7 DOWNTO 0) := NOT b_side;
                c := c_flag_in;  v := v_flag_in;
            WHEN OTHERS => NULL;
        END CASE;
        n := t(7);
        z := set_if_zero (t);
        z_out <= t (7 DOWNTO 0);
        out_flags <= v & c & z & n;
    END PROCESS coding;
END behavioral;
```

FIGURE 9.34
Behavioral description of Parwan arithmatic logic unit.

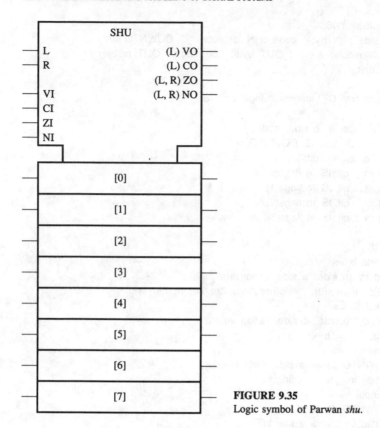

FIGURE 9.35
Logic symbol of Parwan *shu*.

The VHDL description of the status register, shown in Figure 9.38, uses a process statement that is sensitive to the input clock. The *internal_state* variable in the *behavioral* architecture of the *status_register_unit* holds the value of the register. On the falling edge of the clock, this variable is assigned to the nibble output of the status register.

9.5.4.4 ACCUMULATOR. The accumulator of Parwan is an 8-bit register with synchronous loading and zeroing inputs. As shown in Figure 9.39, loading of external data into the register is done on the falling edge of the clock when the *load* input is active and the *zero* input is disabled. Simultaneous activation of the *load* and *zero* inputs causes synchronous resetting of the register.

Figure 9.40 shows the dataflow description of the accumulator. In the *dataflow* architecture of the *accumulator_unit*, when *load* is '1', on the falling edge of *ck*, a guarded signal assignment assigns zero or the *i8* input to the 8-bit output, *o8*.

9.5.4.5 INSTRUCTION REGISTER. The instruction register (*ir*) is an 8-bit synchronous register with an active high load input. The load input enables the clock and causes the register to be loaded on the falling edge of the clock input. The logic symbol of *ir* is shown in Figure 9.41.

```
┌ENTITY shifter_unit IS
│   PORT (alu_side : IN byte;   arith_shift_left, arith_shift_right : IN qit;
│           in_flags : IN nibble; obus\kern1pt_side : OUT byte;  out\kern1pt_flags : OUT
nibble);
└END shifter\kern1pt_unit;
--
┌ARCHITECTURE behavioral OF shifter_unit IS
├BEGIN
│   ┌coding: PROCESS (alu_side, arith_shift_left, arith_shift_right)
│   │   VARIABLE t : qit_vector (7 DOWNTO 0);
│   │   VARIABLE v, c, z, n : qit;
│   │   ALIAS n_flag_in : qit IS in_flags(0);
│   │   ALIAS z_flag_in : qit IS in_flags(1);
│   │   ALIAS c_flag_in : qit IS in_flags(2);
│   │   ALIAS v_flag_in : qit IS in_flags(3);
│   ├BEGIN
│   │   IF arith_shift_right = '0' AND arith_shift_left = '0' THEN
│   │       t := alu_side (7 DOWNTO 0);
│   │       n := n_flag_in;
│   │       z := z_flag_in;
│   │       c := c_flag_in;
│   │       v := v_flag_in;
│   │   ELSIF arith_shift_left = '1' THEN
│   │       t := alu_side (6 DOWNTO 0) & '0';
│   │       n := t (7);
│   │       z := set_if_zero (t);
│   │       c := alu_side (7);
│   │       v := alu_side (6) XOR alu_side (7);
│   │   ELSIF arith_shift_right = '1' THEN
│   │       t := alu_side (7) & alu_side (7 DOWNTO 1);
│   │       n := t (7);
│   │       z := set_if_zero (t);
│   │       c := c_flag_in;
│   │       v := v_flag_in;
│   │   END IF;
│   │   obus_side <= t;
│   │   out_flags <= v & c & z & n;
│   └END PROCESS coding;
└END behavioral;
```

FIGURE 9.36
Behavioral description of the Parwan shifter unit.

Figure 9.42 shows the VHDL description of the instruction register that corresponds to its logic symbol. In the *dataflow* architecture of *instruction_register_unit*, a guarded block statement is used to gate the input clock with the *load* input.

9.5.4.6 PROGRAM COUNTER. The program counter is a 12-bit synchronous up-counter with one reset and two load inputs. The *load_page* input synchronously loads

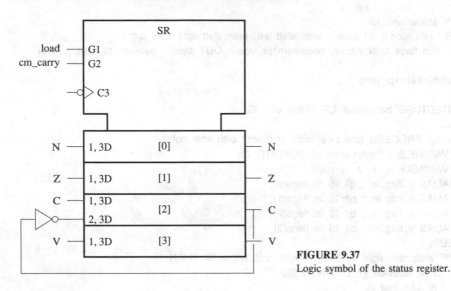

FIGURE 9.37
Logic symbol of the status register.

```
ENTITY status_register_unit IS
    PORT (in_flags : IN nibble; out_status : OUT nibble;
          load, cm_carry, ck : IN qit );
END status_register_unit;
--
ARCHITECTURE behavioral OF status_register_unit IS
BEGIN
    PROCESS (ck)
        VARIABLE internal_state : nibble := "0000";
        ALIAS internal_c : qit IS internal_state (2);
    BEGIN
        IF (ck = '0') THEN
            IF (load = '1') THEN
                internal_state := in_flags;
            ELSIF (cm_carry = '1') THEN
                internal_c := NOT internal_c;
            END IF;
            out_status <= internal_state;
        END IF;
    END PROCESS;
END behavioral;
```

FIGURE 9.38
Behavioral description of the Parwan status register.

input data into the most significant four bits and the *load_offset* loads input data into
the least significant eight bits of the register. The synchronous reset input resets the
entire register. The logic symbol of this unit appears in Figure 9.43.

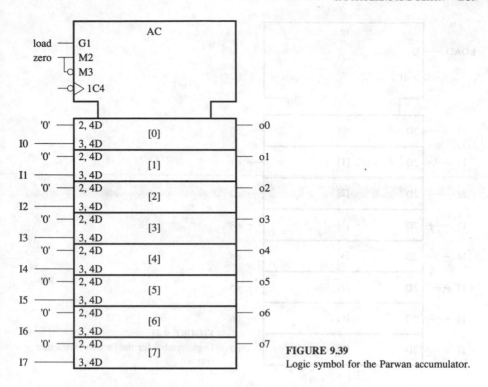

FIGURE 9.39
Logic symbol for the Parwan accumulator.

```
ENTITY accumulator_unit IS
   PORT (i8 : IN byte; o8 : OUT byte; load, zero, ck : IN qit);
END accumulator_unit;
--
ARCHITECTURE dataflow OF accumulator_unit IS
BEGIN
   enable : BLOCK (load = '1')
   BEGIN
      clocking : BLOCK ( (ck = '0' AND NOT ck'STABLE) AND GUARD )
      BEGIN
         o8 <= GUARDED "00000000" WHEN zero = '1' ELSE i8;
      END BLOCK clocking;
   END BLOCK enable;
END dataflow;
```

FIGURE 9.40
Dataflow description of the Parwan accumulator.

The VHDL description of the program counter in Figure 9.44 consists of a process statement that is sensitive to the input clock, *ck*. This code gives the highest priority to *reset*, followed by *increment*, and then by the load inputs. The *behavioral* architecture of the *program_counter_unit* allows for the simultaneous loading of page

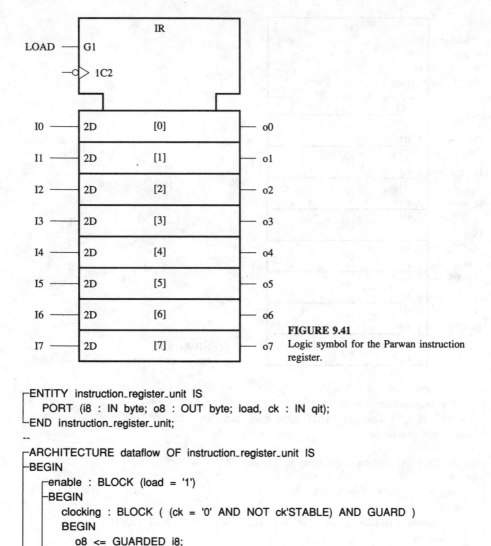

FIGURE 9.41
Logic symbol for the Parwan instruction register.

```
ENTITY instruction_register_unit IS
    PORT (i8 : IN byte; o8 : OUT byte; load, ck : IN qit);
END instruction_register_unit;
--
ARCHITECTURE dataflow OF instruction_register_unit IS
BEGIN
    enable : BLOCK (load = '1')
    BEGIN
        clocking : BLOCK ( (ck = '0' AND NOT ck'STABLE) AND GUARD )
        BEGIN
            o8 <= GUARDED i8;
        END BLOCK clocking;
    END BLOCK enable;
END dataflow;
```

FIGURE 9.42
Dataflow description of the Parwan instruction register.

and offset parts of the register. The *inc* function of the *basic_utilities* package performs the incrementing of the internal state of this description.

9.5.4.7 MEMORY ADDRESS REGISTER. The memory address register (*mar*) is a 12-bit register with two synchronous load inputs. The *load_page* input loads the par-

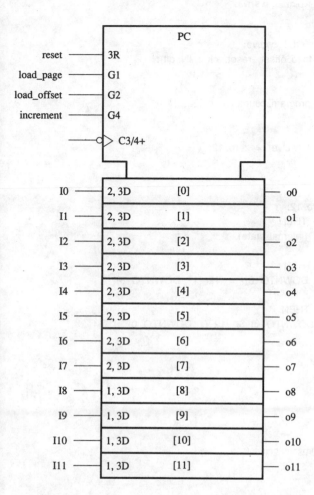

FIGURE 9.43
Logic symbol for the Parwan
program counter.

allel data into the most significant nibble of the register and the *load_offset* loads
data into its least significant byte. The logic symbol of this unit is presented in Figure 9.45.

Figure 9.46 shows the VHDL description of *mar*. A process statement that is
sensitive to events on *ck* constitutes the statement part of the *behavioral* architecture of
memory_address_register. The if statement in the statement part of this process allows
simultaneous loading of *mar* page and offset parts. The *internal_state* that holds the
contents of the register is assigned to the output of this unit on the falling edge of
each clock pulse.

9.5.5 Data Section of Parwan

We completed our description of the components in the data section of Parwan in the
previous section. The data section specifies the interconnection of these components
and defines the Parwan's bussing structure. The inputs of this unit are the data bus,

```
ENTITY program_counter_unit IS
    PORT (i12 : IN twelve; o12 : OUT twelve;
            increment, load_page, load_offset, reset, ck : IN qit);
END program_counter_unit;
--
ARCHITECTURE behavioral OF program_counter_unit IS
BEGIN
    PROCESS (ck)
        VARIABLE internal_state : twelve := zero_12;
    BEGIN
        IF (ck = '0' ) THEN
            IF reset = '1' THEN
                internal_state := zero_12;
            ELSIF increment = '1' THEN
                internal_state := inc (internal_state);
            ELSE
                IF load_page = '1' THEN
                    internal_state (11 DOWNTO 8) := i12 (11 DOWNTO 8);
                END IF;
                IF load_offset = '1' THEN
                    internal_state (7 DOWNTO 0) := i12 (7 DOWNTO 0);
                END IF;
            END IF;
            o12 <= internal_state;
        END IF;
    END PROCESS;
END behavioral;
```

FIGURE 9.44
Behavioral description of the Parwan program counter.

the clock signal, and the signals from the control section. Control signals specify the operation of the components in the data section, control their clocking, and enable bussing of data to their inputs. The outputs of the data section are the data and address buses, bits of *ir*, and four status flags. The entity declaration in the Parwan data section (*par_data_path*) is shown in Figure 9.47.

In the port clause of this figure, *databus* is declared as a bidirectional bus that uses the *wiring* resolution function. Bidirectionality enables data in and out of *par_data_path* via this bus and the use of the resolution function allows all devices connected to the bus to drive it simultaneously. A device outputting data via this bus drives it with the output data, while all other devices drive its bits with high impedance 'Z'.

The names of the *par_data_path* control inputs are the same as those we use for the inputs of the control section and the same as those shown in Figure 9.29. A register control signal name is formed by appending the register name to the name of the register signal. For example, *load_page_mar* input of *par_data_path* connects to the *load_page* input of *mar* register in Section 9.5.4.7. A bus connection signal name

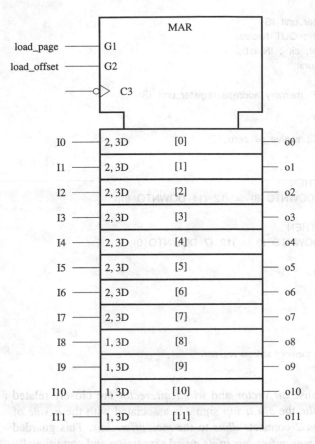

	MAR	
load_page ——	G1	
load_offset ——	G2	
——▷	C3	

I0 ——	2, 3D	[0]	—— o0
I1 ——	2, 3D	[1]	—— o1
I2 ——	2, 3D	[2]	—— o2
I3 ——	2, 3D	[3]	—— o3
I4 ——	2, 3D	[4]	—— o4
I5 ——	2, 3D	[5]	—— o5
I6 ——	2, 3D	[6]	—— o6
I7 ——	2, 3D	[7]	—— o7
I8 ——	1, 3D	[8]	—— o8
I9 ——	1, 3D	[9]	—— o9
I10 ——	1, 3D	[10]	—— o10
I11 ——	1, 3D	[11]	—— o11

FIGURE 9.45
Logic symbol for the Parwan
memory address register.

is formed by the source of the bus followed by "*on*" followed by the name of the bus, e.g., *source_on_bus*.

The declarative part of the *structural* architecture of *par_data_path*, in Figure 9.48 includes the declaration of the data section components and the configuration specification of these components. The declared components are bound to their respective descriptions in Section 9.5.4. This declarative part also contains declarations for buses and signals for connecting components of the data section. The 8-bit *dbus* and the 12-bit *mar_bus* are declared as guarded signals which implies selection logic for their multiple sources.

The statement part of the *structural* architecture of *par_data_path*, shown in Figure 9.49, uses component instantiations, signal assignments, and guarded blocks to specify the connections shown in Figure 9.27. The first part of Figure 9.49 shows the connection of *dbus* to the *a_side* of *alu*, *mar_offset_bus*, and to *databus*. Statements used for these connections are labeled *dbus1*, *dbus2*, and *dbus3*, respectively.

For connecting *dbus* to *alu*, a *qit_vector* type conversion converts the resolved *dbus* type (*wired_qit_vector*) to *qit_vector* for the *alu_a_inp* target. This explicit type conversion is necessary because the base types of *qit_vector* and *wired_qit_vector* are

```
ENTITY memory_address_register_unit IS
    PORT (i12 : IN twelve; o12 : OUT twelve;
          load_page, load_offset, ck : IN qit);
END memory_address_register_unit;
--
ARCHITECTURE behavioral OF memory_address_register_unit IS
BEGIN
    PROCESS (ck)
        VARIABLE internal_state : twelve := zero_12;
    BEGIN
        IF (ck = '0' ) THEN
            IF load_page = '1' THEN
                internal_state (11 DOWNTO 8) := i12 (11 DOWNTO 8);
            END IF;
            IF load_offset = '1' THEN
                internal_state (7 DOWNTO 0) := i12 (7 DOWNTO 0);
            END IF;
            o12 <= internal_state;
        END IF;
    END PROCESS;
END behavioral;
```

FIGURE 9.46
Behavioral description of the Parwan memory address register.

different; this is possible because *qit_vector* and *wired_qit_vector* are closely related types. In the instantiation of *alu*, the *alu_a_inp* signal is associated with the *a_side* of *alu*. The statement labeled *dbus2* connects *dbus* to the *mar_offset_bus*. This guarded block statement uses *dbus_on_mar_offset_bus* in its guard expression and conditionally connects *dbus* to the least significant bits of *mar_bus*. This assignment corresponds to the right hollow triangle shown at the input of *mar_offset_bus* in Figure 9.27. Connection of *dbus* to *databus* is done by the statement labeled *dbus3*, which is also a guarded block. The assignment in this block corresponds to the hollow triangle in Figure 9.27 that connects Parwan to its memory. In the latter two assignments, type conversions were not needed since the types of both sides of the assignments were *wired_qit_vector*. Both these assignments are guarded because their targets are multi-source buses.

In the part of Figure 9.49 that describes register connections, a Parwan register is instantiated and its connections are specified. For example, the instantiation of *ir* (r2: ir) is followed by assignments that place its outputs (*ir_out*) on *ir_lines* and *mar_page_bus*. The statement labeled *ir1* connects all eight bits of *ir* outputs to the *ir_lines* outputs of *par_data_path*. The statement labeled *ir2* is a guarded block statement that uses *ir_on_mar_page_bus* in its guard expression. The guarded signal assignment within this block conditionally places the least significant nibble of the output of *ir* on the most significant nibble of *mar_bus* (*mar_page_bus*). In this assignment, the type of *ir_out* signal is converted from *qit_vector* to the type of its target bus by using the *wired_qit_vector* type conversion.

```
ENTITY par_data_path IS
  PORT (databus : INOUT wired_byte BUS := "ZZZZZZZZ";
              adbus : OUT twelve;
              clk : IN qit;
              -- register controls:
              load_ac, zero_ac,
              load_ir,
              increment_pc, load_page_pc, load_offset_pc, reset_pc,
              load_page_mar, load_offset_mar,
              load_sr, cm_carry_sr,
              -- bus connections:
              pc_on_mar_page_bus, ir_on_mar_page_bus,
              pc_on_mar_offset_bus, dbus_on_mar_offset_bus,
              pc_offset_on_dbus, obus_on_dbus, databus_on_dbus,
              mar_on_adbus,
              dbus_on_databus,
              -- logic unit function control inputs:
              arith_shift_left, arith_shift_right : IN qit;
              alu_code : IN qit_vector (2 DOWNTO 0);
              -- outputs to the controller:
              ir_lines : OUT byte; status : OUT nibble
              );
END par_data_path;
```

FIGURE 9.47
Entity declaration of the Parwan data section.

The last part of Figure 9.49 contains the instantiation of the *alu* and *shu* combinational logic units. The port map aspects in these instantiations specify connections of these units according to the structure in Figure 9.27.

9.5.6 Control Section of Parwan

The description of the Parwan control section consists of a series of states each of which keeps its selected control signals active for exactly one clock period. These states are states of a state machine. In the description of this state machine, we use a style similar to the one from the *multiple_state_machine* in Chapter 7 (Section 7.2.2, Figure 7.37). In the example presented in Chapter 7, a single block statement whose guard expression was used to detect the edge of the clock, contained all the blocks for the states of the state machine. With the Parwan controller, however, the clock edge detection is repeated in every state. A hardware implication of this description style or the description style in Chapter 7 is one in which a flip-flop corresponds to each of the states, and a combinatorial logic block at the output of each flip-flop provides the necessary conditions for activating other flip-flops and for issuing control signals for the data section or the memory. Figure 9.50 shows a typical control flip-flop hardware. The logic block in this figure is designated by a bubble.

```
ARCHITECTURE structural OF par_data_path IS
    COMPONENT ac
        PORT (i8: IN byte; o8: OUT byte; load, zero, ck: IN qit);
    END COMPONENT;
    FOR r1: ac USE ENTITY WORK.accumulator_unit (dataflow);
    COMPONENT ir
        PORT (i8: IN byte; o8: OUT byte; load, ck: IN qit);
    END COMPONENT;
    FOR r2: ir USE ENTITY WORK.instruction_register_unit (dataflow);
    COMPONENT pc
        PORT (i12 : IN twelve; o12 : OUT twelve;
              increment, load_page, load_offset, reset, ck : IN qit);
    END COMPONENT;
    FOR r3: pc USE ENTITY WORK.program_counter_unit (behavioral);
    COMPONENT mar
        PORT (i12 : IN twelve; o12 : OUT twelve;
              load_page, load_offset, ck : IN qit);
    END COMPONENT;
    FOR r4: mar USE ENTITY WORK.memory_address_register_unit (behavioral);
    COMPONENT sr
        PORT (in_flags : IN nibble; out_status : OUT nibble;
              load, cm_carry, ck : IN qit );
    END COMPONENT;
    FOR r5 : sr USE ENTITY WORK.status_register_unit (behavioral);
    COMPONENT alu
        PORT (a_side, b_side : IN byte; code : IN qit_vector; in_flags : IN nibble;
              z_out : OUT byte;  out_flags : OUT nibble);
    END COMPONENT;
    FOR l1 : alu USE ENTITY WORK.arithmatic_logic_unit (behavioral);
    COMPONENT shu
        PORT (alu_side : IN byte; arith_shift_left, arith_shift_right : IN qit;
              in_flags : IN nibble; obus_side : OUT byte;  out_flags : OUT nibble);
    END COMPONENT;
    FOR l2 : shu USE ENTITY WORK.shifter_unit (behavioral);
    SIGNAL ac_out, ir_out, alu_out, obus : byte;
    SIGNAL alu_a_inp : byte;
    SIGNAL pc_out, mar_out : twelve;
    SIGNAL dbus : wired_byte BUS;
    SIGNAL alu_flags, shu_flags, sr_out : nibble;
    SIGNAL mar_bus : wired_twelve BUS;
    SIGNAL mar_inp : twelve;
```

FIGURE 9.48
Declarative part of the *par_data_path structural* architecture.

The inputs of logic blocks come from other state flip-flops and from external inputs that influence state transitions in the control section. The outputs of logic blocks are the control signals, some of which become inputs to the data section. State flip-flops issue various control signals by providing active sources for them. If several

```
┌BEGIN
│   ┌   -- bus connections --
│   │   ┌dbus1: alu_a_inp <= qit_vector (dbus);
│   │   ┌dbus2: BLOCK (dbus_on_mar_offset_bus = '1')
│   │   ├BEGIN   mar_bus (7 DOWNTO 0) <= GUARDED dbus;
│   │   └END BLOCK dbus2;
│   │   ┌dbus3: BLOCK (dbus_on_databus = '1')
│   │   ├BEGIN   databus <= GUARDED dbus;
│   └───└END BLOCK dbus3;
│   ┌obus1: BLOCK (obus_on_dbus = '1')
│   ├BEGIN   dbus <= GUARDED wired_qit_vector (obus);
│   └END BLOCK obus1;
│   ┌databus1: BLOCK (databus_on_dbus = '1')
│   ├BEGIN   dbus <= GUARDED databus;
│   └END BLOCK databus1;
│   └mar_bus1: mar_inp <= qit_vector (mar_bus);
│   ┌   -- register connections --
│   ├───r1: ac PORT MAP (obus, ac_out, load_ac, zero_ac, clk);
│   ├───r2: ir PORT MAP (obus, ir_out, load_ir, clk);
│   ├─ir1: ir_lines <= ir_out;
│   ├─ir2: BLOCK (ir_on_mar_page_bus = '1')
│   ├BEGIN
│   │       mar_bus (11 DOWNTO 8) <= GUARDED wired_qit_vector (ir_out (3 DOWNTO 0));
│   └───└END BLOCK ir2;
```

FIGURE 9.49
Declarative part of the *par_data_path structural* Architecture. (*continued on following page.*)

control flip-flops issue a control signal, the actual control signal is formed by ORing its various sources together. The *par_data_path* unit uses the result of this OR function as input. Signals used to activate control flip-flops also may have multiple sources; therefore, OR functions also are needed at the inputs of control flip-flops.

Figure 9.51 shows an example for the structure of the control section of the Parwan CPU. As shown in this example, all states are synchronized with the same clock and their outputs contribute to the logic for issuing control signals or for activating other control flip-flops. In this figure, state i is conditionally activated by itself or by state k. State i conditionally activates state j, and state k always becomes active after the clock period during which state j is active. Control signal *csx* is always issued when state k is active, or when state i is active and certain conditions are held on a, b, and c inputs. Control signal *csy* becomes active when control is in state j, and certain conditions are held on the d and e inputs.

Figure 9.52 shows the entity declaration of the Parwan control section. Its generic clause contains delay values for memory read and write signals. Its port clause includes outputs to the data section, *ir_lines*, status inputs from the data section, and external memory handshaking and interrupt lines.

The declaration part of the dataflow architecture of *par_control_unit* shown in Figure 9.53 declares a guarded signal for each of the control outputs of the control

```
r3: pc PORT MAP
    (mar_out, pc_out, increment_pc, load_page_pc, load_offset_pc, reset_pc, clk);
pc1: BLOCK (pc_on_mar_page_bus = '1')
BEGIN
    mar_bus (11 DOWNTO 8) <= GUARDED wired_qit_vector (pc_out (11 DOWNTO 8));
END BLOCK pc1;
pc2: BLOCK (pc_on_mar_offset_bus = '1')
BEGIN
    mar_bus (7 DOWNTO 0) <= GUARDED wired_qit_vector (pc_out %(7 DOWNTO 0));
END BLOCK pc2;
pc3: BLOCK (pc_offset_on_dbus = '1')
BEGIN
    dbus <= GUARDED wired_qit_vector (pc_out (7 DOWNTO 0));
END BLOCK pc3;
r4: mar PORT MAP (mar_inp, mar_out, load_page_mar, load_offset_mar, clk);
mar1: BLOCK (mar_on_adbus = '1')
BEGIN   adbus <= GUARDED mar_out;
END BLOCK mar1;
r5: sr PORT MAP (shu_flags, sr_out, load_sr, cm_carry_sr, clk);
sr1: status <= sr_out;
    -- connection of logical and register structures --
l1: alu PORT MAP (alu_a_inp, ac_out, alu_code, sr_out, alu_out, alu_flags);
l2: shu PORT MAP (alu_out, arith_shift_left, arith_shift_right, alu_flags, obus, shu_flags);
END structural;
```

FIGURE 9.49
Statement part of the *par_data_path structural* architecture. (*continued from previous page*)

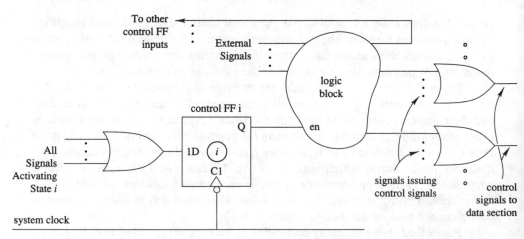

FIGURE 9.50
Typical hardware surrounding a control flip-flop. The logic block in this figure is designated by a bubble.

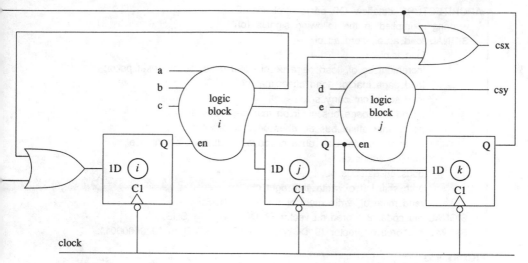

FIGURE 9.51
Example for the structure of Parwan control section.

```
ENTITY par_control_unit IS
   GENERIC (read_delay, write_delay : TIME := 3 NS);
   PORT (clk : IN qit;
            -- register control signals:
            load_ac, zero_ac,
            load_ir,
            increment_pc, load_page_pc, load_offset_pc, reset_pc,
            load_page_mar, load_offset_mar,
            load_sr, cm_carry_sr,
            -- bus connection control signals:
            pc_on_mar_page_bus, ir_on_mar_page_bus,
            pc_on_mar_offset_bus, dbus_on_mar_offset_bus,
            pc_offset_on_dbus, obus_on_dbus, databus_on_dbus,
            mar_on_adbus,
            dbus_on_databus,
            -- logic unit function control outputs:
            arith_shift_left, arith_shift_right : OUT qit;
            alu_code : OUT qit_vector (2 DOWNTO 0);
            -- inputs from the data section:
            ir_lines : IN byte; status : IN nibble;
            -- memory control and other external signals:
            read_mem, write_mem : OUT qit; interrupt : IN qit
            );
END par_control_unit;
```

FIGURE 9.52
Parwan control section entity declaration.

```
ARCHITECTURE dataflow OF par_control_unit IS
  -- oring is implied in the following signals (oi)
  SIGNAL load_ac_oi, zero_ac_oi,
         load_ir_oi,
         increment_pc_oi, load_page_pc_oi, load_offset_pc_oi, reset_pc_oi,
         load_page_mar_oi, load_offset_mar_oi,
         load_sr_oi, cm_carry_sr_oi,
         pc_on_mar_page_bus_oi, ir_on_mar_page_bus_oi,
         pc_on_mar_offset_bus_oi, dbus_on_mar_offset_bus_oi,
         pc_offset_on_dbus_oi, obus_on_dbus_oi, databus_on_dbus_oi,
         mar_on_adbus_oi,
         dbus_on_databus_oi,
         arith_shift_left_oi, arith_shift_right_oi,
         read_mem_oi, write_mem_oi : ored_qit BUS;
  SIGNAL alu_code_oi : ored_qit_vector (2 DOWNTO 0) BUS;
  SIGNAL s : ored_qit_vector (9 DOWNTO 1) REGISTER := "000000001";
```

FIGURE 9.53
Declarative part of the *par_control_unit dataflow* architecture.

section. These signals use the *oring* resolution function in the *basic_utilities* package. The "*_oi*" as the last part of their names identifies them as signals on which oring is implied. The *oring* resolution function ORs multiple drivers on these signals and uses the result for the signal value. Signal *s* of this figure is also a guarded signal with *oring* resolution function. Nine bits of *s* represent the states of the control section, and the *oring* resolution function accounts for the OR gates at the inputs of the state flip-flops.

The statement part of the *dataflow* architecture of *par_control_unit* begins with the assignment of *oring* resolved signals to the actual outputs of the *par_control_unit* shown in Figure 9.54. In fact, this connects the outputs of the implied OR gates to the actual outputs of the control section.

In the remainder of this architecture, guarded block statements for describing the states of the Parwan controller are used. The guard expression of the block statement of state i is $s(i)='1'$, where s is the resolved signal designated for representation of the states of the controller (see the style used in Section 7.2.2).

Figure 9.55 shows the *s1* block for state 1. In this block, a fetch begins by placing *pc* on *mar* bus, and then initiating the transfer of this data into *mar*. If the interrupt input is active, the *pc* reset input is issued and control returns to state 1. If the CPU is not interrupted, state 2 becomes active on the falling edge of the clock. Also on this edge of the clock, *mar* receives its new value. In coding the data registers and control states, we have made certain that they are all synchronized with the falling edge of the clock.

When in state 2, the *mar* bus has received the new value that was scheduled for it in state 1. State 2 of Parwan, as shown in Figure 9.56, completes the fetch operation by placing *mar* on *adbus* and issuing a *read_mem*. The contents of memory that appear on *databus* must be placed in *ir*. For this purpose, the *databus_on_dbus* control signal is issued, the *a_input* function of *alu* is selected, and the load input of *ir* (*load_ir*) is enabled. On the edge of the clock, control state 3 becomes active and

```
┌─BEGIN
│   -- implied or assignments to output signals
│   load_ac <= load_ac_oi;
│   zero_ac <= zero_ac_oi;
│   load_ir <= load_ir_oi;
│   increment_pc <= increment_pc_oi;
│   load_page_pc <= load_page_pc_oi;
│   load_offset_pc <= load_offset_pc_oi;
│   reset_pc <= reset_pc_oi;
│   load_page_mar <= load_page_mar_oi;
│   load_offset_mar <= load_offset_mar_oi;
│   load_sr <= load_sr_oi;
│   cm_carry_sr <= cm_carry_sr_oi;
│   pc_on_mar_page_bus <= pc_on_mar_page_bus_oi;
│   ir_on_mar_page_bus <= ir_on_mar_page_bus_oi;
│   pc_on_mar_offset_bus <= pc_on_mar_offset_bus_oi;
│   dbus_on_mar_offset_bus <= dbus_on_mar_offset_bus_oi;
│   pc_offset_on_dbus <= pc_offset_on_dbus_oi;
│   obus_on_dbus <= obus_on_dbus_oi;
│   databus_on_dbus <= databus_on_dbus_oi;
│   mar_on_adbus <= mar_on_adbus_oi;
│   dbus_on_databus <= dbus_on_databus_oi;
│   arith_shift_left <= arith_shift_left_oi;
│   arith_shift_right <= arith_shift_right_oi;
│   read_mem <= read_mem_oi;
│   write_mem <= write_mem_oi;
│   alu_code <= qit_vector (alu_code_oi);
```

FIGURE 9.54
Assigning signals with implied oring to the *par_control_unit* outputs.

ir will have its new value. Also in state 2, the increment function of *pc* is selected so that its value gets incremented on the next falling edge of the clock.

When state 3 becomes active, as shown in Figure 9.57, the newly read instruction is in *ir*. State 3 starts the process of reading the next byte from the memory. At the same time it checks for the number of bytes in the current instruction. If the instruction is a two-byte instruction, the next byte becomes its address and control state 4 is activated to continue the execution of two-byte instructions. On the other hand, if the current instruction is a nonaddress instruction and does not require a second byte, state 3 performs its execution and activates state 2 for fetching the next instruction.

Nonaddress (single-byte) instructions perform operations on the accumulator and flags. For their execution, appropriate *alu* and *shu* functions are selected, and the target register or flag is enabled. For example, for *asr* (arithmetic shift right), the following steps are taken:

1. the *b_input* function of *alu* is selected so that the *alu* output becomes the contents of *ac*,

```
┌s1: BLOCK (s(1) = '1')
├BEGIN -- start of fetch
│   -- pc to mar
│   pc_on_mar_page_bus_oi <= GUARDED '1';
│   pc_on_mar_offset_bus_oi <= GUARDED '1';
│   load_page_mar_oi <= GUARDED '1';
│   load_offset_mar_oi <= GUARDED '1';
│   -- reset pc if interrupt
│   reset_pc_oi <= GUARDED '1' WHEN interrupt = '1' ELSE '0';
│   -- goto 2 if interrupt is off
│   ck: BLOCK ( (clk = '0' AND NOT clk'STABLE) AND GUARD )
│   BEGIN
│       s(1) <= GUARDED '1' WHEN interrupt = '1' ELSE '0';
│       s(2) <= GUARDED '1' WHEN interrupt /= '1' ELSE '0';
│   END BLOCK ck;
└END BLOCK s1;
```

FIGURE 9.55
State 1: starting a fetch.

```
┌s2: BLOCK (s(2) = '1')
├BEGIN -- fetching continues
│   -- read memory into ir
│   │ mar_on_adbus_oi <= GUARDED '1';
│   │ read_mem_oi <= GUARDED '1' AFTER read_delay;
│   │ databus_on_dbus_oi <= GUARDED '1';
│   │ alu_code_oi <= GUARDED ored_qit_vector (a_input);
│   │ load_ir_oi <= GUARDED '1';
│   -- increment pc
│   │ increment_pc_oi <= GUARDED '1';
│   -- goto 3
│   ┌ck: BLOCK ( (clk = '0' AND NOT clk'STABLE) AND GUARD )
│   ├BEGIN
│   │   s(3) <= GUARDED '1';
│   └END BLOCK ck;
└END BLOCK s2;
```

FIGURE 9.56
State 2: completing a fetch.

2. the *arith_shift_right* function of *shu* is selected so that it shifts its inputs (contents of *ac*) one place to the right,

3. the *load_sr* signal (load input of status register) is enabled so that new values of flags, generated by *shu*, are loaded into *sr*, and finally,

4. the load input of *ac* (*load_ac*) is enabled so that this register gets loaded with the output of *shu* (shifted *ac*).

```
┌─s3: BLOCK (s(3) = '1')
├─BEGIN
│    -- pc to mar, for next read
│    pc_on_mar_page_bus_oi <= GUARDED '1';
│    pc_on_mar_offset_bus_oi <= GUARDED '1';
│    load_page_mar_oi <= GUARDED '1';
│    load_offset_mar_oi <= GUARDED '1';
│    -- goto 4 if not single byte instruction
│    ┌─ck: BLOCK ( (clk = '0' AND NOT clk'STABLE) AND GUARD )
│    ├─BEGIN
│    │    s(4) <= GUARDED
│    │        '1' WHEN ir_lines (7 DOWNTO 4) /= "1110" ELSE '0';
│    └─END BLOCK ck;
│    -- perform single byte instructions
│    ┌─sb: BLOCK ( (ir_lines (7 DOWNTO 4) = "1110") AND GUARD)
│    ├─BEGIN
│    │    alu_code_oi <= GUARDED
│    │        ored_qit_vector (b_compl) WHEN ir_lines (1) = '1' ELSE
│    │        ored_qit_vector (b_input);
│    │    arith_shift_left_oi <= GUARDED
│    │        '1' WHEN ir_lines (3 DOWNTO 0) = "1000" ELSE '0';
│    │    arith_shift_right_oi <= GUARDED
│    │      '1' WHEN ir_lines (3 DOWNTO 0) = "1001" ELSE '0';
│    │    load_sr_oi <= GUARDED
│    │        '1' WHEN ( ir_lines (3) = '1' OR ir_lines (1) = '1' ) ELSE '0';
│    │    cm_carry_sr_oi <= GUARDED '1' WHEN ir_lines (2) = '1' ELSE '0';
│    │    load_ac_oi <= GUARDED
│    │        '1' WHEN ( ir_lines (3) = '1' OR ir_lines (1) = '1' OR ir_lines (0)='1' )
│    │                    ELSE '0';
│    │    zero_ac_oi <= GUARDED
│    │        '1' WHEN ( ir_lines (3) = '0' AND ir_lines (0) = '1' ) ELSE '0';
│    │    ck: BLOCK ( (clk = '0' AND NOT clk'STABLE) AND GUARD )
│    │    BEGIN
│    │        s(2) <= GUARDED '1';
│    │    END BLOCK ck;
│    └─END BLOCK sb;
└─END BLOCK s3;
```

FIGURE 9.57
State 3: preparing for address fetch, execution of single byte instructions.

State 4 becomes active when a full-address or a page-address instruction (instructions requiring two bytes) is being executed. The preparations for reading the address byte (second byte of the instruction) were done in state 3. State 4, shown in Figure 9.58, completes the read operation and makes the newly read byte available at the input of the offset part of *mar*. Because *load_offset_mar* has become active, this byte will be clocked into *mar* on the next falling edge of the clock. If the instruction being executed is a full-address instruction (*lda*, *and*, *add*, *sub*, *jmp*, or *sta*), the page number from *ir* becomes available at the input of the page part of *mar* to be clocked

```
┌s4: BLOCK (s(4) = '1')
├BEGIN -- page from ir, offset from next memory makeup 12-bit address
│      -- read memory into mar offset
│      │ mar_on_adbus_oi <= GUARDED '1';
│      │ read_mem_oi <= GUARDED '1' AFTER read_delay;
│      │ databus_on_dbus_oi <= GUARDED '1';
│      │ dbus_on_mar_offset_bus_oi <= GUARDED '1';
│      │ load_offset_mar_oi <= GUARDED '1'; -- completed operand address
│      -- page from ir if not branch or jsr
│      ┌pg: BLOCK ( (ir_lines (7 DOWNTO 6) /= "11") AND GUARD)
│      ├BEGIN
│      │   ir_on_mar_page_bus_oi <= GUARDED '1';
│      │   load_page_mar_oi <= GUARDED '1';
│      │   -- goto 5 for indirect, 6 for direct
│      │   ck: BLOCK ( (clk = '0' AND NOT clk'STABLE) AND GUARD )
│      │   BEGIN
│      │       s(5) <= GUARDED '1' WHEN ir_lines (4) = '1' ELSE '0'; -- indir
│      │       s(6) <= GUARDED '1' WHEN ir_lines (4) = '0' ELSE '0'; -- direct
│      │   END BLOCK ck;
│      └END BLOCK pg;
│      -- keep page in mar_page if jsr or bra (same-page instructions)
│      ┌sp: BLOCK ( (ir_lines (7 DOWNTO 6) = "11") AND GUARD)
│      ├BEGIN
│      │   -- goto 7 for jsr, 9 for bra
│      ├ck: BLOCK ( (clk = '0' AND NOT clk'STABLE) AND GUARD )
│      │   BEGIN
│      │       s(7) <= GUARDED '1' WHEN ir_lines (5) = '0' ELSE '0'; -- jsr
│      │       s(9) <= GUARDED '1' WHEN ir_lines (5) = '1' ELSE '0'; -- bra
│      │   END BLOCK ck;
│      └END BLOCK sp;
│      -- increment pc
│      │ increment_pc_oi <= GUARDED '1';
└END BLOCK s4;
```

FIGURE 9.58
State 4: completing address of full address instructions; branching for indirect, direct, *jsr*, and *branch*.

into this register with the next clock. If the instruction being executed is *jsr* or *bra* (page-address instructions), the *mar_page* register retains its current value. This is because these instructions only address within the current page.

State 4 activates states 5 or 6 for handling indirect or direct addressing modes of full-address instructions and it activates states 7 or 9 for *jsr* or *bra* instructions, respectively.

The falling edge of the clock that activates state 5 also loads a full 12-bit address into *mar*. State 5, shown in Figure 9.59, handles the indirect addressing mode. In this state, the memory location pointed to by *mar* is read on the *databus*, and is made available on the input of the *mar_offset* register. Activation of *load_offset_mar* causes *mar* to be loaded with the byte from the memory on the next negative edge of the

```
┌s5: BLOCK (s(5) = '1')
├BEGIN -- indirect addressing
│    -- read actual operand from memory into mar offset
│    mar_on_adbus_oi <= GUARDED '1';
│    read_mem_oi <= GUARDED '1' AFTER read_delay;
│    databus_on_dbus_oi <= GUARDED '1';
│    dbus_on_mar_offset_bus_oi <= GUARDED '1';
│    load_offset_mar_oi <= GUARDED '1';
│    -- goto 6
│    ck: BLOCK ( (clk = '0' AND NOT clk'STABLE) AND GUARD )
│    BEGIN
│       s(6) <= GUARDED '1';
│    END BLOCK ck;
└END BLOCK s5;
```

FIGURE 9.59
State 5: taking care of indirect addressing.

clock. As shown in Figure 9.9, indirect addressing mode only affects the offset part of the address. State 5 activates state 6 which is the same state that was activated by state 4 if direct addressing mode was used.

State 6 becomes active when the instruction being executed is *jmp*, *sta*, *lda*, *and*, *add*, or *sub*. When in this state, *mar* contains the complete operand address. Figure 9.60 shows three nested blocks in the block statement of state 6. These blocks are labeled *jm*, *st*, and *rd*.

The guard expression of the *jm* block is TRUE for the *jmp* instruction. In this case, the *pc* load input, *load_pc*, is enabled to cause the contents of *mar* to be loaded in *pc*. This is followed by activation of state 2 for fetching a new instruction from the memory location pointed to by the new contents of *pc*.

The guard expression of the *st* block becomes active if the opcode of the *sta* instruction is detected on the most significant bits of *ir_lines*. In this case, a write to memory is initiated and contents of *ac* are routed through *alu* to reach the *databus* so that they can be written into the memory.

The third block (*rd*) nested in the block statement of state 6 handles *lda*, *and*, *add*, and *sub*. For these instructions, the actual operand is read from the memory location pointed to by *mar*. When the *databus_on_dbus* control signal is issued, this operand becomes available on the *a_side* of *alu*. (Recall that *dbus* is directly connected to the *a_side* of *alu* in Figure 9.27.) Based on the instruction being executed, a selected signal assignment selects an appropriate function of *alu*. For example, for the *add* instruction, the *a_add_b* function is selected. This causes the adding result of *ac* and data on *a_side* of *alu* to become available on the output of *alu*. This result is loaded in *ac* by issuing the *load_ac* control signal. Activation of *load_sr* in the *rd* block of state 6 updates flags with values that resulted from the *alu* operation. Upon completion of full-address instructions, control branches to state 1 for the next instruction fetch.

State 4 of the Parwan controller caused a memory read operation and targeted the information read from the memory into *mar_offset* register. If the *jsr* instruction

```
s6: BLOCK (s(6) = '1')
BEGIN
  jm: BLOCK ( (ir_lines (7 DOWNTO 5) = "100") AND GUARD)
  BEGIN
    load_page_pc_oi <= GUARDED '1';
    load_offset_pc_oi <= GUARDED '1';
    -- goto 2
    ck: BLOCK ( (clk = '0' AND NOT clk'STABLE) AND GUARD )
    BEGIN
      s(2) <= GUARDED '1';
    END BLOCK ck;
  END BLOCK jm;
  --
  st: BLOCK ( (ir_lines (7 DOWNTO 5) = "101") AND GUARD)
  BEGIN
    -- mar on adbus, ac on databus, write to memory
    mar_on_adbus_oi <= GUARDED '1';
    alu_code_oi <= GUARDED ored_qit_vector (b_input);
    obus_on_dbus_oi <= GUARDED '1';
    dbus_on_databus_oi <= GUARDED '1';
    write_mem_oi <= GUARDED '1' AFTER write_delay;
    -- goto 1
    ck: BLOCK ( (clk = '0' AND NOT clk'STABLE) AND GUARD )
    BEGIN
      s(1) <= GUARDED '1';
    END BLOCK ck;
  END BLOCK st;
  --
  rd: BLOCK ( (ir_lines (7) = '0') AND GUARD)
  BEGIN
    -- mar on adbus, read memory for operand, perform operation
    mar_on_adbus_oi <= GUARDED '1';
    read_mem_oi <= GUARDED '1' AFTER read_delay;
    databus_on_dbus_oi <= GUARDED '1';
    WITH ir_lines (6 DOWNTO 5) SELECT
      alu_code_oi <= GUARDED
          ored_qit_vector (a_input) WHEN "00",
          ored_qit_vector (a_and_b) WHEN "01",
          ored_qit_vector (a_add_b) WHEN "10",
          ored_qit_vector (a_sub_b) WHEN "11",
          ored_qit_vector (b_input) WHEN OTHERS;
    load_sr_oi <= GUARDED '1';
    load_ac_oi <= GUARDED '1';
    -- goto 1
    ck: BLOCK ( (clk = '0' AND NOT clk'STABLE) AND GUARD )
    BEGIN
      s(1) <= GUARDED '1';
    END BLOCK ck;
  END BLOCK rd;
END BLOCK s6;
```

FIGURE 9.60
State 6: reading the actual operand, and executing *jmp*, *sta*, *lda*, *and*, *add*, and *sub* instructions.

is being executed, the address in the *mar_offset* register becomes the address of the top of subroutine. State 7, shown in Figure 9.61, continues the execution of *jsr*. This state writes the contents of *pc* to the top of the subroutine (pointed by *mar*) and at the same time targets the address of the top of the subroutine (twelve bits of *mar*) for the *pc* register.

Following state 7 on the falling edge of the clock, state 8 of Figure 9.62 becomes active to complete the execution of *jsr*. In this state, *pc* now contains the first location of the subroutine. Since the actual subroutine code begins in the location after the top-of-subroutine, state 8 issues the *increment_pc* signal and activates state 1 for fetching the first instruction of the subroutine.

Control reaches state 9, shown in Figure 9.63, when state 4 is active and a branch instruction is being executed. When state 9 becomes active, the branch address is in the *mar* register. State 9 loads *mar* into *pc* if a match is found between the branch directive (bits 3 to 0), and the status register bits (v, c, z, and n flags). If the branch

```
┌─s7: BLOCK (s(7) = "1')
├─BEGIN  -- jsr
│    -- write pc offset to top of subroutine
│    mar_on_adbus_oi <= GUARDED '1';
│    pc_offset_on_dbus_oi <= GUARDED '1';
│    dbus_on_databus_oi <= GUARDED '1';
│    write_mem_oi <= GUARDED '1' AFTER write_delay;
│    -- address of subroutine to pc
│    load_offset_pc_oi <= GUARDED '1';
│    -- goto 8
│    ck: BLOCK ( (clk = '0' AND NOT clk'STABLE) AND GUARD )
│    BEGIN
│        s(8) <= GUARDED '1';
│    END BLOCK ck;
└─END BLOCK s7;
```

FIGURE 9.61
State 7: writing return address of subroutine; making *pc* point to top of subroutine.

```
┌─s8: BLOCK (s(8) = '1')
├─BEGIN
│    -- increment pc
│    increment_pc_oi <= GUARDED '1';
│    -- goto 1
│    ck: BLOCK ( (clk = '0' AND NOT clk'STABLE) AND GUARD )
│    BEGIN
│        s(1) <= GUARDED '1';
│    END BLOCK ck;
└─END BLOCK s8;
```

FIGURE 9.62
State 8: incrementing *pc* to skip the location reserved for the return address.

```
  ┌s9: BLOCK (s(9) = '1')
  ├BEGIN
  │   load_offset_pc_oi <= GUARDED
  │       '1' WHEN (status AND ir_lines (3 DOWNTO 0)) /= "0000" ELSE '0';
  │   -- goto 1
  │   ck: BLOCK ( (clk = '0' AND NOT clk'STABLE) AND GUARD )
  │   BEGIN
  │       s(1) <= GUARDED '1';
  │   END BLOCK ck;
  └END BLOCK s9;
```

FIGURE 9.63
State 9: conditional loading of *pc* for the branch instructions.

condition is not satisfied, *pc* retains its value—this value points to the memory location that follows the branch instruction. In any case, control returns to state 1 for fetching the next instruction.

The last block statement in the *dataflow* architecture of the *par_control_unit* assigns zeros to all state designators (bits of *s*). As described in Chapter 7, this causes a state to be reset after it activates its next state. Figure 9.64 shows this block.

This completes the *dataflow* description of the Parwan controller. The general outline of the circuit corresponding to the descriptions presented above is shown in Figure 9.65. This circuit diagram uses the same notations we employed in Figure 9.50.

9.5.7   Wiring Data and Control Sections

The complete dataflow description of the Parwan processor consists of the *par_data_path* in Section 9.5.5 and the *par_control_unit* in Section 9.5.6. The entity declaration of this CPU is shown in Figure 9.66. This declaration is similar to the one shown in Figure 9.14 for the behavioral description of the Parwan CPU, except that the latter does not use a generic clause.

Figure 9.67 shows the general outline of the *dataflow* architecture of the *par_central_processing_unit*. This description specifies interconnections between the *structural* architecture of the *par_data_path* and the *dataflow* architecture of the *par_control_unit*.

```
  ┌ck: BLOCK ( clk = '0' AND NOT clk'STABLE )
  ├BEGIN
  │   s (9 DOWNTO 1) <= GUARDED "000000000";
  └END BLOCK ck;
└END dataflow;
```

FIGURE 9.64
A zero driver is placed on all states, ending the *dataflow* description of the *par_control_unit*.

FIGURE 9.65
General outline of the Parwan controller.

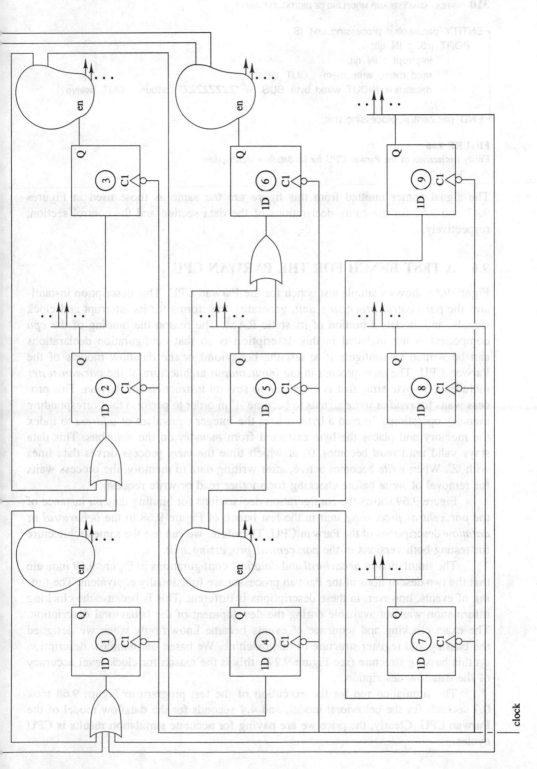

```
ENTITY par_central_processing_unit IS
  PORT (clk : IN qit;
         interrupt : IN qit;
         read_mem, write_mem : OUT qit;
         databus : INOUT wired_byte BUS := "ZZZZZZZZ"; adbus : OUT twelve
         );
END par_central_processing_unit;
```

FIGURE 9.66
Entity declaration of the Parwan CPU for its dataflow description.

The signal names omitted from this figure are the same as those used in Figures
9.47 and 9.52 for the entity declarations of the data section and the control section,
respectively.

9.6   A TEST BENCH FOR THE PARWAN CPU

Figure 9.68 shows a simple test bench for the Parwan CPU. This description instantiates the *par_central_processing_unit*, generates waveforms for its interrupt and clock
signals, and models a portion of its static RAM. The reason the binding of the *cpu*
component is not included in this description is so that configuration declarations
can be written to configure it to test the behavioral or the dataflow models of the
Parwan CPU. The *mem* process in the *input_output* architecture of the *parwan_tester*
includes a 64-byte array that is initialized to several instructions of Parwan. This process waits for *read* or *write* signals to become '1' in order to perform the corresponding
memory operations. To read a byte, it uses the integer equivalent of *address* to index
the memory and places the byte extracted from *memory* on the *data* bus. This data
stays valid until *read* becomes '0', at which time the *mem* process drives data lines
with 'Z'. When *write* becomes active, after writing data to memory, the process waits
for removal of *write* before checking for another read or write request.

Figure 9.69 shows the configuration declarations for binding the *cpu* instance of
the *par_central_processing_unit* in the test bench of Figure 9.68 to the *behavioral* or
dataflow descriptions of the Parwan CPU. Therefore, we can use the same architecture
for testing both versions of the *par_central_processing_unit*.

The simulation of *behavioral* and *dataflow* configurations in Figure 9.69 indicate
that the two descriptions of the Parwan processor are functionally equivalent. The timing of events, however, in these descriptions is different. This is because the clocking
information was not available during the development of the behavioral description.
The exact clocking and sequence of events became known only when we designed
the bussing and register structure of this machine. We based our dataflow description
on this bussing structure (see Figure 9.27); this is the reason for clock level accuracy
of the dataflow description.

The simulation run for the execution of the test program in Figure 9.68 took
0.7 seconds for the behavioral model, and 4.4 seconds for the dataflow model of the
Parwan CPU. Clearly, the price we are paying for accurate simulation results is CPU
cycles.

```
ARCHITECTURE dataflow OF par_central_processing_unit IS
    COMPONENT par_data_path
    PORT (databus : INOUT wired_byte;   adbus : OUT twelve;
          clk : IN qit;
          load_ac, zero_ac,
          . . .
          alu_code : IN qit_vector (2 DOWNTO 0);
          ir_lines : OUT byte; status : OUT nibble
          );
    END COMPONENT;
    FOR data: par_data_path USE ENTITY WORK.par_data_path (structural);
    COMPONENT par_control_unit
    PORT (clk : IN qit;
          load_ac, zero_ac,
          . . .
          alu_code : OUT qit_vector (2 DOWNTO 0);
          ir_lines : IN byte; status : IN nibble;
          read_mem, write_mem : OUT qit; interrupt : IN qit
          );
    END COMPONENT;
    FOR ctrl: par_control_unit USE ENTITY WORK.par_control_unit (dataflow);
    SIGNAL load_ac, zero_ac,
          . . .
    SIGNAL alu_code : qit_vector (2 DOWNTO 0);
    SIGNAL ir_lines : byte;
    SIGNAL status : nibble;
BEGIN
    data: par_data_path PORT MAP
            (databus, adbus,
             clk,
             load_ac, zero_ac,
             . . .
             alu_code,
             ir_lines, status
             );
    ctrl: par_control_unit PORT MAP
            (clk,
             load_ac, zero_ac,
             . . .
             alu_code,
             ir_lines, status,
             read_mem, write_mem, interrupt
             );
END dataflow;
```

FIGURE 9.67
The general outline of *dataflow* architecture of the Parwan CPU.

```vhdl
ARCHITECTURE input_output OF parwan_tester IS
    COMPONENT parwan PORT (clk : IN qit;   interrupt : IN qit;
            read_mem, write_mem : OUT qit;
            databus : INOUT wired_byte; adbus : OUT twelve );
    END COMPONENT;
    SIGNAL clock, interrupt, read, write : qit;
    SIGNAL data : wired_byte := "ZZZZZZZZ";
    SIGNAL address : twelve;
    TYPE byte_memory IS ARRAY ( INTEGER RANGE <> ) OF byte;
BEGIN
    int : interrupt <= '1', '0' AFTER 4500 NS;
    clk : clock <= NOT clock AFTER 1 US WHEN NOW <= 140 US ELSE clock;
    cpu : parwan PORT MAP (clock, interrupt, read, write, data, address);
    mem : PROCESS
        VARIABLE memory : byte_memory ( 0 TO 63 ) :=
            ("00000000", "00011000", "10100000", "00011001", --lda 24, sta 25
             "00100000", "00011010", "01000000", "00011011", --and 26, add 27
             "11100010", "11101001", "01100000", "00011100", --cac, asr, sub 28
             "00010000", "00011101", "11000000", "00100100", --lda i 29, jsr 36
             "11101000", "11100000", "10000000", "00100000", --asl, nop, jmp 32
             "00000000", "00000000", "00000000", "00000000",
             "00001100", "00011111", "00000000", "00000000", --(24, 25, 26, 27)
             "00001100", "00011111", "00000000", "01011010", --(28, 29, 30, 31)
             "10000000", "00010010", "00000000", "00000000", --jmp 18
             "00000000", "11100010", "10010000", "00100100", --    , cma, jmp i 36
             "00000000", "00000000", "00000000", "00000000",
             "00000000", "00000000", "00000000", "00000000",
             "00000000", "00000000", "00000000", "00000000",
             "00000000", "00000000", "00000000", "00000000",
             "00000000", "00000000", "00000000", "00000000",
             "00000000", "00000000", "00000000", "00000000" );
        VARIABLE ia : INTEGER;
    BEGIN
        WAIT ON read, write;
        qit2int (address, ia);
        IF read = '1' THEN
            IF ia >= 64 THEN   data <= "ZZZZZZZZ";
            ELSE· data <= wired_byte ( memory (ia) );
            END IF;
            WAIT UNTIL read = '0';
            data <= "ZZZZZZZZ";
        ELSIF write = '1' THEN
            IF ia < 64 THEN   memory (ia) := byte ( data );
            END IF;
            WAIT UNTIL write = '0';
        END IF;
    END PROCESS mem;
END input_output;
```

FIGURE 9.68

A simple test bench for Parwan behavioral and dataflow descriptions.

312

```
┌CONFIGURATION behavior OF parwan_tester IS
│   FOR input_output
│     FOR cpu : parwan
│       USE ENTITY behavioral.par_central_processing_unit(behavioral);
│     END FOR;
│   END FOR;
└END behavior;
```
                                (a)
```
┌CONFIGURATION dataflow OF parwan_tester IS
│   FOR input_output
│     FOR cpu : parwan
│       USE ENTITY par_dataflow.par_central_processing_unit(dataflow);
│     END FOR;
│   END FOR;
└END dataflow;
```
                                (b)

FIGURE 9.69
Configuring *input_output* architecture of the Parwan tester (a) for testing *behavioral* architecture of the *par_central_processing_unit*, (b) for testing *dataflow* architecture of *par_central_processing_unit*.

9.7 SUMMARY

This chapter showed how VHDL can be used to describe a system at the behavioral level before the system is even designed, and at the dataflow level after major design decisions have been made. The behavioral description aids designers as they verify their understanding of the problem, while the dataflow description can be used to verify the bussing and register structure of the design. A design carried to the stage where a dataflow model can be generated is only a few simple steps away from complete hardware realization. For completing the design of Parwan, flip-flop and gate interconnections should replace the component descriptions in the Parwan dataflow model.

Descriptions in this chapter cover the major language issues discussed in the earlier chapters. A complete understanding of these descriptions requires good comprehension of the VHDL syntax and semantics. Readers who understand all the descriptions in this chapter to the point where they can develop similar models can consider themselves proficient in the VHDL hardware description language.

REFERENCES

1. Hill, F. J., and G. R. Peterson, "Digital Systems: Hardware Organization and Design," 3rd ed., John Wiley and Sons, New York, 1987.
2. Armstrong, J. R., "Chip-Level Modeling with VHDL," Prentice-Hall Inc., Englewood Cliffs, N.J., 1988.

PROBLEMS

9.1. Make a list of eight simple instructions you think would be useful and possible to add to Parwan.

9.2. In Parwan assembly code, write a program to move a block of data that is stored in the memory. The data begins at location 4:00 and ends at 4:63, and is to be moved to page 5 starting at 5:64.

9.3. A block of data in the Parwan memory begins at location 1:00 and ends at 1:63. Write a program in Parwan assembly language to find the largest positive number in these locations.

9.4. Show the VHDL description of the Mark-1 machine whose ISPS description appeared in Figure 1.3 of Chapter 1.

9.5. Write a procedure for reading Parwan memory from an external file. Assume address and data in this file are in hexadecimal number representation and are arranged as shown here:

   page:offset data

Name this procedure *read_memory* and use this subprogram declaration:

   PROCEDURE read_memory (addr : IN qit_vector; data : OUT qit_vector;
         found : OUT BOOLEAN; file_name : IN STRING);

The *read_memory* procedure searches an entire memory file for an address that matches its *addr* argument. If the address is found, it returns the *qit* equivalent of the data appearing on the same line of the file as the address. If the address is not found, the *found* parameter is returned as FALSE. File name is used as the parameter so that the file declaration can take place each time the procedure is called.

9.6. Write a procedure for writing Parwan memory to an external file such that the address is passed to this procedure as a *qit_vector* of size 12, and the data as a *qit_vector* of size 8. Each time the procedure is called, one line containing address and data should be appended to the end of the file. This information is written to the file in hexadecimal using the format shown here:

   page:offset data

Name this procedure *write_memory* and use this subprogram declaration:

   PROCEDURE write_memory (addr : IN qit_vector; data : IN qit_vector;
            VARIABLE memory_file : OUT TEXT);

The *memory_file* parameter in this procedure should be associated with a file object which is declared outside the procedure.

9.7. Rewrite the Parwan test bench such that the memory read and write are done from and to external files instead of to a declared array as they are shown in Figure 9.68. For this purpose, use the procedures developed in Problems 9.5 and 9.6. When a read from the memory is to be done, a call should be made to the *read_memory* procedure and the data read by the procedure should be placed on the *databus*. When a memory write is to be done, a call to *write_memory* should append the address and data to the end of a memory write file. Use this test bench to verify correctness of the changes that you will be making to Parwan in the problems that follow.

9.8. Modify the behavioral description of the Parwan controller such that the *jsr* instruction can use indirect addressing.

9.9. Suggest a set of instructions for a more complete interrupt handling than what is presently available in Parwan.

9.10. Parwan can be modified to use only three bits for distinguishing between various non-address instructions. We can, therefore, reserve bit 3 of the instruction register as an opcode bit for extending Parwan instructions. In addition, two more non-address instructions can be added to the Parwan instructions. Modify the behavioral description of Parwan such that non-address instructions use 11100xxx opcode. For xxx use 000, 001, 010, 011, 100, and 101 for *nop*, *cla*, *cma*, *cmc*, *asl*, and *asr*, respectively.

9.11. Use the method suggested in Problem 9.10 to add an instruction for immediate loading of the accumulator. This instruction can use one of the extra opcodes that become available by modifying opcodes of non-address instructions. For *ldi* (load accumulator immediate), you may use the 11101000 opcode. The second byte of an *ldi* contains the byte that is to be loaded into the memory. Modify the behavioral description of Parwan for the execution of this instruction.

9.12. Add a stack pointer to the register and bussing structure of Parwan for the implementation of a software stack. Restrict the stack to the last page of the memory. Use the method of opcode expansion suggested in Problem 9.10 to make room for a new instruction, and use 11101001 for an *lds* instruction that loads the stack pointer with the data in the next instruction byte. Show all bus connections, registers, and necessary control signals.

9.13. Use the method suggested in Problem 9.10, and the stack pointer of Problem 9.12 to add two new non-address instructions, *push* and *pop*. Use 11100110 for *push* and 11100111 for *pop*. Modify the behavioral description of Parwan for the execution of these instructions.

9.14. Use the stack implementation in Problem 9.12 to modify the *jsr* instruction such that it pushes the return address onto the top of the stack. Add a new *rts* instruction that causes a return from the subroutine. For this instruction, use the opcode expansion method suggested in Problem 9.10, and use 11101010 for its opcode. Modify the behavioral description of Parwan for the execution of these instructions.

9.15. Modify the dataflow description of Parwan for implementing *jsr* as specified in Problem 9.8.

9.16. Show the dataflow implementation of the opcode extension scheme suggested in Problem 9.10. Show all required bus connections and modify the controller of Parwan.

9.17. Modify the dataflow description of Parwan for the implementation of the *ldi* instruction as specified in Problem 9.11. Show all required bus connections and modify the Parwan controller.

9.18. Modify the Parwan dataflow description for the implementation of *lds*, *push* and *pop* instructions (see Problem 9.12 and Problem 9.13). Show all required bus connections, write a description for the stack pointer (*sp*), and insert this unit in the data path description of Parwan. Also, modify the Parwan controller so that it properly executes these instructions.

9.19. Modify the Parwan dataflow description to implement a version of *jsr* that uses the stack in Problems 9.12 (also see Problem 9.14). Show all required bus connections and modify the Parwan controller to properly execute this instruction.

9.20. Use the stack in Problem 9.12 to implement a better interrupt handling for Parwan. The new system should have an *int* input which becomes '1' when interrupt is requested. The CPU identifies an interrupting device by reading the address of its interrupt service routine from location 0:00 of the memory. To service an interrupt, the CPU jumps to predefined memory locations for each of the interrupt sources. Assume an external priority logic determines the device with highest priority and generates its service routine address. Your solution to this problem should also include implementation of a *return_from_interrupt* instruction.

APPENDIX
A

BASIC
UTILITIES
PACKAGE

The code for the *basic_utilities* package shown in this appendix appears here in its final form as it was developed and explained in the book. All the types, procedures, and functions presented in the chapters of this book have been added to this package as we proceeded through the book. Thus, the code in this appendix presents the *basic_utilities* package as it now stands with all the code for the examples and tools that were presented in the book. Here is the package:

```
PACKAGE basic_utilities IS
    TYPE qit IS ('0', '1', 'Z', 'X');
    TYPE qit_2d IS ARRAY (qit, qit) OF qit;
    TYPE qit_1d IS ARRAY (qit) OF qit;
    TYPE qit_vector IS ARRAY (NATURAL RANGE <>) OF qit;
    SUBTYPE tit IS qit RANGE '0' TO 'Z';
    TYPE tit_vector IS ARRAY (NATURAL RANGE <>) OF tit;
    TYPE integer_vector IS ARRAY (NATURAL RANGE <>) OF INTEGER;
    TYPE logic_data IS FILE OF CHARACTER;
    TYPE capacitance IS RANGE 0 TO 1E16
    UNITS
        ffr; -- Femto Farads (base unit)
        pfr = 1000 ffr;
        nfr = 1000 pfr;
        ufr = 1000 nfr;
        mfr = 1000 ufr;
        far = 1000 mfr;
        kfr = 1000 far;
    END UNITS;
    TYPE resistance IS RANGE 0 TO 1E16
    UNITS
        l_o; -- Milli-Ohms (base unit)
        ohms = 1000 l_o;
```

316

```
      k_o = 1000 ohms;
      m_o = 1000 k_o;
      g_o = 1000 m_o;
  END UNITS;

  FUNCTION fgl (w, x, gl : BIT) RETURN BIT;
  FUNCTION feq (w, x, eq : BIT) RETURN BIT;
  PROCEDURE bin2int (bin : IN BIT_VECTOR; int : OUT INTEGER);
  PROCEDURE int2bin (int : IN INTEGER;  bin : OUT BIT_VECTOR);
  FUNCTION inc (x : BIT_VECTOR) RETURN BIT_VECTOR;
  PROCEDURE qit2int (qin : IN qit_vector; int : OUT INTEGER);
  PROCEDURE int2qit (int : IN INTEGER;  qin : OUT qit_vector);
  FUNCTION bit2qit_vector (bin : BIT_VECTOR) RETURN qit_vector;
  FUNCTION qit2bit_vector (qin : qit_vector) RETURN BIT_VECTOR;
  FUNCTION inc (x : qit_vector) RETURN qit_vector;
  PROCEDURE apply_data (
    SIGNAL target : OUT BIT_VECTOR;
    CONSTANT values : IN integer_vector;  CONSTANT period : IN TIME);

  PROCEDURE assign_bits (
    SIGNAL s : OUT BIT; file_name : IN STRING; period : IN TIME);
  PROCEDURE assign_bits (
    SIGNAL s : OUT qit; file_name : IN STRING; period : IN TIME);
  FUNCTION "AND" (a, b : qit) RETURN qit;
  FUNCTION "OR" (a, b : qit) RETURN qit;
  FUNCTION "NOT" (a : qit) RETURN qit;
  FUNCTION wire (a, b : qit) RETURN qit;
  FUNCTION "*" (a : resistance; b : capacitance) RETURN TIME;
  --
  FUNCTION oring ( drivers : qit_vector) RETURN qit;
  SUBTYPE ored_qit IS oring qit;
  TYPE ored_qit_vector IS ARRAY (NATURAL RANGE <>) OF ored_qit;
  --
  FUNCTION anding ( drivers : qit_vector) RETURN qit;
  SUBTYPE anded_qit IS anding qit;
  TYPE anded_qit_vector IS ARRAY (NATURAL RANGE <>) OF anded_qit;
  --
  FUNCTION wiring ( drivers : qit_vector) RETURN qit;
  SUBTYPE wired_qit IS wiring qit;
  TYPE wired_qit_vector IS ARRAY (NATURAL RANGE <>) OF wired_qit;
  --
  FUNCTION oring ( drivers : BIT_VECTOR) RETURN BIT;
  SUBTYPE ored_bit IS oring BIT;
  TYPE ored_bit_vector IS ARRAY (NATURAL RANGE <>) OF ored_bit;
  --
  FUNCTION anding ( drivers : BIT_VECTOR) RETURN BIT;
  SUBTYPE anded_bit IS anding bit;
  TYPE anded_bit_vector IS ARRAY (NATURAL RANGE <>) OF anded_bit;
END basic_utilities;

PACKAGE BODY basic_utilities IS
  FUNCTION "AND" (a, b : qit) RETURN qit IS
    CONSTANT qit_and_table : qit_2d := (
                               ('0','0','0','0'),
                               ('0','1','1','X'),
                               ('0','1','1','X'),
                               ('0','X','X','X'));
  BEGIN
    RETURN qit_and_table (a, b);
```

```
└END "AND";

┌FUNCTION "OR" (a, b : qit) RETURN qit IS
│   CONSTANT qit_or_table : qit_2d := (
│                                   ('0','1','1','X'),
│                                   ('1','1','1','1'),
│                                   ('1','1','1','1'),
│                                   ('X','1','1','X'));
├BEGIN
│   RETURN qit_or_table (a, b);
└END "OR";

┌FUNCTION "NOT" (a : qit) RETURN qit IS
│   CONSTANT qit_not_table : qit_1d := ('1','0','0','X');
├BEGIN
│   RETURN qit_not_table (a);
└END "NOT";

┌FUNCTION wire (a, b : qit) RETURN qit IS
│   CONSTANT qit_wire_table : qit_2d := (
│                                   ('0','X','0','X'),
│                                   ('X','1','1','X'),
│                                   ('0','1','Z','X'),
│                                   ('X','X','X','X'));
├BEGIN
│   RETURN qit_wire_table (a, b);
└END wire;

┌FUNCTION "*" (a : resistance; b : capacitance) RETURN TIME IS
├BEGIN
│   RETURN  ( ( a / 1 l_o) * ( b / 1 ffr ) * 1 FS ) / 1000;
└END "*";

┌FUNCTION fgl (w, x, gl : BIT) RETURN BIT IS
├BEGIN
│   RETURN  (w AND gl) OR (NOT x  AND  gl) OR (w  AND  NOT x);
└END fgl;

┌FUNCTION feq (w, x, eq : BIT) RETURN BIT IS
├BEGIN
│   RETURN  (w AND x AND eq) OR (NOT w  AND  NOT x  AND  eq);
└END feq;

┌PROCEDURE bin2int (bin : IN BIT_VECTOR; int : OUT INTEGER) IS
│   VARIABLE result: INTEGER;
├BEGIN
│   result := 0;
│   FOR i IN bin'RANGE LOOP
│     IF bin(i) = '1' THEN
│        result := result + 2**i;
│     END IF;
│   END LOOP;
│   int := result;
└END bin2int;

┌PROCEDURE int2bin (int : IN INTEGER;  bin : OUT BIT_VECTOR) IS
│   VARIABLE tmp : INTEGER;
├BEGIN
│   tmp := int;
```

```
   FOR i IN 0 TO (bin'LENGTH - 1) LOOP
     IF (tmp MOD 2  =  1) THEN
       bin (i) := '1';
     ELSE bin (i) := '0';
     END IF;
     tmp := tmp / 2;
   END LOOP;
 END int2bin;

FUNCTION bit2qit_vector (bin : BIT_VECTOR) RETURN qit_vector IS
   VARIABLE q : qit_vector (bin'RANGE);
 BEGIN
   FOR i IN bin'RANGE LOOP
     IF bin(i) = '1' THEN q(i) := '1'
     ELSE
       q(i) := '0';
     END IF;
   END LOOP;
   RETURN q;
 END bit2qit_vector;

FUNCTION qit2bit_vector (qin : qit_vector) RETURN BIT_VECTOR IS
   VARIABLE b : BIT_VECTOR (qin'RANGE);
 BEGIN
   FOR i IN qin'RANGE LOOP
     IF qin(i) = '1' THEN b(i) := '1'
     ELSE
       b(i) := '0';
     END IF;
   END LOOP;
   RETURN b;
 END qit2bit_vector;

FUNCTION inc (x : BIT_VECTOR) RETURN BIT_VECTOR IS
   VARIABLE i : INTEGER;
   VARIABLE t : BIT_VECTOR (x'RANGE);
 BEGIN
   bin2int (x, i);
   i := i + 1; IF i >= 2**x'LENGTH THEN i := 0; END IF;
   int2bin (i, t);
   RETURN t;
 END inc;

PROCEDURE qit2int (qin : IN qit_vector; int : OUT INTEGER) IS
   VARIABLE result: INTEGER;
 BEGIN
   result := 0;
   FOR i IN 0 TO (qin'LENGTH - 1) LOOP
     IF qin(i) = '1' THEN
       result := result + 2**i;
     END IF;
   END LOOP;
   int := result;
 END qit2int;

PROCEDURE int2qit (int : IN INTEGER;   qin : OUT qit_vector) IS
   VARIABLE tmp : INTEGER;
 BEGIN
   tmp := int;
```

```
      FOR i IN 0 TO (qin'LENGTH - 1) LOOP
        IF (tmp MOD 2  =  1) THEN
          qin (i) := '1';
        ELSE qin (i) := '0';
        END IF;
        tmp := tmp / 2;
      END LOOP;
   END int2qit;


   FUNCTION inc (x : qit_vector) RETURN qit_vector IS
      VARIABLE i : INTEGER;
      VARIABLE t : qit_vector (x'RANGE);
   BEGIN
      qit2int (x, i);
      i := i + 1; IF i >= 2**x'LENGTH THEN i := 0; END IF;
      int2qit (i, t);
      RETURN t;
   END inc;


   PROCEDURE apply_data (
      SIGNAL target : OUT BIT_VECTOR;
      CONSTANT values : IN integer_vector; CONSTANT period : IN TIME)
   IS
      VARIABLE buf : BIT_VECTOR (target'RANGE);
   BEGIN
      FOR i IN values'RANGE LOOP
        int2bin (values(i), buf);
        target <= TRANSPORT buf AFTER i * period;
      END LOOP;
   END apply_data;


   PROCEDURE assign_bits (
      SIGNAL s : OUT BIT; file_name : IN STRING; period : IN TIME)
   IS
      VARIABLE char : CHARACTER;
      VARIABLE current : TIME := 0 NS;
      FILE input_value_file : logic_data IS IN file_name;
   BEGIN
      WHILE NOT ENDFILE (input_value_file) LOOP
        READ (input_value_file, char);
        IF char = '0' OR char = '1' THEN
          current := current + period;
          IF char = '0' THEN
            s <= TRANSPORT '0' AFTER current;
          ELSIF char = '1' THEN
            s <= TRANSPORT '1' AFTER current;
          END IF;
        END IF;
      END LOOP;
   END assign_bits;


   PROCEDURE assign_bits (
      SIGNAL s : OUT qit; file_name : IN STRING; period : IN TIME)
   IS
      VARIABLE char : CHARACTER;
      VARIABLE current : TIME := 0 NS;
      FILE input_value_file : logic_data IS IN file_name;
   BEGIN
      WHILE NOT ENDFILE (input_value_file) LOOP
```

```vhdl
        READ (input_value_file, char);
        current := current + period;
        CASE char IS
          WHEN '0' => s <= TRANSPORT '0' AFTER current;
          WHEN '1' => s <= TRANSPORT '1' AFTER current;
          WHEN 'Z' | 'z' => s <= TRANSPORT 'Z' AFTER current;
          WHEN 'X' | 'x' => s <= TRANSPORT 'X' AFTER current;
          WHEN OTHERS => current := current - period;
        END CASE;
      END LOOP;
  END assign_bits;

  FUNCTION oring ( drivers : qit_vector) RETURN qit IS
    VARIABLE accumulate : qit := '0';
  BEGIN
    FOR i IN drivers'RANGE LOOP
      accumulate := accumulate OR drivers(i);
    END LOOP;
    RETURN accumulate;
  END oring;

  FUNCTION anding ( drivers : qit_vector) RETURN qit IS
    VARIABLE accumulate : qit := '1';
  BEGIN
    FOR i IN drivers'RANGE LOOP
      accumulate := accumulate AND drivers(i);
    END LOOP;
    RETURN accumulate;
  END anding;

  FUNCTION wiring ( drivers : qit_vector) RETURN qit IS
    VARIABLE accumulate : qit := 'Z';
  BEGIN
    FOR i IN drivers'RANGE LOOP
      accumulate := wire (accumulate, drivers(i));
    END LOOP;
    RETURN accumulate;
  END wiring;

  FUNCTION oring ( drivers : BIT_VECTOR) RETURN BIT IS
    VARIABLE accumulate : BIT := '0';
  BEGIN
    FOR i IN drivers'RANGE LOOP
      accumulate := accumulate OR drivers(i);
    END LOOP;
    RETURN accumulate;
  END oring;

  FUNCTION anding ( drivers : BIT_VECTOR) RETURN BIT IS
    VARIABLE accumulate : BIT := '1';
  BEGIN
    FOR i IN drivers'RANGE LOOP
      accumulate := accumulate AND drivers(i);
    END LOOP;
    RETURN accumulate;
  END anding;

END basic_utilities;
```

APPENDIX
B

SIMULATION ENVIRONMENTS

In this appendix, sample session runs for four VHDL simulation systems are presented. The purpose of this presentation is to provide a quick reference for the users of these software packages and, also to illustrate the general features of VHDL simulation environments. For all four packages, the same example is used; this example illustrates only the main features of a simulation system. Interactive use of the system, setting breakpoints, formatting outputs, using the VHDL tool in a CAD design environment, stepping through the simulation, debugging the code, and many other advanced features are not discussed here.

The following type fonts help the readability of run session dialogues:

Operating system and simulation software prompts are shown by: system prompt.

User commands are shown by: **user command.**

Responses from the host machine and run results are shown by: *host response*.

Response from the VHDL simulation system is shown by: vhdl response.

We use the following font for comments: our comments.

B.1 A SESSION OF THE VDS VHDL ENVIRONMENT

This section presents a sample session for simulating a small example using the VHDL Development System (VDS) of Cadence Design Systems.[1] The simulation was performed on a SUN-4 machine. For this simulation, you need these files:
FILE: and2.vhd; – Input file name.

```
ENTITY and2 IS
   PORT (x1, x2: IN BIT; z: OUT BIT);
END and2;
ARCHITECTURE run_demo OF and2 IS
BEGIN
   z <= x1 AND x2 AFTER 5 NS;
END run_demo;
```

FILE: test.vhd; – A simple test bench.

```
ENTITY tester IS END tester;
ARCHITECTURE io OF tester IS
   COMPONENT and2 PORT (x1, x2 : IN BIT; z : OUT BIT);
   END COMPONENT;
   FOR ALL : and2 USE ENTITY WORK.and2(run_demo);
   SIGNAL a, b, c : BIT;
BEGIN
   c1 : and2 PORT MAP (a, b, c);
   a <= '0', '1' AFTER 100 NS, '0' AFTER 200 NS, '1' AFTER 300 NS;
   b <= '0', '1' AFTER 150 NS, '0' AFTER 250 NS, '1' AFTER 350 NS;
END io;
```

FILE: test.rcl; – Report control file.

```
SIMULATION_REPORT test IS
BEGIN
   REMOVE_PAGE_ID;
   SELECT_SIGNAL : a, b, c;
   SAMPLE_SIGNALS BY_EVENT IN NS USING '.';
END test;
```

Session Run Follows:

```
nu>
nu>    ls
and2.vhd   test.rcl   test.vhd
nu>
nu>
```

We will assume that environmental variables have already been set.

---

[1]Cadence Design Systems; 555 River Oaks Parkway; San Jose, CA 95134, Tel: 408-943-1284

```
nu>
nu>
```

Originally the WORK library of the *VDS* system is empty.

```
nu>  vds dir
Standard VHDL 1076 Support Environment Version 3.1 - 1 April 1991
Copyright (C) 1991 Cadence Design Systems, All rights reserved.

VHDVDS-I-NO_UNITS - No units found in <<navabi>>.
nu>  vhdl and2.vhd
Standard VHDL 1076 Support Environment Version 3.1 - 1 April 1991
Copyright (C) 1991 Cadence Design Systems,  All rights reserved.

nu>
nu>
```

AND2 Entity and Architectures are compiled into the WORK library. The *dir* command shows contents of this library.

```
nu>  vds dir
Standard VHDL 1076 Support Environment Version 3.1 - 1 April 1991
Copyright (C) 1991 Cadence Design Systems,  All rights reserved.
Library <<navabi>>

AND2                          Entity           22:22:00 03-APR-1991
AND2(RUN_DEMO)                *Architecture     22:22:04 03-APR-1991

nu>
nu>
```

For analyzing the TOP unit the -top option has to be specified with the *vhdl* command.

```
nu>
nu>  vhdl -top test.vhd
Standard VHDL 1076 Support Environment Version 3.1 - 1 April 1991
Copyright (C) 1991 Cadence Design Systems,  All rights reserved.

nu>
nu>  vds dir
Standard VHDL 1076 Support Environment Version 3.1 - 1 April 1991
Copyright (C) 1991 Cadence Design Systems,  All rights reserved.
Library <<navabi>>

AND2                          Entity           22:22:00 03-APR-1991
AND2(RUN_DEMO)                *Architecture     22:22:04 03-APR-1991
TESTER                        Entity           22:23:06 03-APR-1991
TESTER(IO)                    *Architecture     22:23:10 03-APR-1991
nu>
nu>
```

The top unit has to be built before simulation. Use the *build* command for this purpose.

```
nu>
nu>  build -repl 'tester(io)'
```

```
nu>
nu>
```

Successful execution of the *build* program generates a Kernel.

AND2	Entity	22:22:00 03-APR-1991
AND2(RUN_DEMO)	*Architecture	22:22:04 03-APR-1991
IO	Kernel	22:24:03 03-APR-1991
TESTER	Entity	22:23:06 03-APR-1991
TESTER(IO)	*Architecture	22:23:10 03-APR-1991

```
nu>
nu>
```

The Kernel can now be simulated using the *sim* command.

```
nu>   sim io
```

```
VHDSIM-N-SIGTRAN Signal Tracing turned on
VHDSIM-N-QUIESCE Quiescent state reached with no response after 355 ns

nu>
nu>
```

Simulation generates a run file from which a report can be generated. Report generation is done by the *rg* command.

```
nu>   rg io 'test.rcl'
```

```
nu>
nu>
```

The *io.rpt* file is created in the present directory.

```
nu>   ls
and2.vhd  io.rpt    test.rcl  test.vhd
nu>
nu>   cat io.rpt
```

Vhdl Simulation Report

Kernel Library Name: <<navabi>>IO
Kernel Creation Date: APR-03-1991

```
            Kernel Creation Time: 22:24:22
                   Run Identifer: 1
                Run Date: APR-03-1991
                 Run Time: 22:24:22


          Report Control Language File: test.rcl
              Report Output File : io.rpt


            Max Time: 9223372036854775807
               Max Delta: 2147483646
```

Report Control Language :

```
  SIMULATION_REPORT test IS
  BEGIN
    REMOVE_PAGE_ID;
     SELECT_SIGNAL : a, b, c;
     SAMPLE_SIGNALS BY_EVENT IN NS USING '.';
  END test;
```

Report Format Information :

```
  Time is in NS relative to the start of simulation
  Time period for report is from 0 NS to End of Simulation
  Signal values are reported by event   ( '.' indicates no event )
```

TIME	----------------------------SIGNAL NAMES---------------------		
(NS)	A	B	C
0	'0'	'0'	'0'
100	'1'	...	...
150	...	'1'	...
155	...	...	'1'
200	'0'	...	...
205	...	...	'0'
250	...	'0'	...
300	'1'	...	...
350	...	'1'	...
355	...	...	'1'
nu>			
nu>			

Simulation of the two-input AND gate is completed.

```
  nu>
  nu>
```

B.2   A SESSION OF THE V-SYSTEM/WINDOWS
VHDL ENVIRONMENT

This section presents a sample session for simulating a small example using the VHDL simulation environment of Model Technology Incorporated.[2] The V-System/Windows

---

[2]Model Technology Inc.; 15455 NW Greenbrier Pkwy, Ste 210; Beaverton, OR 97006; Tel: 503-690-6838

requires an Intel 80286, 386 or 486 based Personal Computer. The simulation run shown here was performed on Microsoft Windows running on a 286-based PC. Files used in this run are shown here:

FILE: and2.vhd; – Input file name.

```
ENTITY and2 IS
    PORT (x1, x2: IN BIT; z: OUT BIT);
END and2;
ARCHITECTURE run_demo OF and2 IS
BEGIN
    z <= x1 AND x2 AFTER 5 NS;
END run_demo;
```

FILE: test.vhd; – A simple test bench.

```
ENTITY tester IS END tester;
ARCHITECTURE io OF tester IS
    COMPONENT and2 PORT (x1, x2 : IN BIT; z : OUT BIT);
    END COMPONENT;
    FOR ALL : and2 USE ENTITY WORK.and2(run_demo);
    SIGNAL a, b, c : BIT;
BEGIN
    c1 : and2 PORT MAP (a, b, c);
    a <= '0', '1' AFTER 100 NS, '0' AFTER 200 NS, '1' AFTER 300 NS;
    b <= '0', '1' AFTER 150 NS, '0' AFTER 250 NS, '1' AFTER 350 NS;
END io;
```

Session Run Follows:

After invoking V-System from the Windows environment, a window with the "Front" prompt appears.

```
Front>
Front>
```

Initially, the WORK library is empty. The *vdir* command shows the entries in this library.

```
Front>    vdir
Front>
Front>
```

Compile *and2.vhd* into the library. For this purpose, either type in the command, or use dialogue boxes from the windows.

```
Front>    vcom and2.vhd
# -- Loading package standard
# -- Compiling entity and2
# -- Compiling architecture run_demo of and2
Front>
Front>
```

The new design has been added to the library. Use *vdir* to list items in the WORK library.

```
Front>    vdir
# ENTITY and2
Front>
Front>
```

Compile *test.vhd* into the WORK library.

```
Front>    vcom test.vhd
# -- Loading package standard
# -- Compiling entity tester
# -- Compiling architecture io of tester
# -- Loading entity and2
Front>
Front>
```

The new design has been added to the library.

```
Front>    vdir
# ENTITY and2
# ENTITY tester
Front>
Front>
```

Start the simulation by issuing the *vsim* command at the prompt.

```
Front>    vsim
```

In the "Simulation Parameter" window specify *test* for *primary*, and *io* for *secondary*. When done, the "Vsim" window opens, and the following appears:

```
Vsim>
# Loading C:\VHDL\STD.standard
# Loading WORK.tester[io]
# Loading WORK.and2[run_demo]
Vsim>
Vsim>
```

At the prompt, list the signals to be observed.

```
Vsim>    list a b c
```

A "List" window opens with the initial values of the *a*, *b* and *c* signals. To start the simulation, use the *run* command at the Vsim prompt in the "Vsim" window. Use 1000 for the maximum time.

```
Vsim>    run 1000
```

In the "List" window values of signals appear. Simulation stops at 355 nanoseconds.

```
ns   a b c
 0   0 0 0
100  1 0 0
150  1 1 0
155  1 1 1
200  0 1 1
205  0 1 0
250  0 0 0
300  1 0 0
350  1 1 0
355  1 1 1
```

Simulation of the two-input AND gate is completed. Exit from open windows.

```
Sim>    exit
Front>  exit
```

B.3   A SESSION IN THE VLK VHDL ENVIRONMENT

This section presents a sample session for simulating a small example using the VLK VHDL simulation environment of Open Solutions Incorporated.[3] The simulation was performed on a SUN-4 compatible machine. For this simulation the following files are needed:

FILE: and2.vhd; – Input file name.

```
ENTITY and2 IS
   PORT (x1, x2: IN BIT; z: OUT BIT);
END and2;
ARCHITECTURE run_demo OF and2 IS
BEGIN
   z <= x1 AND x2 AFTER 5 NS;
END run_demo;
```

FILE: test.vhd; – A simple test bench.

```
ENTITY tester IS END tester;
ARCHITECTURE io OF tester IS
   COMPONENT and2 PORT (x1, x2 : IN BIT; z : OUT BIT);
   END COMPONENT;
   FOR ALL : and2 USE ENTITY WORK.and2(run_demo);
   SIGNAL a, b, c : BIT;
```

---

[3]Open Solutions, Inc.; 15245 Shady Grove Road, Suite 310; Rockville, MD 20850; Tel: 301-963-5200

```
    BEGIN
      c1 : and2 PORT MAP (a, b, c);
      a <= '0', '1' AFTER 100 NS, '0' AFTER 200 NS, '1' AFTER 300 NS;
      b <= '0', '1' AFTER 150 NS, '0' AFTER 250 NS, '1' AFTER 350 NS;
    END io;
```

Session Run Follows:

```
    nu>
    nu>    ls
    and2.vhd    test.vhd
    nu>
    nu>
```

Use the *setwork* command to create the working library in your current directory.

```
    nu>    setwork
    Setting WORK to dls_navabi
    Setting dls_navabi to /u1/navabi/vhdl_vlk/user
    nu>
```

Compile *and2.vhd* into the WORK library.

```
    nu>    compile and2.vhd
    ......
```

The following units have been compiled:

```
    and2
    and2-run_demo
    nu>
```

New files for the ENTITY and ARCHITECTURE of *and2* have been added to the present subdirectory.

```
    nu>    ls
    and2.vhd        and2.vhdlview    and2-run_demo.vhdlview
    test.vhd
    nu>
```

Compile the test bench contained in the *test.vhd* file.

```
    nu>    compile test.vhd
    ......
```

The following units have been compiled:

```
    tester
    tester-io

    nu>
```

New files have been added to the present subdirectory.

```
nu>    ls
and2.vhd              and2.vhdlview         and2-run_demo.vhdlview
test.vhd              tester-io.vhdlview
nu>
```

Build the simulation model using the *build* command.

```
nu>    build tester
Building complete.
To execute the simulation model, type 'simulate tester'
nu>
```

A simulation file is added to the working subdirectory.

```
nu>    ls
and2.vhd         and2.vhdlview       and2-run_demo.vhdlview
test.vhd         tester.sim*         tester-io.vhdlview
nu>
```

The circuit can now be simulated. Use the *simulate* command.

```
nu>    simulate tester
%KER-I-Elab, Elaborating.
%KER-I-Init, Initializing.
%KER-I-Simul, Simulating.
%KER-I-TimeHi, Simulation terminating; time reached Time'High.
%KER-I-Complete, Simulation Complete.
nu>
nu>
```

A trace file has been added to the present working directory.

```
nu>    ls
and2.vhd          and2.vhdlview       and2-run_demo.vhdlview
test.vhd          tester.sim*         tester-io.vhdlview
tester.trace
nu>
```

Use the *format* program to create a file listing signals in the trace file.

```
nu>    format tester -preview
nu>
```

A control file has been created.

```
nu>    ls
and2.vhd          and2.vhdlview       and2-run_demo.vhdlview
test.vhd          tester.sim*         tester-io.vhdlview
tester.trace      tester.control
nu>
nu>
```

The control file contains a list of signals, and can be edited if necessary to remove or add signals.

```
nu>     cat tester.control
DISPLAY 1 # /tester(io).a
DISPLAY 2 # /tester(io).b
DISPLAY 3 # /tester(io).c
nu>
nu>
```

Use the *format* program to generate the wave file listing values of signals in the control file.

```
nu>     format tester
%FMT-I-Create, Creating formatted wave file: tester.wave.
%FMT-I-Width, 3 signal(s) formatted, requiring 27 columns.
nu>
nu>
```

The waveform file lists events and transactions on signals.

```
nu>     cat tester.wave
Formatted Simulation Output
Signal          Signal
Number          Path Name
----------------------------
          1   : /tester(io).a
          2   : /tester(io).b
          3   : /tester(io).c
T(fs) + Delta       1    2    3
----------    --    ---  ---  ---
         0+  0:   '0'  '0'  '0'
         0+  1:  *'0'*'0'  '0'
   5000000+  0:   '0'  '0'*'0'
 100000000+  0:  *'1'  '0'  '0'
 105000000+  0:   '1'  '0'*'0'
 150000000+  0:   '1'*'1'  '0'
 155000000+  0:   '1'  '1'*'1'
 200000000+  0:  *'0'  '1'  '1'
 205000000+  0:   '0'  '1'*'0'
 250000000+  0:   '0'*'0'  '0'
 255000000+  0:   '0'  '0'*'0'
 300000000+  0:  *'1'  '0'  '0'
 305000000+  0:   '1'  '0'*'0'
 350000000+  0:   '1'*'1'  '0'
 355000000+  0:   '1'  '1'*'1'
nu>
nu>
```

Simulation of the two-input AND gate is completed.

```
nu>
nu>
```

B.4 A SESSION OF THE VHDL XL SYSTEM

This section presents a sample session for simulating a small example using the VHDL XL System of Cadence Design Systems.[4] The simulation was performed on a SUN-4 machine. For this simulation the following files are needed:

```
FILE: and2.vhd; -- Input file name.
ENTITY and2 IS
    PORT (x1, x2: IN BIT; z: OUT BIT);
END and2;
ARCHITECTURE run_demo OF and2 IS
BEGIN
    z <= x1 AND x2 AFTER 5 NS;
END run_demo;
```

FILE: test.vhd; – A simple test bench.

```
ENTITY tester IS END tester;
ARCHITECTURE io OF tester IS
    COMPONENT and2 PORT (x1, x2 : IN BIT; z : OUT BIT);
    END COMPONENT;
    FOR ALL : and2 USE ENTITY WORK.and2(run_demo);
    SIGNAL a, b, c : BIT;
BEGIN
    c1 : and2 PORT MAP (a, b, c);
    a <= '0', '1' AFTER 100 NS, '0' AFTER 200 NS, '1' AFTER 300 NS;
    b <= '0', '1' AFTER 150 NS, '0' AFTER 250 NS, '1' AFTER 350 NS;
END io;
```

Session Run Follows:

Invoke the VHDL shell

```
unix>  vsh
VHDL-XL 1.1     Mar 26, 1992   14:42:18
    * Copyright Cadence Design Systems, Inc. 1990, 1991.    *
    *     All Rights Reserved.        Licensed Software.    *
    * Confidential and proprietary information which is the *
    *     property of Cadence Design Systems, Inc.          *
```

Create directory to use as work library.

```
vhdl-xl[1]  mkdir sample
```

Define logical WORK as *sample* directory

```
vhdl-xl[2]    define_library WORK sample
```

Analyze the contents of file and2.vhd

---

[4]Cadence Design Systems; 555 River Oaks Parkway; San Jose, CA 95134; Tel: 408-943-1284

```
vhdl-xl[3]    analyze and2.vhd
VHDL-XL 1.1    Mar 26, 1992   14:42:42
   * Copyright Cadence Design Systems, Inc. 1990, 1991.    *
   *      All Rights Reserved.         Licensed Software.    *
   * Confidential and proprietary information which is the    *
   *        property of Cadence Design Systems, Inc.    *
Analyzing file "/home/sample/and2.vhd"
   entity declaration:          And2
   architecture body:            Run_Demo
Analysis of 9 lines is complete.  No errors were detected.
CPU time = 0.0 secs for analysis + 0.2 secs for compilation
End of VHDL-XL 1.1      Mar 26, 1992   14:42:43
```

List the contents of the work library

```
vhdl-xl[4]    list_units work
And2                 entity_declaration
And2.Run_Demo    architecture_body
```

Analyze the contents of file tester.vhd

```
vhdl-xl[5]    analyze tester.vhd
VHDL-XL 1.1    Mar 26, 1992   14:42:56
   * Copyright Cadence Design Systems, Inc. 1990, 1991.    *
   *      All Rights Reserved.         Licensed Software.    *
   * Confidential and proprietary information which is the    *
   *        property of Cadence Design Systems, Inc.    *
Analyzing file "/home/sample/tester.vhd"
   entity declaration:          Tester
   architecture body:            Io
Analysis of 17 lines is complete.  No errors were detected.
CPU time = 0.1 secs for analysis + 0.2 secs for compilation
End of VHDL-XL 1.1      Mar 26, 1992   14:42:56
```

List contents of WORK library

```
vhdl-xl[6]    list_units WORK
And2                 entity_declaration
And2.Run_Demo    architecture_body
Tester               entity_declaration
Tester.Io            architecture_body
```

Invoke simulation

```
vhdl-xl[7]    simulate -d WORK.tester.io
VHDL-XL 1.1    Mar 26, 1992   14:43:14
   * Copyright Cadence Design Systems, Inc. 1990, 1991.    *
   *      All Rights Reserved.         Licensed Software.    *
   * Confidential and proprietary information which is the    *
   *        property of Cadence Design Systems, Inc.    *

Elaborating  ...
Simulating  ...
```

Current File is /home/sample/tester.vhd

Specify signals to monitor

```
debug[1]    monitor a,b,c
```

Continue simulation until completion

```
debug[2]    continue
```

0	ns	A	=	'0'	B	=	'0'	C	=	'0'
100	ns	A	=	'1'	B	=	'0'	C	=	'0'
150	ns	A	=	'1'	B	=	'1'	C	=	'0'
155	ns	A	=	'1'	B	=	'1'	C	=	'1'
200	ns	A	=	'0'	B	=	'1'	C	=	'1'
205	ns	A	=	'0'	B	=	'1'	C	=	'0'
250	ns	A	=	'0'	B	=	'0'	C	=	'0'
300	ns	A	=	'1'	B	=	'0'	C	=	'0'
350	ns	A	=	'1'	B	=	'1'	C	=	'0'
355	ns	A	=	'1'	B	=	'1'	C	=	'1'

```
88 simulation events 14 simulation cycles
CPU time: 0 secs in elaboration + 0 secs in simulation
Data structure takes 58308 bytes of memory
End of VHDL-XL 1.1     Mar 26, 1992   14:43:22
```

Exit VHDL shell

```
vhdl-xl[8]    exit
End of VHDL-XL 1.1     Mar 26, 1992   14:43:25
```

APPENDIX
C

STANDARD
MSI 74LS
PACKAGES

Several 7400 standard packages are presented in this appendix. The delays used are simplified and are based on the typical values listed in the TTL Logic data book.

C.1   74LS85 4-BIT MAGNITUDE COMPARATOR

```
ENTITY ls85_comparator IS
    GENERIC (prop_delay : TIME := 11 NS);
    PORT (a, b : IN qit_vector (3 DOWNTO 0);   gt, eq, lt : IN qit;
          a_gt_b, a_eq_b, a_lt_b : OUT qit);
END ls85_comparator;
ARCHITECTURE behavioral OF ls85_comparator IS
BEGIN
    PROCESS (a, b, gt, eq, lt)
        VARIABLE ai, bi : INTEGER;
    BEGIN
        qit2int (a, ai);
        qit2int (b, bi);
        IF ai > bi THEN
            a_gt_b <= '1' AFTER prop_delay;
            a_eq_b <= '0' AFTER prop_delay;
            a_lt_b <= '0' AFTER prop_delay;
        ELSIF ai < bi THEN
            a_gt_b <= '0' AFTER prop_delay;
            a_eq_b <= '0' AFTER prop_delay;
            a_lt_b <= '1' AFTER prop_delay;
        ELSIF ai = bi THEN
            a_gt_b <= gt AFTER prop_delay;
            a_eq_b <= eq AFTER prop_delay;
            a_lt_b <= lt AFTER prop_delay;
        END IF;
    END PROCESS;
END behavioral;
```

C.2 74LS157 QUADRUPLE 2-LINE TO 1-LINE MULTIPLEXER

```
ENTITY ls157 IS
   GENERIC (prop_delay : TIME := 18 NS;
   PORT (g_bar, s : IN qit;
         a4, b4 : IN qit_vector(3 DOWNTO 0);
         y4 : OUT qit_vector(3 DOWNTO 0));
END ls157;
ARCHITECTURE dataflow OF ls157 IS
BEGIN
   PROCESS (a4, b4, g_bar, s)
   BEGIN
      IF g_bar = '0' THEN
         IF s = '0' THEN
            y4 <= a4 AFTER prop_delay;
         ELSE
            y4 <= b4 AFTER prop_delay;
         END IF;
      ELSE
         y4 <= "0000";
      END IF;
   END PROCESS;
END dataflow;
```

C.3 74LS163 SYNCHRONOUS 4-BIT COUNTER

```
ENTITY ls163_counter IS
   GENERIC (prop_delay : TIME := 18 NS);
   PORT (clk, clr_bar, ld_bar, enp, ent : IN qit;
         abcd : IN qit_vector (3 DOWNTO 0);
         q_abcd : OUT qit_vector (3 DOWNTO 0); rco : OUT qit);
END ls163_counter;
ARCHITECTURE behavioral OF ls163_counter IS
BEGIN
   counting : PROCESS (clk)
      VARIABLE internal_count : qit_vector (3 DOWNTO 0) := "0000";
   BEGIN
      IF (clk = '1') THEN
         IF (clr_bar = '0') THEN
            internal_count := "0000";
         ELSIF (ld_bar = '0') THEN
            internal_count := abcd;
         ELSIF (enp = '1' AND ent = '1') THEN
            internal_count := inc (internal_count);
            IF (internal_count = "1111") THEN
               rco <= '1' AFTER prop_delay;
            ELSE
               rco <= '0';
            END IF;
         END IF;
         q_abcd <= internal_count AFTER prop_delay;
      END IF;
   END PROCESS counting;
END behavioral;
```

C.4   74LS283 4-BIT BINARY FULL ADDER

```
ENTITY ls283 IS
   GENERIC (prop_delay : TIME := 14 NS; prop_delay1 : TIME := 16 NS);
   PORT (c0 : IN qit; c4 : OUT qit;
         a4, b4 : IN qit_vector (3 DOWNTO 0);
         s4 : OUT qit_vetor (3 DOWNTO 0));
END ls283;
LIBRARY tutorial;
USE tutorial.t_utilities.ALL;
ARCHITECTURE behavioral OF ls283 IS
BEGIN
   adder : PROCESS (a4,b4,c0)
      VARIABLE atemp,btemp,ytemp : INTEGER := 0;
      VARIABLE stemp : qit_vector(3 DOWNTO 0) := "0000";
   BEGIN
      qit_to_int (a4,atemp);
      qit_to_int (b4,btemp);
      IF (c0 = '1') THEN
          ytemp := atemp + btemp + 1;
      ELSE
          ytemp := atemp + btemp;
      ENDIF;
      IF ytemp > 15 THEN
          c4 <= '1' AFTER prop_delay;
      ELSE
          c4 <= '0' AFTER prop_delay;
      END IF;
      int_to_qit (ytemp,stemp);
      s4 <= stemp AFTER prop_delay1;
   END PROCESS adder;
END behavioral;
```

C.5   74LS373 OCTAL D-TYPE TRANSPARENT LATCHES

```
ENTITY ls373_register IS
   GENERIC (prop_delay : TIME := 15 NS);
   PORT (clk, oc_bar : IN qit; d8 : IN qit_vector (7 DOWNTO 0);
         q8 : OUT qit_vector (7 DOWNTO 0));
END ls373_register;
ARCHITECTURE dataflow OF ls373_register IS
   SIGNAL state qit_vector (7 DOWNTO 0);
BEGIN
   reg: BLOCK ( clk = '1' )
   BEGIN
      state <= GUARDED d8 AFTER prop_delay;
   END BLOCK reg;
   q8 <= state WHEN oc_bar = '0' ELSE "ZZZZZZZZ";
END dataflow;
```

C.6   74LS377 OCTAL D-TYPE FLIP-FLOPS

```
ENTITY ls377_register IS
   GENERIC (prop_delay : TIME := 17 NS);
   PORT (clk, g_bar : IN qit; d8 : IN qit_vector (7 DOWNTO 0);
         q8 : OUT qit_vector (7 DOWNTO 0));
END ls377_register;
```

```
ARCHITECTURE dataflow OF ls377_register IS
   SIGNAL GUARD : BOOLEAN;
BEGIN
   GUARD <= NOT clk'STABLE AND clk = '1' AND (g_bar = '0');
   q8 <= GUARDED d8 AFTER prop_delay;
END dataflow;
```

C.7 74LS299 UNIVERSAL SHIFT-REGISTER

```
ENTITY LS299 IS
   GENERIC (prop_delay : TIME := 27 NS);
   PORT (clk, clr_bar, lin, rin : IN qit;
         s, g_bar : IN qit_vector (1 DOWNTO 0);
         qq : OUT qit_vector (7 DOWNTO 0));
END LS299;
ARCHITECTURE behavioral OF LS299 IS
   SIGNAL iq : qit_vector (7 DOWNTO 0);
BEGIN
   clocking : PROCESS (clk,clr_bar)
   BEGIN
      IF clr_bar = '1' THEN
         iq <= "00000000";
         ELSE IF (clk'EVENT AND clk = '1') THEN
            CASE s IS
               WHEN "01" =>
                  iq <= rin & iq (7 DOWNTO 1);
               WHEN "10" =>
                  iq <= iq (6) & iq (5 DOWNTO 0) & lin;
               WHEN "01" =>
                  iq <= qq;
               WHEN OTHERS => NULL;
            END CASE;
         END IF;
      END IF;
   END PROCESS clocking;
   tri_state: PROCESS (iq, g_bar)
   BEGIN
      IF g_bar = "00" THEN
         IF s /= "11" THEN
            qq <= iq;
         ELSE
            qq <= "ZZZZZZZZ";
         END IF;
      ELSE
         qq <= "ZZZZZZZZ";
      END IF;
   END PROCESS tri_state;
   qa <= iq(7);
   qh <= iq(0);
END dataflow;
```

C.8 74LS541 TRANCEIVER

```
ENTITY ls541 IS
   GENERIC (prop_delay : TIME := 10 NS);
   PORT (g_bar : IN qit_vector (1 DOWNTO 0);
         a8 : IN qit_vector (7 DOWNTO 0);
         y8 : OUT qit_vector (7 DOWNTO 0));
END ls541;
```

```
ARCHITECTURE dataflow OF ls541 IS
BEGIN
    y8 <= a8 AFTER prop_delay WHEN g_bar = "00" ELSE
    "ZZZZZZZZ";
END dataflow;
```

DESCRIPTIONS
OF PARWAN

This appendix shows complete descriptions for the entities relating to the Parwan CPU that we only presented as code fragments in Chapter 9. Section D.1 contains the complete behavioral description of Parwan. This description was presented in Figures 9.15 to 9.26. The complete dataflow description of Parwan Controller presented in Figures 9.52 to 9.64 is shown here in Section D.2.

D.1 PARWAN BEHAVIORAL DESCRIPTION

```
LIBRARY cmos;
USE cmos.basic_utilities.ALL;
LIBRARY par_library;
USE par_library.par_utilities.ALL;
USE par_library.par_parameters.ALL;
--
ENTITY par_central_processing_unit IS
    GENERIC (read_high_time, read_low_time,
                write_high_time, write_low_time : TIME := 2 US;
                cycle_time : TIME := 4 US; run_time : TIME := 140 US);
    PORT (clk : IN qit;
            interrupt : IN qit;
            read_mem, write_mem : OUT qit;
            databus : INOUT wired_byte BUS := "ZZZZZZZZ"; adbus : OUT twelve
            );
END par_central_processing_unit;
--
```

```
ARCHITECTURE behavioral OF par_central_processing_unit IS
BEGIN
    PROCESS
        VARIABLE pc : twelve;
        VARIABLE ac, byte1, byte2 : byte;
        VARIABLE v, c, z, n : qit;
        VARIABLE temp : qit_vector (9 DOWNTO 0);
    BEGIN
        IF NOW > run_time THEN WAIT; END IF;
        IF interrupt = '1' THEN
            pc := zero_12;
            WAIT FOR cycle_time;
        ELSE    -- no interrupt
            adbus <= pc;
            read_mem <= '1';   WAIT FOR read_high_time;
            byte1 := byte (databus);
            read_mem <= '0';   WAIT FOR read_low_time;
            pc := inc (pc);
            IF byte1 (7 DOWNTO 4) = single_byte_instructions THEN
                CASE byte1 (3 DOWNTO 0) IS
                    WHEN cla =>
                        ac := zero_8;
                    WHEN cma =>
                        ac := NOT ac;
                        IF ac = zero_8 THEN z := '1'; END IF;
                        n := ac (7);
                    WHEN cmc =>
                        c := NOT c;
                    WHEN asl =>
                        c := ac (7);
                        ac := ac (6 DOWNTO 0) & '0';
                        n := ac (7);
                        IF c /= n THEN v := '1'; END IF;
                    WHEN asr =>
                        ac := ac (7) & ac (7 DOWNTO 1);
                        IF ac = zero_8 THEN z := '1'; END IF;
                        n := ac (7);
                    WHEN OTHERS => NULL;
                END CASE;
            ELSE    -- two-byte instructions
                adbus <= pc;
                read_mem <= '1';   WAIT FOR read_high_time;
                byte2 := byte (databus);
                read_mem <= '0';   WAIT FOR read_low_time;
                pc := inc (pc);
                IF byte1 (7 DOWNTO 5) = jsr THEN
                    databus <= wired_byte (pc (7 DOWNTO 0) );
                    adbus (7 DOWNTO 0) <= byte2;
                    write_mem <= '1';   WAIT FOR write_high_time;
                    write_mem <= '0';   WAIT FOR write_low_time;
                    databus <= "ZZZZZZZZ";
                    pc (7 DOWNTO 0) := inc (byte2);
                ELSIF byte1 (7 DOWNTO 4) = bra THEN
                    IF
                        ( byte1 (3) = '1' AND v = '1' ) OR
                        ( byte1 (2) = '1' AND c = '1' ) OR
                        ( byte1 (1) = '1' AND z = '1' ) OR
                        ( byte1 (0) = '1' AND n = '1' )
                    THEN
```

```
                        pc (7 DOWNTO 0) := byte2;
                    END IF;
                ELSE -- all other two-byte instructions
                    IF byte1 (4) = indirect THEN
                        adbus (11 DOWNTO 8) <= byte1 (3 DOWNTO 0);
                        adbus (7 DOWNTO 0) <= byte2;
                        read_mem <= '1';  WAIT FOR read_high_time;
                        byte2 := byte (databus);
                        read_mem <= '0';  WAIT FOR read_low_time;
                    END IF; -- ends indirect
                    IF byte1 (7 DOWNTO 5) = jmp THEN
                        pc := byte1 (3 DOWNTO 0) & byte2;
                    ELSIF byte1 (7 DOWNTO 5) = sta THEN
                        adbus <= byte1 (3 DOWNTO 0) & byte2;
                        databus <= wired_byte (ac);
                        write_mem <= '1';  WAIT FOR write_high_time;
                        write_mem <= '0';  WAIT FOR write_low_time;
                        databus <= "ZZZZZZZZ";
                    ELSE -- read operand for lda, and, add, sub
                        adbus (11 DOWNTO 8) <= byte1 (3 DOWNTO 0);
                        adbus (7 DOWNTO 0) <= byte2;
                        read_mem <= '1';  WAIT FOR read_high_time;
                        CASE byte1 (7 DOWNTO 5) IS
                            WHEN lda =>
                                ac := byte (databus);
                            WHEN ann =>
                                ac := ac AND byte (databus);
                            WHEN add =>
                                temp := add_cv (ac, byte (databus), c);
                                ac := temp (7 DOWNTO 0);
                                c := temp (8);
                                v := temp (9);
                            WHEN sbb =>
                                temp := sub_cv (ac, byte (databus), c);
                                ac := temp (7 DOWNTO 0);
                                c := temp (8);
                                v := temp (9);
                            WHEN OTHERS => NULL;
                        END CASE;
                        IF ac = zero_8 THEN z := '1'; END IF;
                        n := ac (7);
                        read_mem <= '0';  WAIT FOR read_low_time;
                    END IF; -- jmp / sta / lda, and, add, sub
                END IF; -- jsr / bra / other double-byte instructions
            END IF; -- single-byte / double-byte
        END IF; -- interrupt / otherwise
    END PROCESS;
END behavioral;
```

D.2 CONTROLLER OF PARWAN DATAFLOW DESCRIPTION

```
LIBRARY cmos;
USE cmos.basic_utilities.ALL;
LIBRARY par_library;
USE par_library.par_utilities.ALL;
USE WORK.alu_operations.ALL;
```

```
--
ENTITY par_control_unit IS
   GENERIC (read_delay, write_delay : TIME := 3 NS);
   PORT (clk : IN qit;
              -- register control signals:
              load_ac, zero_ac,
              load_ir,
              increment_pc, load_page_pc, load_offset_pc, reset_pc,
              load_page_mar, load_offset_mar,
              load_sr, cm_carry_sr,
              -- bus connection control signals:
              pc_on_mar_page_bus, ir_on_mar_page_bus,
              pc_on_mar_offset_bus, dbus_on_mar_offset_bus,
              pc_offset_on_dbus, obus_on_dbus, databus_on_dbus,
              mar_on_adbus,
              dbus_on_databus,
              -- logic unit function control outputs:
              arith_shift_left, arith_shift_right : OUT qit;
              alu_code : OUT qit_vector (2 DOWNTO 0);
              -- inputs from the data section:
              ir_lines : IN byte; status : IN nibble;
              -- memory control and other external signals:
              read_mem, write_mem : OUT qit; interrupt : IN qit
              );
END par_control_unit;
--


ARCHITECTURE dataflow OF par_control_unit IS
   -- oring is implied in the following signals (oi)
      SIGNAL load_ac_oi, zero_ac_oi,
                 load_ir_oi,
                 increment_pc_oi, load_page_pc_oi, load_offset_pc_oi, reset_pc_oi,
                 load_page_mar_oi, load_offset_mar_oi,
                 load_sr_oi, cm_carry_sr_oi,
                 pc_on_mar_page_bus_oi, ir_on_mar_page_bus_oi,
                 pc_on_mar_offset_bus_oi, dbus_on_mar_offset_bus_oi,
                 pc_offset_on_dbus_oi, obus_on_dbus_oi, databus_on_dbus_oi,
                 mar_on_adbus_oi,
                 dbus_on_databus_oi,
                 arith_shift_left_oi, arith_shift_right_oi,
                 read_mem_oi, write_mem_oi : ored_qit BUS;
      SIGNAL alu_code_oi : ored_qit_vector (2 DOWNTO 0) BUS;
      SIGNAL s : ored_qit_vector (9 DOWNTO 1) REGISTER := "000000001";
BEGIN
   -- implied or assignments to output signals
      load_ac <= load_ac_oi;
      zero_ac <= zero_ac_oi;
      load_ir <= load_ir_oi;
      increment_pc <= increment_pc_oi;
      load_page_pc <= load_page_pc_oi;
      load_offset_pc <= load_offset_pc_oi;
      reset_pc <= reset_pc_oi;
      load_page_mar <= load_page_mar_oi;
      load_offset_mar <= load_offset_mar_oi;
      load_sr <= load_sr_oi;
      cm_carry_sr <= cm_carry_sr_oi;
      pc_on_mar_page_bus <= pc_on_mar_page_bus_oi;
      ir_on_mar_page_bus <= ir_on_mar_page_bus_oi;
      pc_on_mar_offset_bus <= pc_on_mar_offset_bus_oi;
```

```
    dbus_on_mar_offset_bus  <=  dbus_on_mar_offset_bus_oi;
    pc_offset_on_dbus  <=  pc_offset_on_dbus_oi;
    obus_on_dbus  <=  obus_on_dbus_oi;
    databus_on_dbus  <=  databus_on_dbus_oi;
    mar_on_adbus  <=  mar_on_adbus_oi;
    dbus_on_databus  <=  dbus_on_databus_oi;
    arith_shift_left  <=  arith_shift_left_oi;
    arith_shift_right  <=  arith_shift_right_oi;
    read_mem  <=  read_mem_oi;
    write_mem  <=  write_mem_oi;
    alu_code  <=  qit_vector (alu_code_oi);
-------------
 ┌s1: BLOCK (s(1) = '1')
 ├BEGIN -- start of fetch
    -- pc to mar
    pc_on_mar_page_bus_oi  <=  GUARDED '1';
    pc_on_mar_offset_bus_oi  <=  GUARDED '1';
    load_page_mar_oi  <=  GUARDED '1';
    load_offset_mar_oi  <=  GUARDED '1';
    -- reset pc if interrupt
    reset_pc_oi  <=  GUARDED '1' WHEN interrupt = '1' ELSE '0';
    -- goto 2 if interrupt is off
    ck: BLOCK ( (clk = '0' AND NOT clk'STABLE) AND GUARD )
    BEGIN
      s(1)  <=  GUARDED '1' WHEN interrupt = '1' ELSE '0';
      s(2)  <=  GUARDED '1' WHEN interrupt /= '1' ELSE '0';
    END BLOCK ck;
 └END BLOCK s1;
-------------
 ┌s2: BLOCK (s(2) = '1')
 ├BEGIN -- fetching continues
    -- read memory into ir
    mar_on_adbus_oi  <=  GUARDED '1';
    read_mem_oi  <=  GUARDED '1' AFTER read_delay;
    databus_on_dbus_oi  <=  GUARDED '1';
    alu_code_oi  <=  GUARDED ored_qit_vector (a_input);
    load_ir_oi  <=  GUARDED '1';
    -- increment pc
    increment_pc_oi  <=  GUARDED '1';
    -- goto 3
    ck: BLOCK ( (clk = '0' AND NOT clk'STABLE) AND GUARD )
    BEGIN
      s(3)  <=  GUARDED '1';
    END BLOCK ck;
 └END BLOCK s2;
-------------
 ┌s3: BLOCK (s(3) = '1')
 ├BEGIN
    -- pc to mar, for next read
    pc_on_mar_page_bus_oi  <=  GUARDED '1';
    pc_on_mar_offset_bus_oi  <=  GUARDED '1';
    load_page_mar_oi  <=  GUARDED '1';
    load_offset_mar_oi  <=  GUARDED '1';
    -- goto 4 if not single byte instruction
    ck: BLOCK ( (clk = '0' AND NOT clk'STABLE) AND GUARD )
    BEGIN
      s(4)  <=  GUARDED '1' WHEN ir_lines (7 DOWNTO 4) /= "1110" ELSE '0';
    END BLOCK ck;
    -- perform single byte instructions
```

```
sb: BLOCK ( (ir_lines (7 DOWNTO 4) = "1110") AND GUARD)
BEGIN
    alu_code_oi <= GUARDED
        ored_qit_vector (b_compl) WHEN ir_lines (1) = '1' ELSE
        ored_qit_vector (b_input);
    arith_shift_left_oi <= GUARDED
        '1' WHEN ir_lines (3 DOWNTO 0) = "1000" ELSE '0';
    arith_shift_right_oi <= GUARDED
        '1' WHEN ir_lines (3 DOWNTO 0) = "1001" ELSE '0';
    load_sr_oi <= GUARDED
        '1' WHEN ( ir_lines (3) = '1' OR ir_lines (1) = '1' ) ELSE '0';
    cm_carry_sr_oi <= GUARDED '1' WHEN ir_lines (2) = '1' ELSE '0';
    load_ac_oi <= GUARDED
        '1' WHEN ( ir_lines (3) = '1' OR ir_lines (1) = '1' OR ir_lines (0)='1' ) ELSE '0';
    zero_ac_oi <= GUARDED
        '1' WHEN ( ir_lines (3) = '0' AND ir_lines (0) = '1' ) ELSE '0';
    ck: BLOCK ( (clk = '0' AND NOT clk'STABLE) AND GUARD )
    BEGIN
        s(2) <= GUARDED '1';
    END BLOCK ck;
END BLOCK sb;
END BLOCK s3;
-------------
s4: BLOCK (s(4) = '1')
BEGIN -- page from ir, and offset from next memory makeup 12-bit address
    -- read memory into mar offset
    mar_on_adbus_oi <= GUARDED '1';
    read_mem_oi <= GUARDED '1' AFTER read_delay;
    databus_on_dbus_oi <= GUARDED '1';
    dbus_on_mar_offset_bus_oi <= GUARDED '1';
    load_offset_mar_oi <= GUARDED
        '1'; -- completed operand (dir/indir) address
    -- page from ir if not branch or jsr
    pg: BLOCK ( (ir_lines (7 DOWNTO 6) /= "11") AND GUARD)
    BEGIN
        ir_on_mar_page_bus_oi <= GUARDED '1';
        load_page_mar_oi <= GUARDED '1';
        -- goto 5 for indirect, 6 for direct
        ck: BLOCK ( (clk = '0' AND NOT clk'STABLE) AND GUARD )
        BEGIN
            s(5) <= GUARDED '1' WHEN ir_lines (4) = '1' ELSE '0';  -- indir
            s(6) <= GUARDED '1' WHEN ir_lines (4) = '0' ELSE '0';  -- direct
        END BLOCK ck;
    END BLOCK pg;
    -- keep page in mar_page if jsr or bra (same-page instructions)
    sp: BLOCK ( (ir_lines (7 DOWNTO 6) = "11") AND GUARD)
    BEGIN
        -- goto 7 for jsr, 9 for bra
        ck: BLOCK ( (clk = '0' AND NOT clk'STABLE) AND GUARD )
        BEGIN
            s(7) <= GUARDED '1' WHEN ir_lines (5) = '0' ELSE '0';  -- jsr
            s(9) <= GUARDED '1' WHEN ir_lines (5) = '1' ELSE '0';  -- bra
        END BLOCK ck;
    END BLOCK sp;
    -- increment pc
    increment_pc_oi <= GUARDED '1';
END BLOCK s4;
-------------
s5: BLOCK (s(5) = '1')
```

```
-BEGIN -- indirect addressing
   -- read actual operand from memory into mar offset
   mar_on_adbus_oi <= GUARDED '1';
   read_mem_oi <= GUARDED '1' AFTER read_delay;
   databus_on_dbus_oi <= GUARDED '1';
   dbus_on_mar_offset_bus_oi <= GUARDED '1';
   load_offset_mar_oi <= GUARDED '1';
   -- goto 6
   ck: BLOCK ( (clk = '0' AND NOT clk'STABLE) AND GUARD )
   BEGIN
      s(6) <= GUARDED '1';
   END BLOCK ck;
-END BLOCK s5;
-------------
-s6: BLOCK (s(6) = '1')
-BEGIN
   -jm: BLOCK ( (ir_lines (7 DOWNTO 5) = "100") AND GUARD)
   -BEGIN
      load_page_pc_oi <= GUARDED '1';
      load_offset_pc_oi <= GUARDED '1';
      -- goto 2
      ck: BLOCK ( (clk = '0' AND NOT clk'STABLE) AND GUARD )
      BEGIN
         s(2) <= GUARDED '1';
      END BLOCK ck;
   -END BLOCK jm;
   --
   -st: BLOCK ( (ir_lines (7 DOWNTO 5) = "101") AND GUARD)
   -BEGIN
      -- mar on adbus, ac on databus, write to memory
      mar_on_adbus_oi <= GUARDED '1';
      alu_code_oi <= GUARDED ored_qit_vector (b_input);
      obus_on_dbus_oi <= GUARDED '1';
      dbus_on_databus_oi <= GUARDED '1';
      write_mem_oi <= GUARDED '1' AFTER write_delay;
      -- goto 1
      ck: BLOCK ( (clk = '0' AND NOT clk'STABLE) AND GUARD )
      BEGIN
         s(1) <= GUARDED '1';
      END BLOCK ck;
   -END BLOCK st;
   --
   -rd: BLOCK ( (ir_lines (7) = '0') AND GUARD)
   -BEGIN
      -- mar on adbus, read memory for operand, perform operation
      mar_on_adbus_oi <= GUARDED '1';
      read_mem_oi <= GUARDED '1' AFTER read_delay;
      databus_on_dbus_oi <= GUARDED '1';
      WITH ir_lines (6 DOWNTO 5) SELECT
         alu_code_oi <= GUARDED
            ored_qit_vector (a_input) WHEN "00",
            ored_qit_vector (a_and_b) WHEN "01",
            ored_qit_vector (a_add_b) WHEN "10",
            ored_qit_vector (a_sub_b) WHEN "11",
            ored_qit_vector (b_input) WHEN OTHERS;
      load_sr_oi <= GUARDED '1';
      load_ac_oi <= GUARDED '1';
      -- goto 1
      ck: BLOCK ( (clk = '0' AND NOT clk'STABLE) AND GUARD )
```

```
            BEGIN
              s(1) <= GUARDED '1';
            END BLOCK ck;
        END BLOCK rd;
    END BLOCK s6;
---------------
s7: BLOCK (s(7) = '1')
BEGIN    -- jsr
    -- write pc offset to top of subroutine
    mar_on_adbus_oi <= GUARDED '1';
    pc_offset_on_dbus_oi <= GUARDED '1';
    dbus_on_databus_oi <= GUARDED '1';
    write_mem_oi <= GUARDED '1' AFTER write_delay;
    -- address of subroutine to pc
    load_offset_pc_oi <= GUARDED '1';
    -- goto 8
    ck: BLOCK ( (clk = '0' AND NOT clk'STABLE) AND GUARD )
    BEGIN
        s(8) <= GUARDED '1';
    END BLOCK ck;
END BLOCK s7;
--------------
s8: BLOCK (s(8) = '1')
BEGIN
    -- increment pc
    increment_pc_oi <= GUARDED '1';
    -- goto 1
    ck: BLOCK ( (clk = '0' AND NOT clk'STABLE) AND GUARD )
    BEGIN
        s(1) <= GUARDED '1';
    END BLOCK ck;
END BLOCK s8;
--------------
s9: BLOCK (s(9) = '1')
BEGIN
    load_offset_pc_oi <= GUARDED
        '1' WHEN (status AND ir_lines (3 DOWNTO 0)) /= "0000" ELSE '0';
    -- goto 1
    ck: BLOCK ( (clk = '0' AND NOT clk'STABLE) AND GUARD )
    BEGIN
        s(1) <= GUARDED '1';
    END BLOCK ck;
END BLOCK s9;
---------------
ck: BLOCK ( clk = '0' AND NOT clk'STABLE )
BEGIN
    s (9 DOWNTO 1) <= GUARDED "000000000";
END BLOCK ck;

END dataflow;
```

APPENDIX
E

VHDL LANGUAGE GRAMMAR

This appendix contains the formal grammar of the standard 1076-1987 VHDL language in BNF format.[1] In this format, productions are on the left hand side of an equivalence, two colons and an equal sign are used for equivalence, vertical bars for oring, square brackets for optional parts, and curly brackets for parts that zero or more of them may be used.

As in the chapters of this book, we have used uppercase letters for the language reserved words. The language productions are ordered alphabetically with page numbers corresponding to pages in the book where an example production is presented.

abstract_literal ::= decimal_literal | based_literal   [27]

access_type_definition ::= ACCESS subtype_indication   [365]

actual_designator ::=   [32]

```
    expression
    | signal_name
    | variable_name
    | OPEN

actual_parameter_part ::=   parameter_association_list                              [92]

actual_part ::=                                                                     [92]
    actual_designator
    | function_name ( actual_designator )

adding_operator ::= + | - | &                                                       [38]

aggregate ::=                                                                       [158]
    ( element_association { , element_association } )

alias_declaration ::=                                                               [158]
    ALIAS identifier : subtype_indication IS name ;

allocator ::=                                                                       [---]
    NEW subtype_indication
    | NEW qualified_expression

architecture_body ::=                                                               [32]
    ARCHITECTURE identifier OF entity_name IS
    architecture_declarative_part
    BEGIN
    architecture_statement_part
    END [ architecture_simple_name ] ;

architecture_declarative_part ::=                                                   [52]
    { block_declarative_item }

architecture_statement_part ::=                                                     [52]
    { concurrent_statement }

array_type_definition ::=                                                           [140]
    unconstrained_array_definition   |   constrained_array_definition

assertion_statement ::=                                                             [228]
    ASSERT condition
    [ REPORT expression ]
    [ SEVERITY expression ] ;

association_element ::=                                                             [106]
    [ formal_part => ] actual_part

association_list ::=                                                                [106]
    association_element { , association_element }

attribute_declaration ::=                                                           [165]
    ATTRIBUTE identifier : type_mark ;

attribute_designator ::=  attribute_simple_name                                     [166]

attribute_name ::=                                                                  [166]
    prefix ' attribute_designator [ ( static_expression ) ]
```

attribute_specification ::=
    ATTRIBUTE attribute_designator OF entity_specification IS expression ;   [166]

base ::= integer   [123]

base_specifier ::=   B | O | X   [123]

base_unit_declaration ::=   identifier ;   [123]

based_integer ::=
    extended_digit { [underline] extended_digit }   [123]

based_literal ::=
    base ├ based_integer [. based_integer] ┤ [exponent]   [123]

basic_character ::=
    basic_graphic_character | format_effector   [123]

basic_graphic_character ::=
    upper_case_letter | digit | special_character| space_character   [123]

binding_indication ::=
    entity_aspect
    [generic_map_aspect]
    [port_map_aspect]   [82]

bit_string_literal ::=   base_specifier " bit_value "   [75]

bit_value ::=   extended_digit { [underline] extended_digit }   [75]

block_configuration ::=
    FOR block_specification   [112]
    { use_clause }
    { configuration_item }
    END FOR ;

block_declarative_item ::=
    subprogram_declaration   [52]
    | subprogram_body
    | type_declaration
    | subtype_declaration
    | constant_declaration
    | signal_declaration
    | file_declaration
    | alias_declaration
    | component_declaration
    | attribute_declaration
    | attribute_specification
    | configuration_specification
    | disconnection_specification
    | use_clause

block_declarative_part ::=
    { block_declarative_item }   [52]

block_header ::=   [---]
    [generic_clause
    [generic_map_aspect ;]]
    [port_clause

```
            [ port_map_aspect ; ] ]
block_specification ::=                                                  [113]
  architecture_name
  | block_statement_label
  | generate_statement_label [ ( index_specification ) ]

block_statement ::=                                                      [181]
  block_label :
    BLOCK [ ( guard_expression ) ]
      block_header
      block_declarative_part
    BEGIN
      block_statement_part
    END BLOCK [ block_label ] ;

block_statement_part ::=                                                 [182]
  { concurrent_statement }

case_statement ::=                                                       [155]
  CASE expression IS
    case_statement_alternative
    { case_statement_alternative }
  END CASE ;

case_statement_alternative ::=                                           [155]
  WHEN choices =>
    sequence_of_statements

character_literal ::= ' graphic_character '                              [132]

choice ::=                                                               [155]
  simple_expression
  | discrete_range
  | element_simple_name
  | OTHERS

choices ::= choice { | choice }                                         [155]

component_configuration ::=                                             [112]
  FOR component_specification
    [ USE binding_indication ; ]
    [ block_configuration ]
  END FOR ;

component_declaration ::=                                                [65]
  COMPONENT identifier
    [ local_generic_clause ]
    [ local_port_clause ]
  END COMPONENT ;

component_instantiation_statement ::=                                   [105]
  instantiation_label :
    component_name
      [ generic_map_aspect ]
      [ port_map_aspect ] ;

component_specification ::=                                              [65]
  instantiation_list : component_name
```

```
composite_type_definition ::=                                              [158]
  array_type_definition
  | record_type_definition


concurrent_assertion_statement ::=                                         [230]
  [ label : ] assertion_statement


concurrent_procedure_call ::=                                              [243]
  [ label : ] procedure_call_statement


concurrent_signal_assignment_statement ::=                                  [37]
      [ label : ] conditional_signal_assignment
  | [ label : ] selected_signal_assignment


concurrent_statement ::=                                                    [72]
  block_statement
  | process_statement
  | concurrent_procedure_call
  | concurrent_assertion_statement
  | concurrent_signal_assignment_statement
  | component_instantiation_statement
  | generate_statement


condition ::=  boolean_expression                                          [134]


condition_clause ::=  UNTIL condition                                      [234]


conditional_signal_assignment ::=                                          [133]
  target  <= options conditional_waveforms ;


conditional_waveforms ::=                                                  [134]
  { waveform WHEN condition ELSE }
  waveform


configuration_declaration ::=                                             [111]
  CONFIGURATION identifier OF entity_name IS
    configuration_declarative_part
    block_configuration
  END [ configuration_simple_name ] ;


configuration_declarative_item ::=                                        [113]
  use_clause
  | attribute_specification


configuration_declarative_part ::=                                        [113]
  { configuration_declarative_item }


configuration_item ::=                                                    [113]
  block_configuration
  | component_configuration


configuration_specification ::=                                            [66]
  FOR component_specification USE binding_indication ;


constant_declaration ::=                                                  [136]
  CONSTANT identifier_list : subtype_indication [ := expression ] ;


constrained_array_definition ::=                                          [140]
  ARRAY index_constraint OF element_subtype_indication
```

```
constraint ::=                                                    [140]
  range_constraint
  | index_constraint

context_clause ::=   { context_item }                            [127]

context_item ::=                                                 [127]
  library_clause
  | use_clause

decimal_literal ::= integer [ . integer ] [ exponent ]          [137]

declaration ::=                                                  [148]
  type_declaration
  | subtype_declaration
  | object_declaration
  | file_declaration
  | interface_declaration
  | alias_declaration
  | attribute_declaration
  | component_declaration
  | entity_declaration
  | configuration_declaration
  | subprogram_declaration
  | package_declaration

design_file ::= design_unit { design_unit }                     [127]

design_unit ::= context_clause library_unit                     [127]

designator ::= identifier   |   operator_symbol                 [93]

direction ::= TO | DOWNTO                                        [140]

disconnection_specification ::=                                 [196]
  DISCONNECT guarded_signal_specification AFTER time_expression ;

discrete_range ::= discrete_subtype_indication | range          [140]

element_association ::=                                         [158]
  [ choices => ] expression

element_declaration ::=                                        [65]
  identifier_list : element_subtype_definition ;

element_subtype_definition ::= subtype_indication             [140]

entity_aspect ::=                                              [82]
      ENTITY entity_name [ ( architecture_identifier) ]
  | CONFIGURATION configuration_name
  | OPEN

entity_class ::=                                              [166]
  ENTITY | ARCHITECTURE   | CONFIGURATION
  | PROCEDURE   | FUNCTION   | PACKAGE
  | TYPE   | SUBTYPE | CONSTANT
  | SIGNAL   | VARIABLE | COMPONENT
  | LABEL
```

entity_declaration ::=   [30]
  ENTITY identifier IS
    entity_header
    entity_declarative_part
  [BEGIN
    entity_statement_part]
  END [entity_simple_name] ;

entity_declarative_item ::=   [205]
  subprogram_declaration
  | subprogram_body
  | type_declaration
  | subtype_declaration
  | constant_declaration
  | signal_declaration
  | file_declaration
  | alias_declaration
  | attribute_declaration
  | attribute_specification
  | disconnection_specification
  | use_clause

entity_declarative_part ::=   [205]
  { entity_declarative_item }

entity_designator ::=   simple_name | operator_symbol   [166]

entity_header ::=   [58]
  [formal_generic_clause]
  [formal_port_clause]

entity_name_list ::=   [167]
  entity_designator { , entity_designator }
  | OTHERS
  | ALL

entity_specification ::=   [166]
  entity_name_list : entity_class

entity_statement ::=   [253]
  concurrent_assertion_statement
  | passive_concurrent_procedure_call
  | passive_process_statement

entity_statement_part ::=   [253]
  { entity_statement }

enumeration_literal ::= identifier | character_literal   [133]

enumeration_type_definition ::=   [133]
  (enumeration_literal { , enumeration_literal })

exit_statement ::=   **[227]**
  EXIT [loop_label] [WHEN condition] ;

exponent ::= E [+] integer | E - integer   [137]

expression ::=   [37]

```
  | relation { AND relation }
  | relation { OR relation }
  | relation { XOR relation }
  | relation [ NAND relation ]
  | relation [ NOR relation ]

extended_digit ::= digit | letter                                    [123]

factor ::=                                                            [38]
  primary [ ** primary ]
  | ABS primary
  | NOT primary

file_declaration ::=                                                 [147]
FILE identifier : subtype_indication IS [ mode ] file_logical_name ;

file_logical_name ::=  string_expression                             [147]

file_type_definition ::=                                             [147]
  FILE OF type_mark

floating_type_definition  ::=  range_constraint                      [365]

formal_designator ::=                                                [106]
  generic_name
  | port_name
  | parameter_name

formal_parameter_list ::=  parameter_interface_list                  [93]

formal_part  ::=                                                     [106]
  formal_designator
  | function_name ( formal_designator )

full_type_declaration ::=                                            [133]
  TYPE identifier IS type_definition ;

function_call ::=                                                    [89]
  function_name [ ( actual_parameter_part ) ]

generate_statement ::=                                               [71]
  generate_label :
    generation_scheme GENERATE
    { concurrent_statement }
    END GENERATE [ generate_label ] ;

generation_scheme ::=                                                [72]
  FOR generate_parameter_specification
  | IF condition

generic_clause ::=                                                   [102]
  GENERIC ( generic_list ) ;

generic_list ::= generic_interface_list                             [102]

generic_map_aspect ::=                                               [106]
  GENERIC MAP ( generic_association_list )

graphic_character ::=                                                 [365]
```

basic_graphic_character | lower_case_letter | other_special_character

guarded_signal_specification ::=   [194]
guarded_signal_list : type_mark

identifier ::=   [30]
letter { [underline] letter_or_digit }

identifier_list ::= identifier { , identifier }   [52]

if_statement ::=   [95]
  IF condition THEN
    sequence_of_statements
  { ELSIF condition THEN
    sequence_of_statements }
  [ELSE
    sequence_of_statements]
  END IF ;

incomplete_type_declaration ::=   TYPE identifier ;   [---]

index_constraint ::= (discrete_range { , discrete_range })   [141]

index_specification ::=   [142]
  discrete_range
  | static_expression

index_subtype_definition ::= type_mark RANGE <>   [143]

indexed_name ::=   prefix (expression { , expression })   [141]

instantiation_list ::=   [82]
  instantiation_label { , instantiation_label }
  | OTHERS
  | ALL

integer ::= digit { [underline] digit }   [365]

integer_type_definition ::= range_constraint   [365]

interface_constant_declaration ::=   [99]
  [CONSTANT] identifier_list : [IN] subtype_indication [:= static_expression]

interface_declaration ::=   [99]
  interface_constant_declaration
  | interface_signal_declaration
  | interface_variable_declaration

interface_element ::=   interface_declaration   [99]

interface_list ::=   [99]
  interface_element { ; interface_element }

interface_signal_declaration ::=   [100]
  [SIGNAL] identifier_list : [mode] subtype_indication [BUS] [:=
  static_expression]

interface_variable_declaration ::=   [100]
  [VARIABLE] identifier_list : [mode] subtype_indication [= static_expression]

iteration_scheme ::=
  WHILE condition
  | FOR loop_parameter_specification

[94]

label ::= identifier

[67]

letter ::= upper_case_letter | lower_case_letter

[365]

letter_or_digit ::= letter | digit

[365]

library_clause ::= LIBRARY logical_name_list ;

[126]

library_unit ::=
  primary_unit
  | secondary_unit

[126]

literal ::=
  numeric_literal
  | enumeration_literal
  | string_literal
  | bit_string_literal
  | NULL

[365]

logical_name ::= identifier

[126]

logical_name_list ::= logical_name { , logical_name }

[126]

logical_operator ::= AND | OR | NAND | NOR | XOR

[38]

loop_statement ::=
  [loop_label :]
    [iteration_scheme] LOOP
      sequence_of_statements
    END LOOP [loop_label] ;

[94]

miscellaneous_operator ::= ** | ABS | NOT

[38]

mode ::= IN | OUT | INOUT | BUFFER | LINKAGE

[59]

multiplying_operator ::= * | / | MOD | REM

[38]

name ::=
  simple_name
  | operator_symbol
  | selected_name
  | indexed_name
  | slice_name
  | attribute_name

[158]

next_statement ::=
  NEXT [loop_label] [WHEN condition] ;

[227]

null_statement ::= NULL ;

[239]

numeric_literal ::=
  abstract_literal
  | physical_literal

[365]

object_declaration ::=

[39]

    constant_declaration
    | signal_declaration
    | variable_declaration

operator_symbol ::= string_literal   [38]

options ::= [GUARDED] [TRANSPORT]   [181]

package_body ::=   [100]
  PACKAGE BODY package_simple_name IS
    package_body_declarative_part
  END [package_simple_name] ;

package_body_declarative_item ::=   [100]
  subprogram_declaration
  | subprogram_body
  | type_declaration
  | subtype_declaration
  | constant_declaration
  | file_declaration
  | alias_declaration
  | use_clause

package_body_declarative_part ::=   [100]
  { package_body_declarative_item }

package_declaration ::=   [97]
  PACKAGE identifier IS
    package_declarative_part
  END [package_simple_name] ;

package_declarative_item ::=   [99]
  subprogram_declaration
  | type_declaration
  | subtype_declaration
  | constant_declaration
  | signal_declaration
  | file_declaration
  | alias_declaration
  | component_declaration
  | attribute_declaration
  | attribute_specification
  | disconnection_specification
  | use_clause

package_declarative_part ::=   [99]
  { package_declarative_item }

parameter_specification ::=   [94]
  identifier IN discrete_range

physical_literal ::= [abstract_literal] unit_name   [138]

physical_type_definition ::=   [138]
  range_constraint
    UNITS
      base_unit_declaration
      { secondary_unit_declaration }
    END UNITS

port_clause ::=
  PORT (port_list) ;   [58]

port_list ::= port_interface_list   [59]

port_map_aspect ::=   [75]
  PORT MAP (port_association_list)

prefix ::=   [65]
  name
  | function_call

primary ::=   [65]
  name
  | literal
  | aggregate
  | function_call
  | qualified_expression
  | type_conversion
  | allocator
  | (expression)

primary_unit ::=   [58]
  entity_declaration
  | configuration_declaration
  | package_declaration

procedure_call_statement ::=   [148]
  procedure_name [(actual_parameter_part)] ;

process_declarative_item ::=   [227]
  subprogram_declaration
  | subprogram_body
  | type_declaration
  | subtype_declaration
  | constant_declaration
  | variable_declaration
  | file_declaration
  | alias_declaration
  | attribute_declaration
  | attribute_specification
  | use_clause

process_declarative_part ::=   [227]
  { process_declarative_item }

process_statement ::=   [227]
  [process_label :]
    process [(sensitivity_list)]
      process_declarative_part
    BEGIN
      process_statement_part
    END process [process_label] ;

process_statement_part ::=   [227]
  { sequential_statement }

qualified_expression ::=   [---]
  type_mark ' (expression)

```
      | type_mark ' aggregate

range ::=                                                            [140]
   range_attribute_name
   | simple_expression direction simple_expression

range_constraint ::=   RANGE range                                   [138]

record_type_definition ::=                                           [158]
   RECORD
     element_declaration
     { element_declaration }
   END RECORD

relation ::=                                                         [250]
   simple_expression [ relational_operator simple_expression ]

relational_operator ::=   =  |  /=  |  <  |  <=  |  >  |  >=          [250]

return_statement ::=                                                 [151]
   RETURN [ expression ] ;

scalar_type_definition ::=                                           [132]
   enumeration_type_definition      | integer_type_definition
   | floating_type_definition       | physical_type_definition

secondary_unit ::=                                                   [52]
   architecture_body
   | package_body

secondary_unit_declaration ::=   identifier = physical_literal ;     [138]

selected_name ::=   prefix . suffix                                  [65]

selected_signal_assignment ::=                                       [178]
   WITH expression SELECT
     target  <= options selected_waveforms ;

selected_waveforms ::=                                               [178]
   { waveform WHEN choices , }
   waveform WHEN choices

sensitivity_clause ::=   ON sensitivity_list                         [235]

sensitivity_list ::=   signal_name { , signal_name }                 [227]

sequence_of_statements ::=                                           [94]
   { sequential_statement }

sequential_statement ::=                                             [227]
   wait_statement
   | assertion_statement
   | signal_assignment_statement
   | variable_assignment_statement
   | procedure_call_statement
   | if_statement
   | case_statement
   | loop_statement
   | next_statement
```

```
    | exit_statement
    | return_statement
    | null_statement
```

sign ::= + | -   [38]

signal_assignment_statement ::=   [41]
  target <= [TRANSPORT] waveform ;

signal_declaration ::=   [66]
  signal identifier_list : subtype_indication [signal_kind] [:= expression] ;

signal_kind ::= REGISTER | BUS   [194]

signal_list ::=   [197]
  signal_name { , signal_name }
  | OTHERS
  | ALL

simple_expression ::=   [102]
  [sign] term { adding_operator term }

simple_name ::= identifier   [27]

slice_name ::= prefix (discrete_range)   [141]

string_literal ::= " { graphic_character } "   [246]

subprogram_body ::=   [93]
  subprogram_specification IS
    subprogram_declarative_part
  BEGIN
    subprogram_statement_part
  END [designator] ;

subprogram_declaration ::=   [93]
  subprogram_specification ;

subprogram_declarative_item ::=   [93]
  subprogram_declaration
  | subprogram_body
  | type_declaration
  | subtype_declaration
  | constant_declaration
  | variable_declaration
  | file_declaration
  | alias_declaration
  | attribute_declaration
  | attribute_specification
  | use_clause

subprogram_declarative_part ::=   [93]
  { subprogram_declarative_item }

subprogram_specification ::=   [93]
  PROCEDURE designator [(formal_parameter_list)]
  | FUNCTION designator [(formal_parameter_list)] RETURN type_mark

subprogram_statement_part ::=   [93]
```
```

{ sequential_statement }

subtype_declaration ::= [157]
SUBTYPE identifier IS subtype_indication ;

subtype_indication ::= [140]
[resolution_function_name] type_mark [constraint]

suffix ::= [127]
simple_name
| character_literal
| operator_symbol
| ALL

target ::= [41]
name
| aggregate

term ::= [72]
factor { multiplying_operator factor }

timeout_clause ::= FOR time_expression [234]

type_conversion ::= type_mark (expression) [274]

type_declaration ::= [133]
full_type_declaration
| incomplete_type_declaration

type_definition ::= [132]
scalar_type_definition
| composite_type_definition
| access_type_definition
| file_type_definition

type_mark ::= [157]
type_name
| subtype_name

unconstrained_array_definition ::= [144]
ARRAY (index_subtype_definition { , index_subtype_definition })
OF element_subtype_indication

use_clause ::= [98]
USE selected_name { , selected_name } ;

variable_assignment_statement ::= [95]
target := expression ;

variable_declaration ::= [95]
VARIABLE identifier_list : subtype_indication [:= expression] ;

wait_statement ::= [231]
WAIT [sensitivity_clause] [condition_clause] [timeout_clause] ;

waveform ::= [178]
waveform_element { , waveform_element }

waveform_element ::= [178]
value_expression [AFTER time_expression]
| NULL [AFTER time_expression]

APPENDIX
F

VHDL
STANDARD
PACKAGES

This appendix presents standard VHDL packages. Section F.1 presents the STAN-DARD package and Section F.2 presents the TEXTIO package. In all the descriptions in this book, we assume that all types and functions in the STANDARD package are visible and that you must explicitly declare the TEXTIO package when you need it.

In this appendix, we have deviated from our convention of using uppercase letters for VHDL keywords and standards, and use uppercase letters only for VHDL keywords. This is done to make the entities defined by the package more apparent.

F.1   THE STANDARD PACKAGE

The STANDARD package defines primitive types, subtypes and functions and it re-sides in the STD library:

```
--  Package STANDARD as defined in Chapter 14, Section 2 of the IEEE Standard
--  VHDL Language Reference Manual (IEEE Std. 1076-1987).
--
PACKAGE standard IS
    TYPE boolean IS (false,true);
    TYPE bit IS ('0', '1');
    TYPE character IS (
        nul, soh, stx, etx, eot, enq, ack, bel,
        bs,  ht,  lf,  vt,  ff,  cr,  so,  si,
        dle, dc1, dc2, dc3, dc4, nak, syn, etb,
```

```
       can,  em,   sub, esc, fsp, gsp, rsp, usp,
       ' ', '!', '"', '#', '$', '⊕', '&', '",
       '(', ')', '*', '+', ',', '-', '.', '/',
       '0', '1', '2', '3', '4', '5', '6', '7',
       '8', '9', ':', ';', '<', '=', '>', '?',
       '@', 'A', 'B', 'C', 'D', 'E', 'F', 'G',
       'H', 'I', 'J', 'K', 'L', 'M', 'N', 'O',
       'P', 'Q', 'R', 'S', 'T', 'U', 'V', 'W',
       'X', 'Y', 'Z', '[', '\ ', ']', '^ ', '_',
       '"', 'a', 'b', 'c', 'd', 'e', 'f', 'g',
       'h', 'i', 'j', 'k', 'l', 'm', 'n', 'o',
       'p', 'q', 'r', 's', 't', 'u', 'v', 'w',
       'x', 'y', 'z', '{', '|', '}', ' ', del);
    TYPE severity_level IS (note, warning, error, failure);
    TYPE integer IS RANGE -2147483648 TO 2147483647;
    TYPE real IS RANGE -1.0E38 TO 1.0E38;
    TYPE time IS RANGE -2147483647 TO 2147483647
      UNITS
        fs;
        ps = 1000 fs;
        ns = 1000 ps;
        us = 1000 ns;
        ms = 1000 us;
        sec = 1000 ms;
        min = 60 sec;
        hr = 60 min;
      END UNITS;
    FUNCTION now RETURN time;
    SUBTYPE natural IS integer RANGE 0 TO integer'HIGH;
    SUBTYPE positive IS integer RANGE 1 TO integer'HIGH;
    TYPE string IS ARRAY (positive RANGE <>) OF character;
    TYPE bit_vector IS ARRAY (natural RANGE <>) OF bit;
  END standard;
```

F.2 TEXTIO PACKAGE

The TEXTIO package defines types, procedures, and functions for standard text I/O
from ASCII files and it resides in the STD library:

```
--   Package TEXTIO as defined in Chapter 14, Section 3 of the IEEE Standard
--   VHDL Language Reference Manual (IEEE Std. 1076-1987).
--
PACKAGE textio IS
      TYPE line IS ACCESS string;
      TYPE text IS FILE OF string;
      TYPE side IS (right, left);
      SUBTYPE width IS natural;

      FILE input : text IS IN "std_input";
      FILE output : text IS OUT "std_output";

      PROCEDURE readline (VARIABLE f:IN text; l: INOUT line);

      PROCEDURE read (l: INOUT line; value: OUT bit; good : OUT boolean);
      PROCEDURE read (l: INOUT line; value: OUT bit);

      PROCEDURE read (l: INOUT line; value: OUT bit_vector; good : OUT boolean);
```

```
        PROCEDURE read (l: INOUT line; value: OUT bit_vector);

        PROCEDURE read (l: INOUT line; value: OUT boolean; good : OUT boolean);
        PROCEDURE read (l: INOUT line; value: OUT boolean);

        PROCEDURE read (l: INOUT line; value: OUT character; good : OUT boolean);
        PROCEDURE read (l: INOUT line; value: OUT character);

        PROCEDURE read (l: INOUT line; value: OUT integer; good : OUT boolean);
        PROCEDURE read (l: INOUT line; value: OUT integer);

        PROCEDURE read (l: INOUT line; value: OUT real; good : OUT boolean);
        PROCEDURE read (l: INOUT line; value: OUT real);

        PROCEDURE read (l: INOUT line; value: OUT string; good : OUT boolean);
        PROCEDURE read (l: INOUT line; value: OUT string);

        PROCEDURE read (l: INOUT line; value: OUT time; good : OUT boolean);
        PROCEDURE read (l: INOUT line; value: OUT time);

        PROCEDURE writeline (f: OUT TEXT; L : INOUT line);

        PROCEDURE write (l: INOUT line; value : IN bit;
                            justified: IN side := right; field: IN width := 0);

        PROCEDURE write (l: INOUT line; value : IN bit_vector;
                            justified: IN side := right; field: IN width := 0);

        PROCEDURE write (l: INOUT line; value : IN boolean;
                            justified: IN side := right; field: IN width := 0);

        PROCEDURE write (l: INOUT line; value : IN character;
                            justified: IN side := right; field: IN width := 0);

        PROCEDURE write (l: INOUT line; value : IN integer;
                            justified: IN side := right; field: IN width := 0);

        PROCEDURE write (l: INOUT line; value : IN real;
                            justified: IN side := right;
                            field: IN width := 0; digits: IN natural := 0);

        PROCEDURE write (l: INOUT line; value : IN string;
                            justified: IN side := right; field: IN width := 0);

        PROCEDURE write (l: INOUT line; value : IN time;
                            justified: IN side := right;
                            field: IN width := 0; unit: IN time := ns);

--      FUNCTION endfile (VARIABLE f: IN text) RETURN BOOLEAN;
--      This function is implicitly defined when a file type is declared.

END textio;
```

Cindy Fiedler

TESOL TECHNIQUES
AND PROCEDURES

J. Donald Bowen
Harold Madsen
Ann Hilferty

NEWBURY HOUSE PUBLISHERS, Cambridge
A division of Harper & Row, Publishers, Inc.
New York, Philadelphia, San Francisco, Washington
London, Mexico City, São Paulo, Singapore, Sydney

Library of Congress Cataloging in Publication Data

Bowen, J. Donald (Jean Donald), 1922–
    TESOL techniques and procedures.

    Bibliography: p.
    Includes index.
    1. English--Study and teaching--Foreign speakers.
I. Madsen, Harold S.   II. Hilferty, Ann.   III. Title.
IV. Title: T.E.S.O.L. techniques and procedures.
PE1128.A2B64   1985   428'.007   84-27293
ISBN 0-88377-291-4

Cover design by Leslie Bartlett
Book design by Sally Carson

NEWBURY HOUSE PUBLISHERS
A division of Harper & Row, Publishers, Inc.

 Language Science
Language Teaching
Language Learning

CAMBRIDGE, MASSACHUSETTS

Printed in the U.S.A.

63-20444

First printing: September 1985

15 16 17 18 19

To our students,
who taught us as much as we taught them.

ACKNOWLEDGMENTS

In writing this book we have incurred many debts that are difficult to recognize. Good ideas are typically elaborated by many users over periods of time, and consequently in their current form tend to become coin of the realm, with their developmental history largely forgotten.

Nevertheless, when we knowingly appropriated an idea, we have entered a brief biblio note in parentheses in the text. Source notes then appear in full bibliographical form in the reference section beginning on page 392 of this book. Less frequently, as the situation seems to warrant (e. g., in the historical section), we use footnotes to further elaborate on a point, though an effort was made to minimize this practice.

Of greater concern are the occasions when we have unknowingly omitted a credit that is obvious to the colleague we have slighted. We apologize in advance and hope the omissions are minimal.

We do owe a debt of gratitude to Professor Shen Zi-wen, on leave from the Shanghai University of Science and Technology, who spent unnumbered hours in several libraries attempting to perfect our lists of references. Our sincere thanks, too, to Kay Bowen, who typed and retyped this long and difficult manuscript, with never a complaint, giving concurrent editing.

FOREWORD

Surrounded on every hand by advertisements whose promise exceeds their fulfillment, how can one do other than applaud a product that delivers twice as much as its title lays claim to? *TESOL Techniques and Procedures* is a book directed to teachers of English for speakers of other languages, but it builds on a universe of research and practice in language teaching, and as far as principles go is adaptable to the teaching of Italian or Arabic or Burmese or any other second language. English teachers can simply thank their good fortune that the exemplification is in English and no adaptation is called for.

A better-qualified team of authors would be hard to find. I have appreciated Donald Bowen's work for thirty years, as a fellow linguist and Hispanist and most closely as a co-worker on the Modern Spanish project of the Modern Language Association (see page 35n). His experience as director and teacher in programs of English as a second language began in 1959, after some years in the field of Spanish, and has extended to countries as distant as Egypt and The Philippines. Since 1963 he has been a principal figure in the ESL program at the University of California, Los Angeles. No one could speak with more authority—as observer, innovator, and practicer-of-what-he-preaches—in this special and far-flung area of English language teaching.

Harold S. Madsen, currently chairman of the Linguistics Department at Brigham Young University, began his professional career in TESL as a generalist. His overseas experience in Ethiopia, Egypt, and Bahrain posed problems that have propelled his interest toward language testing. He is now a testing specialist. Another interest that he has developed is the history of language teaching, a subfield he has dipped into very substantially.

Ann Hilferty had early experience as a Peace Corps Volunteer in Nigeria, from 1962 to 1965. When she returned it was with a fully developed interest in TESL. She has been involved in teacher training, administration of ESL programs, and teaching reading and writing skills in Boston. Recently she spent four years in China, where she continued an interest in research and gave vital leadership to an ESP program, Guangzhou English Language Center, during its important formative years.

You will have noted that all three authors have substantial experience overseas, but also considerable experience in the United States. They are fully equipped to share information and advice on the many aspects of second language teaching which are addressed in this text.

With such varied talent it is no surprise that this book is a *vade mecum* through all the broken terrain that menaces the beginning teacher or still bewilders the veteran. Language teaching has a history—it will not do for us to be ignorant of it, lest we lose sight of the things that endure and are tempted to embrace novelty for novelty's sake. Our authors give us this perspective, from the Roman period onward, with critical appraisal of developments in the present century. Though the audiolingual movement stands as a watershed (inevitably, as never before or since has so much energy and capital been invested in one set of principles), the authors put their faith in a "prudent eclecticism," drawing the best from each of the methods that have proved to have their own particular worth.

But it is substance more than method that distinguishes this book. Each classroom problem is approached from opposite ends, holistically and analytically, not only for the double insight but because students differ in their styles of learning. All the major problems are confronted—and most of the minor ones that can be foreseen—and every possible device that will make the student's grasp more secure, from simple comprehension to abstract discussion, is described in ways that will make the teacher's planning easier. Nor are the negative influences neglected—administrative and budgetary restrictions that nip some of our ambitions—for if we are to make the most of our resources we must know how far we can go.

Our authors envision the teacher at all levels, and the student whose objectives may include all or only part of the skills associated with a second language: the chapters devoted to oral matters do not overbalance those related to written; due attention is given to the enormous importance of literacy in today's world of communication, and there is a healthy emphasis on the interdependence of modalities.

One gets the sense from the book of *being in the world*. The classroom is an extension of all the ways of learning language that are born of necessity, and motivations from outside are exploited to the full: community involvement, materials that are not contrived but intrinsically useful, social meanings that so often transcend the exchange of desiccated information. All this is introduced without cheapening the competence of the instruction: the authors are linguists; their guidance in the analysis of technical problems is professionally scientific. The teacher will learn here how to apply the analytical tools of every discipline—including every major school of linguistics—that has had something worthwhile to say about language teaching.

In short, we have here a text that can be trusted both for background and for fresh ideas—the teacher with less than ideal preparation will come abreast of the field and the one with jaded palate will receive new stimulation and a sense of worth. Second language teaching deserved this book. It comes at the right time.

July 1985   Dwight Bolinger

CONTENTS

Section I   METHODOLOGICAL PERSPECTIVES

Section II   ORAL COMMUNICATION

A. Performance Skills: Oral Discourse

B. Component Skills

Section III   WRITTEN COMMUNICATION

A. Performance Skills: Written Discourse

B. Component Skills

Section IV   PLANNING AND EVALUATION

INTRODUCTION

There are at least two types of textbooks used in the methodology course of an ESL teacher training program. One is a collection of the best articles that have been produced by knowledgeable professionals in the field. The resulting anthology presents a broad spectrum of opinion, which the editor(s) of the volume organize into sections or units, introduced by descriptive headnotes and followed by summaries, discussion topics, projects, footnotes, etc. The anthology is essentially a library convenience, bringing selected articles together so the students can spend more time reading and less trying to locate what they are expected to read. A good anthology has much to contribute to a program, especially in helping to promote the eclecticism prized by most teachers and teacher trainers today. Limitations, however, include possible duplication of seminal ideas, excessive variety, and a resulting lack of cohesiveness.

The other kind of text is produced by a single author or by joint authors who share a common philosophy and are thus able to provide coherence and balance in their presentation. In addition to presenting relevant theoretical concepts, such a book often furnishes sample presentations and materials to assist the teacher trainee. The teacher of the methods course may choose one or the other of these two kinds of texts. Often both are employed, a decision that can profit from the strengths of both approaches.

A classic earlier anthology is Allen and Campbell's *Teaching English as a Second Language: A Book of Readings* (1965, 1972), while a very solid recent collection is Celce-Murcia and McIntosh's *Teaching English as a Second or Foreign Language* (1979). Well-received early volumes written to exemplify a single ESL methodology include Fries' very influential *Teaching and Learning English as a Foreign Language* (1945), and Dacanay's *Techniques and Procedures in Second Language Teaching* (1963). The long popularity of the latter has been attributed in part to its practicality and abundance of examples. The methods text we are presenting attempts to build on the strengths of these earlier works.

In surveying the needs of ESL methods classes, we recognize the value of the multiple viewpoints provided by anthologies. But we feel that such collections, though always helpful, may be less essential nowadays, with the widespread access that we have to TESL-related journals (Chapter Two, pages 52, 55) and to ERIC indexes. We hope that we have produced a text that will be cohesive and self-sufficient.

First, we attempt to provide the same abundance of practical examples found in the Dacanay text, but updated for contemporary use. Next, our *Techniques and Procedures* are based on a set of working assumptions which we feel derive from collective experience in second language instruction and from language research. A third feature is the historical perspective provided in initial chapters. This is intended to help teachers evaluate new methods, recognize and avoid fads, and appreciate the potential of various teaching approaches. An additional feature not common to most methods texts is a section on curriculum planning, testing, and evaluation.

In Figure I.1 we show (in the form of an inverted tree diagram) an outline of our text. With one exception, the last branch from every node leads ultimately to a chapter.

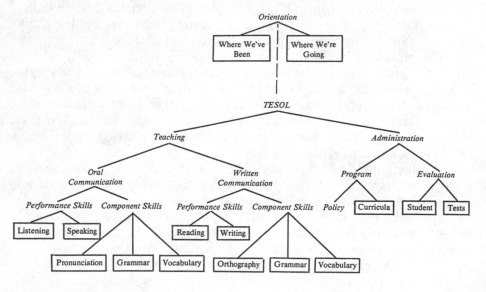

Boxes represent Chapters.
(Numbered 1–15 left to right.)

FIGURE I.1   Outline for *TESOL Techniques and Procedures*

WORKING ASSUMPTIONS

While a wide variety of language teaching methods have been promoted in recent years, most methodologists today prefer an eclectic or pragmatic approach rather than one that is highly restricted or codified. During the past decade, TESOL practitioners have assumed increasing responsibility for the direction of the discipline. Of course the contributions of psychology, sociology, and linguistics have continued to be significant. But classroom applications from experimental research are certainly limited and often tentative. While it is not feasible to wait for definitive answers to each methodological issue, it is helpful to identify significant areas of agreement, such as the widely accepted pragmatic approach to methodology mentioned above. The "prudent eclecticism" of this text reflects that view.

The following set of assumptions seems to be compatible with classroom experience and research findings. They undergird the pedagogy we recommend:

1. All normal persons can learn a second language.
2. Exposure to the language being studied is indispensable.
3. Practice by language learners is necessary.
4. People are different in the way they learn a second language.
5. Learner motivation is essential to effective language learning.
6. Learning is enhanced by lesson content that is realistic and useful.
7. Communication is recognized as the normal function of language use.
8. The array of methods advanced over the centuries has produced "very few inherently bad ideas . . . in language teaching." (Kelly 1969, p. 363)
9. Teachers (competently trained) and materials (appropriately prepared) can assist students in the language-learning process.
10. Language-related research must be interpreted and applied in terms of practical classroom experience.

OVERVIEW OF THE TEXT

Few if any of the above working assumptions are new. And as the reader of Chapter 1 will quickly notice, there are very few ideas in the field of language teaching that are genuinely new. Designations, mottoes, fads come and go; but the substance of language instruction is remarkably stable. Terminology changes more often than procedures. Such terms as "realistic, natural, contextualized, congruent, cohesive, comprehensible" all share the meaning of mirroring the language as it is actually used. It is true that emphases change, however, both within the language-teaching tradition, and idio-syncratically with individual teachers. We think this is a good thing, especially if the teacher is firmly grounded with a good perspective of where the profession is. But we think that this knowledge has too often been missing, and the resulting deficiency has been the cause of much duplication that could have been avoided.

With the many demands on teachers, we can't expect that they also become pedagogical historians. But there is a minimum acquaintance that should be a part of a teacher-training program. We have introduced this minimum as the initial section of our study: a section on perspectives— looking first back and then ahead, to get a clearer feeling for where we have been and where we are going.

Then we present the materials and skills sections: ten chapters on different modalities of communication—first oral and then written. These appear in separate sections, not because we advocate the classical audiolingual ordering, but because we feel that it will be easier to discuss and teach these skills if they are considered separately. We also separate for individual treatment "performance skills" and "component skills." In the performance domain, we emphasize the use of the language for realistic (and ultimately *real*) communication. Performance skills are fundamentally integrative, as the term "discourse" suggests. Component skills, on the other hand, have to do more with individual features which students (native or nonnative) need to be aware of. We call attention to the matched structure of the component skills chapters: pronunciation/orthography, the grammars of spoken and written English, as well as the vocabularies of speaking and writing. While we feel separate treatment is justified, at the same time we should remain aware of the parallels that help both to distinguish and to relate these skill areas.

The fourth section of the book deals with curricula and evaluation. Curriculum planning looks ahead and attempts to martial the resources that will assure an effective classroom. Evaluation, both of students and of teachers, provides the feedback that tells us if we are reasonably successful as professionals, and if not, how to identify our problems and design solutions. Evaluation is of course a very large field in language learning as in general education. While our presentation is obviously not adequate for the professional evaluator, it should be sufficient for the "general practitioner" assigned as a teacher in the classroom.

A word about the exercises: It has been suggested that we should mark each exercise for the optimum competence/proficiency level that it is designed for. At first we resisted this suggestion, rationalizing that the teacher knows her students better than text authors can, and that what is called high intermediate in one type of class might correspond to high beginner in another. We nevertheless succumbed to the argument that if the authors in all their planning cannot place an exercise on a reasonably simple (but abstract) competence scale, how could classroom teachers, especially those attending or recently graduated from a teacher training program, be expected to provide this kind of judgment? Figure I.2 provides our model and key.

Illustrative exercises are coded to give readers a rough idea of the relative sophistication for each exercise. Teachers are thereby alerted to the possible need for making exercises simpler or more complex.

CLASSROOM MANAGEMENT

The bulk of this volume treats the concerns of foreign or second language teaching. There are, however, considerations of a more general nature—

			Code
Sequenced Levels	Beginning Beginner	BB	1
	Low Beginner	LB	2
	High Beginner	HB	3
	Low Intermediate	LI	4
	High Intermediate	HI	5
	Limited Advanced	LA	6
	Terminal Advanced	TA	7

Autonomous Levels

False Beginner

Newly Arrived Student*

Citizens/Residents**

Refugees***

Vietnamese/Cambodian   Cuban/Hungarian

*Typically weak in Oral Skills
**Typically weak in Written Skills
***Run the gamut, but some groups typically non-academic and ill prepared

FIGURE I.2   Key to Recommended Level of Assignment for the Exercises in *TESOL Techniques and Procedures*

considerations which are relevant to any formal teaching context. These concerns apply to any organized classroom, and they are crucial to a teacher's success. At the risk of overstating the obvious, we mention them in this general introduction.

The teacher first of all should look to the physical comfort of her students in the classroom. The room should be well lighted and ventilated, not too hot and not too cold. It should avoid or at least minimize external noise. The teacher should consider seating arrangements that are possible in the class, and select one or more that encourage informal participation by, and interaction among, the students.

The teacher should welcome her students and should project a friendly, sympathetic approach. (This may well be the most important suggestion we offer in this text.) The teacher should have the ability to lead the student to more effective expression without telling him that his utterance was completely inadequate. She should encourage students, but should avoid comments that border on the realm of insincere praise. Specifically, she should not commend work unless it is better than average, or even outstanding. She should know how to inspire motivation and should be generous with her rewards when they're deserved.

She should begin the class with a brief review of material recently covered, tying new and old lessons together.

The teacher should go to class with at least one, and preferably several, contingency lessons that she can use if necessary when the electricity goes out and the tape recorder or the overhead projector won't work, or when she finds out that the students have already mastered the material she is planning to teach.

The teacher should maintain eye contact with her students and not be gazing out the window when she is talking to or listening to students. Students should be addressed respectfully and in a friendly way that indicates the teacher's interest and concern.

Discipline is a word that has come to mean the authoritarian maintenance of order by almost any means necessary. It implies control and the subjugation of the students' behavior to the will of the teacher. We would like to point out that discipline is built on the word "disciple," which is one who accepts and follows a teacher or a doctrine. It involves moral as well as mental instruction of the students, so they will be well adjusted and easily able to take their place in the world outside of the classroom. A good teacher can inspire a student to do this.

Section I
Methodological Perspectives

There is a long and notable history in the profession of language teaching. We are the beneficiaries of many hundreds of years of experience in teaching and learning languages. There are specialized studies on our collective experience over the centuries, but they are not widely known or consulted, and not much has filtered down to the working level of current practitioners. Partly for that reason we have devoted the first chapter of the present book to a quick summary of this tradition and effort.

The Aimara Indians of Peru and Bolivia are said to represent man's relationship to his world of space and time by visualizing a human figure facing the past with his back to the future. The past he knows; the future is still a mystery which he cannot see. In contrast, the technologically oriented western society would represent man facing the future, because that's the direction he moves in while making his plans for subduing the earth. He expects and looks for guideposts to tell him that his plans have been adequate to his purposes. The past he keeps as a memory, but he doesn't see it—he remembers it and takes it into account when he plans.

The second chapter looks at contemporary society, noting the assumptions professional teachers live and work by and the nature and kind of questions they ask in hopes of improving their efforts through a better understanding of the variables they can control and exploit. So we include a discussion of recent research findings and the further questions that have been raised.

If we can look back, as the Aimara do, and then look forward, as western society does, and in this way keep abreast of new research findings, we can serve the profession well, contributing insights and experience to the pool of information from which textbooks and manuals are made. The teacher who has the perspectives of where we've been and where we're going can combine insights from the past with options for the future to become "prudently eclectic," approaching the task of helping students learn (which some call "teaching") with more confidence and more alternatives, to be able to influence the growth and maturity of the student audience.

CHAPTER ONE

WHERE WE'VE BEEN: INSIGHTS FROM THE PAST

INTRODUCTION

Objectives in Reviewing Historical Methods

References to language methodologies of the past often seem intended to serve as foil for today's innovation. It is fashionable to criticize the "mindless pattern drills" and the "boring repetition" considered inherent in yesterday's Audiolingual approach, or to smile condescendingly at the quaint notion from the nineteenth century of "exercising one's mental faculties" through rigorous Grammar-Translation instruction. In retrospect, the shortcomings of various earlier methodologies are quite obvious, as those of today's methods will certainly be to future generations. The purpose of this chapter, however, is *not* to review with our excellent hindsight the failings of certain language teaching practices of the past. Nor is it to chronicle past methodologies simply because, like Everest, they "are there." One aim is to help the ESL/EFL teacher avoid diachronic provinciality by examining insights from language specialists and teachers of the past, some of whom were giants in their time and indeed in ours. Another is to broaden the language teacher's range of resources and enable him to evaluate contemporary methodologies more knowledgeably and honestly, and therefore more effectively.

Seriously evaluating a language method implies a depth of preparation not demanded of all who teach language. We recall an EFL teacher-training program in a developing country where financial resources and the language training of prospective teachers were both severely limited. The British teacher trainers reluctantly but wisely, it seems to us, greatly restricted their aims in order to maximize teacher effectiveness in the limited time available for training. While basic do's and don'ts were provided, along with remedial language instruction, the principal focus was on training the teachers to use the EFL textbook series which had been especially written for use in that country. In a short time they became reasonably proficient in presenting the lessons of one specific text. By contrast with the program of information and familiarization presented to these *teacher trainees*, the one envisioned for users of this book is a preparation enabling professionally educated language teachers to profit from any of a number of texts and to evaluate, select, and amend materials or teaching procedures appropriate for any of a large number of local circumstances.

Rationale in Surveying Historical Methods

Historical perspective should be useful in avoiding blind adherence to the most recent language cult on the scene, as well as restrictive polarization. A leading psychologist has lamented:

So many people insist on being *either* pro-Freudian *or* anti-Freudian, pro-scientific behaviorist or anti-scientific cognitive psychology, etc. In my opinion all such loyalty-positions are silly. Our job is to integrate these various truths into the whole truth, which should be our only loyalty. (Maslow 1962)

In a landmark address early in the decade of the seventies, Carroll warned TESOL of the same problem:

Our field has been afflicted, I think, with many false dichotomies, irrelevant oppositions, weak conceptualizations, and neglect of the really critical issues and variables. When I summarized (Carroll, 1965) two extreme points of view in language teaching as being, first, the "audiolingual habit theory" and second, the "cognitive-code learning theory," I had no real intention of pitting one against the other. I was only interested in pursuing what each theory would imply if pushed to the limit. Indeed, even at that time I meant to suggest that each theory had a modicum of truth and that some synthesis needed to be worked out. Instead, the trend has been for points of view to become crystallized and polarized. (Carroll 1971, p. 102)

Still today the dichotomies persist despite continued pleas for a more balanced perspective (Stevick 1974, p. 194; Prator 1979, p. 13).

A related matter which an improved historical perspective promises help in coping with is the notion that "newer is better" and that accepting one method implies an automatic rejection of all that preceded it. As a result, innovation is sought for its own sake. This long-standing bias in favor of newness has discouraged cumulative development in the profession, necessitating our discovering anew and refining once again abandoned techniques and methods which should never have been eliminated. One reason for this could be an inclination for many to view language teaching primarily as an art. Alterations in methodology are thus analogous to shifting preferences in fashion, architecture, music, literature, and the graphic arts. Some have seen the changes as reflecting major educational and social trends, others as a rejection of procedures that have become excessively formalized and petrified (Kelly 1969). But for those of us who see language teaching as incorporating characteristics of both art and science, it is apparent that language professionals, by drawing upon tested and accepted practices of the past, can help vitalize and stabilize teaching practice.

After surveying over twenty centuries of language teaching, Kelly concludes that "very few inherently bad ideas have ever been put forward in language teaching" (Kelly 1969, p. 363). Reflecting on the numerous concepts and teaching approaches this encompasses, those seeking the "one best method" would certainly be put off by such an observation. But Kelly's view is compatible with the finest thinking and research on language teaching. A third of a century after the publication in 1900 of the monumental *Report of the Committee of Twelve*, the conclusions of this comprehensive language teaching study were still hailed (as they well ought to be even now) as "practically incontrovertible" (Geddes 1933). One of these conclusions was that no single method is superior to all others. It was deemed advisable to select a teaching approach compatible with a student's age and the goals of instruction. Similarly, in our day, Carroll has suggested that instead of attempting to pit method against method to determine overall superiority, it is more advisable to investigate what the conditions are that cause each method to succeed best (Carroll 1959 [original copyright 1953], pp. 187–189; see also pp. 178–179). The historical survey of language methods can complement such experimental evaluation, since extended real-life application of a method acts as an effective crucible for assessing its practical results under specific circumstances. It seems to us perfectly clear that newly conceived "modern" methods can be better evaluated in the light of similar and contrasting historical methods.

Because our survey must for practical reasons be selective, we choose to spend the bulk of the time on positive contributions which have accrued. In doing so, we parallel the emphasis in contemporary humanistic psychology:

It becomes more and more clear that the study of the crippled, stunted, immature, and unhealthy specimens can yield only a cripple psychology and a cripple philosophy. The study of self-actualizing people must be the basis of a more universal science of psychology. (Maslow 1954)

Also, we devote a substantial proportion of the discussion to the past hundred years since developments here necessarily have more direct relevance to current methodological concerns.

To understand methodological concerns, we need some form of agreement on the meaning of "method." Often in the literature "method" refers to an entire movement held together, rather loosely, by some philosophical principle or cluster of procedures and proscriptions. For instance, the so-called Direct Method can be taken to include all the separate "direct-type" methodologies from François Gouin's 1880 formulation to James Asher's Total Physical Response; or a more restricted version—lopping off the Natural Method approach at the beginning of the movement and the Audiolingual at the end. We will differentiate, as Anthony (1963) does, between movements and specific methods more limited in scope and often associated with a single individual. The macro-view could include the Grammar-Translation movement, the micro-view the Berlitz or the St. Cloud method.

Before embarking on this historical survey, the reader would probably benefit from a word or two of caution. In an introduction to the educational writings of Comenius, Piaget notes that "nothing is easier, or more dangerous, than to treat an author of three hundred years ago as modern and claim to find in him the origins of contemporary or recent trends of thought" (Comenius [1957], p. 1). And historian Toynbee warns of the "parochialism" and "impertinence" of interpreting the past in terms of a very limited and local present (1946, pp. 36–41). One should be very cautious, then, in identifying causal relationships between past and present methodologies or even in assuming that familiar-looking techniques of another era match contemporary techniques very closely. Practices of the past, however, can provide us with additional resources and improved perspective.

Our need to rely on secondary as well as primary sources in preparing this historical survey leads to the possibility of occasional bias in the selection and interpretation of historical language teaching practices—particularly among those writing during the monolithic Audiolingual era, when to most there appeared to be only one right way to teach a second language. We have consistently striven to resist any doctrinaire interpretation provided by authors of historical surveys.

THE CLASSICAL PERIOD

Roman Instruction

Greek was studied by Roman youth as early as the second century B.C. Roman parents recognized the value of beginning second language instruction when the child was very young, and of providing this through native speakers. The bilingual training of their children began informally in the relaxed atmosphere of their home. (This seemed logical to the Romans since prior to 300 B.C., they had no formal schools and for a considerable time, literacy, numeracy, and morality were taught by the father in the home.) Greek nurses, slaves, or tutors provided years of immersion in the target language, instruction which often began at infancy.

When the boy entered school, he was fluent in both Greek and Latin. During part of this era, bilingual instruction was also provided at school. This occurred initially in the tool subjects and was followed by simultaneous instruction in the Greek *grammaticos* course together with the Latin *ludi magister* course; after this there was instruction by the Greek *rhetor* and the Latin *orator*. In the primary (or *ludus*) school, for boys and girls 7 to 12, students learned to read, write, and count. In these private-venture schools, they learned reading by first mastering the alphabet, then applying letters in syllables, observing proper pronunciation, and then reading words and connected discourse. Writing consisted of taking dictation.

Some texts provided vocabulary that was alphabetized and also organized semantically under various topics. Included, too, were appropriately simple narrative or conversational readings in such subjects as mythology, historical sketches, fables, and conversation. We include an example of the latter, translated by Titone:

The *paterfamilias* moves toward his family and says,
"Good morning, Caius," and he embraces him.
The latter returns the greeting and says,
"Nice to meet you. Would you like to come along?"
"Where?"
"To see our friend Lucius. We are going to pay him a visit."
"What's the matter with him?"
"He's sick."
"Since when?"
"Since a few days ago."
"Where does he live?"
"Not very far from here. If you like we can go there." (Titone 1968, p. 7)

As we see, this consists of fairly natural exchanges that incorporate examples of question forms.

Bilingual Greek-Latin instruction stretching from the home to the apex of formal schooling provided for social interaction, trade and practical intercourse with Greek-speaking communities outside Rome, and esthetic-philosophical application. With many students fluent in their second language before entering school, those who could afford advanced education moved from the literacy training of the primary school into rigorous grammatical and rhetorical instruction emphasizing polished and eloquent expression, modeled on the most prestigious Greek writers. During the Republic, when preparing young men for service in the Forum was politically meaningful, oratory was an important attainment. Cicero, in the first century B.C., wrote eloquently on the training of the cultured *doctus* orator. Later, during the early Empire, rhetoric received great emphasis in the increasingly literary education of the well-to-do Roman youth.

Quintilian's Influence

Marcus Fabius Quintilian, A.D. 35–95, one of the greatest teachers of this early period, drew upon his extensive experience as a teacher of rhetoric in developing his principles of second language instruction. He based his well-known text *Institutio Oratoria* on his own teaching experience as well as on the most effective Roman texts of the past. He appears to have been influenced by the writings of the Roman orator Cicero (106–34 B.C.), particularly Cicero's important educational treatise, the *De Oratore*.

Advocating an immersion concept, Quintilian suggested Greek as the initial medium of instruction for Roman youth. The student would listen to an Aesop fable and then give it orally in his own words. Subsequently, he would write out a simple paraphrase. Following a similar procedure, he would paraphrase a Greek poet; later he would be required to produce an essay based on a quotation from the ancients. On matters of correctness, Quintilian recommended following the usage of the educated majority; he urged learning words in contemporary use rather than learning obscure or archaic forms. In short, this master teacher promoted practical, contextualized instruction underpinned with valid usage principles.

THE MEDIEVAL PERIOD

Moving into the medieval period in Europe, we find Greek on the decline with Latin emerging as the language of the schools, the church, and even of government and commerce. In fact, the medieval scholar came to regard Latin as "the logically normal form of human speech" (Bloomfield 1933, p. 6). While this new "world language" underwent changes, it was still a "living language and was acquired (for a time at least) in a simple and natural way through hearing, speaking and reading" (Newmark 1948, p. 1). Thorough, constant instruction was provided by Christian clergy through the upper (higher monastic and cathedral) levels.

Oral classroom activity took various forms, including disputation and oral evaluation. To the extent they were available, Latin classics were read. And grammatical analysis became prominent, with rule mastery as significant as communicative skill. This of course was no accident, since grammar headed the list of the seven liberal arts of the medieval curriculum.

A note on these seven liberal arts: In the late Imperial period near the end of the fourth century, Martianus Capella reduced the medieval scholar Varro's list of the liberal arts to seven: grammar, rhetoric, logic, arithmetic, geometry, astronomy, and music. These seven liberal arts were adopted by the Christian church to be taught in monastic and cathedral schools, remaining virtually unchanged for about six hundred years. After these came the study of ethics (or metaphysics) and finally theology. Grammar, rhetoric, and logic constituted the *trivium*, the remaining four subjects the *quadrivium*. Prior to the thirteenth century, the trivium, notably grammar, constituted the usual preparation for studying theology. "Grammar" included not only the study of syntax but also literary analysis and "vocal expression." Rhetoric included both effective oral expression and eloquent written expression. Logic (or dialectic) concentrated on proper reasoning, identification of errors in thinking, development of strong arguments, and discussion of theological issues.

Of far-reaching effect was the publication of two Roman grammars. One was a fourth-century Latin primer *De octo partibus orationis* by Aelius Donatus, which was used for over a thousand years. The other was an early sixth-century grammar by Priscian. They are believed to have established the pattern for Latin grammars throughout the Middle Ages as well as for vernacular grammars that began to appear in the late fifteenth century and later. Both used a catechetical presentation involving countless questions and answers on grammar.

Much later (in the twelfth century), Alexander de Villa Dei's grammar, *Doctrinale Puerorum*, added principles of syntax and even drew upon usage. This popular text, which was in rhyme, extolled grammar as "the doorkeeper of all the other sciences, the apt expurgatrix of the stammering tongue, the servant of logic, the mistress of rhetoric, the interpreter of theology, the relief of medicine, and the praiseworthy foundation of the whole quadrivium" (Cubberley 1948, p. 155).

Grammarians of the twelfth and thirteenth centuries became involved with logic. Despite the honored place grammar had held throughout this period, it was finally eclipsed in the later Middle Ages by logic.

In comparing foreign language approaches in Europe during the Middle Ages with the approach in classical Rome, we see that particularly in Romance countries the initial (conversational) phase tended to be omitted. Whereas Roman youth ideally learned to speak their second language at home and then gained literacy through listening to Greek prose read aloud followed by their own paraphrasing of it, the major introduction of European youth to Latin was through grammar, following a modest preliminary exposure to grammar in the primary schools.[1] Instruction in rhetoric culminated their second language training. One reason for beginning almost at the outset with grammar was that in Romance countries, Latin was regarded simply as a more cultivated form of the vernacular; but this approach was utilized by the clergy through other non-Latinized parts of Europe as well, where a Latin tongue was not spoken.

In teaching rhetoric, medieval instructors drew upon both classical and ecclesiastical models, although there was some suspicion of the former. In fact, their rhetorical approach has been termed eclectic, despite the pervasive ecclesiastical influence (Kelly 1969, pp. 401–402). The purposes for which the second language would be used influenced the approach and the cultural content of instruction. There was a practical need for effective argumentation and written expression in both theology and philosophy; grammar appeared appropriate for the precision and analysis inherent in logical argument; rhetoric, including powerful literary models, was deemed essential for good writing.

---

[1] These elementary schools ranged from the lower monastic and conventual to the song, choir, parish, and chantry varieties. Even the more thorough "Inner Monastic" school, for those intending to take vows, provided rather limited language instruction: Latin pronunciation, reading of Latin psalms (utilizing an alphabet approach as in the classical period, and memorization, since only the teacher had a text), as well as writing by copying religious maxims with a stylus onto wax tablets (Cubberley 1948, pp. 150–152).

Given our late twentieth-century conception of the nature of language, medieval objectives in grammatical analysis may appear unsound. But there is logic and practicality in the overall system: One learns the vernacular at home, followed by a systematic study in school of its classical sister form, Latin. This largely oral instruction complements subsequent studies in rhetoric, which is undergirded by a thorough understanding of grammar. And writing skills are developed with reference to well-written prose similar to that which the student will ultimately have to produce himself. Moreover, instruction has twin practical (and not unfamiliar) objectives: preparing the student to function in school, where Latin is the medium, and enabling him to function in his profession.

THE RENAISSANCE

Language Instruction in Europe

The Renaissance found Latin as firmly established as ever, the language of the schools and of virtually all educated men in the West. Grammar reemerged as the central focus of foreign language (Latin) instruction.[2] In England, Latin grammar schools had developed. And modifications occurred in the teaching of grammar. For one thing, grammar and literature tended to become two separate subjects. Secondly, strong advocates arose, such as Erasmus, for an inductive approach to grammar.

In time, there began to be an expectation that educated men would acquire a foreign language in addition to Latin. Such instruction was offered not in the schools but privately by native-speaking immigrants and through practical contacts while traveling abroad. During the Middle Ages, the first instruction in modern foreign languages had been provided not by the Church but by the troubadours of southern France and northern Italy. Later, trade, exploration, and travel broadened Renaissance interest in language. Greek was an important early addition; Hebrew and Arabic were added later. By the sixteenth century, noblemen traditionally studied French, and within a hundred years the upper middle class did so as well, English now being introduced as another foreign language.

Some grammars and dictionaries of exotic languages were compiled. In addition, studies of old and contemporary European languages were made (Bloomfield 1933, pp. 7–8).[3]

---

[2]Bruni saw Latin as the sure foundation of all true learning, and to attain this learning he felt "we must never relax our careful attention to the grammar of the language." "Grammar," said Aeneas Sylvius, "is the portal to all knowledge whatsoever." Guarino concurred: "The foundation of education must be laid in grammar. Unless this be thoroughly learnt, subsequent progress is uncertain—a house built upon treacherous ground" (Eby and Arrowood 1940, pp. 910–911).

[3]In 1492 Antonio de Nebrija completed his impressive Spanish grammar. By 1530, John Palsgrave, an Englishman, published *L'éclaircissement de la langue française*, a textbook for the study of French. And the relationship between English and German was presented in a grammar published by Offelen in 1687.

Two significant developments in the Renaissance were the reaction of certain important scholars and educators against ineffective and stultifying language teaching practices as well as the advancing of carefully conceived teaching methods.

The Influence of Erasmus and his Contemporaries

Very prominent among this group was the eminent Dutch scholar Desiderius Erasmus (1466–1536). Significantly influenced by Quintilian, Erasmus held that the system of the language could be discovered inductively through exposure to discourse. He viewed grammar and rhetoric merely as means and not ends. (Thompson, in his introduction to the *Collected Works of Erasmus*, reminds us that in Erasmus' time *grammar* and *rhetoric* were about as broad as *language* and *literature* are today [Erasmus (1978), 23:xliii]). Grammar rules, reserved for advanced work, would be disclosed only with accompanying examples and after each grammar point had been learned in context. Similarly, generalizations on usage could be determined by examining the language, not by a priori assumptions. Erasmus held that "a true ability to speak correctly is best fostered both by conversing and consorting with those who speak correctly and by the habitual reading of the best stylists" (Erasmus [1978], 24:669).

Erasmus advocated that Latin be learned during childhood, preferably at home with a private teacher, while Greek would be learned through the medium of Latin formally in school. *Speaking* the foreign language would begin at the outset. Good oral communication was most important; next was reading and then writing. He advocated learning the language through exposure to interesting and practical conversations and stories accompanied by visuals such as pictures and charts.

Erasmus' three stages of language instruction began with conversation, naming, and describing—during the somewhat informal speaking phase at home. The second stage continued the conversational emphasis using stories based on history and mythology, dialogues on domestic subjects, and descriptions using pictures that enabled students to increase their vocabulary without using translation. Grammar instruction was still very limited and always accompanied by simple, down-to-earth examples. In the third stage, reading received increased emphasis—in part to exemplify excellent expression. Now more time was spent on grammar and language practice, but in appropriate perspective.

Retention of what was studied would be facilitated by understanding fully the content of the lesson, by following a systematic sequence (e.g., simple to complex), and by reintroducing the matter. A wide variety of rhetorical exercises would be utilized, such as transforming verse into prose, imitating the style of a prominent writer, translating, or recasting propositions in various forms (Erasmus [1978], 24:671, 679). Finally, training in language would complement the acquisition of a liberal education, Christian principles, morality, and judgment. And testing should receive the same care that is given to instruction.

Contemporaries of Erasmus such as Martin Luther (1483–1546) likewise sought teaching reforms. Luther asserted that excessive drill on rules was detrimental. Philipp Melanchthon (1497–1560) opposed the prevailing formalized Latin instruction, declaring that grammar must not be considered an end in itself. The Sicilian Lucas di Marinis, renamed Lucio Marineo in Spain, charged that students at the University of Salamanca were both fearful of and generally incompetent in Latin grammar, which they studied in formidably lengthy textbooks. Acquainted with the writings of both Quintilian and Erasmus, he published in 1532 a simple 67-page text designed to help students enjoy Latin and develop quicker mastery of oral production.[4]

But it was Michel de Montaigne (1533–1592), the son of a French nobleman, who provided the most dramatic account of the contrast between a newly espoused direct approach and the formalized approach of the day. In his essay "On the Education of Boys," he described his acquisition of Latin at home. Montaigne indicated that his father provided a Latin tutor for him; and up to the time he was six, his parents and even the servants conversed with him solely in Latin. At this age he knew no French, but his Latin was so nearly perfect that scholars were reluctant to attempt any improvement. And this was achieved, said Montaigne, "without any book, without grammar or teaching, without any rod and without fears" (Montaigne [1946], p. 150).

He then enrolled in one of the most prominent classical schools in France, the College de Guyenne. But since Latin was not presented orally, it was not long before he was unable to speak it. Little wonder that Montaigne advocated learning language from native speakers and educating young nobles by having them visit foreign countries where they could assimilate not only the language but also the culture of the people.

Reaction against concentrating on grammar and rule memorization took various forms. The English scholar Roger Ascham (1515–1568) focused on classical texts, having the student repeatedly translate a piece until it was mastered. Not until this point was grammar instruction utilized. Also using translation as a starting point, the German scholar Wolfgang Ratke, or Ratichius (1571–1635), advocated inductive language teaching. And in the early seventeenth century, William of Bath, or Bateus (1564–1614), likewise employed translation but concentrated on vocabulary acquisition. A cornerstone principle of his 1611 text was acquisition of vocabulary through contextualized presentation: Bath's text included 1200 proverbs incorporating common Latin vocabulary, and it presented homonyms in sentence context.

---

[4]In the introduction, Marineo wrote:

Judging these few things to be enough for beginners and the rest not necessary, I leave it to others fruitlessly to weary the minds of their students. For if, after they have made acquaintance with the form of words, they will spend that time which others spend on rules of grammar, in hearing the authors from whom those same rules are taken, they will certainly advance more, and become not grammarians but Latinists" (Newmark 1948, p. 2).

The Influence of Comenius
and Other Seventeenth-Century Educators

Jan Ámos Komenský, known as John Amos Comenius (1592–1670), was a Moravian bishop and the most influential educator of the seventeenth century. He regarded contemporary Latin instruction as unacceptable and ineffective. He started with Bath's contextualized vocabulary principle and over the years elaborated a remarkable approach to language teaching which included a systematic, graded presentation of syntax, inductive instruction in grammar, and lexical mastery through controlled vocabulary and visual association. His 1631 text, *The Golden Gate to Languages Unlocked*, included a hundred chapters, which introduced a thousand sentences in Latin sequenced in order of complexity and so arranged as to generate the concord and inflections being taught. The vocabulary was limited to 8,000 of the most common Latin words. Commonplace topics were employed such as fire, metal, stone, trees, bees and honey, deformities, the house and its parts, the family, prudence, and the state. Throughout this book, which was soon translated into sixteen languages, Comenius stressed that an understanding of the subject content must parallel one's mastery of linguistic forms.

Mastery of the material in this 1631 text was to be achieved through ten readings of each chapter. These readings included translating into the vernacular, writing out the material in the vernacular and Latin, and listening to the teacher reading the text in Latin while translating the unseen passage into the vernacular. Later readings involved looking at word derivations, studying inflections and synonyms, applying grammar rules, and then memorizing the passage.

Comenius helped to insure this further in his 1657 book, *The World in Pictures*, in which on the page opposite a picture a relevant text was included. He held that "words should not be learned apart from the objects to which they refer" (Comenius [1896], 356). A sample text accompanying a visual in his picture book reads as follows:

The Mason	Faber Murarius
layeth a Foundation	ponit Fundamentum,
and buildeth Walls,	& struit Muros,
Either of Stones . . .	sive e Lapidibus . . .
Or of Bricks . . .	sive e Lateribus . . .

(Comenius, 1887, reprint, pp. 80–81)

Comenius held that the subject matter of lessons should have appeal to students (e.g., avoid presenting Cicero and other "greats"), that modern languages should have priority over classical languages, that language should be learned "by practice" rather than by rules (though rules were seen as complementing practice), and that the subject matter of initial exercises should already be "familiar" to students (Comenius [1896], pp. 356–359).

In brief, Comenius' contributions were unique and monumental.[5]

In 1658 Charles Hoole translated Comenius' picture text into English and stressed in his own language text the need to appeal to the senses and to one's understanding rather than simply to rote memory.

The English philosopher John Locke (1632–1704) reflected the influence of both Montaigne and Comenius. He attacked the foolishness and pedantry of schoolmasters and protested the teaching of Latin to students going into trade or commerce. He recommended French as a second language for children, urging that it be presented conversationally in a natural way. He felt the same approach was appropriate for Latin and opposed analytical, grammatical approaches. He favored easy introductory texts such as Aesop's Fables accompanied by interlinear translation, and said that if grammar was to be taught at all, it should be taught last of all (Locke [1964], pp. 119–124).

In 1693 he published *Some Thoughts Concerning Education*. Rejecting contemporary approaches to language teaching which concentrated on grammar, he argued that the second language should be mastered so it could be used "without thought of rule of grammar." He continued:

And I would fain have any one name to me that tongue, that any one can learn or speak as he should do, by the rules of grammar. Languages were made not by rules or art, but by accident, and the common use of the people. And he that will speak them well, has no other rule but that; nor any thing to trust to but his memory, and the habit of speaking after the fashion learned from those that are allowed to speak properly. . . . (Locke [1964], p. 129)

We see in Locke's promoting French as a foreign language worthy of study a reflection of the seventeenth-century inclination to give more and more attention to vernacular language. For instance, Ben Jonson's text, *The English Grammar*, written about 1600 and published in 1640, is considered by some to be the first genuine grammar of the English language (Carpenter 1963, p. 93). The dominance in education of Cartesian logic, which conceptualized all things in relationship to a basic model, spawned the notion of a universal underlying grammar for all languages, which could be perceived in one's native language. This helped spur the growing trend to translate texts into the vernacular as a key methodological procedure. Reaction against rule memorization and grammatical analysis also helped promote a "cognitive" grasp of contextualized prose, via translation.

---

[5]One historian summarizes the significance of Comenius' influence:

Comenius stands in the history of education in a position of commanding importance. He introduces the whole modern conception of the educational process, and outlines many of the modern movements for the improvement of educational procedure. What Petrarch was to the revival of learning, what Wycliffe was to religious thought, what Copernicus was to modern science, and what Bacon and Descartes were to modern philosophy, Comenius was to educational practice and thinking. The germ of almost all eighteenth- and nineteenth-century educational theory is to be found in his work. . . . (Cubberley 1948, p. 415)

In summary, the Renaissance as a whole provided formal rule-oriented instruction in Latin. This deductive presentation focused on grammar. Though cognitive in its basic approach, it was lacking in efficiency and practical application. There were a number of reformers, however, who throughout this period began to effect impressive changes. Practical matters were broached. The learning of modern foreign languages was encouraged, though generally outside the existing system of schools. Well-conceived pedagogical procedures were introduced. Motivation began to be given more prominence, as reflected for example in texts using interesting, contemporary topics. Effective procedures were advanced, such as the use of contextualized, graded vocabulary aided by visual association. Reformers sought to facilitate understanding by using easier, more relevant texts and by appealing to the senses. There was likewise considerable effort to put grammar in proper perspective: first, by postponing instruction in it; second, by developing oral proficiency first and even engaging in "direct" language activities such as translation before introducing it; and finally, by utilizing an inductive rather than a deductive approach. In short, inefficient grammar-rule course work of this period was at times countered by the sound language instruction of reformers.

THE EIGHTEENTH CENTURY

The eighteenth century witnessed the demise of Latin as the medium of instruction, although it was still considered an important study because of the supposed mental discipline it provided, not to mention the force and beauty of verbal expression instilled as a result of studying classical writers. This same century also witnessed the birth of English grammar and the enthronement of reason and prescription in grammar.

While some usage rules, such as the shall-will dictum, can be traced to the seventeenth century, generally such rules were formulated in the prescriptive, Latin-based corrective grammars, which appeared during the eighteenth century in greater and greater numbers. Leonard's detailed analysis of texts on the English language which were written at this time reveals that fewer than fifty publications on grammar, rhetoric, criticism, and linguistic theory appeared from 1700 to 1750; during the second half of the century, however, there were over two hundred. Most of these, he says, "were concerned in whole or in part with solecisms, barbarisms, improprieties, and questions of precision in the use of English" (Leonard 1929, p. 12).

Grammar became important in its own right for the supposed intellectual stimulation it provided. Along with an emphasis on grammar, the translation techniques that had been developed in the 1600s continued to be popular during the Age of Reason.

Various reformers in France strove for revision of language teaching methods.[6] And in Germany, similar interests were manifested. The efforts of Weitenauer, Meidinger, and Basedow illustrate the range of teaching innovations advanced at this time. For example, in 1762 Ignatius Weitenauer (1705–1783) published the book *Hexaglotton* on the teaching of foreign languages. This text used contrastive techniques to teach a dozen foreign languages and Latin as well. Sample passages were used to show how interlinear translation, grammar summary, glossary, and verb particle lists could be employed to help learn the target language. This was one of the most systematic and thorough approaches to date, and his text appears to be one of the first to provide guidance in pronunciation.

The aim of Johann Valentin Meidinger (1756–1820) was to speed up language learning by starting with grammar rules and using these as the means of translating *into* the foreign language. (The usual practice at this time was to translate from the foreign language into the native language.) His instruction reflected a cognitive orientation. In emphasizing grammar, Meidinger was in step with the times. Since all languages were felt to have correspondence in a "first cause," it seemed appropriate to concentrate on grammar—even vernacular grammar—from which the grammars of all other languages could supposedly be deduced.

Perhaps the most creative German reformer was Johann Bernard Basedow (1723–1790), a language teacher of considerable renown. He founded a unique teacher-training institution and model school. Drawing upon practical experience, he taught that languages should be learned first by speaking and later by reading. Instruction in French and in the vernacular preceded that in Latin, and formal grammar study was to be delayed till later. Learning was facilitated through an impressive variety of involvement activities: Titone mentions his use of "conversation, games, pictures, drawing, acting plays, and reading on interesting subjects" (Titone 1968, p. 19).

Besides the efforts of these and other European reformers, language instruction in the eighteenth century was also influenced by the writers of the new vernacular grammars.

The most influential English grammar of this era was written by Robert Lowth: *A Short Introduction to English Grammar* (1762). It drew upon the terminology of Latin grammars and attempted to teach "correct" usage by providing numerous examples of "errors" from many of England's best

---

[6]Cesar Dumarsais (1676–1756) advocated that languages be taught naturally with an emphasis on use or practice. For Latin, contextualized material was to be presented with interlinear translation. And Pierre Chompre (1698–1760) proposed a direct approach to teaching Latin and other foreign languages. Claude-François Lysarde de Radonvilliers (1709–1789), tutor of Louis XV's children, used interlinear translation but recommended that a close literal translation be avoided in favor of one that represented the thoughts of the author. P. J. F. Luneau de Boisgermain (1732–1804) expanded on Radonvilliers' concepts, and indicated that by avoiding a grammar approach the student could learn the language on his own through "direct practice" (Titone 1968, pp. 16–21).

writers, including Addison, Dryden, Pope, and Shakespeare. Not recognizing usage "as the sole arbiter in linguistic matters" (Baugh 1935, p. 353), grammarians such as Lowth sought through logic and analogy to expunge the corruptions in English and purify the language by ruling on hosts of expressions and grammatical forms. This point of view was passed on to nineteenth-century grammarians such as Lindley Murray, who incorporated Lowth's text almost verbatim in his best-selling grammar book covering orthography, etymology, syntax, and prosody or mechanics.[7]

While a rather strained and contrived grammatical analysis was the rule in most classrooms, there were a few, such as Joseph Priestly (1733–1804) and George Campbell, who rejected the imposition of Latin forms on other languages and the wholesale manufacturing of usage rules. Having studied Oriental languages, Priestly recognized the impracticality of explaining the grammar of one language from that of another.[8]

Finally, significant twentieth-century linguistic insights have their roots in concepts expounded during the latter part of the eighteenth century and even earlier. For example, knowledge of Sanskrit led to the recognition that most European languages must have developed from a common source. The Indo-European language theory was enunciated by Sir William Jones in 1786. A corollary is the recognition of change as a natural linguistic phenomenon. (On the recognition of change as a natural linguistic phenomenon, see Sledd 1959, pp. 3–4 and Bloomfield 1933, pp. 12–13.) A more immediate impact was felt from the publication in 1755 of Samuel Johnson's dictionary with its listing of variant meanings for a given word and the use of quoted contexts to amplify meaning.

---

[7]Murray also drew upon two other important eighteenth century texts: William Ward's *Grammar of the English Language* (1765) and Charles Coote's *Elements of the Grammar of the English Language* (1788). Most of Murray's subsequent editions followed a four-part division: Part I, orthography, included three chapters—one on the nature of the letters of the alphabet, another on the nature of syllables, and a third on words and spelling. Part II consisted of a nine-chapter section of etymology; word classification and parsing were the chief concerns. Parsing included identifying the part of speech by name, indicating its properties, stating its relation to other words, and giving the rule for constructing it. Part III was devoted to syntax: the function and relationship of words in the sentence. Part IV, on prosody, typically included punctuation, utterance, figures, versification, and sometimes pronunciation (accent, quality, emphasis, pause, tone). An appendix included rules for writing—the first portion being devoted to single words and phrases, the second to sentence construction. Definitions and rules were provided, presumably to be memorized; then follow-up exercises were included for drill.

[8]In 1761 Priestly wrote:

I am surprised to see so many technical terms of Latin grammar retained in the grammar of our own tongue, where they are exceedingly awkward and absolutely superfluous; being such as could not possibly have entered into the head of any man, who had not been previously acquainted with Latin. (Darian 1972, pp. 21–22)

Campbell, whose *Philosophy of Rhetoric* appeared in 1776, likewise rejected Latin and logic as arbiters of usage:

It is not the business of grammar, as some critics seem preposterously to imagine, to give law to the fashions which regulate speech. On the contrary, from its conformity to these fashions of speech, and from that alone, it derives all its authority and value. (Darian 1972, p. 23)

THE NINETEENTH CENTURY

Grammar-Translation

While the roots of Grammar-Translation are clearly visible in the eighteenth century, and even much earlier, this approach did not emerge full-blown until the early decades of the nineteenth century. During the second half of the century, when Grammar-Translation was receiving wider and wider acceptance, it was challenged by the Natural Methodologists and later still by linguists who advocated instruction based on phonetic principles. The culmination of this counter-movement resulted in the Direct Method approach. During the controversy between Grammar-Translation and the Direct Method, a voluminous literature on methods appeared, and professional organizations were created. By the end of the century, no one method was dominant, and Grammar-Translation was losing support.

Some trace the antecedents of Grammar-Translation methodology to ancient times, citing advanced translation exercises by Roman poets in the second and third centuries B.C., experimental instruction in third century A.D., and works such as Aelfric's Latin grammar about A.D. 1000, in which the author indicated his text would provide an introduction to English grammar as well as to Latin. Translation as an advanced exercise was used by early Roman poets such as Livius Andronicus, Ennius, and Naevius. It was used for a time as a language-teaching device in Alexandria and Gaul (Kelly 1969, pp. 15, 172). Darian notes that Aelfric, an Anglo-Saxon abbot (from about 955 to 1020) wrote his Latin grammar in English for school children (1972, p. 18).

Records indicate that at least in one locale during the fourteenth century, dictation was given in the vernacular for translation into Latin, and later complaints about translation as a language learning exercise show that the practice continued to have some currency. William Lily, assisted by Erasmus, wrote the first English grammar in modern English. Published in 1513, this work juxtaposed the Latin paradigm with the English translation. During the Renaissance simple English paragraphs (*vulgaria*) describing everyday situations were carefully analyzed (construed) in the classroom and then translated into Latin, for grammatical and even for rhetorical training. ("Construing" consisted of examining each word or phrase, explaining its grammatical use, and then identifying equivalents in the mother tongue.)

This continued into the seventeenth century, accompanied by the publication of phrase (idiom) books, bilingual dictionaries, guides on translation, and grammars. As we have seen, by the eighteenth century it was accepted that basic understanding of a foreign language grammar should be gained by analytical mastery of the vernacular grammar. And by the end of the eighteenth century this proclivity coupled with an even more pervasive "construing" at all levels of language instruction provided an appropriate milieu for Grammar-Translation.

A key transition figure was Meidinger (discussed earlier), who helped formalize the new methodology. *Grammatical rules and paradigms were provided as the basis for translating native-language sentences into the foreign language.* James Hamilton (1764–1829) was among those, however, who argued for an *inductive* approach to language instruction, indicating that the student's initial exposure must be to readings in the target language. He employed the Gospel of St. John in applying his approach, but found the text too difficult for most students.[9]

Influential textbooks soon appeared which helped facilitate Grammar-Translation instruction.

In 1811 a widely imitated textbook writer named Johann Heinrich Seidenstucker (1785–1817), like Plotz who would follow him, published an easier book than those used by Hamilton and his followers. It consisted of unrelated sentences (e.g., "The door is black," "The horse of the father was kind") tailored to illustrate syntactic rules in such a way that they could be comprehended by youth. One section of the book provided rules and paradigms; the other, French sentences for translation into German and German sentences for translation into French.

Texts by authors such as Franz Ahn and H. S. Ollendorf utilized similar formats, the chief weakness being contrived and unnatural sentences, unlikely to promote genuine language competence. Titone provides sample items: "The cat of my aunt is more treacherous than the dog of your uncle," "My sons have bought the mirrors of the duke," "Horses are taller than tigers" (1968, p. 28).

Probably the most prominent of the Grammar-Translation advocates was the German writer Karl Plotz (1819–1881).[10] Utilizing the two-part rule/translation format, his texts attempted to use the vernacular to master the foreign language. A student of Plotz has described this method:

Committing words to memory, translating sentences, drilling irregular verbs, later memorizing, repeating and applying grammatical rules with their exceptions—that was and remained our main occupation; for not until the last years of the higher schools with the nine-year curriculum did French reading come to anything like prominence, and that was the time when free compositions in the foreign language were to be written. (Bahlsen in Titone 1968, p. 28, and Newmark 1948, p. 6)

The widespread availability of textbooks and increasing enrollment in language classes contributed to the acceptance of Grammar-Translation: It

[9]Following the Hamiltonian System, Jean Joseph Jacotot (1770–1840) published a text in 1823 which incorporated Fenelon's *Telemacque*. Both of these men influenced Toussaint-Langenscheidt, whose *Unterrichtsbriefe* was designed for self-instruction (Newmark 1948, p. 5).

[10]Newmark summarizes Plotz's impact on nineteenth-century language instruction:

To some an idol, to others the embodiment of every linguistic malfeasance in language pedagogy, [Plotz] dominated through his French and English textbooks the schools of Germany until long after his death. He was an indefatigable worker, a complete master of the language he attempted to teach, and the last and most influential representative of the grammar-translation method. (1948, p. 5)

was an easy method for the teacher to use. Classes could be taught in the students' native language with little teaching skill or foreign-language speaking skill needed by the instructor. Objectives were limited and attainable. Vocabulary lists, printed grammar rules, and sample sentences to translate, followed by reading selections, provided maximum control for teachers and students.

Appeals of Grammar-Translation included the cognitive, systematic use of grammar rules as a basis of instruction (not unlike the generative-transformational grammar appeal in the post-Audiolingual era). The directness of translation and the utilization of students' native-language proficiency were also appealing features. And not to be overlooked was the esthetic argument: Language learning could be intimately entwined with some of the most beautiful and profound literature of the ages, thus avoiding the plastic and vapid contexts (decried by contemporary ESL experts such as Widdowson 1981, and Oller 1984) that plague us even in the latter decades of the twentieth century.

Principal limitations were tedium, inefficiency of instruction, and limited results in terms of communication—notably, limited oral proficiency.

The Natural Method

The excesses of Grammar-Translation began to spark reactions which collectively came to be known as the Natural Method movement. Drawing upon the writings of Rousseau and educational reforms of Pestalozzi, these reformers challenged the value of translation and the efficacy of formal grammar study. Nor were they interested in phonetic analysis. Since children learn "naturally" to speak before they read, some recommended that oracy precede literacy and that receptive skills precede productive ones. Proponents of the Natural Method tended to avoid the use of books in class, though later adherents, in attempting to formulate a systematic overall philosophy, allowed that textbooks could be utilized for inductive insights. Like the child in his home, the student was to be immersed in language and allowed to formulate his own generalizations. Most felt that the age of a student was immaterial, all persons learning the same way regardless of age or educational background. Activity, games, and demonstration were advocated to enhance motivation and understanding.

The prestigious *Report of the Committee of Twelve*, commissioned in the 1890s by the National Education Association in the United States, described the Natural Method:

In its extreme form, it consists of a series of monologues by the teacher, interspersed with exchanges of question and answer between instructor and pupil—all in the foreign language; almost the only evidence of system is the arrangement, in a general way, of the easier discourses and dialogues at the beginning, and the more difficult at the end. A great deal of pantomime accompanies the talk. With the aid of gesticulation, by attentive listening, and by dint of repetition, the beginner comes to associate certain acts and objects with certain combinations of sound, and finally reaches the point of reproducing the foreign words or phrases. When he has arrived at this stage, the expressions already familiar are connected with new ones in such a way that the former give the clue to the latter, and the vocabulary is rapidly extended. . . . The mother tongue is strictly banished. . . . Not until a considerable familiarity with the spoken idiom has been attained is the scholar permitted to see the foreign language in print; the study of grammar is reserved for a still later period. Composition consists of the written reproduction of the phrases orally acquired.

Forerunners of the Natural Method movement, including Lemare, Dufief, and Payne, emphasized induction and self-reliance. Writing in 1819, P. A. Lemare recommended that rules not be given to students. While not rejecting translation, he did reject the notion of teaching discrete segments of language. Four years later N. G. Dufief wrote that immersing the student in language and allowing him to deduce the rules was nature's way. Joseph Payne in 1830 likewise rejected the notion of explaining the language to students (see Kelly 1969, p. 40).

By 1833 Harvard's brilliant language scholar George Ticknor (1791–1871) emphasized spoken language, as well as acquisition by immersion, but resisted pushing the "natural approach" too far. He felt there was no single language teaching approach applicable to all learners. While an inductive, oral presentation might be useful for children, other approaches would better suit adults and persons of varying language background.

Two decades later a major figure in this reform movement, Claude Marcel, enunciated his antitranslation position and recommended student initiative in language learning through an inductive approach.

In his 1867 text, which set forth his system of instruction, he essentially rejected all formal systematic use of grammar instruction or dictionaries. While stressing reading, he began with ear training through the teacher's reading aloud to students. This was followed by graduated reading practice. Only then was the active task of speaking required. Little emphasis was given to writing, the last subskill taught. He recommended that students read twenty-five to thirty books in order to master reading the second language. Though covering all four skills, he gave greater attention to the "receptive," particularly reading, and as a result he is sometimes identified with the "reading method" advocates of the late nineteenth century.

At about this time, Gottlieb Heness, later joined by Lambert Sauveur, conducted language schools in New England, where they gave special attention to conversational techniques. Heness opened his initial one in 1866 at New Haven, Connecticut: a private modern language school. Then with Sauveur he opened another in Cambridge, Massachusetts, and conducted summer schools attended by prominent language teachers, including Henry Wadsworth Longfellow. Heness capitalized on cognates, felt no compulsion for pictures except with children, urged rapid oral exchanges to avoid even mental translation, and urged teacher inventiveness so that chance influences from the environment (sneezes, wagon noises, flower scents, lightning, etc.) could be incorporated in the lesson.

The involvement-focused conversational instruction of the Frenchman François Gouin (published in 1880) provided a more systematic approach than had previously been apparent in the Natural Method movement. Anticipating the contemporary Total Physical Response technique, Gouin involved students actively in *doing* what they spoke about, first in their native language and then in the target language. Familiar subjects and connected conversational discourse characterized the language that his students acted out. The approach followed an insight Gouin gleaned from observing a small child reenacting a visit to a mill while simultaneously verbalizing his actions (Gouin 1896, pp. 34–38).[11]

Proponents of nature's way offered a serious challenge to advocates of Grammar-Translation but encountered criticisms themselves: notably in respect to their lack of system, the heavy demands on teachers to create their own teaching procedures, the rather extensive linguistic proficiency needed by teachers, alleged "showmanship," their seeming lack of esthetic concern, and a supposed absence of intellectual "discipline." At the end of the century the Committee of Twelve failed to recommend the Natural Method but did acknowledge its motivational value. Viewing the method in the final quarter of the twentieth century, our judgment is certainly less severe. Although lacking suitable textbooks and teacher guidelines, the movement had a laudable interest in fostering the teaching of natural, contextualized language in everyday situations, incorporating both verbal and nonverbal activity.

The Phonetic Method

Throughout the second half of the nineteenth century there had been considerable linguistic activity. Descriptive phonetics was pursued by a number of scholars of the period. One linguistic issue was phonetic spelling: Advocates ranged from Leopold Bahlsen, who felt that all languages should be represented phonetically, to Brigham Young in America, who had many local books and records transcribed into a locally developed phonetic script called the Deseret Alphabet.

This international linguistic activity resulted in the emergence of the Phonetic Method (or Structural or New Reform Method). Now the anti–

[11]We have access to Gouin's procedures in his 1880 *L'art d'enseigner et d'étudier les langues* and in his *Erstes Übungsbuch für das Deutsche.* Unlike most contemporaries, he was not interested in reading or in written exercises. Nor was he attracted to phonetics or the use of realia and pictures. Instead, he utilized lessons of a maximum 20 to 30 short sentences constituting a brief narrative that could be acted out. There were several such selections in a series, and several of these in a general series. One elementary series is titled "The Well." Three exercises make up the little series: (1) The maid goes to draw water at the well; (2) The maid lets down the bucket into the well; (3) The maid winds up the bucket. After an explanation in the native language, the teacher dramatizes the narrative with a foreign language explanation. Each movement is then isolated in order to focus on the verb of that particular action. Individual students carry out the same activity—initially with native language sentences accompanying their movements (Gouin, pp. 129–130). Gouin's "natural" or "psychological" method had as a central concern the association of ideas. The *Report of the Committee of Twelve* describes in detail the "Psychological Method," which was "invented by Gouin and brought into general notice by Betis."

Grammar-Translation reform movement gathered momentum, at the same time paving the way for the Direct Method. It was Wilhelm Viëtor (1850–1918) and followers such as Ripman of Great Britain and Alge of Switzerland who in the latter decades of the century criticized most sharply the still-prevalent Grammar-Translation approach, and who created linguistically based language-teaching models as alternatives to the existing system.

Viëtor charged contemporary instruction with failing to provide skills of expression. He utilized oral expression as the basis of instruction, stressing pronunciation, avoiding grammatical rule giving, and seeking to impart a practical mastery of language forms for use in-country; cultural information was also provided. The teacher would read a passage aloud, explaining unfamiliar words as students followed along. After discussing questions on the passage, students would paraphrase the story aloud. Next would come written answers to questions, phonetic work on new words, and ultimately recitation. Gestures, pictures, and interesting contexts were to be used in making applications of familiar material. Graded reading would come later.

The Committee of Twelve noted the method's focus on pronunciation and seemed impressed by the European scholars supporting this movement, which by the end of the century had not yet been introduced into America. [12]

Contemporary reservations included the method's lack of esthetic and intellectual focus as well as its heavy requirements for linguistic expertise on the part of teachers. American language experts of the day were also concerned that objectives were too broad for their limited foreign language offerings. A concern nowadays would be the method's heavy emphasis on pronunciation, although its cultural-communicative features seem modern indeed.

As the century ended, Grammar-Translation was still dominant but was losing ground, particularly in northern Europe and the United States. The Phonetic or New Reform Method with its weight of linguistic authority had begun to coalesce with the Natural Method (including the Psychological). Shortly to be labeled the Direct Method, this combined movement was greatly aided by an international congress of modern language teachers. At their 1898 congress held in Vienna, they agreed to utilize some element of the

---

[12]The Committee Report commented in part:

The phonetic method resembles the "natural" and the "psychological" schools in that it takes the modern spoken language as a basis and at first relies mainly on oral instruction, using as far as possible the foreign language itself as a medium of communication. Unlike most "conversational" courses, however, it is very systematically constructed. It begins with a training of the ear and the vocal organs, the pupils being thoroughly drilled in the vowels and consonants of the strange tongue. . . . printed texts are used, but only in phonetic notation. The ordinary spelling is carefully kept from the students during the elementary period. . . . Objects, pictures, and maps are constantly displayed, and every effort is made to familiarize the class with the surroundings, the institutions, the habits, the character, and the mode of thought of the people whose language they are learning. . . . Inflections and syntax are studied inductively. Composition consists first of the oral and written reproduction of matter already heard or read, then of combinations of familiar phrases. Systematic grammar is reserved for a late stage, and translation comes last of all. (*Report of the Committee of Twelve*)

Direct Method in every beginning-level lesson, e.g., dialogues or dramatization. Two years later at Leipzig they agreed to extend the practice to advanced classes as well. According to Mackey, such practices included "almost exclusive use of the second language in the class, the use of texts in modern prose, material on the foreign culture, [and] inductive grammar. . . ." (1965, p. 146). Such a dramatic challenge to the older approach resulted in a large body of literature debating pros and cons as well as increased experimental applications of the new method.

THE TWENTIETH CENTURY—1900 TO WORLD WAR II

Despite these developments, Grammar-Translation continued to enjoy widespread acceptance from the turn of the century until World War II. For example, a review of language instruction in the United States during the 1920s and 1930s reports that "though many individual teachers placed varying degrees of emphasis on speaking and understanding, certainly the most common type of instruction was the 'grammar and translation' method, used in much the same form for both ancient and modern languages (Moulton 1963, p. 22).

The Direct Method, however, was on the rise. Already introduced into countries such as England and Belgium, it became in 1902 the official language teaching method in both France and Germany. But it had no place in American classrooms until the 1920s (Geddes 1933, p. 38).

The Direct Method

Supporters of the Direct Method tended to favor instruction in modern foreign languages rather than in classical languages. While some judicious use of translation was approved (examinations sometimes included a translation section), most Direct Method teachers rejected translation as the cornerstone of language instruction. They tended to favor an incubation period of listening prior to teaching students how to speak, and quite generally the teaching of receptive skills prior to productive skills.

Speech, not writing, was viewed as the basis of language. Training in phonetics was advocated for teachers, but pronunciation—not phonetics—was to be taught in class; the phonograph was commonly utilized. A strict oral-aural approach was used at beginning levels (with oral readings introduced later on). And contrastive analysis began to be emphasized. Books could be used with caution later on though some disapproved, either because the printed word might weaken pronunciation skills or because texts were so prominent in Grammar-Translation classes. While some saw the value of occasional grammatical explanations, most vehemently rejected such practice. Unlike many predecessors they began to advocate graded sequencing of materials from easy to difficult, and they agreed that language was a skill or habit. Its social application made awareness of the foreign culture important. Rejecting the Natural Methodologists' claim that young and old learn the same way, Direct Methodologists favored modifying their teaching approaches according to the age or background of students.

As impressive as these principles sound, they were not easily implemented. Lack of teacher training and materials, the relatively unstructured coursework, unrealistic requirements for lesson preparation, exacting requirements for teacher expertise in the foreign language, exhausting drains on teacher energy during lesson presentations—these and other limitations often caused frustration and exhaustion among early adherents.

But interest continued to run high. Many visits were made to institutions using the Direct Method, and a great deal was written on the subject.

Typical in America and Europe was an inclination to modify the new method in order to adapt to teacher ability and local needs. For example, in a 1937 New York State foreign language syllabus we read: "Few advocates of the direct method are now so extreme as to reject all use of the mother tongue. . . ." Advocating a "common sense method," officials outlined a number of Direct Method practices to be followed, together with some modified Grammar-Translation practices (*Syllabus in Modern Foreign Languages*, 1937, pp. 10–21). Mackey describes increasing Direct Method modifications at this time and shows how in country after country, major compromises were effected: In Germany it became the "eclectic method" after it was blended with a rather traditional and systematic teaching of grammar; in France, a similar blending of old and new came to be known as *methode active*. In Switzerland, Belgium, and England, modifications also appeared (with teachers in England gradually "drifting back" toward Grammar-Translation) (Mackey 1965, pp. 146–147).

Then during the second decade of the twentieth century, massive language teaching experimentation was conducted in the United States. The Modern Foreign Language Study was organized in 1924; the seventeen-volume final report issued in 1929 avoided championing any single method:

Despite a certain amount of experimentation that has been done, there is little concrete and wholly trustworthy evidence to show to what extent a given classroom method is, in itself, productive of superior or of inferior results. . . . So many factors are involved in every teaching situation that none of the various efforts made by the study to secure unequivocal testimony in regard to the comparative results from different teaching methods were wholly successful. (Coleman 1929, pp. 276–277)

The most controversial aspect of the study came in Algernon Coleman's report (volume 12: *The Teaching of Modern Foreign Languages in the United States*). Coleman recommended that since 85 percent of high school students studied a foreign language for only two years, it was advisable to limit course objectives essentially to reading proficiency. This was objected to by educators such as Mercier of Harvard who asked why it was "necessary to right about face, according to the Coleman Report . . . toward the position from which Vietor invited us to turn some fifty years ago?" (Mercier 1930).

Despite the impetus of the Coleman report to focus on reading, the Direct Method was recognized prior to World War II along with Grammar-Translation as one of the two dominant methods then in use.[13] Moreover, in Coleman's important 1929 report on the Modern Foreign Language Study, we learn that there was a "distinct trend" in U.S. secondary schools "away from translation as a means and as an end, and toward some form of 'direct' approach" (Coleman 1929, p. 276). But the Coleman Report's recommendation that at least one skill—namely reading—be mastered well during the secondary student's brief exposure to a foreign language probably helped ensure the continuing dominance of Grammar-Translation up to America's involvement in World War II.

The Influence of Early Methodologists

The balance of this chapter will sample the teachings of two prominent early twentieth-century methodologists who broke with the Grammar-Translation tradition. Because of various compromises with "Direct" tenets and because the Reform was in reality a broad movement rather than a rigid, narrowly defined method, the approaches of these leaders will overlap but not coincide with mainstream Direct Method principles.

SWEET. No more influential and creative scholar-teacher can be found than Henry Sweet (1845–1912), a renowned British philologist and phonetician, who knew over a dozen languages and who published on speech sounds and pedagogy both prior to and following the turn of the century. His *History of English Sounds* and *Handbook of Phonetics* appeared during the decade prior to Viëtor's famous pamphlet of 1882, which served as a call to arms in the Reform Movement. During the 1890s alone, he published over half a dozen books—ranging from phonetics and grammar to historical linguistics and language teaching methods.

Referring to traditional methods of his time, he described his position as "a mean between unyielding conservatism on the one hand and reckless radicalism on the other" (Sweet 1964, p. vii). For example, he insisted on beginning with spoken rather than literary language but refused to join reformers in condemning translation. "A good method," he said, "must, before all, be comprehensive and eclectic" (Sweet 1964, p. 2). In teaching pronunciation, one cannot rely merely on imitation, he claimed; nor can

[13]Nearly half a century ago, the Direct Method and Grammar-Translation were viewed as the dominant methods in America:

There are two fundamentally different methods—the direct and the indirect—with several subclassifications. The direct method seeks to eliminate the mother tongue, endeavoring from the beginning to associate directly the object and the foreign word, the thought and the foreign expression. The indirect [Grammar-Translation] method bases its work on the pupil's knowledge of his own language and depends largely upon preliminary grammatical instruction, translation and explanation in the vernacular. (*Syllabus in Modern Foreign Languages*, 1937)

minor errors simply be ignored (he advocated using minimal pairs [bill/bell] to generate more native-sounding speech). Kinesthetic mastery is needed, said Sweet, who suggested techniques such as touching one's "adam's apple" or plugging one's ears in order to differentiate between voiced and voiceless phonemes. He described the complementary features of syntactic form and semantic meaning and differentiated between lexical and syntactic items. "Association" was viewed as a cornerstone of language learning; and repetition, while essential, was not to be emphasized to the point of boredom. Memory was seen as dependent on interest and "attention."

Sympathetic with Direct Method interest in pronunciation and use of the foreign language in class, he did not hestitate, nevertheless, to point up early theoretical limitations such as the supposition that the same process is involved in first and second language learning, or the tendency to focus too exclusively on easily represented objects and actions. He advocated systematic grammar instruction but with natural language samples, and after a "feel" for the grammar had been acquired. And he taught that language instruction must be based on sound linguistic and psychological principles.

Anticipating the Audiolingual era, he described speech as the basis of the literary language and as the logical model of language instruction, particularly at the more elementary levels. Noting the striking contrasts among languages, he pointed up the fallacy of applying rules from one language, such as Latin, in describing another. He saw language as being partly rational (describable by rules) and partly arbitrary—grammar tending toward the former and lexis the latter. Sweet divided his "progressive method" into five stages (Sweet 1964, pp. 116–122) ranging from an early oral emphasis to an advanced literary level.[14]

Sweet has wielded a powerful influence in second language teaching. His work in phonetics served as a basis for the International Phonetic Alphabet (IPA). His 1900 text, *The Practical Study of Languages*, was a pedagogical work of such significance that it was republished and studied for over half a century after his death. The Direct Method itself experienced refinements as a result of the insights and influence of this man.

PALMER. Among Sweet's younger contemporaries was a man who devoted his career almost entirely to teaching and pedagogical investigation. Harold E. Palmer (1877–1949), a prolific and capable writer, saw, like Sweet, the necessity for a rational, systematic approach to language teaching. But at the same time he championed a careful eclecticism that would facilitate the learning of persons differing in age, temperament, language background, and the like. His "multiple line of approach" rejected

---

[14]The first, "mechanical," was to generate fluency in pronunciation as well as mastery of a number of irregular forms contextualized in sentences. The "grammatical" stage followed, with natural language specimens exemplifying syntactic categories, presented in order of difficulty. Next came the "idiomatic and lexical" stage with its systematic acquisition of essential idioms and vocabulary. The "literary" stage drew upon *literature* for more advanced language mastery, and the "archaic" involved moving from contemporary to less familiar forms in older literature.

allegiance to any one theory as well as to the notion that inherent conflicts exist between methods. For him, the "complete" method included any teaching practice except "bad" ones, and it enabled the teacher to draw upon multiple techniques or needed pedagogical improvements in order to fulfill his task. He compared the exaggerated claims of some narrowly defined methods with those of patent medicine vendors with their cure-all claims (Palmer 1964, pp. 105–115).

But unlike Natural Methodologists, he was not satisfied with an intuitive approach. He felt a logical, scientific plan could be prepared (consider one of his hundred or more publications: *The* Scientific *Study and Teaching of Languages* [emphasis added]). Palmer felt that language teachers needed training in all branches of linguistics and not simply in phonetics, as many proponents of the Direct Method advocated. The theoretical underpinning should be provided by linguistics, psychology, and pedagogical principles (Palmer 1964, pp. 35–36; 1968, pp. 163–189; and Palmer and Redman 1969, pp. 60–62).

His creativity takes many forms. He developed his own phonetic system, which he used until he discovered in 1907 the one devised by the Phonetic Association. His smallest meaningful *lexical* units he called miologs (-ly, re-, etc.), monologs (words), and polylogs (because of, wake up, etc.). He developed a syntactic system called Ergonics, and gave attention to semantics as well as to vocabulary, morphology, syntax, and phonology (Palmer 1968, pp. 17–23).

A proponent of oral and conversational approaches to language teaching (consider selected titles by Palmer: *Colloquial English, Oral Method of Teaching Languages*, and *The Teaching of Oral English*), Palmer advocated teaching receptive skills (listening and even reading) up to three months before having students speak. Basic principles included providing students with appropriate learning strategies, giving them systematic language practice, carefully sequencing language study, and providing appropriate balance in the four skill areas.

His sequencing or gradation included ears before eyes, reception before production, oral repetition before reading, choral work before individual work, drill exercise before free production, concrete before abstract meaning; and where a difference in native language–foreign language alphabets existed, delaying use of the new alphabet until the student had a reasonably good grasp of the target language.

Teaching practices included utilizing multiple avenues to convey meaning (such as "spatialization" where words are related to actions and objects, context, definition, and even translation), appropriate use of vernacular explanations, use of pattern drills and substitution tables, and capitalizing on the difference between intensive and extensive reading—a distinction thought to be original with Palmer. Moreover, like Sweet, he helped refine and broaden the Direct Method in England. A survey of this gifted teacher's theoretical concepts and practices reveals striking parallels not only with post-war Audiolingualism but also with today's most current language teaching methods.

Sweet and Palmer were of course not alone. Such people as Walter Ripman and Michael West in England, Leonard Bloomfield and Otto Jespersen in the United States, Adolf Bohlen in Germany, and François Closset in Belgium provided linguistic and methodological contributions which hastened the decline of Grammar-Translation instruction.[15] Chapter Two will describe the development of that new approach along with the challenges to it that ultimately arose.

Until we reach and discuss the contemporary scene, we will not offer a definitive summary. But even at this point it should be apparent that an extraordinary amount of trial and error, reflection, analysis, and experimentation has been invested in the endeavor of language teaching by international scholars throughout the ages. Collectively they have made major contributions toward the solution of problems facing the profession today (including an eclectic selection of techniques, notions, and applications of communicative functions). Recognizing the contemporary relevance of historical contributions, we can mine them (as Stevick did the Cummings Device—Chapter Two) for insights and applications. Moreover, we can utilize historical insights in evaluating and applying "new" methodologies as they make their appearance.

At the same time, we are compelled to recognize those factors that transcend methodology: the teacher's personal mastery of the language principles she is teaching, the students' role in and varied capacities for language acquisition, the varying objectives of instruction from class to class, and finally, *the magic of the chemistry in teacher-student interactions, which overrides any method that the teacher might possibly select.*

But recognizing these factors doesn't negate the importance of utilizing sound methodology. Chapter Two leads us into a careful evaluation of contemporary techniques and methods.

---

[15]The nineteenth century witnessed not only the flourishing of the Grammar-Translation Method, as we have seen, but also the Natural Method, the Reading Method (given initial impetus by Marcel, and in the twentieth century by Michael West in England and the Coleman Report in the United States), the Psychological Method, and the Phonetic Method (Mackey even identifies a separate Grammar Method and Translation Method [1965, p. 153]). Moreover, the fusion of Natural and Phonetic Methods into the Direct Method spawned varieties, as noted earlier, such as the Eclectic Method, *Méthode Active*, and the Eclectic Direct Method in Britain involving experts such as Palmer himself.

Others include the Berlitz Method (a type of Direct Method originating in the nineteenth century and in use commercially even today), the Basic Method (or Basic English or Simplification Method), Tan Gau, the Unit Method, Language Control Method, Practice-Theory Method, Cognate Method, Dual-Language Method, Situation Method, Conversation Method, Graded Direct Method, and many named after specific teachers or language experts (for brief descriptions of some of the latter, see Mackey 1965, pp. 151–155, and Titone 1968, pp. 97–111; for more extended descriptions, see Kelly 1969, Darian 1972, Newmark 1948, and Larudee 1964).

DISCUSSION

1. Why should language practitioners be concerned with the history of language teaching?

2. What are some of the meanings of the word "method" as regards language teaching?

3. Describe the contribution of Marcus Fabius Quintilian to second language teaching.

4. Discuss Erasmus' three stages of language instruction.

5. What does the experience of Michel de Montaigne indicate with respect to language learning?

6. Who was the most influential educator of the seventeenth century? Identify some of his books.

7. Describe the activity referred to as "construing" and indicate whether it is associated more directly with Grammar-Translation or the Natural Method.

8. Tell what you can about the Committee of Twelve.

9. What was the most controversial recommendation of the Coleman Report?

10. Name two major scholars who worked in the late nineteenth and early twentieth centuries and outline their contributions.

CHAPTER TWO

WHERE WE'RE GOING: OPTIONS FOR THE FUTURE

Recently, a U.S.-born EFL teacher visited the United States from China, for the first time in thirty years. At the TESOL conference he attended, he observed with interest the many new language teaching methods that had surfaced since he had left his native country. At the same time he found what he described as a maturity among language teachers that he had not seen before in America: often a mild skepticism about the latest teaching fashions, a tendency not to embrace them uncritically, but instead to probe them in order to discover what insights they could add to their own teaching procedures. In short, he found that a pragmatic eclecticism had replaced the Audiolingual approach of post–World War II years.

Our visitor noted, however, that despite the years of criticism of Audiolingualism, it was still the single most visible teaching method in America, if not in the world. Some form of this approach seemed to him to undergird much of today's eclectic language teaching. In surveying contemporary trends in methodology, we will determine to what extent our visitor's observation is true. In fact, a careful assessment of the Audiolingual approach itself will help us determine just where we are and where we're headed in ESL teaching.

THE EMERGENCE OF AUDIOLINGUAL METHODOLOGY

Just as the Direct Method was an extension and refinement of the Natural Method, so Audiolingualism had its theoretical roots in the Direct Method.

But the transition between these two approaches was not a simple one. While the Direct Method continued to make inroads in Europe, its progress was slow in the United States. The Coleman Report had persuaded educators that since it was not practical to teach all language skills, at least the reading skill could be mastered reasonably well. This helped perpetuate Grammar-Translation as the handmaiden of reading. It wasn't until the involvement of the United States in World War II that we find a climate suitable for the development of Audiolingual methodology.

World War II Influences

Involved in a conflict that would quickly fling Americans into Europe, the Pacific, and Asia, U.S. government and military organizations recognized that large-scale and intensive training would be needed to provide language expertise for this globe-spanning operation. And it was speaking ability that was needed, even more than ability to read. Since the nation's foreign language teaching effort had been relatively limited and academic or literary, the military turned to linguists and anthropologists for assistance in describing the exotic languages that would need to be learned, and for help in preparing teaching materials and training courses. They capitalized on the Intensive Language Program developed by the American Council of Learned Societies just a few months before America entered the war. Moulton reports that "before the Program was over, just about every trained linguist in the country, young or old, had become involved in it one way or another" (1963, p. 23). The military contracted with a number of American universities to provide special language training designed by Army linguists. This undertaking was known as the Army Specialized Training Program (ASTP).

Just as linguists had lent their prestige and support to the Direct Method several decades earlier, they now provided similar support to what some began to call the "Army Method." Less than a year after America's entry into the war, Leonard Bloomfield published a guide on learning languages for which teaching materials were unavailable. And linguists across the country prepared grammars, phrase books, dictionaries, and other teaching materials.

The so-called Army Method developed by these language scholars consisted primarily of a shift in emphasis from the written to the spoken language and of immersion in intensive, practical instruction. While this approach was in the immediate national interest, it also reflected the convictions of many American linguists who had long been engrossed in anthropological research, particularly on little-known American Indian languages. Franz Boas, Leonard Bloomfield, and others had determined that these so-called primitive languages constituted a valuable resource not only for linguistic investigation but also for insights on how to teach a language.

What they had been analyzing was the spoken language, not the written; and what they advocated for instruction was speech, not writing. Reading and writing could be presented later, if sufficient time were available. But when literacy skills were taught, these needed to be based on oral skills: "A student who does not know the sound of a language, finds great difficulty in learning to read it. He cannot remember the foreign forms so long as they figure for him as a mere jumble of letters" (Bloomfield 1933, p. 505).

The low priority of literacy training stemmed not only from the oral emphasis of the Army's linguists but also from the fact that some of the languages to be learned for military purposes had not been written down or had difficult characters to master, such as Thai, Burmese, Korean, Japanese, and Chinese. Therefore, training manuals for these languages (22 in all) were prepared, under titles such as *Spoken Thai* and *Spoken Burmese*.

If the most noticeable characteristic of ASTP schools was oral work, the second was abundant drill. Since language was regarded as a set of subconscious habits, it was decided that the Army's language training programs must provide intensive drilling, which could lead to "overlearning" and subconscious habits in the new language. In class, students imitated native-speaking "drill masters," repeated material chorally and individually, engaged in dialogs that had been memorized in or out of class, responded to drill exercises, answered questions, and produced variations on drills and dialogs. Pronunciation drill included minimal-pair practice, borrowed from the language analysis tool kit of the linguists. In these small classes, activity ranged from phonemic analysis and transcription to dictation, and conversation practice was aimed at providing mastery of colloquial speech.

A survey of ASTP German classes indicated a range of 12 to 25 contact hours weekly, with an average of 16. General instruction averaged 5 hours, and drill averaged 11. There was a basic phase and an advanced phase, the former lasting 9 months and the latter about 11 months. Five 1-hour demonstrations each week covered pronunciation, grammar, and vocabulary. About six 2-hour sessions were held weekly with a native "informant" or "drillmaster" and only ten students per group. The drillmaster read pairs of questions and answers at normal speed, followed by choral and individual reading. Printed copies were then provided, and these were practiced in groups of five, with students providing corrections to each other. After blackboard explanations, class members were divided into pairs to practice dialogs, which were based on everyday situations and on material related to the history, culture, and geography of Germany. Extensive use was made of pictures and objects. Records, simulated broadcasts, and talks by German-speaking guests were used. The "language table" arrangement insured conversation in the target language, even at mealtime. From time to time, advanced classes occasionally engaged in a form of spontaneous or impromptu role play, with the teacher in a key role: "For example, a detachment of paratroopers lands in France with the purpose of cutting German communication lines. The teacher plays the first native they meet, a sympathetic Frenchman who wants to help, and they interrogate him" (Darian 1972, pp. 86–88).[1]

To sum up, speaking and drill were played up, grammar and translation were played down. Pattern practice helped provide inductive mastery of grammar. There was no translation from English into the foreign language; but some courses permitted occasional translation from the foreign language into English, at the advanced level. The students' native language could be used to provide instructions as well as explanations of structure and meaning.

Some literacy training was used to complement oral instruction. In Western European language courses, reading often began simultaneously with oral instruction—for example, as printed versions of question and answer drills. In Oriental and Eastern European language classes, reading was introduced 1 to 6 weeks after the beginning of the course, and then only in a romanized alphabet. Writing was not an official part of Army language courses, but as we have noted, dictation was occasionally used to reinforce oral instruction.

Developments Following the War

Within a year after its inception, ASTP had 15,000 people being trained in fifty-five colleges and universities. Their rapid acquisition of foreign language proficiency quickly gained widespread recognition for the Army's language programs—both through articles in scholarly journals and through interest in the popular press. In addition to keen interest in the new "Army Method," there developed during and following the war a market for American foreign language speakers abroad and an interested clientele at home. English emerged as the undisputed international language, introducing to the American scene English as a second or foreign language. Moreover, technology gave birth to new recording devices—mainly the wire recorder and later the tape recorder—and with these the language laboratory.

The convergence of three important conditions acted as a powerful catalyst in launching the new methodology: the involvement of linguists, widespread teacher interest, and corroboration from psychologists. We have already noted the extraordinary involvement of linguists in developing this approach. Theirs was a total commitment to the new oral-aural method-

---

[1]Among the present authors, Bowen in 1943–44 had nine months of ASTP Spanish instruction at Rutgers University. The program was referred to as "Language and Area Training." A six-hour academic day was normal, with approximately two hours devoted to area (geography, history, culture, economics), usually in Spanish. A four-man teaching team was made up of two native Spanish-speaking instructors and two for whom Spanish was a second language. Soldier students roomed together and ate together. Part of the area training and all of the inevitable military science lectures were in English. Classes consisted of twelve members. New technology was supposed to have been applied, but some of the members of the teaching staff, unsympathetic to the changes in approach, largely ignored the official guidance and went back to parsing verbs. Fortunately instructors rotated, so all four sections of Spanish worked with all of the instructors.

ology.[2] At the same time, large numbers of language teachers became persuaded that an oral approach was needed; many of these had been skeptics before serving as language drillmasters in the Army program. Behavioral psychologists, whose research complemented that of the linguists (Rivers 1964), concluded that language learning resulted from conditioning or habit formation through responding to specific stimuli. To them, the mimicry and error-free practice of Audiolingualists seemed ideally suited to language acquisition. This confluence of scholarly and practical wisdom was irresistible.

While traditionalists voiced their reservations, the principal difficulty in implementing the new method in the schools was translating it from an almost totally oral intensive form into a four-skill nonintensive college course.[3] Few seemed to recognize the limitations inherent in a slim three-hour offering. So intense was the disappointment, in fact, that for a time after the war, the new method seemed all but doomed. However, some key institutional support[4] and national reaction to Sputnik saved the day. The 1958 National Defense Education Act (NDEA) funded the training of large numbers of language teachers in the new method; once again linguists were tapped to

[2]The term "audiolingual" was coined by Nelson Brooks of Yale University to replace "oral-aural," a label that had not been as easily understood when referred to orally (Scherer and Wertheimer 1964, p. 5).

[3]The remarkable success of the military language schools had stemmed from both internal and external factors: "(1) carefully selected students, (2) highly motivated students, (3) common housing, (4) small classes, (5) many contact hours, (6) native-speaking or bilingual teachers, (7) a generous supply of teaching aids, (8) a nontechnical approach to phonology, with English as a reference point, (9) area studies relating the target language and the culture of its speech community to the students' culture" (Scherer and Wertheimer 1964, p. 3).

[4]Some of the earliest organizations to adopt and help develop Audiolingual methodology were the Army Language School (1941), Navy Language School (1941), Air Force Russian Language Program (1946), and the Foreign Service Institute of the Department of State (1947). Also cited as supportive was the use of Direct Methods by commercial language schools such as Berlitz, the basically Audiolingual programs of some institutions of higher learning such as Middlebury and Cornell's foreign language offerings, and Michigan's English Language Institute, where English was taught as a second language. Finally, the Modern Language Association's resolutions beginning in 1946 and continuing into the 1950s breathed new life into Audiolingual methodology.

In the ferment then referred to by some scholars (e.g., William Riley Parker) as the New Key, and with the experience that traditional language instruction was not and probably could not be successfully used for orally oriented instruction, a plan was devised at a special conference called by the Modern Language Association in 1956 to produce a new kind of text, with professional support and assistance that would be compatible with the new ideas being applied to university-level language teaching. The result was a textbook marketed under the title *Modern Spanish*, which had a profound effect on teaching methodology and on subsequent textbooks for Spanish and for other foreign languages taught in the United States. *Modern Spanish* went through three successive editions and gained a wide acceptance after it appeared in 1960. The production of this Spanish textbook was financially supported by (at that time) an unprecedented grant from the Rockefeller Foundation of just over $40,000! At that time both the fact of a grant and the amount were novel features destined to become dwarfed by the munificence and ready availability of future grant support. More important than the initiative, the language teaching profession retained and exercised the right of final editing, though the publisher gave up this right very reluctantly, since publishers make it their business to know which kinds of books will succeed on the market and which kinds won't. The Spanish project broke the circle where publishers continued making the kinds of books that had sold in the past, effectively stifling initiative to make even modest changes. Previously, since it was the publisher's money at risk, publishers had called the tune.

interact in the training of language teachers. This decade also witnessed the exporting of teachers and directors of English programs to many foreign countries, where the new oral approach would be implemented. Audiolingual methodology was now firmly established.

Reasons for Audiolingual Success

What was the source of Audiolingual success and vitality? Detractors attributed it to novelty (a methodological Hawthorne effect) or to the supposed gimmickry of the new tape recorders in burgeoning language laboratories. Some felt its success was due primarily to the dramatic increase in time spent on language teaching in Army programs and to the limited objectives or the small classes. A great many felt it was the emphasis on oral activity.

But the linguists thought otherwise. To them it was the "scientific" nature of the linguistic approach. Audiolingual giants such as Fries strived to set the record straight:

> For at least ten years some of us have been trying to explain that the fundamental feature of the "new approach" to language learning is not a greater allotment of time, is not smaller classes, is not even a greater emphasis on oral practice, although many of us believe these to be highly desirable. The fundamental feature of this new approach consists in a scientific descriptive analysis as the basis upon which to build the teaching materials. (Fries 1949; see also Fries 1945, pp. 3, 5, 7)

He added that it was the "linguistic scientists' " descriptive techniques, contrastive analysis, choice and sequence of materials, and methodological procedures growing out of the materials that were all-important.

Looking at Audiolingualism in historical perspective, we can see that one reason for its success was its great prestige almost from the beginning, and the almost unprecedented and essentially unanimous support from research scholars in a variety of disciplines as well as from teachers and the public at large. (As suggested earlier, part of its prestige can be attributed to the success of U.S. Army programs during the war, when selected and well-motivated students spent many hours a week studying limited aspects of the language, with capable instructors.) Even internationally, the best-received alternative was the Direct Method, which was very close in form to the Audiolingual Method.

Secondly, it was accompanied by carefully prepared materials—an advantage not enjoyed by those who had used the older Natural Method or even by earlier users of the Direct Method. Related to this were the well-developed teaching syllabi, which removed virtually all guesswork for the teacher. This in turn bolstered teacher training and inservice programs. And finally, it employed a variety of historically proven teaching practices: It was skill oriented, with a practical oral emphasis as practiced by Quintilian, Erasmus, and many others. It provided contextualized language practice in true-to-life situations including dialog, which had been used with success by many since the early Roman period. It provided a wide variety of activities to help maintain interest, and it made extensive use of visuals as Comenius and others had done with such good results. In addition, it arranged for abundant practice.

THE REEMERGENCE OF ECLECTICISM

The Eclipse of Audiolingualism

Just as the foundation of Audiolingualism had been laid by linguists, so the first significant challenge to this method also came from linguists. The publication in 1957 of Noam Chomsky's work on transformational-generative grammar electrified the linguistic community with its dramatic and powerful challenge to structural linguistics. Two years later Chomsky attacked the language acquisition theory of behavioral psychology. This twin assault challenged existing descriptions of language as well as the most basic notions of how language is acquired. With Chomsky's underscoring of this position the following decade at the Northeast Conference on Language Teaching, the profession began to realize that the theoretical underpinnings of Audiolingualism were threatened. Their basic notion of language as a set of habits was apparently unfounded. The new view saw it as rule-governed, with language acquisition a creative process requiring considerable learner initiative rather than learner manipulation through mimicry, memorization, and overlearning.

These theoretical salvos constituted the initial onslaught. The anti-Audiolingual movement gained momentum as public focus shifted to the excesses of Audiolingual adherents and real or imagined limitations of the methodology. Taught by capable teachers, Audiolingual classes had been exciting, action-filled experiences, largely fulfilling Wardhaugh's perception of effective pedagogy:

I see a need for lots of examples, lots of variety, and lots of context-oriented work. . . . All linguistic activity must be associated with meaningful activity so any techniques designed to encourage meaningful activity are obviously important in language learning. Consequently, movement, involvement, and situation, and the concomitants of these—laughter, games and stories—are important in teaching. (1969, pp. 111, 114)

But many less sensitive teachers pushed drill to the extreme—a natural consequence of the "overlearning" concept. And all too many employed mind-jarring strings of unrelated sentences for pattern practice, uncontextualized minimal-pair drills, anemic dialogs with thinly disguised doses of structure. It was easy to justify a heavy amount of dialog memorization and pronunciation drill on discrete features of the language. In their worst form, Audiolingual classes ignored meaning, denied creative responses from students, and concentrated on linguistic form rather than on communication. Such excesses resulted in boredom and painfully slow progress. This could be contrasted with the exaggerated claims of some Audiolingual hucksters.

Certain critics not only concentrated on Audiolingual excesses but also embellished them by redefining Audiolingual tenets: Meaning was supposedly absent in this methodology; use of the native language or translation was supposedly taboo; presumably only speaking was taught; and communication was supposedly as alien as communism, "mindless" drill being the only means and end of Audiolingualism.

But the method was not simply victim to unprincipled attack. Faulty theoretical assumptions such as the habit-formation notion of language learning contributed to some of the excesses mentioned above and to unproductive emphases. One of these was the "phobia," as Bolinger puts it, of the student's making a mistake.[5] The resulting "control" was often stultifying. The grammar-based Audiolingual approach moved cautiously from supposedly simple to more and more linguistically complex features, often without adequate consideration for what might be needed in everyday situations. This reflected the "scientific" approach of the method's linguist midwives. Another limitation was an almost exclusive reliance on induction. As suggested above, faulty *emphases* more than fundamental methodological weaknesses plagued the system: too much phonology, too little concern as a rule for the written word; high interest in language form, low interest in student creativity and initiative in acquiring the language.

With the authority of this monolithic approach seriously challenged and its prestige tarnished, many teachers began to cast about for acceptable alternatives. They were surprised when the new linguists insisted that transformational-generative grammar was of little immediate use in formulating a new instructional approach. As early as 1965, Carroll identified two contrasting methodological options as being the Audiolingual habit theory and a Cognitive-Code learning theory. He advocated that the best features of each be utilized, since both incorporated valid procedures. But the tendency was to magnify the shortcomings of Audiolingual practices and strike out for something new. There were those who rushed to embrace each new approach.[6] Others continued using Audiolingual methodology, seemingly oblivious to the theoretical turmoil. But a number began to recommend a "prudent eclecticism" (e.g., Marckwardt and others).

[5]Bolinger, in a balanced presentation, looks at implications of Audiolingual tenets inherited from earlier methods as well as those stemming from structural linguistics (1968, pp. 30–41). He notes that structuralists in hand with behavioral psychologists fostered undue reliance on an inductive approach to grammar; they gave great emphasis to the oral, to the benefits of drill, and the supposed stimulus-response nature of language. However, most Audiolingual limitations, he feels, are weaknesses of "practice and proportion."

[6]Prator refers to "great prophets" of language methodology who "have built up large and often blindly enthusiastic groups of followers and who have been able to impose their somewhat closed systems of thought on a generation or more of disciples by their personal prestige and authority" (1979, p. 6). New prophets or gurus arose in the post-Audiolingual era, but only a minority of teachers accepted them blindly or without reservation.

What were some of the alternative approaches available from which an eclectic approach could be derived? There were commercial language schools such as Berlitz, Yazigy, and English Language Services. And there were distinctive commercial language materials such as those designated as St. Cloud, Situational Reinforcement, and Microwave. The latter, along with Stylized Mnemonics, Language Learning Games, and Total Physical Response (TPR) resemble elaborate techniques more than they do distinctive teaching methodologies. Extensions of Total Physical Response include a variety of delayed speaking procedures, the most prominent being Winitz and Reeds' Aural Discrimination Method, or Winitz's Comprehension Approach (1981). But the methods most widely heralded at this time included Suggestology, the Silent Way, and Counseling-Learning. In addition, broad movements and principles gained widespread acceptance. These included humanistic education and communicative competence. Then from Europe came a bold new approach to language teaching known as the Notional-Functional Syllabus. All these proved useful in connection with the new eclecticism. The following pages elaborate on them and suggest what insights each has contributed.

Commercial Language Schools

Contemporary commercial language schools have had limited influence, since relatively little has been published on them in professional journals. And the modest information available suggests that with a few exceptions they do not differ significantly in their approach from Audiolingualism.

Begun over a century ago, the Berlitz schools number in the hundreds and are found worldwide. The approach used is reportedly similar to the Direct Method, since only the target language is permitted to be spoken by teachers and students. And oral instruction utilizing normal conversational situations is required from the outset. The Yazigy schools of Brazil seem to follow an Audiolingual approach, utilizing quantities of dialogs based on everyday situations. Their materials are richly illustrated, and a newsletter keeps consumers abreast of international developments. With home offices in Washington, D.C., English Language Services was developed during the peak of Audiolingualism to help meet TEFL needs overseas by providing teachers, programs, and materials for government and private agencies. Schools and programs, such as the three mentioned here briefly, helped maintain Audiolingualism as a component of the new eclectic approach.

Commercially Marketed Systems

Certain commercially developed materials have been presented as new teaching methods. And they have attracted some attention since they are readily available for use in the classroom.

ST. CLOUD. Used more by foreign language teachers than ESL/EFL instructors is the St. Cloud method. A primary appeal is its total contextualization of language in a stream of multimedia presentations. The visual emphases of Comenius and Audiolingual methodology are employed so as to transcend mere linguistic accuracy: The aim is to convey semantic meaning, cultural insights, and even nonverbal communication.

The basic device in this modified Direct Method instruction is the filmstrip, which is used with a tape followed by choral repetition. Reading material is introduced after sixty hours of oral work. The St. Cloud method was developed about three decades ago at a teacher training college in St. Cloud, France.

Limitations include a very structured approach allowing for little teacher or student initiative. Not as communicative as some more recent approaches, St. Cloud is less successful with advanced students and college age students than with those who are younger and less advanced. In addition to its success in conveying meaning, this method tends to produce good pronunciation and assistance for weaker nonnative teachers.

SITUATIONAL REINFORCEMENT. A principal feature of Eugene J. Hall's commercially developed Situational Reinforcement approach is to have students become actively involved in what they are talking about. The purpose of this activity is similar to the media immersion in St. Cloud and the physical responses in Asher's method discussed later, and that is to convey and reflect meaning. Another aim of Hall is to provide "authentic communication" through cognitive choices rather than mere mechanical repetition.

Reacting against the strict Audiolingual sequencing of structures from simple to complex, Hall has abandoned completely the idea of a grammar-based and grammar-sequenced presentation. His situational focus moves students from dialogs and readings on familiar, concrete objects to the discussion of more abstract matters. The brief grammar points discussed grow out of the situation.

One limitation is excessive repetition in the dialog presentation. And the U.S. orientation in the texts could be a limitation in some overseas settings. Also, the unstructured format gives some students the impression they are not making any real progress. But students find it easy to become involved in the realistic situations, and meaning is presented readily through the activity strategy. Finally, an advantage approaching that of St. Cloud is the relative ease with which these materials can be used by the novice teacher.

MICROWAVE DEVICE. Once produced commercially as a new method by imitators, the Microwave Device has always been regarded by its author to have a more limited though still useful role. It was conceived of in 1964 by Earl Stevick after reading Thomas Cummings. The Microwave or Cummings Device consists of a simple strategy utilizing a small cluster of questions and answers to generate a maximum amount of information (for example, the relatively small repertoire needed by a hotel desk clerk).

Preparing teaching materials for the Foreign Service Institute and Peace Corps, Stevick saw the feasibility of preparing an embassy guard, for instance, with a limited stock of specific linguistic information which could be quickly learned and yet enable him to generate new vocabulary and engage in bona fide communication. The format of a Microwave consists of an utterance (usually a question) and four to eight responses. The cycle of instruction when the device was initially conceived included an M-phase (mimicry, manipulation, mechanics) and a C-phase (communication, conversation, and continuity).

An acknowledged limitation is its being only a single technique in a larger language learning operation. Principal advantages of Microwave are its efficiency and communicative potential.

What features do these methods stress that are not typically present in Audiolingual instruction? Developed during the heyday of Audiolingualism, the St. Cloud method provides just a slight shift in emphasis—more attention to conveying semantic meaning, visually. Hall's Situational Reinforcement also underscores the conveying of meaning, but through acting out what is spoken. His more radical departure is in totally rejecting a grammar-sequenced approach to instruction. Likewise indifferent to grammatical sequencing, Microwave is intended for immediate communication in the real world.

Innovative Methods

Novel approaches with a rather limited number of followers to date include Lipson's Stylized Mnemonics, Terrell's Natural Approach, Harrison's Structured Tutoring, Asher's Total Physical Response, and the Winitz-Reeds Comprehension Method.[7] Following a brief summary of these methods, a somewhat more extensive review will be made of three major contemporary methods.

STYLIZED MNEMONICS. Alexander Lipson's mnemonic method begins with translation (a device not entirely foreign to Audiolingual methodology). After a cluster of useful sentences is learned, simple stylized drawings are introduced to represent oft-expressed ideas and vocabulary: for example, to "like" something is pictured by a heart; "doesn't like" would consist of a large "X" through a heart. These are then utilized to cue increasingly complex story lines.

The sometimes bizarre situations are typically culturally relevant, engrossing, unpredictable and communicative. Limitations include its being tailored for a linguistically homogeneous group and a bilingual instructor. (See Lipson 1971.)

NATURAL APPROACH. A rather recent innovation is Tracy Terrell's Natural Approach in which listening predominates at first and speech is never forced. Errors are not directly corrected, except in written assignments. Class time is devoted exclusively to communicative activities; grammar work (largely self-correcting exercises) is done outside class.

---

[7]For a more detailed treatment, see Madsen (1979), Blair (1982), or Oller and Richard-Amato (1983).

Learning comes through a wide variety of Affective Acquisition Activities that capitalize on student interests and feature *meaning* rather than language form. Motivation to speak is a key concern; and speech is held to follow natural stages from yes/no and one-word answers to complete sentences and connected discourse.

Students learn how to tolerate a certain amount of language flow that is not completely comprehensible, with an expectation that at times they simply need to get the gist of what they hear. They may respond orally when they feel comfortable in doing so; and responses in the native language are permitted. Early on, there is considerable interest in vocabulary expansion and little emphasis on grammar. (See Terrell 1982, Krashen and Terrell 1983.)

Advantages include the high interest and low anxiety of classroom procedures. But, as with Lipson's method, the effectiveness depends in large measure on the teacher's ingenuity.

STRUCTURED TUTORING. In his Structured Tutoring program, instructional psychologist Grant Harrison uses adult or peer volunteer tutors who are warm and supportive. Materials have a heavy grammar emphasis and are carefully sequenced. Reading and writing are introduced the second week of instruction. The situation is nonthreatening. Instruction is obviously self-paced and virtually cost-free—the only expense being the purchase of the teaching handbook. The tutoring takes place one-on-one.

Advantages include essentially anxiety-free learning, an easy-to-follow instructional book, and virtually free teaching. Limitations include disjointed instruction when the volunteer tutors drop out of the program, the limited number of native English speakers in some overseas locations, and highly controlled teaching materials that leave little room for teacher/student initiative. (See Harrison 1976.)

TOTAL PHYSICAL RESPONSE. Widely known, Asher's Total Physical Response (TPR) has frequently been incorporated as an instructional technique but seldom as a full-blown method. Like Postovsky, Gary, and others, he advocates delaying speech and concentrating on listening. Controlled experiments show rapid, permanent acquisition of language through the method's use of commands accompanied by physical actions appropriate to the commands (Stand up; walk to the blackboard; draw a house on the board).

Asher notes that essentially all structures can be nested in the imperative. And even abstract terms are introduced: For example, with terms such as honesty, government, and justice written on cards, a student can be told, "Give me 'justice'." An important feature is the student's acquiring the language in communicative "chunks" rather than in discrete, structure-based fragments. In addition, a substantial amount of transfer has been noted from listening skills to reading and writing. "Fine tuning" is to be facilitated through complementary procedures such as the Winitz and Reeds Comprehension Method, to be discussed next. (See Asher 1977, 1982.)

Advantages include its low anxiety characteristics and communicative focus. But since it has been applied essentially to beginners, many have questioned its suitability for intermediate and advanced students.

COMPREHENSION METHOD. Winitz and Reeds' Comprehension Method, as we have seen, complements Asher's TPR approach. It defers speaking and writing until the language is firmly established through listening. Errors in speaking and writing are ignored. Students simply look at a quadrant of pictures while listening to sentences; then they select the picture referred to. Cassette tapes and booklets of pictures using this method are available commercially (Winitz 1978).

Rules and grammar are not explicitly taught. Sentences listened to are increasingly complex. Reading is said to require minimal explicit instruction, and students do not need to speak in the foreign language until they have mastered the basic structures and vocabulary of the target language. (See Winitz 1981.)

Advantages include low-anxiety learning, self-pacing, and (it is claimed) rapid language acquisition. Limitations include the absence of a complete four-skill offering, lack of variety in presentation, and little or no provision for flexibility in meeting student interests and interaction needs at intermediate and advanced levels.

Three Major Contemporary Methods

SUGGESTOLOGY. Developed in Bulgaria by a psychiatrist named Georgi Lozanov, Suggestology (or Suggestopedia) has been used in such varied countries as the Soviet Union and Canada. The method was developed to tap our latent ability to learn languages, by counteracting the crippling fears and inhibitions that supposedly impede language learning. An initial means is through generating great confidence in the program and the competence of the instructor. Another is through a relaxed, nonthreatening atmosphere. Assurances of progress are made. Ideally, the experience is totally positive: Each step is seen as natural, and easily within one's grasp. The experience is made pleasurable not only by a sense of progress in learning the new language but even through physical comfort and esthetic satisfaction.

While some associate Suggestology with hypnotic states, Lozanov denies his method utilizes hypnosis. But he does claim it greatly accelerates learning through "hypermnesia" and that it greatly enhances creativity. This occurs in part by deprogramming negative attitudes toward learning. And he rejects linear instruction as well as the tendency of many to divide elements of the language into bits to be learned in discrete pieces. Similarly, he holds that language growth does not occur in a vacuum; esthetic interests and even ethical awareness develop simultaneously.

To begin with, classical Suggestology avoids the "threatening" classroom in favor of a living room atmosphere with carpeted floors and easy chairs; this is intended to generate a freer flow of conversation, as might occur in one's home. Music and other art forms are introduced for relaxation designed to facilitate the acquisition of language. Suggesting the ease with which the language can be acquired, the teacher introduces dozens of lines of dialog every few days. Homework is minimal, and the emphasis is on communication. Given a new name the first day of class, students are immersed in the new language and begin living out their new identity.

The lengthy dialogs are presented with simple explanations of language features, then with oral interlinear translation, varied intonations, and finally (with scripts put aside) to the accompaniment of classical music.

During the first portion of this three-part dialog introduction—the *explicative* reading—the teacher covers everything that might cause students difficulty: new vocabulary items, pronunciation, grammar. Explanations are simple and informal; students may ask questions. In the second portion—the *intonational* reading—the teacher presents the dialog with three special intonations, while the students follow along in their handouts: one line in normal voice, the next hushed, and the following line in a strong, almost declamatory voice—none of the intonations bearing any special relation to the meaning of the lines being read. During the third portion of the dialog presentation—the *concert*—students are invited to put away their dialog transcripts, relax, and listen to an expressive reading of the dialog accompanied by beautiful classical music.

Subsequent interaction activities utilize lexical and thematic material from the dialogs, elaborating the material through songs and games, readings, and translation. Homework consists merely of skimming over the dialogs presented in class. When students express a desire to do so, they engage at last in rather spontaneous role play activity. (See Lozanov 1978, 1979.)

Experience with this method has shown positive affect, surprising fluency, and communicative ability in a short amount of time. Limitations include the need for linguistically homogeneous students and bilingual teachers of the right temperament and philosophical persuasions. Also students often leave the course with some deficiencies in grammar and phonology. An almost fatal flaw has been the inclination of some Suggestologists and promoters to publish unscientific and exaggerated claims for the method. Resulting criticism (Scovel 1979, Wagner and Tilney 1983) has seriously undermined its prestige.

THE SILENT WAY. Introduced almost two decades ago by Caleb Gattegno, the Silent Way was not discovered by the profession until the mid-1970s. Unlike teachers of other methods, Silent Way teachers speak under 10 percent of the time. But this is not simply to provide students with more time to *talk*, a key objective in Audiolingual classes. Students are felt to need time to reflect and digest what they have heard. Instruction, however, is anything but leisurely. There is considerable discovery and individual initiative, and students often learn from one another. The teacher does not answer questions. No oral corrections are made. Student errors, it is felt, can help students develop criteria of correctness. As important as the language learning that takes place with this method, says Gattegno, is the change in students that enables them to accept one another as "contributors" to their own life, and to accept responsibility for their own learning.

Intensity and austerity characterize the method. For some time, only a few wooden rods and phonic wall charts constitute the visuals employed. The native language of students is always avoided.

Initial instruction involves a very limited amount of vocabulary, the focus being on the "melody" and structure of the language. The various colored rods are used to present simple vocabulary inductively, to show spatial relationships and prepositions, comparatives, tense—in short, every aspect of language including the conditional and the subjunctive.

As instruction begins, the teacher may pick up one of the colored wooden cubes and say, "A rod." She repeats this with rods of different colors, and then she adds "A blue rod," "A red rod," etc., to the students' repertoire. Next, she motions for two students to come forward. She says to one, "Take a red rod." When this action is performed, she says, "Give it to him." Meaning is enhanced through mime, gesture, and assistance from fellow students. Without verbal explanation, the teacher then changes places with one of the students, and the student begins to make requests. The teacher gradually speaks less often and the students more; but the teacher is always fully in charge of what is taking place. Utterances are quickly expanded to ten-, twelve-, and fifteen-word sentences.

Very important is training in the "rhythm" of the language. Taped passages are used even before students have acquired enough language to understand the meaning of what they are listening to. But a feel for the target language is sought through contrast and repeated exposure.

"Visual dictation" is handled with a wall chart and a pointer, with reference to words already introduced. Tapping several words in a row introduces not only possible new combinations but also appropriate speech rhythms and sound-symbol correspondences needed for reading. The teacher may produce an utterance herself, after which the students point to the words on the chart that she has uttered.

When the time comes for more extensive vocabulary expansion, Silent Way worksheets, drawings, pictures, and transparencies are utilized. While no textbook is used during the entire basic skills development period, controlled readers and anthologies are ultimately used in teaching reading and advanced skills. (See Gattegno 1972, 1976.)

Used internationally to teach a wide variety of European, Asian, and Middle Eastern languages, the Silent Way has achieved impressive results. Earl Stevick cites this method along with Counseling-Learning as providing invaluable insights to teachers of a second language (1974; see also Stevick 1976, 1980). But unsettling for many are Gattegno's dogmatic pronouncements, which largely ignore research contributions in the field. Another limitation is the "rod manipulation" technique, which some adult education and inner-city learners reject as irrelevant to their needs.

COUNSELING-LEARNING. This method, also known as Community Language Learning, was introduced two decades ago by Charles Curran, and like Silent Way was virtually unknown in ESL circles until a decade ago. More than any other contemporary method, this approach reflects a concern for the development of positive human relationships. Interestingly, this is aimed at improving the *teacher's* sense of worth and belonging as well as that of the student. Besides personal enrichment, such enhancement is seen as contributing to more effective teaching and improved learning. Rejected in favor of shared task-oriented activities are stances emphasizing doubting, questioning, diagnosing or mere "intellectualizing." Teachers are to recognize each individual's need for personal fulfillment, and therefore communication in language classes should stem from joint learner efforts directed toward completing a given task.

Curran envisions a cycle of development following this pattern: The teacher recognizes student need for fulfillment as well as the fact that such fulfillment stems in large measure from interacting with others and thus obtaining mutual understanding and appreciation. An essential classroom strategy, therefore, is interaction generated by cooperative efforts of learners in completing tasks. To facilitate such interaction, the teacher removes himself from his usual role while persuading students to emerge from their protective stance of noninvolvement. This realignment of roles is hopefully accompanied by increased trust and mutual interest, and it is reportedly aided by the individual's increased personal fulfillment.

The actual instruction appears simple, on the surface. Students (referred to as "clients") sit in a circle. The teacher or teachers (called "knowers" or "counselor-teachers") stand outside the circle. During the initial stage, students are simply invited to converse with one another on any topic. The teacher, standing behind the student, translates these utterances (sotto voce) into the foreign language, and the student repeats the translation. Typically, the student's translated message is taped (but not her original native language utterance).

Questions cannot be answered by the "nonexistent" teacher. As in the Silent Way, there are periods of silence when students mull over what they have heard. Recorded material is played back near the end of the period; portions may be written on the board and grammar points briefly clarified.

Over a period of time, learners proceed through five stages. In the initial (or Embryonic) stage they are very dependent on their counselor-teacher. At the next stage (Self-Assertion), they speak directly to fellow class members in the foreign language, receiving assistance only when they hesitate or ask for it. In the third (or Birth) stage there is greater independence on the part of learners and an improved oneness of purpose in the functioning of knower and clients. Students speak even more freely in the fourth (or Reversal) stage, with confidence that peers understand what is being said. Now the counselor-teacher injects corrections without being asked, knowing that student-clients are secure enough to accept the improvements offered. Finally, in stage five (the Independent or Enrichment period), the counselor intervenes to refine what is being communicated, by adding idioms and more sophisticated or socially appropriate means of expressing what is said. Now color-coded signals are used to indicate error, availability of more appropriate idiom, and appropriateness of utterance.

Counseling-Learning students tend to be very pleased with the control they have over their own learning. And they tend to be impressed with the mutual assistance provided by peers and the mutual trust and respect that develops among students and between students and teacher.

Advantages of Counseling-Learning include the high motivation of learners. LaForge has noted the impressive initiative assumed by students taught with this method, the flexibility they have to move at their own pace, their inclination to assist lagging peers, and their speed of acquisition. Students comment favorably on the freedom permitted and the control they have over the learning process. But what are its limitations? As with the Silent Way, it sometimes fails to meet the expectations of learners, notably adults seeking quick, practical training. It requires a teacher who is expert in both target and native languages and who is sensitive enough to provide the counseling situation that this approach requires. Finally, it is best suited for a linguistically homogeneous class.

Differences between Audiolingualism and Contemporary Options

It is obvious that in the post-Audiolingual period there is no paucity of methodological alternatives. It is clear, too, that these several options vary from each other in certain specific ways: Approaches by Lipson, Lozanov, and Curran utilize translation; most of the others avoid it. Hall's and Curran's ignore grammar sequencing; the St. Cloud and Structured Tutorial retain it. Speaking is delayed for a significant period of time in the Natural Approach, Total Physical Response, and Comprehension Method; in most others, speaking is introduced immediately. Harrison's method utilizes one-on-one instruction; others, such as Gattegno's and Curran's, rely heavily on student interaction.

Despite such variation, however, there are prominent differences in emphasis between these contemporary options and the emphases of Audio-lingual methodology.

With the abandonment of habit-formation theory, the dread of student errors tended to vanish. Most began to regard mistakes as natural and sometimes self-correcting over a period of time (Lozanov, Winitz-Reeds, Terrell, for example). "Mistakes," says Gattegno, "are precious indicators of the discrepancy between what is and what should be." Control over a language was to come by "exploring" it, and such exploration inevitably results in occasional errors.

A corollary was the tendency to abandon teaching materials that employed careful grammatical control. While this typified most new methods, it was particularly evident in those such as Hall's (in which structure was rejected in favor of situation) and Curran's (in which whatever students decided to communicate became the corpus of instruction). Audiolingual emphasis on form, then, gave way to an emphasis on meaning: Consider the language generated by Lipson's stylized drawings, and the focus on simply understanding oral communication in the Natural Approach, TPR, the Comprehension Method, and others.

Understanding the learner's active role in acquiring his language, contemporary methodologists began to place more responsibility on the student-learner. The most dramatic example is Counseling-Learning, which gives the student unprecedented control over the nature of language used, amount and kind of teacher assistance desired, and pace employed. The Natural Approach likewise provides great flexibility of student participation, and the Silent Way is noted for generating self-reliance on the part of learners. Related to this is the role of the teacher. Central in Audiolingual methodology, the teacher in a number of contemporary methods occupies a less dominant position (consider, for example, methods such as St. Cloud and Counseling-Learning).

With an increased emphasis on the student's role in acquiring language, strategies emerged to lessen classroom anxiety and promote a warm, accepting climate, which might stimulate a desire for involvement and investment of one's self. The three delayed-speaking methods and Harrison's tutorial approach, as well as Suggestology and Counseling-Learning, are particularly well suited to reducing anxiety.

Individually and collectively these contemporary methodologies provide viable alternatives to Audiolingualism—both theoretically and practically. To be sure, Audiolingual contrasts with the older Reading Method and with Grammar-Translation are more dramatic. For both Audiolingualism and contemporary methods emphasize the spoken word (to some, the "heard" word), activity, variety, visuals, culture, use if necessary of the native language, and development of practical language skills. This is fortunate in that it provides teachers with an opportunity to retain useful ingredients of the former approach and integrate important features of the new.

This is indeed what has been happening since Audiolingualism headed into a decline. No single method has generated the near unanimous support of linguists, psychologists, and methodologists that the Audiolingual approach did. (A few, however, have provided a guru, such as Gattegno, whose teachings are accepted with something closely akin to unquestioning religious faith.) But there is broad acceptance of the new methods' "cognitive" features. The result has been a trend toward a "prudent eclecticism." As might be expected, these new approaches often bear some resemblance to their Audiolingual progenitor; but given their special emphases, they are in effect new methods.

NEW DIRECTIONS

Some Contemporary Movements

Today's teachers are also able to gain insights from broad movements not directly associated with any given method.

HUMANISM. Some influence is felt, for example, from the *humanistic* movement in psychology and education.[8] Humanists express interest in the total person and not simply in the intellect. As in the voluminous literature on motivation, the interaction of emotions and intellect is closely examined. It has been shown, for example, that learning is significantly enhanced when the student sees the relevance of what he is studying to his personal life (Galyean 1976a, 1976b; see also Stevick 1976, pp. 38–40). In fact, Rappaport holds that memory is intimately related to the emotional responses of the learners (1971, p. 270). Humanistic instruction, therefore, strives to provide a blend (or "confluence" as the educators label it) of the cognitive and the affective. Since humanistic education is concerned not only with increased language proficiency but also with the many facets of personal growth, its content ranges from the academic to exploration of values, development of esthetic sensitivity, improvement of self-image, and a greater capacity to relate effectively with others.

We can see humanistic reflections in various contemporary methodologies, one of the most notable being Counseling-Learning. It is mirrored somewhat too in the communicative competence movement.

COMMUNICATIVE COMPETENCE. Making its appearance in the 1970s, communicative competence focuses on sociolinguistic concerns. *Linguistic* competence is seen merely as an adjunct to communication. Besides mastering linguistic forms, we need to know "when, how, and to whom it is appropriate to use these forms" (Hymes 1972a, 1972b); we need to be adaptable and able to cope with other cultures. Persons with communicative competence are supposedly able to engage in socially appropriate exchanges. This includes knowing what is appropriate to discuss in a conversation. Such competence involves understanding the implications of nonverbal communication.

Training in communicative competence often involves problem solving and carrying out tasks in the community. Activities may include asking for clarification, seeking information, utilizing the truth factor in responses, discerning social appropriateness, talking one's way out of difficulty, agreeing and disagreeing, offering excuses, and hiding intentions (see Rivers 1972a, 1972b).

The principles and practices of this movement had become so widely accepted by the early 1980s that most programs could be said to incorporate

[8]Underpinning humanistic educational concepts is Abraham Maslow's humanistic psychology (Maslow 1954, 1962, 1965; Goble 1970) with its principle of self-actualization.

some elements of communicative competence. It appears also to have influenced the creation of Notional Syllabuses.

NOTIONAL-FUNCTIONAL SYLLABUSES. Undoubtedly the most significant and prestigious language teaching approach to emerge in the post-Audiolingual era is the Notional Syllabus. Commissioned by the Council of Europe, scholars such as Wilkins, Richterich, van Ek, and Trim began in the early 1970s to design a system of language instruction based on the objectives or "functions" of communication.

This contrasts with the usual grammar-based course or the occasional situational course:

> The grammatical syllabus seeks to teach the language by taking the learner progressively through the forms of the target language. The situational syllabus does so by recreating the situations in which native speakers use the language. While in neither case would it be denied that languages are learned for the purposes of communication, both leave the learner short of adequate communicative capacity. . . . The notional syllabus is in contrast with the other two because it takes the desired communicative capacity as the starting point. In drawing up a notional syllabus, instead of asking how speakers of the language express themselves or when and where they use the language, we ask what it is they communicate through language. We are then able to organize language teaching in terms of the content rather than the form of the language. (Wilkins 1976)

On the broadest level, the communicative needs of various groups of learners are identified. Then the basic social purposes or functions of communication are isolated for each group. These in turn are broken down into various concepts or "notions" expressed by language, such as time, quantity, and space. The next level is more focused: These "specific notions" amount to topics of communication. And serving as a basis for specific notions are "exponents." They consist essentially of linguistic elements, notably grammar and vocabulary.

A common core called "Threshold Level" has been worked out as a basis of instruction for all foreign language learners. The six basic functions include imparting and seeking factual information, expressing and finding out intellectual and emotional and moral attitudes, getting things done, and socializing. The seven general notions include the temporal, qualitative, and relational. The specific notions range from home and free time to relations with other people and the weather.

Advantages cited for Notional Syllabuses include imparting communicative rather than simply linguistic competence, higher motivation, and a broader range of language functions and grammar than is available through situational approaches. But respected scholars at the same time express reservations. Some question the need to pit the Notional against the Structural Syllabus; the former could enhance the latter instead of replacing it. Some see the Notional Syllabus as simply another set of isolates:

The notional syllabus leaves the learner to develop . . . creative strategies on his own: it deals with the *components* of discourse, not with discourse itself. As such it derives from an analyst's and not a participant's view of language, as does the structural syllabus. (Widdowson 1978)

Others are concerned with the elusive nature of language function, suggesting the arbitrary nature of the so-called categories and the difficulty of relating form and function. For example, the sentence "It's rather cold in here, isn't it?" could be an attempt to further a social relationship, a mere statement of fact, or a request for action: "Close the window." (See Rutherford 1978; and also Wilkins 1976, pp. 60–61.) And the lack of suitable teaching and testing materials is still another concern.

But a great many see this as a move in the right direction, feeling that applied research and creative effort can overcome present limitations. The compelling logic of this new system as well as the prestige of those associated with the approach (not to mention the broad base of support it has accumulated) suggest that it will be an increasing source of influence on language pedagogy in the years to come.

Influences Beyond Method

In attempting to determine influences on language teaching methods and options for the future, we need to look briefly at the state of our discipline.

INTERNATIONAL DEVELOPMENTS. Political events overseas continue to impact on ESL/EFL instruction at home. Refugees from abroad, notably from Southeast Asia but not limited to this area, constitute a new clientele with special needs. Commercial and government-produced materials (e.g., those from the Center for Applied Linguistics) help shape instruction. Altered relations with countries such as the People's Republic of China, Iran, Afghanistan, Angola, and Ethiopia affect the number and type of EFL instructors needed overseas. Equally important are fluctuations in language policy abroad. The exporting of American and British technology and the flourishing of English as a world language signal the need for EFL teachers with special emphases in business, science, and technology.

THE BILINGUAL MOVEMENT. The far-reaching bilingual effort has major implications for the type of instruction carried on in the public schools of the United States. Given impetus by the influx of Cuban refugees in 1963 and the Bilingual Education Act in 1968, this dynamic movement seeks to enhance linguistically and culturally the education of minority students. Specialists in this area tend to favor a "maintenance" or enrichment bilingual program over a "compensatory" or transitional one designed to provide remedial help only. The cultural content alone of good bilingual programs can help shift the emphasis of English instruction from form to content.

LEGAL ACTIONS. Legal developments, such as the Civil Rights Act mentioned above, have had and will undoubtedly continue to have significant influence on teaching and testing. Earlier the Supreme Court had rejected the "separate but equal" concept of segregation, and in 1971 rejected de facto segregation. Then in 1974 the Court issued its landmark Lau decision, ruling that schools which did not provide special instruction and materials for nonnative speakers were in effect discriminating against them (see Nakano 1977). Court cases during the past decade have also helped reduce discrimination from test practices in the public schools.

ACCREDITATION. Another kind of legal action is that of achieving accreditation in the various states. Despite pressure from Teachers/Teaching English to Speakers of Other Languages (TESOL), the process has been slow. Bilingual education has frequently upstaged ESL; certification agencies are comfortable with the status quo (which permits teachers from other disciplines to handle ESL classes); and often there is little local initiative and savvy to accomplish the task of meeting subject discipline, college of education, and state board requirements. While there is an ample supply of well-qualified teachers, the certification problem permits large numbers of untrained people to staff ESL classes. As a result, "seat-of-the-pants" techniques very often displace sound contemporary procedures.

TEACHER PREPARATION. Despite the publication of the TESOL teacher training guidelines, practices vary considerably in teacher preparation institutions. (Figure 2.1 represents contemporary trends.) Notice the discrepancy between recommended procedures and actual procedures (Figure 2.2). One reason for this is that many institutions provide only a fragmented program, lacking the funds to offer even such basics as methods and student teaching. The strong linguistic element suggests that ESL teachers may be slow to abandon a grammar-based syllabus.

PROFESSIONAL ORGANIZATIONS AND JOURNALS. Although accreditation and teacher training are still at an early stage of development, professional organizations are mature and very healthy. TESOL, less than two decades old, is a vital international organization with well over 10,000 members. Regional affiliates, special interest groups, a good periodical (the *TESOL Quarterly*), and conventions that bring together researchers, trained teachers, administrators, and volunteers—these are welding the profession together, disseminating methodological concepts, and providing for invaluable professional interaction at all levels.

NAFSA'S ATESL serves junior college and university admissions people, counselors, and instructors of foreign students attending American institutions of higher learning. America's Center for Applied Linguistics (not a membership organization) also provides valuable publications and assistance for language teachers. IATEFL, TESOL's important and broadly based British counterpart, has a practical orientation and caters to overseas EFL instructors. It publishes a pedagogically oriented periodical, the *English Language Teaching Journal* (ELTJ). The Regional English

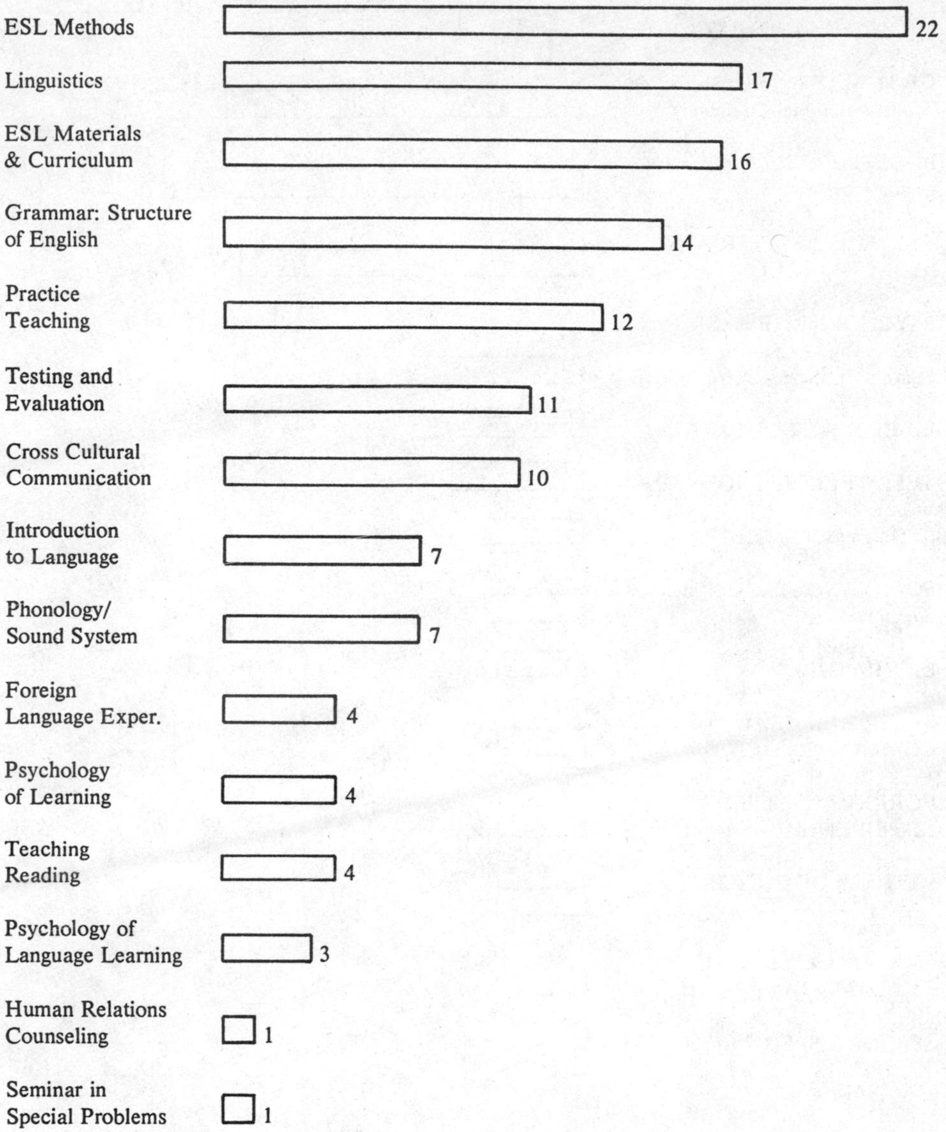

ESL Methods — 22

Linguistics — 17

ESL Materials & Curriculum — 16

Grammar: Structure of English — 14

Practice Teaching — 12

Testing and Evaluation — 11

Cross Cultural Communication — 10

Introduction to Language — 7

Phonology/ Sound System — 7

Foreign Language Exper. — 4

Psychology of Learning — 4

Teaching Reading — 4

Psychology of Language Learning — 3

Human Relations Counseling — 1

Seminar in Special Problems — 1

Total N = 22

Frequencies shown indicate the number of TESL experts who recommended that area.

Source: Robert B. Nolan, Coordinator, Adult Education Service Center, Northern Illinois University, De Kalb, Illinois 60115.

FIGURE 2.1   Relative Frequencies of Recommended Areas of TESL Teacher Training

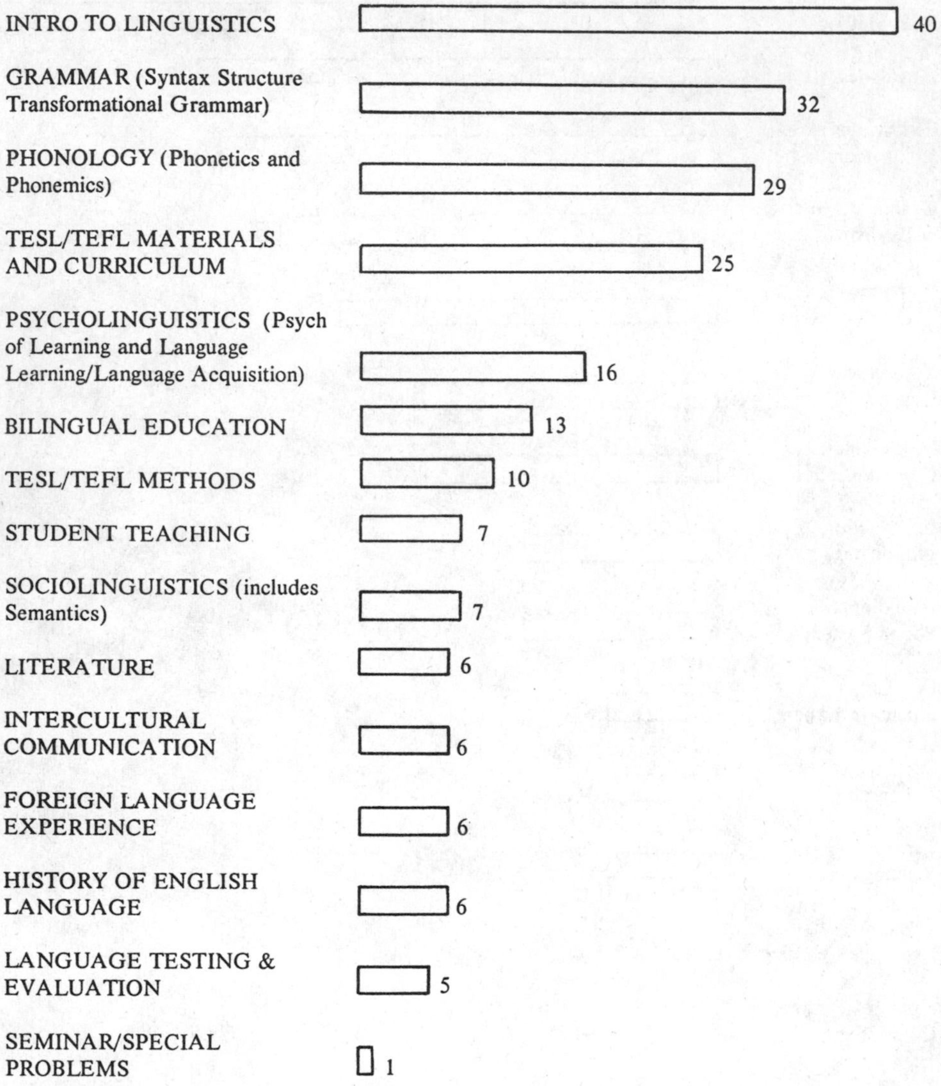

INTRO TO LINGUISTICS	40
GRAMMAR (Syntax Structure Transformational Grammar)	32
PHONOLOGY (Phonetics and Phonemics)	29
TESL/TEFL MATERIALS AND CURRICULUM	25
PSYCHOLINGUISTICS (Psych of Learning and Language Learning/Language Acquisition)	16
BILINGUAL EDUCATION	13
TESL/TEFL METHODS	10
STUDENT TEACHING	7
SOCIOLINGUISTICS (includes Semantics)	7
LITERATURE	6
INTERCULTURAL COMMUNICATION	6
FOREIGN LANGUAGE EXPERIENCE	6
HISTORY OF ENGLISH LANGUAGE	6
LANGUAGE TESTING & EVALUATION	5
SEMINAR/SPECIAL PROBLEMS	1

Number of Programs Surveyed = 44

Source: Blatchford, Charles. *Directory of Teacher Preparation Programs in TESOL and Bilingual Education 1976–1978.*

FIGURE 2.2   Comparative Frequencies of TESL Major Requirements at United States and Canadian Universities

Language Centre (RELC) is one of the strongest regional centers overseas. Located in Singapore, it services countries from India to Japan, with frequent publications, annual conferences, and the helpful *RELC Journal*. Other important periodicals include the research-oriented *Language Learning* (University of Michigan, Ann Arbor); the U.S. government (USIA) sponsored *English Teaching Forum* with its practical articles; and the useful British journal *English Language Teaching and Linguistics Abstracts*.[9] (Peripheral support is received from the U.S. organization The National Council of Teachers of English, and from various foreign language publications such as the *Modern Language Journal*.)

Collectively, these professional organizations and journals constitute a powerful influence in the exchange of methodological insights.

PLURALISTIC CURRICULUM DEVELOPMENT. Trends in curriculum development reflect new approaches to methodology. In Chapter One, we noted an insightful turn-of-the-century pronouncement that various methods serve different purposes. Breaking with the monolithic Audiolingual tradition, the profession is beginning almost subconsciously to adopt this view. Not only do U.S. minorities have various bilingual options available, but a major international movement is well underway to provide English for various specialized or specific purposes (ESP). This thriving ESP movement recognizes that strikingly different ESL/EFL approaches are needed in teaching English for those in electronics or engineering than in teaching English for people in accounting or zoology. Current research is examining, for example, the rhetorical contrasts in the literature of various disciplines. ESP specialists are currently being recruited or trained for overseas positions. And the literature on Europe's new methodological contribution uses the plural—Notional Syllabuses—underscoring the need to provide different instruction to groups with varying language needs. This surely represents one of the most striking developments in the post-Audiolingual period.

MATERIALS. While they always play a significant role in language instruction, materials have a particularly significant place in an era when many inadequately trained instructors are permitted to teach, and when no single, clearly defined method has been agreed upon. Today's materials reflect the new "cognitive" approaches, and we are starting to see texts attempting to utilize the Notional Syllabus concept. Materials have fortunately moved away from the bland presentations of the 1950s and 1960s: Today's have a richer cultural base. Often realistic or even a bit exotic, they are seldom as dull as formerly. And they tend to incorporate multiethnic and nonsexist material.

[9]First language, foreign language, and international research organizations likewise provide useful articles, book reviews, and conference sessions (e.g., the NCTE, ACTFL, MLA, NFMLTA, AILA, and others). Periodicals include the *English Journal*, the *Modern Language Journal, FL Annals*, and the *International Review of Applied Linguistics*. Smaller ESL/EFL publications with practical articles include the Canadian *TESL Talk* and BYU Hawaii's *TESL Reporter*.

TECHNOLOGY. Technological advancements promise some innovative approaches for tomorrow's schools. The language laboratory was a major breakthrough during the Audiolingual period. But the break with this important method was so final that the ESL lab has never regained its former vitality, even though some new "cognitive" software is available. Emerging labs (and they constitute only a fraction of those formerly in operation) appear to be much broader in scope, covering the four skills rather than concentrating on pronunciation and structure drills as in time past. And it seems to us that overhead transparencies and slides are utilized much more frequently than movies or film strips.

On a number of campuses, computer-assisted instruction such as the PLATO and TICCIT programs have been used experimentally. These provide for low-anxiety, self-paced work; and linked with courses that provide valuable peer interaction, CAI can add variety and efficiency to instruction. But few of these "mainframe" programs are cost effective for smaller institutions and public schools.

Most excitement is presently being generated by experimental teaching applications of microcomputers and videodiscs. The trend is to move away from expensive mainframe computer applications to microcomputer applications. Computer interest is so keen in the area of ESL and foreign languages that a new acronym, CALI, has been created—Computer Assisted Language Instruction—and with it a new organization and periodical, the Computer Assisted Language Instruction Consortium with its *CALICO Journal.*

Presently the computer (hardware) has outpaced the instructional programs (software), but interest is so keen that more and more teachers and materials developers are receiving instruction on how to develop CALI programs. They are aided by ingenious software-writing programs such as "Apple Pilot" and "Super Pilot."

CALI advantages are numerous: It permits self-pacing; it facilitates student interaction and initiative; it releases the teacher from time-consuming drilling; it almost invariably sparks student interest; it greatly facilitates revision of exercise materials; and it reduces tedium and anxiety. Its disadvantages are few: Some CALI writers fail to tap the potential of the computer, using it only as an electronic "page turner." Some simply transfer outdated textbook material to the computer. Others emphasize the "games" aspect with minimal attention to bona fide language needs. And some erroneously assume that the computer can replace the instructor; but human interaction is of course essential. The computer, however, can constitute a valuable teaching adjunct.

A very promising computer-related feature is the interactive videodisc, which permits the use of tailormade films or high-interest movies to teach language. Options range from native language "help" segments and freeze-framing to movies that branch into different scenes depending on choices the viewer makes.

One further and very significant application of technological hardware is in the area of research. Assistance in this area ranges from powerful mainframe computers to programmable calculators and microcomputers. "Floppy disk" software packages in statistics for personal computers or "SPSS" and other programs for major computers demanding great "memory" capacity enable language specialists to conduct research never dreamed of a few decades ago. For example, the million-word Brown corpus can be accessed for the use and context of the modal "would" in a large sampling of scientific writing. Test research using regression equations or factor analysis can be conducted. Experimental work with a variety of independent and moderator variables can be conducted using analysis of variance or covariance—procedures far too complex and time consuming to be practical with hand calculators.

RESEARCH AND THEORETICAL FORMULATIONS. This leads us to our final consideration, and that is research and the formulation of theories applicable to language teaching. Ronald Wardhaugh has said, "Good teaching practice is based on good theoretical understanding. *There is indeed nothing so practical as a good theory*" [Wardhaugh's emphasis] (1969, p. 116). Broad areas that have received considerable attention include language instruction, language acquisition, and language testing.

Research paradigms. We should mention at the outset that a contemporary interest (and in some quarters a contemporary *debate*) focuses on the basic research paradigm to select in carrying out one's language research. On the one hand, we have the compelling and lengthy tradition of quantitative empirical research with its appeals of being objective, repeatable, and designed for problem solving. Recognized scholars in our discipline, investigating a wide variety of research questions (e.g., Tucker and Sarofim 1979, Bachman and Palmer 1982) and texts on research methodology (Tuckman 1978, Hatch and Farhady 1982) employ the still dominant quantitative research method.

But a relatively new research paradigm is enabling us to ask new questions, to examine classroom processes, and to determine, for example, *why* and *how* learners process language. This qualitative, mentalistic or "hermeneutic" approach taps a variety of procedures: Language acquisition and language pedagogy research has utilized the ethnographic techniques of anthropologists (Ochsner 1979, Long 1980) so that processes and interaction can be observed (Nystrom 1983, Gaies 1983, Allwright 1983), participant observation recorded—notably by means of diary studies (Schumann and Schumann 1977, Bailey 1980), and even mentalistic language-processing strategies investigated, through introspection and retrospection (Cohen and Hosenfeld 1981, Radford 1974). Such investigations are often hypothesis generating, relying on insights derived from the learner rather than suppositions posed by the researcher.

There is no reason to suppose that accepting one research method means rejecting the other. Sociologist Patton in his classical advocacy of qualitative research points out the handicaps of restricting oneself to a single research paradigm, one of these being the limitation in the kinds of questions we can ask (1978, pp. 199–238). Others, too, such as Ochsner (1979, p. 71) and Gaies (1983, p. 215) see qualitative research as complementing the traditional quantitative empirical approach.

Classroom-centered research. The empirical researcher normally identifies independent variables such as an "experimental" approach and a "control" (or traditional) approach plus a dependent variable—namely, the contrasting scores obtained for students following a limited period of instruction. By contrast, the classroom-centered researcher focuses on classroom *processes* more than she does on classroom *results.* Data used tends to be "naturalistic" in the sense that classroom processes are not directed or controlled; teachers are not told what to teach or how to conduct their classes. Instead, the researcher looks at teacher talk or student interaction, perhaps utilizing discourse analysis techniques.

Qualitative *or* quantitative research procedures may be used; but the focus is on what actually occurs in the classroom, including the language processing strategies employed by students. The latter may be determined by such means as having students maintain journals, or by having them monitor their language processing as it takes place (introspection), or through interview procedures in which students reflect on how and why they processed the language as they did (retrospection).[10]

Contrastive Analysis. While classroom-centered research, discussed above, is *person*-focused, the earlier contrastive analysis research was *language*-focused. During the Audiolingual period, linguists examined features of the native language which contrasted with features of the foreign language, indicating that these would be areas most likely to cause difficulty for foreign language learners. By the early 1970s, this contrastive analysis theory had been to an extent supplanted by error analysis, which examined not only the impact of transfer errors but also those related to the target language, including overgeneralization. Errors were classified according to source, such as interference and developmental errors. Later in the 1970s, Schachter and others resuscitated a weak form of contrastive analysis, demonstrating the limitations of error analysis in such matters as avoidance of unfamiliar structures (Schachter 1974).

Order-of-acquisition research. Over a decade ago, those interested in language acquisition became increasingly interested in investigating the sequence in which various morphemes were acquired. Studies of first language learners began to reveal that there was a predictable order in which children acquired certain morphemes (Brown 1973). And second language researchers soon began investigating the same phenomenon. Despite some cautions (Larsen-Freeman 1975), a "natural order" theory was posited for second language learners as well when it was found that a predictable

---

[10]For illustrations of this kind of research and for additional discussion of the forms that classroom-centered research takes, see Seliger and Long (1983) and the June 1983 *TESOL Quarterly.*

sequence was likewise present for second language adults and for second language child learners (Bailey, Madden, and Krashen 1974; Dulay and Burt 1974).

The Monitor Model. Puzzling exceptions to the first and second language acquisition order discussed above as well as differences in oral and written performance or grammar test and free conversation performance led Krashen to formulate the Monitor Model theory on how second language students master a foreign language. It appeared that when the new language was "picked up" in a natural way without a conscious orientation toward grammatical structures and language form, adult mastery of morphemes paralleled that of first language children (Krashen, Sferlazza, Feldman, and Fathman 1976).

Language development which comes in a subconscious way by being exposed to communicative situations is referred to in this theory as "acquired," while language development stemming from conscious attention to linguistic form is labeled as "learned." The "acquisition" process appeared to generate fluency in the language and to contribute to communicative ability, particularly oral proficiency. The "learning" process, on the other hand, was seen to provide a more limited function in language production, notably to assist in "monitoring" or editing language features that had been consciously learned. But monitoring required adequate time, conscious attention to form, and mastery of the linguistic rules.[11] Subsequent research, however, suggests that the "learning" process in traditional instruction may play a greater role in language development than suggested in the original Monitor theory (Long 1983).

Input hypothesis. Refinement of the Monitor Model led to a more detailed formulation of *how* language is "acquired." Of first importance is "comprehensible input," notably in the listening modality. Language acquisition comes from receiving input which is understood (i) together with a little input that is perhaps one step beyond the level the learner is now on (l); Krashen's simple formula illustrating this principle of embedding new material in a comprehensible context is, then, "i + l" (Krashen 1982b).

Input studies. Widespread interest in the Input Hypothesis has increased second language research into the nature of input the ESL or FL student receives in the classroom—an investigation which had begun over a decade ago (Larsen-Freeman 1976, Gaies 1977, Henzl 1979, Long 1981, Schinke-Llano 1983).

Research has shown that even in native language situations where children are learning to speak, parents intuitively modify what they communicate to their offspring (see Freed 1980), yet this "Caretaker Speech" includes occasional "i + l" material. Caretaker Speech tends to focus on the "here and now," and it is characterized by short phrases, simple sentences, and repetition.

---

[11]Helpful summary presentations of the Monitor Model are found in Krashen (1977) and in Krashen (1982b).

"Foreigner Talk," the equivalent of Caretaker Speech, is normally an intuitive modification made when one converses with persons who are obviously nonnative speakers of one's native language. It includes careful articulation, a slower speech rate, lexical and syntactic adjustments as well as some repetition (see Hatch 1979, Freed 1980). Similar but not identical to Caretaker Speech, Foreigner Talk that occurs in the classroom is "Teacher Talk"; and while this can aid comprehension and language acquisition, not all teacher input is as helpful as might be supposed (see Chaudron 1983).

Interaction studies. Since those acquiring a second language are not merely passive agents in the process, it has been found that appropriate learner-teacher *interaction* provides the ideal environment (or "optimal input") for L2 acquisition. Important early investigations focused on turn-taking as a basic ingredient in conversational interaction (Sacks, Schegloff, and Jefferson 1974). Since then a variety of interaction patterns have been studied, including contrasts between classroom questions and answers and out-of-class questions and responses (Long and Sato 1983). This research study revealed an in-class predominance of display over referential questions and thus not only a contrast with normal informal interaction but a continuing emphasis on accuracy over communication.

Error treatment. Our earlier methods discussion has shown an increasing inclination to regard errors as a natural by-product of student initiative and discovery in using the language. Contrastive analysis, as we have seen, classified and quantified student errors. Subsequent research has looked at the effect of errors and at error treatment in the classroom.[12] Error treatment studies have identified the kinds of correction tendered, such as direct or indirect, the proportion of errors dealt with in class, and the amount of consistency in treatment of student errors, including situations in which error correction is made. In his summary of error treatment research, Gaies concludes that

research to date in error treatment can only serve to encourage the search for classroom practices which promote a selective treatment of errors, since one of the consistent findings of such research is that errors are not treated in the second language classroom as universally as might be supposed. (Gaies 1983)

Attitude and motivation research. A very substantial body of studies is concerned with the effect of learner attitudes on second language acquisition—attitudes toward the language, the culture represented by the language, the teacher, etc. Gardner has noted that at least initially, in language learning, motivational variables are more important even than intelligence and language aptitude. Research by Gardner and Lambert (1959, 1972) posited two kinds of motivation—integrative and instrumental—the former reflecting a desire to identify with the target culture and

---

[12]Consider also the research that looks at error "repair," most of which is self-initiated, for example, the work done by Schegloff, Jefferson, and Sacks (1977).

the latter the need to fulfill a practical objective such as obtaining employment. Integrative motivation was seen as a more significant influence in language learning than was instrumental motivation.

Subsequent studies have suggested that the relative importance of integrative and instrumental motivation as predictors of language learning outcomes depends upon a number of variables including whether the L2 is being learned in an L1 or L2 environment (Lukmani 1972), the degree of perceived support from the L2 community for learning the L2 (Genesee, Rogers, and Holobow 1983), and learner attitudes toward the L2 community (Oller, Baca, and Vigil 1977; Gardner, Gliksman, and Smyth 1978). Graham (1985) has proposed an additional refinement of the instrumental motivation factor which he calls assimilative motivation and which he claims is largely responsible for the development of nativelike speech in young second language learners.

Schumann (1978) outlines a broad framework of social and psychological variables, including attitude and motivation, which he claims are important in determining the success of second language learners. These include such factors as the dominance relationship between the L1 and L2, the degree of enclosure of the learner in an L1 environment, the cohesiveness of the L1 community, the congruence of the first language and culture with the one being acquired, the ego-permeability of the learner, and the degree to which the learner undergoes language and culture shock.

Cognitive styles. Research into cognitive styles attempts to identify the various ways individuals conceptualize and structure their environment (Goldstein and Blackman 1978; see also Witkin and Goodenough 1981), and closely related to this are investigations into learning-style differences, including modality preference (such as aural or visual), tempo (ranging from reflective to impulsive), and problem-solving strategies (Sperry 1972). Varying learning styles have been found to differ in efficiency (Bourne and others 1971) and to relate in some ways to differences in personality (Ellis 1978). Some studies reveal a need for "alternate methods to match the educational cognitive styles of different students" (Schultz 1977).

Investigations have also looked at Locus of Control (differences in students according to assessment of responsibility for success or failure [Vasquez 1978]) and into the popular dichotomy of right-brained and left-brained children (Ornstein 1973, Fadely and Hosler 1983; also see the neurological discussion below).

Among the styles identified in language classes, we have High versus Low Input Generators (Seliger 1983)—the "HIGs" being more effective learners than the "LIGs"—and Field-Dependent versus Field-Independent learners (see Ramirez and Castaneda 1974). FD students have been shown to depend on external frames of reference during cognitive processing, while FI students tend to utilize internal, self-generated strategies in cognitive tasks (Witkin and Goodenough 1981). Performance on certain tasks (such as a cloze test) appear to be easier for Field Independent learners (Stansfield and Hansen 1983).

Neurological research. Perhaps no area even remotely related to second language instruction has resulted in more quackery and pure nonsensical recommendations than have the often misinterpreted findings of those engaged in neurological research. Outlandish "applications" of research include having second language students write with the left hand to activate the right hemisphere (RH); and "insights" include the supposed finding that newly acquired left hemisphere (LH) dominance has spawned institutionalized religion and dictatorships.[13]

Briefly, neurological research findings show that language processing in the brain tends to predominate in the left hemisphere, particularly in adults. But LH damage to very young children can result in RH processing of language functions. Hemisphere dominance can be more appropriately viewed in terms of processes rather than specific language matter. And the RH may well complement the functions of the LH, particularly in beginning second language situations. Also, it appears that the RH may be utilized more extensively by bilinguals who learn their second language quite some time after they do their first one than by those who acquire their first and second languages at about the same time (Seliger 1982, Genesee 1982).

Nevertheless, as interesting as such findings are, Scovel notes that the subjects involved in the studies reported and the skills investigated do not parallel those encountered in the ESL classroom:

I am highly critical of any direct application of neurological research to foreign language teaching, just as applied linguists of a generation ago were correctly suspicious of direct applications of the then comparatively new science of linguistics to second language instruction. (1982)

Second language testing research. Among the many topics covered in contemporary ESL/FL test research has been the creation and validation of measures that reflect both in format and results current concern for bona fide communicative contexts. Reducing redundancy in a prose passage has been found to be a very effective device in differentiating between native and nonnative language ability. Experimental techniques include adding noise to a taped passage, deleting short segments from a taped lecturette, identifying the second word in orally presented sentences, and interpreting a blurred written passage.[14] Extensive research has been carried out with other reduced redundancy procedures in wide use, such as the dictation and cloze (Oller 1971, 1973). (For an explanation of these test types see Chapter Fourteen of this text.)

Evaluation and refinement of tests to meet special purposes has also been carried out—tests to measure the language dominance of children who speak

---

[13]The first anecdote was furnished by an amused Seliger (1982) and the second by a bemused Scovel (1982), both of whom caution the profession about unwise interpretations and applications of neurological findings.

[14]For a summary discussion of these and other reduced redundancy tests, see Madsen (1981).

two languages, a listening test with printed *native* language options, oral proficiency tests for highly trained civil servants, and many others.

Still other studies look at language bias in language tests (Briere 1973, Leach 1979), test affect on examinees (Madsen 1982), the relative merits of discrete-point and integrative tests (Farhady 1983), the efficacy of a socially appropriate measure of communicative competence (Farhady 1980), whether or not a general factor of language proficiency undergirds various types of tests (Carroll 1983), and the construct validation of oral proficiency tests (Palmer, Groot, and Trosper 1981).

With the advent of the personal computer, there have been developments in computer assisted testing to facilitate diagnostic analysis of strengths and weaknesses, instant results, record keeping, and interactive capabilities. But far more significant is the development of computerized adaptive testing utilizing latent trait procedures such as the Rasch model, to calibrate test items independent of examinees, to facilitate item banking, dramatic reduction of exam length with improved precision of testing as well as potential identification of item and person bias (Wright 1977, Larson and Madsen 1985).

Second language pedagogy research. We noted in Chapter One that by the turn of the century, no empirical evidence had been found in support of any one instructional method. But investigations of method superiority continued into the 1960s. Since then there have been additional forms of pedagogical inquiry including studies of the characteristics of effective language teachers (Moskowitz 1976), extensive work in the area of monitoring teacher talk and teacher interactions (Flanders 1960, Fanselow 1977), abundant contemporary classroom-centered research in which learner interaction and learner strategies are investigated (Rubin 1975, Bailey 1983), and attempts to extrapolate principles and guidelines from language acquisition research (Krahnke and Christison 1983).

While one occasionally reads of a full-scale ESL methods experiment (Wagner and Tilney 1983) and of recommendations for methods research (Richards 1984), there has been a major trend away from global evaluations of methods (Allwright 1983). In fact, research even at the level of technique has its uncertainties:

We do not yet have, and cannot expect to have in the foreseeable future, a situation where teachers can, with confidence born of a background of solid experimental results, tell their trainees what techniques to use and what not to use. (Allwright 1983)[15]

---

[15]Gaies elaborates:

As Allwright ... has already discussed, there has been a perceptible trend away from global categorizations of second language classroom instruction. We have simply rejected the notion that classrooms differ simply along a single variable such as *method*. The failure of experimental research to demonstrate the clear-cut superiority of any one method has undoubtedly been a factor in this, as has been the sheer difficulty of conducting such research. Classroom process research rejects as simplistic any univariate classification of the second language instruction experience. (1983, p. 206)

The implication is that pedagogical decisions will derive from descriptive reports of classroom research, from broad-based research findings in various language-related areas, and as Scovel has suggested, from "common sense, experience, and sensitivity" (1982).

CONCLUSIONS AND PROGNOSIS

In conclusion, we see that following the Audiolingual period, there has developed a tendency to retain sound practices from the Audiolingual approach (such as the oral focus, activities, variety, visuals, etc.), and slough off practices that had come under criticism (such as extensive memorization, lengthy pattern drill—especially phonological drill—and uncontextualized practice). At the same time, we find an inclination to graft on useful procedures from new methodologies and movements: tolerance of some errors, more realistic and contextualized practice, increased student initiative and decreased teacher domination, communicative activities even in early stages of instruction, and a conscious affective ingredient. These have been advanced by teacher training institutions, professional conventions, workshops and periodicals, and by contemporary textbooks. Only a rather small minority have adopted a specific new methodology fully without modification.

But what can we anticipate for the future?

For one thing, there has been little negative reaction to the present "cognitive" approaches. Consequently, we can expect that they will continue to be utilized in the immediate future. The most serious challenge is that of the Notional Syllabuses. Despite limitations, they will probably increase in popularity. An optimistic view of the future suggests that they will be integrated into the existing cognitive methodologies, just as elements of Total Physical Response, Counseling-Learning, Communicative Competence and others have been assimilated. (We recall Widdowson's suggestion that the Notional Syllabuses could help the Structural Syllabus realize its fuller potential.) A more pessimistic assessment says that, as in the past, teachers hungry for something new to cure their tired instruction will turn their back on cognitive approaches and follow the newest Messiah.

But we lean toward the optimistic view.

One reason is that during the post-Audiolingual period, a major methodological adjustment was made without abandoning all or even most Audiolingual practices. (To be sure, many users of "cognitive" procedures are unaware of this and would be incensed to have it suggested that any vestige of Audiolingual methodology contaminated their program. Of course, looked at individually, the *effective* techniques retained from Audiolingual methodology belong to the ages.)

Another reason is that *almost unawares we have come to accept a methodological pluralism.* We speak of cognitive methods and Notional

Syllabuses and English for Specific Purposes—all in the plural. With little fanfare or debate, we have come to recognize that varying situations call for differing approaches. By not labeling the variant forms of cognitive methodology, we are able to modify them without the trauma associated with changing or abandoning a method. This compares with parting from a friend as contrasted with abandoning a spouse.

Related to this pluralism is a healthy tendency to accept practical and theoretically sound practices from any new methodology. There is a parallel in the bilingual movement's full acceptance of multilingual and multicultural backgrounds. Innovative methods, such as those reviewed in this chapter, are now seen and very likely will continue to be seen as valuable resources that can enable us to vitalize and refine our approach to language teaching.

The optimistic view suggests that like the physical sciences, language teaching is now able, more than ever before, to incorporate findings into its methodological system without abandoning the entire existing system. At the same time, we are realistic enough to recognize that a minority will always clamor after the newest fad or panacea, embracing it totally and zealously until a still newer methodology is announced.

Our hope for the future is that the increasingly well-informed and well-trained body of professionals in our discipline will be inclined to accept and utilize valuable insights from the past as well as from our burgeoning present-day resources. By so doing, we will at last be able to enjoy the cumulative development that we have denied ourselves for so long.

The chapters that follow strive to reflect this broad-based approach. Not aligned with a narrow loyalty position, the teaching suggestions are based on the pluralistic cognitive thrust of contemporary methodology.

DISCUSSION

1. What influence on language teaching did World War II have? Explain why. What do the letters ASTP stand for?

2. Why was the language laboratory so unsuccessful as a language learning aid?

3. Explain and summarize the NDEA program.

4. Why did Audiolingualism lose favor as a teaching philosophy? What are some of the real limitations of Audiolingualism?

5. Name (and describe) some of the alternative approaches available to teachers who were or became dissatisfied with Audiolingual methods.

6. Describe the methods promoted by Lozanov, Gattegno, Curran.

7. Explain what is meant by "communicative competence" in a language learning context. "Notional-functional syllabuses."

8. Name and briefly describe the editorial philosophy of six contemporary journals or similar publications devoted to language teaching.

9. How is the *CALICO Journal* different from those cited above? What promising field does it develop?

10. How does E(nglish) for S(pecial) P(urposes) promise to promote methodological pluralism?

Section II
Oral Communication

We have chosen to analyze language in terms of contrasts on two axes of classification, the x axis representing communicative initiative, i.e., perceptive versus productive, and the y axis representing modality, i.e., aural versus visual. The field produced by these two axes lays out the four performance skills. Figure II.1 illustrates the relationships.

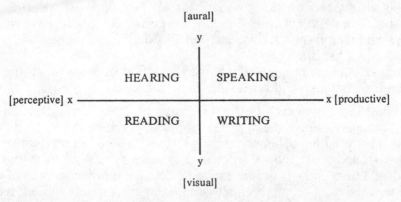

FIGURE II.1

The performance skills are HEARING and SPEAKING (both with comprehension) and READING and WRITING (both with social appropriateness). The performance skills for oral discourse (listening and speaking) are cultural universals: all people have oral language. The performance skills for written discourse (reading and writing) are cultural accretions, very much a part of the culture of literate societies, but learned, usually as a part of formal education. As we shall see later, this difference has important consequences for second language training. By their nature, the performance skills are measured by integrative instruments, because each skill is made up of subskills that can be individually measured, with discrete-point instruments.

(The terms "integrative" and "discrete-point" will be explained in Chapter Fourteen. For now, integrative tests examine bundles of individual skills working together; discrete-point tests measure the individual skills one at a time.)

In addition to the four performance skills, there are four component skills. Two of these (PRONUNCIATION and ORTHOGRAPHY) are appropriately associated with each of the two modalities (aural and visual). The other two component skills (GRAMMAR and VOCABULARY) are general, applying to both oral and written communication. Thus there are separate chapters for grammar and vocabulary in both oral and written communication. A figure showing this treatment is located on page x.

Aural-Visual

Some of the differences which impel us to separate treatment of the two sets of modalities are:

Aural (Oral) Language	Visual (Written) Language
1. Unidimensional, unidirectional	Bidimensional, multidirectional
2. Normal listener feedback	Delay or absence of feedback
3. Paced	Tempo ad libitum
4. Accuracy depends on monitor that must anticipate to act	Can be pondered, strengthened, corrected, edited, revised
5. Physical facility: speech tract and hearing mechanism	Physical facility: eyes and hand
6. Complex equipment necessary to arrange for storage and retrieval	Simple to arrange for storage and retrieval

The oral language exists in the dimension of time. Writing occurs on a plane, on paper, a stone, metal plates, papyrus, parchment, etc., and can be scanned in any pattern of length and height (though time-honored convention for English and most Indo-European languages specifies left to right for individual letters and words and top to bottom for successive lines of text). Oral language may be more effective in expressing emotions, but written language is much more effective for presenting charts, tables, etc. Imagine, for example, doing a crossword puzzle by oral language alone.

Perceptive-Productive

The second, the x axis, differentiates between sending and receiving skills. When sending a communication, the individual has major control over the features and structural patterns being employed. When receiving, he loses much of the initiative. Still, most people have a wider perceptive range than productive range. This is partly because of necessity and partly because of the normal sequence of learning. A word (or sound or construction) is often acquired by first being perceived and later by being produced. Notice that we have avoided the terms "active" and "passive." We maintain that all skills are active and that the term "passive" ignores the selectivity, interpretation, etc., engaged in by the receiver in listening-reading acts.

In summary, the four performance skills represent what the student does with the language as a real communicant. In a survival situation, one forgets the niceties of cultivated language and relies on utterances or written expressions that may be ill-formed, but certainly will be limited: consider the restricted speech of a tourist or military dependent living temporarily in a foreign country but needing to get directions or make a purchase.

But in many social or academic or business situations careful attention is paid to the language components of pronunciation, grammar, vocabulary, and even orthography. Their mastery can bring refinement and recognition of the more subtle nuances needing expression. As teachers, we will be concerned not only with strategies for survival, but obviously too with facilitating the acquisition of a broad range of communicative ability.

But before we can initiate successful plans for achieving this goal, we need at least tentative answers to a number of questions: Were the structuralists on sound theoretical ground in sequencing learning from listening to speaking, then reading, and finally writing? Or should we deliberately mix modalities and initiatives with the expectation that essentially the same underlying rules and patterns are activated by each of the four skills? If so, will attention given to patterns in any skill mutually support the other three? Is the visual modality more or less important than the aural?

If our program doesn't provide time to master all four skills, should we settle for just one or two? Is the order of learning grammatical structures or vocabulary the same for a second as for a first language learner? To what extent should language form be sublimated or ignored as compared with language function? Is an inductive approach to be preferred to a basically deductive one? Do students differ in styles of learning?

Experimental research has provided few definitive answers to questions such as these, yet responses are required in order to confidently proceed with instruction. Answers will be based largely on assumptions and insights arrived at from the accumulated experience of language teachers. The assumptions we follow are eclectically drawn, and pragmatic in that they are based on experience.

Language learning involves very complex sets of activities. Since it is not feasible to discuss all of them, we have selected representative activities that can serve as guidelines on which an instructional program can be based.

A

PERFORMANCE SKILLS:
Oral Discourse

CHAPTER THREE

LISTENING

INTRODUCTION

Though the listening function in language use can be isolated, it is typically linked to speaking in normal patterns of vocal interchange, with regular shifts of roles in oral discourse between speaker and hearer. Certainly role shifts are a typical feature of language use, and one that is particularly applicable to language education. Nevertheless there are situations where listening is exclusively employed, as when a radio or television presentation or a movie is the focus of a listener's attention. A similar relationship prevails when a subject attends an actual dramatic performance, or listens to a live lecturer.

Listening per se is occasionally referred to as a "passive" skill. This interpretation oversimplifies the definition of listening; a listener is far from passive as he receives, analyzes, and interprets the oral signals that come his way, recreating the message of the speaker.

The order in which language skills are acquired by native speakers, and frequently assumed as most appropriate for second language learners, is first listening and then speaking, with reading and writing coming later, usually as part of a formal educational program. Whatever the theoretical priority of listening, we do not believe that the other oral skill, speaking, need be delayed for long. Any effective long-term procedure will provide a give and take, mixing receptive and productive activities to suggest, if not to match, real-life communication. For purposes of analysis, however, we separate the various skills associated with language use and language learning, so we can discuss classroom procedures with dispatch and clarity.

Perhaps at this point we should define listening as more than just being in the environment of speech sounds. More carefully specified, listening is attending to and interpreting oral language. The student should be able to hear oral speech in English, segment the stream of sounds, group them into lexical and syntactic units (words, phrases, sentences), and understand the message they convey.

We can analyze different approaches to listening, depending on the kind of involvement specified for the listener. We distinguish *interactive* and *noninteractive*, a contrast that describes whether the listener just listens and retains the message or listens and does something. Beginning with the pattern with least overt involvement, we mentioned radio and television programs, where the listener just "witnesses." This type of listener participation we designate as noninteractive (excepting, of course, the listener-call-in talk shows), though the listener is no doubt involved mentally. But he doesn't participate in any way that immediately affects the speaker, or source of the program.

A live lecture is similar, though there is usually at least a minimum of listener feedback, if nothing more than laughter at appropriate points in the lecture, nodding of heads to signify understanding and agreement, quizzical looks when communication is broken or when the listener(s) do not agree with the speaker, and maybe applause when the lecture ends. These responses can be termed interactive, but nonverbal.

ACTIVITIES FOR BEGINNERS

Class Management

One way to maximize students' experience in listening is for the teacher, from the very beginning, to regularly use second language terms for *class management*. It takes virtually no time to teach students to react correctly to such instructions as "Everybody sit down; Listen carefully; Answer; Again; Repeat; Write it on the blackboard; Open/Close your books; Turn to page 31; Take out a piece of paper and a pencil; Can somebody clean the blackboard; See who's at the door," etc. Terms like these can simply be used in context whenever they are appropriate, at most with a supporting gesture (though teachers should not forever use a standardized gesture that comes to be the cue the students respond to). There's no need to devote special classroom time to practicing these management terms. Just use them; the bright students will help the slower ones if necessary.

ESL classes in English-speaking countries rarely have to be encouraged to use English as the language of the classroom; the decision is forced by the fact that there's no other common language that all of the students can understand. But English taught in other countries can benefit from this advice, as can foreign language classes in the United States, where all the really important and relevant communication often takes place in the native language of the students.

Physical Response Activities

A clearer example of an interactive but nonverbal relationship can be seen in the procedure called "Total Physical Response," or TPR in methodological parlance (Asher 1977). Here the response is overt, predictable, and under the specific control of the instructor. In this activity the instructor gives the student(s) a series of command forms, which are carried out physically: "Stand up; Walk to the window; Open the window; Run in place; Return to your seat; Sit down," etc. Students initially associate the command with an appropriate activity by having the instructor go through the actions with them the first time or two. By then at least some of the students will have learned the appropriate association between word and action (Code 1–3).

It isn't advisable to always have a student move to another part of the room, especially when large classes are involved. Imagine the chaos if fifty or sixty students tried to open the window simultaneously, or the boring alternative of having fifty or sixty students perform the opening in sequence. Fortunately there are meaningful alternative actions that can be done at each student's seat. This is one clear advantage of the activity: it can be tailored to the level and experience of the class, from early beginning to advanced courses. Let's look at a drill (the students would of course "listen" to what we look at) designed for a fairly early elementary class.

EXERCISE 3.1

FOLLOWING ORAL INSTRUCTIONS

Instructions: Carry out the requests of your instructor. (Code 3–4)

Teacher	Student
1. Take out your geography book.	(Complies)
2. Open it to page 36.	
3. Find the third paragraph.	
4. Look at the second line.	
5. Find the fifth word.	
6. Raise your hand when you are ready to go to the blackboard and write the word you have found.	

The instructor can give the commands one at a time, waiting until one is accomplished before giving the next, or can give the whole series and expect the class, or the student(s) involved, to remember them.

The TPR procedure can be repeated as many times as necessary when new actions and vocabulary are introduced to the students, providing of course that the new items lend themselves to interpretation by physical actions. It might be difficult to instruct the student in command form to enjoy, to understand, to appreciate, etc. What action would be expected? And how could the performance be evaluated?

At a somewhat more advanced level there can be interesting variations on this activity. One possibility is to give different instructions to different students, following the pattern of instructions in Exercise 3.1, and have a line of answers, copied one at a time on the blackboard by individual students. The teacher sees to it that, without the students noticing, the blackboard contributions are reasonably aligned, vertically or horizontally. Or each assigned task can carry a number that reflects the arrangement of the words in a preplanned sequence. As a follow-on activity the students read off the words, until someone in the class notices that the words, recited in order, make up a sentence that carries a meaningful, perhaps a surprising message—for example, announcing an unexpected party or field trip, or some class privilege.

This mixes a little writing and a little reading into the listening context, but this is of no great consequence. Students are not expected to become listening and hearing specialists before an introduction to other language skills, and this activity implies a class of more than early beginning competence.

Another procedure, which can be described as a drawing task, offers an interactive nonverbal activity, one that provides excellent and educationally relevant practice in listening skills. Asking the students to follow a set of directions can be an important part of class lessons at various levels of proficiency. The following, a fairly complicated series of directions, is designed for a more advanced class.

EXERCISE 3.2

FOLLOWING SPOKEN DIRECTIONS—A DRAWING TASK

Instructions: Do exactly what the voice on the tape requests. (Code 4–6)

1. Take a piece of notebook paper of standard size (about 8-1/2 by 11 inches) and place it in front of you, with the long dimension running horizontally.
2. In the middle of the page draw a circle, about an inch in diameter (about the size of a United States 25¢ coin).
3. Directly over and touching this circle draw another circle, just a little smaller in size.
4. Directly over these circles draw a third; make it a bit smaller than the second one. This is the beginning of a snowman.

5. Make a face on the top circle, by drawing eyes, nose, and mouth.
6. Draw a tall hat on the head; avoid covering the face.
7. Draw two arms that look as if they were made by using two brooms.
8. Give your snowman a name, and write that name just below the figure you have drawn.
9. Write your own name on the back of the sheet.
10. Hand your paper to your teacher.

[Technical Note: When giving the instructions, or recording them to be given later, the sentence numbers are not read; they are for convenience in reference. Note that the emphasis is added only for the teacher's convenience in grading the exercise. While reading instructions to the students, emphasis should not be used.]

This directions task can be evaluated by counting the number of accurate compliances. The sample exercise yields 20 points, distributed among the ten sentences as indicated by the underlined words.

Notice that the directions imply that the exercise (instructions and items) has been prerecorded on tape. This is a useful procedure because the students will know that they can't disturb the class by making oral requests for a repetition of something they're not sure of, so they will usually listen more attentively. Also the teacher can be sure of the pacing, which will make the exercise more valid for comparing different classes, or for evaluation of the same class at different times.

This is a very flexible kind of exercise; it can be varied from a distinctly simple activity to one that is very demanding, applying as parameters: (1) complexity of tasks, (2) length of exercise, (3) length of sentences delivering instructions, (4) frequency status of vocabulary used, (5) speed of delivery of instructions. Spoken directions can be produced that are suitable to almost any level of student achievement, from soon after beginning study of a new language to sophisticated advanced levels.

There are various kinds of discrimination that a student can be asked to perform in an interactive but nonverbal exercise format. With a general introduction such as "Point to . . . ; Draw a line under . . . ; Enclose in a circle . . . ;" etc., a student can be given language experience limited to listening skills. An example is:

EXERCISE 3.3

INSTRUCTIONS UTILIZING SHAPES AND COLORS

Instructions: Color the shapes on the sheet according to the directions. (Code 2–3)

Teacher	Student

Teacher

1. Color the small triangle green.   (Complies)
2. Color the bottom half of the large square red, the top half blue.
3. Leave the small circle white but go over the circumference with a blue pen (or crayon).
4. Draw a purple circle around the small square.
5. With two crossing straight lines, connect the opposite corners of the parallelogram (with two sloping lines). Moving from left to right, the falling slope should be orange and the rising slope brown.

Sample form:

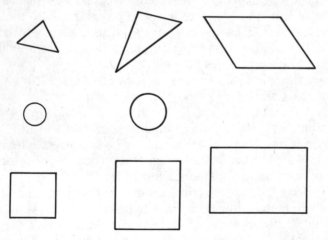

As an alternative to having the teacher provide the outline shapes as a handout, they could be drawn by each student from a set of oral directions, with one student or the teacher doing this work at the blackboard. When the teacher has verified the acceptability of the shapes drawn by the students, the blackboard model can be erased. Then, the oral directions are begun (Code 3–4).

Again the complexity of the task can be considerably varied to meet the ability and experience levels of a wide variety of classes. We think this is a desirable feature of an exercise format that can be applied in different kinds and levels of classwork. We also believe that this kind of exercise shouldn't necessarily avoid an occasional unfamiliar word (e.g., parallelogram), since there is a context to help the student guess accurately. This is the way most future vocabulary growth will be accomplished, so why not allow an occasional guess at a new word.

Limited Verbal Response Activities

Nonverbal interactive exercises like these provide for student response by other than the use of productive language skills (compliance with commands or requests to perform physical routines, to draw diagrams or pictures, etc.). Such activities can be enlarged by other types of exercises, in particular exercises that are verbal and interactive, but involve a minimum of response in the target language. The response in these exercises is limited to yes/no, true/false, simple answers to WH-questions, usually answers that consist of one word. This type of exercise is most useful if it can be molded to suit the circumstances of the individual students, keeping in mind the importance of the truth factor in real-life communication.

A sample can be seen in:

EXERCISE 3.4

SIMPLE QUESTION SEQUENCES

Instructions: Give a true answer. (Code 2–3)

Teacher	Student(s)
1. Benito, do you live with your family?	Yes.
2. Are there other children in your family?	Yes.
3. How many?	Four.
4. How many are boys?	Two.
5. You have two brothers then?	Yes.
6. And you must have two sisters?	Yes, I do.
7. Are your mother and father at home?	Yes.
8. How many in your family altogether?	Eight.
9. Really. Your father and mother are two. You have four brothers and sisters; that makes six. And with you it comes to seven. Who's the eighth?	My grandmother.

The questions can be varied in other ways, e.g., to determine where in the family Benito comes: oldest, second oldest, youngest (the baby); the ages of his various siblings; how many cousins he has; whether or not he knows them all; etc., ad infinitum. The only suggestion is that questions for listening practice should elicit fairly simple answers, so the students' attention can be focused primarily on listening (Code 3–4).

Benito's family is used in this exercise to illustrate the question sequence. In a real class, actual students should be used, and verifiable answers expected. The exercise can be repeated with students asking the questions, perhaps with a directed-dialog format. (See Chapter Four, page 109.)

What if the student can't answer? Other simple questions can probe the reasons: "Do you know what 'sister' means?" (No.) "You know what a brother is, don't you?" (Yes.) "Well, a sister is like a brother, only she's a girl."

Another effective procedure is to rely on other students to identify meanings. If the questions are reasonable, they'll be listening. Without the anxiety that often accompanies the responsibility to answer, they may do much better than the student who's on the spot. So, ask another student, maybe one with the same first language, and invite her to tell Benito what "sister" means in their first language.

Students should be helped to concentrate on the meaning of what they hear; consequently the demand for "productive" activity is minimized. This implies no expectation of full-sentence or complete-sentence answers. In fact, such answers should be avoided, using instead the shortest answer that will provide the information requested. This is, after all, the normal pattern of communication in real life.

Congruence Exercises

A very useful type of oral communication exercise that can readily be adapted to training in listening is the congruence exercise. Briefly, the student hears an utterance that may or may not make sense, as judged on the basis of reason and logic. He judges the sentence *congruent* if it in some way is logical and reasonable, *noncongruent* if it doesn't make any kind of sense. Frequently, minimal-pair words (we'll talk about minimal pairs at length in Chapter Five) are employed in a context where only one of them works. For example, *best* and *vest* are a minimal pair involving /b/ and /v/. We can alternately put these in a sentence that is logical with one, illogical with the other. If the sentence is "It's the best in the west," the judgment should be *congruent*; but if "It's the vest in the west" is heard, it is *noncongruent*—it makes no sense. Advertising people often pick a deliberately noncongruent statement, like the second one above, because they know their clients will make the association of the *vest* they want to sell with the word *best*. This association will be remembered because it is clever, and people will buy vests.

Congruence exercises can be designed to illustrate and/or practice numerous facets of language use. Often they can be employed to clarify discrete problems. The following exercise deals with phonemic contrasts in the English stressed vowel system:

EXERCISE 3.5

CONGRUENCE AS A CUE TO REALITY

Instructions: Number your paper from 1 to 8. Then for each sentence you hear, write S if the sentence makes sense; write N if the sentence doesn't make sense. (Code 2–3)

	Teacher	Student
/ɛ ~ ey/	1. Don't_____ for him another minute. (wet/wait)	1. N/S
/ɪ ~ ɛ/	2. You can't_____ there; it's marked "reserved." (sit/set)	2. S/N
/ɛ ~ æ/	3. Her_____ is more interesting than her future. (past/pest)	3. N/S
/ɛ ~ ə/	4. The river will _____ if it keeps raining. (fled/flood)	4. N/S
/ɛ ~ æ/	5. Could you _____ me a thousand dollars? (land/lend)	5. S/N
/iy ~ ɪ/	6. Hey _____ , get out of that apple tree. (keyed/kid)	6. N/S
/u ~ uw/	7. _____ at these want ads before you buy a car. (Look/Luke)	7. S/N
/u ~ uw/	8. If we all_____ our money, we can pay the rent. (pull/pool)	8. N/S

[Technical note: For a listening exercise the students would of course *hear* these sentences. To show how this exercise functions, two options are listed for each sentence—one correct, one wrong. The appropriate answer will of course depend on which options are presented to the students. The column of symbols on the left is included for the teacher's information, listing the specific vowel contrasts that the sentences deal with.]

Skill-Building Activities

Teaching an acceptable level of comprehension in English involves more than helping students learn to recognize and produce unfamiliar vowels and consonants. Also included is a very complicated stress system, which if not learned well will be a frequent source of misunderstanding. We have been surprised at the large number of students who have reached advanced levels of instruction with no real awareness of how the English stress system works. The following sentences are another application of the congruence format, this time to illustrate one important feature of stress in English:

EXERCISE 3.6

ENGLISH STRESS IN CONTRASTIVE CONTEXTS

Instructions: Number your paper from 1 to 8. Then for each sentence you hear, write *S* if the sentence makes sense; write *N* if it doesn't make sense. (Code 3–4)

Teacher	Student
1. Are they in the same class? No, he's a first year student and she's a third year student.	1. S
2. What did he say about the new VW? That it will have both advántages and disadvántages.	2. N
3. Do you wanna play hóuse? Yes, but just a small one.	3. N
4. Don't plug in your razor here; it says direct current. That's OK. This razor is AC/DĆ.	4. N
5. Are they in the same class? No, he's a first year stúdent and she's a third year stúdent.	5. N
6. What did he say about the new VW? That it has both advántages and dísappointments.	6. N
7. Do you wanna pláyhouse? Yes, but just a small one.	7. S
8. Don't plug in your razor here; it says direct current. That's OK. This razor is AC/DĆ.	8. S

In English a contrastive stress (typically louder and often pronounced on a higher pitch) is regularly placed on new information in a context.

Note sentence 1 in the drill just presented. We have two people in the context, one male and one female. We know they are students, but we don't know if they study in the same grade, so we ask if they are in the same class.

The answer includes information already known by the person who asked, and also some new information: that the boy is in a first year class and the girl in a third year class. The two ordinal numbers (first and third) are stressed, as a mark that they carry the specific new information requested. In sentence 2 the new information is the prefix *dis-*, added to something old: the word *advantages*, which occurred earlier in the sentence. So we contrastively stress *dis-* to show that this normally unstressed syllable should be stressed when it alone carries new information. We judge the sentence in which *dis-* is not stressed as noncongruent. Note sentence 6, where *dis-* is stressed. But this time the word it is added to is not already in the context; therefore the *dis-* is not the only part of the word that is new, and the contrastive stress should have been the syllable *-point-*. So sentence 6 is also noncongruent.

Note how this feature of contrastive stress is used to interpret the basic meaning of the following pair of similar sentences:

1. John hit Bill and then Jóe hit him.

2. John hit Bill and then Joe hit hím.

In sentence 1 Bill gets hit twice, first by John and then by Joe. In sentence 2 Bill gets hit by John, but then John is hit by Joe—exactly the same words, but a substantial difference in meaning. The difference is the location of the sentence stress in the last clause of each sentence: *Jóe* in sentence 1 and *hím* in sentence 2. A specific exercise can reveal whether the student can hear and interpret contrastive stress in these sentences:

EXERCISE 3.7

CONTRASTIVE STRESS
IDENTIFYING MEANING DIFFERENCES–A

Instructions: Number your paper from 1 to 10. For each number you will hear a statement and then a question. Answer the question on the basis of the information given in the statement. (Code 3–5)

Teacher	Student
1. Ralph hit Tim, and then Steve hit hím. Who got the second hit?	Ralph
2. Helen pinched Mary, and then Eileen pinched hér. Who got the second pinch?	Helen
3. Jim shoved Mel, and then Ál shoved him. Who got the second shove?	Mel
4. Jack tripped Bill, and then Don tripped hím. Who was tripped the second time?	Jack

5. Ben kicked Ali, and then Husséin kicked him. Who got the   <u>Ali</u>
second kick?

6. Sohair ran at Anita, and then Káy ran at her. Who got run at the   <u>Anita</u>
second time?

7. Mack shouted at Greg, and then George shouted at hím. Who   <u>Mack</u>
got shouted at the second time?

8. June insulted Bea, and then Dórothy insulted her. Who got the   <u>Bea</u>
second insult?

[Technical note: This exercise should be prerecorded to guarantee consistency in presentation. Other patterns of stress placement can be recorded for variety when this exercise is repeated.]

The information carried by English contrastive stress is frequently ignored in teaching English. Indeed, teachers are often not aware of the contrasts involved, though many (especially native English-speaking) teachers use these patterns in their own speech.

EXERCISE 3.8

CONTRASTIVE STRESS
IDENTIFYING MEANING DIFFERENCES–B

Instructions: Finish each sentence by supplying a logical completion, consistent with the placement of the stress in the first part of the
sentence. (Code 3–6)

Teacher	Student
1. He didn't lose his new pén; (he lost . . .)	He lost his péncil.
He didn't lose his néw pen; (he lost . . .)	He lost his óld one.
2. She didn't break her chína bowl; (she broke . . .)	She broke her gláss bowl.
She didn't break her china bówl; (she broke . . .)	She broke her plátter.
3. She didn't forgét her textbook; (she lost . . .)	She lóst it.
She didn't forget her téxtbook; (she forgot . . .)	She forgot her láb manual.
4. They didn't just kíck the ball; (they threw . . .)	They thréw it.
They didn't just kick the báll; (they kicked . . .)	They kicked each óther.

Note that this exercise requires a fairly sophisticated oral response, though the information needed is either supplied or clearly implicit. But it does require the ability to manipulate one aspect of the stress system. Competent scholars have pointed out that the intelligibility of spoken English is reduced more by errors in stress than in mistaken sounds.

A highly conspicuous example that illuminates the continuing need for exercises to improve listening skills is the lack of recognition and acceptance of informal levels of communication in many traditional classes. Over and over again we hear the testimony of second language speakers who have come to the United States (or Britain, or Australia, etc.) that they have experienced serious problems of language adjustment. Students with ten years of English instruction and even more find that when they arrive they have major difficulties trying to comprehend even simple sentences of spoken English.

Why? Apparently the kind of English they have been exposed to in their classes does not reflect real language use. The reason for this deficiency seems to be related to educational tradition. In first language classes the teachers rightly assume sufficient control by their students of informal English. The purpose of native language instruction is to expand the style and register levels of formal English, to develop a larger and wider knowledge of concepts, to foster an understanding and appreciation of the artistic use of language and literature; in short, it is a liberal arts approach.

This pattern of instruction fails to meet the needs of second language students, because they lack the background knowledge that is taken for granted in native English-speaking students, particularly an intimate acquaintance with informal spoken English. Couple this with the common feeling that informal language is somehow of inferior quality and really should be replaced, especially in the language classroom, by more prestigious, formal varieties, and we have problems.

ESL students in an English-speaking country can self-test their listening skills by trying to follow a conversation in situations where their presence is not conspicuous (as in eavesdropping on a conversation between native speakers). Another check can be the dramatic programs on television or radio. If students have difficulty, a need for improved spoken language competence may be indicated. Another informal evaluation is: do native speakers in communicating with ESL students use a slowed-down, more formal variety of English? If so, it may mean that the native English speakers perceive their second language listeners to be linguistically deficient.

If we were asked to pick out the one feature of English that most troubles foreign students who come to an English-speaking country for advanced-level educational training, we would without hesitation name the combination of weak stress and the vowel *schwa*. Both of these features of spoken English are well-kept secrets as far as many visiting students are concerned, and most visitors whose English has been acquired in foreign schools report a difficult adjustment when they first come to the United States, Britain, etc. A good part of this listening deficiency is due to complete innocence about the stress and vowel combination in weak-stressed syllables.

These features are very often slighted in second language study of English, especially in the many one-syllable particles that English uses, such as *and, to, for, than, the, was,* etc. When treated as vocabulary items or for their grammatical functions, they are spoken in isolation, and citation forms are used. But when they are "buried" in a context, the no-longer-stressed vowel is exchanged for schwa. Thus a sentence like "But he came to the dance" retains full vowels for the stressed vowels (in *came* and *dance*). All the others are "reduced" to schwa (or in the case of "he," to the vowel /iy/). Note also that the /h/ is dropped from "he" when this pronoun is not right at the beginning of a sentence or after a phrase break. This can be shown in writing by replacing the "h" with an apostrophe, but this is not often done, whereas in spoken English it is the normal pattern. We can of course resort to phonetic transcription, in which case we would write: /bət iy kéym tə dhə dǽnts/ The unstressed vowels are shown by spelling them /ə/ or /iy/. The substitution of schwa for a full vowel, a process included in what we call *reduction*, is so all-pervasive that most nonspecialist English speakers are unaware of the process, and indeed will often deny that they use reduced schwa, or at best will admit they do so only when speaking carelessly.

This pattern needs serious consideration; it has a massive effect on listening skills. The following exercise may be useful, learning to hear by practicing both listening to and speaking these lines from a child's starter verse.

EXERCISE 3.9

WEAK-STRESSED VOWELS—CHILD'S STARTER VERSE

Instructions: As you listen to (and repeat) this verse, be sure to notice the reduced vowels in weak-stressed words (broken underline). They are very briefly pronounced. (Code 1–3)

> One for the money,
> Two for the show,
> Three to get ready,
> And four to go.

The combination of reduction (i.e., substitution of schwa for the vowels) and the very short and rapid pronunciation of the affected syllables is to a great extent responsible for the problems of oral comprehension that plague newcomers who have not been informed of vowel reduction in English. This is a major problem that deserves a high priority in both listening and speaking activities.

Special drills can be devised to help students sharpen their listening skills, with additional attention on examples of weak-stressed schwa. Schwa is especially difficult to identify when it occurs internally in a sentence and appears adjacent to another vowel. Note the following sentences which involve and contrast the names *Ann* and *Anna*:

1. Have you seen Ann? Have you seen Anna?

2. Is Ann coming tomorrow? Is Anna coming tomorrow?

These sentences differ only by the schwa in *Anna*, and it is not hard to identify them accurately in the sentence pairs above. But if the schwa occurs internally and is adjacent to another vowel, it is much more difficult to hear:

3. Is Ann over the flu? Is Anna over the flu?

and, if the adjacent vowel is another schwa, the difficulty is greatly increased. Native speakers of English find the distinction easy; for most second language students it is a demon.

4. Has Ann applied for the job? Has Anna applied for the job?

This is well worth an exercise:

EXERCISE 3.10

WHEN WEAK-STRESSED SCHWAS COME TOGETHER

Instructions: Number your paper from 1 to 6. Then write the name you hear in each sentence. (Code 1–3)

Teacher	Student
1. Has Ann applied for the job?	Ann
2. Has Ann applied for the job?	Ann
3. Has Anna applied for the job?	Anna
4. Has Anna applied for the job?	Anna
5. Has Ann applied for the job?	Ann
6. Has Ann applied for the job?	Ann

[Technical note to recording voice: These sentences must be spoken without special emphasis on the point of contrast, which is after all a weak-stressed vowel. In no case should a break or a glottal stop be allowed to separate the name from the next following word. Use a natural conversational style.]

Other pairs of names can be used in this pattern, such as Rose and Rosa, Eve and Eva, Christine and Christina, Diane and Diana, Marie and Maria, etc. Or names can be selected that differ in sex; with this feature the clue to a correct use of a short-answer response is:

Did Glen appear happy?	Yes, he did.
Did Glenna appear happy?	Yes, she did.

Other pairs can be slipped in with the sequence randomized to avoid mechanical identification and response: Paul and Paula, George and Georgia, Norm and Norma, Will and Willa, etc.

One of the difficulties ESL students consistently encounter is hearing and identifying the weak-stressed particles that abound in spoken (and written) English. These particles are almost always reduced (with a schwa replacing the full vowel that would appear in a citation form). The following exercise includes an effort to show how the little words tend to be overlooked. They must be heard, and heard in a style that matches conversational English. Otherwise not only the pronunciation but also the grammar is distorted.

EXERCISE 3.11*

PERCEPTION OF PARTICLES

Instructions: On a piece of paper make a check every time you hear *and*. (Code 2–4)

Three years have gone by.

Yes, the sun's come up over a thousand times.

Summers and winters have cracked the mountains a little bit more and the rains have brought down some of the dirt.

Some babies that weren't even born before have begun talking regular sentences already; and a number of people who have thought they were right young and spry have noticed that they can't bound up a flight of stairs like they used to without their heart fluttering a little.

All that can happen in a thousand days.

Nature's been pushing and contriving in other ways too: a number of young people fell in love and got married.

Yes, the mountains got bit away a few fractions of an inch; millions of gallons of water went by the mill; and here and there a new home was set up under a roof.

*We are pleased to acknowledge this exercise as the suggestion of a former student, Kazumi Higa.

How many times does the word *and* occur in this passage from *Our Town* by Thornton Wilder? The teacher can ask for a show of hands as she says "One or more? Two or more? Three or more?" and so on until all the hands are down. It will probably come as a surprise to a lot of students that *and* was used eight times. But these occurrences are not unusual. Words like *and, to, the, in,* etc., don't carry much context information, and we don't notice them until they're missing.

If the class is quite good at hearing particles, the exercise can be made more challenging by changing the task: this time instead of making a check mark, the students can listen for and identify the word following the *and*; then write down this following word (Code 3–6). This time the students should be told how many instances there are of the word designated for the exercise. The two exercises go well together. The student has just had a confirmation (or correction) of his attempt to hear and count all occurrences of *and*; now he listens more closely and tries to become more aware of the context of the passage.

We recommend the relevant passage be recorded, in a very informal style, with care taken *not* to give any kind of special emphasis to the word being "sleuthed." If the passage is recorded, there is less chance that students will interrupt, and the teacher can feel confident of comparable results if the exercise is given to other groups or classes.

We wish to make clear our reason for including the preceding exercise: in calling attention to weak-stressed (and reduced) particles we may have the unwanted side effect of increasing the stress with which they are pronounced as their importance is acknowledged. This is not an exercise that should be repeated; it is rather intended as a demonstration to show just how inconspicuous the particles are when properly pronounced. It is an awareness exercise, and once awareness is achieved, it has served its purpose.

COMMUNICATIVE CLASSROOM ACTIVITIES

Listening skills are important to any language learner who will be involved with the spoken language, but they are especially important to students. Success in schoolwork is crucially dependent on the students' ability to understand lectures and other class activities.

The exercise following is an example of the type of lecture-style activities students need to prepare for:

EXERCISE 3.12

LECTURE ON TEMPERATURE AND DENSITY

Instructions: Listen to the following excerpt from a physics lecture; then be
ready to answer a few questions. You may make written notes if
you wish. (Code 5–6)

Matter can exist in three forms: solid, liquid, and gas. The different forms are the
consequence of temperature, or heat. The most frequently used measure of heat is
the centigrade thermometer, calibrated in centigrade degrees by establishing and
comparing the temperature of water when it freezes and when it boils. This distance
is divided into 100 equal intervals or steps, which we mark on our thermometers,
with the point of freezing marked zero degrees and the point of boiling marked 100
degrees. The term *centigrade* comes from Latin, where it means "a hundred steps."

There are additional conditions that are part of the "official" definition of the
centigrade scale, such as measurement under normal atmospheric pressure at sea
level, utilizing pure water, etc.

Most substances occupy less space when they are cold than they do when they are
hot; indeed they vary on a scale of density that depends on temperature. A substance
in liquid form is more dense than the same substance in gaseous form; the same
substance in solid form is likewise more dense than when in liquid form. This is the
normal behavior of almost all substances.

The exception is *water*, which reaches its maximum density at 4 degrees
centigrade. Both ice and steam (the solid and gaseous forms) are less dense than the
liquid form: water. This is very fortunate for us humans, because if water were like
other substances, becoming more dense at lower temperatures, the earth would be
uninhabitable. Because water expands when it freezes, ice floats instead of sinking.
The floating ice melts when exposed to bright sunlight or warm surroundings,
whereas if it were more dense, it would have sunk to the bottom of the ocean (and
other bodies of water). These bodies would then be eternally frozen just a few feet
under the surface, and the earth would be one great deep freeze right through the
twelve-month year. This would also tie up immense quantities of water, then
unavailable for other purposes, but more important, the temperature would be too
cold for the earth to support life as we warm-blooded mammals know it.

The centigrade scale is sometimes referred to as the celsius scale, in honor of a
young Swedish astronomer named Anders Celsius (1701–1744), who invented the
centigrade thermometer in 1742 when he was 41 years old.

COMPREHENSION QUESTIONS

Instructions: Answer the following questions in as brief a manner as possible.
If you took notes, you may refer to them. (Code 6–7)

Teacher	Student
1. What three forms do substances occur in?	1. Solid, liquid, gas.
2. In what form are substances usually least dense?	2. Gas.
3. In what form are substances usually most dense?	3. Solid.
4. What substance is an important exception?	4. Water.
5. What do we call gaseous water?	5. Steam or water vapor.
6. What do we call frozen water?	6. Ice.
7. At what centigrade temperature does water freeze?	7. Zero degrees.
8. At what centigrade temperature does water boil?	8. One hundred degrees.
9. Who invented the centigrade thermometer?	9. Celsius.
10. What was his profession?	10. Astronomy.

To designate this as a listening exercise the questions have to be fairly simple so it is not primarily a speaking (or writing) exercise or a memory test.

Often the same lecture can be used for more than one drill. The lecture on density, for instance, can be the source of a cloze dictation.

EXERCISE 3.13

CLOZE DICTATION

Instructions: Listen to the following paragraph and write the missing words in the blanks. (Code 5–7)

The centigrade _scale_ is sometimes referred to as the celsius scale, in honor of a young _Swedish_ astronomer named Anders Celsius (born in 1701), who _invented_ the centigrade thermometer in _1742_. He died in 1744 when he was _43_ years old.

In 1736 Celsius was a _member_ of an expedition to Lapland, to measure an _arc_ of the meridian. He was especially _interested_ in observations of the aurora borealis, a subject on which he _published_ a book in 1733. He supervised the _building_ of an observatory in Uppsala in 1740 and became its first _director_.

[Technical note: The blanks are of course not filled in on the student worksheet. They are filled in here to provide the recording voice and the teacher with a complete text. The passage should be read at usual speed without special pauses for the blanks.]

You will notice that the first paragraph is copied almost exactly as heard in the last paragraph of the lecture, but the second paragraph is new material, as yet unheard by the students. The decision to follow one or the other, or both (as here) of these patterns is left to the instructor. Doing the exercise satisfactorily depends on oral comprehension, but also on memory. We think that no harm is done by this "mixing" of components. They normally work together anyway, and this is a useful way of getting accustomed to the greater complexity of full-fledged communication.

As we have seen (in Exercise 3.12), comprehension questions can be used to check listening skills. The queries can be pitched to different levels of understanding or sophistication. Note the following, more demanding in terms of handling data:

EXERCISE 3.14

INFERENTIAL SKILLS–A

Instructions: Evaluate the following statements based on information given in the physics lecture. If the statement follows logically from the lecture mark it *true*; if not, mark it *false*. Use *T* and *F*. (Code 6–7)

__F__   1. Temperature is an incidental feature of not much concern in physics.

__T__   2. Using zero and one hundred degrees to mark freezing and boiling is essentially arbitrary.

__T__   3. The word centigrade shows the influence Latin has on scientific terminology in English.

__F__   4. Scientists in European countries do not communicate very much.

__T__   5. Water is a unique substance in many ways.

Because the chapter on listening comes early in the text, or perhaps because we have so often heard the sequence "listening-speaking-reading-writing," we may sometimes think listening is an early course activity that is discontinued when a class moves on to intermediate and advanced levels. This is not a valid assumption. Listening exercises go right along with the student as he accumulates more experience and develops more confidence. The difficulty of advanced-level assignments is of course increased to be commensurate with advanced status. The exercise that follows is an example of a "higher-level" comprehension activity.

EXERCISE 3.15

INFERENTIAL SKILLS–B

Instructions: Sometimes people say something they don't really mean. The insincerity may be signaled by intonation (tone of voice) or the circumstances make a literal interpretation preposterous, so that it can't be taken literally. Listen to the following exchanges and then tell (or write) what you think the speaker really meant. (Code 6–7)

What is Said	What is Meant
1. Wife: George, I think I'm pregnant again. Husband: Now, isn't *that* a pleasant thought.	That's terrible. This is no time to have another baby.
2. Man visiting laundry: Could you please show me the machine that pulls the buttons off my shirts and blows them through my socks?	I am dissatisfied with your laundry service: you are too hard on clothes.
3. My wife bought some meat today. We take delivery next week when the escrow closes.	Meat is enormously expensive. A purchase is comparable to a real estate transaction.
4. Shy girl to clown: You tickle me. Clown: What a strange request. Still, I'll do it.	I am amused by your routine. I'm not often asked to tickle anyone, but I'm a good sport, so I'll tickle you.
5. I never wake up Grumpy in the morning. If I do she fumes at me all day.	First meaning: When I awaken I'm happy. Realigned meaning: When I wake Grumpy (my wife) up, she's unhappy the rest of the day.
6. Will you call me a taxi? Sure. "You're a taxi."	Please summon a taxi for me. Realigned meaning: You = taxi.
7. Will you help me out? Sure. Which way did you come in?	Assist me, please. I'll be glad to see you go.

The ability to "read between the lines" will make it possible to enjoy more intimate relationships with friends in your new culture. You will notice that the difference between what is expected and what is said is often the basis of one kind of humor in English. But it is more: seeking new and suggestive meanings is an important function of literary criticism. It is well to be sensitive to the possibilities of these "double meanings."

Listening, then, is not a set of activities that will be phased out as the course progresses. At many levels of instruction, perhaps all, listening exercises are appropriate. Students involved in learning about the culture of a new language group need to be good observers, and this need impinges on literature. We may tend to think of literature as something read, but much literature is intended to be heard. Plays especially should be heard, and also short stories that have considerable dialog. Arthur Miller, Mark Twain, etc.—many authors are ideally heard, at least part of the time.

Less ambitious experiences are also available. Many radio stations prepare or otherwise provide themselves with short narrative selections, apparently designed as filler, to be used for the odd minute or two not occupied by programs and advertising. Each one is short, consisting of a few bars of a musical theme, followed by a minute or two of narrative on some topic of current interest, such as "Ma Bell" (the telephone company), "Sunshine Robbery" (air pollution), "The Coming of the Ice Age" (changing weather patterns), etc. A local broadcast studio was quite willing to supply copies of this series, called "The Odyssey File," to the small departmental media center for TESL at UCLA. Teachers of ESL classes have put these selections to good and frequent use. In fact they have built up sets of material to accompany the listening activities, such as comprehension questions, paraphrase possibilities, cloze-test-type reconstructions, etc. The Odyssey File presentations have been popular with students, and teachers appreciate having them handy either as the "contingency" section of their lesson plans, or with their introduction and use planned and integrated into the lesson.

An excellent and appropriate activity for the classroom is story telling or story reading by the teacher. Stories can be selected wholly for the pleasure of listening to them, with no assignment based on the plot, characterization, style of writing, or other explication required of the student. We suggest that manipulation activities be completely eliminated (no retelling, summary, description, setting, etc.), limiting discussion to questions students may wish to ask about things they don't fully understand.

The selection of stories will be of great significance—they must suit the interests of the students, and these of course depend on age, proficiency in English, etc. We suggest stories not too complicated linguistically and not too long. The teacher may want to read for short periods on successive days, rather than trying to finish a story in one day. Whenever interest flags, the reading should be brought to an immediate end. We suggest stories like "The Lady and the Tiger" or "The Cask of Amontillado." If a story doesn't go over well, abandon it and try another. The teacher should read in a way that enchances the story, using a clear, well-modulated voice. She should permit questions at any time and indeed should encourage them.

EXERCISE 3.16

STORY READING

Instructions: Listen to the story that your teacher will read to you. Raise your hand any time you don't understand something and feel you would like to ask a question or have something retold or explained. But remember, you don't need to understand every last detail to enjoy the story. Useful questions that might be employed are: (Code 6–7)

Student	Teacher
1. What does the word "cask" mean?	A wooden container for liquids, like a small barrel.
2. What is a "cellar"?	A cool place under ground for storage of food and drink.
3. Did he really leave the man in the cellar?	Yes, he really did.

COMMUNITY INTERACTION ACTIVITIES

Though students have met and studied English in the classroom, they want and need to take their skills into the community. The students form part of the community, and all have roles to play. Our first responsibility as community participants and members is to find out what's going on.

Eavesdropping is a good way to inform oneself of community activities and at the same time get good experience in listening comprehension. It must be done discreetly and publicly, so as not to constitute an invasion of privacy. Anywhere in crowds is a good place to eavesdrop: in a registration line at a university, at a counter in a department store, on a municipal bus, in a theater or concert hall before the program begins, at an athletic event. Assignments can be made by the ESL teacher, for student participation and reports. Students should seek answers to such questions as: description of participants, circumstances, locale, purpose of the conversation, content of exchanges, and any unusual features of the discourse. Then they can report to their teacher and classmates, after which, especially if the exercise is combined with speaking activities, they can field questions from other students. The teacher can grade these efforts by judging completeness, accuracy, relevance, etc.

EXERCISE 3.17

EAVESDROPPING

Instructions: Listen to a conversation somewhere in a public place and be prepared to answer some general questions about what was said. (Code 6–7)

1. Who was talking?	Two girls.
2. About how old were they?	Maybe 16 to 18.
3. Where were they when you eavesdropped?	At a "Hamburger Haven."
4. What were they talking about?	Babysitting.
5. What did they say?	That they don't get paid enough.
6. Did they become aware that you were listening?	No.

The telephone is another device that can give realistic practice in listening. On the telephone there are no gestures to supply visual feedback. As a consequence the speaker needs and expects verbal feedback (Uh huh; Yes; Is that so; etc.) or some brief indication that the listener is still there and attentive. Often the caller can't talk to the person he called; he may then ask the person who answered the telephone to take a message. Details of that message are important: Who? What? When? What time? How many? etc. "Dennis called at 2:00 P.M. and asked if you could lend him your geography textbook for a couple of hours. He'd like you to call him back after 5:00 P.M. today."

In another telephone exercise the student tries to reconstruct a conversation of which he heard only the local half, and that from across the room.

EXERCISE 3.18

CONVERSATION RECONSTRUCTION

Instructions: After hearing only the local half of a telephone conversation, try to supply the information requested. (Code 6–7)

_____   Oh hello, Andy. Long time no hear.

_____   No, she's not. I don't know where she went.

_____   Well, yes. I heard her say earlier that she had decided not to go to Baltimore this week.

_____   That's right. She won't have her lesson.

Teacher	Student
1. Who called?	Andy somebody.
2. What time?	About ten this morning.
3. Who did he want to talk to?	I think Beverly.
4. Where is Beverly?	I don't know.
5. Did she go to Baltimore?	No, she decided not to go.

The telephone can be used in other ways. In some cities there are recorded messages available at specified numbers, such as time and weather messages, movie announcements, marine weather, racetrack results, airlines flight information, bird watchers' messages, aquarium and planetarium programs, etc., even a poem-a-day rendition! Students can be asked as an assignment to copy verbatim one or more of these messages. They can relisten as many times as necessary to copy the message accurately. Further applications may be interesting to the class; a student can read his message to the class while others take notes. Then they can write reports (paraphrases of the message) as if passing on the information they heard to other friends.

One special kind of paraphrase is translation into the student's first language. This involves a minimum of productive skills from a (literate) student, and gives him a chance to utilize his comprehension and memory skills without taxing the productive skills he is just beginning to develop. We should provide students with practice in translation as a very legitimate language activity that has been unjustly restricted for the wrong reason (assuming it was an artistic skill not to be chanced by mere students). Most student translations are not and need not be "artistic," just communicative. Students must hear, understand, process, and interpret what they learn. Translating into their own language is not too demanding (except maybe for their teacher).

A chapter on listening should recognize the possible contribution of the language laboratory to effective language instruction. A language lab can be a specially equipped room with booths for individual students, or it can be as simple as a single tape player that everyone in the class listens to at the same time, or it can even be a cassette player, which many students own or have access to. While the booths offer a certain amount of privacy which is helpful to some students, others prefer not to be isolated, and indeed seem to get lonesome in their booths, interacting only with a machine.

There are some things the lab can do very well, better than the teacher, and there are other things the lab cannot do at all. The most attractive feature is the ease with which a variety of voices can be brought to the student—to expand his listening experience. Also, voices on tape never tire, and they therefore provide a consistent model (though some instructors might question the desirability of a model that never varies, since the student must be taught to function over a range of performance styles).

The lab by itself can model, but it can't evaluate. Nor can the student be left to do his own evaluation. Some argue that if the student is capable of evaluating, he probably doesn't need the instruction. A certain amount of evaluation, at least of listening skills, can be built into a taped lesson: The student can be given a series of choices, such as selecting the best paraphrase of two possibilities, making a congruence decision, etc., and he can be directed to write these down. Then, after the student has committed to paper his judgments on a series of items, the voice on the tape can read off a list of correct responses, so the student can tally the items he got correct and have an evaluation of his own performance.

One excellent use of the lab is suggested in the technical notes that are part of this chapter. Exercises, even for use in class, are often best presented by tape recording. This assures an approved and a consistent presentation. After an exercise is introduced in the class, it can be made available in the lab, for the student who is interested enough to want to go hear it over again. We recommend *not* making this a class assignment, because it may then come under the opprobrium of required activities. Better leave it as an option that will help a few people rather than as a forced activity that many, or even all, will resent.

A presentation of a recorded lecture makes an ideal lab assignment, and it is highly relevant to a student's needs as a participant in the learning process. He needs practice in interpreting and understanding lectures, an activity that is the essence of academic education. Also there are applications that involve culture and literature, as students listen to performances that can be of a high artistic quality. Many are available, done by professional artists. Seeing a play can be a valuable substitute. Hearing poetry read by a skilled reader, or by the author himself or herself, can give an immediacy to the experience that may otherwise be hard to come by in the average classroom.

The lab has been proposed as an experience that can provide individualized instruction. So it can: Lessons can be prepared to treat simple problems of pronunciation, or grammar, or vocabulary, or culture, lessons that meet individual students' special needs. The difficulty is preparing or otherwise providing for the lessons. One fifteen-minute lesson often is the result of an investment of 20 to 25 or more man-hours by a knowledgeable and skilled author, or team of authors. And the lesson, in addition to providing accurate and effective content, must fit the needs and level of the student, or it won't be usefully individualized. The teacher who assumes responsibility for an individualized laboratory program, unless she has access to adequate materials, is very brave indeed—or is not well informed as to the size of the responsibility being undertaken. The potential for effective instruction is there, but the task of providing adequate materials is monumental.

We'd like to offer a few suggestions that may be worked into procedures that yield a substantial benefit from the accumulating hardware that is becoming available in the language lab (though we don't feel able at the present time to establish complete sets of principles and procedures for incorporation). Suggestions: videotaping classroom lessons, presentations, lectures and/or lecturettes; participation and observation of role playing; taped conversations; visits to other classes and reports of what was observed; listening to current news broadcasts (possibly recordings, so they can be heard as many times as a student wishes) with reports and analyses; etc. The list can be indefinitely long.

There are, obviously, more aspects to listening activities in a language classroom than could be discussed in the present chapter. And indeed listening will creep into other discussions in subsequent chapters; it cannot be kept out. There would be an unavoidable artificiality in trying to separate the many skills that make up language competence. To divide and keep separate the next chapter, on speaking, will be a case in point. There isn't any listening without someone speaking, and speaking without somebody listening is an empty gesture. But, following the precedent of many other methodologists, we feel that a discussion which dwells on each functional skill is valuable for understanding each skill, as long as we keep in mind the relation of the parts to the whole.

DISCUSSION

1. Why is the use of the target language for class management procedures to be recommended?

2. What are the limitations of TPR?

3. What advantages does a drawing task offer?

4. Explain how a congruence drill works.

5. How is new information signaled by contrastive stress?

6. Why do some teachers avoid informal English in the classroom?

7. Comment on the ethics of eavesdropping in public as a language practicing device.

8. How does vowel reduction affect intelligibility?

9. Cite several ways the telephone can be used to provide language practice.

10. What are some of the advantages and limitations of a language lab?

CHAPTER FOUR

SPEAKING

INTRODUCTION

In a methodology class on second language teaching we think listening and speaking clearly belong together, and we have so arranged the present book, with both skills treated in an early unit which we call *Oral Communication*. The relative order for discussing listening and speaking is of less consequence, though separate treatment for listening and speaking is consistent with somewhat different pedagogical approaches. For instance, while listening can be initiated by providing speech sounds in a student's environment, there's no comparable means to condition a student to speak.

(There are serious and competent scholars [e.g., Asher (1977)], who would disagree with us, claiming that the best overall pedagogy involves a student's submersion in active listening which should precede by a substantial period of time his or her participation as a speaker. Asher's technique of keying a physical response to listening practice is well considered and designed. We accept it, but feel that it should be only one of the arrows in the teacher's quiver.)

How *do* you get a student to speak? It is certainly not practical to wait until the spirit moves someone to utter a word or phrase or sentence (though Curran [1976] seems to suggest that procedure). Classroom time is too valuable to spend very much of it quietly waiting. Probably the easiest way is to ask the student to speak, and if necessary tell him what to say. This kind of guidance in the beginning assumes some use of a language that the student understands, quite often the student's native language; otherwise the message may not be delivered.

Another way is to ask the student a question. He will try to answer if he realizes he's been queried, if he knows what the question is asking, and if he can control the phonology, grammar, and lexicon necessary to frame an appropriate answer. But in the beginning stage students don't know these things: they are precisely the subject matter to be learned. Successful learners should be able to produce their thoughts in a way that will make their message accessible to native speakers of English who have no special training in linguistics or in the native language of the speaker.

Imitation and Repetition

One very common technique is to model (say) the questions and the answers and have the students repeat the latter, or perhaps both, signalling the meaning in some way (with realia, pictures, gestures, even translating). There's a paradox inherent in this technique. We are ultimately teaching oral communication, yet imitation and repetition are antithetical to communication, the essence of which is unpredictability. Unless you can tell your communicant something he doesn't already know, there's no point in communicating with him. When he hears a sentence repeated it carries no new information and therefore is contextually meaningless.

One of the few times we use repetition in real life is when we fail to hear or understand, and in that function it is socially meaningful; but as a regular feature of speech, repetition gets shopworn very easily. Another occasion is when we learn a poem to recite or a part in a play to prepare for a dramatic performance. This is also not typical in normal communication.

We have to reconcile the student's need for practice and the desirability of having real communication in our classroom discussions, which are successful in direct proportion to their being convincingly realistic.

A lot of communication can take place, however, from the very beginning with nonverbal assistance. A teacher can establish a context, and with the help of a standardized set of gestures soon have students producing sentences in the new language that is being studied. Very often, and this is standard audiolingual methodology, the teacher models a sentence and the students repeat it. The teacher uses whatever means are at hand (gestures, pantomime, translation, guessing, etc.) to inform the students of the meaning, which the student learns with the pronunciation.

When a number of sentences are learned, the student begins to see, or is helped to see, patterns on various levels of analysis: sounds, arrangements, structures, lexicon, meanings, etc. He observes, or is told, the meanings of the utterances and how to make changes, so that he can express similar meanings in similar sentences.

If teacher and student(s) work at it, they will be able to express all of their really basic needs in the new language. In many cases, including most ESL classes in the United States, there is no choice. The class *has* to use English, because limited though it may be, it is the only language common to all the students in the class.

The technique of repetition by the student, beginning with an imitation of what he hears, has come to be so thoroughly imbedded in some versions of language teaching pedagogy that often it is used far beyond the time it is really needed. It is doubtful that an extended period of repetition makes a significant difference in the quality of oral production, especially since any out-of-class practice has to depend on the student's memory of what the sentence sounded like. The once-frequently-observed requirement that a renewed model be supplied before any student imitation seldom had the effect of erasing (or even diluting) the influence of the native tongue—a source of much of the error noted. Gattegno leans prominently in the other direction, an absolute minimum of modeling, and the student has to catch as catch can, learning from more alert classmates what he failed to grasp from his teacher. Most teachers will want to compromise somewhere in the middle—some repetition practice, but not to excess, and it will be minimized as the class progresses.

The initial efforts of the student will likely include mistakes, especially in pronunciation and grammar, where his own first language imposes itself on his attempts to produce words and sentences in the second language. We know one student who requested some "dapes" from a department store clerk in the camera section of the store. "Dapes" is not a word in English, so the clerk should have corrected the intention to "tapes," which they did stock. But the clerk, missing the expected aspiration for an initial /t/, failed to understand, until the client enlarged to "recording dapes."

ACTIVITIES FOR BEGINNERS

Phatic Communication

A logical place to begin speaking and authentically communicating is with a category of items that are easy to teach and which fit into the regular class routine, expressions described by the term *phatic communication*. These are the familiar expressions of greeting, gratitude, small talk, introductions and making acquaintance, leave-taking, etc. The important function of these terms is to provide lubricants for social interaction: to recognize and acknowledge the presence and societal status of people within easy communication range.

They communicate attitudes rather than just bare facts. When early in the day we meet someone we know, we say "Good morning. How are you?" and we expect the answer "Fine thanks. How are *you*?" If we are on more intimate terms, we might say "Hi Doug. How's it goin'?" which normally elicits a "Just fine" or "Not bad" or something similar.

An honest answer in these situations would be surprising, because none is expected. They are just formulas that acknowledge arrival, recognition and attention, appreciation, departure, etc.

Phatic expressions are mostly frozen sentence partials or sentences that are not normally analyzed for integration into the grammar. We rarely if ever use grammatical permutations, such as "I have been seeing you; I will have been pleased to meet you; Saw you later," etc.

phatic

EXERCISE 4.1

PHATIC EXPRESSIONS FOR INITIAL LESSONS: INFORMAL AND FORMAL CONTEXTS

Instructions: Repeat the dialog after your teacher or the tape. Make your participation realistic by taking first one part and then another. Practice until you have memorized the dialog. (Code 1)

A. Betty: Hello, Bill.
    Bill: Hi, Betty. How're ya doin'?
    Betty: Pretty good. What's new?
    Bill: Oh, not much.

B. Mr. Jones: Good morning.
    Mr. Evans: Good morning. How are you?
    Mr. Jones: Fine, thanks. How are *you*?
    Mr. Evans: Fine, thank you.

C. Bill: Well, I gotta go.
    Betty: OK. See you around.
    Bill: Bye-bye.

D. Mr. Jones: Nice day, isn't it?
    Mr. Evans: Yes, beautiful weather.
    Mr. Jones: Well, I must go. See you later.
    Mr. Evans: Goodbye.

E. Betty: Bill, this is Sally, my new roommate.
    Bill: Nice t'meetcha, Sally.
    Sally: Same here.
    Betty: I gotta run. Be seein' ya, Bill.

F. Mr. Jones: Ms. Thomas, I'd like you to meet Mr. Evans, our office manager.
    Ms. Thomas: How do you do.
    Mr. Evans: How do you do, Ms. Thomas. I'm pleased to meet you.

G. Bill: Have some punch, Betty?
    Betty: Thanks a lot.
    Bill: Don't mention it.

H. Mr. Jones: Can I offer you a cup of coffee, Ms. Thomas?
    Ms. Thomas: Yes, thank you very much.
    Mr. Jones: You're welcome.

Teaching these greetings, etc., involves little more than modeling and practice, then incorporation into the personal interactions of those involved. Notice that the exchanges are very brief; this facilitates easy retention. Note also that there is a considerable amount of cultural data, either expressed or implied; teaching the dialogs assumes a treatment of this data if the students are to understand what they have learned. Mr. Jones and Mr. Evans say "Good morning," but students need to be made aware that the day is divided into three periods, which correspond to *good morning, good afternoon*, and *good evening*, with a similar expression, *good night*, that is used only for taking one's leave after dark, or when retiring. These concepts should be explained (or illustrated), practiced, and incorporated.

When a teacher selects or produces dialogs, even in the simplified situations shown in Exercise 4.1, an effort is made to have realistic, useful exchanges. The sentences learned in dialogs will subsequently be used many times in real communication, so utterances should be useful and extendable to a variety of real situations.

One way to promote reality in dialogs is to observe the "truth factor." Change the dialogs (soon after they are learned, or right from the beginning) to reflect real people and the real situations that characterize their lives. Let your students talk honestly and accurately.

In the dialogs cited as Exercise 4.1, there is considerable additional linguistic and cultural information that the student must learn. Most conspicuous is the difference in register observed by young people and adults, shown by contrasts in the two columns. As soon as they are introduced, students use first names, while adults often begin an acquaintance with titles (Mr., Ms., Mrs., Miss) and family names. Students' expressions tend to be less formal, utilizing sentence fragments more frequently than do adults (Have some punch?; Nice to meet you; Be seeing you), often written (when writing them is appropriate) with informal pronunciations shown by special spellings (seein' ya, t'meetcha, etc.). Also shown are alternate forms that have no appreciable change of meaning (Hi versus Hello; Be seeing you versus See you around).

Students need to be told that some of these expressions may have very different meanings in different cultural settings: Americans assume that the expression "Thank you very much" after an invitation to partake of food or drink is an acceptance. Not so the Amharic speaker: his "Thank you very much" means "No, thank you very much" or "Thanks anyway."

How is a dialog taught? Many teachers feel the class should start with some form of choral repetition, perhaps dividing the class into halves, with each half repeating a character's part, then switching so everybody gets to practice all the roles. In a class of children the teacher may want to individualize the roles and associate them with puppets, stick figures on the blackboard, or live models chosen from the class, while she moves behind each "performer" to model his or her lines. Then the "performers" present what they have just learned. If the "performer" can't remember an utterance, the teacher can offer a new model or can give an indirect instruction ("Ask her if she'd like a cup of coffee," etc.).

A resourceful teacher will try to find occasions to bring back in later lessons words and ideas that have been presented to the class, changing the contexts gradually until eventually the expressions have something like their full range of meanings.

Let's perform again the brief exchanges that were introduced as Exercise 4.1, this time with a slight modification:

EXERCISE 4.2

DIALOG ACCOMMODATION

Instructions: The teacher should call on students to play out the roles of the mini-dialogs of Exercise 4.1. Participants should accommodate the dialog to their own name and sex. They should be prepared to play the informal as well as the formal roles, insofar as possible using an appropriate pronunciation. (Code 1–2)

Small talk (light conversation or chitchat designed to acknowledge a person's presence and/or status) in English frequently takes the form of comments about the weather. Other cultures use other topics; Arabic, for instance, makes family news the subject of small talk. The Egyptian may wonder why the great amount of concern about the weather (which in Egypt doesn't change much), and in any case, nobody can influence weather in any meaningful way. Filipinos use another question with the same purpose of establishing rapport: "Where are you going?" for which the expected answer is the literal equivalent of "Just over there," with never an expectation of an actual destination. An American housewife who didn't understand the "real meaning" of "Where are you going?" asked us why Filipinos were so nosy! She obviously hadn't communicated meaningfully across this culture boundary.

Skill-Building Activities

Almost any improvement in pronunciation is a strong plus for understanding and speaking. This is probably never more true than for the weak-stressed vowel schwa in English. The schwa is not overly common as a sound in the world's languages, and its frequent occurrence under weak stress in English seems to be an idiosyncrasy not shared by many other languages. The frequency of schwa in English is astonishing. One recent phoneme count shows schwa occurring 25 percent of the time for all vowels (one in every four) in a relatively conservative pronunciation of a rather formal text (Bowen 1980). The frequency of occurrence rises to almost 40 percent when the same passage is interpreted more informally, illustrating how the use of schwa is even more important in colloquial-style English.

Probably no other single sound or single feature will more greatly enhance the intelligibility of a student's spoken English, so it is well worth a serious effort to understand and master this most English of sounds. In Chapter Three (pages 85–88) the schwa is discussed and practiced in the context of listening skills. That presentation should perhaps be reviewed, as it is very relevant to the present discussion.

The weak-stressed schwa is the neutral vowel in English. It is the normal replacement for the "full" vowels when the process of reduction takes place. The full forms *to, for, have, from, them, there,* and many hundreds of others appear with schwa when weak-stressed. It substitutes for other weak-stressed vowels in *prŏduce, ĕlectric, ŭnique, ĭndeed,* etc., and is a regular alternate in words with morphophonemic shifts: *cónduct–condúct.*

Indeed, schwa is difficult because it is different. It is extremely short and lightly pronounced. Note the following:

What in the name of heaven is he doing?

This sentence (and most others) can be interpreted at least two ways:

Formal: hwέt ɪn dhə néym av hέvən ɪz hiy dúwɪng
Informal: wέʔ ən dhə néym ə hέvn əz iy dúwən

The syllables marked for strong stress don't change much. Almost all of the others do; they change to schwa, unless schwas are already there, in which case they are given a still more light and rapid pronunciation.

Weak-stressed schwa is pronounced lightly and quickly. This will be difficult for students whose mother tongue has evenly stressed syllables. There is a vast difference in the length of English syllables (discussed under prosody in Chapter Five, page 133) and the schwa is found in the very shortest. Note the two sentences:

a. Is Glenna outside?

b. Is Glenna around?

The schwa is so short that it may not be heard by an uninformed student. Sentence *a* has a schwa before the diphthong /aw/. Sentence *b* brings together two schwas, both weak-stressed and is even more difficult to interpret. The students who experience trouble with schwa may hear *Glen* instead of *Glenna.* The following exercise will provide practice in both hearing and pronouncing weak-stressed schwa:

EXERCISE 4.3

PRONOUNCING WEAK-STRESSED SCHWA

Instructions: Ask questions according to your teacher's instructions. Don't make a break between words. (Code 1–3)

Teacher	Student
1. Ask if Georgia's around.	Is Georgia around?
2. Ask if Willa's around.	Is Willa around?
3. Ask if Glen's around.	Is Glen around?
4. Ask if Norm's around.	Is Norm around?
5. Ask if Will's about.	Is Will about?
6. Ask if George's ahead of us.	Is George ahead of us?
7. Ask if Norma's across the street.	Is Norma across the street?
8. Ask if Glenna's above average.	Is Glenna above average?
9. Ask if Kenyatta's alive.	Is Kenyatta alive?

A speaking activity that can be very appropriate for several levels of student achievement is picture description. In one pattern the student does not have to understand complicated directions or cues. He simply tells what he sees. Or leading questions can guide his observation to specific features he must interpret. This is a useful skill that sharpens both observation and language.

Here is an example:

EXERCISE 4.4

ANSWERS CUED BY PICTURES

Instructions: Answer according to each picture. (Code 1-2)

	Teacher	Student
	1. Is it raining?	Yes.
	2. The boy is taller than the girl. True or false?	False.
	3. What's on the table?	Books.
	4. What is she doing?	Swimming.
	5. What is this man?	A sailor.

Translation is a much-maligned activity for language study, but we feel it is not at all inappropriate. Many of our students will be asked at some time in their lives to provide translation services, usually on a rather basic level. We think a little preparation for this eventuality is not amiss, and suggest slips with written instructions for each student in his native language for him to ask another student, or the teacher, a question in English and then report to the class what the answer was.

EXERCISE 4.5

TRANSLATED QUERIES

Instructions: Follow the instructions on the written slips. Report to your classmates what you find out. (Code 2–4)

Task	Report
1. Pregúntele a su vecino a la derecha que cuánto tiempo hace que se encuentra en los Estados Unidos.	My neighbor on my right says he has been in the United States for 6 months.
2.	
3.	
4. etc.	

These slips must be made up in advance, and the teacher should be sure to have enough and enough languages represented, so every student can have one. We should not include just the languages commonly known in the United States and ignore speakers of exotic languages. This activity is of course not appropriate for situations where the students are not yet literate (too young or uneducated), or when the teacher is unable to get the directions translated into exotic languages. Chances are that if there are students from an unusual language background, there will also be literate adults, though they may be hard to locate.

COMMUNICATIVE CLASSROOM ACTIVITIES

Early in this chapter we suggested the possibility of getting students to talk by asking them to do so. One of the most effective ways to do this is by means of a procedure called "directed dialog." Very simply put, this means that the teacher gets a conversation started by suggesting that one student make a comment to, or ask a question of, another student, the teacher offering the content of the remarks. This technique can be very effective indeed, since to use it properly the students must be able to manipulate the grammar, especially the grammar of person-marked verb forms and personal pronouns, which is a challenge to many students. Following is an example of a directed dialog:

EXERCISE 4.6

DIRECTED DIALOG

Instructions: Listen to the instructions and suggestions the teacher will give to individual students. The students addressed should carry out the instructions to the best of their ability. (Code 3–5)

Ellen, ask Lee if she's ever been to Hawaii.	Ellen: Have you ever been to Hawaii, Lee?
Lee, answer.	Lee: No, I haven't.
Ellen, ask her if she knows anyone in the class who has been there.	Ellen: Do you know anyone in the class who has been there?
Answer, Lee. (Use a gesture or omit if not needed.)	Lee: I think Ann has.
Lee, you're not sure? Ask her.	Lee: Ann, you've been to Hawaii, haven't you?
(Let Ann answer without a request, if she can and will.)	Ann: Yes, I was there two years ago.
Ellen, ask her how long she was in Hawaii and what took her there.	Ellen: What does it mean to ask "what took her"?
Who can help interpret "what took her"?	Ralph: I think it means "Why did she go there."
Is that right, Nita?	Nita: Yes, I think so.
OK, Ellen. Now your question.	Ellen: How long were you in Hawaii, Ann, and why did you go?
	Ann: Two weeks; it was our vacation.

This exercise can very easily be carried on for as long as students maintain an interest in the discussion. It has several very good features: It can be used to elicit full-sentence statements or questions (without the unnatural full-sentence answer that some teachers require for regular classroom response exercises, justifying their procedure by pointing out that otherwise students get no practice working with full-sentence structures). Also, directed dialogs are very flexible; they can be made easy or difficult to fit the needs and abilities of classes through a wide range of proficiency. Furthermore, they are natural sequences that "fit the occasion"; the teacher uses "you" and the student conforms with an appropriate "I": "Tell him you'd like to know . . ." becomes "I'd like to know . . ." The teacher uses "her" and the student says "you": "Ask her to lend you a . . ." becomes "Can you please lend me a . . . ?" (Note that there is a comparable adjustment in word order, from the normal subject-verb of the teacher's wording: ". . . if *she* has been to Hawaii" to an inversion when the student asks "Have *you* been to Hawaii?") Another advantage: it is easy to adapt to the individual ability and proficiency of the students, giving complex instructions to the students who can handle them.

It's relatively easy to involve several students, and the discussion can get quite complex without disorienting the students. It's not unnatural: in real life we do ask people to carry oral messages for us, so it is not limited to purely classroom situations. Finally, the directed-dialog technique lends itself to a very useful procedure: *fading*. Fading involves the withdrawal of the teacher stimulus and participation in an activity as student interest mounts and the activity no longer needs to be sustained by teacher direction. More and more responsibility is passed on to the students. In some classes it might be possible to pass on the role of dialog director to a good student or students.

Survival English

Sometimes people have advance notice of an assignment that will take them to another country and culture, with time to get at least partially prepared linguistically. This is quite often true of a student who studies English, sometimes for many years, with the expectation of eventually using the language for study, travel, employment, etc. This is fortunate because it usually takes extensive and serious practice to learn to communicate efficiently in a second language. Since others do not have the assurance of sufficient time to learn under ideal circumstances, what should the person thrust into a multilingual situation try to do?

Such a predicament calls for Survival English, a concept which almost inevitably rests, partially at least, on local situations. Often there will be dominating characteristics of the physical area that will indicate priorities. In Hong Kong there will be a special need for talking about ferries; In San Francisco, bridges; in the Philippines, jeepneys; in Egypt, the river; in New York, the subway; in Los Angeles, the freeways, etc.

The survival student should concentrate on the problems that are real to him in his personal situation. If he depends on trains, he'll need expressions about departures, stations, destinations, tickets, etc.; if he has a car, he'll need road and traffic information. Regardless of where he is, he should learn to count and should master directional terms necessary to communicate with a taxicab driver, such as "right, left, straight ahead, stop here, how much," etc. He should try to learn clock time, colors, days of the week, and other vocabulary sets that will make shopping, moving around the city, etc., easier.

He should learn a few question forms, in particular those that suggest a simple answer, one he can handle: "How many streets (or blocks)? Do I turn right or left? What is the name of the street I turn on?" etc. Choice questions may be helpful, for example, "north or south, right or left, this side of the street or the other," etc. Finally, he should learn to use gestures, pointing, finger counting, etc., that will support his attempts at oral communication, and he should have the means of enlarging his vocabulary when bilinguals are available, by asking: "How do you say *pangalan* in English?" or "What does *medan* mean?" And he should be prepared to facilitate communication with phrases such as "Speak slower, please; Could you say that again . . ."

An important skill should be cultivated by any person who has to communicate at the survival level: the ability to construct a simplified paraphrase. This skill is useful in many circumstances, but is especially appropriate when asking directions of a stranger. The student should design his questions in such a way as to maximize chances for a simple answer. Questions need to be highly specific, asking for one piece of information at a time, in order to reduce the number of different answers that could be semantically appropriate. Some of the WH-questions (*who, what, where, when*) are likely to produce simpler and more specific answers than others (*how* or *why*). Choice questions can be kept simple, if the choice is clearly limited: "Would you like Coke or Seven-Up?" And of course *yes-no* questions, if clearly stated, produce the simplest answers of all: two possibilities that are clearly distinguished in pronunciation and meaning.

The following exercise is intended to develop the skill of the simplified paraphrase in formulating questions:

EXERCISE 4.7

GETTING DIRECTIONS—PARAPHRASE SKILLS

Instructions: Make the following sentences simpler and shorter. Don't change the meaning. (Code 2–3)

Questions by John	Paraphrase by Eduardo	Answers by Giacomo
1. What's the best highway route from here to Naples?	Does this road go to Naples?	Che? What? Yes, sí.
2. How long would it take us to drive there?	(How many hours to Naples?)	(Three.)
3. Is there train service in case we decide not to drive?	(Is there a train to Naples?)	(Yes.)

4. Does this highway go straight through, or do we have to get another road?	(This road goes right to Naples?)	(Yes.)

Questions by Hussein	Paraphrase by Beni	Answers by John
5. I've looked all over this map and I can't find Corda Drive.		What did you say?
	Do you know Corda Drive?	Yes, I've heard of it.
6. Take a look at this map and show me where it is.	(Show me Corda Drive on this map.)	(Near here.)
7. Does it run North-South or East-West?	(Does it go this way or this way?)	(This way.)
8. If you can find it, point out exactly where it is.	(Can you find it?)	(Yes. Right here.)

A survival English exercise is not pronunciation practice. It is not a time to correct mistakes unless these mistakes are absolutely crucial to the minimum level of understanding that the concept of survival implies. The teacher might make a few inconspicuous notes about problems that could become part of a future pronunciation lesson, but interrupting the exchanges of messages in a survival exercise should if at all possible be avoided.

Hopefully the period of necessity for survival English is short and does not lead to a proficiency plateau from which no further improvement is expected. The student should recognize his needs and work toward supplying them. How can he judge his progress? One indication that he may not have achieved a successful mastery is that natives of the language or the location, when addressing him alone, will use a careful and distinct pronunciation and short, simple sentences, introduce more redundancy, and possibly increase the loudness of articulation. This special variety of the language, often called "foreigner talk," is popularly believed to be more easily understood. If used exclusively, or even extensively, it can postpone the day of native-like speaking and comprehension.

We acknowledge that when a student is addressed with foreigner talk, this is not of itself sufficient evidence of failure to master spoken English. It may be that the student is performing somewhere between a low level of proficiency (characterized by strongly accented and simplified speech) and an acceptable level showing satisfactory progress toward fluent control of the spoken language. But the degree of fluency in English that elicits foreigner talk should be recognized as a way station, not as a destination. It is, in short, a sign that the serious student must continue his efforts to produce more accurate and more normal-sounding utterances.

If a student is faced with a genuine survival situation, a pattern such as the reduction of full vowels to schwa when weak-stressed, pervasive though it is, may not be the most important detail to concern the student. If he cannot be understood by one person, he should try another: people (including native speakers) vary widely in their ability to tolerate vagueness and variation when they function as listeners. If one approach doesn't work, try another. If the student wants to communicate the word *comparable*, /kámpərəbəl/ and is not understood, he might try /kəmpɛ́rəbəl/ . It might be a matter of dialect, as in the case of the two pronunciations of *comparable*, and the listener will "connect" when he hears another oral interpretation.

Stress patterns that diverge from expected norms can be surprisingly difficult for native speakers to interpret. The divergent stress pattern frequently functions as a disguise, even in a context that should partially, at least, disambiguate the situation. Some examples from nonnative English:

/shíkəgòw, vəríyəs, grənyúwlər, fórbədən, kámpəshən, səkrífəs, səbówdɪzh, sətɛ́lət, stəbórn/.

(Answers, if you need them, are at the end of the chapter.)

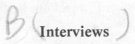

The student who seriously wants to improve his second language proficiency should be concerned with the accuracy of his pronunciation. He should ask his teacher and his knowledgeable friends to inform him when he makes a bad mistake while speaking. Sometimes this will interrupt the conversation, but usually the critic will find a natural break in the communication flow to offer his comment. The student who benefits from this special treatment should thank his critic to make sure the contribution is appreciated. This way a student has the free service of several tutors who can help him polish his oral proficiency, because as his pronunciation improves, so will his listening comprehension.

This suggestion should not be considered a substitute for a good phonetics or pronunciation class. If the student really wants to improve, he should have the assistance of a specialist.

Interviews

Conducting interviews is an excellent way to employ speaking skills. With the teacher's help and guidance, the class can work out a set of questions that can be addressed to a visitor. The teacher should explain what kinds of questions are appropriate. Many people don't like to be asked how old they are, what they weigh, how much money they earn, etc., but there are plenty of other queries that can be used. Examples are:

EXERCISE 4.8

INTERVIEWER EXPERIENCE

Instructions: Ask the following questions of a visitor to your class. (Code 3–4)

1. How long have you lived in Los Angeles?
2. Are you a teacher?
3. Where do you work?
4. What's your favorite sport? Game? Hobby?
5. Have you visited Manila?
6. What did you notice that was different there?
7. What have you noticed that is different *here*?

Then the student or students that interviewed the visitor can present him or her to the full class, mention whatever things seem to be of general interest to the class, and then let the class ask other questions. Most visitors will enjoy becoming part of the class for a few minutes, and they can be a valuable addition to a language lesson.

The student can also profit from experience on the other side of the interview situation. In the following exercise, the teacher conducts a mock employment interview, the student taking the part of the applicant. No special preparation need be given for this assignment. Let the chips fall where they may, and see what happens.

EXERCISE 4.9

INTERVIEWEE EXPERIENCE

Instructions: Answer the following questions that might be put to you in a job interview. (Code 3–5)

Teacher	Student
1. What work experience have you had?	I've had a position as office boy with an American company (Amoco) in Cairo. I've also had experience as a tourist guide specializing in the Giza pyramids and the Sound and Light presentation offered there.

2. Where are you in school?   I'm a third-year university student.
3. Are you interested in part-time or full-time work?
4. Can you drive a car?
5. Do you have a license?
6. Can you type? How many words a minute?
7. Do you have any other office skills?
8. What languages do you speak?
9. Could you work evenings?
10. What is your immigration status?
11. Do you have a U.S. work permit?

Show and Tell

One of the familiar and reliable activities that regularly take place in elementary school classes for native speakers of English is called "Show and Tell." The name of the procedure is suggestive. The pupils are encouraged to bring a favorite toy or object of any kind to class; they are given the full class's attention and an opportunity to show their classmates what they have brought. They also tell them about it: how they got it, where it came from, what it is used for or what it can do, etc. Other pupils handle the object, try it out, ask questions about it, etc. Older students can also play "Show and Tell." They bring items or objects appropriate to their age and interest level: a pocket calculator, a frisbee, an electronic toy, or an editorial from the newspaper. "Show and Tell" capitalizes on student interest and provides a good opportunity for self-expression. To increase class interest, foreign students should be encouraged to bring something from their own countries.

EXERCISE 4.10

SHOW AND TELL

Instructions: Give each student one or more opportunities to show the class something that interests him, to tell the class about it, and to answer any questions his classmates might wish to ask. (Code 3–5)

Douglas: This is my new pocket calculator. It will add, subtract, multiply, divide, do square roots and percentages. It has one memory bank. It will run on house current if you have an adaptor, or it can take three double A cells.

Other Students	Douglas
1. How much did it cost?	$11.95 plus tax.
2. Where did you get it?	Thrifty Drug.
3. What company makes it?	Rockwell International.
4. Where was it made?	In Japan.

Still another technique, the assignment of oral reports, can support the teacher's efforts to pass on to the students another part of the responsibility for class activities. Three- to five-minute talks can be assigned, written, edited (with whatever help the teacher can give), and presented. We recall a class at the Foreign Service Institute which trained U.S. Air Force personnel for military mission assignments in Latin America. With great regularity they were asked at an early meeting in their host country to "say a few words" of introduction. We anticipated their need and made this speech of introduction one of our early, serious assignments. It did double duty to satisfy a training assignment and to provide helpful experience for this modest but not unimportant early opportunity to impress favorably one's counterpart and colleagues.

Providing for this assignment produces an exercise consisting of an outline reminder of the topics to be covered, e.g.:

EXERCISE 4.11

WORD/PHRASE OUTLINE FOR ORAL PRESENTATION

Instructions: Following the suggested order of topics, make a brief oral report describing your life. (Code 6–7)

1. Birth
2. Family
3. Childhood
4. School
5. Work Specialization
6. Marriage
7. Travel
8. Present Activities
9. Plans

If this seems to make excessive demands on the students, reassure them with help to individual students in working out their text, which they can become thoroughly familiar with, even memorize, for a more polished presentation. Subsequent assignments can include oral reports on other subjects, particularly subjects of current political interest. Eventually, as skills increase, the class can host modest debates between class members. We have seen this technique be so successful that the students could not confine themselves to the second language in the classroom. When people *want* to say something, it's hard to impose arbitrary limits or restrictions on the amount or, within reasonable limits, the content of what they can say. It's a worthwhile and appropriate classroom technique.

EXERCISE 4.12

INFORMAL DEBATE

Instructions: You and a classmate will conduct an informal debate by taking turns making a statement and then challenging the statement in a rebuttal. Whatever one says, the other will disagree. Then the one that made the statement tries to justify it. (Code 6–7)

Example:

Jan: The railroads in the United States should be allowed to drop their passenger service and concentrate on long hauls to move goods.

Sally: I disagree. They offer poor service purposely, so people like you will support the companies' desire to abandon passenger trains. They should make their passenger service better, and people will choose the train more frequently. Etc.

As fluency and proficiency improve, students can be given more demanding types of exercises. For advanced-level students the give-and-take of arguments about aspects of the economy, history, or philosophy of the reference country can be a rich lode to be mined.

At an appropriate time after study skills have been presented in the chapters on written discourse (Chapters Eight and Nine), the preparation for an oral debate could be profitably combined with techniques for gathering information from written sources.

COMMUNITY INTERACTION ACTIVITIES

Eventually the teacher should devise activities which will transcend the classroom and take the students out into the community, where they can try their skills in realistic settings. Many assignments can be devised that will require oral communication between the student and the community. Typically these will be task-oriented. The following exercise involves the purchase of a ticket for a trip by train:

EXERCISE 4.13

BUYING A RAIL TICKET

Instructions: You are at the railroad station in Slough and you want to buy two tickets to Cardiff. Find out what trains go from London to Cardiff, whether or not they stop at Slough, what classes of travel are available, how long the express train takes to get to Cardiff, what the cost of tickets is. (Code 5–7)

Student	Teacher
1. Can you go by train to Cardiff from here?	Yes; there's a London to Wales line.
2. What classes of travel are available?	First and second class.
3. How long does an express train take to get from Slough to Cardiff?	Two hours and forty-five minutes.
4. What trains go from London to Cardiff?	Numbers 2, 8, 12, and 14.
5. Do they all stop at Slough?	No.
6. Which ones do?	Numbers 8 and 12.
7. What's the cost of a second-class ticket?	£11.60.
8. I'd like two second-class tickets, please.	That'll be £23.20.
9. What platform do we board the train from?	Number 1.

The same information is processed into another form for a report.

EXERCISE 4.14

PASSING ON INFORMATION

Instructions: Pass on to your traveling companion the important information you gained in the preceding interview. (Code 5–7)

1. There are four express trains today from London to Cardiff.
2. Two stop at Slough; one at 10:45 A.M., the other at 2:30 P.M.

3. I bought two tickets for the earlier train.
4. We should plan to be at the station by 10:15.
5. The train is boarded from Platform 1.

In most communities there are many opportunities to utilize local resources for communication experience. Information about dry cleaners, shoe repairs, self-service laundries, auto repair shops, employment agencies, fast food establishments, the public library, fire stations, car-wash facilities, state highway patrol, ambulance service, self-storage facilities, airport transportation, emergency plumbing repairs, U-haul trailers, automobile road service, nurseries, stock brokers, tree surgeons, pool service companies, etc.—there's almost no end to the possibilities of organizations and institutions that can be studied and then reported on orally to the class, with a question period for the students to ask the "reporter" more about the subject of his report.

EXERCISE 4.15

GATHERING INFORMATION FROM THE COMMUNITY

Instructions: Go to the community institutions or agencies listed below and get information about the services they offer that would be useful or interesting to a foreign student. Then prepare a dialog that illustrates the information you got. Show the dialog to your teacher for any corrections necessary; then be prepared with a classmate to perform the dialog before the class. (Code 4–6)

1. The post office:

Student	Postal Clerk
a. How much does it cost to mail a letter to an address in the U.S.?	$.22 for the first ounce. $.17 for each additional ounce.
b. About how many grams are there in an ounce?	About 28.
c. What's the overseas rate for letters?	Air or surface mail?
d. I'd like to know both.	Airmail is $.40 for the first half ounce and $.35 each additional half ounce. Surface rates are $.30 for the first ounce, $.17 each additional ounce.
e. Are there airgrams for foreign letters?	Yes. They cost $.36.

2. A bank.
3. A movie theater.

4. The bus company.
5. A car-rental office.
6. The International Student House.

If the class is located in a non-English-speaking country or environment, two alternatives are possible: (1) Collect information from an English-speaking institution (the American Embassy or Consulate, an American company, an international organization (UNESCO office, World Health Organization, etc.), or get the information from a local (first language) source, but still make your report in English, with help in its preparation from your teacher).

In addition to the necessary linguistic competence to handle specific situations, a student needs to develop a sense of what is socially appropriate. There are times when it will not be possible to accept invitations, even though one might want to. The following exercise offers practice declining invitations:

EXERCISE 4.16

MAKING EXCUSES

Instructions: Graciously decline the following invitations and supply a valid reason why you cannot accept. Make your regrets sound sincere. (Code 6–7)

1. Sunday dinner at an American home:

Kim Soong	Mrs. Browning
a. (Ring)	Hello.
b. Hello. Is this Mrs. Browning?	Yes.
c. Mrs. Browning, this is Kim Soong. I'm calling to thank you most sincerely for the invitation to dinner next Sunday, and to tell you I'm very sorry I won't be able to accept.	Oh, I'm sorry too. We've looked forward to meeting you. Gari has told us so many interesting things about you.
d. I'd like so much to come, but I've promised my parents I would go to San Jose and meet my aunt and uncle, who live there. They haven't seen anyone from our family since they left Korea fifteen years ago.	I understand, Kim. We'll try to find another time when you can come.

e. Thanks, Mrs. Browning. It was very   Goodbye.
   nice of you to invite me. Goodbye.
2. Friday night at the symphony orchestra.
3. An invitation to a football game.
4. Saturday evening picnic on the beach.
5. A ride up to see the Sequoias.
6. An invitation to attend the Laguna Festival of Arts.

In an advanced-level language class, course material should encourage more sophisticated awareness of intentions expressed indirectly. A would-be speaker must be able to appropriately interpret a response that is not the immediate sum of its grammatical and lexical parts. Note the following exchange:

Husband: George came by, said that he won't be able to make this month's payment on the money he borrowed from us.

Wife: That's the third straight month. He's turned out to be a fine friend.

The wife's comment is inconsistent if we look at the literal meaning of what she is saying. She is obviously not happy with their "fine friend." This could be more clearly signaled in its oral form, if high pitch and contrastive stress are placed on the word *he*.
   Here's another example:

Wife: The gardener came by, said he'd get around to us tomorrow.

Husband: I'll bet he will.

We don't know the intention of this rejoinder unless we hear it spoken. If the sentence stress is on *bet*, it's sarcastic; if the sentence stress is on *will*, it is an honest expression.
   In the following exercise the student is asked to correctly interpret the content of the sentences:

EXERCISE 4.17

RECOGNIZING INTENTION

Instructions: Listen to (or read) the following mini-dialogs and be prepared to explain the real attitude of the persons speaking. (Code 6–7)

1. Wife: I liked that furniture salesman.
   Husband: So did I. He really gave us a good deal.
2. Teen-age son: The manager at the used car lot assured me that the Plymouth had only one previous owner, an elderly lady who drove it very little and treated it like a jewel.
   Father: That's a man you can really trust.
3. Wife: The bill collector said he'd hit you with a suit.
   Husband: That's just what I need—another suit.
4. First golfer: My wife takes care of the little decisions; I handle the big ones.
   Second golfer: Like where you can play golf, after you get her permission.
5. Weekend farmer: These trees need iron.
   Brother-in-law: Bury some nails in the ground close to the trees.
6. Boyfriend: You say you've got a new tie pin?
   Girlfriend: No, no—not a tíe pin; a Thâi pín. It's worn on a girl's dress, not on a man's tie.
7. Woman in doctor's office: Hepatitis?! That's all I need.
8. Man at community airport: One more flying lesson. That's all I need.

An exercise of this type lends itself to a limited discussion of certain cultural points. Without an awareness of the beliefs and practices implied in the mini-dialogs, the humor may be difficult or impossible to detect. Some of the considerations, keyed by number are:

1. This is a sincere expression. The salesman created a good impression by convincing his customers that he had their welfare at heart.
2. This statement recalls the widely accepted belief that used-car salesmen in our society are notoriously dishonest, that they will say anything, right or wrong, true or false, to make a sale.
3. This is a pun, a play on two of the meanings of the word *suit*. The husband seems to be avoiding an unpleasant conclusion by an attempt to be humorous.
4. This is a reference to the henpecked American husband, who (judged from the vantage point of some other cultures) allows his wife to make all the significant decisions shaping their lives. (Note it doesn't have to be true, just traditional.)

5. This is straight talk; some trees do need iron, and it can be supplied by burying nails in the soil nearby.
6. This is another pun: two possible meanings are disambiguated by different stress patterns in their pronunciation. /táy pìn/ versus /tây pín/ . The first is a "tie pin," a small clamp to hold a man's tie in place. The second is a "Thai pin," a pin from Thailand, normally made to adorn a lady's dress.
7. I've already had more problems than I can take care of.
8. To get my pilot's license.

Oral communication at a more advanced level should include instruction in the affective use of language. There are ways to be polite and ways to be brusque. Partly this is done by intonation (tone of voice), but partly by the words and expressions chosen. This can be illustrated by the following exercise:

EXERCISE 4.18

EXPRESSING POLITENESS/ANNOYANCE

Instructions: You will be asked to participate in a role-play for one of the following situations. (Code 5–7)

Example:

A husband is irritated by his wife's neglect to record the checks she writes on their joint account. The account is overdrawn for the third time this year. He expresses his annoyance; she tries to mollify him and promises him (for the third time) that it won't happen again.

Husband: Clare, you've done it again.
Wife: Done what, Dear?
H: You've written checks and not made a record of them.
W: Did I? I was so sure I'd remember this time.
H: Three checks have bounced. Our credit will be ruined!
W: Really? Three?
H: That'll be $30, ten for each bad check.
W: I'm so sorry.
H: What good does that do?
W: I'll surely see that it doesn't happen again.

1. A rebellious teen-age daughter has been told by her mother that she can't go out this weekend. The daughter complains and tries to get her mother to change her mind.
2. The daughter slips out of the bedroom window on Saturday night, hoping her absence won't be noticed. Her father is waiting when she gets home.

3. Your teacher is giving you a test, and the instructions include a warning that there will be no talking of any kind among the students. During the test your friend asks you for an eraser, and you tell him you don't have one. The teacher doesn't notice him but does notice you, and asks you to bring your test paper to her and then leave the room. You go up to her and try to explain.

4. You've just had an accident that was clearly your fault, because you didn't signal a lane change or check by looking back to make sure the lane you moved into was available. You did look in the mirror, but the car you hit was by then out of the range of your mirror. You try to find out how fast the lady was traveling, in hopes of proving she was above the posted speed limit and therefore jointly responsible for the accident.

5. You are an insurance salesman. You have tried to sell a friend an accident policy, but your friend says he (or she) never has accidents and therefore doesn't need insurance. Driving down the street the next day you brush by a person in a pedestrian lane. The person brushed by is very frightened, but no harm was done, so you don't stop, because you've now noticed the pedestrian is the friend you tried to sell an accident policy to. You're not sure you were recognized, but hope not. That night your friend calls. You approach the telephone nervously, wondering how you'll explain your discourtesy for not stopping. The friend recalls you wanted to write an accident policy, and says he (or she) has had a change of mind, because some darned fool nearly killed him (or her) at noon that day as he (she) was crossing the street.

6. You are a negotiator representing labor in a coal mine. Others are management representatives, and one is a government labor specialist. There is an argument about safety in the mine, with you claiming there is a deadly gas in the mine and the management representatives claiming the mine has been tested and found free of gas. The government specialist offers to check the mine again.

7. In the courtroom with a trial going on, you are called to testify as a witness to an automobile accident. The responsibility for the accident depends on which car went through the red light. Both drivers claim their light was green. The two cars are a VW bug driven by a student and a Cadillac El Dorado driven by a well-dressed lady. You are not sure, because your attention was on the cars instead of the traffic light, but you think the VW was at fault.

8. You accidentally upset a crystal goblet, spill its contents on your hostess, and break the goblet when you jump to retrieve it. Try to apologize in a way that will be appropriate. Your hostess is a little upset, but tries to put her guest at ease.

9. Have students write up other situations, check them to see for sure that they are usable, then put them in a hat and have students draw to see who prepares which role-play.

Role-play and the preparation of skits (short, small-group dramatic efforts), if interesting and instructive, can be presented to the class. These are excellent activities that involve several students at once, with several groups proceeding simultaneously, and consequently more students getting active practice in the speaking skills.

EXERCISE 4.19

ROLE-PLAY

Instructions: Assign parts and act out the following situations. Encourage initiative and creativity, with different outcomes when a situation is repeated. Try to keep the discussions friendly and polite. (Code 7)

1. A nearby family has a small boy who repeatedly tugs sharply at your sleeve and then pretends he was not the one who annoyed you. You speak to his mother and ask her to do a better job of supervising him. The boy protests his innocence, and his father, a boor, backs him up and tells you to quit bothering the child.
2. You try to get a waiter's attention, but he has too many tables to attend to, and he tries to ignore you. You finally get up and walk over to where he is and tell him he is waiting on tables of guests that arrived after you did. He is offended, and the rest of the night consists of poor service and further complaints. You leave a very small tip, and the waiter tries to embarrass you publicly as you leave.
3. Your teacher makes a flagrantly false statement and you try to suggest it is erroneous without causing any offense. The teacher is sensitive and prefers to think you are trying to make him look inadequate in the eyes of the other students.

An activity which we call "gambits" affords an enjoyable opportunity to develop linguistic and social skills. They allow full rein for the students to use creative imagination. They consist of statements and questions at various levels of formality and politeness which students analyze to describe situations they express. Following are examples:

EXERCISE 4.20

GAMBITS

Instructions: The statements and questions below are brief conversational exchanges that suggest problems in interpersonal relations. Put some of these together and then describe the likely participants and situations that would motivate the exchanges. (Code 7)

1. a. Polite interruption

Formal: Pardon me. ⎫ Did you realize you're ⎧ stepping on my foot?
           Excuse me. ⎭   ⎨ standing in the light?
                                         ⎩ blocking the way?
                                           taking my tray?

Neutral: Do you know you're ⎫
           You're   ⎭

Informal to rude: Pardon me! ⎫
                     Excuse me! ⎪
                     You're   ⎬
                     Hey, you're ⎭

1. b. Response to polite interruption

Formal: Oh, I'm terribly sorry. I didn't realize. ⎫
           I beg your pardon.   ⎭

Neutral: I'm sorry.

Informal to rude: Sorry. ⎫
                      Okay, okay. ⎭

1. c. Polite rejoinder

That's all right. ⎫
Don't worry.   ⎭

2. a. Requests for repetition

Neutral: Pardon me? ⎫ I didn't hear what you said.
           Excuse me? ⎬
           Sorry?   ⎭

Informal to rude: What?   ⎫
                     What say? ⎭

2. b. Response

Neutral: Oh, I'm sorry. I said _____ .

3. a. Asking for clarification

Formal/neutral: I'm afraid I didn't understand ⎧ you
                                                ⎨ what you said.
                                                ⎩ what you mean(t).

                          Can you ⎧ explain what you mean(t)? ⎫
                                  ⎩ tell me again?   ⎭

Informal to rude: What do you mean? ⎫
                     What?   ⎭

3. b. Response
      Formal/neutral: Oh, I'm sorry. $\left\{\begin{array}{l}\text{Let me try to explain it again.}\\ \text{I meant \underline{\hspace{2cm}}.}\end{array}\right.$

                     I meant _____ .

One activity that bears fruit in terms of improving speaking skills is an acquaintance with popular literature. Learning rhymes, poems, songs, proverbs, sayings, etc., brings the student a little closer to the culture. Additionally, the rhythms learned along with the poems and even the songs are usually valid examples of the suprasegmental elements in the language. Actually we have made a start on popular poetry with the "One-for-the-money" rhyme presented in Chapter Three. It has proved to be a good device to interpret, get accustomed to, and practice weak stress.

Limericks

Another rich vein that can be mined with profit is the limerick, which is a universal poetic form in the English-speaking world. Here are a couple of examples:

> There <u>was</u> a young <u>lady</u> from <u>Prin</u>,
> Who was <u>known</u> as <u>exceedingly</u> <u>thin</u>;
>   While <u>sipping</u> a <u>malt</u>,
>   She com<u>mitted</u> a <u>fault</u>:
> She <u>slipped</u> through the <u>straw</u> and fell <u>in</u>.

We have underscored the strong-stressed syllables to illustrate the rhythm, though our interest in these and comparable verses is on the *un*stressed syllables, which so often give second language students trouble. The second example is a bit more difficult, but has the same underlying rhythm pattern:

> There once was an old man from Lyme
> Who married three wives at a time,
>   Saying: one is absurd,
>   So three is preferred,
> 'Cause bigamy, sir, is a crime.

Students with a bent for or an interest in writing verse might try to compose a limerick, following the rhyme scheme aabba, with the b's representing short lines, as in the models. The best should be recited to the class.

It's both easy and profitable to combine speaking practice with other skills. For example, to get source material for an oral report, the student can be given a reading or a listening assignment. In preparation the teacher can dictate for written copying some of the probably unfamiliar lexical items, using the alphabet names of the letters to verify correct spellings. (This should not be overdone; some lexical items should be left for the student to guess from context.)

In addition to oral reports, the student can benefit from telling anecdotes or jokes. The ability to talk about an incident, tell an anecdote, joke, etc., is a valuable social skill. The student should prepare his oral contribution carefully, with help from his teacher.

After the other students have heard the report they can be invited to ask questions. If they hesitate, the teacher should ask one of *them* a question, with a difficulty level appropriate to the individual addressed. When a question is not satisfactorily answered, involvement of other students is suggested: "Ron, do you agree with Jimmy?" (Be sure to sometimes use this procedure when a satisfactory answer has been given, so the question itself will not signal the teacher's disapproval of the answer.) This exercise will have much of the give-and-take of a real subject-matter course, which is what is intended.

A somewhat unusual assignment is provided by playing the game "Rumor." The class is lined up and the teacher whispers a message (length and difficulty level appropriate to the class) to the student on the end of the line, who listens and repeats it, again in a whisper, to the next student, continuing down the line. What emerges is seldom recognized. The teacher should then ask the students to write down what they heard and passed on, a procedure that will expose any deliberate sabotage as the message traveled.

We have treated what we call the oral communication performance skills and we now move on to the related component skills: pronunciation, grammar, and vocabulary. These are somewhat more traditional areas of concern for language students, and we recognize their importance. But we have enjoyed talking about listening and speaking in their own right. Hopefully students will continue to be concerned with the oral communication skills, and will try to refine them by specific attention to the components without which there would be no communication.

(Answers to illustrative examples on page 113: Chicago, various, granular, forbidden, compassion, sacrifice, sabotage, satellite, stubborn.)

DISCUSSION

1. How do arrangements to provide listening experiences differ from arrangements to provide speaking experiences? How can a teacher get her students to speak?

2. What is "phatic communication"? What is its purpose?

3. Why is schwa so hard to produce for many students?

4. How does the "directed dialog" technique work? What advantages does it offer?

5. What is the technique called "fading"? How is it employed?

6. What characteristic of a "paraphrase" makes it useful in a second or foreign language class?

7. What is the role of pronunciation accuracy in survival English?

8. What is foreigner talk and to what use can it be put in language teaching?

9. What are gambits and how are they used in a classroom? How do they teach socially appropriate responses?

10. How can popular literature be used in a language class? What advantages does it offer?

B

COMPONENT SKILLS

CHAPTER FIVE

PRONUNCIATION

INTRODUCTION

We now turn from the performance skills of oral communication to the component skills. Whereas we have focused on communication *per se*, although we could not completely ignore sounds, structures, and words, we emphasized the information that could be transmitted, not worrying too much about accuracy of pronunciation, catholicity of structure, or fitness of lexicon—as long as we somehow got our message across. We judged performance by the standards of basic communication, not elegance. But if this remains the totality of instruction and context is always given precedence over form, students are led to a permanent plateau of pidgin from which very few emerge.

For many students pidginization can be avoided by incorporating in the instruction phonological, grammatical, and lexical refinements in the component skills, to perfect their use and to establish a commitment to a wider range of linguistic styles and registers. This makes an overall contribution to exact, clear, unambiguous expression and makes movement in the direction of native-speaker competence more likely.

As part of a liberal arts curriculum the component skills have an interest for their own sake (we are always eager to better understand how our society functions), as well as for what they contribute as handmaidens to efficient communication.

An important question that needs a thoughtful answer is: How much time should be devoted to pronunciation? The answer will depend on several factors: level of instruction, age range of the students, aims of the course, availability of materials, training of teachers, intensity of involvement, interest of students, etc.

Some students find extended correction tedious, so the instructor should be sensitive to flagging interest, moving on to something else when pronunciation exercises no longer produce noticeable progress. For most curricula the answer to the "how much" question can be five to ten minutes of class time per meeting for as long as the need and willingness of the students last. This takes into account the morale of the class and the recognized needs of the students.

Priorities

Another problem the teacher must solve is how to decide what errors to correct, and especially how to determine what order to observe among the errors that have been listed for treatment. In other words, when confronted with numerous kinds and examples of mistakes, where should the teacher begin? To deal with all levels at once is manifestly impossible. We suggest a sequence built on the following criteria:

1. *Fluency*: First of all the student should strive for a smooth flow of language. This will help avoid a broken-up sequence of syllables that are hard to understand and difficult to correct. The normal rate of speech should be a first priority for any analysis or practice of pronunciation. The teacher should adopt a clear, quick signal that tells the student to "put it all together." The signal we recommend is for the teacher to hold his hands in front of him, the cupped surfaces facing each other like a couple of parentheses, gradually moving the hands toward each other. Other corrections should wait until "normal tempo" is established.

2. *Stress* placement: Exercises coming later in this chapter will try to explore this very complex area. Studies have shown that misplaced stresses result in comprehension failures more readily than wrong sounds. Try the following on your students (or yourself) as sample problems:

/sənsínətiy, kənfídənchəl, prɛ̀pərǽtəriy/

Correct a syllable at a time, if necessary: given /səkrǽmənow/ , try /sæk/ , not /sək/ ; /sæ̀krəménow/ . **Again** /sæ̀krəménow/ . **Now** /mɛn/ , not /mən/ ; /sæ̀krəmɛ́now/ ·

3. *Rhythm* and *intonation*: Students occasionally ask for teacher approval by pronouncing their problem phrase with a question intonation.

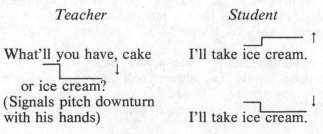

Teacher	*Student*
What'll you have, cake or ice cream? (Signals pitch downturn with his hands)	I'll take ice cream. ↑ I'll take ice cream. ↓

4. *Vowels* and *consonants* are next, sequenced among themselves to give priority to the ones that cause misunderstanding, then those that mark a heavy accent, and last (and usually dispensable) all others, to introduce refinements.

Category 4 problems can be determined with relative specificity if students have the same background language, but not so easily if they are from a multilingual background, which is the case in most classes in the United States, Canada, Britain, Australia, etc. So what does the teacher do?

It would be nice if we could follow the order of the priorities we have listed. But it is difficult to talk about such features as fluency, stress, pitch, and rhythm before considering consonants and vowels, since the features cannot be disembodied. Our compromise is to first list the segmental sounds (the consonants and vowels) and then take up combinations of sounds and features, specifically the vowels and stress patterns.

Consonant Patterns

To illustrate the relative simplicity of the phonological inventory we include in tabular form the English consonants. These are not always pronounced in the same way, so the table conceals some of the complexity. There are important variants, such as the different ways of pronouncing the sound /t/, such as *tack, tree, butter, bottle, button, winter, stay, cat*, etc. In general, symbols near each other on the chart represent sounds that are likely to be confused by some students: e.g., symbols in the same box, in the same row, or in the same column, particularly if the student's language lacks one of a pair of sounds.

English Consonants*

	Bilabial	Labio-Dental	Dental	Alveolar	Palatal	Velar	Pharyngeal
Stops	p b			t d		k g	
Affricates					ch j		
Fricatives		f v	th dh	s z	sh zh		h
Nasal	m			n		ng	
Lateral				l			
Retroflex					r		
Semiconsonants					y	w	

Stress and Vowel Patterns

Every natural language will have areas of complexity that are responsible for some of the problems experienced by second language students. These areas are different for different languages. Two notorious problem areas in English are the vowel systems and stress patterns. The interplay between the two increases the complexity of both.

American English, for most dialects, has fourteen vowel and diphthong contrasts. We display them with a nine-box grid with three rows marking relative height of the tongue (high, mid, low) and three relative horizontal positions (front, central, back), with lip participation described as spread for the front six boxes and rounded for the back three. The figure to the left below labels these concepts:

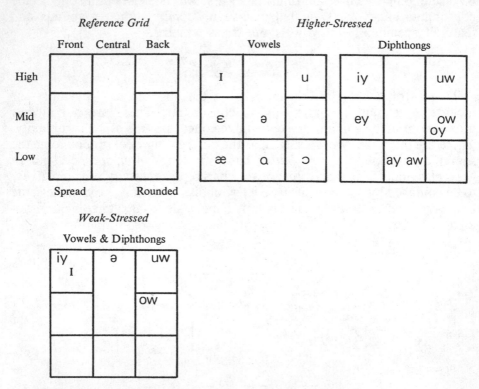

The boxes under the label "higher-stressed" list the inventory of vowel and diphthong contrasts of American English, seven of each, shown for clarity in separate sets of boxes. Finally, on the right the nine-box grid is repeated to show which of the vowels and diphthongs (there are five) can occur with weak stress.

Note that the five weak-stressed vowels and diphthongs tend to be high on the grid. This tendency seems to push all the weak-stressed forms toward the top, but most especially the schwa, which is lifted to the top of the oblong slot assigned as its domain. This placement reflects the tendency to associate *high* and *weak*, which does indeed characterize the reduced vowels of the weak-stressed system.

Perhaps we can clarify the relationships with some examples. Let's first try to describe in broad outline some of the stress contrasts in modern English.

EXERCISE 5.1

LEVELS OF STRESS IN ENGLISH LEXICAL ITEMS

Instructions: Repeat after your teacher the pairs of words. Pay attention to the second syllable in each pair. It is longer in the second word. Say the list again. Can you hear and mimic the difference? Now say the list in the opposite order. (Note that to show the weak-stressed vowels we have listed the forms under *Student* in a respelling that indicates more clearly where the weak-stressed vowels occur.) (Code 1–3)

Teacher		Student	
/ˊ ˅/	/ˊ ˋ/	/ˊ ˅/	/ˊ ˋ/
driver	driveway	dráyvər	dráyvwèy
carpet	carport	kárpət	kárpɔ̀rt
office	offset	ɔ́fəs	ɔ́fsɛ̀t
feeble	female	fíybəl	fíymèyl
acre	acorn	éykər	éykɔ̀rn
shortage	shorthand	shɔ́rtɪj	shɔ́rt·hæ̀nd
comic	comrade	kámɪk	kámræ̀d
sunny	sundial	sə́niy	sə́ndàyl
issue	fishhook	íshuw	físhhùk
pillow	pillbox	pílow	pílbɑ̀ks

Students should note, or have their attention drawn to, the different emphasis or stress in each pair. The second syllable of the first word is always one of the weak-stressed vowels, in this list /ə, iy, ɪ, ow, uw/ as in off*i*ce, sunn*y*, com*i*c, iss*u*e, pill*o*w. The second syllable of the second word has a vowel from the list of strong-stressed: /ey, ay, ɔ, ɛ, æ/ , etc. Words in the left-hand column are stressed *strong-weak* /ˊ ˅/ ; words in the right-hand column are *strong-medial* /ˊ ˋ/ .

Let's look at another set of words, which have similar contrasting stress patterns, but are identically spelled. Most of these words (all of the ones cited in this exercise) end in the suffix spelled *-ate*. The stress patterns are /ˊ ˅ ˅/ and /ˊ ˅ ˋ/ , identical except for the last syllable, which is weak in column A and medial in column B.

EXERCISE 5.2

MEDIAL AND WEAK STRESS IN A PATTERN
OF ENGLISH HOMOGRAPHS

Instructions: Read the words in vertical lists (in column A and column B) after your teacher, being careful to preserve the correct stress pattern on each word. Then read column C twice, the first time maintaining the stress pattern of column A, the second time following the stress pattern of column B. Then read column C a third time, this time horizontally, alternating stress patterns that identify and distinguish nouns or adjectives in columns A and C_1 and verbs in columns B and C_2. (Code 2–5)

A	B	C	
1. doctorate	decorate	duplicate	
		C_1	C_2
/dɑ́ktərət/	/dɛ́kərèyt/	/dúwpləkət ~ dúwpləkèyt/	
2. consulate	calculate	correlate	
3. adequate	allocate	alternate	
4. literate	illustrate	intimate	
5. delicate	dedicate	delegate	
6. desperate	demonstrate	desolate	
7. obstinate	obligate	animate	
8. passionate	penetrate	advocate	
9. temperate	tolerate	estimate	
10. ultimate	indicate	intimate	

The last syllable of the -*ate* words draws our attention: it will have either the diphthong /ey/ or the simple vowel /ə/ . In these forms the /ey/ will always be pronounced with a medial stress, and /ə/ will always take weak stress. This correlation between vowel quality and stress is a crucially important feature of English structure, one that L2 students of English should be actively aware of. It will recur constantly in a description of English pronunciation.

Students will perhaps notice, or their attention can be called to, the fact that items in column A are nouns or adjectives, column B are verbs, and column C can be either, depending on the pronunciation. Column B, the verbs, participate in a derivational pattern that produces a postverbal noun:

decorate–decoration

Column A items do not fit this pattern. There is no *doctoration or *adequation. Column C *verb* forms do participate as verbs, but of course they can also appear as adjectives or nouns. Keeping in mind the membership of forms in noun, adjective, or verb classes, try the following exercise orally. If it is too difficult, try it as a written assignment.

EXERCISE 5.3

FORM CLASSES AND MEANINGS
OF POLYSYLLABLES ENDING IN -*ATE*

Instructions: From the definitions given, try to produce meaningful sentences, using the appropriate pronunciation for the -*ate* word cited. Reference letters/numbers identify -*ate* forms that appear in exercise 5.2. (Code 5–7)

Definition	Reference		Example
1. To draw pictures	illustrate	(B)	He wants to illustrate children's books.
2. Highest academic degree	doctorate	(A)	
3. Very close, as a friend	intimate	(C1)	
4. To protest as a group	demonstrate	(B)	
5. Frail, of uncertain health	delicate	(A)	
6. To go through	penetrate	(B)	
7. A key just like another key	duplicate	(C1)	
8. To draw pictures for a movie cartoon	animate	(C2)	
9. To give authority to another person	delegate	(C2)	
10. Able to read and write	literate	(A)	

Note that if the definitions are verbal, the word defined will appear in columns B or C; if nominal or adjectival, in columns A or C. The exercise combines grammar and vocabulary study, though the crucial clue is in the pronunciation.

In an advanced class, or an excellent intermediate class with high achievement potential, the teacher could assign this exercise as a small-group activity, in which stronger students could help weaker ones, especially in composing and writing example sentences.

If the class still finds exercise 5.3 too difficult for their level of competence, the use of a good monolingual dictionary can be specified, especially with a small-group approach. One or two students can be designated "lexical specialist" to identify the form class affiliation(s) and the meaning(s) of the item(s) under scrutiny.

It might prove useful to students if they know that -*ate* endings are very common. In one reverse English word list (a lexical tool that alphabetizes words from the end rather than from the beginning of each word), approximately 5,000 -*ate* words are listed, including the patterns presented in this section and other patterns (*rate, date, late, rebate, debate, phosphate,* etc.). It is interesting to note that in this list verbs are much more numerous than adjectives or nouns. Though we do not have an accurate count that permits us to list percentages, a guess that a new and unfamiliar word is pronounced like a verb will be more frequently correct than a noun-adjective guess.

One more exercise should suffice to demonstrate the complexity (and perhaps consequently the flexibility) of the uses of stress in English. This is the distinction between noun compounds and noun phrases. An example of this contrast is the name of an item that can almost always be found in a classroom: *blackboard*, which is usually green and is not a board. In contrast a *black board* is indeed a board that is black. Listen to the contrast:

bláckboàrd–blâck bóard

The first example is a word—a compound word but a word. Since it is a separate word, its meaning may not be (and usually is not) derived from the combined meanings of the simple words that make up the compound (cf. the second example, which is two separate words).

These forms are distinguished in oral communication by whether the first or the last syllable gets the highest stress. We will use this contrast between noun phrase and noun compound as an illustration of a congruence exercise, a very flexible and productive type of exercise that was introduced in Unit 3.

EXERCISE 5.4

CONGRUENCE EXERCISE:
NOUN COMPOUNDS VERSUS NOUN PHRASES

Instructions: If the sentence makes sense, respond *OK*. If it doesn't make sense, respond *No*. (Code 3–6)

	Teacher	Student
1.	The steak was served on a hot pláte.	OK
2.	The steak was cooked on a hótplate.	OK

3. Put that hótplate in the dishwasher.	No
4. Serve the steak on a hótplate.	No
5. That hot pláte uses a lot of electricity.	No
6. That hot pláte is no longer a hot pláte.	OK

Note that this exercise is much easier than those found earlier in this chapter. It is part of a strange paradox that the priority features of English pronunciation are much more complicated and sophisticated than later features and sounds. For this reason pronunciation courses and programs typically start with contrasts between sounds that share some of the same characteristics.

DETERMINING WHAT TO TEACH

We have to have a rationale for the decisions we make on what to teach. We have presented one that assigns priority to some of the sound features we identify as suprasegmental. But we find it difficult to exploit these before handling some of the vowel and consonant problems. When we have done what we can with an introduction to the suprasegmentals, have made students aware of them, achieved correction of errors (in a priority order as recommended earlier in this chapter), then we turn to the vowels and consonants. How do we proceed? We can observe the mistakes students make (or have made in the past) and try to organize them on the basis of the importance they have in disrupting communication.

Some problems we notice: the Filipino merchant says "Pibe pesos"; the Japanese airline steward says "Have a present fright"; the Egyptian street vendor says "Beaches are five bounds"; the Chinese waiter asks "You want flied lice?"; the German breakfast diner says "One fried ache and toast"; etc. We hear these and are amused. Sometimes we figure out what is meant, sometimes we are left wondering.

Error Analysis and Contrastive Analysis

This method of determining what needs classroom attention in pronunciation is referred to as *Error Analysis* (EA). We hear mistakes and design our materials and teaching to correct them. Mistakes which are serious we will probably hear, but often a teacher will miss errors because they are unexpected, or because she has developed a tolerance for the kinds of mistakes that are common with a particular foreign language influence on English, or for other reasons that we don't even understand. Still we can expect that flagrant errors will be caught by the teacher.

But why wait until errors appear? Can't we anticipate and try to prevent them, to correct them before they happen? This is the aim of *Contrastive Analysis* (CA), through which the teacher, having carefully studied and compared the phonological systems of two languages, the students' native language and the classroom target language, anticipates the errors that are likely, alerts the students, and tries to prevent the mistakes before they are made. We see no conflict in applying both of these procedures, and in fact we believe they ultimately lead to about the same list of problems. If the predictions of the analysis are valid, they will certainly match the errors that are noticed. Both theories fall short in actual application. Teachers do not hear all the errors their students make, and CA predicts errors which somehow never seem to occur. Used together, EA can provide a confirmation for CA, and CA can provide listening guidance for EA. The important thing is to define the errors and hopefully to list them in an order of decreasing importance so the most crucial ones can be given early attention in the classroom.

When the problems are defined, how do we go about converting them into pronunciation lessons? We recommend that the student be given a chance to listen to a correct model and imitate it. Some sounds prove to be relatively easy, and the students' approximation will be quite satisfactory. Some students need little or no additional instruction, but others will need lots of help. If the imitations are defective, guidance is indicated.

Most experienced teachers have a store of explanations and often some favorite gimmicks that they call upon to provide this guidance. Perhaps the student has not mastered the flapped /t/ in words like *Betty*. The student pronunciation separates the two syllables *Bet-* and *-ty* (as the English spelling falsely suggests) and pronounces them as if they were two words: *bet* and *tea*. For some students words in their own language can be cited. The flapped /t/ in *Betty* can be compared with, even identified with, the /r/ in the Spanish pronunciation of *beriberi* (which sounds like "Betty, Betty"). By means of this comparison the student is told that English *t* in some environments sounds like his *r*. This is true, but it seldom occurs to a Spanish-speaking student to compare two sounds that are written so differently.

There'll be repercussions: when the Spanish speaker comes against the word *berry* (or *bury*), he must be told that his flapped sound is not a satisfactory substitute for the English /r/. We may call this the "growled /r/" and caution the student that while his tongue tip turns upward, it must not touch any part of the top of his mouth.

We are strongly tempted to continue with this inventory, but we must remember that this is a chapter on how to teach pronunciation, not a pronunciation course which presumes to provide answers to all of the problems involved. There are several standard manuals which try to make this kind of list. Our purpose in this chapter will be served by talking about typical problems and making suggestions for diagnosis and treatment. What follows is an application of the /r–t/ contrast in a pronunciation activity:

EXERCISE 5.5

MINIMAL-PAIR SENTENCES:
INTERVOCALIC AND POST-TONIC /-r-/ VERSUS /-t-/

Instructions: You will hear six sentences that are identical except for one
different sound in a single word. If you hear *witty* in the sentence,
respond *clever*; if you hear *weary* in the sentence, respond *tired*.
(Code 2–5)

Teacher	Student
1. He's very witty after four years in college.	Clever
2. He's very weary after four years in college.	Tired
3. He's very weary after four years in college.	Tired
4. He's very weary after four years in college.	Tired
5. He's very witty after four years in college.	Clever
6. He's very weary after four years in college.	Tired

This is called a minimal-pair sentence exercise. It has a meaning, carries a
message. The two alternatives are both reasonable, both appropriate to the
context, and about equally plausible. This is the pronunciation drill par
excellence. It is a far better application of the minimal-pair concept than
some widely used variants of a few years ago, where the students' task was to
hear two words, or one word twice, and judge "same" or "different." Or
equally nonproductive, he would hear three one-word pronunciations and
would identify whether the first, the second, or the third was different from
the other two. These were hopelessly mechanical and of little value.

It is well to remember that unfamiliar sounds in a foreign language may be
extremely difficult for a student to distinguish (and to produce). Anyone who
has studied Arabic is aware of the difficulty of differentiating the five or six
separate pharyngeal sounds. Other languages pose comparable problems.
We have seen teachers who blame a student for carelessness or laziness
when he fails to make a distinction. Chances are he simply cannot hear the
distinction and needs help, not blame. He needs to listen to and to hear the
contrast, make any necessary prescribed adjustment, and then have the
advantage of informed practice.

Some of the problems of English are quite general for speakers of many
languages of the world. Speakers of languages that do not include schwa in
their vowel inventory are likely to be confused in the identification of this new
vowel, since it appears right in the middle of the pattern and is about equally
distant from all the other vowels in the system. The following exercise deals
with the problem of failing to make a clear and consistent distinction between
/ə/ and /ɑ/ :

EXERCISE 5.6

MINIMAL-PAIR SENTENCES: /ə/ and /ɑ/ BEFORE /r/

Instructions: You will hear six sentences that are identical except for one different sound in a single word. If you hear *firm* in the sentence, respond *store*; if you hear *farm* in the sentence, respond *land*. (Code 1–3)

Teacher	Student
1. The children inherited the firm.	store
2. The children inherited the farm.	land
3. The children inherited the firm.	store
4. The children inherited the farm.	land
5. The children inherited the farm.	land
6. The children inherited the farm.	land

Actually the following /r/ helps differentiate the /ɑ/ from the /ə/ , because /r/ following /ə/ tends to make the area of its articulation rise. The pattern can be plotted on the vowel grid as follows:

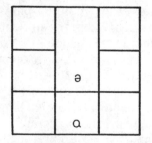 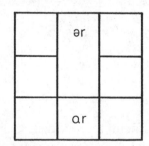

Note that it is not necessary to always have six sentences, or that the sentences be one sentence pair repeated. In fact the exercise will be more interesting if more meaning is packed into it:

EXERCISE 5.7

MINIMAL-PAIR SENTENCES: /ə/ AND /ɑ/

Instructions: You will hear one or the other of two interpretations of the following six sentences. If you hear *pup* in the sentence, respond *dog*; if you hear *pop* in the sentence, respond *dad*. (Code 1–3)

Teacher	Student
1. Has your pup finished eating?	dog
2. When does your pup usually go to sleep?	dog
3. My pop trembles when he is angry or afraid.	dad
4. My pop sure cleaned his dinner plate.	dad
5. My pup gets all excited when the fire alarm goes off.	dog
6. Your pop sure chased that salesman away!	dad

Notice that the sentences have to make sense with either pair-item inserted. If they don't, the student, even good students, will tune out the unlikely sentence and choose the alternative that does make sense. If for example we had the sentence "My pup wrote out a check for the milkman," most students would interpret "dad," because they recognize this as the only form that makes sense.

A few other comments on this type of exercise: We have to avoid expressions like "Where's the pup?" because we don't ordinarily use *the* with *pop*. *Dad* and *dog* are good paraphrase identifiers because they are short and either likely to be known or easy to teach and useful once learned. They are a little bit weak in being somewhat similar: both have a consonant/simple vowel/consonant syllable structure with identical first consonant. But the disadvantage is slight; the forms are different enough that they will not likely be confused. Their being short is an advantage that saves time in drilling.

We will of course want to drill more minimal-pair sentences with additional word pairs. In selecting pairs we look for simple words, hopefully already known to the students, but if not, then words easy to learn and useful once known. *Tugs/togs* (hard pulls/clothes) meet the simplicity test but fail on usefulness. Better prospects are "He gave me a little *hug/hog*" (affection/piglet); "Someone *shut/shot* up the consulate" (closed/fired on); "He *rubbed/robbed* me" (massaged/stole from); etc. This is weak because of the low frequency of "massaged," but what other word could be used to mean "rubbed"?

The examples given in the above paragraphs indicate ways of practicing the recognition of easily confused sounds, especially those not present in the familiar language. Practice in recognizing may also result in developing an ability to produce the unfamiliar sounds, but this is not a universally accepted conclusion, and many would dispute the value of carryover from recognition to production. We agree. There is no sure way to skill in pronunciation that does not include production of the sounds of a new language. The main difficulty is in numbers. Students can "understand" as members of a group, but they need individual help when they speak. There are of course drills in chains, and these may be helpful, but it is a rare student who can evaluate his own production, who can be his own judge, to determine if a pronunciation is acceptable. If this limitation is acknowledged, we cannot wholly rely on group work in active pronunciation.

How can individual, monitored pronunciation practice be given? We see no way to avoid at least some student-by-student practice under the tutelage of an informed teacher. One procedure that we find useful is to place a student before the class. The teacher has established the contrast to be practiced (Let's say it is the consonant pair /t ~ ch/) and has agreed on a minimal-pair sentence: "The woman answered tearfully/cheerfully." We identify which sentence is produced by using as paraphrase identification "sad" and "happy." (Note we do not select "sad" and "glad" because they sound too much alike.)

[Technical note: The /t/ and /ch/ are acoustically similar and easy to confuse, especially if the /t/ is strongly aspirated and the two consonants occur before a strong-stressed high front vowel: *tearfully/cheerfully*.]

The teacher then positions herself at the back of the room where only the performing student can see her. The others face front so the teacher can communicate visually and privately with the student who will be speaking. The teacher signals to cue the student's sentence by a facial expression (a smile or a frown), or by thumb signals (thumbs up or thumbs down), or by holding up an appropriate moonface (😊   🙁), by cue cards, etc.

The student performs as instructed, and the rest of the class responds with a paraphrase. If the interpretation is not clear, the teacher can request by a show of hands who voted for which interpretation. The teacher controls the decisions since she makes the first move. If the class correctly interprets the teacher's intention, communication is flowing efficiently. If the class, or some part of it, does not interpret correctly, then the teacher has to assess responsibility: if the teacher agrees with the "rights," the speaker is absolved; if the teacher agrees with the "wrongs," the performing student is at fault.

EXERCISE 5.8

PRODUCTIVE/RECEPTIVE ACTIVITY: /t/ VERSUS /ch/

Instructions: One of your classmates will stand before you to receive a private signal from your teacher, who will be behind you at the back of the room. As your classmate pronounces a sentence, say "sad" or "happy" to indicate whether you understood *tearfully* or *cheerfully*. Your teacher will tell you if your classmate and you have performed satisfactorily. (Code 2–4)

Teacher	Student 1 (Ben)	Other Students	Teacher
1. (Thumb up)	The girl answered cheerfully.	happy	Everybody right.

2. (Thumb up)	The girl answered cheerfully.	happy	Everybody right.
3. (Thumb up)	The girl answered cheerfully.	sad	Ben's right, others wrong.
4. (Thumb down)	The girl answered cheerfully.	happy	Ben, you did say "cheerfully," which means *happy*. But I signaled you to say the word "tearfully," which means *sad*. So the rest of you heard him correctly; "happy" was what you heard.
5. (Thumb down)	The girl answered tearfully.	sad/happy	Which of you say sad? Which say happy? Sad is correct.
6. Etc., with others taking Student 1 part.			

One precaution must be taken when students are instructed to perform by speaking sentences. Their production must match what is normal and natural for a native speaker. They must not be permitted to speak slowly, overpronouncing the /t/ and the /ch/ to make an artificial distinction. Start with easy, short sentences that have the crucial word last or first; later bury the pair in the middle of a longer sentence: "The children cheerfully/tearfully answered."

GENERAL PROBLEMS

Regardless of the contrastive relationship that exists between English and the individual student languages, one can look to English alone and find complexities that will inevitably cause problems. We propose to complete this chapter discussing typical problems in English, analyzing them, and suggesting remedies.

Reduction

We have earlier remarked that weak-stressed schwa is very important and frequent in English, but at the same time unusual in the languages of the world. This means that it must have priority attention by a student of English. For this reason it has been included in Chapters Three and Four as well as

Five. In its weak-stressed form schwa is very lightly pronounced and is frequently overlooked by students unaccustomed to the very brief and light pronunciation that is its characteristic. This is especially true in words of three or more syllables where an internal schwa is followed by an /r, l, w/, etc. Words in this pattern frequently show a reduction in the number of syllables they carry. This alternation in form and format will be a major problem of recognition and interpretation for many students. A few examples are:

Spelling	Produced with 3 Syllables	Produced with 2 Syllables
finally	fáynəliy	fáynliy
casual	kǽzhəwəl	kǽzhəl
manual	mǽnyəwəl	mǽnyəl
liberal	líbərəl	líbrəl

This pattern of reduction, especially as in *liberal*, where a /ər/ makes up the middle syllable, illustrates just how weakly a weak-stressed /ə/ is made and how easily it can disappear if the phonological environment encourages reduction.

The students need to hear the shortened form and associate it with what they are used to, in this way building a tolerance for variation within the acknowledged patterns of English. One way to improve hearing is to practice saying the forms:

EXERCISE 5.9

OMISSION OF INTERNAL SCHWA IN INFORMAL SPEECH

Instructions: Listen to your teacher pronounce one of the alternate pronunciations of each word. Identify which one you hear, labeling it as "formal" or "informal." Then pronounce the form in the *other* way (formal if you judged informal, and informal if you judged formal). (Code 2–4)

Word	Teacher		Student	
1. corporal	/kɔ́rpərəl/	formal	/kɔ́rprəl/	is informal
2. funeral	/fyúwnərəl/	formal	/fyúwnrəl/	is informal
3. doctoral	/dɑ́ktrəl/	informal	/dɑ́ktərəl/	is formal
4. numeral	/núwmrəl/	informal	/núwmərəl/	is formal
5. several	/sɛ́vrəl/	informal	/sɛ́vərəl/	is formal
6. admiral	/ǽdmərəl/	formal	/ǽdmrəl/	is informal
7. natural	/nǽchrəl/	informal	/nǽchərəl/	is formal

8. general	/jɛ́nərəl/	formal	/jɛ́nrəl/	is informal
9. different	/dífərənt/	formal	/dífrənt/	is informal
10. federal	/fɛ́drəl/	informal	/fɛ́dərəl/	is formal

Schwa has been observed as an alternate of the other English weak-stressed vowels: we get   /əlɛ́ktrək, məstéyk, prəmówt, rɛ́gyələr/ alongside   /iylɛ́ktrɪk, mɪstéyk, prowmówt, rɛ́gyuwlər/, etc. But we can find one context where weak-stressed /iy/ and /ə/ are always maintained. This is shown in the following congruence exercise:

EXERCISE 5.10

CONTRAST OF WEAK-STRESSED /iy/ AND /ə/

Instructions: Listen to the following sentences and decide which are reasonable. Write *OK* or *No*. (Code 3–6)

	Teacher	Student
/tiy/	1. The light plane flew at *68*,000 feet.	No
/tə/	2. An airliner can fly at *6–8* thousand feet.	OK
/tə/	3. Ann can jump a creek that's *7–8* feet wide.	OK
/tiy/	4. Ahmed works *78* hours a day.	No
/tiy/	5. Julie bounded up the stairs *46* steps at a time.	No
/tə/	6. The rocket reached an altitude of *6–8* thousand feet in a matter of seconds.	OK
/tiy/	7. The wall was *78* feet tall, and he went over it as if it weren't there.	No
/tə/	8. Raymundo can work *7–8* hours without stopping for lunch.	OK
/tiy/	9. Lisa works the *49*-hour shift.	No
/tiy/	10. The shallow end of Paolo's swimming pool is *45* feet deep.	No

---

A clear pattern of reduction is seen in the correlation of stress and vowel quality. Full vowels appear in stressed syllables, but are replaced by schwa when the stress is removed or shifted elsewhere. Another pattern of vowel reduction which involves schwa can be seen in related words with a shift in lexical stress:

democrat   /démǝkrǽt/
democracy   /dǝmákrǝsiy/

The vowels, stressed or unstressed, are represented by the same symbols when spelled (in the first column): *e, o, a*. But when transcribed in the second column, one notes that a full vowel appears with a higher stress, but a schwa appears in the syllable from which the stress has been removed: /dém-/ and /-krǽt/   become /dǝ̆-/ and /-rǝ̆-/ when the stress is shifted. (Note also that the consonants between vowels tend to go with the vowels in stressed syllables.)

There are many words like *democrat/democracy*:

EXERCISE 5.11

SCHWA AND THE LOCATION OF A HIGHER STRESS

Instructions: Your instructor will pronounce a word, like *democrat*. Repeat that word and then supply a related word with the suffix *-ocracy*. (Code 2–4)

Teacher	Student
1. democrat	démocràt, demócracy
2. bureaucrat	búreaucràt, bureáucracy
3. mobocrat	móbocràt, mòbócracy
4. autocrat	áutocràt, àutócracy
5. theocrat	théocràt, theócracy
6. plutocrat	plútocràt, plutócracy
7. aristocrat	arístocràt, àristócracy

There are many thousands of examples that illustrate this widely spread pattern. Now try an exercise that relates pronunciation and writing:

EXERCISE 5.12

VISUAL AND AURAL EQUIVALENTS IN ENGLISH

Instructions: Listen to the following list of words, each composed of four syllables. Decide on the form of an underlying two- or three-syllable word on which the longer word is based, and write both words: the longer, then the shorter. (Code 3–5)

	Teacher	Student		Reference
1.	stəbílətiy	stability	– stable	stéybəl
2.	stərílətiy	sterility	– sterile	stérəl
3.	fəsílətiy	facility	– facile	fǽsəl
4.	əbílətiy	ability	– able	éybəl
5.	vərílətiy	virility	– virile	vírəl
6.	frəjílətiy	fragility	– fragile	frǽjəl
7.	fətágrəfiy	photography	– photograph	fówtəgrǽf
8.	təlégrəfiy	telegraphy	– telegraph	téləgrǽf
9.	ləthágrəfiy	lithography	– lithograph	líthəgrǽf
10.	stənágrəfiy	stenography	– stenograph	sténəgrǽf

(The student's columns are filled in with the expected forms. The reference column is not part of the exercise, but is included because there are variant pronunciations to some of these words. The one that is intended for the student response is listed.)

Reduction is a principle that has many other examples and applications. But our present purpose is to illustrate kinds of learning problems and teaching techniques, not to attempt to solve all the pronunciation problems that involve reduction. Still, the standout problem is a stressed vowel; any one of them becomes a schwa (/V/ → /ə̌/), and the student who learns to control schwa and its distribution will be liberally rewarded with notable improvement, especially in recognition, but also in the production of English, since schwa occurs so frequently.

But reduction is not the only process utilized by spoken English. Two other concepts need to be illustrated and understood. They are: assimilation and contraction.

Assimilation

Assimilation is a technical term in phonetics which can be defined as the process whereby a sound, influenced by a contiguous or neighboring sound, tends to become like it in position and/[or] type of articulation. An illustration shows how this process works:

1. Horse sounds like *horsh* in the expression *horseshoe.*

2. Swiss "   " *swish* " "   "   *Swiss chalet.*

In these two examples, the sequence /s + sh/ becomes /sh + sh/. This is a matter of pronunciation: any contiguous words that produce a sequence of /s + sh/ will become /sh + sh/. A further modification can be heard in the noun compound *horseshoe*: the two /sh/ sounds reduce to one. However, both seem to be retained in the noun phrase *Swiss chalet*. Note that in like manner /s/ and /z/ in *this* and *his* become /sh/ and /zh/ in *this ship* and *his share.* It's very difficult and seems unnatural when an English speaker tries to avoid these assimilations.

Assimilation can be described (as in the dictionary citation above) as an interrelation between sounds, especially contiguous sounds. Another term, one that is explanatory and helpful in describing the process, is "feature spreading." In the examples *horseshoe* and *Swiss chalet*, the feature that is spread is "place of articulation." Alveolar sounds are attracted to the palate in a pattern of regressive assimilation as the influence moves to the left, anticipating the characteristic of the next sound. Thus /s/ becomes /sh/. English has other patterns of assimilation, one of which is well recognized and carefully taught, but this time *progressive* assimilation occurs, as the influence moves to the right: this is the /z/-morpheme that pluralizes nouns (and participates in other patterns). The feature spread in this case is "voicing of articulation": the basic /-z/ becomes /-s/ when the preceding consonant sound is voiceless, as in *ship, hat, cake,* which become /shɪps, hæts, keyks/.

(This is the famous /-z, -s, -əz/ pattern of endings that is found in noun plurals, noun possessives, singular verbs, contractions of *has* and *is*, etc. This pattern has been a favorite with "linguistically trained" teachers for the past 20 or so years. Along with it we usually also see the comparable pattern for regular past tense and past perfect forms ending in /-d, -t, -əd/ .) In this phonotactic sequence (the arrangements of the sounds), it is interesting to note the generation of schwa between consonants that are not allowed to cluster (/sz, jz, zz, td, dd/, etc.). As the English neutral vowel, the schwa appears between the noncombinable consonants, producing an additional syllable, thus avoiding the problem of nonpermitted consonant clusters:

/bes + z → bɛ́səz; jəj + z → jə́jəz; bæt + d → bætəd; treyd + d → tréydəd/

Different languages have different patterns of assimilation. Even though the influence and the change seem entirely logical, they are still language specific. A pattern typical to English can be called *palatal assimilation.* Certain alveolar consonants (sibilants and stops), specifically /s, z, t, d/ or certain combinations of these (namely /ts, dz/), followed by a /y/-sound are affected by a pattern of assimilation that is both regressive and progressive. A label for this is *reciprocal* palatal assimilation. This pattern is designated palatal because the /y/ draws the preceding consonant to the palatal position; then the /y/ itself is "swallowed up" by the resulting sound. This pattern accounts for numerous pronunciations that appear in the balloons of comic strips, which make an effort to sound natural and realistic, with such spellings as "watcha, whodja, didja," etc.

This pattern is well worth explaining to students, especially adults and serious teenagers, because it is not well understood. In summary it is as follows:

$$\left.\begin{array}{c} s \\ z \\ t \\ d \\ ts \\ dz \end{array}\right\} + y \rightarrow \left\{\begin{array}{l} \text{sh} \\ \text{zh} \\ \text{ch} \\ \text{j} \\ \text{ch} \\ \text{j} \end{array}\right.$$

sh He's coming this year.
zh Does your mother know about it?
ch Is that young man the mayor?
j   Would you mind moving over?
ch He always lets your dog in.
j   She really needs your help.

The palatal assimilation series, like any assimilation conditioned by contiguity, is in effect only when the specified sounds are in contact with each other. This fact suggests an exercise format: breaking the sentence between the two words that bring the sounds together. The student can repeat the full sentence as a way of confirming what he is not sure he learned. Unlike the model, the student is not permitted to break between the members of the assimilation pattern; he therefore doesn't avoid the assimilation:

EXERCISE 5.13

PALATAL ASSIMILATION IN ENGLISH

Instructions: You are not sure you heard the sentence right, so you repeat your version so your teacher can confirm or correct the sentence. Do not follow your teacher in breaking the sentences into two halves. Pronounce each sentence in a single continuing phrase. (Code 4–6)

Teacher	Students incorporate:
1. Whose . . . yellow dog is that?	/zh/
2. Pat's . . . yearbook was published late.	/ch/
3. His . . . yard is seldom cleaned.	/zh/
4. Would . . . you take a look at my bicycle?	/j/
5. Miss . . . Young is coming tomorrow.	/sh/
6. This . . . yogurt's dried up.	/sh/
7. Ed's . . . yacht came in this morning.	/j/

Contraction

The last concept that needs discussion is *contraction*. Unlike assimilation, which normally occurs when any combination of words brings two relevant sounds together, that is, meets phonotactic requirements, contraction is basically a grammatical process. Certain forms will normally contract; other very similar combinations will not: e.g., *it is* becomes *it's*, but *it was* does not contract, at least not in the same way. Also note that *is* normally does not contract when it is final in a sentence:

Is he staying?   No, he's coming
Is he really coming? Yes, he is. (Not "Yes, he's.")

One might seek an explanation, saying that the results would be identical; both *it is* and *it was* would be *it's*, and indispensable information would be lost. But we lose the same information even without contraction in "They cut the cake," which can be either past or nonpast. And since *it's* can derive from *it is*, or *it has*, we lose another kind of information.

There are traditional contractions which have long been recognized and accommodated in the writing system of English. *It's* is an example, with an apostrophe to mark the point where sounds and letters are omitted. There are other, basically nonrecognized contractions that have not been legitimized in the spelling system, except for the special purpose of comic-strip conversation, and from there borrowed by some native-English speakers for the purpose of writing informal letters to close friends and family members.

Virtually all native speakers of English use these contracted forms in appropriately informal situations, though some speakers, particularly those with pretentions to a formal education, will try to avoid them when they remember to do so, or when the situation is a rather formal one.

Basically these forms are a verb (*going, want, have, has, got, supposed, used*) plus particle *to*, producing *gonna, wanna, hafta, hasta, gotta, supposta, usta*. A more limited pattern of *give* and *let* before *me* produces *gimme* and *lemme*.

A drill can readily be constructed by reinterpreting formal utterances as informal, which compares the two forms and gives students a chance to hear and work with informal, an opportunity largely denied in the past due to the belief that informal contractions are vulgar and unacceptable in "refined" speech.

EXERCISE 5.14

INFORMAL CONTRACTIONS

Instructions: Carry out instructions given by your teacher, to pass on bits of information to your classmates. Use informal forms like *gonna, gotta, wanna,* etc. (Code 2–4)

Teacher	Student
Tell your classmates that:

1. You have to leave early today,   I hafta leave early today.
2. because you want to catch the 3:30 train upstate.   . . . wanna . . .

3. You feel you have got to keep a promise.   ... gotta ...
4. You and the candidate used to know each other well,   ... usta ...
5. and you do not want to disappoint him now.   ... don't wanna ...
6. After all, you are supposed to be close friends.   ... we're supposta ...
7. Anyway you are going to go and do what you can to   ... I'm gonna ...
   help him.

But with contractions there's more to learn than just how to pronounce them. We have to know when the pieces will contract. Certain conditions have to be met. In general, the verb-plus-*to* contracts if another verb follows, if the candidates for contraction are in the same phrase, and if in the basic sentence form no noun or adverb intervenes.

EXERCISE 5.15

DECIDING WHEN PARTICLE CONTRACTIONS
WILL BE USED

Instructions: The following sentence pairs illustrate sequences of a verb plus the particle *to*, some of which contract, and some of which do not. Repeat each sentence without a pause between the words. (Code 2–5)

Teacher	Student
1a. He's not the man I'm going... to town to see.	He's not the man I'm going to town to see.
b. He's not the man I'm going... to see in town.	He's not the man I'm gonna see in town.
2a. He's not the man; I want ... to be mayor.	... wanna ...
b. He's not the man I want ... to be mayor.	... want to ...
3a. I have ... two hens to feed.	... have two ...
b. I have ... to feed my two hens.	... hafta ...
4a. That's the fuel I used ... to fill my tank.	... used to ...
b. When I had lots of fuel, I used ... to fill my tank.	... usta ...
5a. He's the man I had supposed... to be the new principal.	... supposed to ...
b. He's the man that's supposed... to be the new principal.	... supposta ...

6a. Was he the pilot who got . . . to fly the   . . . got to . . .
    president to Europe?

 b. Is he the pilot who's got . . . to fly the   . . . gotta . . .
    president to Europe?

7a. That's all the food left from the fire, all   . . . has to . . .
    he has . . . to eat this winter.

 b. The food won't last longer than a year;   . . . hasta . . .
    he has . . . to eat it this winter.

8a. She's going and he's going . . . too, I   . . . going too . . .
    think.

 b. She's going and he's going. . . to think   . . . gonna . . .
    she's mentally unbalanced.

We'd like to note and discuss one more complication associated with the schwa + r. We have pointed out that r has an effect on schwa, but have not described that effect. The two sounds are blended together into a single r-colored vowel. This can be appreciated if you compare the pronunciation of the words *fear, fair, far, for* with *fur*. In the case of the first four it is possible to hear three sounds: the /f/, then the vowel, and then the /r/. With the fifth (*fur*), only two sounds can be heard: the /f/ and the /ər/ sound. In some analyses of English this sound is represented by a hybrid symbol composed of a schwa with the arm of an r protruding from its right side: /ɚ/ . We have not adopted this symbol, but we appreciate the problem that it attempts to solve. It is especially nettlesome when two schwa-r (/ər/) combinations come together, as in *treasurer, murderer*, etc. The final syllable is greatly obscured and seems to be signalled by a slight increase in the length of the first /ər/ sound. Practice these forms in the following exercise:

EXERCISE 5.16

ENGLISH FINAL /-ərər/

Instructions: Give the word that correctly finishes the sentence. (Code 2–4)

Teacher	Student
1. A man who murders is a. . . .	murderer.
2. A man who inquires is an. . . .	inquirer.
3. A man who gathers is a. . . .	gatherer.
4. A man who hires is a. . . .	hirer.
5. A man who delivers is a. . . .	deliverer.
6. A man who discovers is a. . . .	discoverer.

7. A man who showers is a. . . .   showerer.
8. A man who looks after the treasure is a. . . .   treasurer.

Second language learners of English will often miss the additional syllable, or will insert a glottal stop between the last two syllables (as, indeed, first language speakers may reasonably do).

English is characterized by fairly complex consonant clusters. Some of these are inherent and some are generated by the morphology. A most complicated initial cluster is made up of /s/ plus /p, t, k/ plus /r, l, y, w/. Some languages (e.g., Polish, Czech) allow more complex clusters than English does. Speakers of those languages have little trouble with English. Some languages (e.g., Hawaiian) have no clusters at all. To handle words like *spring, string, skew, spew, scratch*, the Hawaiian needs help, and we can give it to him in a dual-purpose exercise. Normally we'd consider only one problem in an exercise, but the following offers us a chance to deal with two that are very closely related:

EXERCISE 5.17

CONSONANT CLUSTERS AND WEAK-STRESSED SCHWA

Instructions: Listen as your teacher models two similar-sounding sentences and identifies each one with a paraphrase. Then she will give you one of the paraphrases and you should repeat the sentence that it refers to. (Code 2–4)

Teacher	Student

1. The train flashed by.
2. The terrain flashed by.
The first is railroad and the second landscape.
Repeat the one that means railroad.   The train flashed by.

Now repeat the one that means landscape.   _____

(The sentence referring to railroad requires a cluster of /tr-/, but the one that refers to landscape requires the insertion of a schwa between the /t/ and the /r/, producing an additional but very short syllable.) Here are some more:

3. He's sporting a new wife.   (displaying)
4. He's supporting a new wife.   (maintaining)
5. He spoke in the form he was used to.   (manner)
6. He spoke in the forum he was used to.   (arena)

We should be careful in teaching and practicing clusters, especially the complicated ones that are generated by English morphology, that we do not lay responsibility on our students for more complex patterns than are observed by native speakers. For instance, the rules tell us we should say /fɪfths/, /tɛksts/, /məntths/ . Native speakers regularly reduce these to /fɪfs/, /tɛks/, /mənts/ . A similar performance by our second language students should be acceptable.

The last subject we wish to touch on in English pronunciation is *rhythm*. It is extensive and complex. We will point out the problem without really attempting to solve it. Most of the pronunciation manuals describe at least the basis of the problem, which is the recurring unit of regularity in English prosody: the strong-stressed syllable or, by the exercise of poetic license, a syllable promoted to strong stress for the sake of the rhythm. We can illustrate this by citing popular poetry with underlines to identify the syllables that occupy stress positions and form the center of a poetic foot. Whether that foot is one syllable or three or four syllables, it is granted approximately the same amount of time. The higher-stressed syllables sound very long; the weaker syllables sound very short, especially when there are three or four of them in a single foot. Note the following lines:

Mary / Mary / quite con- / trary / how does your / garden / grow?
With / silver / bells and / cockle / shells and / pretty maids / all in a / row.

The foot *bells* is quite long. *All in a* divides the same amount of time among three syllables; hence they are faster. This rhythm pattern contrasts sharply with that of many languages which follow the pattern of allowing each syllable a relatively stable standard amount of time. This has a profound effect on the two kinds of rhythm patterns.

In this chapter we have been concerned with three things: (1) recently developed techniques for teaching pronunciation in contexts, (2) the means of analyzing needs and establishing priorities for various problems as they emerge in the classroom, and (3) neglected patterns of pronunciation whose introduction into the curricula would more efficiently serve the needs of aural recognition and oral production, so that students will be better prepared to perform the function of listening and, if this is one of their goals, be able more adequately to speak without conspicuous reminders that they are second language students.

We turn next to another component skill—the presentation of English structure, as it impinges on the oral skills of listening and speaking.

DISCUSSION

1. What are some of the factors that help decide how instruction in pronunciation should fit into second language instruction?
2. Discuss the ways in which stress and vowel quality are interdependent.

3. What order of treatment should be observed? In what order should different categories of corrections be undertaken?

4. What is the difference between "noun compounds" and "noun phrases"?

5. How do error analysis and contrastive analysis work together to help the teacher offer effective guidance to her students?

6. What kind of minimal-pair drill can be most highly recommended? Why?

7. Discuss reduction as a problem in pronouncing English.

8. Describe the patterns of palatal assimilation that are common in English.

9. Discuss and compare assimilation and contraction as phonological processes that affect English pronunciation.

10. What is the difference between inherent and morphologically generated consonant clusters?

CHAPTER SIX

GRAMMAR—
ORAL LANGUAGE

INTRODUCTION

In many ways it would seem preferable to discuss the grammar of the written language first, and of the oral language later: (1) Our grammatical tradition comes almost exclusively from the written language. It is only recently that we have recognized and described the structural characteristics that apply only to the oral language. That this is inherent in the history of the language is shown by the derivation of the word *grammar: gram* comes from the Greek word *graphein* "to write." (It is interesting to note that the connotations accompanying these early forms suggest "magic, occult sciences," reflecting the awe in which writing was once held.)

(2) Grammar-translation and reading as the approved methods of language teaching earlier in this century succeeded in establishing a firm association between grammar and reading, which has produced a grammatical analysis of written English. (3) The records we have of early and/or classical languages are in written form and are almost exclusively concerned with the written language. Only in comparatively recent times has technical equipment been available that is capable of making an exact record of speech. (4) The grammar of oral discourse is more easily derived from the grammar of written discourse than vice versa. We can in many instances derive oral usage from written by specific deletion rules, always simpler than building up sentence partials to full-blown, complete grammatical utterances.

Of course much of English grammar applies to both the written and spoken media, and since the overall design of our book presents oral language as the primary condition of human communication and the written language as derived, we will conform to that pattern in describing the grammar of English and will deal first with oral communication.

DEFINITIONS OF GRAMMAR

Perhaps we should start by defining grammar. A simple definition is: the rules by which we put together meaningful words and parts of words of a language to communicate messages that are comprehensible. There are two aspects of grammar:

(1) Know the rules.
(2) Apply the rules.

Either condition can appear alone. Many native speakers can apply the rules without knowing them well enough to describe them. The rules are internalized for subconscious application when communicating. On the other hand, some second language learners know and can explain the rules, but are not able to apply them, and because of this are able to communicate only partially or not at all.

The speaker (and listener) must be able to monitor what he hears in order to effectively express what he wishes to say and to interpret what he hears. But oral language is paced and monitoring may not proceed expeditiously enough to do its job. The remedy is experience and practice, with the necessary minimum of guidance.

Grammar can be understood in different ways by different people with different purposes. (The lists of definitions and examples cited here closely follow the presentation in Stockwell, Bowen, and Martin 1965). (1) To some it is a matter of etiquette: students are given prescriptive rules that help them achieve correct usage. This philosophy is evident in classes for native speakers of English. The most visible purpose seems to be the correction of certain forms and constructions that are considered erroneous or substandard, such as the distinctions between *He went to lie down* and *He went to lay down*; *He doesn't* and *He don't*; *I'm not* and *I ain't*, etc., along with deviant patterns of pronunciation such as *chimbly* and *fambly*. Some forms are correct and should be used; others are wrong and should be eliminated. This is called a *usage grammar* or sometimes a *school grammar*.

(2) Others think of grammar as a massive compendium of sentences and examples, explaining in great detail the rules and the exceptions, usually reaching back to early literary sources for examples. Often these are multi-volume studies, containing thousands of pages, and usually following classical models. This is called a *scholarly grammar*.

(3) For others, grammar is a study of language that deals with the forms and structures of words (morphology) and with their customary arrangement in phrases and sentences (syntax). There are of course several ways of looking at the forms and arrangements of words in sentences. One way

utilizes "signals" which identify some of the relationships, such as (a) *word order* ("This man clearly can't see"—a blind man, versus "This man can't see clearly"—a man in a fog); (b) intonation ("Oh, Henry" versus "O. Henry," a vocative versus a simple name citation); (c) *function words* ("I've got to see Bill and/or John"—both/either), and (d) *affixation* (emigrate versus immigrate, contribution versus distribution, etc.). This is called a *signals grammar*.

(4) Another view of grammar defines sentence patterns as a sequence of slots into which specified fillers (usually lexical items or phrases) can be placed. Thus a sentence pattern could be specified by naming the slots and supplying lists of fillers appropriate for each slot. For example:

Animate Subject	*Transitive Verb*	*Direct Object*
(1) Jim	visited	Anna Marie.
(2) Albright	studied	engineering.
(3) The boy	ate	an apple.
(4) The student	looked over	the lesson.
(5) The cat	climbed	the stairs.

This is called a *slot-and-filler grammar*.

(5) Another view of grammar holds that each choice of lexical item will bear a partly predictable relationship to the following item (or silence, if the item under consideration closes the sentence/discourse). When a listener internalizes the same patterns as the speaker, he is able to follow the discourse, moving ahead by means of predictions that are either confirmed or corrected. Naturally the confirmations help comprehension, whereas the corrections require the listener to back up until he finds himself and then start again. The ratio of confirmations to corrections should increase as the student moves ahead in his language study. This is called a *finite-state grammar*.

(6) Still another kind of grammar looks at the lexical items in an utterance and notes patterns in the words and phrases that reveal an organization. In the sentence *Ring the bell* we get virtually 100 percent agreement that "the" is more closely associated with *bell* than with *ring*. The pattern can be analyzed as:

(6) (*you*) *ring the bell*.

On each level we have the "immediate constituents." On the final level we have the "ultimate constituents." This is called an *immediate-constituent grammar*.

(7) The last definition we present (though certainly not one that completes the list of possible candidates for a definition of the term grammar) is a set of "rewrite rules" followed by a set of "transformational rules" that ideally can correctly (i.e., grammatically) produce any sentence in the language, but no utterances that would be judged nonsentences. This is called *generative grammar*.

Obviously this sketchy list and brief description of types of grammar is not complete. But looking at several established applications of "grammar" gives us helpful insights as teachers and students. It can help us understand what a *pedagogical grammar* should be and what help it can offer the text writer and the classroom teacher. The most useful grammar for second or foreign language instruction will no doubt be eclectic, selecting features from various grammatical traditions according to the needs of different aspects of language instruction and the contributions each type of grammar makes.

Other views of grammar carry their own names, definitions, functions, and emphases. These include "systemic," "stratificational," "junction," and one that has inspired many hopes among language teachers: "case grammar." These haven't so far convincingly demonstrated their application to language instruction, so we briefly acknowledge them and move on.

APPLICATIONS OF GRAMMAR

Why do we need a grammar? We *did* manage to learn our *first* language without a course in the grammar of English. Actually we don't need one. The study of the theory of language (linguistics) and of the structure of the student's native language (grammar) is justified in an academic program for the same reason botany and astronomy are. We can appreciate the flowers and be inspired by the stars without special instruction in botany and astronomy. But if one goal of our education is to *understand* the world we live in, we must include such instruction.

There are other reasons for including grammar in the study list. Grammar can be helpful in the study of foreign or second languages (without which experience a person can hardly claim to be educated), acting as a traffic officer, whose signals and rules will help keep a student on the right road. One's own understanding of these signals and rules will allow him to self-monitor his progress and avoid practicing errors. We correct and improve our linguistic performance by a monitoring device that serves as a grammatical check of every sentence we speak (and probably of every one we listen to), which, when it works properly, assures our ability to follow the rules of discourse. The rules are easier to apply if one understands how the full structure works; they are more difficult to apply if they are arbitrary statements that have to be remembered and used in an apparently capricious way.

Let's now take a look at each of the specific approaches to grammar listed above and try to determine their possible applications to language instruction:

(1a) *Usage grammar* is more relevant and appropriate for second than for first language students. For second language students the need to be informed of correct and noncorrect usage is crucial, since they approach the necessary learning tasks without the experience of having lived in the language and thereby having internalized usage data. We are reminded of the second language student who, realizing that "The man went away/The man went by" were rather similar in meaning, remarked "Did you see that man in a red shirt that just passed away?", when she meant ". . . passed by?" The second language student has to learn English usage, usually in the confines of the classroom, where imagination replaces experience. Usage grammar is to a large degree the source of the necessary corrections supplied to the student. It has mainly served as a written discourse grammar, but has been adjusted to oral usage.

(2a) *Scholarly grammar* provides a check on adequacy or comprehensiveness; it lets us see if we have covered all of the important material that needs to go into the lessons. These studies also perform a very useful service by helping the teacher find effective and relevant examples and illustrative materials.

(3a) *Signals grammar* provides attention to the structural forms and processes of the language being studied. Students are sensitized to the so-called structure or function words, to recognize them when they hear or read, to use them when they speak or write. To wait until this information comes to awareness by "osmosis" would be less than efficient pedagogy. The students can use the awareness of form and function to monitor their own use of these features in communication. A signals grammar is, or can readily be, oriented to listening and speaking.

(4a) *Slot-and-filler grammar* illustrates structural patterns and provides experience in sentence construction. The considerable difficulty in finding filler options that are compatible not only with linguistic requirements, but also with other lexical items, which we often refer to as "co-occurrence potential," will be troublesome, as shown by the very weak sentence drawn from the illustrated lists under section 4 above: "The cat looked over engineering." Nevertheless, since at the early levels of instruction items are offered by the text and the teacher, the student is not left to his own devices. He is spoon fed, so to speak, given only workable examples. With further experience and contact, the student will hopefully develop the perceptual categories that will equip him to make consistent and acceptable judgments. How this skill is developed may be interesting to the research-oriented psycholinguist, but most language teachers will be happy enough to see it happen without the need to explain.

It is interesting to note that the exercise type that is most characteristic of Audiolingual teaching comes directly from slot-and-filler grammar—the ubiquitous substitution drill. Extensive practice with substitution drills and exercises helps develop the feelings a student needs if he is to achieve a reliable judgment that enables him to utilize analogy to extend his mastery of this principle of language learning. Slot-and-filler has mainly been applied to oral language.

(5a) *Finite-state grammar* is above all a listener's grammar. It encourages the listener to predict what the speaker will say as the speaker talks. This skill, which capitalizes on the normal redundancy that occurs in live speech, is crucial in developing oral comprehension, when the student cannot slow up or "reread," though it can also be utilized in reading, especially extensive reading. Note in the following simple substitution drill how easy it is to be misled:

(7) I bought this house.		I bought this house.
a. Like.		I like this house.
b. Car.		I like this car.
c. Park.		(? I park this car.
		(? I like this park.

The grammar plus the lexical co-occurrence potential fail to differentiate between the two possibilities.

Some items are very easy to predict, and will take very few alternative answers, or even only one answer:

(8) He often wears a bow _____ , which has become his political

_____ .

(9) You can do the exam with either pen or _____ , but be sure to

mark the right _____ .

(10) He liked John's _____ , so he offered him the _____ .

The two blanks in (8) are *tie* and *trademark*; in (9): *pencil* is certainly the most likely answer, but for the second blank *choice, answer, alternative*, and maybe others are acceptable. The first blank in (10) could be any of a large number of possibilities, such as *appearance, honesty, manner, promise*, etc., and for the second blank, *position, job, promotion*, etc.—lots of possibilities, but not so open-ended as the first blank in sentence (10).

(6a) *Immediate-constituent grammar* analyzes sentences from a text to illustrate, if not explain, the degrees of closeness as words are built up to phrases and ultimately sentences. The experience of working with immediate constituents familiarizes the student with expansion techniques to develop a feel for "structural equivalence" such that the following two sentences can be recognized as illustrations of the same basic sentence structure:

(11)   John   came   home.

(12) The boy has arrived at the house.

It is common knowledge that the grammars briefly mentioned above do not satisfy the linguistic theorists for reasons that have been discussed at great length in other places. Students usually learn their grammar one small piece at a time; they do not need (and indeed could not immediately assimilate) an entire system. Their requirements are better served by a limited explanation that incorporates new data into the students' previously elaborated (interlanguage) system, whatever form it takes. In other words, the ESL or EFL students are learning language, not grammar. There will be time enough to discuss grammatical analysis in graduate school.

Perhaps the term "interlanguage" deserves expansion, since it is an important concept. As the name suggests, it stands between two languages. It is the incomplete form of a second language mastered by a student as he learns. It is an imperfect copy of the target language, through which the student works his way toward proficiency. There are typically several levels of interlanguage. If a student gets discouraged with his rate of achievement, he may quit trying to improve his expression, and his new language is likely to fossilize, stop progressing.

(7a) *Generative grammar*, consisting of phrase structure rules (for rewriting basic sentence structures) and transformational rules (for deriving realignments, expansions, deletions, etc., applied to the basic sentence strings) offer what many contemporary scholars think is a comprehensive set of procedures for a self-consistent grammar that can explain the enormous complexity of natural languages. This is not an ideal place to discuss conceptual linguistic models in detail, since our interest is in applications rather than theoretical purity. It is noted, however, that we don't hesitate to utilize insights offered by "dated" grammars if they promise useful understanding and effective guidance.

The Verb Auxiliary

One example of a genuine contribution of generative grammar to structural understanding is the English verb auxiliary and its relation to numerous kindred structures in the analysis of English. A simple description of a sentence analysis in the form of simple phrase structure rules is

Rule 1.	S	→ NP	+ Pred
Rule 2.	NP	→ Det	+ N
Rule 3.	Pred	→ Aux	+ VP
Rule 4.	VP	→ V	+ ...

Rule 1 says that a S(entence) is made up of a N(oun) P(hrase) and a Pred(icate). The NP that comes before a Pred in simple declarative sentences will be the Subj(ect) of the sentence. But since other NP's in the sentence will be identical in form to the subject, the identical structure will be shown by referring to all of them as NP's.

Rule 2 simply says that NP will be made up of a Det(erminer) and a Noun. Other rules will define "Determiner" as a Definite or Indefinite Article, a Demonstrative, a Possessive, and sometimes, as before a person's name, as nothing at all, or ϕ.

Rule 3 specifies that the immediate constituents of the predicate are the Aux(iliary) and the V(erb) P(hrase), which includes the verb stem and any other constituents of the verb phrase. In English sentences there will always be a verb stem in the verb phrase to enter into a construction with the Aux.

$$\text{Aux} \rightarrow \text{Aux 1} + \text{Aux 2}$$

If we can specify the Aux as having two components, we will have a very powerful and useful generalization, a rule that relates and explains several otherwise "different" constructions. The verb auxiliary is described in the following chart:

The Structure of the English Verb Auxiliary

Components					Constructions	
Aux 1		Aux 2		Stem	Subj	Pred
Te	(Modal)	(Perf)	(Cont)			
1) -d				eat	John	ate.
2) -d	can			eat	John	could eat.
3) -d	can	have + -en		eat	John	could have eaten.
4) -d	can		be + -ing eat		John	could be eating.
5) -d	can	have + -en	be + -ing eat		John	could have been eating.
6) -d		have + -en		eat	John	had eaten.
7) -d		have + -en	be + -ing eat		John	had been eating.
8) -d			be + -ing eat		John	was eating.
9) -d + do				eat	John	*did* eat.

The rewrite "phrase structure" rule that describes the Aux is as follows:

Rule 5.   Aux → Te (+ Modal) (+ Perf) (+ Cont)

This means that every Aux has the component Te(nse) (which will be Past or Non-Past). In the illustrative chart above, Past is selected. In addition to *Tense* the Aux can optionally include any one or any combination of *Modal, Perfect,* or *Continuous* (in that order). Any or all may appear, but none need to.

We have distinguished Aux 1 from Aux 2. Aux 1 is the moveable part of the Aux, as can be seen when Aux 1 is moved to a position before the subject to form yes-no questions (see chart):

    (2) John could eat.   → Could John eat?

    (3) John could have eaten. → Could John have eaten?

    (6) John had eaten.   → Had John eaten?

    (8) John was eating.   → Was John eating?

Note that in 3 only *could* is fronted; *have* stays put, but *have* in 6, now in Aux 1, does move forward.

The same components operate in the same way to produce WH-questions, negation, affirmation, question tags, short answers, etc., showing the essential unity of these structures—which was not previously appreciated. It also explains the overwhelming number of different forms for short answers and tag questions. In spite of seeming complexity, they have all become very simple in their structural conception.

The information listed on the above pages is necessary to understand an analysis of oral communication or oral discourse. In general, what we might call typical patterns of oral communication make use of basic sentence structures (the output of a phrase structure grammar) plus a number of transformations, usually the rather simple ones such as those just mentioned. There are a few other transformations extensively used in oral discourse, such as the incorporation of a sentence functioning as the direct object of the verb *say* or its equivalents, e.g., "He says (that) John is coming; He said for you to come; He mentioned (that) his father loaned him the money," etc.

We will also look at another, special transformational structure with the forbidding name of "pseudo-cleft" sentences. These structures are particularly numerous in oral discourse, so familiarity with them is an important preparation for the student.

But first let's look at several applications of grammar to language learning.

The grammars briefly outlined in this chapter are not equally useful as general statements of what a grammar is and what may be expected of it. Quite the contrary. Most grammarians, now generally called linguists, have written because they felt they could improve on their predecessors' work. And often they have, though some grammars have had weaknesses that showed up after the excitement of the "new" wore off. The main defect charged by the generativists (an important recent school of innovators) is that former studies lack explicitness, that the current descriptive rules could only be utilized by someone who had native-speaker competence, a vague requirement that seemed to indicate a defect in the description of the grammar. But native-speaker competence is precisely what we are attempting to teach, so we can hardly restrict our students to those who already have it.

The "generative" explanation of the English verb *auxiliary* is a great improvement on previous explanations because of its simplicity. There is no need to explain why sometimes a modal, sometimes *have*, and sometimes *be* is moved to the front of a sentence in question form: it's a natural consequence of the ordering of the elements in the Aux: the first that appears on the left gets inverted. The model also explains in a simple way the noncontiguous co-occurrence of forms that seem to be related in the sentence: They are chosen together (*have* + *-en, be* + *-ing,* etc.), but the components separate in the formation of the construction. It further explains affix incorporation and *do*-support. (Affix incorporation refers to the fact that verb affixes are chosen with a preceding verb stem [e.g., *have* + *-en*], but combine with a following verb stem when the sentence is put together. *Do*-support refers to the automatic insertion of *do* when there is no available verb stem for the tense affix to incorporate with [e.g., Past *he eat* = Past + *do* + *he eat* = Did he eat?]. Many such insights are available in a recent pedagogical grammar by Celce-Murcia and Larsen-Freeman (1983).)

Applications of Grammar to Pedagogy

A pedagogical grammar seeks to offer corrections of errors in previous grammars. *Shall/will* is better understood since language scholars have replaced the erroneous (and overly complex) "futurity-determination" rule, and we are no longer encumbered by the preposition-can't-come-at-the-end-of-the-sentence rule.

With new theories of language we have discontinued many of the classroom activities that contributed little to language learning success, such as reciting verb paradigms, quoting rules paying attention to minor patterns for the sake of their rarity (Take a good look at the example; you might not see another for decades!).

Grammar drills have been the weakest component in our teaching. Contrasts like the *will* and *going-to* futures were exchanged for each other in substitution drills without the students' understanding the contrast in meaning. The present perfect was assumed to indicate a completed action in the present, the present progressive was said to describe an action in progress, even when clearly these were not so, and no clear distinction was made between stative and action verbs. Count and mass nouns were not well defined, with mass nouns curiously described as singular in form but plural in meaning. We now have a better idea of how the article system works with nouns. We also have an improved understanding of indefinite and personal pronouns. We are making progress on the definitions of prepositions, to more accurately predict their occurrence.

As a result of other improved grammatical studies, we have a better notion of the relation of the *be*-passive and the *got*-passive, and the limitations of reflexive pronoun construction in English. We have better definitions and descriptions of how our modal and quasi-modal systems work.

Sentence Analysis

Sentence analysis, surprisingly, was one of the strengths of the old school grammars. True, the definitions were not perfect, but teachers and students got along with them. "A noun is the name of a person, place, or thing" is acceptable if we are generous in our definition of *things*. A pronoun is not a word that takes the place of a noun (or we would say "The *he* is coming"), a definition that at best applied only to third-person pronouns, but we tolerated this vagueness. The older style Reed and Kellogg sentence diagramming did quite well at illustrating sentence patterns.

In summary, contemporary second language students of English are much better equipped to learn oral English, and we look forward confidently to more effective instruction in the future, as ESL students learn to knowledgeably interpret what they hear and read and to monitor the production of messages in their new language.

Substitution exercises have undoubtedly been overused in teaching grammar in the past, but they still have a role to fulfill. Many of the concordance patterns required by noun-verb and noun-pronoun correlations are of a mechanical nature that will benefit from familiarizing practice.

The generativists have sought to be explicit, and they have made important gains, but their grammars, technical though they may appear (a characteristic that frightens off many language scholars and teachers), are far from complete, as they will acknowledge. And an incomplete grammar is just as inadequate as an inexplicit one from the language teacher's point of view.

So generative analysis is not the present exclusive best answer to language teaching needs (deciding on an inventory of points/patterns/structures/ functions to be taught, the order in which they should be presented, the relationships that should be emphasized, etc.). So we still rely on practice, precedent, and the inner voice for most of our decisions. Scholars *try* to update their frame of reference, but the result is often a victory for a well-turned phrase rather than a vigorous, significant, testable step forward. So when the process of offering meaningful sentences to improve grammar drills "wears out" and we no longer feel comfortable with the descriptor *realistic*, we think up a new term, such as *contextualized*, which for a time seems more satisfactory, until it becomes too familiar, when we turn to another term: *cognitive, functional*, or what have you.

Sample Illustrative Exercises

We now present sample student activities suggested by the different grammars that have been briefly described.

(1b) *Usage grammar exercises*. Recalling that usage grammar is greatly concerned with correcting or avoiding errors, the activities below illustrate ways to develop awareness. We have chosen to work with two problems of English structure that most second language students find rather difficult: two-word verbs and prepositions.

EXERCISE 6.1

CONGRUENCE JUDGMENTS—TWO-WORD VERBS

Instructions: You will hear ten sentences. Some of them have a mistake; some of them are correct. Write *X* if the sentence has a mistake; write *OK* if the sentence is correct. (Code 2–4)

Example:

a) Here's your coke; drink up it.   X

b) John will be getting in shortly.   OK

Teacher	Student
1. He turned his head and looked the street up.	X
2. She's stepping out tonight.	OK
3. Put down the light when you leave.	X
4. I can cope Brown with, but not his sister.	X
5. The plane took on fuel and took off.	OK
6. He ran across the message months later.	OK
7. Come now; you're putting on me.	X
8. He's not the person I was at looking.	X
9. She stumbled and fell; that brought on it.	X
10. In spite of her promise, she told him on.	X

Some teachers would disapprove of this type of drill because it displays errors, and a few students may somehow remember the erroneous models they have been exposed to, and forget the correct sentences. A good follow-up for this exercise is a discussion of why the items are wrong, and what can be done to make them right, so the student can more effectively monitor his own speaking performance.

EXERCISE 6.2

ERROR IDENTIFICATION
AND CORRECTION—PREPOSITIONS

Instructions: You will hear ten sentences. Some of them are correct; others
have an error of prepositional usage. Write *OK* if the sentence is
correct. When you hear an error, write down the preposition that
is wrong, and alongside, the correction. (Code 3–4)

Example:

a. John will be here by 11:00.   OK

b. He's coming in the 10:30 train.   in → on

Teacher	Student
1. Congratulations on your graduation.	1. OK
2. Now you can get married at your birthday.	2. at → on
3. And you can get a job and be to your own.	3. to → on
4. Where at do you plan to live?	4. at → φ
5. Is that near by the airport?	5. by → φ
6. Hang on a minute till I can look at the map.	6. OK
7. No, it's not close on the airport.	7. on → to
8. Anyway, the big planes are equipped for noise suppressors.	8. for → with
9. Will you have to travel a long distance to work?	9. OK
10. Good luck for your new job.	10. for → on (with)

This exercise is an improvement over the preceding in that it builds a
context, with the sentences forming a loose kind of paragraph.

[Technical note: To assure a correct and consistent model, we suggest that
exercise 6.2 (and probably 6.1) be given from a recording, with the teacher
using the pause button to be sure all students have sufficient time to write the
answer. Alternatively the exercise can be conducted orally, with the teacher
calling on students *after* the item has been spoken or played from the tape.]

(2b) *Signals grammar exercises.* This view of grammar is concerned with
specific grammatical devices that reflect relationships between sentence

components of various kinds. We will present sample exercises for two of these relationships: the affixes that are copied in question tags and a pattern of intonation that identifies subjects and objects.

Question tags can be described by four features: (1) Aux 1 is copied in its full (noncontracted) form, (2) the subject is copied as a pronoun, (3) application of the Subj-Aux inversion rule (the Aux is moved to a position in front of the subject), and (4) application of the polarity rule (switching positive and negative in the tag to oppose the statement).

Many speakers of languages from India are accustomed to an invariable question tag; they are notorious for using a single tag in English, "isn't it," regardless of what the grammar calls for. They could perhaps benefit from the following exercise.

EXERCISE 6.3

VARIANT FORMS OF QUESTION TAGS

Instructions: Change the following statements to tag questions. (Code 3–4)

1. He'd do it if he could.
2. She'll come in first.
3. John can't go tomorrow.
4. He went wherever he wanted to.

5. He ate what he could.
6. You're having a party.
7. I think I'm expected to come.

8. You've finished the guest list.

9. You won't be needing me.
10. You want to come.

1. He'd do it if he could, wouldn't he?
2. She'll come in first, won't she?
3. John can't go tomorrow, can he?
4. He went wherever he wanted to, didn't he?
5. He ate what he could, didn't he?
6. You're having a party, aren't you?
7. I think I'm expected to come, aren't I?
8. You've finished the guest list, haven't you?
9. You won't be needing me, will you?
10. You want to come, don't you?

Note that in No. 7 the speaker avoids the negative with *am* (ain't, amp't) etc., and settles for the plural marked *are*.

This exercise is somewhat mechanical and tedious. But it is complex, and a good teacher knows that it takes a lot of practice to inculcate a new pattern, especially one that is complex. We should keep in mind the meaning of the tag questions, and especially in oral discourse recognize a difference in meaning that corresponds to the two common intonation patterns which tag questions appear with. The teacher-model sentences simply state a fact, and are assumed to be accurate statements. If the tag is pronounced on a rising intonation, the speaker is signaling that he doesn't know if it's a true statement and he wishes to have that information.

He's coming.   He's coming, isn't he?   (I don't know; please tell me.)

If the tag is pronounced with a falling intonation:

He's coming, isn't he?   (Please confirm my assumption.)

the speaker assumes he has correct information and only wants confirmation. A "no" answer would not be too much of a surprise to the first questioner, but would to the second. An alternate form of this exercise could be cued by directed instructions to ask:

"Tell her he'd do it if he could, and then ask 'wouldn't he?'."

The next exercise illustrates the importance of intonation in interpreting the meaning of sentences. It demands understanding, or confusion results:

EXERCISE 6.4

INTONATION AS A SIGNAL

Instructions: Listen to the tape and copy down the one numeral that the teacher corrects for the following two groups of telephone numbers. Compare the number of errors made in the first group of six to the number in the second group of six. (Code 3–5)

Student Voices	Teacher	Student's Copy Correction
1. Is Doug's telephone number 505-8876?	No, it's 505-8886.	_____
2. Is Chris's number 462-6188?	No, it's 472-6188.	_____
3. Is Donna's number 642-5360?	No, it's 641-5360.	_____
4. Is Russ's number 472-8234?	No, it's 472-8134.	_____
5. Is Evelyn's number 371-8772?	No, it's 271-8772.	_____
6. Is Marianne's number 829-2051?	No, it's 829-3051.	_____
7. Is Dora's number 522-0298?	No, it's 522-0198.	_____
8. Is Mel's number 965-0287?	No, it's 966-0287.	_____
9. Is Al's number 477-2324?	No, it's 577-2324.	_____

10. Is Lisa's number 344-4746?   No, it's 344-4745.   _____

11. Is Edie's number 920-3089?   No, it's 920-3099.   _____

12. Is Jim's number 921-8078?   No, it's 923-8078.   _____

[Technical note: These should be recorded at a brisk pace to insure that the student will more likely rely on the contrastive stress as marked by underlines.]

If you follow a typical student through this exercise, especially if he relies on contrastive stress, as authentic English speakers normally do, he probably made more errors on the second group of six.

(3b) *Slot-and-filler grammar exercises.* This view of English grammar has had a significant effect on language teaching. Just as the analyst attempts to identify important patterns—those with the widest application—the classroom manager takes the same slots and fillers and makes them into substitution drills. A very typical application is referred to as substitution frames.

EXERCISE 6.5

SUBSTITUTION FRAMES

Instructions: By choosing items from each of the six columns, see how many well-formed sentences you can construct. (Code 2–3)

1	2	3	4	5	6
My	father	bought	a	car	last Sunday
	uncle	won		boat	in 1979
	teacher	found		camper	earlier today
Her	mother	sold	an	overcoat	φ

If our calculations are accurate, over 500 sentences can be formed by the 19 slot fillers listed on just four lines. Column 4 is the only one in this frame that requires an obligatory choice—between *a* and *an*, determined by the phonetic feature of a vowel or consonant sound at the beginning of the next following word. The zero given as the last item in column 6 sanctions the omission of the adverb slot.

While all the sentences formed from this table are well-formed (i.e., grammatical), not all are equally useful. Few of us are ever going to "find" a boat or camper or car (unless the context involves finding one to purchase).

"Painted" might have been a more productive choice for the third item in column 3, but then "overcoat" would be a problem.

A striking impression that comes from this exercise is the infinitely large number of patterns one would have to recognize and practice to get even a minimal view of English grammar.

Of course it is not necessary to fill every slot in a substitution exercise. Sometimes we change words in only one slot (simple substitution). Sometimes a change in one slot requires a change in another (not surprisingly called correlative substitution). These latter are useful for practicing concordance patterns.

EXERCISE 6.6

CORRELATIVE SUBSTITUTION

Instructions: You will be given substitutions for the first word in the sentences below. Make two other changes that will be necessary to produce well-formed sentences. (Code 3–5)

Teacher	Student
1. John told Miss Heffernan he would bring his assignment tomorrow.	John told Miss Heffernan he would bring his assignment tomorrow.
2. Jane	Jane told Miss Heffernan she would bring her assignment tomorrow.
3. The class	The class told Miss Heffernan they would bring their assignment tomorrow.
4. I	I told Miss Heffernan I would bring my assignment tomorrow.
5. You and John	You and John told Miss Heffernan you would bring your assignment tomorrow.
6. Jim and I	Jim and I told Miss Heffernan we would bring our assignment tomorrow.

These drills have a major defect. They're not contextualized; they are mechanical constructions that can be called out in class without students necessarily understanding their message, which is in any case minimal and uninteresting. It might bring the class back to life to insert at some point in the drill a few questions that the class, or the best students at least, could answer ~erving the truth factor:

1. Who's Miss Heffernan, Bill? I don't know.
2. What do we know about her? That she's a teacher.
3. Right. Anything else? Maybe that she's understanding, that she sometimes is willing to give her students another day on their homework.
4. Very good answer, Bill.

It can be very salubrious to insert even a modest communication element to keep students on their toes.

(4b) *Finite-state grammar exercises*. This grammar has perhaps contributed less to current methodology than have the others discussed above. But it does show that people often hear what they expect to hear and what the context suggests they should hear, regardless of the actual utterance. An illustrative exercise can show this:

EXERCISE 6.7

EXPECTATIONS IN CONTEXT

Instructions: Listen to the following sentences, and when called on, repeat what you have heard. Your teacher will at times ask for confirmation of your interpretations. (Code 4–6)

Teacher	Student
1. I like a nice cream dessert. Repeat, Nita.	I like an ice cream dessert.
a. How many agree with Nita?	(Show of hands)
b. How many disagree?	(Show of hands)
c. What did you hear, Alicia?	I like a nice cream dessert.
d. How would you say that to emphasize the words that are different in yours and Nita's interpretations?	I like a *nice* cream dessert.
2. He often wears a skirt and tie. (As for no. 1)	
d. What made you think you heard *shirt*?	The use of the pronoun "he."
3. Soup's on. Let's seat, everybody.	
4. I don't see much of them. They come in fréquently in the summer.	
5. How many were in the pie-eating context? Any reasonable answer, Anu.	
6. Well, how did you do on the mid-term text?	

Note that while we classify this relationship of expectation as grammatical, it most often involves an error in interpretation based on mishearing a juncture ("a nice . . ." versus "an ice . . ."), or a mistaken lexical identification because of co-occurrence probabilities ("soup's on" with "let's eat"; "he" with "shirt," etc.), though of course the gender association in the latter is at least partly grammatical. Actually students are doing what we want them to do: letting associations help them in understanding oral language. But they must do it efficiently.

In any case this type of exercise should not be overused, rather should be administered in short doses, usually when unexpected. If the students become suspicious, they will be more alert to inconsistencies in the grammar and lexicon. When students perform satisfactorily, you should still ask the "cornering" questions (that reveal whether or not they caught the inconsistency) so that querying won't become a clue by default.

(5b) *Immediate-constituent grammar exercises.* IC grammar, or phrase structure grammar as it is also called, describes quite satisfactorily sentence constituents that are adjacent to each other. Its concept of "slots" is much more flexible than slot-and-filler grammar. An immediate constituent may be a single word, like "he," or much more complex, as in "the other old man sitting on the bench."

We can start our analysis with a sentence described as consisting of a subject and a predicate. Virtually all English sentences start (in immediate constituent analysis) with this structure:

Subject + *Predicate*

The train   runs fast.

We now specify a form for subject: Det(erminer) *the* and N(oun) *train.* Likewise for the predicate: Intran(sitive) V(erb) *runs* and Adv(erb) *fast.* Other constituents could be derived from Subj or Pred, such as "I" and "ran in the marathon yesterday." Both example sentences are included in the structure "Intransitive Predication" with subclasses (not independent slots) to be described by further identification of constituents. An effective pattern to utilize IC elements in an exercise is what we call a "Moving-slot substitution exercise." An example follows:

EXERCISE 6.8

MOVING-SLOT SUBSTITUTION

Instructions: Listen to your teacher's pronunciation of a sentence; then repeat it yourself. Then listen for words or phrases that can be inserted in the original sentence to replace comparable words or phrases. The material inserted may or may not "trigger" additional changes elsewhere in the sentence. (Code 4–6)

1. The   old   man   walked slowly   down the lane.
2. _____ across the street.
3. _____ young _____ .
4. _____ briskly _____ .
5. _____ girl _____ .
6. _____ marched _____ .
7. _____ soldiers _____ .
8. _____ .
9. _____ up the hill.
10. _____ climbed _____ .
11. _____ .
12. _____ leisurely _____ .
13. _____ strolled _____ .

This type of drill fails to fulfill the congruence requirements of a good exercise. It is somewhat akin to parlor games, and like these games, it is a test of mental agility. Keep in mind that the student hears the original sentence and the clues. He has to figure out where the word or phrase goes by judging the best fit for the placement of the new cue item on the basis of the message given. If the last sentence heard is:

The young man walked briskly across the street

and the cue is "girl," we would expect:

The young girl walked briskly across the street,

and not:

The young man walked briskly across the girl

even though "girl" as a noun could, grammatically speaking, fit either slot. In practice this is seldom a problem, even though the student doesn't have a chart showing by alignment which word or phrase is to be replaced.

We might ask if this exercise is worth spending time on, since it often lacks congruence. We'd say it surely shouldn't be overdone, but an occasional exercise will add interest, will keep the class's attention, and it's fun.

Another kind of exercise that reflects IC grammar (and Audiolingual pedagogy) is a translation-cued pattern exercise. It is used in the exercise that follows so that the cues will not give away the English pronoun forms that constitute the learning point, the raison d'être of the exercise.

EXERCISE 6.9

POSSESSIVE FORMS IN ENGLISH

Instructions: Translate the following brief exchanges from Spanish to English. (Code 2–4)

Teacher		Student	
1. ¿Es éste su libro de él?	Sí, es suyo.	Is this his book?	Yes, it's his.
2. ¿Es éste su libro de ella?	Sí, es suyo.	Is this her book?	Yes, it's hers.
3. ¿Es ésta su pluma de él?	Sí, es suya.	Is this his pen?	Yes, it's his.
4. ¿Es ésta su pluma de ella?	Sí, es suya.	Is this her pen?	Yes, it's hers.
5. ¿Es éste su coche de ellos?	Sí, es suyo.	Is this their car?	Yes, it's theirs.
6. ¿Es éste su coche de ellas?	Sí, es suyo.	Is this their car?	Yes, it's theirs.
7. ¿Es ésta su casa de ellos?	Sí, es suya.	Is this their house?	Yes, it's theirs.
8. ¿Es ésta su casa de ellas?	Sí, es suya.	Is this their house?	Yes, it's theirs.
9. ¿Es éste su libro de usted?	Sí, es mío.	Is this your book?	Yes, it's mine.
10. ¿Es ésta su pluma de usted?	Sí, es mía.	Is this your pen?	Yes, it's mine.
11. ¿Es éste mi libro?	Sí, es suyo.	Is this my book?	Yes, it's yours.
12. ¿Es ésta mi pluma?	Sí, es suya.	Is this my pen?	Yes, it's yours.

This exercise illustrates the disparate application of the concept of gender in the possessive constructions of Spanish and English: In Spanish the gender class of the thing possessed is marked while in English it is the gender class of the possessor that is made explicit. Giving the performance clues in Spanish leaves the students responsible for producing both English forms: the short and the long, whereas if the pattern were cued in English, the student could easily provide the second form mechanically from the first. Note that when first or second person pronouns are used their contextualization must be assumed by an appropriate change in person reference.

(6b) *Generative grammar exercises.* Most of these exercises related to grammars are intended to illuminate grammatical features that are analytical rather than communicative. Perhaps that's inevitable or at least most likely in a discussion of grammatical structures and relationships. We can ask if we should be studying grammar, when the main purpose of the training is to learn to communicate in a new code. If we are to justify the study of grammar, we need to understand how it contributes to communication when two language structures differ extensively. Such an explanation is noted in the use of reflexives in English and other languages. In English the reflexive is applied only to animate nouns (as subjects); in Spanish there is no such restriction: inanimate nouns are quite welcome in a reflexive sentence. English speakers fail to understand the grammatical basis for the difference and have been known to criticize Spanish speakers as irresponsible, since they use a Spanish construction that literally translates "The vase broke itself; The key lost itself," curiously forgetting that the same result could be claimed for the equivalent English expressions which employ the *got*-passive: "The vase got broke(n); The key got lost." Grammatical analysis can help us see and explain such apparent anomalies, and a patterned translation exercise can show the equivalence and explain the difference in the application of the reflexive in the two languages.

Generative analysis has claimed that immediate constituent patterns are not adequate for analyzing natural language; two illustrative sentences have become famous as examples of this inadequacy:

> Mary is easy to please.
> Mary is eager to please.

The sentences are almost identical, with common members in slots 1, 2, 4, 5, and both with high-frequency adjectives in slot 3. Yet the native speaker intuitively feels that they are representatives of different patterns, and he is proved right when transformed sentences are tested. Only one of the two can take an *it*-transformation:

> It is easy to please Mary.   To please Mary is easy.
>   or
> *It is eager to please Mary.   *To please Mary is eager.

Another example of the difference:

> Mary pleases easily.
> *Mary pleases eagerly.

An example that puts the shoe on the other foot:

> *Mary is easy to please her friends.
> Mary is eager to please her friends.

The following exercise expands the pattern:

EXERCISE 6.10

EASY–EAGER

Instructions: Beginning with two sentences (see examples *a* and *b* below), we have added on a further comment that specifies whether Mary or someone else has done the painting. When you hear another adjective, use it to replace "easy" and "eager." Then add an appropriate comment that tells whether Mary or someone else did the painting. (Code 5–6)

Examples:

a. Mary is easy to paint. Many people have painted her.
b. Mary is eager to paint. She has painted many people.

Teacher	Student
1. . . . anxious . . .	Mary is anxious to paint. She's always painting.
2. . . . hard . . .	Mary is hard to paint. Still, many have tried to paint her.
3. . . . impossible . . .	Mary is impossible to paint. Many have tried, but no one has done a satisfactory job.
4. . . . difficult . . .	Mary is difficult to paint. It takes a real artist to paint her well.
5. . . . easy to fool . . .	Mary is easy to fool. Anyone can mislead her.
6. . . . anxious to fool . . .	Mary is anxious to fool. She loves to deceive people.
7. . . . hard to fool . . .	Mary is hard to fool. It's very difficult to mislead her.

The grammar of spoken English naturally has much in common with the grammar of written English. It is after all the same language in each case. But there are differences, and a discussion of these differences may clarify what is acceptable in each medium.

One way to change speakers that is very typical of spoken discourse is for the current speaker to signal that he has finished and is making the floor available. This can be done by asking a serious question to which an answer is expected (i.e., not a rhetorical question asked merely for effect). Depending on the kind of question, the floor may be surrendered temporarily (e.g., a yes-no question by an attorney examining a witness in court), or more or less permanently (e.g., when a question like "What do you think?" is asked). The appropriate signal for a change in speakers is either /↑/ (final rising juncture) or /↓/ (final falling juncture). The /↑/ is limited to yes-no questions, the /↓/ to statements and other kinds of questions (WH, choice, etc.).

A hanging juncture / | / (neither rising nor falling) signals that the speaker has not finished and is not offering to surrender the floor. It was noted that the infamous Joe McCarthy, the senatorial witch-hunter of the 1950s, when before any kind of public where he could gain publicity, used a very small number of change-of-speaker signals; he preferred the speaker's role because that way he could more completely control the line and content of communication.

But McCarthy is not the only speaker to give up the floor reluctantly. And listeners, at least when there is an interesting discussion going on, are often eager and anxious to become speakers. To stake a claim on the floor, a "candidate" will often offer a quick if tentative "You know" at the slightest opportunity (brief break in the speaker's performance) to see if he can gain the initiative and say what he wants to. The current speaker may be easy or difficult to "interrupt," depending on his personality, enthusiasm for the subject under discussion, etc. It occasionally happens that an unsuccessful would-be speaker tries several times, with the discourse moving to other subjects or aspects, and when he finally gets the floor, he has forgotten what he wanted to say, or his contribution, if he makes it, is "dated," i.e., about something the conversation moved beyond.

Assurance of Attention

The speaker in informal conversation, even if he is long-winded, may feel a need to be assured he has an attentive audience. One way to get this assurance is to ask for it; the speaker interjects an occasional "You know" or "You know what I mean," to which he expects a short response of "Yes"; or more likely, an "Uh huh" is adequate, and the speaker can continue with confidence that he is being listened to. Of course a listener may show he's attentive by nodding his head in affirmation, or just looking interested. A test of the validity of this pattern can easily be made in a telephone conversation. If vocal feedback is not offered to the speaker almost once per sentence, he'll assume that contact has been interrupted and will ask something like "Are you still there?" If there is no answer to this specific query, he'll hang up.

Oral "Punctuation"

So the "You know . . ." interjection has two functions: to test one's request or claim for the speaker's role, and to delay the transmission of any important information until the would-be speaker is assured that he does indeed have an audience. These are characteristics of oral communication, a species of "oral punctuation," that fulfill important functions which are handled in other ways and are therefore not necessary or relevant in written communication.

There are characteristic ways of "italicizing" in oral discourse. One is to separately phrase a word (or words) to be emphasized, giving it a special

meaning. Thus to say "He's a | fine | friend" means "he is a *false* friend," i.e., no friend at all. Contrastive stress typically accompanies this kind of separation of an element from the main content. There are special phrases designed or intended to alert the listener to the fact something especially important is about to be said. The politician's "Let's make one thing perfectly clear" is an example. Other people are usually more subtle, saying something like "To put it bluntly," "To tell the truth," "To say it once and for all," etc. These are actually fixed phrases which serve as *oral emphasizers*. We would rarely use comparable but unsanctioned expressions for this purpose, such as "To recognize the facts," "To inform you accurately," "To supply important information," in informal oral communication.

Along with the oral emphasizers, and having a similar function, are the *oral summarizers*: "To make a long story short," which implies "I am leaving out details that are not too important anyway." A comparable expression alludes to a corporate report, using the expression "bottom line," such as "In any case the bottom line is . . ."

Some speakers insert paragraph markers in their discourse, especially inexperienced teachers when lecturing. These will consist usually of "OK" or "Now." They can be useful as signals of transitions in the discourse, but if, as often happens, they get to be too numerous, they lose their effect and become conspicuous and bothersome.

Simple Transformations

Another characteristic of spoken discourse is a limitation on the complexity of sentence pattern used. This limitation, however, has its own limits. It would be convenient if we could report that basic sentence patterns (simple declarative statements which have had no transformations in their derivation: the output of a phrase structure grammar) and simple transformations were used for oral communication and more complex transformations were employed (along with basic patterns) in written discourse. But the facts are not that simple. Some transformations are widely used in oral discourse: negation, yes-no question, WH-question, affirmation, *there*-inversion, question tags, short answers, the *got*-passive, etc. Between oral and written style, or perhaps between the informal and formal style levels to which these so often correspond, are the two-word verbs, with much more frequent use in oral discourse. We have, however, assumed that these are lexical questions, which therefore will be considered in the next chapter, on vocabulary use in the oral language.

Another example that needs to be added to the generalization that simpler forms are typical of the spoken language is the observation that sentences appearing as the direct object in sentences after main verbs like *say, tell*, etc., are very common in oral discourse. This is true of quoted speech: "He said, 'I'll be there early tomorrow,' " and even more so of reported speech: "He said he'd be there early tomorrow." More formal speech assignment, with verbs like "reported, observed, remarked," etc., is more at home in written discourse.

The Pseudo-Cleft or WH-Nominalization Construction

There is one sentence transformation that is surprisingly complex but still has made itself at home in oral discourse. It is the transformation called "pseudo-cleft" by some analysts, "*WH*-Nominalization'" or "*what*-displacement" by others. It seems to serve the same purpose as the politician's "Now let's make this perfectly clear." It supplies "thinking time" without seeming to, because the speaker *is speaking*, though of course saying nothing.

In form the pseudo-cleft or *what*-displacement is an equational sentence, as a first step adding *be* to establish the equation, and in a second step adding the pro-verb *do* to the left side of the equation, holding a place for the verb phrase of the original sentence. This is complicated but can be explained by an example:

Original Basic Sentence	*Pseudo-cleft Transformations*
1. They'll probably send an investigating committee.	Form A: What they'll probably send is an investigating committee.
	Form B: What they'll probably do is send an investigating committee.

The pseudo-cleft functions to place the hearer's attention on the second sentence of the constituent pair that combine to form a single sentence, but one that is much more complex. Form A is of limited usefulness, can be derived from only certain sentences, and is not much used. Form B is very widely employed in oral discourse. Let's practice some of these:

EXERCISE 6.11

PSEUDO-CLEFT TRANSFORMATIONS

Instructions: You will hear a sentence. Make it a pseudo-cleft sentence by adding at the beginning "What we'll do is . . ." Then include the verb phrase from the sentence you started with. (Code 5–6)

Example:

Teacher	Student
a. We'll sell the car.	What we'll do is sell the car.

Teacher	Student
1. We'll call for an ambulance.	What we'll do is call for an ambulance.
2. We'll try to avoid excessive court costs.	What we'll do is try to avoid excessive court costs.
3. The lawyer will try to get involved.	What the lawyer will do is try to get involved.

4. We'll defend the case without outside legal counsel.

What we'll do is defend the case without outside legal counsel.

5. We'll study all the precedent cases.

What we'll do is study all the precedent cases.

It has been suggested that the pseudo-cleft is used to give prominence to the important part of the sentence by providing a nonconspicuous background, thus "foregrounding" the information content of the original sentence. In addition to this "grammatical" device to gain prominence, the same effect can be achieved by "phonological" signals, in this case by contrastive stress:

Thèy'll prôbably sénd an invéstigàting commîttee.

The two features that identify contrastive stress are present in the above sentence: pitch 4 on the syllable(s) to be highlighted, and immediately thereafter a drop to pitch 1 for the remainder of the sentence. Other ways to call special attention to a concept in a context utilize pacing, intensity, pitch shift, etc. While they are more subtle and therefore more difficult to describe, they are also much less important.

Filled Pauses

Oral discourse is often characterized by filled pauses which are spelled "uh," or in r-less dialects, "er." In either case they represent a prolonged pronunciation of schwa. Overuse of this really meaningless feature becomes conspicuous and distracting, getting in the way of good communication. One American secondary school teacher we knew had the habit of overusing a "filled" pause, vocalizing the schwa. To assure survival and the retention of sanity, his students used to contribute a dime each to a kitty, the total amount to go to the student who guessed most accurately how many times their teacher would use this /ə/ during the class hour. Pencils moved unanimously toward the tally sheets at the appropriate minutes, to collect the data needed to award the kitty. We remember the hesitation phenomena, but not the subject of his lectures.

Normal Deletion Patterns

A final feature of oral communication, one of considerable importance, is the use of deletion and pronominalization. Oral communication, especially on an informal level, illustrates this. Note the following oral discourse:

Jeff: Jack, you've got an economics textbook, haven't you got an economics textbook?

Jack: Yes, I've got an economics textbook. Do you want to see my economics textbook?

Jeff: Yes, I want to see your economics textbook, and I would like to borrow your economics textbook for a couple of hours. Could I borrow your economics textbook for two hours?

Jack: I need to consult my economics textbook to do an assignment my teacher has made in my economics textbook for my class in economics. When I finish my assignment, you are welcome to borrow my economics textbook.

This atrocity is alleviated somewhat when allowable deletions and pronominalizations are used.

Jeff: Jack, you've got an economics textbook, haven't you?
Jack: Yes, I've got one. Do you want to see it?
Jeff: Yes, I'd like to borrow it for a couple of hours.
Jack: I need it to do an assignment. When I finish, you're welcome to borrow it.

The second version is different in two important ways. Identical material is either pronominalized or deleted when a back reference is made. The noun phrase including "economics textbook" appears ten times in the first conversation, once in the second, the initial reference. But in the second version, "one" appeared once and "it" four times. There were other deletions justified by removing conspicuous redundancy.

Let's have an exercise on deletion:

EXERCISE 6.12

DELETION OF REDUNDANT INFORMATION

Instructions: Write the following selections on a piece of paper. Then circle or underline the items you think should be deleted. (Code 4–6)

1a. Did you bring your lunch?
 b. Yes, *I brought my lunch*. How about you, *did you bring your lunch*?
 a. Yes, *I brought my lunch*. Let's eat *our lunches*.
 b. *Do you* think we'll have time to go to the post office before the whistle blows?
 a. *Yes*, I think so, *we'll have time to go to the post office before the whistle blows*.
2a. *Are you* going home for Christmas this year, Sal?
 b. I don't know yet *if I'm going home for Christmas this year*, Jan. I like to *go home for Christmas*, but it is very expensive *to go home for Christmas*.
 a. Yes, it is *expensive to go home for Christmas*. But Christmas comes only once a year.
 b. That's what my family says, *that Christmas comes only once a year*. But my family says the same thing about Thanksgiving, Easter, and Memorial Day: *they come only once a year*.

An alert student might sometime notice that a full repetition of a sentence is made in context, where he might have assumed that a deletion would be in order. An example is:

Younger brother: Did yôu cleàn úp thàt mêss in the garage?

Older brother: Yés Ì clêaned úp thàt mêss in the garáge.

There is a sharp tone of annoyance in the answer of the older brother. He is saying that the younger brother should have cleaned the garage, that he was somehow responsible, but failed to accept his obligation. It is the contrastively stressed repetition that carries this information.

Deletion of Grammatical Slots

A different deletion pattern can be seen in conversation, involving the participants. Since the subject is predictably *you* (normally in questions) and *I* (normally in answers), it can be and frequently is omitted along with *have* and *be* from the aspect markers *have + en* and *be + ing*. So an expression like "Gonna go to the football game this weekend?" or "Been working long?" can be answered "Been thinking about it" or "Been busy all day." Likewise, "Coming with me?" can be answered "Be right there." In the first of these two *Are* and *you* are missing; in the second *I* and the modal *will* are omitted. And of course when the first verb stem is gone, the tense marker is also missing. In an alternate deletion pattern *you* is retained but the first part of the Aux drops out: "You coming?"

Let's try some examples of these patterns:

EXERCISE 6.13

RESTORING DELETED FORMS

Instructions: Write the corresponding full sentence for each of the following sentences that have been shortened by optional deletions. (Code 3–5)

1a. Gonna study tonight for tomorrow's test? — Are you going to study tonight for tomorrow's test?

b. You gonna study tonight? — Are you going to study tonight?

c. Think I will, at least a little. — I think I will, at least a little.

d. Hope to be able to, at least once over lightly. — I hope to be able to, at least once over lightly.

2a. Wonder who that is jogging.
  b. Looks like it might be Darwin.
  c. Suppose it does any good?
  d. Probably does; he's overweight, you know.
3a. Well, gotta go; it's late.
4a. Drat it! Left my key in the car and locked all the doors.
5a. You eaten yet?
  b. Yeah, just finished.
  c. Got anything left?
  d. Had an apple, but I ate it.

I wonder who that is jogging.
It looks like it might be Darwin.
Do you suppose it does any good?
It probably does; he's overweight, you know.
Well, I gotta go; it's late.
Drat it! I left my key in the car and locked all the doors.
Have you eaten yet?
Yes, I (have) just finished.
Have you got anything left?
I had an apple, but I ate it.

These sentence forms are not recommended for the active oral skills of a second language student. But they do occur, so the student should be alerted and given a few illustrative exercises.

Miscellany

The oral language sometimes provides more information and sometimes less than the written. Punctuation is represented rather vaguely in oral form whereas in writing many details can be distinguished, as for example in *man–Mann*, the identical-sounding common noun and person name. Another example can be seen in the noun paradigm. Based on the fullest form, English nouns have two categories (number and possession) to produce four contrasting forms:

	Singular		*Plural*	
	Nominative	*Possessive*	*Nominative*	*Possessive*
	man	man's	men	men's
	boy	boy's	boys	boys'

The pattern with four distinct forms is usually taught in school grammar classes for both *man*-type and *boy*-type forms, though the same information interpreted by ear reveals a quite different pattern for *boy*:

mæn	mænz	mɛn	mɛnz
boy		boyz	

In spite of standardized grammatical assumptions and descriptions, speakers of English manage for a great majority of the count nouns in the language to get along successfully with only two forms of nouns rather than the four traditionally listed.

One reason we study grammar is to clarify distinctions we often do not have clearly in our consciousness. Thus we have to learn that, against what should be a reasonable expectation, the word *must* has completely different meanings in:

> John must go.
> John must have gone.

Another example of a pair of closely similar expressions that must be separately learned and applied:

> Pancho is used to eating beans.   (They're his staple food.)
> Pancho used to eat beans.   (He quit some years ago.)

Note the further complication if an error appears in the sentence:

> *Pancho is used to eat beans!   (?)

Other problems of a grammatical nature arise in learning the spoken language. One that regularly appears is the concordance pattern between predicates and complex subjects, as in:

> One of the students is coming to take you to the library.

The noun *students* occupies the usual subject position and appears to govern the number agreement with the following verb, producing:

> *One of the students are coming to take you to the library.

This error can be treated by removing the phrase "of the students" and then asking the student to pronounce the rest of the sentence. If he understands the concordance rules, he'll change from *are* to *is*. Then restore the phrase "of the students" and the student will probably see the error and correct it.

One of the strong and valid reasons we study grammar is to have the descriptive experience which allows us to correct errors on the basis of familiarity with the rules and subrules that explain the constructions that make up the sentences of English.

Sometimes the apparent and true subjects can be very distant from each other:

> One of the men coming down the street with the Memorial Day parade that honors the nation's soldiers is my father.

But the concordance rule still applies.

And it of course works the other way too, with the noun near the verb singular and the more distant true subject plural:

> The men, each with a son and daughter enrolled in the school, were very anxious to talk to the principal.

Three singular nouns (*school, daughter*, and *son*) are closer to the verb, but the true subject is *men*, almost two lines back. Note, however, that two simple nouns, each singular, tied together with *and* regularly become plural and require a plural verb form:

> The boy and his little sister were slowly approaching the school although they were already late.

In this sentence, two singulars make a plural.

This problem will also appear in the written language, perhaps as a pattern even more difficult to correct, because written sentences are often longer and more complex. But the student has more time to consider when he is writing—the monitor doesn't have to work quite as fast where rereading and polishing are possible.

SUMMARY

We have seen something of the application of "standard" grammar to oral use and we've seen how the grammar that applies to oral discourse is sometimes different from the grammar observed in written discourse—and we will see this again when we reach Chapter Eleven. It would be well to remember, however, that there are parameters other than oral and written, and that it is possible to speak "written discourse" (as in formal lectures) and to write "spoken discourse" (as in personal letters, comic strips), etc. In other words, formality levels can be discerned in both spoken and written English, though it is more common to see formal English in written form and to hear informal English in spoken form.

DISCUSSION

1. Why would it be logical to treat the grammar of the written language before the grammar of the spoken language?

2. In what way are we justified in referring to English grammars instead of English grammar? Discuss the ways different definitions of grammar serve different pedagogical purposes.

3. Explain the verb auxiliary structure to someone who has been taught a more traditional explanation of how the auxiliary works.

4. Discuss some of the changes in how grammar is taught that have been inspired by modern grammatical studies.

5. Illustrate the kinds of exercises that reflect different approaches to grammar.

6. What is a moving-slot substitution drill? In what way is it a mechanical exercise? What skill does it develop?

7. Tell what the limiting feature of the English reflexive is.

8. Discuss change-of-speaker and assurance-of-attention signals.

9. Discuss the simple transformations that are frequently used in oral communication.

10. Explain the meaning and use of "filled pauses." How do they affect the efficiency of communication?

CHAPTER SEVEN

VOCABULARY—
ORAL LANGUAGE

INTRODUCTION

The term *word* is without doubt the most universally recognized of the technical terms used by linguists, language teachers, and the educated public, when there is a need to talk about language. The concept *word* and the term to refer to this concept are indispensable to our understanding of the linguistic process.

As dictionary makers well know, the term *word* may be easy to perceive, but is hard to define. Note the problem in the following attempt at the most general meaning (Webster's New World, second college edition, 1978): "a speech sound, or a series of them, serving to communicate meaning and consisting of at least one base morpheme with or without prefixes or suffixes but with a superfix." The writer continues with a more technical definition that is still less precise: "unit of language between the morpheme and the complete utterance." This definition fails to distinguish *word* from *phrase* or *clause*, even in traditional analysis.

The definition for a written word is no improvement, deriving as it does from the definition of an oral word, thus maintaining the level of technical exposition, but with a note of vagueness expressed by the weasel word "usually": "a letter or group of letters representing such a unit of language, written or printed usually in solid or hyphenated form." Where, we wonder, is the lexicographer's rule that the definition should use simpler language than the term being defined? To benefit from these definitions, the dictionary user must already understand: speech sound, base morpheme, prefix, suffix, superfix, complete utterance, unit, solid form, hyphenated form.

The definition for a written word suggests that it is marked by space in running, written text. This turns out to be the most useful part of the definition, though it suggests that word recognition is related to literacy. But nonliterates can also identify words, so recognition is not exclusively visual.

Compared to the very small number of sounds, the limited number of morphological patterns, the restricted number of basic syntactic constructions, the number of words is very great, indeed—far more than any one person is capable of learning. Teachers have to select from this mass the words that will be most useful to their students.

Structure Words and Content Words

Vocabulary concepts apply to different segments of the lexicon. At their most basic level, words of two kinds can be differentiated: *structure* and *content*. Structure words, also called "function words," are often included as part of the grammar of the language. They are limited in number (not more than a couple of hundred) and are often understood through the relational features they express (pronoun *he* stands for the most recent male in the context; preposition *of* indicates the relationship between container and contents in an expression like "a bottle *of* milk"; modal *could* is part of the verb auxiliary expressing ability or possibility; article *the* attests to the definiteness of focus on a specific individual in "*the* man"; etc.). Structure words are a closed class. It is very rare for a new one to be added to the language.

Structure words are learned early—in part because they recur so frequently, but more importantly because a reasonable sample of them *must* be mastered for a student to comprehend readily and speak meaningfully in any context. They are the mortar that holds the content-word bricks together, with specific patterns indicating relationships between the lexical meanings of the content words, so information can be exchanged.

Exact percentages of structure words vary with the kind of text one considers. The specific words and the order of their occurrence also depend on the text. The pronoun *I*, for example, is much more frequent in the speech of preschool children and in fairy tales than in scientific reporting.

How do we decide which words to include in our language teaching? One suggestion, and it is very appealing, is to teach the words that are most useful, assuming these will be the same as those most used. We can count all the words in a substantial and representative sample of the English language and from it find out what words to teach and in what order to teach them. A number of word counts have been made for precisely this (and for other) purposes. But there are serious questions that must be answered before we can confidently accept the results of the word counts.

Types and Tokens

When one thinks of word counts, there are two ways to look at words, referred to as *types* and *tokens*. Types are what you would get if you counted the entries in a dictionary; tokens are what you would get if you counted the words in a novel. A vocabulary count for pedagogical purposes is interested in both. The types are an inventory of words used in a speech event or a writing. They can be listed alphabetically for convenience in locating a particular word. But in word counts they are by tradition listed by frequency, i.e., by the number of tokens each word has, with the list arranged from most frequent to least frequent.

Let's examine a recent count by Kučera and Francis (1967), which makes possible some interesting comparisons:

Total words in corpus	1,014,232	(the "tokens")
Different words in corpus	50,406	(the "types")

The type-token ratio for this count is 20.12: each word in the "dictionary" of the count appears on an average of just over twenty times.

But they are not spread evenly; the most frequently occurring word, *the*, appears 69,971 times: 6.9 percent of the total tokens in the entire corpus. On the other hand, 22,543 words appear only once, which barely gets them included in the count. This means that an astonishing 44.7 percent of the types account for only 2.2 percent of the total tokens.

Perhaps a more detailed look at some of the figures in the Kučera-Francis count would be instructive. The first (most frequent) 500 words are divided between structure and content words as follows:

	Structure	*Content*
1st 100	97	3
2nd 100	45	55
3rd 100	16	84
4th 100	13	87
5th 100	2	98
Total:	173	327

The percentage of structure words starts very high, but drops off fast. It appears that if the trend established in the first 500 words continues, the total number of structure types in the entire corpus will not exceed 200, which is a minuscule percentage of the 50,406 total—less than .4 of one percent. But this tiny number (of types) accounts for over half of the total words (tokens) used, about 51.2 percent, with the other approximately 50,200 content words sharing the remaining 48.8 percent of occurrences. Clearly the structure words are important. But so are the content words. (Cf. Chapter Twelve.) Mortar without bricks won't make a wall.

Because of vagueness inherent in the distinction structure versus content and because the data supplied by Kučera-Francis are not interpretable with exactness, the comparisons of structure and content words are estimates. A computer is used for the count, and the computer cannot tell whether the word *can* is the structure word (the modal) meaning "ability" or the content word *can*, the noun meaning the tin-coated iron container used for marketing food and other products. Furthermore, *up* in "up the flag" and *off* in "off the pigs" may have content meanings such as "raise the flag" and "neutralize the police." It is not always easy to decide for some words between classification as structure or content.

The important information to get from the comparison of these two kinds of words is that structure words have limited types and numerous tokens and content words, on the other hand, have numerous types but limited tokens. Individual content words range widely in relative frequency, but only rarely do any match the frequency of the main body of structure words. As a class, content words are open-ended, with new lexical items entering into use every day. When a need is felt, a word will be coined, as *brunch* was when late Sunday rising confused the first meal of the day.

The ten most frequently occurring words in the count are listed below, with the number of times each occurs and its cycle of reentry:

Nos. (Rank)	Word (Type)	Occurrences (Tokens)	Average Cycle for Reentry
1.	the	69,971	14.5
2.	of	36,411	27.8
3.	and	28,852	35.2
4.	to	26,149	38.8
5.	a	23,237	43.6
6.	in	21,341	47.5
7.	that	10,595	95.7
8.	is	10,099	100.4
9.	was	9,816	103.3
10.	he	9,543	106.3

In this list the frequencies of occurrence vary enormously: *the* appears seven and a third times for every occurrence of *he*. Yet both are among the ten most frequent words in the count.

Let's look at a wider stretch of this count:

1.	the	69,971	14.5
10.	he	9,543	106.3
20.	I	5,173	196.1
30.	they	3,618	280.3
40.	their	2,670	379.9
50.	if	2,199	461.2
60.	them	1,789	566.9
70.	may	1,400	724.4
80.	over	1,236	820.6
90.	before	1,016	998.3
100.	down	895	1,133.2
200.	almost	432	2,347.8
500.	started	194	5,228.0
1,000.	reach	106	9,568.2
2,000.	guess	56	18,111.3

As content words enter, there's a sharp decline in number of occurrences, and an ever-increasing number of words between entry and reentry.

Let's take a look at the far end of the count. Note the large number of words that occur among the least frequent:

	Frequency (Tokens)	Number of Types at that Frequency	Number of Tokens at that Frequency
7,920 – 8,478	10	559	5,590
8,479 – 9,173	9	695	6,255
9,174 – 9,998	8	825	6,600
9,999 – 11,119	7	1,121	7,847
11,120 – 12,398	6	1,279	7,674
12,399 – 14,218	5	1,820	9,100
14,219 – 16,683	4	2,465	9,860
16,684 – 20,630	3	3,547	10,641
20,631 – 27,863	2	7,233	14,466
27,864 – 50,406	1	22,543	22,543

It is clearly not feasible to teach all of these words and extremely difficult to choose which to teach, not knowing which will be serviceable in students' later lives.

Additions to the Lexicon

To make matters worse, new content words are constantly being added to the lexical inventory (as illustrated by the example *brunch* cited earlier), and some of the older items are being sloughed off, as a regular feature of unconscious vocabulary management. Older generation speakers used to talk about products made of "celluloid," but the general word "plastics" has replaced it, with numerous technical words to expand on what has become a very complex area of technical specialization: (a synthetic or semisynthetic organic substance, a polymeric substance, grouped as phenolic, urea, cellulose, acrylic, polystyrene, and vinyl).

A truly challenging problem is finding the means of identifying which of the thousands (and millions) of these words should be presented to students in a language class. This problem does not occur with the same urgency in first language training, because students have a large working vocabulary gained meaningfully in their own social milieu. How can a comparable experience be arranged for second language learners, who lack and need not only the specialized vocabulary of their individual and professional interests, but also significant parts of a general vocabulary?

Can we depend on frequency counts like the Kučera-Francis one cited above to identify both the general and the special needs of our students, to give us valuable guidance that we can incorporate into our curriculum plans? At the lower frequencies the counts can be quite helpful, and we learn most of the first three or four thousand anyway, so small differences in rank have no real consequence—but at the higher frequencies they disagree among themselves and offer advice that is far less reliable. In one textbook we are familiar with, special care was taken to introduce situations and settings that would be relevant and interesting enough to hold student attention. When the text was about three-fourths drafted, the glossary of words included in the textbook was compared with one of the standard frequency lists. Some surprising omissions were noted, words that intuitively seemed to be highly functional and necessary in everyday life, and most especially in a classroom. These omissions were somehow incorporated, either earlier or subsequently in the text. But the words appearing in the textbook draft and *not* in the frequency count were left in the materials. These "nonlist" words had legitimately found their way into the text, and they could stay there. In other words, the list was used to find omissions that should be corrected, but not to identify words to be selected for deletion.

If students continue studying a language, the words that are important enough to know will in due course be "foregrounded" (by repetition or contrast) as a means of impressing them more permanently on the student's mind.

There are many counts, and typically they have different purposes and show different results. There are counts intended to provide guidance in teaching native speakers reading, the study of literature, composition and writing, spelling, counts for military and political intelligence, counts for secretarial and stenographic training, counts for preschool tutelage, counts for different aspects of English as a second language, and recently counts for different fields of English for special purposes, such as nursing, police work, business, etc.

Limitations and Shortcomings of Word Counts

Though many or most of the word counts represent a scientific approach to analyzing lexical usage, some of them, from the point of view of the ESL teacher, have serious limitations and shortcomings. First, with few exceptions, notably a count by Fries of telephone conversations, the words counted come from written sources, with conversational forms under-represented. The counts are not always reliable for lessons in oral communication. They naturally represent their sources. Some counts include literary and classical texts, especially the Bible, with the resulting incorporation of a number of forms not in current use (*ye, bringeth, lovest, didst, thou*, etc.). The opposite situation also inevitably occurs: the omission of words recently added to the language. So words like *TV* (also spelled *teevee*) (and the British equivalent *telly*), though very frequent, do not appear in any but the most recent of the counts. And *channel* is more familiar because it has an important additional new referent.

Another possible bias is occasioned by a certain amount of arbitrariness in deciding what to count. Compound nouns and phrasal verbs are particularly troublesome. Is *post office* (where the mail is handled) one word or two? Does it make any difference if it is written *postoffice* or *post office*? How about *drug store* and *drugstore*? And how do we count *go up* and *come down*? Are there two words or four? Is *ice cream cone* one or three? Are *city* and *cities* two words or one? How about *go* and *went*?

C. K. Ogden in 1929 devised a communication system by which 850 English words supposedly did the work of 20,000. This of course means that none of the two-word (or phrasal) verbs was separately counted, nor were any of the noun compounds, unless they happen to be spelled as a single word. Yet the burden of learning these complex items remains; obscuring the issue doesn't handle the problems. Quite the contrary, it will aggravate the situation.

Most of the early frequency counts are graphic and mechanical, as are virtually all of the post–computer era counts; everything expressed in letters bounded by spaces is a word. In one of these the expression *Los Angeles-San Francisco* is tallied as three words; (1) Los, (2) Angeles-San, and (3) Francisco.

Perhaps a morpheme count would be of greater use because it would tell us about affix distribution and compound words. In the precomputer era Michael West organized a semantic count. It was a massive effort, involving a small army of trained and skilled people. Each technician analyzed the words of a 32-page folio of the 13-volume Oxford English Dictionary, read the entire five million words in the count, and tallied the ones in his or her folio. Though the most useful count that has become available, this procedure proved cumbersome and complicated, and many problems emerged. For example, the word *diamond* is entered with the meanings "jewel" and "shape" specified, but no percentages are given and no mention of the word referring to the edge of certain cutting tools, a suit of playing cards identified by lozenge-shaped red marks, the inner or entire playing field for baseball, a long-wearing phonograph needle, or the association with a promise of marriage. All of these contribute to the frequency status of the word *diamond*.

The frequency counts make one problem stand out in bold relief: the high frequencies of the very small number of structure words and the low frequencies of the infinitely more numerous content words. Freeman Twaddell, in a very interesting and useful article (Twaddell 1973), points out that we can hardly avoid the structure words, since though limited in number, they are ever-present in English communication. But the content words, while extremely numerous, are in typical texts highly infrequent. How can the teacher possibly decide which to teach? He can't, unless the interests of students are very narrowly defined and all of the students have the same aims and goals, which in most classes is extremely unlikely. Twaddell wisely suggests that the student be taught skills (of vocabulary learning in context) instead of an inventory of words. His suggestions, with our comments, include the following:

1) Be willing to guess the meanings of unfamiliar words. (Provisionally select the meaning that adds least to the discourse in which the unfamiliar word was found.)
2) Tolerate vagueness until the need for precise definitions becomes too great to ignore. (This should not happen very often.)
3) Have exercises that teach the student to skim (a reading skill that will be discussed in Chapters Eight and Twelve).
4) Arrange to have extensive contact with the language, and most of the words needed for each individual situation will occur in the types of meaningful contexts that will help students learn what they need.

WORD COUNT SUMMARY

A summary of the two lexical subclasses made by contrasting conceptual categories follows:

Structure Words	Content Words
few (some two hundred)	many (well over a million)
closed category	open category
part of the grammar	pure lexicon
reflect language structure	reflect culture
mostly high frequency	mostly low frequency
need for grammatical elegance	need for linguistic survival

Another way of classifying vocabulary items, one perhaps more familiar to many teachers, is designated "active-passive." Linguists have noted that native speakers of English (and presumably speakers of other languages, maybe all of them) respond to a wider range of vocabulary than they themselves use when speaking. This condition, felt to be normal for native speakers, should therefore be quite acceptable linguistic behavior for second language speakers.

In many language lessons it seems to be assumed that all the words presented in formal lessons should be internalized. This is not what happened to native speakers as they grew up and developed their language skills. They were (and still are) exposed to a lexical smorgasbord, from which they select(ed) the items most interesting and most useful to them.

This is where active versus passive vocabulary can enter our pedagogy. The teacher presents a lesson, making use of a situation appropriate to the course design and to the particular group of students. She introduces the vocabulary in meaningful contexts, but leaves the students to make their own active/passive choices. This procedure is consistent with the assumption that the words in a student's passive vocabulary, when the need for them arises, will move into the active vocabulary. At least the ground is broken for vocabulary building out of internal resources. An implication is that passive status is one route to full acquisition. This is suggested by Twaddell in his advice to tolerate vagueness until the full lexical acquisition of a form is reached.

We might also expect some movement from the active vocabulary to the passive, as students learn more words and don't consistently review older ones. The vocabulary load responds to a student's current needs, and priorities change, often very rapidly, especially in a stimulating educational environment. We are saying that lessons should be based on situations and circumstances, and that if the situations are well developed, they will bring along with them the necessary lexical items. Recalling how truly vast and open-ended the vocabulary of content words is, we are better off allowing (even encouraging) a measure of lexical independence among students.

APPLICATIONS TO VOCABULARY BUILDING

This is not to say that the lexicon should not be planned and taught. But resources and means of analysis will be more helpful to the students than will following a frequency-guided vocabulary lesson, especially when we get to the 4,000-word vocabulary and higher. Lexical study should include the pieces that make up words: prefixes, suffixes, stems, inflectional patterns (if not adequately treated in the grammar), derivational patterns, enough morphophonemics for the student to be able to associate the *im-* of "improbable" or the *ir-* of "irregular" with the *in-* of "inadequate," word "families" (sign, design, signature, assign, designate, etc.) to help identify common elements. If students are interested, a lesson about lexical borrowing could be useful as a means of understanding the ease with which loan words enter English, and the richness of our vocabulary for having welcomed them in.

One way to learn the meaning of unfamiliar words is to observe how they are used and make intelligent guesses. Over time the guesses are refined and the meaning comes to be specific. Another very good way is to ask about one's surroundings, requesting from friends and acquaintances identifications and definitions. Some near-formula expressions are well worth learning; they can be very helpful in asking about things.

EXERCISE 7.1

DIRECT VOCABULARY BUILDING

Instructions: Pick out things you see around you, preferably things you don't know or don't recognize, and ask what they are, what they are called, what they are used for, etc. Try to remember and use what you learn. (Code 1–2)

Student	Student/Teacher
1. What's that? (points outside)	It's a bulldog.
2. What's that? (points . . .)	A police car.
3. What are these? (Holds . . .)	They're grapes.
4. What's this? (Holds . . .)	A key.
5. a. What's this called? (Points at wrist)	It's called a watch.
b. What's the difference between a watch and a clock?	A watch is worn or carried by a person; a clock is usually bigger.
6. What are those?	They're chickens.
7. Who's that? (Points to a man in uniform)	He's a security guard.
8. What does he do?	He guards the school.
9. Who's your letter from?	From my dad.
10. Did he send any money?	No. I didn't ask him for any.

An alert student, especially one living where considerable English is spoken, will be able to listen to many conversations around him: in restaurants, in stores, on buses. He should inconspicuously eavesdrop, try to grasp the line of information, understand the details of what is being said. This is good practice for listening comprehension under less-than-ideal circumstances. Another opportunity to observe the use of language in context is to take advantage of entertainment media: to watch television programs, see plays and movies, listen to the radio, attend lectures, etc. All of this experience is good communication and vocabulary practice.

LEXICAL DERIVATION

Phrasal Verbs

There are two patterns of lexical derivation that students often find difficult to master. The first of these is characterized by Dwight Bolinger (1971) as "an outpouring of lexical creativeness that surpasses anything in our language" and again as "a floodgate of metaphor." He is referring, of course, to the English *phrasal verbs*.

The phrasal verb is curious in a way. It is made up of a content word and one or more particles (structure words often associated with prepositions or adverbs). It is a derivational formation that has been in the language at least since the mystery plays in the Middle Ages and right now is increasingly active as a word formation process.

Phrasal verbs are especially abundant in oral communication. Native speakers have no difficulty with them, rather use them in preference to the Latinate single-word verbs later borrowed from French. Second language students of English, and most especially speakers of Romance languages, often find phrasal verbs unfamiliar, complicated, and difficult.

Complicated they are, and one complexity involves where the particle goes. With intransitive verbs there's no problem: the particle follows immediately after the verb, as in: "John *came in* and *sat down.*" But for most transitive verbs the particle may be placed before or after the object noun, as in:

Harry *threw out* the trash.   Harry *threw* the trash *out.*

But when the direct object is a pronoun, only the second form is acceptable:

Where's the trash?   Harry *threw* it *out.*

As if this were not enough complexity, there's another class of transitive phrasal verbs where the verb stem and particle must remain together, the nonseparables. And there are other complications, for which the interested reader is referred to the study by Bolinger (1971) (e.g., for an analysis of phrasal verbs with more than one particle).

Let's illustrate some of these patterns by means of a paraphrase "translation" exercise:

EXERCISE 7.2

PHRASAL VERBS—INTRANSITIVE

Instructions: Listen carefully to each sentence. Then paraphrase the sentence by substituting an appropriate phrasal verb for the single verb (or vice versa). (Code 2–3)

Teacher	Student
1. Jacques awoke at 7:15.	He woke up at 7:15.
2. He arose 10 minutes later.	He got up 10 minutes later.
3. He seated himself for breakfast.	He sat down for breakfast.
4. He descended on the elevator.	He went down on the elevator.
5. He departed for his office a little late.	He took off for his office a little late.
6. He ascended to the second floor.	He went up to the second floor.

7. It took a while for John to understand.   It took a while for John to catch on.
8. It won't take too long if we all co-operate.   It won't take too long if we all pitch in.
9. When my number arrives, I'll be ready.   When my number comes up, I'll be ready.
10. At the crucial moment, he fainted.   At the crucial moment, he passed out.

You will notice that in some sentences the phrasal verbs sound better than the single-word equivalent, and also that some pairs of verbal expressions don't mean quite the same thing. In many cases the closest single-verb equivalent is the phrasal verb without the particle, but invariably with a change in meaning, e.g., *sit–sit down, stand–stand up*.

Most students, especially those from abroad who are in the United States for an advanced academic degree, will be more familiar with the higher-register Latinate verb forms (ascend, depart, etc.) than they are with the phrasal verbs. U.S.-reared linguistic minority groups are more likely to be familiar with the phrasal verb forms. This explains the option in the instructions for exercise 7.2. The exercise can go either direction, depending on student needs.

Another much larger group of phrasal verbs are the transitive ones with separable particles. They are illustrated by the following patterned examples:

EXERCISE 7.3

PHRASAL VERBS—TRANSITIVE SEPARABLE

Instructions: You will hear a set of ten sentences, each with a single-word verb. Restate the sentences twice, using a two-word verb, first with the two words together, then with them separated by the direct object. Then you will hear an "echo" question from your teacher, to which you will respond repeating the statement, but this time using a pronoun for the direct object. (Code 2–4)

One-Verb (Teacher)	Adjacent (Student)	Separated (Student)	Echo Question (Teacher)	Pronoun Response (Student)
1. He examined the documents.	He looked over the documents.	He looked the documents over.	What did he do to the documents?	He looked them over.
2. They raised the flag.	They ran up the flag.	They ran the flag up.	What did they do to the flag?	They ran it up.
3. They'll abandon the fort.	They'll give up the fort.	They'll give the fort up.	What will they do to the fort?	They'll give it up.

4.	I distributed the leaflets.	I passed out the leaflets.	I passed the leaf-lets out.	What did you do with the leaflets?	I passed them out.
5.	He mentioned the subject.	He brought up the subject.	He brought the subject up.	What did he do to the subject?	He brought it up.
6.	That's how he'll rear his children.	That's how he'll bring up his chil-dren.	That's how he'll bring his chil-dren up.	What will he do to his children?	He'll bring them up in that way.
7.	That caused the epidemic.	That brought on the epidemic.	That brought the epidemic on.	What did that do to the epidemic?	It brought it on.
8.	She telephoned John.	She called up John.	She called John up.	What did she do to John?	She called him up.
9.	That erased his fortune.	That wiped out his fortune.	That wiped his fortune out.	What did that do to his fortune?	It wiped it out.
10.	He extin-guished the light.	He put out the light.	He put the light out.	What did he do to the light?	He put it out.

[Technical note: Particular care should be given by the teacher to the oral interpretation of the "Echo Questions." The questions must sound appropriately realistic, as when a listener misses some information and requests a repetition of the part of the conversation he missed. The echo question is recognized by its special intonation pattern: The voice starts quite high and goes higher at the end of the sentence.]

Again with this exercise the versions of sentences with a phrasal verb sound more familiar and authentic than do some of the one-word verbs. There is a register difference between nearly all pairs, with one-word verbs on a higher register. Perhaps the same can be said for modality: the phrasal verbs are more likely to be used in oral communication, with their Latinate equivalents more at home in written texts.

As if the intransitive and transitive separable patterns were not sufficiently complex, there's another pattern: the transitive inseparables. These look and act like the pattern in exercise 7.2, except they are always adjacent, even when the direct object is a pronoun. The following exercise presents some of these.

EXERCISE 7.4

PHRASAL VERBS—TRANSITIVE NON-SEPARABLE

Instructions: The teacher will pronounce a series of 10 statements. Student 1 will repeat the sentence using a two-word verb and a rising intonation pattern that serves to query the accuracy of his interpretation. Student 2 confirms Student 1's interpretation, incidentally converting the object noun to a pronoun. (Code 3–4)

One-Word Verb (Teacher)	Two-Word Verb (Student 1)	Pronominalization (Student 2)
1. He was observing the parade.	He was looking at the parade?	Yes, he was looking at it.
2. He'll locate the address.	He'll look for the address?	Yes, he'll look for it.
3. He'll mind his little sister.	He'll look after his little sister?	Yes, he'll look after her.
4. We'll expect Chris next Friday.	We'll look for Chris next Friday?	Yes, we'll look for her next Friday.
5. They selected the house.	They decided on the house?	Yes, they decided on it.
6. They ridiculed Ben.	They laughed at Ben?	Yes, they laughed at him.
7. He hadn't considered Janalee.	He hadn't thought of Janalee?	Yes, he hadn't thought of her.
8. Let's summon the doctor.	Let's send for the doctor?	Yes, let's send for him.
9. Let's await Karen.	Let's wait for Karen?	Yes, let's wait for her.
10. Debbie attended her father's advice.	Debbie listened to her father's advice?	Yes, she listened to it.

As complex as the phrasal verbs are with their moveable and nonmoveable particles, the aspect that gives second language students the most trouble is figuring out the meanings. Bolinger was cited earlier as saying the phrasal verbs are a "floodgate of metaphor." An example of this can be seen in the following pair of sentences:

> The maid cleaned out the refrigerator.
> Their pampered teenage son cleaned out the refrigerator.

The maid defrosted and cleaned the refrigerator; the son ate all of the food. It is not a long jump to compare these two kinds of cleaning out. (Note that the verb "cleaned" alone won't stretch to cover both meanings.) If the student lets his imagination run, he'll find that many of the phrasal verbs will yield their meanings. E.g., in the sentence "He put away the records and got out the expense sheets," the particles tell us more than the verb stems *put* and *got*. To *climb up* and *to climb down* are transparent enough; she *woke* the baby *up* versus she *put* the baby *down* depend on the particles for an easy interpretation.

Remember that phrasal verbs may have more than one meaning, just as any other word in the language may. One does not have to look far to find examples. The transitive/intransitive pairs are clear: "Get out" versus "Get out the vote." In an expression like "Boy, was I burned up" I am obviously not incinerated, so the sentence has to have another meaning. Fire can be compared to anger, and that is the key. Compare "He took down the names" and "He took down the pictures," or "He carried out the garbage" with "He carried out their wishes." They yield to analysis if one includes a dollop of common sense and a little imagination. Fortunately, current dictionaries include many of these as subentries to the content words.

There are some confusing combinations: *up* and *down* are helpful in establishing direction of movement in expressions like *come up* and *come down*, but what do we tell a student who wants to know the difference between *drink up* and *drink down*? If there really is a difference, it is not very conspicuous. *Burn up* and *burn down* are another pair, though in this case you can point out that "burn down" happens to a building but not to a bonfire. *Up* is used often as an intensifier, suggesting a full completion of the activity referred to: to *eat up, finish up, clean up, fill up*, etc.

We have spent enough time on phrasal verbs. They are a problem, but there are also other problems. We add one more exercise because it provides an opportunity to show a picture-cued activity.

EXERCISE 7.5

PICTURE-CUED RESPONSES

Instructions: Using phrasal verbs, describe the activities pictured in the following drawings. (Code 3–4)

[Pictures: a sequence of normal daily activities, e.g., the alarm goes off, a man wakes up, pops out of bed, takes off his pajamas, jumps into a shower, puts on his clothes, shaves off his whiskers, etc.]

Bolinger (1971) indicates that phrasal verbs are a prolific source of nouns in English and cites *stándoff, rúnaway, mákeup, gét-together, drópout, lóckout, fállout,* and many others, derived from the phrasal verbs *stand óff, run awáy, make úp, get togéther, drop óut, lock óut, fall óut*, and hordes of other examples. This identification of function by stress pattern is well established by one-word nouns and verbs: *ímport* from *impórt*, *dígest* from *digést*, etc.

This derivational process is no doubt encouraged by the rather large number of words which have membership in two or more categories with absolutely no change in form: *work, trade, store, shop, sleep, cook*, and many, many more. We so commonly move a word around in our oral grammar that no one is surprised when his little boy brings a cut finger, with a request that daddy "band-aid it." English is indeed a language with fluid boundaries between its grammatical categories, and the phrasal verb is taking good advantage of it.

Noun Compounds

But Bolinger mentions that there is one derivational pattern that is even more prolific than the phrasal-verb adaptation: it is the noun compound (the noun + noun combinations). In spoken form the highest stress is on the first noun; in written form the noun compounds have a tendency to be written as a single word, with no space or hyphen between the two component nouns. But this is only a tendency, not a rule. So some establishments are spelled *drug stores* and others *drugstores*, some *air lines* and others *airlines*, etc. The distinction is erratic and not dependable if written with two separate words. (If written solid, they are almost always compounds.)

But the differentiation in the oral language is what gives most students trouble. And it is an important distinction, because nouns can modify other nouns in English, and the resulting noun phrase must be distinguished from the nearly similar noun compound. English has a complicated system of stress. Ignoring contrastive stress, which complicates the system even more, it is still complex. To simplify somewhat, inform the students that if the first noun of a combination is most highly stressed, it is a compound. If the second is most highly stressed, it is a phrase, just like any other noun phrase (i.e., adjective + noun). These are of course associated with different meanings:

Noun Compound	Noun Phrase
1. hót plate (small electric stove)	hot pláte (a heated plate)
2. récord sale (disks sold cheap)	record sále (best sale ever)
3. dúmb waiter (small elevator)	dumb wáiter (restaurant lout)
4. háir brush (for brushing hair)	hair brúsh (made of hair)
5. héad hunter (collects heads)	head húnter (makes decisions)

[Technical note: Differences in spellings are standardized to avoid suggesting clues that are irrelevant in oral presentation.]

Following is an exercise with a mixed sequence of compounds and phrases from which the teacher can judge whether the contrast is acceptably mastered.

EXERCISE 7.6

NOUN COMPOUNDS AND NOUN PHRASES

Instructions: From the clue you will be given, produce an appropriate response that distinguishes a compound from a phrase. If this is too simple, put the phrase/compound in a short sentence that reveals its correct classification. (Code 3–5)

Teacher	Student
1. a store that sells toys	a tóy store
2. a box to keep firewood in	the wóod box
3. a stop that won't be very long	a short stóp
4. a tree that grows apples	an ápple tree
5. a pie made with apples	an apple píe
6. a pin made in Thailand	a Thai pín
7. a box made of wood	a wood(en) bóx
8. a frankfurter on a bun	a hót dog
9. a pin to hold your necktie	a tíe pin
10. a toy in the form of a store	a toy stóre
11. a baseball position between 2nd and 3rd base	a shórt stop
12. a mine where gold is extracted	a góld mine

This list could be lengthened interminably. The sequence is very productive, and new forms are being constantly added, as it is convenient to have them, to take their place alongside such standard items as *córn flakes, óatmeal, potáto chips*, etc. It should be possible to collect a stock of these items for occasional review practice, since it seems to be a point that is not well internalized, even when students are aware of just how the pattern works.

One feature of vocabulary building that is characteristic of oral language is shortened forms of words. Some would explain these as an application of efficiency in speech, and maybe they are. It is easier to use a short word than a long one, even though the shortening produces a homonym, as is the case of *gas*, shortened from *gasoline*, and *gas*, meaning the nonsolid, nonliquid, vaporous form of fuel often used for domestic cooking, heating, etc. Some of these like *ad* and *fan*, have made their way into the language, leaving little or no trace of their lexical history. It is useful for students to know the source and derivational process that produced these words.

EXERCISE 7.7

SHORTENED FORMS

Instructions: Your teacher will set up a sentence frame, then will suggest a substitute for the first word. When called on, produce the sentence as modified by the substitution. (Code 5–6)

1. *Ad* is a short form of the word *advertisement*.

Using sentence 1 above, substitute in the first blank: Gas, Petrol, Fan, Condo, Coop, Econ, Psych, Trib, The Fed, Med school, Vet.

(Some of these have taken on a life of their own: we say "want ad," never "want advertisement" and "fan" no longer suggests "fanatic.")

One favored way of shortening oral forms is to make up a word by citing the first letter of each of the words of a set phrase. Let's try some:

EXERCISE 7.8

LITERAL ACRONYMS

Instructions: Pronounce the following acronyms by giving the names of the letters that make each up (e.g., say /vîy ày píy/, not /vɪp/). Then finish the sentence by giving the equivalent full form. (Code 4–5)

1. *VIP* stands for *very important person*.

Substitute in the first blank: UN, USA, UK, MD, BA, BS, PhD, TNT, MPH, PE, GI, UCLA, PDQ, MVP, IOU. (How is this last one different?)

Another instance of reduction on the lexical level is nicknames:

EXERCISE 7.9

NICKNAMES

Instructions: As your teacher presents a series of names, make statements following the pattern given. (Code 2–4)

1. *Bill* is a common nickname for *William*.

Substitute in the first blank: Joe, Russ, Nan, Don, Ed, Tom, and Fran. Then substitute: Jack, Dick, Bob, Hal, Liz, Kay, Betty. How are the items in the first substitution list different from the items in the second list?

If a second language speaker of English meets a Mr. Bill Holley (the informal name used by his friends) he may need help looking the name up in the (tele)phone book. It's likely "Bill Holley" won't be there. The new acquaintance must know that *Bill* is a common nickname for *William*, so he must look under *William Holley*, probably with an initial added: *Holley, William I.*

These various kinds of shortened forms are very much a part of informal English and are consequently more often heard than seen, and mostly seen in journalistic contexts. There is every chance that more will appear in the future. TV has made it into the language, and VTR is knocking at the gate.

SPECIAL ENGLISH

In an effort to communicate as widely as possible in English, the Voice of America has devised and now has some years of experience with a means of increasing their radio audience. They are using something called "Special English," to encourage students and others who do not have full competence in the oral language. In Special English there are three means of simplifying standard English: a restricted vocabulary, an intuitive simplifying of the grammar, and a very deliberate oral delivery.

Using Special English has some disadvantages. The announcer must be careful not to sound patronizing, for this repels many people. It gets awkward at times to use clumsy-sounding paraphrases, such as "paid foreign soldiers" in place of "mercenaries." The vocabulary items used are limited in number (around 1500, with supplementary lists for science and other special fields). They are collected in a small paperback volume called *Special English Word Book*, published by the Voice of America (1979, 1st ed. 1964). It is a vocabulary devised to fill the needs of news broadcasting. Two words included are "arson" and "astronaut," each of which occurs two times in the more than one million words of running text collected and studied by Kučera and Francis. This underscores the difficulty of coming up with a single list that would be pedagogically useful to different people for different purposes. Any experiment to limit vocabulary will run into snags at times.

In eliciting information it is advisable to encourage words that are already known or that will be easy to figure out; e.g., use simple question forms to ask for directions and locations; "Does this road go to Prague?" in preference to "Where does this road go?" and "How many kilometers from here to Prague?" rather than "How far away is Prague?" Be sure to emphasize the content words. Perhaps you remember a grammar drill, one in which the student is given some content words like "kilometers/here/Prague" from which the student was to concoct a sentence. The content words alone managed to convey a meaning, where the structure words alone (How many/from/to) convey no meaning at all, or certainly very little. If this sounds like just plain common sense, so be it. Common sense need not be at variance with a native speaker's inherent feel for good communication practice; in fact it shouldn't be.

There is much more that could be said about learning vocabulary, and indeed some of it *will* be said in Chapter Twelve, when vocabulary in the written language is discussed. Meanwhile, we turn to the written language in general, to treat performance skills, and then component skills, from the point of view of reading and writing.

DISCUSSION

1. On what basis are words divided up into structure and content groups? Discuss whether grammar or lexicon is involved in the distinction.

2. Discuss how the decision is made on which words to include in the lexicon of a particular unit of work.

3. What information does a type-token ratio disclose?

4. What is foregrounding and how is it accomplished?

5. What are the limitations of a typical word count?

6. Discuss "phrasal verbs" and "noun compounds" for their contribution to an expanding lexicon.

7. What are the implications of passive and active vocabulary?

8. What was Twaddell's advice on how to learn new words? What use would he put the dictionary to?

9. What are moveable and nonmoveable particles? How do students determine which are moveable?

10. What is "Special English" and how is it used?

Section III
Written Communication

Oral communication is universal among mankind; people everywhere can and do communicate by means of mouth and ear. Infants have a built-in predisposition to learn whatever language (or languages) they are in a meaningful way exposed to. Written communication, on the other hand, is acquired by study after oral communication is well established. There are millions of people living in societies that never have developed the means for written discourse.

Those of us who live in technologically advanced societies may tend to forget that literacy is not a common condition in all places. It can be very revealing to visit countries that use an entirely different writing system, with which the Westerner is totally unfamiliar, such as Arabic, Chinese, Hindi, Burmese, etc. In France or Germany or Poland, and even to some extent in Russia, a visitor whose own language utilizes a writing system derived from Latin can at least produce an oral interpretation of the spelling he sees. But this same person in Addis Ababa gets no hints, not even incorrect ones, from the local spelling. Someone who has had this experience usually finds it easy to sympathize with total illiterates.

To be illiterate in a literate society is a tremendous disadvantage. There is still a lot of visual data to interpret, but no access to directions or instructions. The illiterate depends on colors and shapes of signs, containers, traffic signals, etc. The story has been repeated about the canned milk company that put a picture of a healthy baby on its product. The company was astonished to find that nobody bought the milk because of the widely held assumption that the can contained human meat. Nor were the highlights of the baby's cheeks and forehead interpreted as the bloom of health. Rather they were assumed to be a skin infection, a well-known malady that the local people would do everything possible to avoid.

These incidents are extremes, but they show that not only do writing systems have conventions to follow, but so do illustrations and other aspects of daily life. An American Air Force officer assigned to a military mission in a South American country some years ago ordered a new red car to take with him. He learned just in time that only official firemen were allowed to have red vehicles, which saved him from an expensive repainting.

Through recent centuries the place and purpose of written language skills in second language teaching have varied, sometimes even within the same historical period, according to emphasis on the spoken or written language. Emphasis has shifted back and forth for a number of reasons: availability of written texts or fluent teachers, prevailing pedagogical beliefs, whether conventional or iconoclastic, and, most frequently, social priorities and the practical purposes at hand.

Many examples of such changes are described in Chapter One of this book. From ancient Rome through medieval times, for example, it appears that only the most well-born studied advanced written forms of Greek (and then Latin). Other students' language learning was limited to oral instruction from native-speaking slaves.

Since the Renaissance we find conflicting schools of thought in western language teaching. Although not always expressed as such, polarity between the spoken and written modalities has been central to the conflict, as translation and rote memorization of written texts have alternated and overlapped with emphasis on "natural" and inductive methods based on authentic models of speech.

This overlapping continued into the present century. From the early 1900s, for example, the Grammar-Translation Method was retained in spite of criticisms from eminent scholars in the United States and Europe, until World War II, when military demands left no question about the need for different goals and methods of teaching—methods that would rapidly teach American personnel oral language skills enabling them to discharge government responsibilities in countries around the globe. Speaking skills were paramount in the Audiolingual Approach, an emphasis which was supported philosophically and pedagogically by language scholars in the 1940s, further enhanced by the invention of electronic recording devices, especially the tape recorder in the 1950s, the subsequent development of the language laboratory, and the sympathetic writings of the behavioral psychologists.

Chomsky's challenge in 1966 to the underpinnings of the theory that justified the oral-aural approach in the early 1960s cast a long shadow on the rationale for Audiolingual teaching and spawned much new comment on language teaching in general, some of it not specifically related philosophically to Chomsky's teachings. In any case the argument between emphasis on the written or spoken language continues today, even among the latest recommendations for language teaching—as well as among established schools of thought.

In the 1980s, as in the past, the emphasis in each educational setting will vary according to immediate social needs, available teaching resources, and philosophical positions.

The immigrant new to the English-speaking country needs first to gain survival skills in the spoken language, while for the junior high school student in a non-English-speaking country in a school lacking a highly proficient teacher and a well-equipped language laboratory, the most easily realizable goal might be reading fluency and knowledge of the grammar of the written language.

Throughout the 1970s and continuing into the 1980s the worldwide acceleration of commerical and scientific exchange among nations has produced rapidly growing groups of consumers of foreign languages for special purposes. The resulting demand that the United States develop capabilities in other languages in no way matches the international demand for English as the modern language which provides access to the largest amount of the world's information.

Unlike the acknowledged goal of developing spoken language skills in the shortest time possible to meet the military needs of the 1940s, the study of English for technical and commercial purposes has commanded focus on both spoken and written language, possibly with greater emphasis worldwide on written forms. On the one hand, many programs have been developed to meet the needs for rapid training in technical, academic, or professional fields in settings in which the academic materials are available only in English, even though the learners may not immediately need to use spoken English in either their studies or their professional duties. There are simultaneously, however, substantial numbers of "new" programs in ESL focusing on the spoken word, planning in terms of oral functions, and using authentic oral discourse as the prime source of teaching materials. Such programs are called for to meet the needs of such individuals as visiting foreign scholars, as well as undergraduate and postgraduate students, and such diverse migrant groups as economically depressed Mexican farm laborers, Russian émigrés, and Indochinese refugees.

There need not be competition or conflict between oral and written discourse as to focus. The exigencies and direction of each specific educational situation determine the focus, and the combined thought of the best of our predecessors and our contemporaries provides us with ample resources to meet planning needs.

In written communication, as in oral, we present five chapters: two on performance skills and three on component skills. Unlike the oral performance skills, which the native-speaking child brings to school when he enters, written-language performance skills must be mastered by special study.

The first two chapters of Section III treat *reading* and *writing*, the written-language performance skills. Success, especially for reading, can be evaluated by one of the many available standardized tests. Other, perhaps more significant, measures of success are the ability to function meaningfully in a classroom that employs readings from textbooks and other sources, and that expects a creditable effort to take notes, complete written assignments, and write satisfactory lab reports, term papers, and examinations. For student programs other than English (or other language courses), the instructor will likely grade an assignment or test on the basis of the information the student displays, with allowance for grammatical infelicities and spelling errors, if the student's intentions are clear (and correct). The instructor wants to know how much of the course syllabus (engineering, mathematics, economics, or whatever) has been assimilated.

Although both first and second language students have to learn both reading and writing, they cannot be taught in the same way, because second language students must first (or at least simultaneously) acquire the underlying oral system. It is possible to learn literacy skills without having mastered the oral language: many scholars have done so in Latin (though they substitute the sounds of their own language), and many congenitally deaf people have done so. But neither deaf students nor scholars of classical languages no longer spoken natively represent a normal learning situation.

The writing system of English (and many other languages) correlates with the pronunciation, i.e., is based on the phonology. The system employed by English is basically modified phonemic/morphophonemic. In contrast to writing that is ideographic or pictographic, such as Chinese, the letters of the English alphabet stand for sounds, with some anomalies. There are exceptions, where letters are silent, but often even these have a function, as we will see in Chapter Ten.

Chapters Ten, Eleven, and Twelve present the component skills of the written language: orthography, grammar, and vocabulary. Special emphasis for the last two mentioned will aim to distinguish patterns characteristic almost exclusively of the written modality. Again the aim is to present technical information and develop skills that will enable the serious student to refine his writing and become more effective as a communicator.

A

PERFORMANCE SKILLS:
Written Discourse

CHAPTER EIGHT

READING

INTRODUCTION

Borrowing insights from current research, we refer to reading for second language learners as an acquisition process in four stages: (1) beginning reading (including our beginning beginner and low beginner levels), with emphasis on decoding graphic information to understand fully formed but simple language; (2) elementary reading (including our high beginner and low intermediate levels) with emphasis on reading new combinations of vocabulary and sentence-level structures, developing predictive and confirming abilities; (3) intermediate reading (including our high intermediate and low advanced) with emphasis on developing additional reading skills, reading advanced English passages, and reading with purpose; and (4) advanced reading (our terminal advanced) with emphasis on reading authentic materials for specific purposes.

BEGINNING READING:
EMPHASIS ON MECHANICS AND BASIC SKILLS

The reading beginner in ESL may be a child who is learning to read for the first or a subsequent time, an illiterate adult, a moderately educated older child or adult, or a highly educated older child or adult. Since the most difficult part of beginning reading is understanding the reading task itself, i.e., decoding the system of abstract symbols to discover its relation to the spoken language system, it will take longer for the person who is learning to read for the first time. The length of time will vary with age, maturation, previous experience, and a number of social factors. A moderately well-educated teenager or adult, even one whose first language uses a writing system graphically different from that of English, may be able to master the mechanics, with efficient instruction and appropriate materials, in a minimum of fifty lessons, or approximately four months of well-taught classes with primary emphasis on the mechanics of reading. The well-educated person beginning to study English may master the writing system in a matter of a few hours and, if the same alphabet is used, may even be able to skip it altogether. The older adult who does not yet know how to read may need much more time.

Reading Readiness

For the student, young or old, learning to decode from the written language for the first time, reading readiness exercises can be useful. Reading readiness implies helping students to get ready for reading, to give them the foundation for recognition and interpretation of print or characters. It does not mean postponing formal reading indefinitely, but is designed to ensure the maximum possible success with the first reading so that a favorable attitude toward reading is developed. It means that every teacher should take each student at his own level of development and work from there. Studies have shown that a brief delay of formal reading to allow time for the proper development of readiness skills enables students to catch up with those of their peers who can start earlier.

Simply developing facility in the oral language helps students' preparation for reading. In addition, the following are some of the readiness skills students should develop:

1. *Visual Discrimination.* Directions like *same, different, top, bottom, middle, first, second,* and *last* should be learned and used in referring to objects, letters, and words in exercises for visual discrimination. Students learn the names and the general shape of the letters of the alphabet that the language uses, different forms of the same letters (e.g., upper and lower case forms), and are able to tell whether two letters or groups of letters are the same or different. Some possible discriminations are: (a) What is at the top, at the bottom, in the middle of the page? (b) Which object is the first, the second, the last? (c) Are any of the objects, letters, or words the same as the one in the box? (d) Pair the capital and lower case letters as shown in the example.

2. *Auditory Discrimination.* A student who persistently hears or repeats a sound other than the one being modeled needs to sharpen his auditory perception. This is especially likely to be a problem for students who are developing skills in a second language. The learners in this group are accustomed to the sounds of their own first language, and they may not be hearing the crucial differences between the two languages. Auditory discrimination skills should be developed for the parallel sounds in the native and target languages. Some possible exercises include the following: (a) Minimal Pairs: Are the sounds the same or different? (b) Initial Sounds: Do the names of any of the objects shown in the big box begin with the same

sound as the object in the small box? (c) Rhyme Words: Say the names of the object in the big box to yourself. Answer *yes* if it rhymes with the object in the small box, *no* if it does not. (d) Similar Sentences: Which sentences say the same thing? and (e) Minimal Differences: Which sentence of three or more is different?

3. *Memory Training.* One of the important reading readiness skills is the ability to hold something in the mind for a length of time, to be recalled when necessary. Students' attention often wanders, they pick up unimportant information, or they cannot adequately store and retain information they will need later. Examples of exercises for training the memory follow: (a) Repeat the first sentence of three after all have been heard. (b) Give the order of events in a story heard. (c) Name as many of the objects from memory as possible after a picture, or an array of objects, has been shown for a limited time and then removed from sight. (d) Reassemble a picture series in the order first shown.

Some teachers err by confining the beginning reader to mastery exercises for too long a time, and to the exclusion of comprehension exercises, which should start as soon as the reader is able to read new material which makes sense. At the same time, knowledge of orthographic structure is central to the reading process; since acquisition of this knowledge may well be the most important change the person undergoes in learning to read, it is important that the reader get a good grounding in the mechanics and then study in organized fashion the more complex English orthographic structures as his knowledge of the language increases.

A student may be said to be in control of the basics when he:

(1) regularly makes appropriate (e.g., left-to-right) eye movements for English;
(2) recognizes and discriminates among the vowel and consonant sounds in English;
(3) associates vowel and consonant sounds with letters;
(4) recognizes and discriminates among consonant blends and consonant combinations;
(5) recognizes and discriminates among vowel combinations;
(6) recognizes vowel sounds with /r/;
(7) recognizes selected sight words;
(8) recognizes rhyming words when not spelled with the same letter pattern; and
(9) recognizes upper- and lower-case letters and the basic punctuation marks.

The Reading Passage

Materials at the beginning reading level should include groups of sentences, phrases, and words. And although the primary focus is on decoding graphic information, the decoding should always be done with comprehension.

There are many popular methods for selecting and presenting texts to beginners (Hatch 1979). All of the methods work for some; none has been proven best for everyone. Two methods particularly appropriate for the beginning ESL reader are the Whole Word Method and the Linguistic Method.

The Whole Word Method fastens on the reader's ability to process individual words as perceptual units; the Linguistic Method focuses on the recognition of spelling patterns. Both methods make liberal use of visual cues, a very useful device for teaching beginning reading.

Use of the Whole Word Method, appropriate for students of any age, necessitates teachers' selecting materials primarily for inherent interest and usefulness to the prospective reader. Commercial or teacher-produced readers may be used, but even greater student interest can be mobilized with the Language Experience Approach, or the use of stories elicited from the students themselves. For example, one illiterate adult ESL speaker dictated the following five sentences to his teacher:

EXERCISE 8.1

LANGUAGE EXPERIENCE APPROACH

Instructions: Read the following: (Code 1–3)

> I came to the United States.
> I studied English.
> I got my driver's license.
> I got a job at _____ University.
> I won the Sweepstakes.

The teacher copied the sentences onto the blackboard and had a reading lesson for the whole class. Such a passage might be dictated to a tape recorder instead, and transcribed onto paper or a stencil instead of the blackboard. Although limited to the language a particular student has mastery of at that stage, such a passage almost always contains both phonic and other kinds of spelling patterns. In reading this exercise, in which the student's memory of his own story is a useful mnemonic device, the student will practice both sound decoding and whole word recognition. Over a period of time, the exclusive use of this method diminishes its value because of the limitations of students' experiences and vocabulary.

The Whole Word Method encourages students to develop sight vocabulary as the starting point for learning to read. Developing this skill is an ongoing process that will continue throughout the reader's life.

The Linguistic Method focuses on precise decoding of the spelling patterns of written English, and does not encourage guessing. Materials are prepared especially to assist the reader in learning to recognize and decode into sound (and meaning) those spelling patterns in English which have a consistent pronunciation that parallels their spelling. The very popular poem-stories of Dr. Seuss (1974 and 1976) can complement commercial materials of this nature for younger readers. For older, less-educated learners, materials from the Sullivan Series (1980) have proven useful, helping the reader recognize the most common sound-symbol correspondences and their common exceptions.

The obvious advantage of the Linguistic Method is that it capitalizes on pattern recognition, allowing control of the patterns treated at any one time, and allowing for varying degrees of difficulty in the patterns.

Reading texts generated by students encourage the recognition of whole words, but also provide material for exercises following other approaches. This has the desirable consequence of blurring the distinctions between the two methods. The simple, student-produced passage on page 222 illustrates many of the basic patterns which must be mastered in beginning reading. For example: (1) Eight of the twenty different words in the passage are included in the Dolch Sight Vocabulary: *I, came, to, the, got, my, a, at* (1936). (2) The pronunciation of four of the words is unpredictable according to the common English sound-spelling patterns: *to, the, a, won* (though the first three will be mastered early because they are such high-frequency items). (3) The pronunciation of five of the words conforms to the most common English spelling patterns: *got* (hot, pot), *job* (mob, Bob), *my* (try, by), *at* (hat, cat), *I* (a, e, o, u). (4) The pronunciation of five of the words is moderately predictable, according to some of the less common sound-spelling patterns: *came* (blame, shame), *states* (stakes, dates), *license* (lice, dense), *sweepstakes* (weep, makes), *English* (dish, fish—but also string, thing). (5) The pronunciation of one of the words is potentially confusing: *drivers* (diver, striver—but also river, liver). (6) The pronunciation of two of the words is related to their root words, and illustrates more complex spelling and pronunciation rules: *united, university*. Some time after they have been read, the words of the texts can be regrouped for illustration and practice of the patterns. The student-generated text itself illustrates English sentence structure and its writing conventions. It can also easily be divided into components for practice in phrase reading—either as a continuous text in phrases (a phrase per line) or as phrases on separate cards.

Of course the Whole Word Method need not be limited to texts dictated by students. Any texts, including those plucked from the surroundings, can be exploited for patterns in language. Materials which might be used, for example, include familiar short texts such as:

Verses   Selected Ogden Nash rhymes (1980)
Songs   Selected children's or adult songs such as "Old McDonald Had a Farm," "When I First Came to This Land," and "This Little Light of Mine"

Signs   (especially for older beginners)

Exit	Open
Entrance	Closed
Gentlemen	Beware of Dog
Ladies	30 MPH
No Entrance	Go Slow
Danger, Pedestrians	Do Not Pass
Quiet, Hospital Zone	Stop
Ten Items or Less	Telephone
Express Line	Bus Stop
Hard Hats Only	School Zone

Ads   You've come a long way, Baby.
        We try harder.
        The Toyota Edge

There is no conclusive evidence that either the Whole Word or the Linguistic Method for introducing reading texts works best with all students. Nor is there any assurance that when reading, a student will practice only one or the other exclusively. Current research shows that adult learners usually figure out the sound-symbol patterns no matter what the teacher's approach, and that the average learner just beginning to read ESL decodes spelling patterns, recognizes whole words, guesses from context, and makes predictions. The teacher of beginning reading can facilitate a number of potential learning modes by making materials available for both strategies. Perhaps as important as teaching strategy and the selection of materials are students' interests and the difficulty of materials. At every level the teacher should strive to make available to students reading materials of high interest.

The Reading Lesson

Most reading teachers, at any level and no matter what method of reading instruction they follow, can use a basic lesson pattern adaptable for particular levels and for special purposes. The all-purpose lesson consists of the following four steps:

1. Introduction, including the setting of a purpose for reading the target passage, a background of appropriate information, and the new vocabulary necessary to comprehend the main ideas.
2. The reading. This is usually an oral exercise for the beginners, usually consisting of listening to the passage read, or listening and following along. At later stages the reading should be silent.
3. Comprehension tasks.
4. Review and related exercises.

A more detailed sequence will be presented at each proficiency level. Here is an appropriate reading lesson for the beginner: (a) Teacher reads while students listen. (b) Discussion. (c) Teacher reads while students listen and read along. (d) Discussion. (e) Student(s) read aloud (in small groups or in dyads). (f) Discussion. (g) Students read silently, or practice reading aloud individually.

Some curriculum designers and teachers may not agree that reading aloud is an appropriate exercise for early-level ESL students. We think it is a useful practice, if the students can do a reasonable job of it. Reading aloud is a useful skill, and is one that supports speaking ability. And by observing phrasing, the teacher can use this activity to evaluate reading comprehension as distinct from merely mouthing the words.

Even at the beginning level teachers should engage students in discussion of reading materials, ever encouraging readers to think beyond the decoding processes. The types of questions employed for discussion may be categorized as information, inferential, and interpretive. All reading materials allow information questions: the standard *what, when, where, who, how many*, etc. Answers to these questions can be found in explicit statements in the text. For example, asking another student about the passage on page 222: (1) Where did (Juan) come to live? (2) What did he do? etc.

Some beginning materials also lend themselves to inferential questions. For example, one might ask about the passage: (1) Did Juan know English when he came to the United States? How do we know? (2) Does Juan know how to drive? How do we know? (3) Is Juan rich? How do we know?

A few beginning materials, even simplified readers, actually allow interpretive questions as well—questions asking about the author's opinion or the reader's judgment concerning the content of the article, or creative questions asking the reader to use the reading passage as a jumping-off point for discussion of a related subject. Generally, inferential, interpretive, and creative questions receive more emphasis at the later stages of reading development, while information questions are useful at every level.

Students' attention will be even more engaged with an occasional imaginative exercise composed by the teacher or the students themselves to suit the occasion. Such exercises can be designed around perceived survival needs, social needs, personal needs, or games. Possible materials for such exercises might include the following:

Survival Needs   Public announcements:
                   No classes next Friday.
                   Special meeting on visa renewal after school today.
                   Please report for duty at 6:00 A.M.
Social Needs   Notes:
                   An invitation to a wedding
                   A telephone message
                   Games:
                   Treasure hunt—in teams: a list of objects, or sequen-
                       tial directions to a hidden treasure
                   Strip story or strip dialog

Personal Needs   Short samples of prose and poetry can make superb
cameo reading lessons for beginning readers who are
beyond the word-by-word recognition level.

Selected translations from the short verse forms from
other cultures, e.g., Japanese haiku, are much enjoyed.

Games:

Question chains

Telling lies

Reading games can be devised capitalizing on current American phenomena such as the catchy phrases on bumper stickers, T-shirts, and
campaign buttons. Students can vie in making collections of such phrases
and composing their own.

Proverbs in English, metaphors, and similes can make good reading and
often inspire students to compose their own. It is remarkable how easy and
rewarding it can be to escape from the structural, the functional, the
situational, the survival, into the absurd, the profound, the silly, or the
beautiful—in only one sentence.

Students can contribute to their own phrase reading activities by adding to
lists the teacher starts, such as lists of places:

Phrases with in: in the box

book

drawer

pocket

Adjective pairs: good and hot

nice and cool

big and heavy

cold and gray

They are hackneyed for us, but they won't be for most beginning students.
Skimming through groups of these phrases printed on cards makes good
reading practice. Students can make their own groups of cards, writing a
phrase on each side so they can test each other. All such exercises serve
double duty as reading practice and vocabulary building as well.

There is an abundant supply of short passages for beginners in—

1. commercial texts,
2. teacher-written recombinations of materials covered in class,
3. student-written materials, using the Language Experience Approach,
4. narrative games such as strip stories, and
5. group-written stories.

There should be many occasions at this level for reading aloud by teacher
and students. The advantages of having stories read aloud while students
either listen or listen and follow along silently are many: the appeal to
multiple channels of learning, the pleasant experience, and, with the aid of
punctuation, the reinforcement of the sound system of English with its

correspondence to the written language. Students should be encouraged to read aloud as well, while they are still consolidating their mastery of the mechanics—although upon reaching the later stages of reading they should be discouraged from making a regular practice of reading aloud, or of moving their lips while reading silently.

Selection of Basic Vocabulary for Reading Materials

Most graded or simplified readers contain words found on standard frequency lists. These lists are useful, but should be regularly supplemented by additional words and phrases that are of immediate interest and utility to the reader. Survival needs for the older learner and word games for both older and younger suggest other appropriate sources. It should, of course, be obvious that one does not take a list of words and concoct a reading. The words come from the reading, not vice versa. Beginning reading materials should be constructed with a sensitivity to the utility, interest, and value of the words that make up the text. But in case of conflict the text comes first.

All students should soon learn to read names, addresses and telephone numbers important to them, common street signs, and other public labels. Many students will be interested in reading such matter as advertisements, directions on food and medicine labels, instructions on vending machines, simple how-to-do-it instructions, and menus.

Automatic Recognition of Sight Vocabulary

Reading specialists are showing a renewed interest in vocabulary. Many teachers of reading to native speakers make sure that, regardless of preference for introductory methods and materials, their beginning readers learn automatic recognition of the basic sight vocabulary. This emphasis is even more important for the second language learner.

Although there is disagreement on the exact figures, it is generally agreed that 200 to 300 words in English account for 50 to 70 percent of all the words on a typical written page. Clearly it is of great advantage for readers to automatically recognize these words—and the common phrases in which they frequently appear. The Dolch Word List used in reading classes for native speakers, or an appropriate comparable list, should be presented to beginning readers in ESL classes. Punctuation marks and other graphic conventions such as spacing and indenting should also be learned much in the same way as sight words.

Analyzing Phrase and Sentence Structure

Reading phrases and sentences divided into phrase structures, the student should soon become aware of the signalling differences between a phrase, which might be acceptable as a complete statement in spoken English, and a sentence, which is the required minimal unit in written English, except in recorded conversation.

Phrase reading exercises can be useful in weaning the reader from word-for-word reading, and can help increase speed. Combined with specific time limits, speeded-up phrase reading exercises can be designed which help shorten the duration of eye fixations.

At the beginning stage such exercises might include repeat-and-copy exercises, the use of flash cards, lists on the blackboard, matching phrases, etc.

Understanding Sentence Punctuation

Reading aloud by teacher and by students (when they have achieved enough proficiency not to bore their fellow students) can illustrate intonation, stress, pause, and juncture—particularly those features signalled by commas and periods. It is not uncommon for readers literate in other languages to fail to pay adequate attention to these symbols. At the early mechanical stage the punctuation symbols are, indeed, a reasonably consistent representation of part of our pronunciation system. We recommend that students learn the punctuation marks and spacing conventions—as sight "vocabulary."

Extensive Reading

From early on, appealing reading material at appropriate levels of difficulty should be made enticingly available to encourage students to read on their own without the stricture of pressure from the teacher. Specific time available during which students can read if they choose usually helps to develop the habit.

Commercial graded readers for ESL serve the purpose well. Teachers' reading aloud of new materials often piques interest. Reading *half* of an interesting story to the class, or all but the exciting end, can motivate a stampede for the bookshelf during free reading time.

Analysis of Word Structure

The English in course textbooks, along with contributions from Survival English and word games, provides ample sources for the analysis of word structure for the beginning student. The student should be acquainted with examples from the major categories of word building in English, an exercise in analysis that will continue at progressively more difficult levels as long as he continues to use English.

The list of items for word formation exercises does not have to be extensive. The aim is to initiate a familiarity with the most regular and the most productive lexical patterns of English, in order to lay a foundation for a strong network of associations among English words which will continue to enlarge as the student makes advances in English.

Exercises in word building at the beginning level might include reading and writing, for example, in:

1. Pattern practices, e.g., possessive endings and regular and irregular verb forms: *keep, kept*; *sweep, swept*; *sleep, slept*; *weep, wept*; *creep, crept*; *leap, leapt.*
2. Collocations, e.g., lists of synonyms for the words in the passage; lists of analogues such as additional compound words, and lists of related words such as those in exercise 8.1:

university	universe
English	England
driver	driving, driveway
won	win, winner

Some useful classifications for word formation, with examples from Exercise 8.1, include:

1. root words	university, united
2. regular syntactic suffixes	driver's, states
3. present and past verb forms	study, studied
4. derivational affixes	driver, English, university
5. common irregulars	came, got, won
6. contractions	isn't, won't
7. compound words	sweepstakes
8. comparative forms	bigger
9. idioms	Come off it!

Reading exercises may be combined with writing from the beginning, not only as a tool in comprehension or language-building exercises, but also in conjunction with writing as two component skills, both needed to complete an assignment such as information gathering for a creative (expressive) language task.

Illustrations should be used lavishly at the beginning level.

ELEMENTARY READING: EMPHASIS ON BUILDING

The beginning reader learns to read the sight words and decode the common spelling patterns of English, in order to read simple passages both aloud with accuracy and silently with comprehension. Following this stage, the student must learn independence from the grapho-phonic cues that functioned in the initial identification of words, and further develop skills to be used in comprehending more varied and difficult reading.

When do students practice actual reading? Smith, Goodman, and Meredith (1970) contribute a serious indictment of the reading class at large:

although skill in reading can be developed only through practicing reading, in an average hour of reading instruction students usually read for only ten minutes.

Teachers of reading in the ESL class should take warning from such critiques. In programs where reading is an important goal, the developmental needs of readers should be considered, and time should be planned for actual reading activities in monitored, and occasionally timed, situations.

Personal Reading Strategies

The reading strategies of good readers differ markedly from those of poor readers, and the strategies of native speakers of English typically differ from those of second language speakers. These differences might offer further suggestions for the second language class. (1) First language speakers are faster than second language learners at a number of component reading tasks: interpreting individual words and syntactic structures, anticipating sequences of words, and pronouncing individual words. (2) Second language learners read more slowly, needing longer eye fixations to process information, and thus putting overloads on their short-term memories. (3) Native speakers rely more heavily on semantic than on syntactic clues, and attend to word stress and sentence stress, while second language learners divide their time more or less equally between function and content words and don't discriminate efficiently between stressed and unstressed words. Many of them read at the word level only, relating word groups no further than the previous or the following sentence. They read surface meanings and seldom form opinions of what they read. In addition to strategic problems, second language learners are likely to have the handicaps of interference from their first languages and unfamiliarity with the subjects of written passages, in many cases a background of irrelevant teaching methods, and an academic orientation in which reading is not valued.

A look at some of the characteristics of good and poor readers can suggest how the second language reader might be helped (Allington 1978, Hosenfeld 1979, Weber 1977):

Characteristics of Good Readers	Characteristics of Poor Readers
1. Balance grapho-phonic and semantic-syntactic systems	Overuse grapho-phonic cues and underuse semantic-syntactic and context cues
2. Keep the meaning of the passage in mind while proceeding	Analyze the sound system instead of the meaning
3. Read in broad phrases	Translate in short phrases and spend extra time decoding, so lose the meaning of the passage as they read along
4. Skip unimportant words	Read all words as equal in importance

5. Have positive self-concepts as readers	Have negative self-images as readers
6. Replace unknown words with fillers which do not alter the general meaning	Stop at unknown words and look them up

Our analysis of these observations of the reader and the reading process leads us to the conclusion that teachers should: (1) give students class time in which to practice reading, and coordinate additional reading; (2) offer transition exercises between the stage where reading is primarily a mechanical task and the stage of fluent, independent reading, in which the student can develop efficient reading habits and comprehension skills. If students are to have enough time to read, independent reading must be incorporated as an integral part of the reading period.

Selecting Materials

The first rule of materials selection is student interest and usefulness. Often interest and usefulness are related. The second rule has to do with level of difficulty.

Although there is not a hard-and-fast rule as to appropriate level of difficulty, and it is argued by many that high student interest can automatically "simplify" many a difficult reading selection, there are a number of ways of roughly estimating the appropriateness of a reading selection for a particular student or class. There are two methods that are particularly useful for an ESL class: (1) Have the student(s) read the text out loud. If 85 percent of the words are read correctly, the text is at an appropriate level. (2) Make a modified cloze test out of part of the passage. The text is at an appropriate level if the student gets a score of approximately 50 percent accuracy with the use of the appropriate word method of correction. This level of accuracy corresponds to the "Instructional Level" of reading materials expressed as indicating for native speakers 85 to 90 percent comprehension of meaning and 70 to 75 percent correctness in interpretation.

For the teacher who wants a text to be used by the entire class, a perfect selection is virtually impossible. However, high student interest in content may be almost as important as proficiency level in predicting whether a person can "read" a particular passage. Therefore the teacher should be as concerned with interest level as with level of linguistic and semantic difficulty in selecting reading materials.

Although scholars disagree widely as to an optimum number of new words for language learners to try to master per day, there are some useful guidelines for making decisions about the percentage of new words to allow in a text from the elementary level on.

As an easy reading task for native speakers, Edward Fry (1963), recommends a ratio of less than 5 percent. In other words, on the instructional level, Fry suggests introducing only one new word in twenty for guided reading practice. This would allow as many as one hundred new words in an article two thousand words in length. Fry labels as the Frustration Level an introduction of more than 10 percent new words, or two new words out of twenty. He cautions that such materials be avoided as selections for class lessons. Since Fry's reference is to native speakers, we suggest introducing only one new word in thirty-five for second language learners.

In terms of vocabulary, teachers should be clear in what they mean by "new words" in elementary texts. For reading purposes, teachers should (1) look for passive acquaintance, not mastery, of the new word, (2) not count as new any words the students will likely be able to figure out from word analysis or context, and (3) accept a probable vague understanding of the word, rather than seeking a dictionary definition. Only words or phrases which involve completely new concepts or are central to the meaning of the passage should be introduced before a reading exercise is undertaken.

Silent Reading

Silent reading is the essential first step in breaking students from the habit of devoting all attention to the precise decoding of the shapes and sounds of letters. Phrase reading, timed reading, and guessing activities are likewise useful.

As an example of a possible text selected for the elementary reader we have adapted a reading passage prepared initially for third grade native speakers with reading problems. The passage contains 110 words, only 9 of which are not included in the "Dale List of 769 Easy Words" (1948). In ascertaining whether the vocabulary load is too heavy for the class, the teacher may consider the size of the class's *collective* vocabulary and the fact that proper names can easily be learned as new sight words. In exercises in which students talk about their reading, they can help each other with new words. In addition, prereading activities led by the teacher may include discussion of some of the new terms—not as vocabulary building per se, but as background information.

Adapted for a junior high ESL class, the following text appeals to the students' own experience, describing a girl's having trouble understanding a tape-recorded selection. It lends itself to extensive discussion.

EXERCISE 8.2

ELEMENTARY READING COMPREHENSION*

Instructions: Read the following: (Code 3–4)

Mary listened to the tape that the teacher was playing to the class. "So fast," she thought. She was upset. She listened to every sentence, but could understand only one or two words in each. Suddenly the tape stopped and she heard the teacher call on her saying, "Please repeat the first sentence, Mary."

5   She did not remember the first sentence, and that made her feel panicky and ashamed. She put her head down on the desk, looked at the floor and said nothing.

The teacher let the class go to lunch, but asked Mary to stay for a minute. "What is the matter, Mary?" she asked.

9   "I didn't understand any of the reading," Mary said.

*Adapted from *Tutor's Sampler,* Lillie Pope, Deborah Edel, and Abraham Haklay, New York, Book-Lab, Inc., 1973, p. 12.

Sample Reading Lesson, Elementary Level

I. Introduction: Prequestions and Key Words and Phrases
  1. Teacher stimulates student interest by telling them that the story they are going to read is about a schoolgirl with a problem. The problem involves a *tape recorder, sentences*, and *understanding.* The teacher asks students to listen for answers to the following questions:
     a. What is the problem?
     b. What happens to the people in the story?
     c. Can you think of any way(s) to help solve the problem?
  2. Before the students see the passage, the teacher reads the first part to them, stopping and asking questions on selected points.
     a. The teacher stops after line 2 and asks: What does *upset* mean? Why do you think Mary was upset?
     b. After reading the next sentence, the teacher asks: How do you think Mary felt?
     c. After reading lines 5 and 6, the teacher asks: What do you think Mary did?

The teacher does not confirm students' answers as right or wrong. After getting possible answers from students she asks them to open their books and read the story silently in a specified amount of time, say 45 seconds to one minute. When the time is up, the teacher discusses the questions again with the class, acknowledging which of the early answers were closest to the story, but also acknowledging the great number of other possibilities which *might* have been true in a real life situation.

II. Comprehension Tasks—Information, Inferential, and Interpretive or Open-Ended Questions
  1. The teacher asks the following questions, expecting short answers:
     Information: Who is the story about?
                       What happened to her?
     Inference: Why did Mary put her head down on the desk?
     Interpretation: Why do you think Mary failed to understand the sentences?
                       What do you think the teacher next said to Mary?
                       What do you think Mary should do in the future?
                       What do you think the teacher should do?
III. Review and Related Exercises

Clearly this passage lends itself well to a continuation of the language-building exercises described for the beginning level. At the elementary level, both comprehension and accelerated language-building exercises are in order. If the students have specific skills classes in which they learn structure and vocabulary, the reading teacher may be freed from a good deal of this supplementary work. If not, the reading teacher should plan all activities carefully so all the component skills are practiced without comprehension exercises being mistaken for language-building and vice versa.

When the same text is used for both comprehension activities and a source for language building, the comprehension activities should be done first.

Phrase-Spaced Reading

To make a quickie phrase reading passage from an extended passage at this level: (1) Divide a continuous passage of moderate difficulty into phrases. (2) Have students read silently within a given amount of time. (3) Administer a true/false or multiple-choice test of comprehension, and discuss.

At present there is no best guideline in the literature on ESL for selecting constituents as boundaries when creating such exercises. Teachers can devise their own rules of thumb, deciding on length of constituents according to their students' capacities, and the nature of constituents according to phrases that have meaning in themselves and "sound right."

The following passage, offered as an illustration, contains 459 words, of which 16, or 3.5 percent, are not included in the "Dale List of 769 Easy Words." Again, the teacher will have to judge whether such a passage is usable, and, if not, find another or adapt.

EXERCISE 8.3

EARTH'S JOURNEY

Instructions: Read by phrases. (Code 3–5)

Did you know   that right now   you are taking a ride   on a spaceship, the Earth?   All the other people   in the world   are on board, too,   on a trip around the sun,   at more than 18 miles per second.   You and your fellow travelers   have many supplies   along with you for the trip: air, water, land, and energy.   But these supplies   must be used by everyone,   and after they are used   the first time,   they must be reused   again and again.   All of these supplies   are found   in a small area of the Earth: in the air   around the planet   and the thin cover   of earth and water   around the top of the planet, Earth.   Everything living on Earth   depends on the air   and the cover of the Earth.   Everything in the system   is recycled after it is used.   Nothing new is ever added   to this system.   Water on the Earth   turns into small drops   and travels into the air   to make clouds.   Later this same water   comes back to the Earth   as rain (or snow,   hail, or sleet),   provides water for people,   and helps the plants to grow.   It fills rivers, lakes, and oceans,   and then it turns into drops again.   The water you drink   in our spaceship   is the same water   that was drunk by people   hundreds of years ago.   Today our spaceship   is in trouble.   Nothing new is ever added   to our biosphere,   but if we are not careful,   we may use up   some of our valuable supplies,   and we will be in trouble.   Thousands of years ago   there were not many people on spaceship Earth.   If those people   used most of the supplies   in one area of the Earth,   they moved to another part.   Today there are many more people.   We use many more supplies   and we throw many of the natural resources away   after using them.   But if we use all the resources   in one area   we can no longer move   to another area   to use the supplies there.   We have to use   more and more   of our air, water, natural resources,   and energy,   so we must find ways   in which everything we use   can be reused   in the same way   as water is reused   in our biosphere.   We must make sure   that the people who live   hundreds of years from now   will be able to ride on the spaceship   and drink the same water   that the ancient people drank.   If we want to save our spaceship   for the future,   we must help each other   to protect our biosphere   and let Nature   continue to run its course.

Questions: Information, Inferential, Discussion

1. How fast is the Earth moving?
2. Why can we call the Earth a spaceship?
3. What four kinds of supplies do people need?

4. Where are these supplies stored?
5. How are the supplies recycled?
6. What does man have to do to save Spaceship Earth?

1. Why is Spaceship Earth in trouble today?
2. Why wasn't Spaceship Earth in trouble in the past?

1. How are Earth's supplies used differently in different countries?
2. How fast is the speed of Earth? Compare this speed to the speeds of other moving things.
3. What efforts are being made in different countries to deal with the resource problems of Spaceship Earth?
4. What efforts are being made in your area to deal with the resource problems of Spaceship Earth?
5. What other things could people do to help the situation?
6. What do you think the author's opinion concerning Spaceship Earth's problem is?

Word Building—Scanning

Students can learn to distinguish affixes from stems in words that have both, and to identify compound words, idioms, phrasal (two-word) verbs, figurative uses, etc. An appropriate assignment would be to make lists of examples of these items from a reading recently finished.

root words and derivational affixes	biosphere used, reused cycled, recycled invisible valuable evaporate cooperate
compound words	spaceship
idioms	take a ride miles per second make sure that be in trouble run its course
figurative use of words	crust
collocations	rhyme: millions and billions
phrasal verbs	depend on help to add to throw away

Content and Function Words

After students have mastered the basics of the beginning level, they continue to develop control of the mechanics in new ways. Recognition of stressed and unstressed words will help readers decide which words are most important to focus on. The teacher should continue to read to the class at this stage and have the students mark stressed words. (The students will have stopped reading aloud themselves.) Slogans and rhymes are particularly appropriate for these exercises, as they make good use of the prosodic features of English.

Students can participate in variations on this exercise. For example, have students themselves read the phrase silently and underline the word they think is stressed. Later they can compare their choices with those of the rest of the class. Have students read aloud the words they think receive sentence stress, and discuss. Have students find or make up strings of content words used in place of sentences, such as in newspaper headlines, advertisements, telegrams, and notes written informally or in a hurry:

newspaper headlines	Busted Budgets Confront Reagan Creationists Lose First Round
magazine article headline	Japan Leads Way
advertisements	The Toyota Edge Big Bass Breakthrough Canon—Takes Less Gives More
telegrams	Mother arriving Wednesday, Feb. 28, 10:00 am Love
notes	Please bring history notes today. Thanks, A.

Turning the shortened forms into oral sentences provides still another reading practice.

Developing Cognitive Skills in English

Even at the elementary stage the readers should be able to stretch their minds with all the language they know. Pencil and paper tasks allow a wide variety of mind-stretching exercises:

1. simple arithmetical word problems
2. riddles
3. true and false statements
4. word categories game

Everyone's favorite trick questions, appropriately phrased, make good reading and discussion exercises at this level. E.g.:

EXERCISE 8.4

LOGICAL INTERPRETATION

Instructions: Read the following numbered paragraphs. (Code 3–5)

1. A young man was badly hurt in an automobile accident in which his father was killed. When the young man was brought to the nearest hospital for emergency treatment, the doctor in attendance took one look at him and gasped, "My son!" (How could this be?)
2. In a plane crash all were killed. (How many survivors were there?)
3. A lady bought a hat with a yellow flower for $10.00. (If the hat cost $9.00 more than the flower, how much did the flower cost?)

These are particularly good as group exercises. There will inevitably be differences of opinion, and in discussing their opinions students invariably discover the trick in the problem and thus do a nice bit of hypothesizing as well as analyzing the meaning of the text.

True/false items lend themselves beautifully to this type of exercise:

EXERCISE 8.5

ANALYSIS OF MEANING

Instructions: Indicate which are true and which are false. (Code 3–4)

_____ 1. All parents are people.

_____ 2. All poisonous snakes are dangerous.

_____ 3. The opposite of success is failure.

_____ 4. Societies are always made up of human beings.

_____ 5. An American student in China is an alien there.

_____ 6. Good weather ensures safe driving.

(These questions are subject to different interpretations, but this is precisely why they are useful in discussion. The answers depend on the word definitions adopted.)

As the students increase their reading skills at the elementary level, they can begin to read simple charts and graphs, transferring their content into the spoken and written language. This practice is valuable with increasingly difficult materials at all levels of reading.

Reading passages at all levels lend themselves as appropriate sources for language building and vocabulary building. The program design decides whether these activities are done along with reading or at another time. The teacher who is called on to supplement her reading class with other language activities should refer to Chapters Eleven and Twelve on the grammar and vocabulary of the written language.

Extensive Reading

The most valuable thing a reading teacher can do for a student who is approaching proficiency is to encourage and support self-confidence and a sense of value concerning reading in the second language. One of the best ways to do this is to make assignments that the students will enjoy, and give them time to read. This requires preparation and coordination by the teacher, either setting up a reading library of modest dimensions in her own classroom, or providing a guide for outside resources. The teacher should set aside a time during class when the students can go to the reading area to look over the books. Annotated book lists as well as hands-on rummaging help build student interest. Have students make lists of books and other printed materials they think they might like to read. Set another date by which the students are to have spent 5 hours reading a book of their choice. Have students prepare to share with teacher, class, or small group their ideas about what they have read. Prepare a questionnaire on which students can enter basic information about each book after finishing it, mentioning main content, development of plot, reader's opinion: just enough information to individualize the book so it can be recalled readily. Too much of this type of assignment may become burdensome. Another option is to use small discussion groups; still another is to have students fill out questionnaires about books their classmates have reported on.

Students will enjoy keeping records of the books they have read, and there is likely to be cross-motivation when students share information about the books and even compete in filling out prominently displayed charts.

Beginning Study Skills

Study skills have already started to be important at this level. The student should be introduced to a number of uses for the dictionary (checking word meanings, pronunciation, register, parts of speech, histories, idioms, alternate spellings, etc.) and should begin to perform tasks in finding information and reporting.

INTERMEDIATE READING: EMPHASIS ON OVERALL COMPREHENSION AND READING WITH PURPOSE

Have you heard about the newscaster who runs to the coffee shop after his show so he can relax with a cup of coffee and the latest paper to find out what is going on in the world? Or the proofreader who can't wait for the novels she proofs to be put into print so that she can read them and find out what they're all about? These are not far-fetched stories; they are examples of actual incidents which further underline the point that when all one's attention is devoted to the mechanics of reading, full comprehension and retention are almost impossible. (Of course, the well-organized broadcaster must read his materials for comprehension *before* going on the air.)

If efficient reading is in part solving a puzzle with limited information, then the student can best advance, much as a good detective is supposed to, by preparing well beforehand and learning to analyze the evidence—sharpening powers of observation, association, and memory—and becoming a good hunter of clues.

The intermediate, positively motivated student is in a good position to search for clues; the more English already understood, the easier it becomes to hypothesize about new language items. By reading, questioning, and discussing, the reader increases language expectancies. With guidance, these students can take command of the page they read. If they have been answering information questions before, they can now learn to formulate their own questions in the interest of more fully developed reading comprehension.

Most students who persevere through the study of English at the intermediate level have a specific reading goal—a skill they hope to develop and be able to use by the end of this stage of instruction. For those academically bound the goal will include passing examinations, using textbooks efficiently, and frequently turning to professional journals and other reference materials. For others the goal may be the ability to read correspondence of normal difficulty, and newspapers or magazines.

Exercises in reading for academic purposes are exercises in study skills. They overlap with exercises appropriate for other language components at this level, and go hand in hand with further analysis of the structure of written English.

The most important intermediate reading skills are: (1) reading with incomplete information, (2) organizing for careful reading, (3) organizing information, (4) reading critically, (5) developing effective personal reading strategies, and (6) setting effective reading speeds for different kinds of reading.

Reading with Incomplete Information

Reading with incomplete information usually means reading a passage with a sizable number of unfamiliar vocabulary items. The most useful—

and necessary—reading strategy for the second language reader will be to read effectively while tolerating a certain amount of vagueness and uncertainty.

The tendency for many readers is to stop and ponder over each "unknown" word and ask for assistance or look it up in a dictionary. But, as we have seen, this is a typical strategy of the poor reader; not only is the reader who stops frequently at individual words unlikely to find a definition truly appropriate for use in specific passages where items are found, but he also loses many of the advantages gained by the efficient reader who either arrives at a proximate meaning of the word which is adequate for his understanding of the passage, or substitutes a dummy word for the unknown, maybe ignoring it altogether.

Hosenfeld (1977) points out that the reader who gets the meaning of new words from context reaps multiple benefits: (1) he gets the meaning of the words; (2) he connects the meaning with the surrounding sentences; (3) he keeps the meaning of the whole passage in mind; and (4) he recognizes the relative importance of other words.

To help the second language reader who has not already internalized these useful habits, it is important to convince him to accept two principles: (1) It is not necessary to understand the *exact* meaning of every new word in order to understand a passage. (2) It is not necessary to understand some of the words at all.

These points are easy to demonstrate. First, have students read a passage in which a number of words have been deleted and then answer comprehension questions on the passage. Readers will be surprised to find that their comprehension has not been significantly impaired.

The teacher might then profitably conduct an introductory lesson designed to demonstrate that out of as many as thirty to forty "new words" in a lengthy, authentic article, there are probably only four or five that are not explained by either their own construction or the context. And even these few words will probably not have to be looked up by the time the reader has finished reading the entire article.

Skimming and Scanning

Skimming and scanning are examples par excellence of reading with incomplete information. They can be used on an advanced level for organizing information as well as a myriad of tasks in the services of language study in general.

To skim, a reader glides over the surface of a text, reading selected important parts rapidly in order to get an overview of content and organization. To scan, the reader looks through the text rapidly to locate specific information. This rapid reading is done at a speed faster than the speed with which one usually reads a text of average difficulty, and still faster than the slower-than-average speed at which one reads a particularly important and difficult text. Rapid reading serves useful purposes, such as (1) perspective (advance organizing to equip the reader for a later, more thorough reading of a passage), (2) evaluation (helping the reader decide whether the text is worth reading further), and (3) review (allowing a quick survey and review of something read earlier).

For a simple exercise in skimming, refer to the excerpt from the physics lecture in Chapter Three, page 90. (1) After appropriate introduction exercises, have the class read the first sentence of every paragraph and then predict the probable content of the whole passage according to the information in those sentences. (2) From constructing an outline or an associative word list on the blackboard, the teacher can usually reconstruct key features of the articles from students' contributions. (3) For appropriate lead-in exercises, ask questions on the title, "Temperature and Density," or request students to discuss, before reading, specific information in the paragraph. (4) A short comprehension test *before* the reading can be a very good advance organizer if it is given and taken in a nonthreatening spirit. Any of these advance exercises can be given *after* the skimming exercise as well as *before*.

A longer passage such as a lengthy piece of journalism or a chapter from a text can be skimmed by reading all headings and subtitles, then reading the first one or two paragraphs in entirety, then the last one or two paragraphs in entirety, and finally the first sentence of all the paragraphs, from first to last.

A sense of content and general organization can be provided by having students take a specific length of time, e.g., 30 seconds, to *scan* a short article (2 minutes for a longer article) for key words and phrases, which the teacher writes on the blackboard as students offer suggested answers.

While we equip readers to proceed with incomplete information when necessary, at the same time we encourage them to utilize all the information they can get.

EXERCISE 8.6

ORGANIZING IN ADVANCE

Instructions: Follow the directions given. (Code 5–6)

1. Skim title, headings, graphics, etc., to get an overview.
2. Generate prequestions and make predictions as to the answers.
3. Scan the reader's own memory for information related to the main ideas.
4. Read, stopping at major divisions to readjust questions about the text.

Additional exercises can be designed to encourage these activities:

1. Introduce the subject of the article alone (or the title or key phrases, or propositions) and brainstorm in the class or in small groups or dyads.

2. Teacher reads the selection part way through, stopping for students to make predictions concerning the rest of the text.
3. Have students scan for key phrases and discuss before reading.

We recommend relating skimming exercises with long passages to part of the famed SQ3R sequence: "*S*urvey, *Q*uestion, *R*ead, *R*ecite, *R*eview," designed to provide an approach to reading intellectual prose with maximum comprehension. Or we might modify this to SQ2R: "*S*kim, *Q*uestion, *R*ead, and *R*ecite."

At this level students should have practice in the following activities: (1) Read and take notes. (2) Read and fill in an outline. (3) Read and outline. (4) Summarize. (5) Paraphrase. (6) Express information in a different mode, e.g., from prose to chart form, chart to prose form.

Reading Critically

Reading critically presupposes basic skills in understanding and interpreting meaning: (1) understanding literal meanings, (2) paraphrasing the content, (3) getting the main thought and the details, (4) distinguishing among fact, inference, and opinion, (5) seeing relationships, (6) predicting outcomes, (7) drawing conclusions, (8) making generalizations, (9) understanding figurative language, and (10) recognizing propaganda.

To check and give practice in critical reading, the teacher can: (1) Ask the class to distinguish between the author's statements and opinions and the reader's own opinion. (2) Discuss the author's intent, bias, and use of propaganda techniques, if any. (3) Discuss language features and forms.

Personal Attitudes and Reading Strategies

In addition to perfecting the mechanics of reading and developing techniques for dealing with limited information, students will benefit from having positive attitudes about reading English. Some suggestions for helping students build positive attitudes: Facilitate their successful reading experiences. Customize small steps, but not too small—suit the techniques to the individual student. Tactfully help polish the mechanics of students who are behind their peers. Have students read during class and observe them. Make mental notes of problems such as the student who "reads aloud" quietly to himself, and give individual help where needed. Keep records of individual progress, such as records of improvements in timed reading, and discuss each student's record with him toward the middle of the term, while there is still time for working on what is seen as a problem.

Explain the reading course and the teaching techniques if the students are unfamiliar with them. Demonstrate the need for the particular reading skills taught. Give a pretest (i.e., at the beginning of the term) which will show the students' reading levels and provide a basis for comparisons later. Conduct needs assessments which make it clear that the course is related to students' perceived needs. For example, if students are trying to improve their reading in preparation for attending a university in an English-speaking country, find out the average reading load in a particular representative field, and explain the need for faster reading to accommodate such a load. At the end of the term demonstrate the effectiveness of the course by showing pretest and posttest gains both for the class and for individuals.

Culture and Literature

It's worth mentioning that in classes with diverse nationalities and cultures, the teacher can expect differences in attitudes toward reading and different interpretations of value and characterization. The first point can be illustrated by the tendency in some countries for literary men to be or become interested and active in politics. The more typical American attitude is that literary men are on the margin of society. In fact it would be most surprising for a Robert Frost or a Walt Whitman to announce he was going to run for president of the United States. In most Latin American countries a comparable announcement would not be at all surprising.

Likewise there will be different interpretations of the values of, say, the dream world of Walter Mitty. Americans usually enjoy and sympathize with the poor henpecked husband who escapes to a dream world where he takes heroic roles. But to many foreign students, he is a disgusting nincompoop who doesn't have the intestinal fortitude to run his own house and family. It's not a laughing matter to a macho Latin American male. We take our cultural baggage with us when we travel to another culture, a generalization the teacher in the United States should keep in mind.

Maintaining Effective Reading Speeds for Different Kinds of Reading

The inability to vary the speed of reading is a serious drawback for students in the United States in general, and it is a more serious problem for second language readers than for natives. Slow readers do, in fact, make more mistakes than faster readers. Faster readers have the advantage of having to absorb fewer meanings, doing less physical work, and having a supportive rhythm and flow of the language. Regular practice in short, timed reading passages can start the student on the way to a fluent reading speed. A number of reading specialists agree that the minimum speed for effective reading is 200 words per minute, the average: 250 wpm, and the optimum: 400–500 wpm.

EXERCISE 8.7

TWENTY-MINUTE TIMED READING LESSON

Instructions for teacher: (Code 5–7)

1. Get a watch with a second hand.
2. Select a passage of approximately 400 words, aimed at the class mid-reading level, i.e., relatively easy for the class. Write ten comprehension questions, five information and five inferential.
3. Set a 5-minute time limit, and indicate all 10-second periods on the blackboard from :10 to 5:00.
4. When 5 minutes have passed, have students stop whether they have finished the passage or not, and answer the comprehension questions, without looking back at the passage.
5. Review answers to comprehension questions while students check their own papers. Seventy percent accuracy is adequate; at this speed we cannot expect the reader to understand and recall perfectly, and the 70 percent indicates that the reader is capable of a high level of accuracy under different reading conditions.

The significance of the timed reading exercise is an increase in the degree of comprehension and in speed as the class progresses. Twenty of these short exercises over a time should increase students' regular reading speed. Keeping records of students' progress helps both student and teacher.

Text Analysis

Analysis of the syntax of selected texts can help the intermediate student increase sensitivity to advanced written English and its complex patterns, principles of cohesion, and elements of rhetoric and style, and therefore to meaning in general.

Students examining the overall organization of texts may profit from work being done by teachers of ESP, particularly in medicine, the physical sciences, and business.

The academically bound intermediate student may need to develop further skills in English so that language will present no major problems in a full-time study program. The student with problems in reading may appropriately be advised to carry a reduced course load.

At the high end of the continuum of intermediate skills, the reader will begin to tackle authentic or slightly adapted authentic materials. The skills necessary for academic tasks and critical reading are appropriate here. The reader should practice reading appropriate materials efficiently and with comprehension, and develop skills needed for planned professional or academic tasks. In addition to continuing to develop the standard comprehension and reading skills, the student is advised to practice such reading-related tasks as note taking, outlining, summarizing, paraphrasing, citing, and reviewing.

Planning intermediate reading courses can be greatly strengthened by the use of performance objectives. A list of such objectives from one high intermediate reading course in an ESP program (in China) provides a useful example. It is proposed that the student who attains these instructional objectives will have sufficient command of the reading skills to begin full-time university studies in a science program in the United States.

HIGH INTERMEDIATE READING OBJECTIVES

Performance Objectives

The student is to perform the following functions with adequate competence for academic and nonacademic purposes as evidenced by 70 percent accuracy on 14th grade Fry level reading materials used in classroom activities and criterion-referenced tests:

a. extracting explicit and general information,
b. analyzing for logic, overall organization, and viewpoint,
c. appropriately selecting and using text-level reading strategies such as skimming, scanning, outlining, and paraphrasing.

As indicated in the objectives, the level of difficulty of the materials is chosen according to the target skill, i.e., the reading level of an American university undergraduate, rather than according to text analysis or student diagnosis. Reading activities for the course are sophisticated versions of those used at the lower levels, with a few additions. It is useful to do many of the readings in class and to time them, to continue to build toward an efficient reading speed.

Comprehension activities can include multiple choice, fill-in, true/false, and open-ended items as well as matching and rearranging exercises. Exercises in predicting and working with graphics, figures, outlines, and notes are good supplements.

The reading activities are frequently related to writing—particularly in summaries and research writing, and occasionally in composition exercises related to the subject of the reading matter.

EXERCISE 8.8

ENGLISH FOR SPECIAL PURPOSES

Instructions: Read the following: (Code 6–7)

Science and its practical applications in the form of technology, or the "science" of the industrial arts, as Webster defines the term, have had an enormous impact on modern society and culture. For generations it was believed that science and technology would provide the solutions to the problem of human 5 suffering: disease, famine, war, and poverty. But today these problems remain; in fact, many argue that they are expanding. Some even conclude that science and technology as presently constituted are not capable of meeting the collective needs of mankind. A more radical position is that modern scientific methods and institutions, because of their very nature and structure, thwart basic human needs 10 and emotions; the catastrophes of today's world, and the greatest threat to its future, some claim, are the direct consequences of science and technology. A major paradox has been created: scientific rationality, taken as the supreme form of the application of the rational faculties of human beings, and which, along with its practical applications in the form of technological development, have liberated 15 man from ignorance, from the whims and oppression of a relentless nature, and while having subordinated the earth to man, has become the potential instrument of the self-destruction of the human species. War, pollution, and economic oppression are seen as the inevitable spin-off of scientific advance by large sections of the public. The Nazi policies regarding the concentration and eventual 20 extermination of millions of Jews and non-Jews alike, as well as the atomic annihilation of the Hiroshima and Nagasaki bombings, are both seen as the products of an unrestrained scientific rationality.

In recent decades in the West there has emerged a wave of anti-scientific, anti-rational moods, especially among the young people, which threatens a complete 25 rejection not simply of the technological fruits of science, but of scientific rationalism as well, in favor of one or another version of mysticism, irrationalism, and primitivism—or as one philosopher of science has called it, of blood and soil philosophy. Wartovsky has described the argument of the anti-science people as one in which we are admonished to "listen to the blood, get back to our roots, and 30 cast out the evil demons of a blind and inhuman rationality, and thereby we will save ourselves." The only "reasonable thing" to do, according to the opposition-ist, is to reject reason itself—at least in its scientific form. The very rejection of that reason, in "reasonable" terms, is in itself a paradox.

Excerpt from *The Future of Science,* Watts (GELC), 1980.

Exercises on "The Future of Science"

1. *Prequestions*
    a. What does the title mean?
    b. Turn the title into a question.
    c. What do we mean in English when we talk about the "future of something"?
    d. What is the current status of science?
    e. What has been the past history of science?
    f. Why do you think the author is discussing these questions?
    g. What do you think the author is going to say about science?
    h. What do you think the author's position will be on the subject?
    i. What is your opinion?

2. *Multiple Choice Comprehension Questions*
    (1) According to the article, a major paradox has been created in which:
        a. Scientific rationality has provided man with means of both freedom and self-destruction.
        b. Antiscience people reject scientific rationality in reasonable terms.
        c. Scientific rationality has been rejected by proponents of blood and soil philosophy.
        d. (not enough information in the passage to answer)
    (2) The paradox has been caused by:
        a. the failure of science and its practical applications to impact on modern society and culture.
        b. an increase in human problems.
        c. Nazi policies and the bombings of Japan.
        d. (not enough information in the passage to answer)
    (3) The antiscience people:
        a. argue that disease, famine, war, and poverty are increasing.
        b. blame modern catastrophes on science and rationality.
        c. follow versions of mysticism.
        d. (not enough information in the passage to answer)

3. *Reference Queries*
    Each of the following words is numbered according to the line of text in which it appears. In the space beside each (referent) write the word or phrase which identifies what the referent refers to. (Use your own words.)

    a. they (6) _____

    b. its (10) _____

    c. which (13) _____

    d. both (21) _____

    e. one (26) _____

4. *Paraphrase Queries: Ask relevant questions using the terms cited.*

    a. the "science" of the industrial arts (2) _____

    b. blood and soil philosophy (27–28) _____

5. *Redundancy Queries:* Find another way in which the following words are expressed in the text. Fill in word or phrase and line where it is located in the text in the blank spaces below. Some of the questions have more than one possible answer.

    a. science and its practical applications in the form of technology (1) _____

    _____

    b. many (6) _____

c. the application of the rational faculties of human beings (13) _____

_____

d. the human species (17) _____

e. the oppositionist (31–32) _____

6. *Queries on Indirect References:* Identify the following indirect references:

   a. many (6) _____

   b. some (6) _____

   c. some (11) _____

7. *Queries on Subjects:* Identify the subjects of the following verbs:

   a. *thwart* basic human needs and emotions (9–10) _____

   b. *have liberated* man from ignorance (14–15) _____

   c. *has become* the potential instrument of the self-destruction of the human

      species (16–17) _____

   d. *having subordinated* the earth to man (16) _____

   e. *are both seen* as the products of (21–22) _____

   f. *threatens* a complete rejection (24–25) _____

8. *Relocation Queries:* Identify the grammatical functions of the following
   phrases, as: 1) subject of independent clause
                  2) subject of dependent clause
                  3) object of dependent or independent clause
                  4) object of prepositional phrase

   a. Science and its practical applications (1) _____

   b. science and technology (4) _____

   c. science and technology (6–7) _____

   d. unrestrained scientific rationality (22) _____

   e. blind and inhuman rationality (30) _____

9. *Paraphrase Queries:* Paraphrase the following:

   a. A major paradox has been created . . . (11–12 ff.) _____

   _____

   b. In recent decades in the West . . . (23 ff.) _____

   _____

10. *Loaded Language Queries:* Explain the viewpoints expressed by the description of scientific rationality in the following phrases:

a. Science and its *practical* applications in the form of technology (1) _____

_____

_____

b. the *supreme form* of the application of the rational faculties (12–13) _____

_____

c. the *potential instrument* of the self-destruction of the human species (16–17)

_____

_____

d. *unrestrained* scientific rationality (22) _____

_____

e. a *blind and inhuman* rationality (30) _____

_____

Additional exercises in vocabulary building derived from this passage can be found in Chapter Twelve of this book. Such vocabulary building exercises should not be confused with reading exercises. When based on the content of a reading passage, the vocabulary exercises should *follow* the reading exercises.

In many preuniversity or ESP programs the reading skills are practiced in both discrete and synthesizing activities. The separate reading skills are utilized in assigned outlines, summaries, reviews, and research reports.

If students are willing to select some of their own classroom materials related to their respective fields or interests for some of their exercises, the teacher should be prepared to relinquish some control over the activity. For example, if each student in a class summarizes or reviews a different article in a different field, the teacher may comment on the form and organization of the review, but will not be able to judge with complete assurance its accuracy.

ADVANCED READING: EMPHASIS ON READING FOR SPECIAL PURPOSES

The advanced reader will strive to read with understanding comparable to that of a competent native speaker. Reading with full understanding requires extensive knowledge of the culture and familiarity with the society's values and thought patterns as well as its ways of categorizing reality and patterns of conjecturing about those categories, and it requires practice in reading, pondering, and discussing.

Since this level overlaps with the skills a native speaker has to develop, we will not dwell on it other than to describe some of the functions the advanced reader will be aiming at. His goal is to read authentic texts critically. That is, beyond the skills of comprehending the text's content literally, inferentially and suppositionally, the reader should be able to judge the validity and reliability of the content, distinguish between relevant and irrelevant information, and recognize bias or propaganda techniques. The reader should be able to analyze the text without assistance (other than from a monolingual dictionary), to examine elements of mechanics and style, and expose the author's design.

Analyzing the text, the reader should be able to evaluate it, making judgments about its relative merits, and support those arguments. He should be able to engage in discussion about the content of the text at the same level at which it was written.

DISCUSSION

1. What are some of the component skills of "reading readiness"?

2. Describe and differentiate the Whole Word Method and the Linguistic Method of teaching reading.

3. Discuss and illustrate information, inferential, and interpretive questions.

4. Define sight vocabulary and explain how it is used in a reading program.

5. Discuss the characteristics of good and poor readers.

6. Discuss cognitive skills. Why are they developed in a reading program?

7. Why is extensive reading recommended in a reading program?

8. How can one read with incomplete information? How does a good reader react to readings that have vocabulary items that are new and unknown?

9. What are skimming and scanning used for?

10. Indicate how a reader would go about identifying the presence of propaganda or bias in a reading passage.

WRITING

INTRODUCTION

Currently the teaching of writing to native speakers of English in the United States is a major curricular emphasis. General concern about students' needs in writing has led in recent years to the creation of special departments, conferences, and research efforts as well as a proliferation of support courses in universities. This reaction to what one educator has termed "the literacy crisis" in education reflects in part a problem that has existed across languages and across the centuries, the problem of writing well. Current administrative concern about the quality of writing is paralleled by the anxieties of the typical university student, either native or second language speaker, who feels inadequate in the face of the writing task.

Why is this true? Why should a person be able to use a spoken first or second language purposefully with little or no conscious thought, and switch with ease among a number of different styles and registers, but have trouble producing the written forms of the same language?

Writing is more an individual effort than speaking, while at the same time more rule-bound and therefore more error-prone. Although a person is expected to speak correctly, the burden of the spoken communication is shared by the listener or listeners, who provide immediate feedback.

The speaker does not have to pronounce each word exactly according to one standard of pronunciation or one model of structure, while the writer is expected to produce according to one model of spelling, and usually a reduced range of structures, with 100 percent accuracy. If listeners do not understand something said, they can signal the speaker to backtrack and clarify a point. The speaker can cross-check whether the listener is following.

The writer, however, can only try to anticipate difficult areas, and try to make the text clear enough for a one-time-only explanation. The speaker is allowed to start, change and start again, to stutter, to make slips of the tongue, to stall for time by using phrases like "You know," to slip in and out of a number of registers, and to speak in run-ons and sentence fragments. The writer must be consistent in style, avoid ambiguity, and limit redundancy by organizing and writing carefully. What is written is on permanent record. Considering the control of the orthographic system, the careful organization, and the linguistic conservatism required, writing is the most demanding of the language skills.

We have chosen to describe writing for the second language learner as a developmental process, analogous to the process of reading, and to view it from four perspectives, each of which is forefronted at a different time in the building of the writing skills: *Mechanics*, emphasized in the low beginner stages (beginning); *Extended Use of Language*, emphasized in the high beginner and low intermediate stages (elementary); *Writing with Purpose*, emphasized in the high intermediate and low advanced stages (intermediate); and *Full Expository Prose*, emphasized in the terminal stage (advanced).

A proponent of a particular movement or method in language teaching might be more partial, philosophically, to one of the components than the other, e.g., a structuralist to the Mechanics, a cognitivist to the Extended Use of Language, and a functionalist to Writing with Purpose. We believe that all four perspectives are important, and that in a good writing class, no matter what the method or level, some attention will be paid to all of the first three: Mechanics, Extended Use of Language, and Writing with Purpose. The fourth phase, Full Expository Prose, overlaps with writing by native speakers.

Although the writing skill is exploited in many ESL texts primarily as a tool for consolidating students' oral command of English, and for practicing grammar and occasionally rhetoric, we believe that writing should be viewed as a skill in its own right and should continue, at every level, to be developed further. The differences between the spoken and the written language should not be obscured because the writing is so frequently subordinated to purposes of practicing the other language skills. While reading sets up acquaintances among readers and writers, writing teaches the writer that he is an informed and entertaining or instructive person—in a second language.

We anticipate that the four perspectives described in this chapter will suggest emphases for each level of the writing class, which do not exclude each other; we also intend that the perspectives will act as a partial guide for selecting writing activities from among the many controlled, guided, and free types. We believe that there is a place for some kinds of controlled or guided and some free writing activities at every level, but that the teacher has to select and plan courses according to course objectives, student interest, and what seems to her to work best.

BEGINNING WRITING: EMPHASIS ON MECHANICS

Mastery of the mechanics of writing and practice in the basic skills are necessary first steps for child or adult learners who do not yet write in any language. At the beginning level students learn to put thoughts into writing with the major emphasis on mechanics: learning the alphabet, the left-to-right direction of English writing, printing, cursive writing, upper and lower case letters, alphabetizing, basic spelling patterns of English, rules for capitalization, and word and sentence punctuation. The basic skills include writing letters, numbers, words, phrases, and sentences correctly.

Nonliterate students should be guided through the mechanics a step at a time with individual attention. The literate, highly educated "beginner" will probably learn the mechanics at high speed, skipping many of the steps, and in some cases omitting the stage altogether.

Writing Readiness

A checklist for introductory writing skills follows:

The student:
1. has satisfactory command of the reading readiness skills.
2. has command of the motor skills needed for producing legible printing, i.e., left-to-right orientation and the ability to produce shapes which are the building blocks of English letters (practice books for native-speaking children offer suggestions for these exercises).
3. knows and can print the alphabet.
4. recognizes and can produce from written form:

    vowels, consonants and blends   common sight words
    words and syllables   rhyming words
    upper and lower case letters   punctuation
    basic spelling patterns   phrases and sentences
5. has command of the motor skills needed for producing legible cursive writing.

After mastering Step 3 (learning and being able to print the alphabet), the student can name the letters while copying and then spell out loud the words copied.

The speaking, reading, and writing skills are interrelated at this stage of learning, providing mutual reinforcement of items and skills learned, and easily allowing communicative exercises.

After mastering the writing readiness skills, words for writing practice will probably be suggested by the writer's immediate environment and later by his speaking and reading activities. Some of the exercises for beginning reading following the Language Experience Approach can be used also as later writing exercises. (See Chapter Eight.) Also many of the games used for teaching beginning reading and speaking skills can be adapted for writing practice.

As the beginning writer learns to say and read words, and then to copy them, he should soon be able to perform other writing tasks, such as filling in missing letters and later missing words.

When the student is able to write words from memory, creative ideas abound for activities. The student can:

1. list objects in pictures.
2. draw and label his own pictures.
3. make personalized stationery by drawing a personal letterhead on a ditto master.
4. make a monthly calendar or a birthday card for a classmate.
5. draw a picture map of his neighborhood or another familiar area.

As a student's vocabulary increases, alphabetizing tasks provide writing practice:

1. List five words that begin with _____ .

2. Rearrange the following words in alphabetical order: _____ , _____ ,

   _____ , _____ , _____ .

3. Write a girl's name that begins with _____ .

4. Find two objects in the picture whose names begin with _____ .

The beginning learner should know the simple, regular spelling rules, and should practice correct spelling from the beginning. Many of the exercises described in Chapter Ten on orthography will also serve as writing exercises.

Basic Skills

As the beginner's knowledge of English increases he can continue writing, both to consolidate what he is learning to say and read, and to generate new words, phrases, and sentences. He may be asked to make lists of antonyms, synonyms, topical vocabulary lists, or associational pairs or groups of words. Word lists might include:

familiar paradigms like the days of the week or the months
personal lists, such as items on a shopping list, food served at a meal, and packing lists

Word writing games provide good opportunities for students to build their vocabularies while practicing writing. Group games are especially good because the students themselves invariably provide supplementary vocabulary resources.

Game books for both native and second language learners provide new ideas to add to the old faithfuls such as *Twenty Questions*, making many short words out of the letters in a long one, scrambled letters, and crossword puzzles. Many activities in Chapters Seven and Twelve on oral and written vocabulary can be used as writing exercises.

From words students can go on to short word groups such as phrases. One of the first things practiced should be one's signature in cursive form. It is an exciting experience for an illiterate person to learn to write his signature.

The student can also practice writing phrases in writing lists:

Things you'd like to do on vacation
Places it's important to know how to get to
Gifts to give a newlywed couple
Ten typical American sights (sounds, smells)
Things it's important to know how to do in an American city (school, university, state)

Lists of real things can be added:

Names of streets and buildings
Bumper stickers
T-shirt slogans
Campaign button slogans

Extending phrase writing into sentence writing can make the exercises more communicative:

Turn strings of words (as though scribbled on a note pad) into short messages. For example, "football game X Stadium 10:00 am Saturday" can yield a number of different messages when turned into a sentence.

Using a visual such as a picture, a photo, a slide, a filmstrip, or an object, write five descriptive sentences.

Complete open-ended sentences; for example: I'm going to _____ . I like to _____ . My favorite food is _____ . I hope the President will _____ .

Look out the window and write five sentences about things you see.
Make additions to series of sentences, such as:
On Friday I go to school.
On Saturday I play soccer/football.
On Sunday I _____ .
Add sentences to complete short stories:
Harry wanted some milk. He went to the store. The store was closed.
_____ .

Some more closely controlled sentence practice can be provided by exercises on structure (for example, exercises on rewriting or transforming, expanding, and combining sentences). This, however, is normally part of grammar instruction.

The concept of the complete sentence and the features of any distinctive sentence patterns used at this level should be highlighted so students are likely to master the concept inductively, deductively, experientially, or by any other sensible heuristic means.

Each sentence writing activity at the beginner level provides an opportunity for practice of the mechanics of spelling, capitalization, and punctuation. In addition to the sentence exercises, it will be useful to teach the writing of addresses, phone numbers, and, if culturally and functionally appropriate, sums of money.

Dictation is a useful device for checking the mechanics of writing. Everything that the mechanics focuses on is challenged in a dictation, and at the more advanced stages a deeper command of the language is tapped.

EXERCISE 9.1

DICTATION

Instructions for teacher: (Code 1–7, adjustable)

1. Select a short passage (about five sentences) of appropriate linguistic and semantic difficulty for the group.
2. Read the passage aloud once at normal speed while students listen. Answer questions students may have about the meaning of the passage.
3. Read the passage again at normal speed, pausing long enough after each sentence for students to write the sentence down.
4. After finishing the sentence-by-sentence reading, read the dictation through one more time so students can check their writing before handing it in.
5. Either collect and correct the dictations, or uncover the entire passage written on the blackboard for students to correct their own papers.

Writing with a Purpose

The beginner in an English-speaking country, whether young or old, is very likely to have a number of real purposes for which he needs the skill of writing. The purposes are likely to be of a personal, survival, or social nature. Personal tasks for the beginning writer might include: writing shopping lists, guest lists, daily schedules, packing lists, and dates and times on an itinerary; filling out forms; and writing checks.

Communicative games, with their touches of reality, are even better. For example, in a question chain each student in a circle writes a personal question on the top of a piece of paper and passes the paper to the person on the right to be answered. (Each student receives a question from the person on his left.) Each student must answer the question received, then add another question and pass it to the right, and so forth. Alternating question and answer forms requires attention to applicable writing conventions, and students can be encouraged to monitor each other's adherence to the conventions.

The beginning reader who already has some command of English may be able to write more complex sentences. Students' ideas, dictated and recorded or transcribed as described in the Language Experience Approach, Chapter Eight, page 222, can provide usable material for writing exercises. They can serve as models for other writings, or they can be dictated, copied, or used for completion and transformation exercises.

The sentence exercise can be extended somewhat to be used in communication activities: Design games in which students write short notes to friends, and take short messages from real or imagined telephone conversations or from visitors. These exercises develop useful social skills as well as general writing. Practice in taking simple paper-and-pencil tests (including spelling quizzes and simple dictations) will be highly useful to all attending or planning to attend schools where English is the medium of instruction. Although of more immediate practical value to students in an English-speaking environment, such tasks can be useful to those in other linguistic surroundings as well. Situational realism tends to be a good motivator, when the situations are interesting enough, even if they are somewhat contrived.

Free Writing

Free writing is not typically a part of the beginning course. However, enthusiastic students at this level may want to do extra writing on their own. The teacher should encourage and support these students' interest, whether they are "playing with language," or attempting to improve the mechanics of their writing, or both. If the students are playing, consider their work creative, and read and respond to it. If they want to work on mechanics, correct their work as well, and make individualized suggestions if they want to work beyond the pace of the class. The teacher who announces a willingness to read or correct extra student writing will usually find some "takers," and may even find herself setting an extra time aside each week to work with the enthusiastic writers.

Correction

Decisions about correcting writing are simpler for the teacher at the beginning level than at other levels. At this point as a rule of thumb the teacher should emphasize precision and correctness of form in writing and point out all writing errors that have been covered in class, except in writing which both teacher and student have agreed will not be corrected, such as a diary and other free writing activities.

Although the teacher should indeed highlight writing as a skill in its own right, she should also integrate writing with other activities. At the beginning level students should write and read out loud and talk about what they write;

students should read out loud each other's and the teacher's writings. From the beginning they should become used to writing for an audience and seeking feedback. Feedback can be both oral, with students describing their reactions to each other's writing, and written, with students underlining what they think may be errors in form. At a later stage, they can proofread and edit their own and each other's work.

ELEMENTARY WRITING: EMPHASIS ON EXTENDED USE OF LANGUAGE

At the beginning of the elementary level, the ESL student has a vocabulary of fewer than one thousand words and a limited repertoire of sentence level patterns. However, his inventory of language and cultural items is rapidly increasing.

Writing is increasingly important to this student, for study purposes if attending school abroad, and for survival and personal reasons as well if living or planning to stay in an English-speaking country. The student who seriously intends to develop writing skills in English should have writing practice of all kinds, from guided to free, from manipulative to communicative. The student who has only survival needs may require only exercises in writing for specific purposes. For such students, the emphasis at this level is on the Extended Use of Language. The materials the student reads will increasingly differ from the spoken language. The material will contain longer, more complex sentences, sentence groups, and paragraphs. The sentences will introduce new structures and vocabulary, and will exhibit more of a variety of patterns of logic. Since the written passage is allowed less redundancy, the student will have to plan and think critically before and during writing, and polishing or rewriting will become a regular practice in formal writing.

The conservatism of the written language demands intensive work monitored for formal precision; the absolute uniqueness and unpredictability of each piece of writing demands free rein in practice. The ideal in a writing course is to give both kinds of practice, from early on in language learning, preferably in separate writing assignments which receive special treatment from the teacher. Although we encourage full writing, we also encourage a series of writing exercises corresponding to the organizational principles of the course—whether they be functional, structural, or cognitive. The well-planned writing class at the elementary level will include both guided and free writing assignments, each accepted as appropriate in its own realm.

A Diagnostic Test

A short free-writing assignment can serve for diagnostic purposes. In diagnosing elementary student writing, look for problems such as reversed letters, transposed letters or words, incorrect uppercase or lowercase letters, lack of paragraph indentation, lack of familiarity with the basic spelling patterns, and illegible handwriting. Such mechanical problems should be treated with appropriate guidance and practice.

The teacher should also give a quick oral test to make sure that students at this level know the alphabet and can say the names of the letters correctly when spelling words out loud. Students who cannot perform these two basics can usually learn them quickly.

Extended Use of Language: Longer and Varied Sentences

The most important writing exercise at this level is continued composing of sentences, paragraphs, and short essays. Exercises may be planned in sentences, pairs of sentences, and connected sentences, leading to practice in the paragraph and short essay form.

Sentence Pairs

Although lists of sentences can be combined to form longer stretches of writing, the resulting somewhat artificial passages fail either to "hold together" as real writing or to give the writer practice in actually composing extended writing. The following exercises in writing pairs of logically related sentences is a step toward the goal:

EXERCISE 9.2

LOGICAL INTERPRETATION (A)

Instructions for teacher: (Code 4–5)

1. To practice some of the elements of logic of the English language, give students a statement, and have them provide an appropriate following statement.
2. Give students a list of general statements and have them write possible supporting facts for each.
3. Give lists of generalizations and have students provide lists of examples, exceptions, and reasons.
4. Suitable connecting words should be provided when appropriate.

EXERCISE 9.3

LOGICAL INTERPRETATION (B)

Instructions for students: (Code 4–6)

1. Answer a series of related questions.
2. Write a chronology.
3. Give a set of directions to go somewhere or do something.
4. Write a descriptive statement about each person or item in a group.
5. Write sentences describing characteristics of a good language learner, yourself, a set of New Year's resolutions, vacation plans, . . .
6. Write sentences listing and defining the furnishings and apparatus in a lab; list the characteristics of a piece of apparatus.

Simple Paragraphs

Simple paragraph structure should be introduced carefully and taught one step at a time. Separate lessons and practice exercises should be devoted to the concepts of the topic sentence, the main idea and supporting details, and the concluding sentence. Paragraph writing assignments should be suggested by subjects likely to be of immediate interest and use to students. They should at the same time be considered as steps toward building skilled knowledge of the writing system of English.

Extended cloze and scrambled sentences lend themselves particularly well to practice in the parts of the paragraph. The most important practice, however, is simply writing.

To provide practice in writing paragraphs, the teacher can present a sequence, as seems appropriate for the class, from one of the most common ways of arranging information in paragraphs in English: chronological, spatial, climactic, general to specific, and specific to general. Other possible schemes of organization include the four basic modes of writing: exposition, argument, description, and narration; the nine patterns of exposition: facts, process, classification, comparison/contrast, analysis, illustration, cause-effect, definition, and analogy; and a variety of schemes developed for particular ESP courses.

As a semicontrolled writing exercise, the teacher can provide data or have students gather and then present selected data in paragraph form following a suitable rhetorical model. The common pattern of a generalization followed by supporting details provides an easy example, and current charts from newspapers and magazines like *Consumer Reports* and *U.S. News and*

World Report are a ready source of information generally of topical interest to the students. Automobiles, for example, provide an almost universal source of appeal to students. A chart comparing the characteristics of a number of small automobiles may be used as a source of information for paragraph writing.

Some teachers like to accompany exercises in writing free paragraphs with guided exercises providing more structure. For example:

EXERCISE 9.4

QUESTIONNAIRE-BASED ESSAY

Instructions for students: (Code 3–6)

1. Fill out a simple questionnaire and then turn the information into a short essay or biographical statement.
2. Complete the following paragraph: There are three problems the student must deal with when entering high school/university.

   The first _____ . The second _____ . The last _____ .

3. Outline a paragraph as a whole-class activity. Individual students write according to the outline.

At this stage, as the student's command of the language increases, writing exercises indirectly provide practice in the simpler affixation and derivational patterns. Topical lists of words can be made and then used in paragraphs as class, small group, or individual exercises.

Correction

At this stage questions about correcting written assignments arise, and they will be asked again at all subsequent levels of instruction in writing: Should all writing be corrected? Should all writing that is corrected be corrected in the same way? Should all writing that is corrected be corrected by the teacher? How should writing be corrected? What should students do with corrected papers?

Some teachers fear that uncorrected writing leads to fossilization of errors in structure, vocabulary, or mechanics; others feel that heavily corrected writing robs the act of writing of any pleasure and, in effect, applies negative reinforcement. Some of the most conscientious teachers may feel that they are not doing anything for the student unless they identify and mark every error in writing and speech. All of these stances are properly motivated in that they reflect teachers working in the interests of their students. In addition, they are supported by many writers on the teaching of writing, who emphasize the values of continual, frequent production of writing, useful feedback, and revision. But the teacher must also, in pursuit of effectiveness and efficiency, plan a writing course which balances the needs of the student with her own for a reasonable workload. The lack of consensus among teachers reflects a broad division of opinion among scholars on correcting writing.

The most common positions on writing may be sorted, with a great deal of simplification, into the following three groups. (1) The *quality* school of thought holds that writing exercises should be designed and controlled to prevent the possibility of student error, and then should be most strictly corrected to catch every little error that happens in spite of students' caution. For example, at the lowest level students might simply copy printed texts, or copy and make minor changes in the text. All writing would be corrected for all errors. (2) The *quantity* school of thought followers hold that the most important thing is the amount of practice students get in writing. Students are asked to write frequently, and their writing may not always be corrected. Many proponents of this school believe that a language error represents a hypothesis concerning the language; such errors show that the student is learning the language or the skill of writing it, and without errors, learning would not be likely to take place. Some choose to ignore student errors under the optimistic hypothesis that they are the signs of growth in writing ability which will soon make themselves obsolete.

(3) The *middle* schools of thought are composed of many teachers who do not subscribe to either of the other "schools," although some still differ radically from others in their approaches to correcting writing. The approach chosen by the teacher in this group usually varies according to the special purpose of the course or exercise. For example, in a language-building exercise with the focus on a particular grammatical point or general grammatical accuracy, one teacher might feel it important to insist on student accuracy in writing. This teacher would correct structural items carefully. In a creative writing exercise the same teacher might decide that the important focus is imaginative expression or organization of ideas, and that attention to grammatical or spelling accuracy would divert attention from understanding. Some of the different practices "middle school" advocates follow are: (a) Correct certain compositions only for grammar, and certain others only for ideas. (b) Correct compositions only for selected points of grammar, such as those previously discussed and practiced in class. (c) Correct compositions two times: the first for grammar and mechanics, and the second for ideas and organization, or ideas, organization, and style.

It has not yet been demonstrated convincingly that there is any one best kind of writing activity, or any best philosophy for correcting writing. We believe it is neither necessary nor desirable for the teacher who assigns a variety of writing activities to correct all papers or even every word in selected papers. For example, controlled exercises in which only the answers need to be checked can be checked as well by students; this provides regular practice in editing and leads to an increasing awareness of form in writing. (Of course the teacher may want to correct a set from time to time.) The following criteria are suggested for selecting writing exercises for classes and accordingly for deciding what and how to correct:

We recommend first that the teacher try to read and make an appropriate response to every writing assignment collected, whether or not it is also corrected and graded. Second, we recommend a consistent policy for correcting and grading according to the type of writing assignment. In many cases this will mean having different correction strategies for a number of different types of writing assignment. Here are some guidelines for correcting at the elementary level:

1. Controlled Exercises: exercises containing answers which are specifically either correct or incorrect (such as fill-ins, completions, transformations, answers to questions) aim at developing precision, usually of the written form. These exercises should be read and corrected for precision, but the only errors indicated should be those in following directions or answering the target question accurately. These exercises can be corrected by the teacher, or the students themselves can underline the incorrect forms they find.

2. Guided Exercises: exercises which require composing full sentences (such as in writing sentence series, answering a series of questions, or writing a short paragraph or paragraph series) require the performance of a number of skills. These exercises should be read and corrected and/or commented on, but only for the particular purpose each exercise was designed for.

There are a number of systems designed for indicating errors, including composition checklists, systems of editorial symbols, writing in the correct form, and using a tape recorder. We recommend the simplest system that can give clear information. Have students write compositions on every other line, so there will be ample room for correction symbols and comments, and:

1. underline an error in form. Write "WW" above if the word is a wrong word choice. Write "K" above if the word is an awkward word or expression.
2. use a ∧ (a caret) to indicate each omitted word.
3. circle words spelled inaccurately.
4. put a cross through each unnecessary word.

Example sentence:

∧ Student was interest<u>ing</u> to learn t̶h̶e̶ his (freind) willcome.

In addition to structural and mechanical errors, it is important for the teacher to comment on other elements of writing she has been drawing students' attention to. For example, she will help the student with information on paragraph organization, transition between paragraphs, rhetorical organization, register, cohesion, and style. Sometimes these comments are more important than indications of structural and mechanical errors.

There is some question as to how much students benefit from their written work. Our personal experience suggests that many students seem to benefit from teacher's comments and personal correction of their written work, but that asking students to copy overlong papers just to correct a small number of structural inaccuracies is boring and demoralizing. We recommend modified revision of compositions thus corrected. Students are less likely to resent a partial rewriting, writing the correct form in the space above each error, and rewriting selected sentences and other word groups the teacher has commented on. Time should be set aside regularly in class for revision. The teacher can walk around while students are working, an efficient way of checking students' performance and competence errors. If a student immediately understands and can correct the error, the teacher can assume it was merely a slip or a performance error. If the student substitutes still another error for the first, or doesn't understand what is wrong with his first form, the student hasn't grasped the item.

The ideal solution is to prepare the written assignments on a word processor; having a computer on your side is very helpful. Specific corrections can be flexibily corrected with minimum effort, and a perfect copy can be printed up.

It is important that the teacher make clear to students what her correction plan is, especially if she should decide to correct only the items emphasized in class. Some students will join the writing class expecting a different plan of correction, and those who hope that every word they write will be corrected may need an explanation if the teacher's plan is otherwise.

Correcting papers and monitoring students' error corrections in class also provides the teacher with information about writing errors common among students. It is our experience that if students write regularly and their papers are read and commented on, many of their errors disappear after a few weeks without any extra remedial work. Errors or error types that do not disappear after a month or so call for additional practice. If the errors are common to a number of students, a class treatment is in order, such as a special presentation by the teacher and guided exercises concerning the point. For errors that only one or a few students make, it is more efficient for the teacher to make individual suggestions for remedial work.

The mechanics of writing may present surprising hurdles for literate students who read and write a language which is graphically very different from English. Arabic and Farsi writers, for example, who are used to writing with the line above the written symbols, have trouble "staying on the line" in English. They also have trouble with capitalization and correct spelling of vowel sounds, since Arabic script lacks both vowels and uppercase letters. Chinese students beginning to write in English frequently have trouble maintaining consistency in their spelling, being accustomed to logographic systems of characters which do not represent pronunciation. Extra attention will be needed for these students.

The low intermediate student who still has problems mastering the mechanics may be embarrassed to return to beginner-level exercises. In such cases, the student's regular writing exercises should provide the occasion for further attention to the mechanics, and extra writing assignments of that nature may be given.

Alphabetization exercises with new vocabulary words at the elementary level will help with the dictionary work students will be doing in reading class, as well as lay a foundation for reading and study skills.

In addition to gaining practice in punctuation through writing their own paragraphs, students may profit from rewriting unpunctuated passages.

It will be useful for students to hear both their own and model paragraphs read aloud by the teacher with appropriate intonation, phrasing, and pausing as signalled by the punctuation. This practice is especially useful for students in countries where English is not spoken, to help them develop an accurate sense of the relationships between the spoken and the written systems—on the phonological and the syntactic levels. Hearing paragraphs read aloud will also help confirm for the student the systematic differences between spoken and written English, particularly the features of contraction, reduction, and assimilation.

As they acquire proficiency in writing connected English, students should begin to "proofread" their own and each other's papers for mechanical errors such as spelling and punctuation. Have students reread their completed papers, correcting any mistakes they find, and then exchange them with those of other students for additional proofing before papers are handed in to the teacher.

Writing with Purpose

The elementary writer can use his increasing skill for purposeful activities. Survival uses of the writing skill at this level may include performing more school tasks which require writing, and using writing more for the affairs of daily life, such as completing forms, writing applications, and writing notes or short letters to real people.

Free Writing

The lower intermediate student may be ready for free writing as a regular assignment. Have each student buy or make a small notebook and require that she fill a certain amount of it every day with English (for example, half a page or a full page according to the size of the notebook—about 100 words). Allow students to write anything they want, even words copied out of other books, so long as they write in English. The teacher may collect and read notebooks once a week, but should not correct writing errors, and should not share the contents of the journals with other people. The journals are private writings, shared only with the teacher, who responds in a personal way. The purpose of free writing is to get learners used to writing English without fear of failure or ridicule.

Students who are also systematically accruing practice in writing English structure with accuracy, either in the writing class or another part of the English program, usually show steady improvement in their writing in such free exercises, even if the writing is not corrected and revised.

The free writing exercise occasionally provides opportunity for the student living abroad to put into words his feelings about sometimes disturbing experiences, which are read and responded to by a sympathetic person. This can help the English teacher understand some of the "other sides" of the language learning and acculturation situation, and may provide a welcome sounding board for students—as well as language practice.

INTERMEDIATE WRITING: EMPHASIS ON WRITING WITH A PURPOSE

The intermediate writer has a vocabulary of somewhere between 1,000 and 3,600 words, has command of the most common sentence-level structures, and is building up a knowledge of the less frequent words and patterns. You might say the writer's command of English items wavers between active and passive, because there may be frequent performance errors in all the language skills. Students at this level vary enormously among themselves in terms of which language items and skills they are strong or weak in. This necessitates a teaching approach which allows individual focus and attention.

To have gained an intermediate level of proficiency, the student has already put much effort into studying English; but he still has quite a way to go if pursuing fluency. For the serious scholar, as well as the uncommitted student, the intermediate level is usually the terminal level of formal studies in ESL. Upon completing the intermediate level of ESL, the student in a non-English-speaking country, and the non-English major in a university where English is the medium of instruction, frequently reach the point at which they can satisfy external pragmatic requirements such as getting a job that requires a knowledge of English, passing requirements for entrance to an English-medium university, graduating from secondary school, or living in an English-speaking country.

Writing with Purpose

The emphasis at this level is writing with purpose. The ESL class can help the terminal intermediate student with guided practice in advanced survival skills, and the committed scholar with skills needed for special purposes, either academic or professional.

Writing that is more formal is another matter. The controls and guidelines become more sophisticated at this level, and the background work and instructions for assignments, more complex.

An introductory diagnostic writing assignment will give the teacher some idea of the needs of individuals as well as the class in general. However, it may be better to postpone recommendations for remediation, as students at this level may show rapid reduction in performance errors during the first three or four weeks of the term.

Because the typical student sees a future use, or in some cases immediate use, for the language he is studying, the teacher can exploit and expand on many of the exercises for personal, survival, and other purposes suggested for writing at the lower levels. For example, an enjoyable and useful social survival exercise is writing short social notes to conform to brief role descriptions. This exercise can be carried out without any notice, if there are 25 to 30 minutes available.

1. Divide the class into couples or small groups.
2. Create interesting situations that people might conceivably write notes to each other about. For example:
   a. Your friend has just given an excellent talk to the class. Write a note complimenting her. Tell her what you liked about the talk.
   b. Your classmate has helped you feel more comfortable in school. Write a note thanking her for her help. Tell her the ways in which she has helped you.
   c. You have forgotten your wallet and have no money. Write a note to your classmate, explaining the situation and asking if you can borrow some money.
3. Give two different situations to each couple. Have one student in each pair write a note to the other, following the guidelines suggested by one of the roles.
4. Students exchange notes and respond to each other.
5. Discuss the specific roles and the options for carrying them out. Ask students to comment on notes that seem "typically American" and any that appear unusual. Try to get class members to make comparisons of ways the same situation might be handled in other countries.

For many students at this level, the formal letter is immediately useful for purposes of university or job application. An alternative approach to having students write letters which are then analyzed is to begin by discussing a real letter which then serves as a model or guide for a writing assignment.

LETTERS

Instructions: Do the following: (Code 5–6)

1. Read a model letter for a job inquiry or university application.
2. Analyze elements of the layout of the letter.
3. Analyze parts of the job inquiry.
   a. Identify self.
   b. Identify situation.
   c. Express interest in position and institution.
   d. Make polite request.
   e. Specify how you can be reached and indicate when you will check back.
   f. Sincerely yours. . . .
4. Review useful phrases.
5. Have students write similar letters.

Other topics for simulated practice:

university application	billing error
merchandise complaint	hotel reservations

It is useful for students to do a follow-up letter as well. Practice is seldom included in the writing course for responding to a letter, but letters are like an extended conversation. The first one is simply an invitation for the addressee to reply, and students are frequently at a loss as to how to respond to the reply that they are very likely to receive.

If the letter itself is important, to know how to respond to a reply is equally useful. Another helpful practice for students at this level, and one that they usually address quite seriously, is writing a résumé.

RÉSUMÉ

Instructions for teachers: (Code 5–7)

1. Read a number of sample résumés, and select one for a class model. If possible, the résumés should be real ones, e.g., of self and colleagues and former students.
2. Outline the parts of the résumé. Discuss.

3. Have students make a draft of a personal résumé, following the steps of the outline.
4. Students check each other's drafts and then comment.
5. Teacher collects and checks drafts, and makes comments and suggestions.
6. Students revise and present next copies.

Writing a letter or a résumé is a large jump from the paragraphs and paragraph series of the elementary level and the social notes of the intermediate. Both forms are of crucial importance in serious transactions, and should be corrected with great care.

The intermediate student passes the level where learning a simple task enables him to successfully complete target tasks—like letter writing. The purposes have become so complex that only those students who are committed to continued, intense long-term study and practice in the language can hope to be able, eventually, to perform the tasks independent of substantial help from others whose level of proficiency is higher.

The intermediate students refining their English for academic or professional purposes will have to tackle writing exercises at still another level of difficulty: term papers, or essays on subjects for which they will have to gather and organize information. The most effective means developed for teaching essay writing are all variations on the basic pattern of: (1) selecting a topic and gathering appropriate information, (2) organizing the information, (3) writing a rough draft, (4) editing: reading and reorganizing, (5) revising, and (6) proofreading.

Teachers in both first and second language classes have developed a large number of approaches for teaching essay writing. Most of the variations in approach have to do with the amount of teacher/student control in selecting and organizing information, editing, and rewriting. Those who worry that the demand for detailed organization before writing or the imposition of models might discourage the student or stifle the train of thought have a valid concern. On the other hand, academic and professional writing are required to be appropriate in register, form, and logic; and this argues for approaches that develop students' awareness of those conventions, and for giving feedback about their writing. The best approach is to encourage students' patience and develop their various writing skills, while keeping the creative light burning. Fortunately, there are a number of possible approaches, each of which honors the fact that writing anything of length is a job which, like most crafts, has a number of steps. The styles of organizing can be boiled down to three main types:

1. Take content from one's own experience or the results of one's own information gathering, and arrange it into a logical format. This is the most common method, and is perhaps the most useful to the student of general English. A number of ways should be suggested for assisting students with the initial information gathering and organization.

2. Analyze a prose model, reconstruct its outline, and use the outline as a model for writing another passage, using parallel or analogous information. This method is used in current textbooks on writing, many of which are quite good. Although the idea is pedagogically sound, the teacher should insist that such activities not comprise the total reading or writing activities. Not all the students' reading matter should be analyzed for organization, and not all their writing should be subordinated to the structure produced by another writer writing about another subject.

3. Follow an outline prepared by someone else, e.g., teacher or textbook. This has particular value for the student new to the conventions of written English. It is also useful to the student of English for a particular purpose, for example, the science student preparing to do graduate work in an English-medium university which will require writing research papers in English. The organization of each part of such a paper should be analyzed and practiced, one part at a time, over a number of weeks, each part of the outline providing a substantial writing assignment.

EXERCISE 9.7

A MODEL UNIT

Instructions for teacher: (Code 4–6)

The following is a recommended model, when time permits, for writing guided exercises and compositions at the intermediate level:

Class 1 *Presentation of Assignment.* This may be done in a number of ways, including teacher explanation, class brainstorming, class discussion, or research.
Gathering of Information. Students may need teacher-provided texts or texts of their own choice. They may search for information in the school or a public library.
Method of Organization. The teacher provides or elicits some examples: rhetorical outline, model passage, organizational outline.
Writing. The student writes the first draft.

Class 2 Student brings assignment to class, proofreads, and makes corrections. A classmate reads, underlines three to five errors, and writes a comment. The teacher collects and corrects overnight, identifying errors and adding comments.

Class 3 Teacher returns papers. Students correct errors, conferring with each other as they wish, while the teacher gives individual help, answering questions and checking corrections.

There is often a strong temptation at the intermediate level to substitute exercises in structural items for writing practice. Even if the teacher chooses a controlled or guided written exercise as one mode for consolidating students' accuracy in language (as part of a preplanned sequence or as the result of correcting students' compositions), these exercises should not be accepted substitutes for more creative writing, but should be supplementary.

The teacher of intermediate writing to university-bound students should make sure that they are developing the study skills necessary for academic work, e.g., library skills, note-taking, outlining, reporting, and making literary references. It sometimes falls on the shoulders of the writing teacher to guide students in the acquisition of these skills.

There is a strong need for students going on to studies in an English-medium university to know how to paraphrase and summarize, not just as language practice, but in order to make appropriate references in reports and papers. For this reason extensive practice is desirable, preferably in rewriting authentic academic or professional materials that they will later be using.

Increased Speed

Just as they read slowly, second language students frequently write slowly, a disadvantage in English classes and perhaps a deterrent in overall writing practice. Practice in writing faster seems to help students become better prepared for test situations and to release them from some of their own anxiety about writing. As with native speakers, writing fast may allow students to produce more creative ideas in rapid prose, which can afterwards be edited into a form suitable for a specific writing task.

Three less familiar writing exercises can be adapted to provide timed writing exercises with some variety: (1) dicto-comp, usually used to give practice in the mechanical aspects of writing; (2) limited-timed writing, usually used to increase the number of words written per minute; and (3) the extended cloze, used to increase skill in organizing and practicing style.

In the dicto-comp, students listen four times to the teacher reading a short passage (five to fifteen sentences, depending on the level of the class), and then try to write as much of the passage as they can remember.

EXERCISE 9.8

DICTO-COMP

Instructions for teacher: (Code 4–5)

(1) Select a short passage easily within the range of comprehension of the students. (2) Introduce the subject of the passage to the class; write on the blackboard and explain any words or phrases which are likely to be new to them.

(3) Read the passage to the class four times. Students are not to write while the teacher reads, but may ask whatever questions they want to after the first three readings. (4) After the fourth reading, students write down the composition, trying to include all the original ideas and sequences, and using words from the original when they remember them. (5) The teacher evaluates the compositions for correctness of meaning and structural accuracy.

In limited-timed writing the teacher introduces a subject related to the reading activity. After class discussion, students write as much as they can on the subject in seven minutes. If this activity is done once a week, students usually see marked progress in organization of facts and ideas as well as a dramatic increase in the number of words which can be written per minute.

EXERCISE 9.9

LIMITED-TIMED WRITING

Instructions for teacher: (Code 5–7)

(1) Select a topic that is related to the reading passage and somewhat familiar to the students. (2) Phrase the topic in a statement or question that presents two sides that can be argued. For example, an article on nuclear power may suggest the statement: "There are both risks and benefits in the construction of a nuclear power plant." The statement or question should function as the topic sentence for the writing activity. (3) Have students discuss the topic sentence for five to seven minutes. As they discuss, write students' key words and phrases on the blackboard. Try to elicit points of view on each side of the topic, and write the relevant words and phrases in two columns. (4) Have the students think about the topic for one minute in order to organize their thoughts. (5) Have students write on the subject for seven minutes, warning them when the first six minutes are up that they have only one minute left in which to conclude. (6) Collect the papers and correct them primarily for style, content, and structural accuracy.

In an extended cloze exercise, students copy an incomplete short passage and then complete it in their own words. Although the time is limited, the objective is not to increase the number of words per minute, but to increase the speed of organizing thought in a second language and of judging and producing in a style that will be compatible with the first part of the passage.

EXERCISE 9.10

EXTENDED CLOZE

Instructions for teacher: (Code 5–7)

(1) Select a paragraph from a passage easily within the comprehension of the students, preferably a passage that discusses a particularly interesting or controversial idea. (2) Select enough from the beginning of the passage so that the main topic and the direction of the development are clear. (3) Write the beginning on the blackboard and discuss the main topic and direction of development for two minutes. (4) Have students think about the topic for one minute. (5) Give students ten minutes in which to copy the beginning and complete the paragraph. (6) Collect paragraphs and correct for appropriateness of content and idea development.

Timed writing can be practiced with a number of other exercises as well:

Transform information from graphs and tables into prose.
Rewrite one paragraph in a number of registers.

As with reading, we find it helpful to the student to have many different kinds of writing exercises presented in class under timed conditions. It is useful for the teacher to plan a specific number, and specific kinds, of writing assignments to be emphasized each week. For example, in a high intermediate five-hour (one-week) writing class in ESP, the following schedule is appropriate:

Two long writing assignments for the week, one in class (45 minutes) and one at home (1,000 words). Both to be corrected by the teacher for mechanics, organization, and style.
Two timed writing exercises in the week, in class (20 to 25 minutes each). Both to be corrected for ideas and organization.
Two short writing exercises in the week, in class (15 to 20 minutes each) on selected structural or rhetorical features. Both to be corrected for the particular focused feature(s) only.

Teachers who find this too heavy a load of correcting must try to modify the aims while continuing to give the students adequate writing practice and feedback.

The intermediate level should provide materials for the continued study of the differences between spoken and written English. Vocabulary, sentence patterns, register, rhetorical forms, syntactic devices, and principles of cohesion continue to be met in more complex forms. Variations of controlled and guided writing exercises provide useful activities for practicing these characteristics of written English. Paraphrasing and the dicto-comp procedure, somewhat freer forms of guided writing, are particularly useful.

Grading

In addition to correcting according to a plan decided on by the teacher, we recommend grading selected papers using modified objective scoring. This provides detailed feedback for students on various components of their writing skill, and records for students and teachers of the progress individuals and the group are making.

In terms of the teacher's activity, "grading" is a step beyond "correcting." We recommend using a writing checklist tailor-made for a particular class, and assigning numerical values to the subsections and the individual items on the list.

We have found the following grading procedure effective:

1. Grading presupposes that you have already corrected the paper, i.e., indicated errors according to your policy, and written comments indicated on the checklist.
2. After correcting the paper, list abbreviations for each of the checklist categories in a column at the end of the paper. Go through the paper a second time, assigning points to each checklist category and recording the point scores at the end of the paper beside the appropriate abbreviation.
3. Total the points.
4. Make brief comments next to each major category, particularly if the writer has not performed well.

Since grading is a time-consuming process, the teacher with a large workload may choose to apply it selectively, spacing assignments that are graded so that students will get sequential feedback on their work, and selecting writings that reflect the progressively complex stages of the writing program.

ADVANCED WRITING:
EMPHASIS ON FULL EXPOSITORY PROSE

Writing instruction characteristic of the advanced level includes courses for English majors, advanced sections in Intensive English Programs, and advanced programs for special purposes. In most cases these courses will be preparing students for specific purposes such as professional studies or work in post-graduate programs in their fields of specialization, particularly in the fields which require much verbalization, such as law, government, and most business and economics majors.

The typical student in such a course might be a language specialist majoring in linguistics, literature, or English teaching, or a specialist in another field such as business, economics, or medicine. Since the subject of English for English specialists overlaps with English for native speakers and is beyond the scope of this book, we will limit our remarks here to courses for non-English majors.

The needs of students at this level will be similar to those of the intermediate, writing for specific purposes: (1) organizing information and ideas, (2) following stylistic and rhetorical conventions, and (3) diagnosing and remediating composition for a mastery of the system of written English from sentence level through extended prose discourse.

A Diagnostic Test

Writing assignments at the beginning and end of the course—with errors fully indicated, comments included, and graded according to course standards—will yield information both about individuals and about the group. If the group is relatively homogeneous (e.g., from the same country, language background, and field of study), planning the syllabus and individual classes will present fewer problems.

The writing conventions of a particular field are usually expressed clearly and succinctly in the style sheets of major publications in that field. Analysis and discussion of these style sheets provide a useful initial focus, and later act as references for discussions of the papers students write.

Writing Long Papers: Extended Use of Language

Like the intermediate student, the student at the advanced level will profit from writing long papers that resemble assignments they will have to complete in their prospective academic or professional programs. Unless his previous experience is unusually full, the advanced student also will profit from a step-by-step treatment of the long writing assignment broken into stages with correction, feedback, and revision. Initial diagnosis and the first few weeks' writing experience will show whether the student also needs remedial work in structure, rhetoric, or mechanics.

Materials: Types of Textbooks

The careful teacher should use informed judgment in selecting the type of text and/or treatment for her class.

1. The most readily available books contain exercises designed almost exclusively to teach structure. Although they have in common their focus on problems of structure in written English, these books differ from each other rather significantly. The best among them include imaginative communicative exercises and useful summary lists, while the least impressive simply include pattern practices, using lists of unrelated items which provide fragments of information, not communication. Such texts are clearly useful for teaching new language, but address neither the component writing skills nor full writing.

2. The second type of text takes advantage of reading passages as models of prose, and also as sources of material for exercises in vocabulary, complex sentences, paragraphs, and style. These are the most similar to writing texts for native speakers.

3. The third most common type of text treats both structure and rhetoric. Almost all of these texts provide models, some of which are used also for language analysis. In some of the texts the exercises on structure and on rhetoric are clearly distinguished from each other; in others they are mixed and sometimes combined, somewhat haphazardly. Both the second and the third types of text bridge the gap between practice in language and that in writing skills. Some even contain a few exercises in full writing. However, the two texts tend not to distinguish clearly among the relative functions and values of these activities.

4. The rarest kind of writing text, and perhaps the most promising for intermediate and advanced writers, distances itself from concerns of structure and focuses on rhetoric and logic. Such texts might be described as cognitive. They treat the writing task as problem solving, and set the prospective writer the task of identifying characteristics of writing and then using their discoveries about writing in actually composing new essays.

Although the purposes of these texts differ greatly, the following characteristics appear in some of each of the types of text, regardless of purpose: attention to speech first, the use of model passages, and inclusion of vocabulary lists and spelling exercises. After examining a number of texts, one notices how neutral many of the writing exercises are, and how dependent they are on the theoretical frameworks of their books for meaning. Whether using texts or creating one's own exercises, it will be necessary for the teacher to make important distinctions herself. She should: distinguish clearly between language exercises and synthesizing exercises in writing; give detailed treatment of each writing step practiced; begin support courses early in the term; and consider the student as in a developmental series of writing skill stages.

Early in this chapter we suggested that each writing teacher has to select and plan courses according to course objectives, student interest, and what seems to her to work best. We offer the following checklist of questions as a guideline for the teacher in selecting writing exercises for a particular class or student and in deciding what and how to correct:

1. At what stage of writing is the student?
   a. Beginning—Mechanics
   b. Elementary—Extended Use of Language
   c. Intermediate—Purposeful Writing
   d. Advanced—Expository Prose
   e. Other
2. What is the purpose of the writing exercises?
   a. To check/consolidate/practice another language skill
   b. To practice structure
   c. To practice rhetoric
   d. Free writing
   e. Other

3. What information will most help the student in this assignment, and can the teacher provide that information without taking on an unnecessarily heavy workload?
4. Will it be helpful or harmful to the student for the teacher to give more than one kind of information on one writing assignment?
5. Should the assignment be *graded* as well as *corrected*?

Writing is a skill that lends itself to advanced-level training and use in specialized situations. It is a most important part of preparation for academic pursuits. Indeed, without well-developed writing skills, advanced-level training and education seem impossible. Writing is usually named and listed last in a recitation of the four skills, and it belongs last. But this is no excuse for neglecting writing. Indeed, it needs more attention, because it is so typically postponed in the teaching sequence.

DISCUSSION

1. List and describe four perspectives from which writing can be viewed.

2. It is suggested that writing is the most demanding of the language skills. Agree or disagree and state your reasons (the evidence that supports your position).

3. What important differences must be observed when teaching writing to literate versus nonliterate students?

4. Why can it be said that dictation is a useful device for checking mechanics of writing? What else can dictation check?

5. List five or more of the most common ways of arranging material in paragraph writing in English. What are the four basic modes of writing? The nine patterns of exposition?

6. State the arguments for stressing quality of performance in writing assignments, and the arguments for stressing quantity. Can the two emphases be combined?

7. What's the difference between controlled writing and guided writing?

8. What steps should be followed in writing a personal résumé?

9. What specific study skills should the writing teacher take responsibility for, if they are not otherwise provided for?

10. Correcting and grading a composition can best be done with the help of a checklist. Agree or disagree and give reasons for your answer.

B

COMPONENT SKILLS

CHAPTER TEN

ORTHOGRAPHY

INTRODUCTION

The Complexity of English Spelling

Modern English has a reputation as a language whose spelling is nearly chaotic. Partly because of this a years-long program in spelling is a requirement in typical first language instruction in English through elementary and middle schools and often an important element in the language program through secondary school. Second language students of English whose first language has a spelling system that is simple and regular complain about the complexity and irregularity in English spelling.

They are right. English spelling is complex and demanding. Most Americans are familiar with a teaching technique referred to as a spelling bee, which utilizes the format of a contest to identify and reward good spellers, indeed recognizing classroom, grade-level, school, city, regional, and even national champions.

To try to describe a spelling bee to a Spanish speaker is difficult: he will fail to see the point or appreciate the purpose of spelling instruction. His own language lacks even a meaningful equivalent to the English word "spell"; he gets along with *escribir*, the general word for "write," or with the more specific word *deletrear*, which means "to give the letters their individual names, then combine sounds into syllables, then syllables into words." In any case, few Spanish speakers worry about spelling. There are only half a dozen problems in their writing system, and these are often overlooked as people develop a considerable tolerance for alternate spellings. Even in this age of computer identification some Spanish speakers may vary the way they spell their own names, one time writing *Sanchez*, another time *Sanches*, with no great amount of concern about the difference.

Sight Words and Outdated Spellings

English has earned its reputation. Many of our most common words have spellings that are nearly unique as representations of the sounds of the language: *the, one, two, who, some, school, gym, weird, been, many, said, their, laugh, broad, know, honor, cafe,* etc. Examples of less frequently occurring words are: *indict, victuals, sword, bade, colonel.* Language teachers have a term for these: "sight words," and they are usually taught, a few at a time, as individual lexical items, with no attempt to extract patterns that can be expanded to spell other words.

Another problem in English is outdated spellings. Since spelling reforms have been relatively few and far between in English, we have maintained spellings that have long since ceased to be meaningful as clues to pronunciation. The most frequently cited example is probably the series of letters *ough,* found in various words with no practical way to describe which pronunciation is indicated by this complicated spelling; a few examples are:

though	/dhow/	rough	/rəf/
through	/thruw/	cough	/kɔf/
bough	/baw/	hiccough	/hík̇əp/
thoroughly	/thə́rəliy/	trough	/trɔf ~ trɔth/
ought	/ɔt/	lough	/lɑkh/

[Note: Many speakers of standard American English will want to substitute /ɑ/ for /ɔ/ in most instances of /ɔ/ .]

There are numerous other examples in English vowel patterns of a spelling representing several pronunciations in which the main difference is a matter of the frequency of various representations. We cite only two:

eo:

people	/iy/	Borneo	/iyow/
leopard	/ɛ/	neon	/iya/
yeoman	/ow/	pigeon	/ə/
theory	/ɪ/	Napoleon	/yə/

ea:

great	/əy/	bear	/ɛ/
eat	/iy/	heart	/ɑ/
ear	/ɪ/	learn	/ə/
bread	/ɛ/	ocean	/ə/

Some of these spellings are much less frequent than others, and therefore less important, and some are partly conditioned by surrounding sounds. Since they are nearly unique representations, they are probably best taught as sight words.

Looking the other direction, one can identify an English sound and find many ways to spell it. Simple vowel /ɪ/, for example, is most commonly spelled *i* as in *sit*. But it can also be spelled *y* as in *gym, ea(r)* as in *hear, ee(r)* as in *cheer*. These are common patterns. But there are numerous minor patterns, as shown in the following list:

e	pretty	o	women
ee	been	u	busy
ia	marriage	ui	build
ei	weird	i(C)e	give
ie	sieve		

Loanwords and Spellings

Another source of irregularity in English spelling is accounted for by the ready tendency to borrow words and their spellings from other languages. An example can be seen in the two-vowel sequence *au*, which normally signals the pronunciation /ɔ/ as in *naughty, haul*, etc. We borrowed the German word *sauerkraut* and introduced into English the spelling *au* to represent the pronunciation /aw/. Likewise, the spelling *eau* for the sound /ow/ has come with French words like *beaux, bureau, plateau*, etc., to add another bit of irregularity and complexity to English. The letter *c* is given the value /ch/ in borrowing Italian *cello*. On the other hand, the Spanish word *junta* comes into English with the /j/ sound suggested by the spelling rather than keeping the Spanish /x/ (matching English /h/).

The area of onomastics is another rich source of irregularity in English spelling. Without analysis note the following examples of foreign names that have been Americanized without changing the original foreign spelling: *DeJong* /diy yóng/ , *Deschamps* /díshà/ , *Frauchiger* /fráwəgər/ , *Freud* /froyd/ , *McKaughn* /məkóyn/ , *Du Maurier* /duwmàriyéy/ , etc. In the heydey of Ellis Island many immigrants with complicated names were rechristened to avoid spellings the immigration authorities could not understand, e.g., *Otto* from Arabic *Aro*. Today immigrants are likely to keep their own spellings, but their American friends and colleagues will continue to anglicize the pronunciation, often drawing it far away from the original spelling. We were recently surprised when a dermatologist identified as Dr. *Winn* turned out to be a Vietnamese who spelled his name *Nguyen*.

Regularity of English Spelling System

With many unusual examples like these it is easy to overreact and condemn the apparent vagaries of English spelling. It *is* a complicated system, but that complication in large part matches the complexity of the English sound system. In noting this Chomsky has characterized the English spelling system as ideal for its main purpose, which is to represent the language for native speakers of English. In making this statement Chomsky is referring to what is often described as the morphophonemic structure of the language. English spelling is in part, but only in part, a phonemic system (in which each phoneme is characteristically represented by a single letter, e.g., *m* = /m/, i.e., each time you hear /m/ you can be pretty sure the spelling will be *m*). Many languages have a phonemic system for spelling as the major characteristic of their writing system. We can cite as examples Spanish and Finnish, which have had the additional advantage of periodic updating by official or semiofficial government institutions, usually called language academies, established for the purpose of making recommendations on matters of language and usage.

Thus when a Spanish speaker uses the forms *dorm-, duerm-, durm-,* distinct spellings represent the vowel sounds /o, we, u/; though all are from related words with the common meaning "sleep," each different phonemic variant has its own spelling. By contrast, note some parallel examples from English.We have the words *sane, sanity* (/seyn, sǽnətiy/). Obviously *sane* and *sanity* share a common meaning, referring to a normal healthy mind, and this is shown by a common representation for the vowels of the first syllable of each word, even though their pronunciations are different. Another example is *meter, metrical* (/míytər, métrəkəl/), again two words with a common area of meaning. *Meter* is the basis of the *metrical* system of measure and the two words have a common spelling for their first vowel, the letter *e*; but again the pronunciation is different. This difference in pronunciation offers no trouble to a native speaker of English because he knows the words and does not need to be informed of their pronunciation. The case is quite different for a second language student of English, especially a student who has learned to depend on a close correlation between spelling and pronunciation in his own language. He has to be informed of the patterns of difference between the pronunciation (which is not shown by the spelling) in forms like *sane–sanity*; *meter–metrical*; *mine–mineral*; *cone–conical*; *duke–duchess*—with literally thousands of examples of the alternations which are illustrated in these ten forms.

Morphophonemic Alternations

Notice that in each pair of words a simple vowel and a diphthong are matched. Notice also that in both words the vowel in question is a stressed vowel. This feature will become more important and significant when we discuss vowel reduction in a later section of this chapter.

It should be pointed out that these correlations of simple vowels and diphthongs are not small classes of words, but are large, representing tendencies and relationships that are basic to the structure of the language. There are thousands of words involved. Note a few examples from the /ay ~ ɪ/ pattern: *mine–mineral, private–privy, vine–vineyard, oblige–obligatory, alive–living, collide–collision, decide–decision, provide–provision, wide–width, scribe–script, prescribe–prescription, bible–biblical, sacrifice–sacrificial, strike–stricken, vile–vilify, crime–criminal, line–linear, conspire–conspiracy, satire–satirical, wise–wisdom, precise–precision, rite–ritual, site–situated, finite–infinity, five–fifth, ride–ridden, criticize–criticism*. This list could be expanded almost endlessly, and there are other diphthong-vowel patterns. Obviously these alternations are central to the structure of the language.

TEACHING SPELLING

How are these patterns taught? We think by making students aware of the patterns, so they come to expect the alternations. It seems too extensive and diverse a system to try to drill specifically, particularly in the early stages of instruction, and as the above list illustrates, the patterns are very much individual pairs of words.

The morphophonemic alternation of vowel patterns in semantically related word pairs (and families) has spawned a spelling tradition which underlines the importance of coordinating the teaching of spelling and pronunciation. Since with respect to this pattern spellings reflect pronunciations indirectly, once these correlations are appreciated it will become easier to show how English has generalized the pattern to spelling words that are not related in meaning, but show the same alternation of simple vowel and diphthong. This produces a major pattern in English spelling which has introduced a corresponding terminology, followed in most grammars and dictionaries for native speakers of English, with the terms *short* and *long* applied to the five traditional vowels of the English alphabet. The term "short" refers to simple vowels. The term "long" refers to diphthongs, as shown in the following table. For dictionary purposes, the short vowel is shown with a breve, the long vowel with a macron:

Short	Pronunciation	Example	Long	Pronunciation	Example
ă	/æ/	mat	ā	/ey/	mate
ĕ	/ɛ/	pet	ē	/iy/	Pete
ĭ	/ɪ/	bit	ī	/ay/	bite
ŏ	/ɑ/	not	ō	/ow/	note
ŭ	/ə/	rub	ū	/uw/	rube

Another way of showing these relationships is to plot them on a vowel chart:

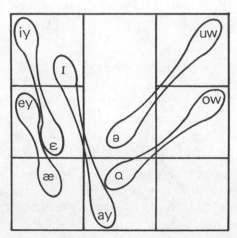

This pattern becomes an important basis for the English spelling system. In monosyllables, a simple vowel is usually followed by a single (or double) consonant (*bad–add, nil–hill, sod–odd, but–putt*, etc.)

EXERCISE 10.1

VOWEL ALTERNATION PATTERN IN ENGLISH

Instructions: Take the following words from dictation, observing the patterns described above. (Code 2–3)

Example:

	fæt	feyt	fat _____ fate _____
1.	ræt	reyt	
2.	mæt	meyt	
3.	kæn	keyn	
4.	sæt	seyt	
5.	pɛt	piyt	
6.	dhɛm	thiym	
7.	twɪn	twayn	
8.	fɪn	fayn	
9.	hɪd	hayd	
10.	rɑt	rowt	
11.	hɑp	howp	
12.	kɑp	kowp	
13.	dəd	duwd	
14.	jət	juwt	
15.	təb	tuwb	

Monosyllabic Patterns

The English short vowels are typically represented in monosyllables by a simple vowel symbol followed by a single or double consonant. The double consonant may be a geminate, two different consonants representing a single sound, a cluster of two consonants representing two sounds, or a complex single consonant representing two sounds. These possibilities are charted as follows:

Sound	S	p	e	l	l	i	n	g
Simple Vowel	Letter	Single C	Geminate	Digraph	Cluster	Complex		
/æ/	a	ad	add	sang	ask	tax		
/ɛ/	e	hen	mess	deck	germ	hex		
/ɪ/	i	sin	hill	with	gift	six		
/ɑ/	o	on	off	dock	cost	box		
/ə/	u	but	putt	such	bust	flux		

The single consonant is the standard of this pattern; geminates double the same consonant. A digraph is two consonants that represent one sound. A cluster is two consonants that represent two sounds, and a complex (there is only one in English, the *x*) is one consonant that represents two sounds. Each of the patterns can be presented and drilled.

A student eventually will get a feeling for the distribution of these possibilities, e.g.: final *c* and *k*, which can occur alone (*sic, flak*), usually combine in a digraph (*sick, back*); *v* finally (*slav*) is rare—usually *e* is added: *have, breve, live, love.* Final *l* (nil) is usually doubled: *hill, hall, hull.*

A much more complex and less predictable pattern is the representation of diphthongs in monosyllables. We have illustrated the VCe pattern, which is extensively used in writing diphthongs. Normally only one consonant follows a diphthong and usually two vowel letters are involved, though there are numerous exceptions.

There are alternate spellings to the VCe for diphthongs, most of which are VVC. Examples are:

		VCe	(V) (S)	VV		VVC	
/ey/	ā	ace	pay, they	ae	Rae	ai	maid
						ea	break
						ei	vein
/iy/	ē	theme	be, key	ee	see	ee	feet
				ea	sea	ea	seat
/ay/	ī	dice, type	by, buy	ie	die	ie	lied
/ow/	ō	home	go, show	oe	toe	oa	road
/uw/	ū	fume	flu, chew, do	ue	blue	ou	soup
				oo	too		

The *ee* and *ea* patterns for /iy/ are far more common than the standard *eCe.* And all the VS patterns allow for open syllables (no final consonant) that are not usually found with simple vowels. These diphthongs are mostly spelled V, VS, or VV. (S stands for semivowel *y* or *w*.)

It can be readily noted that there is considerable overlap; this will translate into pedagogical problems to be solved.

Our recommendation for teaching all the vowel spellings presented above is to take advantage of familiarization and association. Sounds can be presented orally either with individual words or, more appropriately, in sentence contexts; when a series of words that form a particular pattern have been accumulated, they can be incorporated in a spelling lesson that shows a consistent relationship between sound and spelling. Thus *oo* is the appropriate spelling for words with the vowel sound /u/, like *book, good, hoof, stood, foot, wool, look, wood*, etc. On another occasion the teacher can present *oo* with another value: /uw/, presenting illustrative words such as *food, proof, tooth, snooze, choose, coop, cool, school, room, moon, spoon, zoo, too*. These can be presented at first separately, and in a later lesson combined with the /u/-words spelled *oo*. At some subsequent time either as a comment or as a related lesson, forms like *blood* and *flood* should be introduced, pointing out this limited spelling pattern as an overlap.

Homonyms

The reader will undoubtedly have noticed another kind of overlap in the data presented on spelling. Not only does the same spelling represent different sounds, but more difficult for the student who is to produce English words in written form, the same sound can have numerous spellings. Thus we have *eCe, e, ee, ea, (e)y*—all possible spellings for the sound /iy/. The difficulty is increased by the frequent occurrence of homonyms such as *see–sea, meet–meat, cede–seed*, etc. Groups of words with each spelling can be associated together in a single lesson (such as *be, me, we, he*) later compared with *see, bee, fee, tree, free, tee, three, week, peek, heel, green, seed*—and at another time *sea, tea, pea, flea, each, peach, reach, teach, bead, leave, eagle, speak, peak, weak, heal, clean, cream, team, cheap, dean, eat*. All the possibilities of a pattern need not be taught—only the ones that are useful and relevant to the student's progress. Less frequent but regular spellings are: *key, city, valley*. We suggest that early spelling lessons be presented in the following format:

EXERCISE 10.2

SPELLING TEST FOR THE DIPHTHONG /iy/

Instructions: Write the words given as a list on a piece of paper. Each word
will be illustrated in a sentence. (Code 3–4)

Name _____

Date _____

1. see	I see the mailman coming.	see	1. _____
2. tea	She serves tea at four o'clock.	tea	2. _____
3. week	I'll come here next week.	week	3. _____
4. be	I'll be here tomorrow.	be	4. _____
5. Bea	Bea said she'd come.	Bea	5. _____
6. feat	The feat is indeed memorable.	feat	6. _____
7. theme	The theme was turned in late.	theme	7. _____
8. seeds	Do you have the garden seeds?	seeds	8. _____
9. beads	Her beads broke.	beads	9. _____
10. Pete	Do you know Pete?	Pete	10. _____
11. agree	Do you agree with her?	agree	11. _____
12. peach	I'd like a peach.	peach	12. _____
13. beets	Do you like beets?	beets	13. _____
14. meat	Serve the meat.	meat	14. _____

English spelling includes many homonyms and they can be bothersome to
students. The teacher can sometimes encourage acceptance by pointing out
that in this respect the written language contains more information than the
spoken. Special spelling lessons can be prepared to present homonyms. The
format illustrated in the above lesson can be utilized perhaps as a
combination review/new item lesson to present such pairs and triplets as:
*need–knead, bear–bare, reins–rains–reigns, by–buy–bye, toe–tow, so–sew–
sow, through–threw*, etc.

On a more advanced level, homonyms which involve spelling contrasts
with weak-stressed syllables in polysyllabic words can provide much-needed
spelling instruction. The less frequent traditional demons of English spelling

experience can be presented: *stationary–stationery, principal—principle, compliment–complement, current–currant*, etc.

Four vowel sounds have escaped the net established by the principal morphophonemic alternations used to introduce English spelling. To be complete we include them with their common spellings:

/u/	*u*	put, pull, bush	*oo*	foot, look, oops					
/ɔ/	*aw*	law, lawn	*au*	maul, pause	*a*	hall	*o*	for
/aw/	*ow*	cow, how, sow	*ou*	cloud, noun					
/oy/	*oy*	boy, toy	*oi*	boil, toil					

Our recommendation for teaching these spellings is, as expressed earlier, to take advantage of familiarization and association.

Vowel Reduction

Alternate forms of stressed vowels in English words are not the only applications of morphophonemic structure to the English spelling system. Another pattern of even greater consequence to both pronunciation and spelling is referred to as "vowel reduction." This is effectively illustrated by two polysyllabic word pairs from English, shown below in spelling and pronunciation:

telegraph	photograph	/télǝgrǽf/	/fówtǝgrǽf/
telegraphy	photography	/tǝlÉgrǝfiy/	/fǝtágrǝfiy/

Note the contrast in stress pattern in the top and the bottom rows (marked in the third and fourth columns). If we distinguish full vowels from reduced vowels we see that the full vowels /ɛ, æ, ow, ɑ/ always appear with one of the higher levels of stress while the reduced vowels /ǝ/ (and in these words /iy/) are consistently weak-stressed. This illustrates a very powerful morphophonemic pattern in English, one that must be assimilated if the student is ever to develop a feel for the language, which will have to precede the mastery of spelling.

The spelling indicates the pronunciation of the underlying vowels, which will be retained if the syllable is strong- or mid-stressed, but the pronunciation changes to /ǝ/ if the syllable is weak-stressed.

The exercise below gives the student a chance to hear "full" strong-stressed vowels and "reduced" weak-stressed vowels, marking each where it appears in this listening exercise.

EXERCISE 10.3

VOWEL REDUCTION IN ENGLISH

Instructions: Fill in the vowels of the word pairs as you hear them pronounced. (Code 5–7)

Example

able	ability	eybəl	əbɪlətiy

1. stable	stability	st_b_l	st_b_l_t_
2. sterile	sterility	st_r_l	st_r_l_t_
3. facile	facility	f_s_l	f_s_l_t_
4. civil	civility	s_v_l	s_v_l_t_
5. agile	agility	_j_l	_j_l_t_

[Note: If students are not familiar with transcription symbols, they could be asked to circle the syllable that gets strong stress.]

One problem that accompanies vowel reduction is accurately identifying the underlying vowel so it can be spelled correctly. Unfortunately for the student of English spelling, there is no typical representation of weak-stressed schwa. It can be any of the vowels of English, and indeed quite a number of vowel combinations. Selecting the correct vowel letter to represent a syllable with schwa can sometimes be a very difficult problem. Sometimes there seems no way to tell; you just have to know (or learn) the spelling. Other times you can find a related word with a different stress pattern. This allows the vowel otherwise represented as schwa to come up from the deep structure and reveal its identity. Thus if we have a word like *author* and we don't know how to spell the /ər/ syllable, we can depend on a word like *authority* to help us decide on the correct spelling, because the *o* in *authority* will also indicate an *o* in the comparable syllable in *author*. The following drill suggests some comparisons that can be helpful in identifying the correct spelling of schwa.

EXERCISE 10.4

IDENTIFYING UNDERLYING VOWELS
BY COMPARISON WITH RELATED FORMS

Instructions: You will hear a word with a schwa in a weak-stressed syllable, for example the second syllable of *total*. Try to think of a related word where the second syllable is strong-stressed, as in *totality*. From the /æ/ in *totality* you can assume that the vowel in the second syllable of *total* is also spelled with an *a*. (Code 5–7)

		Vowel Letter for V̆ in 1st Column	V́ Sound in 2nd Column
1. author	authority	o	/ɔ/
2. manager	managerial	e	/ɪ/
3. grammar	grammatical	a	/æ/
4. popular	popularity	a	/ɛ/
5. matter	material	e	/ɪ/
6. prior	priority	o	/ɔ/
7. nasal	nasality	a	/æ/
8. labor	laborious	o	/ɔ/
9. similar	similarity	a	/ɛ/
10. regular	regularity	a	/ɛ/
11. column	columnar	u	/ə/
12. supervisor	supervisorial	o	/ɔ/
13. Wagner	Wagnerian	e	/ɪ/
14. Chaucer	Chaucerian	e	/ɪ/
15. Caesar	Caesarian	a	/ɛ/

Many other words can be fed into this pattern. A few examples are: *numeral–numerical, vicar–vicarious, drama–dramatic, plural–plurality, mortal–mortality, mystery–mysterious, minister–ministerial, injure–injurious, polar–polarity, super–superior, janitor–janitorial.*

This will of course be an exercise for advanced-level students. The vowel sounds in the fourth column are for information only, and are not a part of the exercise. Note that part of the group have an *r* following the schwa, which has an effect on the source of the schwa, e.g., polar–polarity /ɛ/ , drama–dramatic /æ/ . The sound of the corresponding syllables will be different, but the spellings of the two words will still match.

In a few cases there are alternate pronunciations of the same word in English which are known to many people. Regardless of which one of a pair any particular speaker prefers, he can get spelling hints for the schwa-vowels from a comparison of the two. Examples are:

comparable	/kǽmpərəbəl – kəmpérəbəl/
formidable	/fɔ́rmədəbəl - fərmídəbəl/
horizon	/hɔ́rəzən – həráyzən/
abdomen	/ǽbdəmən – əbdówmən/
advertisement	/ədvə́rtəsmənt – æ̀dvərtáyzmənt/

Another problem specifically generated by the absence of a typical written representation of weak-stressed schwa, one which troubles native speakers as relentlessly as it does second language students, is the accurate spelling of the endings *-ant/ ent, -ance/-ence*. One consistently sees errors in newspaper copy and even in otherwise carefully edited books. The problem is inherited from Latin and is mostly restricted to the Latinate vocabulary in English. The solution for native English speakers has primarily been to rely on experience in studying Latin or one of the derived Romance languages, where the distinction in the sources of the loanwords lives on.

But this doesn't help students who have not studied a Latin language or have failed to master the appropriate related form, or most of the second-language students of English who come from areas of the world where Romance languages are not widely studied. Another problem is that the numerically superior *-are* verbs in Latin have encroached on the *-ere/-ire* territory to produce misleading results lilke *admittance, assistant, attendance*, etc. Then there is the occasional doublet like *confident* "trusting, assured" and *confidant* "a close friend who shares one's intimacies." Of course there is *confidential* to help, but which form does it relate to?

We suggest the following drill type to meet this kind of problem.

EXERCISE 10.5

SPELLINGS OF SOME WEAK-STRESSED SUFFIXES

Instructions: Your teacher may want to do this exercise orally, or as a written assignment. In either case, supply only the information requested. (Code 3–4)

Missing Letter

1. His assist __ nce was needed.   *a*
2. He's depend __ nt on his family.   *e*
3. Her repent __ nce was sincere.   *a*
4. The old man's resist __ nce was low.   *a*
5. The incumb __ nt usually has an advantage.   *e*
6. She comes from a promin __ nt family.   *e*
7. He lives on a low subsist __ nce level.   *e*
8. The attend __ nce at the theater is off.   *a*

9. The defend __ nt showed no interest in his own defense.   *a*
10. The temper __ nce movement was unsuccessful.   *a*

This is an efficient exercise which can be done quickly. If nothing else it gives experience in familiarizing students with correct spellings, and the format of omitting only the crucial vowel letter allows the ambitious student to look up the words in a dictionary if nothing less than perfection will satisfy him.

A similar exercise on *-able/-ible* would sometimes be helpful, since troublesome forms occasionally arise, such as the synonyms *eatable–edible*.

Morphophonemic Alternation/Reduction of Consonants

We have talked at some length about the morphophonemic alternation and reduction of English vowels. It was appropriate to start our chapter on orthography with these vowel patterns because that's where the major complexity lies. But the terms morphophonemic alternation and morphophonemic reduction of consonants are also relevant to a description of English spelling, though of less overall complexity.

As traditional terminology for simple vowels and diphthongs we have short vowels and long vowels; similarly we refer to hard and soft consonants. There's no real hardness and softness involved, just as there was no length, but the terms suffice to identify certain consonant contrasts. They are mainly applied to the consonants *c* and *g*, which when hard are /k/ and /g/, and when soft are /s/ and /j/. Thus we have numerous pairs like the following:

	c		*g*
/k/	*/s- (sh)/*	*/g/*	*/j/*
electric	electricity	legal	legislation
critic	criticism	logos	logic
public	publicity	regal	regent
romantic	romanticism	centrifugal	centrifuge
classic	classicism	pedagogue	pedagogy
physics	physician	analog	analogy
politics	politician	obligation	oblige
statistics	statistician	allegation	allege

We point these out as patterns ESL students should be aware of. They are not of crucial importance, and they are not exhaustive; there are others such as t/c (this time recognized in the spelling: *intimate/intimacy*).

There are other consonant alternation patterns that are functional, where voiceless/voiced pairs of consonants mark noun/verb contrasts. Sometimes the spelling shows these, sometimes not. Examples with the contrast in final position are:

/-s/	/-z/	/-f/	/-v/	/-th/	/-dh/
use		shelf	shelve	mouth	mouthe
abuse		safe	save	teeth	teethe
loose	lose	calf	calve	wreath	wreathe
house		half	halve	sheath	sheathe
excuse		proof	prove	bath*	bathe*
refuse*		thief	thieve	cloth*	clothe*

*vowel/stress difference in addition to consonant alternation

Consonant reduction involves the appearance of consonant letters in the spelling that are not present in the oral forms of words. Examples are: handsome, surprise, grandpa, cupboard, Wednesday, answer, who, whom, honest, castle, listen, raspberry, receipt, salve, walk, corps. These have to be learned like sight words.

Another pattern of consonant reduction is based on phonotactic rules. Nonpermitted clusters simplify by dropping one of the consonants, only to have it restored in another form of the word, usually when an affix is included that allows the cluster to become a sequence.

EXERCISE 10.6

SEQUENCE FORMS OF CONSONANT CLUSTERS

Instructions: Read a word from the left-hand column, then give one or more related words that utilize the "silent" letter from the word given. (Code 6–7)

1. sign   _____ (signal, signify, etc.)

2. column   _____ (columnar)

3. hymn   _____ (hymnal)

4. know   _____ (acknowledge)

5. mnemonic _____ (amnesia)

6. damn   _____ (damnation)

7. gnostic   _____ (agnostic)

8. thumb   _____ (thimble)

9. muscle   _____ (muscular)

Doubled Consonant Letters

One more consequence of the morphophonemic structure of English spelling must be discussed: the doubling of consonant letters (not sounds) to indicate short vowels. You will remember that a typical pattern for representing the vowels in monosyllables is either a final consonant or two consonants. The long vowel was indicated by a single consonant followed by an *e*. This pattern has important consequences for inflectional or derivational forms of verbs made by adding suffixes such as *-ing* and *-er*. For example, when a verb ends in a single consonant, as *plan*, and *-ing* or *-er* is to be added, one must first double the final consonant of the stem. The correct form is *planning, planner*. If the same suffixes are to be added to the word *plane* (referring to a specialized tool in a wood shop), the *r* can be added directly to produce *planer*, but the *e* is dropped before adding *-ing* for *planing*. If the verb has two vowels before the single final consonant, the *-er* and *-ing* are added directly: *speak, speaker, speaking*. This is a pattern that applies to almost all the verbs in English. If a verb with a simple vowel and two consonants follows, there is no need to double, and the *-ing* and the *-er* can be added directly; e.g., *backing, backer*.

The pattern is consistent, though it is perhaps slightly illogical to use a consonant manipulation to indicate a vowel value. Nevertheless, that's the way it is. Following is a drill to apply these rules:

EXERCISE 10.7

DOUBLING CONSONANT LETTERS BEFORE SUFFIXES

Instructions: Follow the pattern given. The irregular verbs will not have an *-ed* form. (Code 2–4)

	-ing	-er	-ed
1. hop	hopping	hopper	hopped
2. rope	roping	roper	roped
3. sing	singing	singer	—
4. line			
5. push			
6. shout			
7. pin			
8. putt			

9. join _____   _____   _____

10. set _____   _____   _____

Virtually all the verbs of English can be used in this drill, and it will be well to include a representative sample.

This pattern of spelling applies even when the forms are not necessarily verbs, as in *bitter–biter*; *latter–later*; *bonny–bony*. We can generalize by advising the students to remove the final *e* from a word like *game* and add *-ing*. Or in a word like *ram*, to preserve the information that the *a* will be pronounced /æ/ , double the *m* in *ram* and write *ramming*.

There are a few exceptions, some quite common forms such as *giving, having, singeing, changeable, noticeable*, etc., but they are not numerous or frequent.

Another pattern of consonant doubling is quite regular and useful to know about. This is the doubling of the final consonant, especially in monosyllabic personal names—sometimes given names, but most frequently family names. It has the virtue of distinguishing them from their mundane homonyms, which can be especially helpful in cases like *Mudd* and *Hogg*. There are many of these, among which the following can be cited: *Plann, Ladd, Fenn, Conn, Glenn, Penn, Goff, Hiss, Webb, Cobb, Pitt, McCann, Call, Kidd, Todd, Redd, Pett, Flamm, Ross, Ott, Rudd, Russ, Hill, Snell, Budd*. Sometimes a final *s* appears on such names, as in *Hobbs, Nebbs, Gibbs, Mills*. Note that in line with the generalization we have made about the doubling of consonants only after simple vowels, this list of names contains exclusively simple vowels. Thus there is continuity in the pattern of consonant doubling. Note a similar distribution in nicknames: *Edie* compared with *Eddie*; *Petie*, but *Betty*; *Boni* and *Bonnie*; *Jamey* and *Jimmy*.

Doubling consonants in two-syllable words when affixes are added is a little more complex. It depends on the stress. If the second syllable carries word stress, the consonant is doubled; otherwise it is not. Compare refe*r*ence and refe*rr*al, or dete*rr*ed. Note the contrast of "offer–offe*r*ed" and defer–defe*rr*ed."

Syllabication

One painful experience for most Americans is learning where it is possible to break a word that won't quite fit at the end of a line. The almost universal use of a typewriter increases the difficulty, because no squeezing is possible. The rules are: (1) a single consonant between vowels goes with the vowel that has higher stress: blów·er, a·wáy. (2) If there are two consonants between vowels, they will divide if they are a sequence, but if they form a cluster, both will go with the second vowel if it carries a higher stress: re·claím, but rèc·la·má·tion. A higher priority rule says morpheme boundaries will be respected, so -*tion* is not divided. A double consonant letter is usually divided, so for the *cl* in *reclamation* one goes with each syllable.

You will notice that American dictionaries include all the permissible division points in the main entry of each polysyllabic word, with raised dots as point markers. Many people just give up and check every one they can't avoid in typing a paper. Special dictionaries for secretaries and stenographers include nothing else, just a list of words with syllables marked. The conventional dictionary markings are widely accepted by editors, but the written markings don't always correspond to the way we divide words when we pronounce them. Here's a chance to practice:

EXERCISE 10.8

SYLLABICATION

Instructions: Place a caret (a small upside down v that looks like this: ∧) between the letters at the points where you think one syllable ends and the next begins. (Code 3–5)

barrel	future	postoffice	contribution
furnace	beyond	posterior	conscience
galoshes	playground	postulate	connection
furniture	supermarket	stylistic	linguistic

The dictionary has been mentioned as a place to find out how to divide words into visual syllables. Earlier it was mentioned as a source of acceptable spellings. These two types of information are supplemented by other very useful data that a student should learn to make use of: the word class(es) an item belongs to, the definitions it offers, the source language, and the various idioms a word participates in. Meanings are usually marked when archaic, obsolescent, informal, slangy, obscene, etc. A good dictionary is truly an indispensable tool for a serious student.

Mnemonic Devices and Word Games

A final note: given the literally millions of first language students who have used rhymes or other mnemonic devices to remember spellings, we see no objection to the presentation of verses like:

> *i* before *e*,
> except after *c*
> and when sounding like *a*
> as in *neighbor* or *sleigh*.

Then a sentence follows citing the most frequent exceptions, which are not numerous, indicating the rule is useful:

"Neither of the weird foreigners from the heights of science efficiently seized their leisure."

Likewise we have no objection to acrostics as memory joggers, such as:

George Evans' old grandmother rode a pig home yesterday.
A red Indian thought he might eat tobacco in church.

Many people get a lot of satisfaction (and incidentally some excellent practice) playing word games. Some are competitive, like Scrabble, Boggle, Perquackey, or the more homespun "hangman." A noncompetitive and self-challenging activity is crossword puzzles, which are very popular in the United States. We recommend participating in these games, whether for the fun of it—or as assignments for classwork.

DISCUSSION

1. Why is English spelling more demanding than Spanish spelling?

2. Discuss sight words and their function in English spelling.

3. Describe the morphophonemic influence in English spelling and in the structure of the English language. Contrast and describe morphophonemic and phonemic spellings in English.

4. What do the terms "short" and "long" refer to when applied to English spelling? What diacritics are employed to differentiate the two?

5. Why are homonyms bothersome to students?

6. Which form of the language gives more information: the written or the spoken?

7. What does the word "demons" refer to in the context of English spelling?

8. What common feature of spelling can be seen in vowel alternation and vowel reduction?

9. How can a knowledge of Latin help a speaker of English become a better speller of English?

10. What is the main function of doubled letters in English spelling?

CHAPTER ELEVEN

GRAMMAR—
WRITTEN LANGUAGE

INTRODUCTION

Essentially the same grammar applies to written and spoken English. There are differences, but they are differences in application rather than of kind. Since oral language is used in an appropriate physical setting, more deletion patterns are allowed (Goin' home now?—Yeah, can't think of any reason not to). Written English, on the other hand, has more embedding and a greater range of embedding. Spoken English makes moderate use of restrictive relative clauses (He's the one I told you about) and the *wh*-nominalization (What we're going to do is wait right here). On the other hand one would rarely find in informal spoken English a *that*-nominalization functioning in subject slot (That he decided not to come is sincerely regretted by all), or a nonrestrictive relative clause (My brother John, whom you met at the cocktail party yesterday afternoon, is a 32nd degree mason).

A difference in the relative complexity of forms and constructions in the written language is encouraged by the nature of pacing and therefore of monitoring. A speaker or a listener has to maintain a pace of delivery or comprehension that matches the normal rate of oral communication. We note that this is approximately 125 words per minute. A speaker who falls below about 90 words per minute may have difficulty holding his audience. And a listener who cannot process at these same speeds will have a handicap he will not likely overcome.

The written language, on the other hand, allows both the reader and the writer to pace their activities at whatever rate they consider optimum for their own expression and comprehension. And if it is needed, there can be a second (or third, fourth, etc.) chance to read or write a difficult passage, since a private activity is involved.

Has English always had a grammar? We'd say yes, in the sense that words and morphemes always combined to form utterances. But our academic ancestors would have said no, because it wasn't formulated and described. Why was it necessary to develop a formal grammar? The early grammars of English were written for a very specific purpose—to make possible for writers of English the enviable stability enjoyed by the classical languages, particularly Latin. Latin had a grammar and stability. English lacked both. The solution seemed to lie in the provision of a grammar for English.

One of the crucial features which seems to have escaped the attention of the scholars was that Latin was a dead language and English was very much alive. Latin was dead in the sense that there were no native speakers whose innovations and creative use of the language introduced changes.

Latinate Grammars

The familiar grammar of Latin provided the model by which English grammar was designed and written. Indeed Latin was considered to have *the* universal grammar which could serve as a model for describing any other language. The result was the application of certain Latin rules to the description of English, where they didn't fit well. There are still teachers of English presenting the Latin rule which says a preposition may not come at the end of a sentence. The rule was accurate for Latin, but doesn't fit English.

With the appearance in 1795 of a grammar by Lindley Murray (1745–1826), an Englishman ironically born in America, the Latinate tradition was formally established, and it changed very little in the next century. At that time the teachers were ready and willing to prescribe, and the students wanted their prescriptions.

(Incidentally, this is true of most foreign and second language classes at the present time. The students feel the need for guidance and the teachers are ready to interpret the correct set of rules needed to communicate. There's nothing inherently wrong with prescriptive grammar, if the prescriptions are accurate.)

Some of the rules the nineteenth-century grammarians formulated may have reflected an earlier use of the English language, but some seemed to have been dreamed up merely because it was felt a rule was needed. An example is the complex description of the difference between *shall* and *will*, which is much better forgotten than discussed. It wasn't until the first half of the twentieth century, when the structuralists studying nonliterate languages found emphasis on usage unavoidable, that correctness was defined, even for literate situations, as what most people actually say and write. While in a historical context this may be an extreme position, it was necessary to clear the air.

Modality and Register

We need to make a few comments about the difference between oral and written language and the similar, though not identical, difference between formal and informal usage. The following diagram is an attempt to show the overlap:

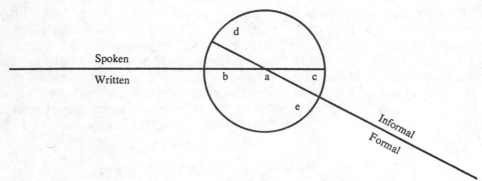

The diagram suggests that language usage is divided 50–50 between the written and the oral modality, with another overlapping 50–50 division between informal and formal styles. The 50–50 balance is not necessarily true and certainly differs for different people. Some literate native speakers rarely do any writing at all, or do very little beyond lists of suggestions for things they need to remember, such as a shopping list. Others—say an editor or a proofreader on a newspaper—spend almost all of their working day involved with the written language.

The value of the diagram is its indication that most written language tends to be formal (bae) and most spoken language tends to be informal (dac). There is such a thing as spoken formal (dab), as in the case of lectures, speeches, and sermons, and there is written informal (cae), especially when it is in imitation of spoken standards, as in plays, dialog, novels, etc., and in personal correspondence through letters, in which spelling and usage may vary considerably from the usual written language.

Informal English is probably making inroads on the written preserve formerly claimed by formal English. This book is reasonably formal, but four paragraphs back we used the contracted form "wasn't," definitely an informal usage that we would have avoided twenty years ago. Perhaps we'll have to acknowledge changes in usage that will recognize a smaller gap between formal and informal.

Pacing and Density

We have already mentioned pacing, which almost by itself assures that oral language will be loose and written language compact. A speaker who stands to lose his audience because of overslow pacing may resort to empty expressions which are designed and used to keep the floor, presumably while he thinks over what he really wants to say. Thus the popular "You know what I mean?" or "Let me put it this way," "It seems to me," and the politician's "Let me make one thing perfectly clear." These communicate virtually nothing, in fact are not intended to communicate, but function merely to maintain contact and initiative. They help both the speaker and the listener by moderating the pace of the communication. They are rare indeed in written English.

The same function can be accomplished in the written medium by the writer, who rewords and reworks his sentence until he feels it effectively communicates what he has to say, and by the reader, who backs up and rereads a sentence or clause or expression as many times as he feels necessary to extract all of the meaning he is interested in. This is a stylistic matter which can be described with the word "density." Density is control in different ways of the level of style in English, especially in written English. Density can also be applied to a description of the structure of the language. The more dense the language is, the more formal it is likely to be (Ohashi 1978). Note the following example: "Look at that man. He's wearing a very strange kind of hat. His hat has three corners. It's colored purple and it's dusty. It's a very unusual hat."

With a density increase which also moves upward on the scale of formality you might say, "Look at that hat that has three corners. It's purple and dusty. It's very unusual." Still more density and more formality can be achieved by saying "Look at that unusual, dusty, purple, three-cornered hat."

If a thought or idea is expressed in fewer words, the resulting condensation will usually be a more formal expression. Note the illustrative pairs of sentences where the shorter sentence is the more compact and consequently the more formal:

1a) No matter what happens, be there on time.
b) Whatever happens, be there on time.

2a) I have to meet the 4 o'clock plane.
b) I must meet the 4 o'clock plane.

3a) A hearty welcome is waiting for you.
b) A hearty welcome awaits you.

4a) She does not like going by ship.
b) She dislikes going by ship.

It is possible to find counterexamples, where the wordier of two more or less synonymous expressions is the more formal: "In my judgment it seems likely that he will arrive very shortly" versus "I think he'll be here soon." This is not an illustration that matches the grammar of the two sentences, but the lexicon.

Accepting density as a criterion, the students can try some paraphrases that shorten the sentences given, and note they are more formal and more suggestive of written language style.

EXERCISE 11.1

FORMAL PARAPHRASES (A)

Instructions: Paraphrase and shorten the following sentences. (Code 3–4)

Teacher	Student
1. When I was walking down the lane, I met my good friend Charles.	Walking down the lane I met my good friend Charles.
2. If it had not been for my father, I wouldn't have gone to college.	Had it not been for my father, I wouldn't have gone to college.
3. Since the weather was good, they went for a walk.	The weather being good, they went for a walk.
4. This was my idea, arrived at without anybody suggesting it.	This was my idea, arrived at without anybody's suggestion.
5. He was not aware of the car that was coming toward him.	He was unaware of the approaching car.
6. He is not well and he needs help.	He is unwell and needs help.

Perhaps it's coincidence that the shorter construction is more formal, but at least the difference is consistent.

Many of the most common words in English have multiple meanings. Those with many meanings tend to be less formal than those with fewer or just one meaning.

EXERCISE 11.2

FORMAL PARAPHRASES (B)

Instructions: Paraphrase with more general vocabulary. (Code 3–4)

1. I went to the post office to obtain some stamps.	get
2. He is approximately six feet tall.	about
3. She was reared by her grandparents.	raised
4. John operates a sawmill.	runs
5. William repairs radios.	fixes
6. We should endeavor to improve our lives.	try

It is something of a paradox that density, which can be expected to shorten utterances, and combining sentences in complex constructions, which will inevitably produce longer sentences, can both be expected to increase formality. If a communication is both dense and lengthy, complexity can readily be recognized. For example, when adding information a speaker/writer can employ what is called a coordinate conjunction, which ties two thoughts together. Like most other devices, coordination can be abused, tying thoughts together that are not sufficiently closely related, resulting in what usually is recognized as a juvenile style of narration.

5) We went down town, and we saw a candy store, and we went in and bought some chocolate drops, and we went to the movies, and. . . .

Belonging together can be understood in more than one way. The association can be expected, or it can be a little surprising or unexpected. We signal which of these relationships we wish the reader to understand by the conjunction we use to join the two sentences together. In the following exercise this difference is illustrated.

EXERCISE 11.3

USING COORDINATE CONJUNCTIONS

Instructions: Combine the pairs of sentences with *and* (if the second sentence is a natural consequence of the first) or with *but* (if the second sentence is somewhat unexpected). (Code 3–4)

Example:

a. The policeman saw the man jump over the fence. He went to investigate.	The policeman saw the man jump over the fence and went to investigate.
b. The policeman saw the man jump over the fence. He did nothing.	The policeman saw the man jump over the fence but did nothing.

1. The ink fell off the table. It didn't spill.   (but)
2. Jack got in a fight. He got his nose bloodied.   (and)
3. He lost control of the car. He somehow avoided an accident.   (but)
4. His algebra book was stolen. He got it back.   (but)
5. I got a flat tire. I had other difficulties which have made me late. (and)
6. The teacher seemed angry. He didn't say anything.   (but)
7. He really studied hard. He didn't get a good grade on the exam.   (but)
8. The car rolled over three times. The driver was buckled in. He was not hurt. (and)

Notice that the relationship works both ways. Expected and unexpected are marked by *and* and *but*. On the other hand, the presence of *and* or *but* tells us what the writer (or speaker) expected.

Note the following pair of complex sentences, which differ only by the use of *and* in one and *but* in the other:

6) The policeman saw the robber run out of the bank and did nothing.
7) The policeman saw the robber run out of the bank but did nothing.

In (6) the narrator records that this is what you can expect from the police in this context, while (7) indicates that for the policeman to do nothing in these circumstances is somehow unusual.

Misreading

Elsewhere in this volume (especially Chapters Eight and Twelve) we have suggested that the student learning to read should concentrate his attention on the content words if he wants to extract the general meaning of a passage quickly. This is especially true for the important skill of skimming. We compared the reading of English to a brick wall, where the bricks are the content words and the mortar represents the structure words. To concentrate one's attention on content words is a valid piece of advice: the bricks do represent the meaning, in a tangible sense, but the mortar is not completely unimportant: without it you don't have a wall, but a pile of bricks.

It is very easy to misread, especially if the reader is trying to increase his reading speed. When not skimming, but when reading for information, the student can't afford to be wrong too many times. When the thread of meaning is lost he has to return and reread the sentence, or perhaps the paragraph. Students are deliberately taught the valuable skill of skimming, very useful as a means of orienting oneself to the content of an unfamiliar passage. Rather than trying to extract specific information, the student is finding out what the selection is about. As his skimming skill improves, he can get more out of the selection. But this is a kind of tentative reading, especially subject to correction if he misreads. The native English-speaking or the advanced-level ESL student knows something is wrong if all of a sudden the selection no longer makes sense. Then he has to back up and reread it (or part of it) and try to correct the misstep he has made. Usually it is a little word he failed to see or take into account, and seeing it is enough to make the correction that returns the selection to meaningfulness.

The following set of drills attempts to reproduce the situation. The sentences on the left will be understood as erroneous because a structure word has been omitted (to guarantee it will be overlooked; in real life it is there but in reading was missed or misread). The student should try to locate the point where the omission is made and to determine what item has been omitted. Only then should reference be made to the corrected sentence on the right (having had it covered) to see if the correction can be confirmed. The errors will be grouped by categories (prepositions, conjunctions, etc.).

EXERCISE 11.4

OMITTED PREPOSITIONS

Instructions: Read the sentences in the left-hand column one by one. Figure out why they're wrong; correct them by inserting the missing preposition. (Code 5–6)

Example:

1. In some cases citizens contribute input for decisions policy.

   In some cases citizens contribute input for decisions on policy.

2. The look-say method doesn't seem to work for a limited number content words.

   The look-say method doesn't seem to work for a limited number of content words.

3. Dinner do you prefer tea or coffee?

   After dinner do you prefer tea or coffee?

4. Some activities may be used help children develop word recognition abilities.

   Some activities may be used to help children develop word recognition abilities.

5. The following questions are not based any particular selection.

   The following questions are not based on any particular selection.

6. Read the book soon; it can be found our library.

   Read the book soon; it can be found in our library.

7. The students should compare their finished work the original very carefully.

   The students should compare their finished work with the original very carefully.

8. He looked the blue horizon and wondered what was beyond it.

   He looked at the blue horizon and wondered what was beyond it.

If this exercise is done from the blackboard in the classroom with the class as a whole, the "answers" could be covered until they are needed for confirmation or correction of student responses. Many times a student will unknowingly make the correction on his initial reading, because he (and all of us) prefer a text that makes sense. Or, reading the sentence, a student will get the sense of the sentence and wonder if there really is an erroneous omission.

Here's another exercise:

EXERCISE 11.5

MODAL AUXILIARIES

Instructions: Read the sentences in the left-hand column one at a time. Figure out why they are wrong; correct them by inserting the missing modal. (Code 4–5)

Example:

1. David says Doug go if nobody else volunteers.	David says Doug will go if nobody else volunteers.
2. You simply see my new dress.	You simply must see my new dress.
3. Where we spend our vacation this year?	Where shall we spend our vacation this year?
4. He might agree to represent us, and then again he not.	He might agree to represent us, and then again he might not.
5. You have a cookie if you're a good boy.	You can have a cookie if you're a good boy.
6. If he had come on time he have cooked dinner.	If he had come on time he would have cooked dinner.
7. Oh, if only I play like that, I'd give half my life.	Oh, if only I could play like that, I'd give half my life.
8. The minister blessed the grave and said "He rest in peace."	The minister blessed the grave and said "May he rest in peace."

As you've seen in the last two exercises, skimming may introduce errors, resulting in incorrect guesses, even though they are very good guesses. (Note, however, that some of the above sentences can take alternate corrections; e.g., sentence 5 takes "might, could," etc.)

In real reading the student may have to refer back several times to clarify an important sentence or paragraph. This is especially true of short relator words (relative pronouns, adverbial conjunctions, etc.).

Here's a sample exercise:

EXERCISE 11.6

RELATOR WORDS

Instructions: If the following sentences (on the left) do not seem to sound just right, try adding a relator word to make them sound more natural. Add only one word per sentence. (Code 4–5)

Example:

1. John's much more settled he got married last year.

   John's much more settled since he got married last year.

2. I'll deliver the peaches he needs the truck to go to work.

   I'll deliver the peaches before he needs the truck to go to work.

3. The steps go along with making curriculum plans are complex.

   The steps which go along with making curriculum plans are complex.

4. Bill came with the key, we got into the house.

   After Bill came with the key, we got into the house.

5. We don't want to; we will go with the expedition.

   We don't want to; nevertheless we will go with the expedition.

6. I've been here Friday morning at ten o'clock.

   I've been here since Friday morning at ten o'clock.

7. I had a lonesome dinner she left for the airport.

   I had a lonesome dinner after she left for the airport.

8. I would go with you to the movies I were not so tired.

   I would go with you to the movies if I were not so tired.

Analyzing Errors

Occasionally a reader is misled by reading a word incorrectly, an error that is picked up very quickly when the sentence is reread. Lots of similar words exist, and the grammar of the language helps make the correction. Suppose we think we read: "The farmer needs more mature for fertilizer this year." This makes no sense unless we can reinterpret the word "mature." If we know the word "manure" the substitution makes sense, because fertilizer and manure in the same context make an understandable semantic collocation, where fertilizer and mature do not. Also the slot needs a noun, not an adjective, so the grammar of the language guides us to a correct reinterpretation.

EXERCISE 11.7

SIMILAR-APPEARING WORDS

Instructions: Correct the following sentences by making them grammatical and meaningful. (Code 4–6)

Example:

1. He was under dress when he confessed.   He was under duress when he confessed.
2. By profession he was a relator.   (realtor)
3. She fried the beacon for breakfast.   (bacon)
4. The diverse were on the ocean floor.   (divers)
5. The water was barely palatable.   (potable)
6. My grandfather fought with the   (cavalry)
   calvary.
7. The man who had run amok was   (wielding)
   welding a heavy bolo.
8. In coercive writing the letters are   (cursive)
   joined together.
9. His abuse was truly fragrant.   (flagrant)
10. Above all we must be untied.   (united)

WRITTEN DELETION STYLES

Special grammar rules are applied in two styles of written English: news headlines and telegrams. Both involve deletions that are based on the same assumptions: that space is limited and unnecessary words are to be avoided. So all words that do not contribute substantially to the message are deleted from the headline or telegram, as long as the resulting expression communicates a message. This approach tends to affect structure words more than content words, though some structure words are retained, usually with a specialized function. Headlines and telegrams must communicate, though sometimes ambiguity creeps in, as shown by an old favorite: "Ship Sails Today," which if a headline will be interpreted as "The ship sails today," but if a telegram, likely means "Ship the sails today."

News Headlines

Sometimes ambiguity is based on orally produced suprasegmental features such as the headline "USSR Hunts Woman Killer." Is this to be read "wôman kíller" (a woman who has become a killer) or "wóman kìller" (a killer of either sex who attacks women)? Possibly the ambiguity was deliberate, a means of attracting readers, which is an important aspect of headline writing in the first place.

Let's look at some of the features (lettered and listed below) of headlines:

1. TMI Records Falsified = The records at the Three Mile Island nuclear plant have been falsified.
   a. Omission of most particles.
   b. Capitalization pattern of titles.
   c. Acronyms and abbreviations welcome.
2. Solzhenitsyn Fund Aide Gets 2 Years in Jail = An aide working for the Solzhenitsyn fund is sentenced to two years in jail.
   d. Heavy prenominal modification.
   e. Use of figures for numbers.
   f. Preference for short words.
3. Hughes' Heirs to Pay Actress = The heirs of Howard Hughes are going to pay off an actress.
   g. Future shown by *to* + verb rather than *will* + verb, possibly a deletion from *be going to* + verb.
   h. Apostrophe used when appropriate.
4. Collins, Sloane Locked in Tight Kentucky Race = Collins and Sloane are opponents in a close political competition in Kentucky.
   i. Use of comma instead of conjunction *and*.

EXERCISE 11.8

INTERPRETING NEWS HEADLINES

Instructions: Expand the following newspaper headlines to produce grammatical sentences that say the same things. (Code 4–6)

Example:

1. Court Upholds Tax on Biased Schools

The (U.S. Supreme) Court upholds a tax on schools that practice racial bias.

2. Man Convicted in Murder of CHP Officer
3. Key House Panel Oks LA Subway Funds
4. Vote Put Off on Campaign-Funding Bill
5. Poland Moves to Defuse Police Brutality Charge
6. Reagan Assailed for Rights Panel Plan

7. Suspected Killer of Marine Charged in 4 More Deaths
8. Governor Will Seek Support to Fight Tax Hike
9. US Adds $2.5 Million for AIDS Research
10. April Consumer Prices Up 0.6%

Telegraphic Style

Telegram style is similar, but differs in a few details: it does not use symbols like % or $, and it avoids numbers given in figures, since a single error can obscure the meaning intended, and errors introduced during transmission are not uncommon; most, hopefully, are self-correcting. No apostrophes are used. Long words are not avoided, since charges are by a word count and long words cost no more than short words.

EXERCISE 11.9

INTERPRETING TELEGRAMS

Instructions: Write grammatical paraphrases for the following telegraphic messages. (Code 4–5)

1. Boy six lbs four ozs 18:00 June ten mother baby fine
2. Arriving Sunday noon Panam two
3. Marilou won first place statewide beauty contest
4. Congratulations beauty crown luck next step
5. Your book appears Friday seventeen April Congratulations
6. Sell Gavin Electronics immediately
7. Lorraine Thompson killed instantly auto accident Sincere condolences
8. House flooded all family safe
9. All American Express checks stolen await instructions
10. Accept latest offer match scheduled Saturday June twelve

COMBINING SENTENCES

One very common feature of written English is the appearance of complex sentences, which are made up of two or more simple sentences. Normally when two sentences are combined, one is embedded in the other. The accepting sentence is referred to as the *matrix* sentence, and the sentence which becomes part of the new complex sentence is called the *constituent* sentence. Note the following example:

8a) The soldiers attacked.
 b) The message arrived.

These two events can be related to each other in terms of a time sequence: the attack began before the message arrived, or it began after. Or the two events occurred simultaneously. If sentence (a) is the matrix and sentence (b) the constituent, we can say:

c) The soldiers attacked before the message arrived.
d) The soldiers attacked after the message arrived.

These two sentences can reverse roles so that (b) is the matrix and (a) is the constituent, in which case we get:

e) The message arrived before the soldiers attacked.
f) The message arrived after the soldiers attacked.

Note that the same information is contained in sentences (c) and (f); also, the same semantic content appears in sentences (d) and (e). Note also that the order of the matrix and constituent (or independent and subordinate clauses, as some would designate them) can be reversed, so that the four illustrative complex sentences could be:

g) Before the message arrived, the soldiers attacked.
h) After the message arrived, the soldiers attacked.
i) Before the soldiers attacked, the message arrived.
j) After the soldiers attacked, the message arrived.

This freedom of placement for adverbial clauses is typical of English, where adverbs can often occur almost at any point in a sentence. Note:

9a) Already he had finished reading the assignment.
 b) He had already finished reading the assignment.
 c) He had finished reading the assignment already.

Here's an exercise to practice making combined sentences from simple sentences:

COMBINING SENTENCES

Instructions: Combine the sentences given below, choosing between *before* or *after* (or allowing either one). State why only *before* or *after* or both can be used. (Code 5–7)

Examples:

Teacher	Student	Rationale
1. We had an early dinner. He arrived.	We had an early dinner before/after he arrived.	The dinner can come either before or after the arrival.
2. John and I had a good talk. We finally got together.	John and I had a good talk after we finally got together.	The talk cannot precede the getting together.
3. I was practically full-grown. I got to know Eduardo.	I was practically full-grown before I got to know Eduardo.	"Practically full-grown" wouldn't "happen" after an acquaintance was made.
4. The company commander received the message. He decided on the attack.		
5. He played a good game of chess. He was 15 years old.		
6. The bell will ring. The class formally starts.		
7. Kenneth's sister will rehearse him. He goes for an interview tomorrow.		
8. The city had to clean up. The storm passed.		

EXERCISE 11.11

REVERSING THE ORDER OF CLAUSES

Instructions: Repeat the drill above, but this time change the order of the
clauses. (Code 4–6)

Example:

1. We had an early dinner.   After/Before he arrived,
   He arrived.   we had an early dinner.
2. (etc.)

Another exercise pattern starts with the complex sentence and identifies
the matrix and constituent sentences from which the complex one is
constructed. Thus we can start with "Before he discovers the loss I will return
the money." This is made up of "I will return the money" and "He
discovers the loss." This can be a helpful procedure for the student who
needs to figure out the relationship of the ideas that underlie the communication.

You will notice that all of our examples are taken from constructions that
involve time clauses, and we have restricted these to constituent sentences
introduced by *before* and *after*. There are of course other introducers, such as
*by the time that, until, after, when, as soon as, once, while, as long as, as,
just as, whenever, as often as*, etc. Some of these are distinguished by very
tenuous shades of meaning, and exercises can be designed to illustrate those
differences.

In addition to differences of sequence, other relationships are possible.
Examples are clauses of cause, purpose, and result, and the hypothetical *if*-
clauses in conditional sentences. The interested reader can refer to any one
of the standard grammars; our purpose here is to show illustrative examples,
not to offer a comprehensive analysis.

Another kind of complex sentence is designated as a relative construction,
where the embedded clause functions as an adjective. For this kind of
complex sentence the matrix and the constituent must contain instances of
the same noun. For example:

10a) I like a student.   I like a student who does his
   b) The student does his work on time.   work on time.

It is essential that the word *student* mentioned in both the matrix and the
constituent sentence refer to the same individual. That these two sentences
do so is shown by the use of *the* as the article modifying the word *student* in
the second sentence. Then a simple formula combines the two sentences.
The second occurrence of the noun is substituted by the relative pronoun

who; then *who* is moved to the beginning of the clause if it is not already there, and the constituent clause is inserted right after the duplicated noun in the matrix sentences. The result is a complex sentence with an adjectival clause, in this case a restrictive clause, since the clause is needed to identify the modified noun in the matrix sentence.

If the word had been a thing, instead of a person, the relative pronoun would have been *which* instead of *who*. Note the following:

11a) I like a car.
   b) The car doesn't break down. } ⟶ I like a car which doesn't break down.

Both *who* and *which* can be substituted by *that*. But that isn't enough complication. Note these sentences:

12a) The boy enjoyed the book. }
   b) Asimov wrote the book. ⟶ The boy enjoyed the book which Asimov wrote.

⟶ The boy enjoyed the book that Asimov wrote.

⟶ The boy enjoyed the book Asimov wrote.

This pattern shows that *that* can substitute for *which*, and in turn *that* can be deleted if the next word is a noun or pronoun. The deletion could not take place if a verb followed, e.g., "The boy enjoyed the book which/that was written by Asimov." We could not say *"The boy enjoyed the book was written by Asimov."

A word about nonrestrictive clauses: they are parenthetical comments, and they don't modify, limit, or restrict the noun they modify in the matrix. Note:

13a) New York is the largest city in
     the U.S.
   b) New York has its share of street
     crime. } ⟶ New York, which is the largest city in the U.S., has its share of street crime.

Which cannot be substituted by *that*, nor can *which* be deleted. New York is identified by its name; we don't need a relative clause to restrict its meaning. Note the following similar sentence, which will be restrictive:

14a) A city will have its share of
     street crime.
   b) The city has over half a million
     people. } ⟶ A city which has over a half a million people will have its share of street crime.

A city (any city—it's not identified) will have its share of street crime provided it fulfills the condition of having half a million inhabitants. The constituent helps identify the modified noun in the matrix. Thus *which* can change to *that*, but *that* cannot be deleted, because a verb follows the relative pronoun (*which* or *that*).

Let's look at some adjective clauses and see if we can distinguish restrictve and nonrestrictive.

EXERCISE 11.12

CLASSIFYING ADJECTIVE CLAUSES

Instructions: Indicate whether each of the following sentences has a restrictive or nonrestrictive adjective clause. (Code 4–5)

Examples:

1. My friend John, who plays the violin professionally, is   <u>nonrestrictive</u>
   coming tomorrow.
2. A friend who plays the violin is coming tomorrow.   <u>restrictive</u>
3. The winners, who were invited, came to the party.
4. The winners who were invited came to the party.
5. Thomas Jefferson, who was from Virginia, founded the
   University of Virginia.
6. My son, who lives in Colorado, is a psychologist.
7. My daughter who has red hair lives in Texas.
8. The university which hopes to grow needs a dynamic
   leader.
9. I like movies that tell a good story.
10. My only son, who is a manpower expert, is coming to visit
    next Christmas.

The alert student may notice (if he sees the sentences) that nonrestrictive adjective clauses are set off by commas to reflect the juncture, or break, that occurs in speaking. If someone notices this feature of written English, congratulate him or her and confirm the use of commas for this purpose. But the commas reflect speech—they are not the determining feature of the construction.

Adverb Clauses and Adjective Clauses

Further deletions which can be applied to adjective clauses account for other modification patterns, for instance postnominal phrases:

15) The road which is in the valley ⟶ The road in the valley is winding.
     is winding.

And we can proceed, with the help of another transformational rule, from postnominal to prenominal modification:

16) There's a baby upstairs. ⎫ ⟶There's a baby that is crying upstairs.
     The baby is crying.   ⎬ ⟶There's a baby crying upstairs.
                            ⎭ ⟶There's a crying baby upstairs.

17) He bought a Chevrolet. ⎫ ——→He bought a Chevrolet which is red.
     The Chevrolet is red.   ⎭ ——→*He bought a Chevrolet red.
                                ——→He bought a red Chevrolet.

Modifiers with -*ing* can form a construction in which they appear before or after the noun to be modified. Most single-word adjectives must be transposed to a position before the noun.

This is an example where further application of rules produces a simpler construction. This is unusual; for the most part the application of further rules produces a more complicated result. This is why we locate a treatment dealing with adverb and adjective clauses in a section of our book that treats complexity. This will be even more obvious with the next section, where we treat noun clauses.

Some noun clause constructions are frequently heard in oral discourse, for example the *wh*-nominalization, with examples like:

18) What we're going to do is find suitable employment for you.
19) What we're gonna do is wait right here till he comes.

Other constructions are almost never heard in spoken discourse:

20) That he is a great author is clearly shown by his success on the market.

This is a nominalization that occurs in subject position. It is perfectly at home in written English, but would sound suspicious in conversation. Nevertheless, the constructions common in written English are especially frequent in language used for science and technology:

21) That copper is present in the sample can be shown by a simple experiment.

Let's try to construct some subject nominalizations:

EXERCISE 11.13

NOUN CLAUSES—SUBJECT (PREPOSED)

Instructions: Embed the first sentence (sentences a) in the second sentence (sentences b) in subject position, following the pattern shown. (Code 4–5)

1a. Hoffa was a crook.   ⎫   That Hoffa was a crook was shown
 b. Something was shown beyond the ⎬——→ beyond the shadow of a doubt.
     shadow of a doubt.   ⎭
2a. He took advantage of his position.
 b. Something will be long-remembered.

3a. He is a hero.
  b. Something has turned his head.
4a. Nancy can't hold a job.
  b. Something is her most serious
    problem.
5a. He is essentially honest.
  b. Something is widely accepted.
6a. He is completely innocent.
  b. Something is taken for granted.

EXERCISE 11.14

NOUN CLAUSES—SUBJECT (POSTPOSED)

Instructions: Embed sentences a in sentences b, following the pattern shown.
             (Code 4–5)

1a. Hoffa was a crook.   } ⟶ It is assuredly true (that) Hoffa was
  b. It is assuredly true.   a crook.
2a. He took advantage of his position. } ⟶ It is apparent (that) he took advan-
  b. It is apparent.   tage of his position.
3a. He is a hero.   } ⟶
  b. It was easy to see.
4a. Nancy can't hold a job.   } ⟶
  b. It became obvious.
5a. He is essentially honest.   } ⟶
  b. Something is widely accepted.
6a. He is completely innocent.   } ⟶
  b. It is taken for granted.

Note that the relator word *that* is optional in the exercise immediately above, but obligatory in exercise 11.13.

   The student and the teacher will by now have noticed that these last two exercises are very mechanical. They can be done by anyone who follows a couple of simple rules; it is not necessary to understand what is being communicated to produce grammatically correct sentences. The same result would occur if we went through the embedding process in reverse, deriving matrix and constituent sentences from complex sentences like those in the right-hand column above.

   The same pattern of sentence construction can be presented in a more meaningful context. Try the following:

EXERCISE 11.15

CONTEXTUALIZED SENTENCES WITH NOUN CLAUSES

Instructions: Benito is collecting information for a theme he will write for his English class, selecting as his subject the trial of Jimmy Hoffa. He lists the charges in the left-hand column, the trial statements in the middle column, and the draft sentences for his theme in the right-hand column. (Code 4–5)

1. Hoffa was a crook.	It is assuredly true.	It is assuredly true that Hoffa was a crook.
2. He broke many laws.	It was proved in his trial.	That he broke many laws was proved in his trial.
3. He tried to buy off witnesses.	It was duly noted.	It was duly noted that he tried to buy off witnesses.
4. He was not above threatening violence.	It was revealed in sworn testimony.	That he was not above threatening violence was revealed in sworn testimony.
5. He illegally transferred union funds.	It was shown by bank records.	It was shown by bank records that he illegally transferred union funds.
6. He perjured himself.	It can be taken for granted.	That he perjured himself can be taken for granted.

Notice that Benito alternates the preposed and postposed structures of the sentences in the third column of his draft to improve the quality of his writing, and to show he has learned the structures presented in exercises 11.13 and 11.14. This exercise is more effective than either of the two preceding because it attempts to contextualize all the exercise sentences so they deal with one related set of ideas, that is, so they have thematic unity.

Much more could be said about nominalization, but our present purposes are served by the sampling just given.

We turn now to a consideration of vocabulary in the written language.

DISCUSSION

1. Why is pacing crucial to oral communication but not to written?

2. How would you explain the assumption, common in the seventeenth and eighteenth centuries, that English had no grammar? What feature or quality did a written and published grammar presumably supply?

3. Discuss "prescriptive grammar." Does it have a role in contemporary teaching?

4. What is the difference between modality and register? Can you give examples of each?

5. Ohashi says that more dense expression produces sentences that are more formal. Does this generalization apply to contractions? Explain your answer.

6. *And* and *but* are both coordinating conjunctions. Explain the differences between them.

7. Why is it difficult at times to locate the missing particle in sentences that are deliberately erroneous?

8. In what details do headline and telegraphic styles differ? Why?

9. What is the difference between matrix sentences and constituent sentences?

10. Which are more formal, nominalized complex sentences with subject preposed (cf. exercise 11.13) or postposed (cf. exercise 11.14)?

CHAPTER TWELVE

VOCABULARY— WRITTEN LANGUAGE

INTRODUCTION

Currently in language teaching in the United States there is increased interest in vocabulary as a component of the second language class or program. Vocabulary is viewed as a significant component of standardized language tests; new texts are being published which support it as a study; and attention is being given by methodologists and program planners to the most effective ways to promote command of vocabulary among learners.

This trend is not novel, but rather is a continuation of an approach to language teaching which can be traced back over generations. The ancient Greeks left records of vocabulary lessons in the form of lists of alphabetized words and semantic groups. Later the Romans were to continue the practice of alphabetical and topical listings, and to contextualize items in simplified readings and present them bilingually in oral lessons. The Renaissance teacher Bath also presented vocabulary in contextualized form using translation. Bath's emphasis on vocabulary acquisition was further elaborated by Comenius, whose program included graded syntax and an inductive approach to grammar, with a strong component of controlled vocabulary taught through visual association.

Vocabulary lists were a familiar part of lessons that followed the Grammar-Translation approach. Students used dictionaries to translate vocabulary items back and forth. Students under the Direct Method identified vocabulary in context at the beginning of each lesson. However, with the accession of the structuralists and the Audiolingual approach, independent vocabulary study was relegated to secondary status, technically not eliminated, but deferred until pronunciation and grammar could be mastered, which often meant postponement sine die.

Contemporary scholars, particularly the cognitivists, communicationists, and functionalists, have focused language teachers' attention once again on vocabulary.

Currently vocabulary is viewed as important in its own right, not just as a set of slot fillers for structural paradigms. Even among some of the structuralists there is emphasis given to vocabulary. Twaddell sees the expansion of vocabulary as indispensable at advanced levels of teaching (1973). The Notional approaches demand classes of specific words appropriate for the particular notions, functions, and needs of specific people, times, places, and tasks. Expanding analysis of language in terms of discourse, register, personal interaction, social situations, rhetoric, cohesion, and coherence has focused anew on meaning in a number of senses, including the meaning of the content word or phrase and the semantic relationships among such words.

In this chapter we will discuss the import of vocabulary or "new words" in written English, discussing the subject at different levels of language learning and the issues of vocabulary for both reading and writing.

The English Language

Vocabulary in English can be looked at in many ways. The fifty to eighty word roots English shares with other Indo-European languages, together with the forty to fifty prefixes, combine and recombine into hundreds of thousands of different words. Words from this stock may occur in single free form, *table*; free form plus bound form, *tablet*; or two or more free forms, *tablespoon*. The same word may shift among word classes, *a walk/to walk*; or be used figuratively, persons from all *walks* of life; or subtechnically, *charm* as a personal quality or as in a property of a particle of matter described in physics. Some of the more colloquial semantic constructions include blends, *smog, brunch*; clipped forms, *fan, ad, coop*; acronyms, *laser, scuba*. Adding color to the list are the continually growing groups of foreign loanwords and phrases in English, some ancient, such as *e.g., i.e., etc.*; some quite recent, *sputnik*; some technical, *Weltanschauung*; and some merely popular, *rodeo*.

STYLISTIC CONSIDERATIONS

When we distinguish some of the characteristics of the vocabulary, we see even more evidence of complexity. First, much of the formal vocabulary in written English is French, Latin, or Greek in origin. Then what *happens* to vocabulary in writing is almost as interesting again as the exotic etymologies of the various words themselves. In standard written English there are "laws" (or at least regulations) which look unfavorably on a root word being repeated in close proximity to itself. For this and other structural reasons, content words in English are frequently substituted, paraphrased or otherwise indirectly referenced.

In more complex writings content words are frequently separated from their immediate constituents by subordinate groups of words such as heavy nominalizations: "That he does not favor the proposed legislation can readily be seen in what he has said in his speeches from the floor." Writing in almost any field where interesting research is being carried out encourages the production of still more new vocabulary.

It is claimed that for ordinary requirements people need 7,000 "passive" and 3,000 "active" words (Keller and Warner 1979). This is not very many; an average twelve-year-old native speaker of English knows approximately 135,000 words, and a university student, approximately 200,000. Where do they get them? They come by ear or by eye. Experts are not agreed on the dominance pattern of learning orally or visually. Some claim a pupil passes from being orally dominant to being visually dominant as early as grade three. Others think it is as late as grade eight. These are probably the outside limits. Whichever the dominant medium, all language learners—including native speakers—continue to learn new vocabulary long after they have mastered structure and syntax.

Where can the ESL learner start to tackle the great mass of English vocabulary? Is there any one best approach for teaching it? Of course the answer to this question lies in each particular teaching situation, and concerns not only words but also students, objectives, teaching resources, and teaching/learning constraints.

APPROACH TO VOCABULARY LEARNING

Probably the best way to build a strong vocabulary is through extensive participation as a respondent in real communication situations. This means talking to lots of people in English—or at least doing a lot of listening—to strengthen competence in oral skills, including a useful supply of words. It also means doing a lot of reading to enlarge one's vocabulary in the written language.

Why do we separately specify oral and written language? Actually we don't have watertight compartments for oral and written performance, but oral language tends to be informal, and written, formal. There are exceptions, such as a formal lecture and an informal letter to a friend, but this doesn't alter the reality of the formal-informal distinction, especially in an academic setting.

The oral-written dichotomy also correlates with the likely means of solving the problems of defining new terms or identifying and remembering an incompletely learned item that the student has been exposed to. Visual feedback, possible when one is there in person, tells the speaker that he has not been understood, so that a repetition, a paraphrase, or an explanation is in order. If, in an oral language exchange, understanding of a specific term is crucial and communication has been broken, the listener can usually inquire as to meaning. On the other hand, there is no visual feedback to the writer when one is reading; but the form is clear and the reader can always rely on the dictionary if he feels he must know what a particular word means.

Inferring Meaning

In both cases (oral and written reception) it's better to try to infer the meaning even though misunderstanding is a risk. Twaddell says to be satisfied with a partial, imperfect understanding; one's comprehension will improve with further intake. Here is an example of what he means:

A historian is writing on a subject that he believes has never been treated in an unbiased way and he intends to correct this fault. The antis and the pros have had their say, so what he is writing is neither an apologia nor a screed, but a fair appraisal that takes both sides into account. The reader has never seen the words *apologia* or *screed* before, but he can guess what they mean. The word *apologia* is probably related to *apology* or *apologize*, which suggests the *pro* point of view, so *screed* must mean the opposite: an unprincipled attack. The student reader can continue on his way without worrying about the exact meanings.

If the reader's curiosity is aroused and he looks up the word *screed*, he will be told that it is related to *shred*, and that it refers to a long list of ideas intended for use as a harangue. This may be enough information to foreground the word so it will be remembered. But should the second language student try to remember the word *screed*? It is of such low frequency that few native speakers of English have bothered to learn it. If a word is important enough to learn, it will reappear, providing the student keeps communicating. Perhaps what we should be worrying about is adequate input, letting the selection of appropriate words take care of itself. Possibly we should provide a smorgasbord and let the student partake of what interests him, without assuming that we are all-wise in our provisions for his lexical care and feeding. This in fact is what happens to native speakers: they are exposed, potentially at least, to a wide variety of words, from which they choose what they need and what interests them. If it were not so, we would not find a difference between active and passive vocabulary.

VOCABULARY SELECTION AND ACQUISITION

Given the fact that there are so many tens of thousands of content words in the lexicon of the language, the best policy seems to be a careful selection of the situations in which the student will likely find himself and let the situations determine the vocabulary that will be used. We can then expect to expose the student to lexical networks of terms that are semantically compatible, each supporting the other. Vocabulary growth will usually be quite satisfactory, with little or no effort to learn specific items. This is one strategy for learning vocabulary. There are others.

Suppose you are reading a selection and you come across a word you can't assign a meaning to, and the word seems crucial to understanding the passage. Your guesses of the meaning seem inadequate and you have tolerated a degree of vagueness which appears to have become extreme; you need to know the meaning of the word. But suppose you're reading the selection called "There's a Unicorn in my Garden." You suspect "unicorn" is some kind of animal, but why should its being in a garden be newsworthy enough to include in the title of the selection? Does it eat the cabbage, like a rabbit? Is it an animal that belongs in a garden, or is it an intruder? Or are you on the wrong track? Maybe it's a unique variety of corn or some other plant— or maybe it's a tool, or a piece of garden furniture. In any case you decide you really need to know the meaning of this word before continuing any further. What should you do?

Glossaries and Dictionaries

The efficient solution is to ask somebody, but if this is inconvenient there are other options. If you are reading from a textbook especially prepared for students of English as a second language, it may have a glossary at the end of the book. This is a list of all, or perhaps the most important or more frequently occurring, words above a floor of the very most common ones that appear in the textbook. Each word appears with a definition or definitions. The advantage of a glossary is that the words can be defined specifically for the context in which they appear in the textbook. If you're reading a book about baseball and you look up the word *diamond*, the definition will describe a playing field. You will not be troubled by other definitions, such as "gemstone, drill tip for industrial tools, a suit used in playing cards, a promise of marriage," etc. If the book doesn't have a glossary or if you're looking up a word from a source other than a textbook, you can always refer to a dictionary—either a bilingual dictionary which gives the equivalent in another language, or a monolingual dictionary that describes the meaning of an English word using other English words. Depending on the size and scope of the dictionary, you may or may not find the meaning that is appropriate to the context you drew the word from. If you have a small pocket dictionary, definitions will be very simple and many words you may want to look up will not be included. If you refer to a desk dictionary, there will be minimum words and minimum definitions. If you consult a library dictionary, such as Webster's Third New International, you will find that an encyclopedic entry is typical, often with much more information than you want, leaving you with the responsibility for finding the right definition for your purposes. In a pocket dictionary the following definition for *unicorn* was given: "fabulous horse-like animal with a single horn." This definition leaves you with the responsibility for interpreting "fabulous," which often means "spectacular"—though in this case it means "found only in fables," in other words, nonexistent. It tells you the animal has one horn, but doesn't describe the horn or tell you where it is located on the animal. A serious deficiency lies in the fact that you may come away from this definition not knowing a unicorn is an imaginary animal. A desk dictionary definition of the word *unicorn* is "a mythical horse-like animal with a single horn growing from its forehead. In biblical usage it is a two-horned ox-like animal, a mistranslation." The second definition is useless, serving only to confuse the issue with a Biblical mistranslation. In an unabridged library dictionary a unicorn is defined as "a fabulous animal, possibly based on faulty old descriptions of the rhinoceros, and generally depicted as in heraldry, with the body and head of a horse and hind legs of a stag, the tail of a lion, and in the middle of the forehead a single long straight horn held to be a sovereign remedy against poisoning." There are several other definitions, including "an ox having his horn buds surgically altered to produce a single median horn; a Scottish gold coin of the 15th and 16th centuries weighing 59 grains and having the figure of a unicorn on its obverse; material reputed to be the horn of the fabulous unicorn, formerly used for ornament, as an antidote, or as a talisman; a team of three horses harnessed with one as leader; an equipage with such a team; a howitzer; any of several plants felt to resemble a unicorn horn." In addition there are definitions that include *unicorn* as a modifier, such as unicorn whale, antelope, beetle, bird, caterpillar, fish, moth, plant, plant family, root, shell. As you can see, this definition goes beyond what an ESL student would need. It is a dictionary for a specialist.

Thesaurus

While we are talking about reference works, we might mention the thesaurus, which is a semantically organized word list, usually with an alphabetically organized key as the second half of the book. The thesaurus is useful for only one purpose: to look up words that you already know but that have slipped your mind. It should never be used to find new words to use in writing. *Unicorn* appears in the thesaurus keyed to the form "rara avis." It is listed with the phoenix, griffin, sphinx, centaur, minotaur, dragon, Loch Ness monster, merman, mermaid, wyvern, etc.—i.e., forms of other imaginary animals.

An idea that helps minimize looking up words in a dictionary, but more particularly in a glossary, is the practice of penciling a small dot in front of an entry every time it is looked up. An occasional glance through the glossary will readily identify those words which have been judged to be important enough to look up, but not important enough to learn. Any word with three or four or more dots in front of it should become the object of special study.

One additional idea is a vocabulary notebook. As words are learned, the interesting ones can be listed in a notebook where it will be convenient to review them from time to time. It will be interesting to know which prove to be useful enough to keep in the active vocabulary, and which slip back into passive.

So far we have looked mainly at vocabulary recognition, an important reading skill. But concern with vocabulary has a wider application.

DERIVATIONAL MORPHOLOGY AND WORD BUILDING

Vocabulary study can be considered valuable in building general language competence over and above the appearance of items in particular contexts in the readings. Particularly useful are the analysis approaches that help describe word formation in English. One widely acknowledged way to build vocabulary is through an understanding and application of word formation processes, sometimes called derivational morphology. Among other things this involves affixation, usually the addition of suffixes to the ends of words or word stems to make new words. An exercise based on derivational word building can be tailored to students at almost any level.

Here's a reading that will be the basis of several illustrative exercises:

An Unpleasant Experience

He was attentive but nervous as the medium began her invocation. Would there be a response? Would it be a contribution to the solution of his problems? Should he take the idea seriously? Was such a consideration consistent with the role of a supposedly enlightened scientist? The medium suggested he assume a restful position, then called for more concentration; otherwise making contact would be impossible. She summoned the dear departed, but no answer.

He had looked everywhere, and found nothing. If he didn't find that piece of paper, her estate would be probated under common law, and he'd have to pay a ridiculous assessment—in legal jargon, the fee of the California Statutory Probate Commission.

They had saved for their declining years, only to have this legal monstrosity forced on them. He knew she had hidden the will in the house, so it wouldn't get lost. Now this little problem seemed so horrendous. Out of their modest estate, he would have to give a faceless official $11,150. It seemed so useless. And there would be delays, and he would have to be bonded, with him bearing the cost of the bond, assuming that the court would even consider naming him executor. Maybe they'd give that job to a bank—more fees and expenses, and to no useful purpose. It all seemed so pointless.

He was still suffering the pain of loss, and he didn't know how to cope with this new set of problems. He realized how depend<u>ent</u> he had become since his sick<u>ness</u>. Why had they been so care<u>less</u> in this detail, <u>when</u> they were ordinari<u>ly</u> so care<u>ful</u> in planning their lives? He decided it was a hope<u>less</u> situa<u>tion</u>. He'd just have to turn over his life to the lawyers and get along the best he could. "Damna<u>tion</u>!"

"Quiet!" the medium said. "I think we're making contact. Call out to your wife."

"Ellen! Ellen! Where are you? Can you hear me? Are you here?"

"Of course I'm here, dummy! Where do you expect me to be? Why are you making so much noise?"

"Where am I? What happened? Ellen, is that you? Oh, hallelujah and God be praised! You can't imagine what a horrible <u>night</u><u>mare</u> I've just had. I hope I never have to go through that again. In fact, <u>I</u> hope <u>I</u> don't have to go through it the first time. By the way, where do you keep our wills?"

[Technical note: The copy of this exercise supplied to students would not underline affixes. Underlining is supplied here to make reference easier.]

EXERCISE 12.1

DERIVATIONAL FORMS (A)

Instructions: Find all the words in the above reading that end in -<u>tion</u> or -<u>sion</u>. Divide them into subgroups depending on the vowel that precedes the -<u>tion</u>. (Code 5–7)

invocation	position	contribution
concentration	commission	solution
damnation		
situation		
consideration		

Add other words to each list, if possible some that are suggested by words in the selection.

probation	addition	persecution
location	tradition	pollution
realization	edition	distribution
imagination	recognition	substitution
information	definition	revolution

Construct sentences that use the words listed. Then work back from the noun derivation to the underlying verb stem (e.g., invocation → invoke; concentration → concentrate) and subclassify the derivation by underlying verb type.

DERIVATIONAL FORMS (B)

Instructions: Find all the examples of words with derivational endings in patterns with at least two examples in the text. (Omit the -<u>tion</u> words.) (Code 5–7)

<u>-ly</u>	-ous	-ful	-less	-ible
supposedly	nervous	restful	faceless	horrible
ordinarily	ridiculous	useful	useless	impossible
seriously	horrendous	careful	pointless	
			careless	

DERIVATIONAL FORMS (C)

Instructions: Find the antonyms among the derived forms. (Code 5–7)

useful   useless
careful   careless

Now add pairs of similar forms where only one is present in the text. Underline the one that appears.

hopeful	hopeless	possible	<u>impossible</u>	pleasant	<u>unpleasant</u>
<u>restful</u>	restless	<u>dependent</u>	independent		
		<u>consistent</u>	inconsistent		

EXERCISE 12.4

DERIVATIONAL FORMS (D)

Instructions: In the text find examples of derived forms where only one example occurs. Add three or four others. (Code 6–7)

-ness		-ity	
sickness	monstrosity	electricity	calamity
sadness	pomposity	simplicity	possibility
greatness	verbosity	publicity	solidarity
togetherness	curiosity	felicity	stupidity
happiness	animosity	elasticity	validity

Find in the selection any derivational affixes that have not been mentioned or listed.

-or	-y	en-
executor	dummy	enlighten

Synonyms

Synonyms are words having the same or nearly the same meaning in the same language. Technically speaking, there are no authentic synonyms. In the past, if two words had the exact same meaning, one of them dropped out or took on a special meaning. But the meanings we refer to are sufficiently close to each other that we consider them synonyms. We have to look hard to perceive a difference between the verbs *shut* and *close*. However, one can say "The market closed higher," but not "The market shut higher." Similarly we can refer to a person who cannot leave his house because he is too ill as a "shut-in," but not as a "close-in." Another example is the pair *ill* and *sick*. We say "It's an ill wind that blows no good," but not "It's a sick wind." We can refer to sick humor, but if we say "ill humor," we're referring to the condition of a person or an animal who is in a bad mood.

CONNOTATION AND REGISTER

Connotation and register combine to give words meaning beyond the lexical assignment of a central interpretation. The following exercise consists of groups of five words that have meaning in common. Some of the words express favorable connotations, some express unfavorable, and some are neutral. See if your students can classify items in the groups appropriately.

EXERCISE 12.5

WORD CONNOTATIONS

Instructions: Classify the following words as favorable (+), unfavorable (−), or neutral (0). The first group is done for you. (Code 4–6)

+ petite	___ adaptable	___ tip	___ odor
0 small	___ changeable	___ gratuity	___ stench
0 minuscule	___ variable	___ service charge	___ smell
− stunted	___ versatile	___ handout	___ aroma
− dwarfish	___ inconsistent	___ honorarium	___ bouquet
___ genius	___ planning	___ friend	___ retainer
___ sage	___ conniving	___ companion	___ supporter
___ intellectual	___ anticipating	___ confidante	___ lickspittle
___ egghead	___ scheming	___ henchman	___ yes-man
___ pedant	___ manipulating	___ minion	___ sycophant

One problem associated with vocabulary that becomes apparent in reading is the misinterpretation of words that are very similar in appearance. Very often these words do not suggest each other when they are heard, but they may when they are seen. Sometimes coincidence aggravates confusing features: e.g., the pair *exotic/erotic* may be confused with each other. The *ex* of *exotic* begins with a syllable that is close in form to the word *sex*, which is suggested by the word *erotic*. How can these be clearly separated? We have one exercise to recommend, but mainly we would call the problem to the attention of teachers as an occasion when misinterpretations may arise. The usual remedy, when a reader gets to a point where the sentence makes no sense, is to back up and look again at what he has just read. Very often a single word will hold the key to the mystery.

EXERCISE 12.6

VISUALLY SIMILAR LEXICAL ITEMS

Instructions: Read the following sentences aloud at a quick pace. (Code 4–6)

erotic/exotic

1a. Something that is strange and strikingly fascinating is said to be e = otic.
b. Something that arouses sexual feelings is e = otic.

physiology/psychology

2a. He's taking a class called Behavioral P = = = = ology.
b. He likes p = = = = ology and the other life sciences.

casual/causal

3a. Wear ca = = al clothes to the picnic.
b. "Therefore" is a ca = = al conjunction.

nuclear/unclear

4a. An = = clear response is difficult to understand.
b. A = = clear response risks destroying civilization.

uniformed/uninformed

5a. An un = = formed policeman is not a rarity.
b. A un = formed policeman is a sworn officer.

hearsay/heresy

6a. You can't convict a man of h = = = = y today.
b. You can't convict a man on h = = = = = y evidence.

deceased/diseased

7a. The d = = eased plant was almost dead.
b. They honored the d = = eased soldier.

heroin/heroine

8a. When the cutter approached, they threw the heroi = overboard.
b. When the hero approached, they hid the heroi = = .

simile/smile

9a. His s = ile revealed a happy personality.
b. His s = = ile was a very apt comparison.

linage/lineage

10a. The lin = ge on the page was calculated.
b. The records of his lin = = = ge go back to 1600.

salon/saloon

11a. She went into the sal = = = n to get a drink.
b. She went into the sal = n to get her hair cut.

ingenious/ingenuous

12a. He's ingen = ous, artless, naive.
b. He's ingen = ous, inventive, clever.

applause/applesauce

13a. The appl = = = e was thunderous.
b. The appl = = = = = e tasted very good.

militating/mitigating

14a. He's guilty, but there are mi = = = ating circumstances.
b. The evidence will surely be mi = = = ating against him.

epitaph/epithet

15a. His epit = = = is on the gravestone.
b. In his anger he hurled an uncomplimentary epit = = = at his former friend.

STRUCTURE VERSUS CONTENT VOCABULARY

In Chapter Seven we discussed oral language vocabulary, various word counts, and the type-token ratios typical of all counts. We pointed out that structure words have very high token counts. The obverse is true for content words: they have enormous type counts and typically light token counts. This is another way of saying there are few structure words, but they occur very often, while there are enormous numbers of content words, though used far fewer times, many thousands of them only once in over a million running words of text. In spite of these figures, the content words tell us more about a communication than do the structure words. Yet many students are likely to look at a familiar structure word for help when they are reading a selection for the first time. They are stuck on the new content words, of which there are so many. Nevertheless, they know *some* content words, and these can help them learn others. The following exercise should be interesting.

EXERCISE 12.7

STRUCTURE AND CONTENT WORDS

Instructions: Read the box on the left below. Then read the one on the right. (Code 5–6)

= = = = = = = = = = = = may
be at or near their = = = =, at least for
the = = = = = = = = = = of this
= = = =. = = = = = = = =
= = = = = = further
= = = = = = = = =, if any, will be
= = = = =. = = = = = are widely
= = = = = = = = = =.

Mortgage rates = = = = = == = =
= = = = = = = = = = lows, = =
= = = = = = = = = = = = remainder
== = = = = year. Experts believe
= = = = = = = declines, = = = = =,
= = = = = = small. Loans = = =
= = = = = = available.

It is clear that the function words by themselves do not communicate at all. But the content words are very suggestive. It is assumed that when a native speaker reads he focuses mainly on the content words, employing the conventions of newspaper headlines or telegraphic style, using the function words when necessary to resolve a questionable interpretation. If the reading is not complex he may not need the function words. The second language learner, on the other hand, has been extensively drilled in the form and use of function words, so he likely goes right on reading them, since they are familiar. He may also read the content words, but by the nature of word frequency counts and occurrences, these will be far less familiar to him. This seems to be one reason why second language learners are not often truly successful at reading. They need practice in skimming, a procedure in which content words are emphasized as the student reads as fast as he can, skipping words assumed to be unimportant or less important.

COLLOCATIONS

Word lists are becoming respectable again as a language learning device. The word list can accommodate any school of thought on language learning and language teaching in which the learning principles of association/mnemonics are accepted.

Most of the techniques mentioned hitherto are in a way lists—but they are lists of words grouped together according to some structural similarity: common roots, derivations, affixation, orthography, pronunciation, and compounding patterns.

Other lists can be made grouped according to semantic or functional relationships, or even according to random association.

Teachers of specific subjects find such lists useful. For example, a physics professor at Northeastern University categorizes nouns from word problems which his large percentage of ESL-speaking students have trouble following. Some of the categories this professor has devised are: (1) words implying rigidity, the ability to transmit force, e.g., plank, boom, strut; and (2) words implying flexibility, the ability to transmit only tension forces, e.g., tow-rope, string, guy wire.

The collocations are especially appropriate in what are called subtechnical terms in English for Science and Technology (EST), since useful practice on relevant vocabulary items is made available. One application is in measurement.

EXERCISE 12.8

MEASUREMENT VOCABULARY

(Code 5–6)

1. 60 seconds = one _____
   60 minutes = one _____
   24 hours = one _____
   7 days = one _____
   4-1/2 weeks = one _____
   12 months = one _____
   100 years = one _____
   100 centuries = one _____

2. 2.54 centimeters = one _____
   12 inches = one _____
   3 feet = one _____
   5-1/2 yards = one _____
   40 rods = one _____
   8 furlongs = one _____
   1760 yards = one _____
   5280 feet = one _____

Another collocation involves color:

EXERCISE 12.9

COLOR

Instructions: Answer the following. (Code 3–4)

1. The dark color at the end of the spectrum is (violet).
2. The next color is (indigo).
3. The next color is (blue).
4. The next color is (green).
5. The next color is (yellow).
6. The next color is (orange).
7. The next color is (red).
8. The primary colors are (blue), (yellow), and (red).
9. The secondary colors are (green), (orange), and (purple).
10. A mixture of all colors is (white).
11. Absence of color is (black).
12. The achromatic colors are (black), (white), and (gray).
13. The warm colors (sometimes called *advancing*) are (red), (orange), and (yellow).
14. The cool colors (sometimes called *receding*) are (purple), (blue), and (dark green).
15. What does "vibgyor" mean? (It's an acronym made from the names of the colors in the spectrum.)

Another collocation can be made up of the converse forms of verbs.

EXERCISE 12.10

CONVERSE FORMS

Instructions: State the converse verb that goes with the form given. (Code 3–4)

1. The converse of *come* is (go).
2. The converse of *buy* is (sell).
3. The converse of *read* is (write).
4. The converse of *give* is (receive).
5. The converse of *bring* is (take).
6. The converse of *rise* is (fall).
7. The converse of *work* is (play).
8. The converse of *speak* is (listen).
9. The converse of *rent* is (rent).
10. The converse of *lease* is (lease).

Another type of collocation is semantic association.

EXERCISE 12.11

SEMANTIC ASSOCIATIONS

Instructions: Complete the following. (Code 4–6)

1. A watch (keeps time).
2. A billboard (displays ads).
3. A waitress (serves customers).
4. The tide (comes in and goes out).
5. A highway patrolman (catches speeders).
6. A senator (makes laws/represents constituents).
7. An author (writes books).
8. An expert (has answers).
9. An engineer (drives trains/builds bridges).
10. A farmer (grows crops).
11. A proofreader (catches errors).

There is a class of words called *homonyms*. They are usually paired, though they may be triplets or quadruplets. They may have the same spelling, but have different semantic interpretations and come from separate sources. The following exercise is an illustration.

EXERCISE 12.12

HOMONYMS

Instructions: Try to give other examples of homonyms. (Code 6–7)

1. "Fair" describes the weather. It can also refer to a (festival).
2. "Bear" is a dangerous wild animal. It can also mean (carry/tolerate).
3. "Left" is to the west when facing north. It can also mean (departed).

Some homonyms have different meanings and spellings, but identical pronunciations:

/rayt/	= right, write, wright, rite
/reyn/	= rain, reign, rein
/dhɛr/	= their, there, they're
/hɪr/	= hear, here
/lÉsən/	= lessen, lesson
/prÍnsəpəl/	= principal, principle
/stéyshənÈriy/	= stationary, stationery

One small area of difficulty facing learners of English is the existence of homographs: pairs of words with the same spelling, but with different pronunciations and meanings. The reader is left to assign an interpretation based on the context. Fortunately there are not very many of these, but they do have a potential for causing trouble.

EXERCISE 12.13

HOMOGRAPHS

Instructions: Your teacher will write a word on the blackboard. Use it in two
sentences, illustrating it with two meanings, each of which will
have a different pronunciation. (Code 6–7)

1. wind	/wɪnd/	There's not much wind today.
	/waynd/	Wind the clock.
2. wound	/wuwnd/	His wound is not serious.
	/wawnd/	I already wound the clock.
3. bow	/baw/	I'll have to bow to the inevitable.
	/bow/	I brought my bow and arrow.
4. row	/row/	He sat in the third row.
	/raw/	The newlyweds had their first row.
5. dove	/dəv/	A dove is a bird of peace.
	/dowv/	He dove into the swimming pool.
6. read	/riyd/	Read the lesson for tomorrow.
	/rɛd/	I already read it.
7. lead	/liyd/	He's to lead the expedition.
	/lɛd/	Lead is a dangerous metal.
8. tear	/tɪr/	We saw a tear in his eye.
	/tɛr/	Did you tear your new shirt?
9. coop	/kuwp/	The chickens got out of the coop.
	/kowɑp/	I shop at the coop.

An important part of the responsibility a student has toward learning near-synonyms is learning to appreciate the relative generality-specificity of words with overlapping meanings. This should help in choosing words for specific contexts.

EXERCISE 12.14

GENERALITY

Instructions: Mark "G" for *general* or "S" for *specific* for the following pairs of words. (Hint: number of meanings) (Code 5–6)

1. eat _____	8. lawn _____	15. home _____
partake _____	grass _____	apartment _____
2. get _____	9. transport _____	16. grain _____
receive _____	train _____	wheat _____
3. fly _____	10. Selectric _____	17. fire _____
soar _____	typewriter _____	oxidation _____
4. study _____	11. copier _____	18. diamond _____
review _____	Savin _____	ruby _____
5. man _____	12. fruit _____	19. arm _____
Irishman _____	grapefruit _____	wrist _____
6. book _____	13. fire drill _____	20. finger _____
report _____	precautions _____	thumb _____
7. pen _____	14. lens _____	21. bush _____
ballpoint _____	magnifying glass _____	rose _____

Another collocation could be made up of adjectives and their antonyms:

EXERCISE 12.15

ANTONYMS

Instructions: Your teacher will say an adjective. Write an adjective with the opposite meaning. (Code 3–5)

1. high _____   10. hot _____

2. white _____   11. weak _____

3. far _____   12. bright _____

4. sweet _____   13. evil _____

5. young _____   14. hard-working _____

6. industrious _____   15. clockwise _____

7. left _____   16. hungry _____

8. rough _____   17. straight _____

9. open _____   18. wet _____

This exercise can be readily adapted to a team game or competition. Divide the class into two groups and line them up in two lines that stretch to the front of the class. The teacher calls out an adjective, and the two students at the head of the two lines vie to see who can give the right answer first. Then the winner goes to the back of his line as the scorekeeper puts a tally mark on the blackboard. The team that loses has to clean the blackboard.

IDIOMS

A particular type of complex lexical item is called an *idiom*. A working definition of an idiom is " a group of words whose total meaning is not the sum of the individual meanings of the words included in the idiom." The implication for an idiom is that it must be learned as a unit rather than as a grammatical construction, because it is impossible to predict its meaning; e.g., the expression "beating around the bush" suggests an action of a person applying blows to all sides of a shrub. This gives no hint to the real meaning, which is "being evasive; avoiding the central issue." In a developing, changing society, language metaphors are often devised and applied because they have the value of freshness and novelty. It can happen that a metaphorical meaning becomes so common that it replaces the earlier meaning. This has happened with the word *channel*, which used to suggest a water course. For most speakers it has come to mean primarily a television broadcasting address. Here's an exercise on idioms.

EXERCISE 12.16

IDIOMS

Instructions: Reread the selection "An Unpleasant Experience" and copy all the expressions you think are idioms. Beside each write what you think it means. (Code 4–6)

God be praised	that makes me happy
dear departed	recently deceased
declining years	retirement
bearing the cost of	paying for
pain of loss	difficulty of adjusting to adversity
of course	emphatically yes
by the way	I'm changing the subject
in fact	to confirm it more emphatically

A prolific source of new vocabulary items in the language is coinage. Sometimes we know the author of a creative word or phrase, as in the case of the expression "gobbledegook," a contribution of Congressman Maverick from Texas, when he was confronted by a paper written by a bureaucrat in Washington. It refers to what should be a modest statement but is made obscure by writing that is pompous and calculated to bury the real meaning, if ever there was any, in an avalanche of big words and twisted syntax. The term gobbledegook takes advantage of two words in English: the rolling, throaty *gobble* of a turkey, and *gook*, which suggests a sticky muck.

A politically movitated expression is "lame duck." This is a reference to a politician who is serving out the remainder of his term after he has announced retirement or has been defeated at the polls. Another political term is "gerrymander," made up of a man's name, *Gerry*, and the last part of *salamander*, a slimy amphibian related to frogs and toads. It refers to the practice of dividing a state or county into unfair and illogical election districts in an attempt to gain political advantage. There are many other expressions that have come into use to serve political purposes: "dark horse, filibuster, scofflaw, pass the buck, muckraker, caucus," etc. Many coinages are created in response to a need; they are used and then discarded when the need is over. One does not hear much of "mugwumps" these days, though it was a useful and significant term about a century ago.

Science has been the source of many coinages, as technical knowledge increased and there was a need to discuss new things and conditions. Advertising specialists excel in inventing new words, which really do sell products. One thinks of "serutan," which happens to be "natures" spelled backwards. It would be interesting to know how many gallons of the product were sold because of the association of nature and medicine.

One characteristic of academic writing which carries over into other writing is the avoidance of repetition of a content word, word stem, phrase, or expression. Note the following paragraph which violates this rule:

To correct the test the teacher should provide a set of answers. If the provision of these answers does not provide all the help needed, acceptable alternatives should be provided.

The repetition of the word *provide* and *provision* is very conspicuous, unnecessarily drawing attention away from the message intended. We suggest the following revision as an improvement:

To correct the test the teacher should supply a set of answers. If the provision of these answers does not furnish all the help needed, acceptable alternatives should be provided.

This reads much more smoothly, and there are no conspicuous repetitions.

EXERCISE 12.17

AVOIDING LEXICAL REPETITION

Instructions: Rewrite the following short selections to eliminate distracting repetition. (Code 4–6)

1. Who's going to present first?
   I am the first presenter.
   What's your presentation on?
   I'm presenting a lesson on modals.
2. We're going on a picnic.
   Didn't you go picnicking last weekend?
   Yes, but that picnic was on the beach. We're going picnicking now to the mountains.
   So many picnics. How do you plan them?
3. A promissory note promised to repay the loan in three months, but it was a promise not kept.
4. I have to write a letter to Doug and a letter to Dale. Doug's letter comes first because I know what to say in his letter. Dale's letter has to be figured out.

Learning new words is often considered in the popular mind to be the primary aim of language study. Perhaps this is because of the obvious intersection of form and meaning in vocabulary items. Most educated people, and even those whose education is limited, are familiar with the dictionary, where they can find out what a word means and be sure how it's spelled. This is especially important in an academic environment, because lexical skills and knowledge are taken for granted, and a failure in their mastery is a substantial handicap. The best that underprepared students can hope for is assignment to a noncredit class where their deficiency can possibly be made up, though this is costly in time and expense.

The university dropout rate confirms the need for success in language study, for both first and second language students. For this reason, quality training in language studies at the elementary and secondary levels is critically needed. Too often vocabulary study has been postponed with the assumption that it is more appropriate to the advanced levels of language pedagogy, where it is in fact an assumed skill.

We turn now to problems of curriculum and evaluation.

DISCUSSION

1. Discuss early interest in vocabulary as an important component of language teaching. How is vocabulary treated in the Audiolingual approach?

2. Why are vocabulary items often substituted, paraphrased, or otherwise indirectly referenced in formal writing?

3. About how many words can a literate adult native speaker be assumed to know?

4. What considerations affect the approach any particular class may take to the planning of vocabulary study?

5. How does one foreground a lexical item? How are vocabulary items chosen for inclusion in a lesson?

6. How do a glossary, a dictionary, and a thesaurus differ from one another?

7. What is meant by the statement "Technically there are no authentic synonyms"?

8. Which communicate more information: structure words or content words? Why?

9. Is there a role for competition in studying vocabulary in the language classroom? Explain.

10. The inability to spell correctly is a serious handicap. Agree or disagree and discuss.

Section IV
Planning and Evaluation

Planning and evaluation are the parentheses that bracket actual classroom presentation. Logically considered, planning should precede instruction, and evaluation should follow. In real life, however, both concepts are combined with instruction because neither planning nor evaluation is ever completed. They are both ongoing processes.

Planning is ideally carried out when some definite assumptions about the course can be made, and specific results can be expected. It illustrates the necessity for tailoring instruction to specific circumstances and makes clear the difficulty of generalizing. Curriculum building is a process that should be part of every instructional context—not a job that will some day cease to be needed when somebody has done the job to perfection.

The reader may ask why a chapter on educational planning and evaluation is included in what is otherwise recognized as a methods textbook. Evaluation is relatively easy to justify, because this activity is expected as part of the responsibility of almost every language teacher. Curriculum planning, on the other hand, is often done by supervisors and/or administrative personnel, or sometimes left to chance. Quality instruction seldom results from this kind of benign neglect. The teacher is often left to plan her own syllabus, but, unless she knows how to proceed, the quality of instruction can likewise suffer. Untrained or uncommitted teachers can avoid planning decisions by leaving them to the writer of the textbook being used: "Just follow the book." Or planning will be done a lesson at a time (each day a new plan), with no attempt to build a consistent and coherent course. This inevitably produces low-quality instruction.

One crucial reason for including material on planning springs from another source. We have noted that many times a successful ESL teacher is drawn into supervisory/administrative positions, and the responsibility for curriculum planning falls to her by reason of her promotion. For the newly appointed supervisor or administrator, an understanding of the content of educational planning can be the difference between success and failure. She should at least appreciate the scope and quality of information that goes into formal planning—the unavoidable responsibility for education—to provide a basis on which to build. Helping the teacher to recognize and utilize needs analyses, inventories of resources, workshops for inservice training, selection of textbook materials, and then harnessing feedback, is the least we can do to strengthen the preparation of the educator whose career begins in language teaching.

CHAPTER THIRTEEN

PLANNING CURRICULA

INTRODUCTION

In this chapter we would like to frame the ESL class with a wide lens, considering its place in the *curriculum* of which it is a part, as well as in the *syllabus* of individual courses. We would like to discuss the background of curriculum and syllabus planning, addressing a number of points not always considered in discussions of methods and materials: (1) the ESL class is contextualized in a sea of philosophical, social, economic, political, and personal realities which affect its definition, design, and implementation. (2) The ESL class has a history over a period of time, often involving "teams" of people and "series" of efforts loosely coordinated chronologically. (3) The living context around an ESL class does not become static after a class begins; ideally the ESL class should be in a continual process of planning, implementation, evaluation, and revision, in keeping with the fluidity of its environment. By reviewing the ESL class in the larger frame of historical context and sequence of planning steps, we seek to offer a thumbnail checklist to help teachers and planners note the point of planning at which they enter the process, assess the adequacy of their resources, and adapt a rough blueprint for further planning, implementation, or evaluation as appropriate.

Definition

A curriculum is a total instructional program composed of syllabuses or individual course programs. In many programs course designers or teachers themselves provide further guidance by planning schemes of work, week-by-week or day-by-day calendars for course activities with suggestions for teaching techniques and supplementary materials. Having a clear mandate and source of support naturally facilitates the construction of a curriculum.

The curriculum allows the teacher to see each course in the perspective of the entire program; the syllabus provides a statement of purpose, means, and standards against which to check the effectiveness of teaching and the progress of students in each course. The course outline provides daily or weekly guidelines as needed by the classroom teacher.

CURRICULUM PLANNING

The curriculum is especially needed for the development of a new program, particularly when no appropriate precedents exist, because it provides the specifications for the effective, integrated organization of the whole. The syllabus for each course provides consistent guidelines for the teacher in planning classes, and for students in setting their own personal goals.

Predictably, current interest in curriculum and syllabus planning has led to a number of models. These differ from each other primarily in the basis for organization and the amount of detail. For example, a syllabus may be organized according to any one of a number of possible approaches, such as structural, functional, or thematic; it may include a bare-bones outline of a course, or much detail, with daily instructions for the teacher. However, although there are differences in descriptions of the curriculum and the syllabus, there is widespread agreement that both are necessary for the development and maintenance of good language programs and courses.

The syllabus planner can proceed with confidence when the following are present:

1. a clear statement of the mission of the educational program
2. an understanding of the conditions under which the program will be supported, administratively and financially
3. the design for a proposed program superstructure, i.e., administrators, teachers, support staff, and their areas of responsibility
4. a calendar for program design and evaluation
5. an analysis of students and their needs
6. a program design which reflects goals, resources, constraints, and funding
7. a statement of the purpose and plan of each particular course in the program

Experienced curriculum planners agree in general that the syllabus, whether or not very detailed, should include the essentials for planning and teaching. We submit the following bare-bones list of syllabus content as the necessary minimum for implementing and evaluating a course:

1. a general statement of course purpose
2. a student profile
3. a statement concerning selected approaches to syllabus design, linguistic analysis, and language teaching

4. instructional goals
5. performance objectives
6. exit criteria specifications
7. a teacher profile
8. class size
9. calendar and hours allocations
10. recommended texts, supplementary materials, and audiovisual aids
11. out-of-class activities, e.g., tutorial activities, Learning Center time, assigned homework time
12. minimal instructional standards, i.e., teacher responsibilities
13. testing and grading

The teacher, in turn, has responsibilities regarding the syllabus. Whether or not she is the person who actually writes it, the teacher fleshes out the syllabus and makes it real. Guided by the syllabus, she makes final decisions about classroom management, a style of relating to students, the number of steps in each point, individualization, the adaptation and supplementing of materials for classroom use, in-class testing, a feedback system, record-keeping, collaboration with other teachers, and the involvement of students in planning. The teacher tries to make the syllabus unfold on schedule, while testing whether the schedule is appropriate in that particular situation. She measures individual students against each other, diagnosing students and adjusting the syllabus as appropriate. She field-tests materials—her own and others—and tries to give objective evaluations. She consults with other teachers, comparing materials, techniques, and solutions to teaching problems. She adjusts for unexpected changes, such as the inexplicable differences from one term to the next among groups of students who should be identical, judging by available measurement instruments. She reports what is needed to do the job, such as materials, training, consulting, support services for students, and student selection procedures. In short, the teacher provides an ongoing evaluation of the syllabus and her implementation of it. Even if the syllabus planner is an experienced and observant teacher, the blueprint design will have to be tried out, and tested in the trying. And even if the syllabus is implemented successfully with one group of students and teacher, variations may be necessary in planning for a different group.

Planning a Small Program

A planner for a small program, often an individual teacher, may have to improvise, inferring a program mission from other things she knows about the system, operating insecurely and in a vacuum when assurance of administrative and financial support is not forthcoming, improvising her own procedural calendar and imposing an internal rule. In such a situation, the needs assessment and needs analysis must be done on site. Whatever the conditions, it is usually a compromise between the needs of the community (or institution) and the abilities of the students.

Background information about the educational program shades into the content of the course syllabus itself. Under optimum conditions a teacher will be able to answer questions about each course she is planning or already teaching and therefore responsible for evaluating:

1. What is the purpose of the course?
2. Who are the students? What are their backgrounds, strengths, personal goals, etc.?
3. What approach to syllabus design has been selected, e.g., notional, functional, situational, communicative, grammar, integrated? What approach to linguistic analysis has been selected, e.g., structural, functional, situational? What approach to language teaching has been selected, e.g., Communicative, Audiolingual, Direct, TPR, the Silent Way, Grammar Translation, etc.?
4. What are the instructional goals?
5. What are the performance objectives (in behavioral terms)?
6. What are the exit criteria specifications? That is, what behaviors will indicate that students have reached the goals of the course? How is this behavior to be measured?
7. What qualifications in terms of language, training, experience, and skills must the teacher have? What is expected of the teacher in conducting the course?
8. What is the optimum class size? What are the advantages and disadvantages of larger and smaller classes? Are complementary strategies used for an over- or an underenrolled class?
9. How much class time is available? How is it divided up? How are testing and vacations scheduled? What are the other time dimensions in the students' academic schedule?
10. What teaching materials are used? Are they commercial, educational, authentic? Are they easily available? Do they need adaptation? Are AV materials and equipment available?
11. How is students' time structured outside of class?
12. What learning activities are teachers minimally responsible for, e.g., minimal number of words to be written and corrected per student per week in a composition class, minimum number of recorded conversations to be analyzed and graded per student per term in a speaking course?
13. What criteria are used to assess students' achievement? Teacher judgment, tests, both? Pre-, mid-, post-? Criterion-referenced, norm-referenced, standardized? Teacher-made, commercial? How are students graded, certified, and promoted?

If the planner/teacher doesn't know the answer to any of these questions, she should seek or propose one. If she knows the answer and is not satisfied with it, she should seek to do something about it.

These lists are suggestive. The teacher and planner can use them as procedural guidelines to be both followed and tested as the course is taught.

A Curriculum Plan

The call for a curriculum does not usually originate from the desk of an educational theoretician. It dates, typically, directly or indirectly back to a higher level in the hierarchy of the state or institution. A neat and attractive theoretical model of the overall process has been developed by Elite Olshtain, presented with her doctoral dissertation (University of California, Los Angeles, 1978).

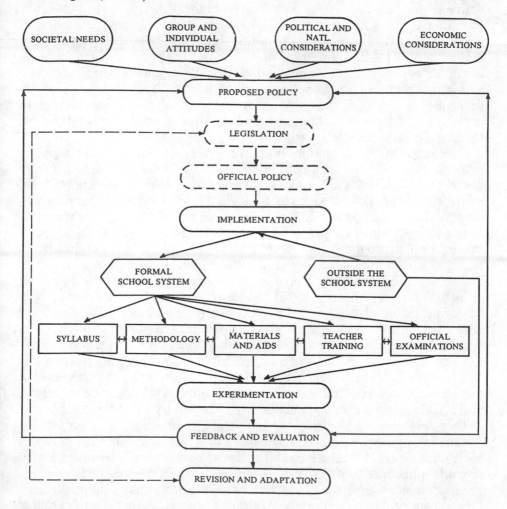

FIGURE 1a   The Theoretical Model

(By permission of the author)

Educational programs begin with a perceived need to which a program of instruction is seen as a partial or full solution. The need may be articulated and the proposal for solution initiated by members at any level of a hierarchy, but at some point the idea must be acted on by the decision makers of the unit involved, whether it be a university department, a school system, or even a national ministry of education. Policy decisions, either explicit or implied in other decisions, must be made.

In some cases the citizen-consumer of education contributes input for policy decisions, such as in American communities where local citizens active in the election of public officials express their views about their educational rights and interests. Cases in point are bilingual education in California in the seventies and the multiethnic, multilingual communities of many Southeast Asian countries. In other cases the policy makers, because of conflicting constituencies, make decisions in the interests of the country which may seem at odds with the desires of the individual, such as decisions to use English as the language of government, commerce, and education in order to avoid national factionalism and to derive an educational advantage by adapting a modern language.

Discussion in these situations is often considerable, and sometimes policy is a matter of negotiation among a number of vested interests. Following negotiation or mandate, a policy decision is made, and authority and responsibility are delegated (to an individual or group) for further development of the policy and finally for implementation. The implementation will have to consider the necessary requirements for designing, maintaining, and evaluating the program, both within its setting and in the context of its accountability to the larger community of which it is a part.

The degree of care with which these preliminary stages are conducted can strongly influence the quality of the resulting language programs. It is somewhere around this point, i.e., between the preliminary steps and the actual design and implementation, that local school administrators, often with assistance from classroom teachers, are "plugged in," not infrequently to a situation in which details of the curriculum and syllabus are incomplete. We recommend that the teacher assess the situation, using the checklists in this chapter, note what may be needed for an optimally effective curriculum, and make decisions that will include what she will try to add to complete it.

In a well-organized situation the policy is articulated in an official statement and responsibility is delegated to a selected, qualified group or individual. Good examples include the Italian government's recent project to upgrade public school English teaching, Israel's comprehensive ESL program in public education, and the Canadian government's many successful language programs, materials development, and research. The Council of Europe's programs are an example of this articulation on an international scale.

The parameters are the same for a local program. In the best of all possible situations, the official policy states intent to support the program financially and administratively, and provides for a number of subpolicies. The implementer coordinates the design of the program and individual courses, preparing a needs analysis, which is used to develop and specify curriculum and syllabus, plans, methodology, materials, teacher training, testing, and evaluation.

For large programs that are well organized and well funded, the person or persons officially delegated with the responsibility of planning the curriculum are usually well-qualified specialists. In new programs for a small number of special people, or programs in school systems with limited resources, the planner may well be one teacher, the only one in the field, or one recruited with or without previous experience in planning. It can be helpful for the planner, whether an administrator or a teacher, to know who the other "team" members have been, as sources of background information and potential support and cooperation in future efforts.

SUMMARY

In summary, we feel it important that teachers and planners never lose sight of the need for planning, evaluation, and revision, and have at their disposal the information and tools necessary to conduct these three steps continually and smoothly. We offer the topic lists in this chapter as thumbnail guides for checking whether there are sufficient background information, commitment for support, and attention to planning detail available to give the program its best chance to succeed. Although the major focus in the rest of this volume has been class content and testing, we feel that classes can succeed only within a positive and well-organized context.

Checklist

There is not room enough in this volume for a fuller treatment of program development. We hope that the steps outlined briefly here might serve as a checklist for planning a program, or for evaluating one already in operation:

A. Background
   1. Perceived social needs
   2. Political and economic considerations, public attitudes
   3. History of constituencies, negotiations
B. Implementation

1. Policy, mission, planning	9. Resources
2. Needs assessment	10. Calendar
3. Needs analysis	11. Program evaluation
4. Entry and exit criteria	12. Methods
5. Goals	13. Materials
6. Objectives	14. Teacher training
7. Student profile	15. Testing
8. Teacher profile	

Starting from the last step, Testing, and working back, planners may first check whether all items are included, and second, whether each has been adequately treated. The complete absence of any item on the list indicates a major flaw in the curriculum or syllabus. If all essential items are included, but some are not articulated with enough detail to be easily described, used, and evaluated, more planning work needs to be done. If all essentials are included and articulated in sufficient detail, decision makers can pose questions amenable to evaluation and likely to lead to new decisions about the program.

Any program founded on a commitment to valued goals, an integrated set of educational beliefs, sufficient background information, and a plan for implementation congruent with the historical environment should succeed. The excellence of a program, whether large or small, lies in the continual, informed, critical judgment with which it is conceived, designed, implemented, and evaluated. At whatever point on the continuum of the history of the program the teacher/planner starts, and wherever the class, the class will become and remain strong so long as there is consistently good critical judgment and sincere effort.

DISCUSSION

1. What are the implications of the statement that planning and evaluation "are both ongoing processes"?

2. How do curriculum and syllabus relate to each other? Which is more important if a new program is being developed?

3. List some of the possible approaches on which a syllabus may be organized. How much detail will a good syllabus have?

4. What seven understandings and precedents should be present to assure a successful syllabus?

5. What should a bare-bones list of essentials for a syllabus include?

6. Educational programs begin with a perceived need to which a program of instruction is seen as a partial or full solution. Who will likely articulate the need?

7. What usually determines whether a single person or a committee of specialists will do the planning?

8. The three critical steps that must be kept in sight are: planning, evaluation, and revision. Justify.

9. What is the best way to use the checklist on page 353?

10. What does history have to do with curriculum planning?

CHAPTER FOURTEEN

EVALUATING STUDENTS

OVERVIEW

We consider testing and evaluation of language skills and competences a very important part of language teaching. For this reason we believe that a chapter on testing is not only appropriate but essential in a book on language teaching methodology. Testing has traditionally provided a measure of growth or achievement by which the success of the students' learning has been evaluated. Additionally, testing provides significant information about student morale and anxiety levels, an opportunity for a special kind of intensive study referred to as "reviewing for a test," and diagnostic tips that come to the teacher as feedback.

Contemporary ESL/EFL tests can be divided into roughly two general categories: those that test *skill* (such as speaking, spelling, or writing) and those that test *knowledge* (such as linguistic information, culture, or literature). Our concern will be almost exclusively with tests of language skill. These skill tests group themselves into measures of *proficiency* (general ability in English or readiness for a particular program as indicated by a placement exam) and measures of *achievement* (progress tests indicating relatively short-term gains). A third kind of skill exam is the *aptitude* test—a prognosis of future ability to learn a language. Since we are writing to the teacher, we will concentrate primarily on classroom achievement tests, the teacher's main evaluation instrument.

Other classifications of language tests include the subcategories *subjective* (essay, précis, translation—which must be evaluated by a trained professional) and *objective* (multiple choice, true/false, single-word answer—which can be scored by a clerk with a key that identifies right answers). Another subcategory, independent of subjective-objective, depends on type of subject participation: *receptive* (listening and reading, where the student is an interpreter) and *productive* (speaking and writing, where the student is a creator). Note that these two are not appropriately described as active/passive, for the student is very active in both types.

Tests can also be designated by modality and the modal interaction required by test items: *spoken* language (listening and speaking) and *written* language (reading and writing). These categories are not watertight compartments that keep linguistic elements from each other. Very often a test will be bimodal, where a spoken cue will be recorded as a written answer (as in dictation). Or a written stimulus can trigger a spoken response (as in oral reading).

There are a few other definitions we need in order to discuss testing in a reasonably comprehensive way. If individual test scores are based on the performance of a group (such as one's class), the test is classified as *norm-referenced*. On the other hand, if scores are based on independent criteria (such as the achievement of course objectives) the test is said to be *criterion-referenced*.

Another contrast of subcategories has become increasingly important: *integrative* tests simultaneously evaluate clusters of interrelated, often undefined, skills such as listening, writing, spelling, punctuation, and penmanship on a dictation test; *discrete-point* tests look at only one factor at a time, such as a punctuation usage, a grammar correlation, etc. Note that multiple choice tests can be either integrative (most reading exams, for example) or discrete-point (most vocabulary tests).

UTILIZING MULTIPLE APPROACHES IN EVALUATION

Evaluating Student Activities

It is advisable to evaluate students in a number of different ways rather than to rely almost exclusively on formal exams. Doing so can help reduce the anxiety often associated with major tests given just once or twice a term, and it can increase student incentive to do the many things we ask of them. Naturally students should be apprised ahead of time of what will be evaluated as well as the relative weight of each activity—something to be determined, of course, by individual teachers or those responsible for the ESL/EFL program.

Possible areas of evaluation might include homework assignments, in-class exercises, reports, projects, team activities, and class discussion or participation. One teacher of our acquaintance decided to evaluate participation periodically by utilizing cards, each of which bore the name of a student. Those performing acceptably had their cards placed unobtrusively in one pile, those unacceptably in another; after class the results were quickly recorded. Whatever the method, it is good to record fairly often how students are doing in each area. Then periodically students can be informed of their performance. Additional areas sometimes evaluated include attendance, punctuality with assignments, and even deportment.

Testing Students Informally

Informal testing ranges from simple interviews (performance being rated with a $+$, $\sqrt{}$, $-$, or a brief narrative comment) to short quizzes. The latter can be used to check on a reading assignment, note-taking (by allowing students to use their notes in answering a few questions), or progress in some area of communication. Quizzes should not take too much class time (normally not more than five minutes two or three times a week) nor too much teacher time for correction. While it is not necessary to announce which days they will be given, it is important to let students know in advance that they will be a regular class activity—not a penalty for misconduct. Quizzes can help students in their studies by allowing them to see areas of emphasis in the course and by diagnosing individual limitations; quizzes can help them prepare for formal tests by acquainting them with the types of questions that will be used. They can even constitute a relatively painless "installment plan" evaluation. At the same time, quizzes can help assure that outside exercises or readings are taken care of promptly. They have even been known to help improve attendance, punctuality of arrival, and discipline at the outset of the class period.

DECIDING ON GENERAL GUIDELINES

While our testing emphasis is on skills evaluation, this in no way suggests that affective goals, including humanistic values, attitudes towards various cultures, or moral views should be ignored.[1]

In every way possible our language tests should complement teacher efforts to create a positive student attitude toward the course. To the extent possible, students should have the opportunity to experience some success and progress in the language (this might mean including some simple quizzes measuring preparation for class, using a few easy items at the beginning of a test, selecting dictation passages of appropriate difficulty, or making sure a major test is not excessively difficult for the majority of the class). Instructions should be simple and clear, with adequate examples of each question type. Adequate time needs to be provided for the test. Tests should be evaluated (see Chapter Fifteen) so that faulty questions can be eliminated. Test research shows a dramatic difference in the amount of anxiety generated by various types of language tests. Teachers should assess which test forms create most anxiety for their students and avoid test types that are most debilitating.

To promote positive student attitudes toward tests, also be careful to announce tests well in advance, cover only what you have covered in class, familiarize students ahead of time with new types of test questions, and try to

[1]The National Council of Teachers of English has urged teachers "to preserve (and, if need be, fight for) the retention of important humanistic goals of education . . . whether or not there exist instruments at the present time for measuring the desired changes in pupil behavior" (*The English Journal* 1970, 501).

have tests reflect the nature of class instruction. This means that in testing writing, students will have an opportunity to write—not simply circle responses on a multiple choice test; students who have learned vocabulary by inferring meaning from context will be tested by looking at vocabulary in context and not simply at isolated lexical items.

Teachers have been known to undermine their own morale by burdening themselves with excessive evaluation. There are several ways to remedy this problem: (1) Make student writing assignments shorter (often a paragraph can reveal as much as several pages); use short quizzes. (2) Let students participate in correcting some of their work. (3) Occasionally scan the exercise or paper for only one or two key errors. (4) Now and then use informal oral evaluation while the balance of the class is engaged in some other activity. (5) Capitalize on evaluating class activities of various kinds and thus reduce the amount of formal testing needed.

TESTING LANGUAGE COMPONENTS

Evaluating the components of the language such as grammar, vocabulary, and pronunciation doesn't necessarily reflect ability to communicate in English. Such evaluation can be useful, however, in showing what progress has been made by students in mastering specific features of the language over a relatively brief period of time.

Grammar

Ability to handle the grammar of English *could* be evaluated in quite a few different ways, such as determining the relative sophistication of structures in student essays and conversations, or analyzing the grammatical errors made in translation, composition, oral presentations, or dictation. These procedures, however, are rather time consuming, subjective, and demanding on the teacher. A more direct approach is Sentence Combining:

(G/1) He will come later. I will ask him then. (I'll ask him when he comes.)

There are two even more efficient ways to test grammar. One is Simple Completion, and the other is Multiple Choice Completion.

Simple Completion. The Simple Completion item type can be illustrated with this two-word verb item:

(G/2) She just sat _____ to eat breakfast. (ans: down)

One limitation is getting unanticipated answers. For example, in G/2 above, one might get "up," if one assumes the person is hospitalized or in bed. Consider, for example, the large number of options possible for the sentence, "He just _____ the store." The teacher might have expected "left," but could get responses such as "saw, found, bought, sold, entered," etc. One option is to accept any correct response. Another is to provide more context:

(G/3) Usually he leaves the store at 5:00, but yesterday he _____ it at 4:30.

Still a third possibility is to use a judicious amount of terminology, assuming that all are familiar with the terms used:

(G/4) (Add a question tag) She's very bright, _____ ?

Normally Simple Completion items request only one word in the blank. Instructions for items like G/4 would have to allow for more than one word. Other Simple Completion items allowing multiple-word responses are the following:

(G/5) I'd go if _____ .

(G/6) Where did they put the box? _____ .

These free-response items provide considerable latitude for students to reply, but they place heavy demands on the teacher. Correct responses to G/5 might include: if I were you / if I owned a warm jacket / if he hadn't borrowed my car / if I could / if she did. To G/6, we might get: In the closet/ Which box? / It's over there, etc.

To provide more control, we can sometimes cue the answer:

(G/7) Yesterday, they _____ (buy) some furniture.

Since there is still more than one possible answer for some verb inflection items like this, it is acceptable to cue the desired answer with multiple blanks and even dialog-type sentences:

(G/8) "What are you doing, Jean?"

"Oh, I _____ _____ (wait) for a bus." (am waiting or 'm waiting)

Since so many textbook exercises use Simple Completion, they can serve as an easy transition to tests of the same type. Texts often provide two or more cues. These are virtually the same as multiple choice items:

(G/9) Complete the following sentence using "do" or "make":
I swept the floor, but I didn't _____ the dishes.

Multiple Choice Completion. While good Multiple Choice Completion questions take longer to prepare than those we have just been discussing, they are faster to correct, and there is only one correct answer possible:

(G/10) He gave the book . . . her.
   A. on   *B. to   C. at   D. —
   D indicates no word is needed.

Naturally, it is important not to write items with more than one correct answer:

(G/11) (unacceptable)
    They have . . . money left.   [either A or B]
    *A. a little   B. little   C. few   D. a few

Also avoid divided usage. In the following sentence, the "rule" requires "had written," but most native speakers also feel comfortable with "wrote."

(G/12) (unacceptable)
    Before he left on vacation, he . . . the letters.
    A. wrote   B. has written   C. writes   *D. had written

In addition, avoid non-English distractors. They are too obvious to some students, and they offend many teachers and administrators:

(G/13) (unacceptable)
    She . . . the package last night.
    A. brung   *B. brought   C. broughted   D. bringed

Finally, do not repeat words in the options that could appear in the stem:

(G/14) (unacceptable)
    I'll wait up . . . (   ).
    A. since you come home.
    *B. until you come home.
    C. while you come home.
    D. as you come home.

Question Types for Special Purposes. Various forms of questions are available to evaluate grammar for special purposes:

1. Testing beginners. Students unable to read in English can be tested individually: "Put this box behind the little one." Besides carrying out commands, they can be asked questions about pictures or simply told "Point to the picture where the tree is as tall as the house."

2. Testing several features at a time. More challenging than Multiple Choice Completion are questions like the following. (They have the psychological disadvantage of incorporating errors in the basic sentence.)

A few of my friends <u>have studied</u> English <u>for</u> several years <u>in United States</u>.
  A   B   C   D

3. Testing grammar in an integrative format.
    a. The Bowen Integrative Grammar Test consists of random sentences spoken aloud so that normal reduction, contraction, and assimilation are incorporated. Students are simply asked to write down the second word of each sentence that they hear:

    /jə lâyktə ǵow/   (Would you like to go?) (ans: you)

b. The Multiple Choice Cloze Test is similar to Multiple Choice Completion, except that a passage of connected prose is chosen. Function words (like determiners, prepositions, conjunctions, and auxiliary verbs) are deleted at random intervals; multiple choice options are written for each blank. See also the discussion on Selected Deletion Cloze, page 376.

4. Manipulating specific structures. Students can be required to make specified changes in sentences such as transforming them from active to passive, from present to past tense, from direct to indirect discourse, etc.

Vocabulary

Selecting what vocabulary items to test obviously depends on student needs. Besides words from readers and other ESL texts, one can collaborate with teachers of other classes in English-medium schools in identifying useful lexical items. Vocational and even social needs should also be considered. In addition, testing will reflect instructional approaches. This means that few teachers will be satisfied with looking at words in isolation. As with grammar, our basic techniques will involve Simple Completion and Multiple Choice.

Simple Completion. One challenge is to provide context that clearly cues only the word being tested:

(V/1)) The _____ is the room in a house where we prepare meals. (ans: kitchen)

The context may even include a very short written dialog:

(V/2) "Here's our chance; we have a good runner on third base."
"Yes, and the next batter hit a home run last time up."
WHAT AMERICAN GAME ARE THEY PLAYING? (ans: baseball)

Another cueing device involves the use of compound words:

(V/3) Don't touch my back! I got a sun_____ yesterday when I went swimming. (ans: sunburn)

A related kind of question is word completion, in which one or more syllables are deleted:

(V/4) She already feels bad about what she did. Your criticism was quite _____necessary. (ans: unnecessary)

(V/5) Becky is a courag_____ little girl. She's not afraid of dying. (ans: courageous)

Multiple Choice Completion. A suitable context is again needed—one that suggests the meaning of the deleted word. For example, if one wanted to test "vindictive," it would not do to use it in a sentence such as "He was a very . . . man." A large number of other words also fit this context. A much more suitable sentence would be

(V/6)   His wife had no desire for revenge, but he was terribly . . .
   A. loquacious   *B. vindictive   C. lethargic   D. jocular

Naturally, avoid cues that give away the answer, like the "an" in this item:

(V/7)   (unacceptable) Even I knew the answer. It was an . . . question.
   A. hard   B. long   C. new   *D. easy

One way is to include the article with the multiple choice option: "a hard," "an easy," etc. Another pitfall is using distractors that mean about the same thing, such as "big" and "large." Some students know they are synonyms and therefore avoid selecting either one. Another error to avoid is using words that do not fit the sentences grammatically; again, some students may get the item right, for the wrong reason:

(V/8)   (unacceptable) He ran . . . down the street.
   *A. quickly   B. beautiful   C. race   D. wide

When possible try to use words that have some semantic relationship to the context. In example V/8, "race" is a pretty good distractor despite its form, because it is often associated with the verb of the sentence—"ran." Also, use options that are about the same level of difficulty. Note how the first option "sticks out" in this set:

   *A. nefarious   B. simple   C. dark   D. soon

Obviously, avoid including more than one correct answer.

Question Types for Special Purposes. There are also strategies suitable to varying kinds of instruction.

1. Testing beginners. Students can be tested individually by having them perform simple tasks: "Bring me the red book." Sometimes tasks can be handled in a group: "Color the cow brown." Beginning students can also be tested by using true/false statements or yes/no questions: "Horses can fly." (false); "Is this a pen?" (yes). Using pictures, the teacher can have students point at or draw a circle around certain objects.

2. Testing synonym recognition. While synonyms can be tested in an open-ended fashion, multiple choice options are generally more successful. These are fairly easy to prepare since context is not as crucial; the synonym can be expressed in a phrase if necessary. Sometimes a key word is used instead of a context.

DEVOUT   A. somewhat liberal   B. rather confused
   *C. deeply religious   D. badly misunderstood

Rather closely related is the testing of definitions; instead of the *stem's* being a prose context, it can consist of just a definition. Another variation is the testing of related words:

"He ate lots of *fruit*."
A. bread   B. carrots   C. cheese   *D. apples

Pronunciation

Separate tests of pronunciation are not frequently used in this post-Audiolingual period. Instead, pronunciation is more often incorporated in tests of speaking. But for those needing a separate measure of progress in pronunciation, the Reading Aloud procedure and the Multiple Choice (pronunciation) Recognition technique can serve the purpose quite well.

Reading Aloud. Two forms of Reading Aloud pronunciation tests consist of unrelated sentences and prose paragraphs. The former is generally more satisfactory for teachers who do not have the time for sophisticated phonological analysis. Also it is useful in providing a quantifiable, simply scored measure of pronunciation. The main limitation with any Reading Aloud measure is that this is a rather specialized skill which many people fail to acquire, even in their native language. Nevertheless, it can give us a useful if rough index of pronunciation ability.

What we test is determined not only by what we have taught but also by the common needs of our students. One feature that causes difficulty in comprehension is faulty word or sentence stress; another is faulty intonation. Distracting "foreign" accent problems are accentuated by failure to reduce unstressed syllables to schwa and by inability to handle consonant clusters, word linking, assimilation, and the like.

After identifying what to test, prepare sentences containing each pronunciation feature. If looking at the /ɪ/ – /iy/ contrast, this kind of sentence is acceptable:

(P/1)   She cut her lip.

Avoid the temptation to pack too many of these sounds into one sentence:

(P/2)   (unacceptable) Those thin bins are for green beans.

This tends to tip the student off to what is being tested; it often results in unnatural English and unfamiliar vocabulary. As a general rule, avoid using minimal pairs, except occasionally for contrastive stress:

(P/3)   That's what he thought, not what he taught.
         The student's paper would not have the stress marks included.

Since most people can observe at least two pronunciation features in a given sentence, it is usually more satisfactory to evaluate two different matters, such as the voiced "th" and the final rising intonation in a sentence such as the following:

(P/4)   Is that his mother?
         The sentence is to be read aloud.

Whether isolated sentences or connected prose is read, it is advisable to give students the opportunity to read through the material a few minutes ahead of time so that they can read aloud as naturally as possible.

Multiple Choice (pronunciation) Recognition. While pronunciation is an active skill, the ability to *recognize* pronunciation tends to reflect student ability to produce speech sounds,[2] and it enables us to test pronunciation in groups rather than individually.

Formerly, sounds were tested in isolation with contrasting words or phrases. Nowadays, in this cognitive era, we prefer to incorporate meaning in the drill and in test items. For example, in checking certain vowel sounds such as those in "cat," "cot," and "coat," we might use an item like this:

(P/5)   (students hear)   The coat is too small.
          (students read)   *A. I can't wear it.   B. I can't sleep in it.
                                    C. It drinks only milk.

A simple two-choice item testing the vowel sounds in "lock" and "look" can be handled as follows:

(P/6)   (students hear)   Lock it up in the library.
          (students read)   A. in a dictionary   *B. with a key

Contrastive stress can be evaluated the same way:

(P/7)   (students hear)   His son walked into the drúgstore.
          (students read)   A. not his daughter   B. not out of it
                             *C. not the bank

And appropriate-response items can be used to test a variety of matters, including intonation:

(P/8)   (students hear)   Would you like/pie or ice cream?
          (students read)   *A. Yes thank you . . .
                              B. Some ice cream, please.

A Guessing Correction can be used when only two options are given (see Chapter Fifteen).

Question Types for Special Purposes. Two ways to test beginners who can't read yet are through Oral Repetition and Pictures.

1. Oral repetition can be used to test any of the features discussed earlier. The teacher reads a sentence aloud: "I want the red one, not the blue one," and the student attempts to duplicate it orally.

2. Pictures can also be used to test pronunciation. Sketches of stairs, stores, and stars could be used to test, "He looked at the stars."

TESTING COMMUNICATION SKILLS

The tests to be discussed in this section are particularly important, because they evaluate not only what has been learned in class, but also how well students can actually communicate in their new language. Illustrations

---

[2]Any indirect measure like this has its limitations, however. Some can recognize sound contrasts, for example, without being able to produce them well.

will be provided on how to evaluate the four skills of listening, speaking, reading, and writing.

Listening

The section on pronunciation just concluded illustrates how to evaluate prelistening skills. For students who have some skill in reading, suggestions in the next two sections can be utilized to test listening comprehension skills.

Multiple Choice Sentence Comprehension. One of the simplest measures of listening comprehension is having students select appropriate responses to sentences that they hear. In preparing multiple choice options, use familiar vocabulary and grammar so the test doesn't become a measure of reading comprehension. And since students have to retain what they have heard in their short-term memory, use only three very short options:

(L/1) (students hear) Will he help her?
       (students read)   A. Yes she will.   B. Yes it helps.
                        *C. Yes he will.

Besides yes/no questions like L/1, we can use WH-questions. Since we are representing conversation, notice that the answer can be simply a phrase:

(L/2) (students hear) Where did she put the brush?
       (students read) *A. In the drawer.   B. Yes she did.
                         C. In a minute.

Questions can be made more challenging by avoiding stereotyped responses. For example, a correct response to L/2 might be "Which brush?" or "Let's ask Tom." Correct answers to yes/no questions don't always include the words "yes" or "no":

(L/3) (students hear) Can we go when he comes?
       (students read)   A. He's coming.   *B. We can.
                         C. Yes he will.

Another kind of sentence comprehension listening item is Appropriate Paraphrase. The stem is usually a statement rather than a question:

(L/4) (students hear) Jack is as tall as Bill.
       (students read)   A. Jack is taller.   B. Bill is taller.
                        *C. They are the same height.

It is acceptable to paraphrase only part of the sentence:

(L/5) (students hear) They're going swimming whether or not it rains.
       (students read) *A. Rain won't stop them.
                         B. They hope it rains.
                         C. Only sunshine is acceptable.

Multiple Choice Passage Comprehension. Since listening involves more than understanding conversation, student comprehension of lectures, radio and TV segments, and business transactions can also be evaluated.

Lecture comprehension can be evaluated by using lecturettes—two or three very short simulated lectures. These should include typical hesitations (and I . . . ah . . .), asides (a Republican wouldn't agree, however), and short digressions. Students should be permitted to take notes on these 5- to 8-minute lecturettes, and questions are prepared on the substantive portion—not on asides or digressions, of course. During the test, students are permitted to use their notes.

In testing listening comprehension of other contexts, students would not take notes, since they would not normally do so in real life situations. Radio dramas, TV commercials, and routine business transactions are good sources of extended discourse contexts. Normally poetry and lyrics to songs are not good sources. Be careful not to ask questions that are extremely detailed. Here is a fairly challenging commercial followed by typical questions:

"Oh look, Ryan! Beef Wellington!"

"Where? Where? I think my mother used to watch him wrestle on TV."

"No. Beef Wellington! My favorite dish! I've never missed a chance to have Beef Wellington!"

"Oh. Okay. Waiter, I'll have the Lobster Newburg, and the lady will have the Bee—"

"Dover Sole, please!"

"Harriet, why did you switch?"

"I don't know. All of a sudden I felt like fish, too!"

"Okay then. Instead of the lobster I'll try the Beef Wellington and bring the lady—"

"Lamb chops."

"Okay, Harriet, why do you keep changing your order?"

"I really want to share a bottle of wine with you."

"So, what's the problem?"

"Well, how can we? I mean, if one of us has meat and one of us has fish?"

"Harriet, Blue Nun can solve the problem."

"I don't want a miracle. I just want some wine."

"No, Blue Nun is a wine, a delicious whole wine that's correct with any dish: Beef Wellington, Lobster Newburg—anything you're eating."

"You're getting sophisticated—"

"I'm glad you noticed. Waiter, make that one bottle of Blue Nun and two straws, please."

(L/6)   Where does this conversation take place?
         A. At a church   *B. At a restaurant   C. At home
(L/7)   What is being advertised?
         A. A place to eat   B. Types of meat to buy   *C. A type of drink to buy

(L/8)   (an advanced question) Why did the woman change her order?
A. So they could have Blue Nun   B. So they wouldn't both have meat or fish   *C. So they could order the same beverage

Question Types for Special Purposes. There are several interesting and effective ways to test the listening of beginning students:

1. True/false items can easily be constructed: "Fire is cold." (F)
2. Native language printed options can be prepared for oral cues in English.
3. Simple tasks can be required of students: "Go to the door" / "Point to the window" / Draw a house and two trees behind it."
4. Pictures can be used, and true/false or yes/no questions asked: "Is it night?" In addition, sets of pictures can be used. A statement can be made about one of the set. Students circle the right picture in group testing, or point to it, if being tested individually.

Speaking

Because eliciting and scoring spoken English appears difficult, this skill is often not directly tested at all. In this section, we present techniques that help control the responses so that scoring can be facilitated.

Controlled Elicitation. Having students read something aloud from the printed page maximizes examiner control of output and eliminates subjective evaluation of student logic, originality, etc. Of course this technique is not suitable for beginners who cannot read, and it cannot measure important speaking skills such as appropriateness. One procedure is to have students read aloud a set of disconnected sentences containing examples of such things as stress, word joining, intonation, and vowel-consonant features. In addition, a rough indication of fluency can be obtained (although it needs to be kept in mind that reading aloud from the printed page is a skill not always acquired even by advanced learners of English). As in tests of pronunciation, one can limit the scoring to two or three features per sentence. Another Reading Aloud procedure is to have the student read a *prose passage* aloud. Ahead of time the examiner marks his or her copy so that each critical feature can be checked.

Directed Response can be tightly controlled, or it can allow some possibility for grammatical adjustments and social appropriateness. The following question represents the simplest and most tightly controlled item:

(S/1) Tell him it's raining (Ans: "It's raining.")

More flexibility is apparent in this Directed Response question:

(S/2) Ask her politely to come here. (Ans: Sue, could you come here for a moment, please?)

A third kind of Controlled Elicitation technique is the Paraphrase. This usually involves presenting to the student connected discourse such as a story and then asking that it be retold in the student's own words. Obviously this involves listening (or reading) in addition to speaking. Scoring can be based on the number of main points covered in the retelling as well as the usual criteria employed for evaluating speaking: fluency and appropriateness, grammar, vocabulary, and pronunciation.

Allowing even more freedom than the technique just discussed is the expository procedure called Explanation. This can involve simple processes:

(S/3) Explain how to use a vending machine to buy a candy bar.

Or it can involve more extended explanations:

(S/4) In just two or three minutes, tell how American children celebrate Valentine's Day.

Still another Controlled Elicitation procedure is Guided Role Play. The teacher takes a fixed role, with lines prepared ahead of time and virtually committed to memory. The situation is explained fully to the student, but his or her lines are essentially spontaneous, guided only by what the teacher says.

Guided Interview. Any of the techniques discussed so far under Speaking Tests can be incorporated in the Guided Interview, which is simply a loosely structured process for generating communicative utterances.

The interview typically starts with easy-to-answer questions: yes/no, either/or, and simple information questions:

(S/5) Are you here to take the English test?
(S/6) Do you live on campus in a dorm or off campus?
(S/7) How long have you been here in the United States?

Some are more open-ended:

(S/8) Tell me how you went about getting your visa.

An occasional question requires the student to ask for clarification:

(S/9) When you leave, take this card to the file. (Ans: Pardon me, where is that?)

A few require responses to statements:

(S/10) I don't suppose you had any difficulty finding the room.

The questions in a Guided Interview should be clustered so that they are semantically related: for example, questions about the person's country and family, residence and study in America, etc. They should progress from easy to more challenging, but with occasional simple questions later in the interview to help bolster the student's confidence. The questions should be presented with the appearance of spontaneity; and alternate questions should be available so that students won't be able to respond satisfactorily simply by consulting those who took the interview earlier. Students should *not* be made aware during the test of items that they miss; and repetition of a question is permissible, although this normally results in a point loss when fluency is being checked. If the student misses three or four items in a row, the interview can be gracefully terminated. Above all, the student should be put completely at ease so that she won't become inhibited in her responses.

Scoring the interview follows the same pattern as that for other oral tests. Rather than using a holistic impression of general proficiency (as is normally the procedure in scoring an essay, for example), it is far more satisfactory to use an objectified approach. Decide ahead of time what your criteria are. Those used for second or foreign language oral tests internationally can serve as a guideline: These include appropriateness, fluency, grammar, vocabulary, and pronunciation (when pronunciation begins to interfere with communication).

A typical objectified scoring system allocates a fixed number of points per item on the interview. This is sometimes two points. Satisfactory responses (though not necessarily native-like responses by any means) are given two points. Those that communicate the idea but have to be repeated or are marred with distracting grammatical flaws may receive only one point. Those that are unintelligible or situationally quite inappropriate receive no points. Open-ended questions that may involve a somewhat extended response (for up to a minute or more) may be given extra points—say 4 or 5. Part-credit scoring similar to that mentioned above can apply to these questions as well.

Question Types for Special Purposes. For beginning students, the following procedures can be used:

1. Directed Response, discussed earlier in this chapter, combines listening and speaking with graduated control of student response.

2. Pictures with simple oral prompts are useful for students not yet literate in English: "Tell what's happening here." / "What did she do?" / "Where are the boys?" We can also use a sequence of sketches, or a map of a neighborhood including dotted lines showing someone's route, to prompt a brief narrative.

Reading

The two most common ways to test reading comprehension are by checking comprehension of sentences and comprehension of reading passages.

Sentence Comprehension. Multiple choice paraphrase of sentences is an effective technique. The options should not be more difficult than the stem, of course:

(R/1) Don will sing if they ask him to.
      A. Don wants to sing.   *B. Don is willing to sing.   C. Don will sing.   D. They want him to sing.

The paraphrase may refer to only part of the sentence:

(R/2)   Even though the plan is quite unworkable, the Senator has every
intention of countering the opposition's efforts against it.
A. The Senator has good intentions.   B. The Senator is joining
the opposition.   *C. The Senator supports the plan.   D. It is
countering the opposition.

Occasionally Appropriate Response questions are used:

(R/3)   Could you tell me which gate the Western flight is arriving at?
*A. What's the flight number?   B. Yes, it's arriving.
C. You certainly could.   D. Yes, at the gate.

A related task is to check the meaning of signs, which might consist of
sentences or simply phrases. The paraphrase technique could be used, or one
might ask where such a sign is found:

(R/4)   No Smoking in Lavatories
A. hotels   B. parks   C. theaters   *D. airliners

Keep in mind the possibility of cultural bias. All students must have the
cultural background needed to answer any given question.

Passage Comprehension. The traditional reading context is a prose
passage from a reader or school book, such as a science text. But there are
other important kinds of passages to consider when preparing a test:
magazine advertisements, classified ads in newspapers, forms of various
kinds (such as credit application blanks), and dittoed handouts from the
school.

Questions on the passage can be multiple choice or simple completion; but
be cautious not to impose a challenging writing task or the test may be as
much a writing test as a reading test. Use a variety of kinds of questions:
simple recall in the wording of the original passage, paraphrase, synthesis of
several sentences or of the entire passage, and implications or author's point
of view. Here is how a paraphrase item might be prepared:

Harlem is the section of New York City that has the largest black population.
People used to believe that the residents of Harlem were culturally deprived. This is
not necessarily true. It is true that many citizens of Harlem suffer from poverty and
inadequate educational and job opportunities. But the Afro-American in Harlem has
a rich cultural heritage.

The key portion we will use is ". . . many citizens of Harlem suffer from
. . . inadequate . . . job opportunities." Our paraphrase is ". . . lots of people
in Harlem have a hard time finding work." Almost every word but Harlem is
different. The paraphrase is also simpler. Here is the resulting question:

(R/5)   In this passage, we see that lots of people in Harlem . . .
A. are culturally deprived.   *B. have a hard time finding work.
C. are not Afro-Americans.   D. are not citizens.

An "implication" question can incorporate paraphrase and synthesis:

The Golden Gate Bridge joins the beautiful city of San Francisco with the suburbs to the north. Each day, about one hundred thousand automobiles cross the bridge, taking people to and from the city. More than half of them cross the bridge during the morning and evening rush hours; with traffic so heavy, the trip is not pleasant. Now, however, there is at least one group of happy commuters. These are the people who travel under the bridge instead of on it. The trip takes only thirty minutes and is not very costly. The ferry they take is the roomy, quiet, comfortable "Golden Gate."

(R/6)   Why do some people take the boat to work?
A. It is much faster than driving.   B. It is not as expensive as driving.   *C. It is more peaceful than driving.   D. They don't need to buy an expensive car.

One problem to avoid in preparing reading comprehension questions is using items that students can answer from general knowledge:

(R/7)   (unacceptable) In this story we find that the Greeks defeated Troy by *A. hiding soldiers in a great wooden horse.   B. pretending to attack another city.   C. attacking when the Trojans were celebrating.   D. taking a famous woman captive.

Other problems include using distractors which are so obviously wrong that they can be logically eliminated, and consistently making the right answer longer than the others (often due to our efforts to eliminate any doubt about its correctness).

Question Types for Special Purposes.

1. Prereading items that get at word attack skills include timed processing of word or phrasal pairs and triplets. Students circle "S" if the pair is the same or "D" if the words are different; e.g., lit, lid / tan, tan.

2. True/false questions can be used to test the reading comprehension of those who might have difficulty coping with multiple choice options: "She is my father" (illogical; therefore the student circles "F" for "false").

3. Pictures that require no writing or additional reading can also be used for students with very limited reading skill. Students simply read in English a statement such as "He came home at night," and then they circle the sketch that matches what they have read.

4. Essay questions and multiple choice items are used to evaluate student understanding of literature. Most suitable on the advanced level, these questions often include reference to plot, theme, characterization, tone, style, and information about various genres and periods of literature. This transcends mere reading comprehension, of course. Essay questions would be used only if students had demonstrated good control of the written word.

Writing

Like other communication skills, writing integrates a variety of features: structural skill, lexical mastery, knowledge of mechanical conventions, sensitivity to appropriate diction, and the ability to handle larger rhetorical functions including paragraphing, unity, and organization; not to mention adapting the presentation to the topic and the audience. Since it is not possible to teach so many things simultaneously and since the higher-level matters are not even reached in many ESL/EFL programs, this presentation will point out how to evaluate some of these subskills separately, as they are being acquired.

Testing Writing-related Subskills. The subskills covered here include grammar, mechanics, diction, and objective measures of rhetorical matters such as unity and organization.

GRAMMAR is often checked by having students combine sentences, since writing transcends the clause level. After students are introduced to coordinators such as *and, but, or, for, nor,* simple coordination can be cued this way:

(W/1) Maria is studying English. _____ She is working in a store, too.
(Ans: Maria is studying English, and she is working in a store, too.)

Another approach to checking sentence combining mastery is to provide specific connectives to be used:

(W/2) He runs his company efficiently. His company makes a lot of money. (so . . . that)
(Ans: He runs his company so efficiently that it makes a lot of money.)

Yet another approach allows more flexibility in the response:

(W/3) He said for you to come this afternoon *unless . . .*

In addition to sentence combining, sentence expansion and sentence reduction can be used. The former has the student add modifiers or additional phrases and clauses. The latter has the student embed clauses:

(W/4) My brother is stingy. My brother won't lend me a dime. (Reduce one sentence to a single word.)
(Ans: My stingy brother won't lend me a dime.)

MECHANICS includes matters such as spelling, punctuation, and capitalization. The simplest way to handle spelling is to dictate words, in context. Students write only the key word:

(W/5) *marriage*: She just told me about her marriage to Jim.

Another option is to have students identify the misspelled word (although some object to students' being exposed to errors):

(W/6) *A. alright B. surprising C. studying D. a lot

Punctuation as well as capitalization can be checked by having students rewrite sentences such as the following:

(W/7) as i was riding my bicycle to work one day last week suddenly i heard a girl shout look out a trains coming

Though more time consuming to prepare, multiple choice sentences are another possibility:

A	B	C	D

(W/8) We sent for / a repair man to take / a look at the / telephone. In the office where I work.

DICTION can be checked in Simple Completion items or in multiple choice sentences such as the following:

(W/9) The newspaper indicated that Uganda's UN representative . . . in a local hospital following yesterday's automobile accident.
A. kicked the bucket *B. died C. passed to the great beyond D. departed mortality

RHETORICAL MATTERS such as unity and organization can be examined indirectly. A rather crude check of unity can be made by selecting a well developed expository paragraph and then adding an irrelevant sentence. For example, the Harlem selection preceding sample item R/5 begins, "Harlem is the section of New York City that has the largest black population." We could insert here: "This is the largest city in the state of New York." Students could be asked to underline the sentence that doesn't belong.

A somewhat crude measure of organizational ability can be had by selecting a well-developed paragraph utilizing good transition words. Sentences are then scrambled and retyped in the new (but illogical) sequence. Students are required to indicate what the correct sequence of sentences is.

Testing Guided Writing. Three forms of guided-writing evaluation will be covered in this section: modifying existing passages, amplifying skeletal drafts, and directing "free" writing.

MODIFYING EXISTING PASSAGES can be carried out several ways. One is to take an existing passage such as that on the San Francisco ferry (preceding sample item R/6). Each sentence is changed to a question:

(W/10) "Does the Golden Gate Bridge join the beautiful city of San Francisco with the suburbs to the north? Each day, do about one hundred thousand automobiles cross the bridge. . . ?" etc.

Then students are directed to rewrite the passage, changing all questions to statements. A variation on this theme is to take a narrative written in the first person and have students rewrite it in the third person.

Other changes that students can be asked to make include putting a dialog such as the Blue Nun commercial (preceding sample item L/6) into regular prose form:

(W/11)   Harriet said, "Oh look, Ryan! Beef Wellington!"
"Where? Where?" Ryan responded. "I think my mother used to watch him wrestle on TV." (etc.) (Ans: Harriet called Ryan's attention to Beef Wellington, which he misunderstood to refer to a wrestler his mother used to watch on TV.) (etc.)

More challenging still is requiring a dialog (usually much simpler than the one above) to be changed to reported speech:

(W/12)   Change the following to reported speech.
MRS. ELLIS   How do you like teaching, Peggy?
MRS. NORRIS   I love it, Jane. I'm teaching part time, you know.
MRS. ELLIS   What days do you teach?
MRS. NORRIS   On Monday, Wednesday, and Friday. . . .
(Ans: Mrs. Ellis asked Mrs. Norris how she liked teaching. Mrs. Norris replied that she loved it, and she added that she was teaching part time. Mrs. Ellis then asked what days her friend taught, and Mrs. Norris said she taught on Monday, Wednesday, and Friday. . . .)

AMPLIFYING SKELETAL DRAFTS provides active responses of a different kind:

(W/13)   Write a paragraph by filling in the needed words.
I – not – school – yesterday / I – absent / visiting – my grandparents / they – beautiful farm – country / farmhouse – beautiful / not – big – very nice / mother – born / grandfather – born
(Ans: I wasn't in school yesterday. I was absent. I was visiting my grandparents. They have a beautiful farm in the country. The farmhouse is beautiful, too. It's not very big, but it's very nice. My mother was born there. My grandfather was born there, too.)

Still more freedom is provided in this skeletal draft:

(W/14)   Write a paragraph on a favorite trip you have taken, by explaining these points. Write one sentence on each question. Use suitable transition words.
1. How old were you?   2. Where did you go?   3. Who went with you?   4. How did you get there?   5. What did you do?   6. What did you enjoy the most?

DIRECTING "FREE" WRITING can be done by providing sufficiently detailed information on which students are to write. This can take the form of situational description, pictures, charts, maps, or lists of information on a topic (for example, if the topic were selecting an apartment, two sets of data on housing could be given: rent, location, furnishings, amenities, etc.—for Apartment A, and for Apartment B).

But guiding the writing is only half the task. Grading it reliably is equally important. Occasionally one can grade a short piece of writing for only one or two points, such as the use of complete sentences and correct tense. This simplifies evaluation, speeds up the task, and boosts the morale of weaker students. Generally holistic scoring will be used. (See Chapter Nine on writing for evaluation guidelines.) Evaluation criteria should be planned in advance and shared with students. No one error (particularly grammatical or mechanical) should lower the grade significantly. Scanning several papers before assigning grades is helpful. We ask ourselves how well the student met the objective of the assignment, how well the paper communicates, and to what extent we are distracted or confused by student errors. Basic questions like these and not a mere listing of mechanical-grammatical errors can guide us in assigning the appropriate A, B, C, D, or E grade. And our written comments can provide encouragement while simultaneously making the composition test a valuable learning experience.

Question Types for Special Purposes.

1. Simple copying (in cursive) of a text is a meaningful task for beginning students.
2. Note-taking is an appropriate kind of evaluation for students who have lecture classes.

TESTING GENERAL COMPETENCE

Proficiency Tests (or tests of general language ability) are used to place students in multilevel programs. But they aren't very sensitive to short term gains from class instruction, nor are they often useful as diagnostic instruments. Nevertheless, many teachers are interested in them, since they can provide a very revealing index of the student's overall ability to communicate in English.

Experimental Proficiency Tests

Several experimental proficiency tests capitalize on the concept of reduced redundancy testing: Examiners have found that by reducing the message content in a given passage, native speakers are still generally able to understand the communication, while nonnative speakers are less able to process it—particularly those with minimal second language skill. One rather widely reported reduced-redundancy exam is the "noise test" that Bernard Spolsky and associates have developed. A form of this consists of taped, dictated sentences to which electronic noise is added, which tends to obscure some of the message, particularly inflectional endings. Another such test is "gapped listening," a taped lecture or narrative with one-second deletions from the message about every five seconds. A third, called the "blur test," features a message that is visually impaired, like the sixth or eighth carbon copy of a typed manuscript. (Bowen's grammar test—the IGT—is also based on the principle of reduced redundancy.)

David Harris's Memory Span test is based on a similar premise to that of the dictation, namely that second language learners will have fewer linguistic "hooks" to hang a message on. It consists of sixteen dictated sentences, ranging in length from eight words at the beginning to twenty words at the end.

Gari Browning (1974) and others (Robert C. Weissberg [1971], Jesse J. Villareal [1969]) have experimented with a test requiring students to judge between short native and nonnative English language statements. And Alan Davies has tried out a test that can evaluate either reading comprehension or reading speed. This Editing Test consists of a prose passage to which irrelevant words are added in random order—but never two adjacent to each other. Students must comprehend the message in order to delete the superfluous lexical items.

Classroom Proficiency Tests

There are several ways to test general English language proficiency in the classroom. One way is to administer a battery of different language tests, such as one testing reading, another writing, another speaking, etc. Some have suggested that a good listening test comes as close as any specific skills test to measuring general competence in English. But the two most widely accepted general proficiency tests are cloze and dictation.

Cloze Tests. Based on the reduced-redundancy principle, cloze tests are rather simple to prepare and score. The cloze consists of a prose passage from which words are deleted. The deletion ratio ranges from one in five to one in ten, with one in seven being the norm. "Selected-deletion" of specific lexical items enables us to test vocabulary or grammar. Deleting function words, for example, produces a test that correlates well with grammar exams. For a test of general proficiency, delete a fixed ratio of words, such as every seventh word; occasional adjustments can be made to avoid items already tested.

Select a passage at the appropriate level of difficulty: that is, slightly below the level students are at. Do not use passages with many proper names, dates, figures and the like. Leave at least the first and last sentence intact. If the passage is too long, edit out part of it, and if necessary construct an introductory sentence that helps put the passage in perspective; the segment used should be unified and should make sense by itself. If the cloze test is being used by itself as a measure of proficiency, it would be good to have close to 50 blanks. Instructions should have students read over the entire passage before filling in any blanks, and students need to be told that inserting more than one word in a blank will result in an error. Using the exact words deleted as an answer key works pretty well; but if the teacher is a native speaker of English she can allow acceptable alternatives. If the test is quite important, the teacher can administer it ahead of time to native speakers. Any word that two or more native speakers write in constitutes an acceptable answer.

Dictation Tests. Like the cloze passage, the dictation passage should be unified and make sense on its own. Again, if the dictation is taken from a longer passage, it may be necessary to compose an introductory sentence. Next, decide where to pause for students to write. This must be decided in advance—ideally at normal structural divisions within the sentence. One key to the success of the dictation as a test of general proficiency is to read the passage in sufficiently large chunks—normally not fewer than five words and seldom over nine words at one time. Mark the passage with a slash (/) so you will know where to pause. Instructions should indicate that the passage will be read once at normal speed, to provide an overview of content; students are not to write at this time. Then it will be read a second time at near normal speed, but this time with pauses for students to write down what they have heard. (All students should be given adequate time to write down what has been dictated.) No phrases will be repeated. However, an optional third reading at normal speed can be given (without pauses). It is customary to write on the blackboard (or test paper) the spelling of a difficult word or two that are central to the passage; and paragraphing as well as punctuation is sometimes given to the students. The most widely accepted correction system is to take off one point for every error regardless of difficulty (except for repeated misspellings of the same word). To score a dictation, one can allocate an arbitrary number of points to it (say, 100). If there are more errors on some papers than the points allocated, one can divide the number of errors by two (or even three) and subtract this number from the total points assigned to the dictation.

In conclusion, prepare tests on the appropriate level of difficulty, with careful instructions and examples, allowing adequate time and in every way assuring positive affect. Let the test be a learning experience, and never use it as a penalty.

After the test has been administered and corrected, take time to evaluate it. The chapter that follows explains how to evaluate your language exam.

DISCUSSION

1. We can expect four benefits from testing: a measure of the success of student learning, information on student morale and anxiety levels, opportunity for intensive learning in review for the test, and diagnostic tips as feedback to the teacher. Align these in order of importance and explain your decisions.

2. Describe the subcategories that tests can be divided into: proficiency-achievement-aptitude, subjective-objective item types, receptive-productive participation, spoken-written modality.

3. Explain norm-referenced versus criterion-referenced tests, integrative versus discrete point tests.

4. Name and describe three ways students can be tested informally.

5. How can the teacher, using tests, provide opportunities for success in the language class?

6. What level of sophistication should the vocabulary and grammar aim at in a test of listening comprehension?

7. How can one be sure that a reading test is not also a writing test?

8. Give an example of a test item with cultural bias.

9. Why is there a tendency for the test maker to write the correct answer to a multiple choice item longer than the distractors?

10. Give an example of a reduced-redundancy exam.

CHAPTER FIFTEEN

EVALUATING TESTS

Every test we administer deserves some kind of evaluation, even if it is rather subjective and intuitive. This includes tests that we don't intend to use again as well as important exams that can be revised and readministered to another group. The reason for this is probably obvious: to improve the quality of our tests by such means as simplifying and clarifying instructions or eliminating items that are unclear or ambiguous. In discussing evaluation procedures, we will look first at informal evaluation and then at some simple statistical procedures.

INFORMAL EVALUATION

Ideally, teachers should maintain a kind of checklist or log on exams that they administer. Even if the actual test is not retained, one can note the nature of the test, its length, time allocated for it, the class it was used in, the date, and scope (quiz, midterm, etc.). Evaluation data might include: (1) the length of time it took to prepare the test, (2) how long it took to score each test, (3) whether or not most students were able to complete it in the time provided, (4) whether or not the instructions and questions were clear, (5) whether or not there was an adequate match of classwork and evaluation. Anecdotal information from students is particularly useful in evaluating items 4 and 5. (6) Reactions to individual questions should be noted so that defective items can be revised or discarded.

Assuming that language and not culture is being evaluated, one should constantly be on the lookout for biased items. This might be a reading selection that is familiar to one segment of the class but not to another (one with a science orientation, for instance). It might be vocabulary items more familiar to boys than to girls (such as "carburetor" or "punt formation"). It could be a sentence that relies on a cultural item (TV personality, geographical location, or custom) for its meaning. Such an item would favor students who had lived in the English-speaking country for quite some time. If teaching a heterogeneous group of ESL students, one should be aware even of "transparent" lexical items that are familiar as cognates to one segment of the class.

A final concern is that of test affect, notably test anxiety. While psychologists note that anxiety can be "facilitating" as well as "debilitating," it is advisable to avoid tests that are excessively stressful. Such tests do not provide the best measurement of language ability, particularly of anxiety-prone individuals.

What can cause a test to create heightened anxiety? Conditions surrounding the test can have an effect: faulty instructions or test directions that are changed while the test is in progress, lack of time to complete the test, or obvious cheating by other students. The actual test is obviously another factor: unfamiliar test formats, questions on material not covered by the teacher, questions too difficult for the level being evaluated. In addition, some forms of questions are far more anxiety producing than others (for example, more than one study has shown cloze tests to be more anxiety producing than oral interviews). It would be useful for the teacher-examiner to determine ahead of time which test formats are particularly distressing to her students. Such information can be solicited from students informally, or a ready-made questionnaire can be administered.[1]

SIMPLE STATISTICAL EVALUATION

While forbidding to some teachers, certain simple statistical calculations are extremely useful, not only in applied research but also in evaluating the strengths and weaknesses of our tests. They contribute a clear, efficient way to inform ourselves about our tests, as well as an international "language" for sharing information about them with others. Finding the average helps us determine whether or not a given test is at about the right level of difficulty; calculating the "spread" shows whether it differentiates adequately between strong and weak students. Validity tells us whether we are actually measuring what we had hoped to measure; and reliability indicates how

[1] The Jones-Madsen Test Affect Questionnaire includes 10 items: (1) How well do you think you did on this test? (2) How pleasant was the experience of taking this test? (3) How difficult did you find the test? (4) How fair do you think this test was? (5) How well did this test correspond with what you have been doing in class? (6) How well do you think the test reflects your knowledge of English? (7) How frustrating did you find the test? (8) Some tests are very reliable in that you would get the same score by taking it a number of times, whereas others are affected more by chance factors. How reliable do you think this test is? (9) Some tests are better than others in differentiating between those who really have a skill and those who don't. Others are affected by extraneous factors such as cleverness in taking tests or general ability or intelligence. To what extent do you think this test discriminates well in this regard? (10) How well do you personally like this test? (This is designed to be administered in the student's native language with a 5- to 10-point Likert scale. Items 1, 2, 3, 7, and 10 measure frustration more directly than do the others.)

consistent the evaluation is (an exam, incidentally, must be reliable in order to be truly valid, but reliability does not guarantee validity). Calculations can be carried out with only a knowledge of basic math, but a simple calculator is helpful in eliminating errors and speeding up the computations.

Finding the Average

There are several ways of describing test results. For example, one *could* list all the scores in a given class. A more efficient way is to let a single score represent the entire collection (or *distribution*) of scores. We do so of course by calculating the average (or *mean*). In explaining this and other procedures, we will use a few conventional symbols that enable us to summarize the steps quite succinctly.

To calculate the mean, we first sum $[\Sigma]$ each score $[X]$ in the class. Then we divide this total by the number of persons $[N]$ for whom we have test scores. Thus the mean $[M] = \Sigma X/N$. If the scores for our class were 80, 70, 60, 50, and 40, we would sum these ($\Sigma X = 300$) and divide by the total number of scores ($N = 5$). In other words, $\Sigma X/N = 300/5 = 60$.

As most are aware, to convert any score (including the mean or average to a percentage), we simply divide the score (X) by the total points possible (T) on the exam (% $= X/T$). Thus to convert a score of 15 on a 20-item test to a percent, we divide 15 by 20: % $= 15/20 = .75$; our result is .75, or in other words 75%.

In evaluating our test, we note that a high mean (such as 85% or 90%, for example) indicates our test was quite easy, possibly too easy for our students. A very low mean (such as 30% or 40%) quite obviously indicates the test was very difficult.[2] In short, the class mean can help us evaluate the suitability of our test. Naturally, it can also reflect the adequacy of our instruction and serve as a reference point for evaluating the performance of individual students. The mean can also be used to compare two groups of students and to measure progress by a given class.

A second measure of central tendency is the *median*. This is the "middle score" in a distribution of class scores. It has two special applications: (1) It gives a more representative measure of a class when there are a few very high or very low scores. (The class *mean* or average tends to be distorted by extreme high or low scores.) (2) It can be determined very quickly without the aid of a calculator or adding machine.

To find the median, simply arrange test scores in order from high to low; then identify the middle score. Using our first set of scores above (80, 70, 60, 50, 40), we can determine by inspection that the median is 60. This happens to coincide with the mean, but generally they are not quite the same. To calculate the median for a larger set of figures, use this procedure: Add 1 to

---

[2]A score close to 30% on a multiple choice test may result simply from students' guessing at items; the test is too hard. Another way of viewing these results is that a high average indicates most students have mastered the material, whereas a low average indicates they haven't learned it.

the total number of test papers, and divide this figure by 2. In other words, $Mdn = [(N + 1)/2]$th score. For a class of 19 students, one would find the $(19 + 1)/2 = 20/2 = $ 10th score (counting either from the bottom or the top of the row of scores).[3]

Measuring the Amount of "Spread"

We have seen that one way of describing and evaluating tests is to calculate a measure of central tendency such as a mean or median. A second procedure is to describe the amount of "spread" or variability that is found in a set of scores. Variability, like central tendency, can be represented by a single figure. Generally a good test produces a fairly wide spread of scores. As might be anticipated, there are a couple of exceptions: (1) Very little spread can be expected if the students are about equal in ability. (2) And often there is little spread even in a class with varying levels of ability if the test is very easy or extremely difficult. In the first instance, everyone has mastered the point(s) being tested, and so all are getting (similar) high scores; in the second instance, virtually no one understands the material being presented, with the result that all get (similar) low scores.

But if real differences exist among one's students and the test checks material studied but not yet fully mastered by everyone, there should be a fairly large spread of test scores. In such a situation, we can compare the ability of various tests to reflect the variability that we know exists.[4] Measures of variability can also be used to compare or contrast the relative homogeneity of two or more classes.

A rough estimate of variability can be obtained by calculating the *range*. This is obtained simply by subtracting the lowest score from the highest score $(R = X_H - X_L)$. Thus if the highest score were 84 and the lowest were 44, the range would be 40. The main problem in using the range to calculate variability is that only one or two extremely high or low scores can obscure the spread that exists among the bulk of the test papers.

The *standard deviation*, on the other hand, takes every score into consideration in representing the spread of scores. Hand calculation is somewhat beyond the scope of this brief presentation.[5] But the standard deviation is programmed into some inexpensive hand calculators, enabling

---

[3]Note that in a class with an "even" number of students (say, 12 persons), the median is a decimal: $(12 + 1)/2 = 13/2 = 6.5$. This means that the median or middle score is half way between the 6th and the 7th score. With scores such as the following, we see that the sixth score is 70 and the seventh score is 72; the median, therefore, is 71: 95, 88, 86, 86, 79, 72, 70, 69, 68, 61, 55, 50.

[4]It is not unusual, for example, to find students spread out on a grammar test but bunched together on a composition; this sometimes indicates that those evaluating the composition are simply not able to differentiate adequately among the essays.

[5]This is the raw score formula:

$$\frac{N\Sigma X^2 - (\Sigma X)^2}{\sqrt{N(N-1)}}$$

the teacher simply to enter in his or her test scores and automatically get the calculation. For those with access to a standard (mainframe) computer or a minicomputer, test scores can be entered and a basic statistical package used to generate the mean, standard deviation, and other statistics as well.

The calculator or computer automatically determines how far each score deviates from the mean, squares each deviation from the mean, averages these squared figures, and then calculates the square root of this average deviation amount. The result (the standard deviation) is a very stable statistic, which is not unduly affected by extreme high or low scores.

Assuming there is a marked difference in the ability of our students and that our test aims at identifying this spread of ability, a "large" standard deviation (see discussion below) shows our test reflects that spread. Given the circumstances we have just described, a "small" deviation would indicate our test was not differentiating among students adequately well. Note that the size of the standard deviation does *not* tell us anything about the ability level of those evaluated—simply the amount of spread in their scores.

When comparing standard deviations of various examinations or subtests, it is helpful to have each test converted to a percentage. While there are not absolute criteria, a standard deviation of 10 or 15 is fairly typical of many ESL tests based on 100 points. A standard deviation on a 100-point test of 3.79, for example, would usually be considered rather small unless the class was quite homogeneous; a standard deviation of 19.16 on a 100-point test would usually be considered very good. But the principal use of standard deviation should be for purposes of comparison. Other factors being equal, a cloze test with a standard deviation of 8.12 would be preferred to one with a standard deviation of 5.23—assuming that both are based on the same number of points. Of course if the same test is used with two groups, our perspective is different: Group A may have a standard deviation of 12.16; Group B may have a higher mean than Group A but a standard deviation of only 6.89. This simply means that Group B is more homogeneous (in this skill area) than Group A, or that Group B is experiencing a "ceiling effect," the exam being too easy for them.

We recommend that this statistic be calculated for every important test. When you evaluate the subtests of an examination battery, the mean and standard deviation of each part and of the total should be obtained.

Determining Validity

If a test actually measures what it claims to measure, we say it is *valid*. Some tests, like an essay examination of writing skill, clearly appear to be measuring what they say they measure; this intuitive characteristic is called *face validity*. If there is a good match between the components of a speaking test, for instance, and the theoretical constructs of oral communicative competence, we can say the test has *construct validity*. *Content validity* can be determined by matching the test with the course of instruction or linguistic subskill on which it is based. *Concurrent validity* and *predictive validity* can be determined statistically by comparing student performance with a standard. Concurrent validity can be arrived at by comparing one's test with a teacher rating or with a test administered about the same time as the test in question. Similarly, predictive validity can be determined by examining the relationship between performance on one's test and subsequent class grades or end-of-term exam.

While we need to be concerned about content and face validity, our emphasis in this section will be to provide a practical way of measuring the validity (concurrent or predictive) of important tests that we prepare.

Typically this is done by administering one's own test and also a comparable ESL test in which we have a great deal of confidence (for example, the TOEFL, which is not practical for some programs due to its expense, infrequency of administration times, inconvenience of location, and delay in exam results). A Pearson correlation (Pearson product-moment correlation) is then calculated. It is important, of course, to correlate performance on one's test with performance on the same kind of test, if possible. Where this is not possible, the next best arrangement is to correlate one's ESL exam with a good general measure of ESL proficiency. As indicated above, course grades or teacher rating can be used; but these are more subjective than the test-test comparison.

Like the standard deviation, calculating the Pearson correlation is somewhat beyond the scope of this discussion.[6] And like the standard deviation, it is programmed into some inexpensive hand calculators so that teachers can simply enter their two sets of student scores and automatically get the Pearson correlation. Also, standard and minicomputers handle the calculation very simply.

When ranked data (like a teacher ranking) is used, one must use the Spearman (rank-difference) correlation formula. After grading the tests, convert the test scores to ranks and arrange in a table like this:

Student	Test Score	Test Rank	Teacher Ranking of Students	d	d²
A	86	1	2	1	1
B	75	2	1	1	1
C	70	3.5	4	.5	.25
D	70	3.5	3	.5	.25
E	68	5	7	2	4
F	60	6	6	0	0
G	50	7	5	2	4

$$\Sigma d^2 = 10.5$$

[6]This is the Pearson correlation formula:

$$\frac{N\Sigma XY - (\Sigma X)(\Sigma Y)}{\sqrt{[N\Sigma X^2 - (\Sigma X)^2][N\Sigma Y^2 - (\Sigma Y)^2]}}$$

Notice how tied scores are handled. In this case, rankings 3 and 4 are tied; simply add these ranks together ($3 + 4 = 7$) and divide by the number of ranks that are tied (here, 2); 7 divided by 2 is 3.5—the rank we assign to the tied test scores. In a parallel column we list the teacher ranking of each student. Then we find the difference between each pair of ranks and put this difference under the "d" column. In the last column we put the square of each difference (the difference multiplied by itself). Finally we get the sum of these squared differences (here, 10.5). This figure is used in the numerator of the formula that follows, and the number of pairs (here, 7) is used in the denominator.

The Spearman formula is

$$1 - \frac{6\,(d^2)}{N\,(N^2 - 1)}$$

Using the example above, we have

$$1 - \frac{6\,(10.5)}{7\,(49 - 1)} = 1 - \frac{63}{336} = 1 - .19 = .81$$

This Spearman correlation can be substituted for the Pearson correlation if one has no calculator or available computer for the latter calculation, but it is a little less accurate than the Pearson when correlating two sets of test scores.

The correlation of two commercial tests of the same skill (such as listening) is expected to be quite high: .85 to .95 or better. Homemade tests are expected to correlate .75 or better with comparable commercial tests, and in the high .60's or better with general proficiency tests. Correlations with teacher ranking or end-of-course grades may end up only in the .50's or .60's. These are very general guidelines. Correlations will vary depending on the range of ability of one's students. People of about the same ability will produce a relatively low correlation; people with a wide range of ability will generate a higher correlation.

The validity of one's language test can be evaluated according to the criteria outlined in the previous paragraph, provided students are reasonably heterogeneous in language skills and provided the test presents a reasonable challenge. (For example, a test of 15 vocabulary items easily memorized by all may not constitute a "valid" assessment of general vocabulary mastery.) Correlations also enable one to compare the validity of various locally prepared grammar tests, for instance, by correlating each one with a standardized grammar test in which we have confidence.

When interpreting correlation results, keep in mind that the correlation coefficient is not a percentage; instead, it is a measure of the tendency for two variables (two sets of *test scores*, in this discussion) to vary together. When persons scoring high on one test tend to score high on another, and persons scoring low on the first score low on the second measure, we have a high correlation.

Note that a perfect correlation is 1.00 (a situation that virtually never occurs in any testing situation), and a 0.00 represents the absence of a correlation. Certain data can even generate negative correlations (age, perhaps, when correlated with language achievement); here a high negative correlation (e.g., a $-.89$) is as important as a high positive correlation is in our usual validation calculations.

One final matter for teachers to consider when interpreting correlations: Squaring our correlation result shows how much of the variance or spread in the main test (which we're using as our criterion measure) is accounted for by our "home-made" test.

Let's illustrate this principle: The students in your class all took a commercial listening test (the Michigan Test of Aural Comprehension—the MTAC) at the beginning of your course. You are certain that the 35-point spread in scores is attributable to differences in students' language ability, since you have confidence in the exam and those administering it. A week later, you administered your own listening test. But you wonder whether its spread of scores might be due in part to factors other than language ability—matters such as IQ, defective tape, cultural bias, cheating, etc. The correlation coefficient between the two tests turns out to be .57; and squaring this (multiplying .57 × .57) gives you .32. Now you know that your worries are well founded. Your test accounts for only about a third of the variance or spread in the MTAC scores—variance that you feel represents actual difference in language proficiency. Fortunately, however, your *revised* listening test correlates .82 with the MTAC. Squaring .82 gives you .67; and this indicates that two-thirds of the variance in their MTAC scores (or "true" spread) can now be accounted for by your test—a very sizable proportion of the variance, indeed.

In short, squaring your correlation is an important additional way to check your test's validity: that is, whether it is in fact measuring what it purports to measure.

Checking Reliability

Reliability is a measure of test consistency, that is, how likely we are to get the same result if an identical test were administered to the same group of students on another occasion. There are several possible ways to check the reliability of a test, some more efficient than others. One logical approach is simply to give the same test a second time and then correlate the two sets of scores. But this wastes a lot of class time and annoys students. In addition, it is flawed by practice effect if the second test is given soon after the first one; or marred by student gains if given much later on (practice effect and learning vary considerably from student to student). Another option is to develop a second form of the same test, then administer these two in close succession and correlate the results. But it is difficult and time consuming for the teacher to develop a good alternate form; and expenditure of class time is again a problem. A slightly indirect but acceptable alternative for tests containing separate items (like a multiple choice test, completion exam, or cloze) involves splitting the test into two parts and correlating one part with the other. The typical way this is done is to find the score for the odd-numbered items (1, 3, 5, etc.) and then find the score for the even-numbered items (2, 4, 6, etc.). Thus two scores are generated for each student, and these are correlated—preferably with the Pearson correlation formula. The result is called a *split-half* reliability coefficient.

Directly related to the size of the reliability coefficient is the number of items on the test. Using the split-half formula, we in effect reduce the number of items by 50 percent. The Spearman-Brown correction formula compensates for this. The correction $= 2 (r)/1 + r$, where r stands for "correlation." If our split-half correlation were .60, we would adjust this as follows: $2(.60)/1 + .60 = 1.20/1.60 = .75$; and our adjusted correlation would be .75.

Reliability coefficients are expected to be higher than the validity figures mentioned earlier. Thus full-length commercial tests would be about .90 or better. Full-length teacher-made tests would hopefully reach the .80's. Shorter (say, half-period) teacher-made tests might only make the .70's. As with validity figures, these are guidelines only.[7]

Determining Efficiency

Still another way of evaluating our tests is to determine their efficiency. No statistical procedures are suggested, but it would be advisable to maintain a record of the time needed to construct the exam, score it, and analyze it. If the affect, validity, and reliability of two exams are roughly the same, it would be logical to opt for that which requires the least time to prepare, administer, and score.

Performing an Item Analysis

Because so much preparation time is needed for multiple choice and completion tests, it is logical to evaluate each item on the test so that good ones can be used again, bad ones discarded and weak items repaired. Moreover, items used on subsequent tests can be arranged in order of difficulty, thus encouraging students as they begin the test and assuring that all will have an opportunity to answer questions they are most likely to know on a speeded test. Item analysis can enhance not only our tests' validity but also their affect.

[7] An approximation of reliability can be obtained for tests like dictations and essays, which are not divisible into separate items. Administer a second dictation of approximately the same length and difficulty. Then correlate the results of these two "tests." This is your estimated reliability coefficient.

An item analysis looks at three things: (1) the difficulty of each item, (2) the ability of each item to discriminate between students of varying ability levels, and (3) the attractiveness of the distractors in multiple choice questions.

CALCULATING ITEM DIFFICULTY. With a simple calculator, it would not take much time to determine the percentage of the class that got each item on the test correct. But to facilitate a complete item analysis for an important test follow this procedure: (1) Correct all of the exams in the class. (2) Arrange them in sequence from high to low. (3) Put the papers in three stacks: the highs in one pile, the lows in another; set the middle group of papers to one side. (4) Then tabulate the responses to each item on a form like the one that follows, the highs in column one and the lows in column two.

We will illustrate how this is to be done. Assume you had test papers from several classes totaling 45 students. This would result in 15 high-group papers and 15 low-group papers (a total of 30); the 15 mid-group papers would be set aside. For test item #9, with choice "C" the correct answer, the tabulation might look like this:

Item 9		High Group	Low Group
	A	///	////
	B		
	©	// // /	// /
	D	/	///
(no answer)	(X)		//

To compute the item difficulty (percentage getting it right), add the number in the high group getting the question right to the number in the low group getting it right and divide by the total students in the sample (high plus low groups):

$$\frac{\text{High correct} + \text{Low correct}}{\text{Total number in sample}} = \frac{H_c + L_c}{N}$$

For our sample this is

$$\frac{11 + 6}{30} = \frac{17}{30} = .57$$

or 57%.

Guidelines on evaluating item difficulty suggest that if over 90% get an item right, it is too easy; and if fewer than 30% get it right it is too difficult. Since 57% got item 9 correct, it is within the range of acceptable difficulty. Items outside this range would be revised or discarded. Those retained would be arranged in order of difficulty with the easier items placed at the beginning of the exam.

CALCULATING ITEM DISCRIMINATION. As we have noted, the discrimination figure is a measure of how well the item differentiates between students in the high group and those in the low group. To calculate discrimination, subtract the number in the low group getting the item right from the number in the high group getting it right, and divide by the total number of papers in the sample (high plus low tests):

$$\frac{\text{High correct} - \text{Low correct}}{\text{Total number in sample}} = \frac{H_c - L_c}{N}$$

To illustrate the procedure, we can use our original tabulation for item number 9: Subtract the 6 in the low group getting the question right from the 11 in the high group getting it right, and divide by 30, the total number in the sample:

$$\frac{11 - 6}{30} = \frac{5}{30} = .17$$

It is generally felt that a discrimination figure of .10 or lower is unacceptable, while one of .15 or higher is acceptable. Discrimination between .10 and .15 is marginal or questionable. Our Item 9 discrimination factor of .17 is therefore acceptable (figures higher than this are still better).

Keep in mind that level of difficulty and discrimination can be calculated for tests such as dictations and essays if points are allocated rather than a letter grade. An example will illustrate this. Suppose one had 30 test papers (10 highs and 10 lows) with a dictation worth 25 points. Add up all the points earned by the high group (for example, 200); subtract the points earned by the low group (say, 100). Divide this by 500 (25 points times the 20 papers in the sample). The result is .20, an acceptable discrimination figure.

One caution: Acceptable discrimination is often not achieved for rather easy and rather difficult questions (those approaching 90% correct or 30% correct); for these items, one should not adhere too rigidly to the discrimination guidelines. And as mentioned earlier in this chapter, there will not be much discrimination in a small class of students with about the same level of language proficiency; thus for homogeneously grouped students, it would not be advisable to adhere too closely to the discrimination guidelines.

EVALUATING DISTRACTORS. Very obvious or illogical distractors can also contribute to weak discrimination. No guidelines have been established to indicate the minimum number of choices to expect for each distractor, but we tend to expect one or two at least in a sample of 25 or more papers. Using this rule of thumb, we find that distractor "B" in sample Item 9 is not functioning as might be expected: No one selected this response. We would inspect the wording of this choice to see if a more suitable option could be written.

As with discrimination evaluation, however, do not follow this rule of thumb too rigidly when examining very easy test questions. Obviously when most low students as well as high students are answering an item correctly, there aren't many left to select the distractors. There are at least three reasons for students' passing over some of our distractors: (1) they have virtually all mastered the language point being tested; (2) we are using an obvious pair (*a* and *the* or *few* and *a few*); no other options are plausible; (3) our distractors are completely illogical.

One or two additional suggestions need to be made in connection with conducting an item analysis. If one's class is very small (say under 10 or 12 students), it may be unwise to divide the group into three, unless the students are quite heterogeneous as far as English language proficiency is concerned. Level of difficulty and distractor evaluation could be calculated for the entire group. If looking at discrimination seems feasible because of the varied proficiency in the class, one might select high and low groups of four apiece from a class of ten students in order to provide more stable results. But even with this precaution, the item analysis of such a small group should be interpreted cautiously and accepted only tentatively.

Using a Guessing Correction

When students take a speeded objective test that doesn't permit most students to complete all items, it is not unusual for many to take a moment at the end to randomly assign an answer to unfinished questions in the hope of improving their score. On a four-option 100-item test, a person with 40 unanswered questions (an extreme case to be sure) would hope to pick up 10 points with his chance responses.

To guard against this, the teacher can employ a simple guessing correction. This consists of the number of right answers minus the number of wrong answers—divided by the options minus one. For the four-item example above, this would be: Correction $= R - (W/3)$. Assuming the student did get 10 right and 30 wrong through his guessing, the result would be $10 - (30/3) = 10 - 10 = 0$. Thus the student would gain nothing by guessing. The formula for three-option questions would be $R - (W/2)$, and the formula for true/false items would be $R - (W/1) = R - W$.

There is no need to apply this formula to unspeeded tests which provide time for most students to attempt all questions.

Taking the time to evaluate one's tests pays good dividends both in improved evaluation and increased student morale. Discarding weak items demonstrates one's sense of fair play as well as his or her concern for creating the best possible evaluation instrument.

DISCUSSION

1. How can test anxiety be minimized in a test? (Give 4 ways.)

2. What do the average class score and the spread of scores indicate about a test?

3. What is test validity? Reliability?

4. What is the difference between mean and median? Which is easier to determine? Why? What can they indicate if very high or very low?

5. What does the standard deviation tell about a set of test scores that the range does not? What is a typical, satisfactory standard deviation on a test that has (or has been converted to) 100 points?

6. What is a "ceiling effect" on a test and what does it indicate?

7. Explain four different concepts of validity.

8. What is a Pearson product-moment correlation? How does it differ from a Spearman (rank-difference) correlation?

9. Reliability can be calculated by test-retest, Form A-Form B, split half. Tell how these differ from each other.

10. What three purposes does an item analysis serve?

REFERENCES

Ahn, Franz. *Ahn-Oehlschaeger's Pronouncing Method of the German Language*. New York: E. Steiger, 1880.

Ahn, Franz. *A New, Practical and Easy Method of Learning the German Language*. 3rd ed. St. Louis, MO: E. Herder, 1897.

Allen, Harold B., and Russell N. Campbell, eds. *Teaching English as a Second Language*. 2nd ed. New York: McGraw-Hill, 1972.

Allington, Richard L. "Reading, Meaning, and the Bilingual Student: Some Suggestions," in Richard L. Light and Alice H. Osman, eds. *Collected Papers in TESL and BE: Themes, Practices, Viewpoints*. New York: New York State English to Speakers of Other Languages and Bilingual Educators Association (1978), 245–248.

Allwright, Dick. "Classroom Centered Research on Language Teaching and Learning: A Brief Historical Overview," *TESOL Quarterly* 16:4 (1983), 191–204.

Anthony, Edward M. "Approach, Method and Technique," *English Language Teaching* 17:2 (1963), 63–67.

Arapoff, Nancy. *Writing through Understanding*. New York: Holt, Rinehart and Winston, 1970.

Arapoff, Nancy. "Writing: A Thinking Process," in *The Art of TESOL: Selected Articles from the English Teaching Forum* Part 2. Washington, D.C.: English Teaching Forum, 1975, 233–237.

Arthur, Bradford. *Teaching English to Speakers of English*. New York: Harcourt, Brace, Jovanovich, 1973.

Arthur, Bradford. "Short-Term Changes in EFL Composition Skills," in Carlos A. Yorio, Kyle Perkins, and Jacquelyn Schachter, eds. *On TESOL '79*. Washington, D.C.: TESOL (1979), 330–342.

Asher, James J. *Learning Another Language through Actions: The Complete Teacher's Guidebook*. Los Gatos, CA: Sky Oaks Productions, 1977. (Expanded Second Edition 1982)

Bachman, Lyle F., and Adrian S. Palmer. "The Construct Validation of Some Components of Communicative Proficiency," *TESOL Quarterly* 16:4 (1982), 449–465.

Bailey, Kathleen M. "An Introspective Analysis of an Individual's Language Learning Experience," in Stephen D. Krashen and Robin Scarcella, eds. *Research in Second Language Acquisition: Selected Papers from the Los Angeles Second Language Forum*. Rowley, MA: Newbury House, 1980, 58–65.

Bailey, Kathleen M. "Competitiveness and Anxiety in Adult Second Language Learning: Looking AT and THROUGH the Diary Studies," in Seliger and Long, 1983, 67–103.

Bailey, Nathalie, Carolyn Madden, and Stephen Krashen. "Is There a Natural Sequence in Adult Second Language Learning?" *Language Learning* 24:2 (1974), 235–243.

Bander, Robert G. *American English Rhetoric*. New York: Holt, Rinehart and Winston, 1971.

Barnard, Helen. *Advanced English Vocabulary* I, II. Rowley, MA: Newbury House, 1971.

Baugh, Albert C. *A History of the English Language*. New York: Appleton-Century, 1935.

Bazzani, Carolyn Good. "More Efficient Reading for ESL Students." Presentation at TESOL Convention, Mexico City (April, 1978).

Been, Sheila. "Reading in the Foreign Language Teaching Program," *TESOL Quarterly* 9:3 (1975), 233–242.

Bejan, Nicolae. "Scientific English as a Separate Register," *English Teaching Forum* 16:2 (1978), 41–42.

Blair, Robert W., ed. *Innovative Approaches to Language Teaching*. Rowley, MA: Newbury House, 1982.

Blatchford, Charles, ed. *Directory of Teacher Preparation Programs in TESOL and Bilingual Education 1976–1978*. Washington, D.C.: TESOL, 1977.

Bloomfield, Leonard. *Language*. New York: Henry Holt and Company, 1933.

Bolinger, Dwight. "The Theorist and the Language Teacher," *Foreign Language Annals* 2:1 (1968), 30–41.

Bolinger, Dwight. *The Phrasal Verb in English*. Cambridge, MA: Harvard University Press, 1971.

Bolinger, Dwight. *Aspects of Language*. 2nd ed. New York: Harcourt, Brace, Jovanovich, 1975. (First published in 1968)

Bourne, Lyle E., Jr., Bruce R. Ekstrand, and Roger L. Dominowski. *The Psychology of Thinking*. Englewood Cliffs, NJ: Prentice-Hall, 1971.

Bowen, J. Donald. "Linguistic Competence and Writing Conventions," in Malcolm P. Douglass, ed. *Claremont Reading Conference, Thirty-eighth Yearbook*. Claremont, CA: Claremont Graduate School, 1974, 83–93.

Bowen, J. Donald. *Patterns of English Pronunciation*. Rowley, MA: Newbury House, 1975.

Bowen, J. Donald. "An Exploratory Study on the Frequency of English Segmental Phonemes," in John F. Povey, ed. *Language Policy and Language Teaching: Essays in Honor of Clifford H. Prator*. Culver City, CA: English Language Services, 1980, 131–138.

Brengleman, Frederick H., ed. *The English Language: An Introduction for Teachers*. Englewood Cliffs, NJ: Prentice-Hall, 1970.

Brière, Eugene J. "Cross-Cultural Biases in Language Testing," in John W. Oller, Jr. and Jack C. Richards, eds. *Focus on the Learner: Pragmatic Perspectives for the Language Teacher*. Rowley, MA: Newbury House, 1973, 214–227.

Brooks, Nelson. "The Meaning of Audiolingual," *Modern Language Journal* 59:5–6 (1975), 234–240.

Brown, H. Douglas. *Principles of Language Learning and Teaching*. Englewood Cliffs, NJ: Prentice-Hall, 1980.

Brown, James I. *Efficient Reading, Revised Form A*. Lexington, MA: Heath, 1971.

Brown, Roger. *A First Language*. Cambridge, MA: Harvard University Press, 1973.

Browning, Gari L. "Testing Pronunciation Indirectly: An Experiment," MA thesis, UCLA, Los Angeles, 1974.

Buckingham, Thomas. "The Goals of Advanced Composition Instruction," *TESOL Quarterly* 13:2 (1979), 241–254.

Carpenter, Charles. *History of American Schoolbooks*. Philadelphia: University of Pennsylvania Press, 1963.

Carroll, George R. "The Battle for Better Reading," in Allen and Campbell, 1972, 178–184.

Carroll, John B. *The Study of Language: A Survey of Linguistics and Related Disciplines in America*. Cambridge, MA: Harvard University Press, 1959. (Original copyright 1953)

Carroll, John B. "The Contributions of Psychological Theory and Educational Research to the Teaching of Foreign Languages," *Modern Language Journal* 49 (1965), 273–281.

Carroll, John B. "Current Issues in Psycholinguistics and Second Language Teaching," *TESOL Quarterly* 5:2 (1971), 101–114.

Carroll, John B. "Psychometric Theory and Language Testing," in John W. Oller, Jr., ed. *Issues in Language Testing Research*. Rowley, MA: Newbury House, 1983, 80–107.

Celce-Murcia, Marianne, and Lois McIntosh, eds. *Teaching English as a Second or Foreign Language*. Rowley, MA: Newbury House, 1979.

Celce-Murcia, Marianne, and Fred Rosensweig. "Teaching Vocabulary in the ESL Classroom," in Celce-Murcia and McIntosh, 1979, 241–257.

Celce-Murcia, Marianne, and Diane Larsen-Freeman. *The Grammar Book: An ESL/EFL Teacher's Course*. Rowley, MA: Newbury House, 1983.

Chaudron, Craig. "Foreigner Talk in the Classroom—An Aid to Learning?" in Seliger and Long, 1983, 127–140.

Cherrington, Marie R. *Improving Reading Skills in College Subjects*. New York: Teachers College Press, Columbia University, 1974.

Chomsky, Carol. "Reading, Writing, and Phonology," *Harvard Educational Review* 40:2 (1970), 287–309.

Chomsky, Noam. "Linguistic Theory," in R. G. Mead, ed. *Northeast Conference on the Teaching of Foreign Languages*. Menasha, WI: George Banta, 1966, 43–49.

Chomsky, Noam. "Review of Skinner's Verbal Behavior," *Language* 35 (1959), 26–58.

Chomsky, Noam. *Syntactic Structures*. The Hague: Mouton, 1957.

Clarke, Mark A., and Sandra Silberstein. "Toward a Realization of Psycholinguistic Principles in the ESL Reading Class," in Mackay, Barkman, and Jordan, 1979, 48–65.

Cohen, Andrew, Hilary Glasman, Phyllis R. Rosenbaum-Cohen, Jonathan Ferrara, and Jonathan Fine. "Reading English for Specialized Purposes: Discourse Analysis and the Use of Student Informants," *TESOL Quarterly* 13:4 (1979), 551–564.

Cohen, Andrew D., and Carol Hosenfeld. "Some Uses of Mentalistic Data in Second Language Research," *Language Learning* 31:2 (1981), 285–313.

Coleman, Algernon. *The Teaching of Modern Foreign Languages in the United States: A Report Prepared for the Modern Language Study*. New York: Macmillan, 1929.

Comenius, John Amos. *The Orbis Pictus*. Syracuse, NY: C. W. Bardeen, 1887.

Comenius, John Amos. "The Method of Language," in John Amos Comenius, *The Great Didactic of John Amos Comenius*. Introduction by M. N. Keatinge. London: Adam and Charles Black, 1896, 355–362.

Comenius, John Amos. *The School of Infancy*. Editing and Introduction by Ernest M. Eller. Chapel Hill, NC: The University of North Carolina Press, 1956.

Comenius, John Amos. *John Amos Comenius on Education*. Introduction by Jean Piaget. New York: Teachers College Press, Columbia University, 1957. (Foreword, 1967).

Cowan, J. R. "Lexical and Syntactic Research for the Design of EFL Reading Materials," *TESOL Quarterly* 8:4 (1974), 389–399.

Cronnell, Bruce. "Spelling English as a Second Language," in Celce-Murcia and McIntosh, 1979, 202–214.

Cubberley, Ellwood P. *The History of Education*, Cambridge, MA: Houghton Mifflin, 1948.

Cummings, Thomas. *How to Learn a Foreign Language*. Privately published, 1916.

Curran, Charles A. *Counseling Learning: A Whole-Person Model for Education*. New York: Grune & Stratton, 1972.

Curran, Charles A. *Counseling Learning in Second Languages*. Apple River, IL: Apple River Press, 1976.

Cuyer, Andre. "The Saint-Cloud Method: What It Can and Cannot Achieve," *English Language Teaching* 27 (1972), 19–24.

Dacanay, Fe R. *Techniques and Procedures in Second Language Teaching*. J. Donald Bowen, ed. Quezon City, PI: Alemar-Phoenix, 1963.

Dale, Edgar, and Jeanne S. Chall. "A Formula for Predicting Readability," *Educational Research Bulletin* xxvii (January 21, 1948 and February 17, 1948), 11–20, 37–54.

Danielson, Dorothy, and Rebecca Hayden. *Using English: Your Second Language*. Englewood Cliffs, NJ: Prentice-Hall, 1973.

Darian, Steven G. *English as a Foreign Language: History, Development and Methods of Teaching*. Norman, OK: University of Oklahoma Press, 1972.

Deighton, Lee C. *Vocabulary Development in the Classroom*. New York: Teachers College Press, Columbia University, 1974.

Diller, Karl C. *The Language Teaching Controversy*. Rowley, MA: Newbury House, 1978.

Dolch, Edward W. "A Basic Sight Vocabulary," *Elementary School Journal* 36 (1936), 456–460.

Doyle, Henry Grattan. "George Ticknor," *Modern Language Journal* 22:1 (1937), 3–18.

Dubin, Fraida, and Elite Olshtain. *Facilitating Language Learning: A Guidebook for the ESL/EFL Teacher*. New York: McGraw-Hill, 1977.

Dulay, Heidi, and Marina Burt. "Natural Sequences in Child Second Language Acquisition," *Language Learning* 24:1 (1974), 37–53.

Dykstra, Gerald. "Toward Interactive Modes in Guided Composition," *TESL Reporter* 10:3 (Spring 1977), 1–4, 18–19.

Eby, Frederick, and Charles Flinn Arrowood. *The History and Philosophy of Education Ancient and Medieval*. New York: Prentice-Hall, 1940.

Eisenberg, Anne. *Reading Technical Books*. Englewood Cliffs, NJ: Prentice-Hall, 1978.

Elkins, Robert J., Theodore B. Kalivoda, and Genelle Morain. "Fusion of the Four Skills: A Technique for Facilitating Communicative Teaching," *Modern Language Journal* 56:6 (1972), 426–429.

Ellis, Henry C. *Fundamentals of Human Learning, Memory, and Cognition*. 2nd ed. Dubuque, IA: Brown, 1978.

Erasmus, Desiderius. *The Colloquies of Erasmus*. Craig R. Thompson, trans. Chicago, IL: The University of Chicago Press, 1965.

Erasmus, Desiderius. *Collected Works of Erasmus*. Vol. 23, 24: *Literary and Educational Writings*, Craig R. Thompson, ed. Toronto: University of Toronto Press, 1978.

Erasmus, Desiderius. "On the Method of Study" ("De ratione studii ac legendi interpretandique auctores liber"), Brian McGregor, trans., in Desiderius Erasmus, *Collected Works of Erasmus*. Vol. 24: *Literary and Educational Writings*, Craig R. Thompson, ed. Toronto: University of Toronto Press, 1978, 661–691.

Eskey, David E. "A New Technique for the Teaching of Reading to Advanced Students," *TESOL Quarterly* 4:4 (1970), 315–321.

Eskey, David E. "Advanced Reading: The Structural Problem," in *The Art of TESOL: Selected Articles from the English Teaching Forum* Part 2. Washington, D.C.: English Teaching Forum, 1975, 210–215.

Fadely, J. L., and V. N. Hosler. *Case Studies in Left and Right Hemispheric Functioning*. Springfield, IL: Thomas, 1983.

Fanselow, John F. "Beyond Rashomon—Conceptualizing and Describing the Teaching Act," *TESOL Quarterly* 11:1 (1977), 17–39.

Farhady, Hossein. "Rationalization, Development and Validation of Functional Testing," presentation at TESOL Convention, San Francisco (March, 1980).

Farhady, Hossein. "The Disjunctive Fallacy between Discrete-Point and Integrative Tests," in John W. Oller, Jr., ed. *Issues in Language Testing Research*. Rowley, MA: Newbury House, 1983, 311–322.

Flanders, Ned A. *Interaction Analysis in the Classroom: A Manual for Observers*. Ann Arbor, MI: The University of Michigan Press, 1960.

Freed, Barbara F. "Talking to Foreigners Versus Talking to Children: Similarities and Differences," in R. C. Scarcella and Stephen D. Krashen, eds. *Research in Second Language Acquisition*. Rowley, MA: Newbury House, 1980, 17–19.

Fries, Charles Carpenter. *Teaching and Learning English as a Foreign Language*. Ann Arbor, MI: The University of Michigan Press, 1945.

Fries, Charles Carpenter. "The Chicago Investigation of Second Language Teaching," *Language Learning* 2:3 (1949), 89–99.

Fries, Charles Carpenter. *Linguistics and Reading*. New York: Holt, Rinehart and Winston, 1963.

Fry, Edward Bernard. *Teaching Faster Reading: A Manual*. Cambridge, MA: The University Press, 1963.

Fry, Edward Bernard. *Reading Drills for Speed and Comprehension*. Providence, RI: Jamestown, 1975.

Furukawa, James M. "Chunking Method of Determining Size of Step in Programmed Instruction," *Journal of Educational Psychology* 61:3 (1970), 247–254.

Gage, N. L. *The Scientific Basis of the Art of Teaching*. New York: Teachers College Press, Columbia University, 1978.

Gaies, Stephen J. "The Nature of Linguistic Input in Formal Second Language Learning: Linguistic and Communicative Strategies in ESL Teachers' Classroom Language," in H. Douglas Brown, Carlos Yorio, and Ruth Crymes, eds. *On TESOL '77*, Washington, D.C.: TESOL (1977), 204–212.

Gaies, Stephen J. "Linguistic Input in Formal Second Language Learning: The Issues of Syntactic Gradation and Readability in ESL Materials," *TESOL Quarterly* 13:1 (1979), 41–50.

Gaies, Stephen J. "The Investigation of Language Classroom Processes," *TESOL Quarterly* 17:2 (1983), 205–217.

Galyean, Beverly. "Humanistic Education: A Mosaic Just Begun," in Gilbert A. Jarvis, ed. *An Integrative Approach to Foreign Language Teaching: Choosing among the Options*. ACTFL Foreign Language Education Series 8, 1976a, 201–403.

Galyean, Beverly. *Language from Within: A Handbook of Teaching Strategies for Personal Growth and Self Reflection in the Language Classes*. Santa Barbara, CA: Confluent Education Development and Research Center, 1976b.

Galyean, Beverly. "A Confluent Design for Language Teaching," in Blair, 1982, 176–188.

Gardner, R. C. "Social Psychological Aspects of Second Language Acquisition," in Howard Giles and Robert N. St Clair, eds. *Language and Social Psychology*, Oxford: Basil Blackwell Publishers, Ltd., 1979, 193–220.

Gardner, Robert C., and Wallace E. Lambert. "Motivational Variables in Second Language Acquisition," *Canadian Journal of Psychology* 13 (1959), 266–272.

Gardner, Robert C., and Wallace E. Lambert. *Attitudes and Motivation in Second Language Learning*. Rowley, MA: Newbury House, 1972.

Gardner, R. C., L. Gliksman, and P. C. Smyth. "Attitudes and Behavior in Second Language Acquisition: A Social Psychological Interpretation," *Canadian Psychological Review* 19 (1978), 173–186.

Gary, Judith Olmstead. "Delayed Oral Practice in Initial Stages of Second Language Learning," in M. K. Burt and H. C. Dulay, eds. *New Directions in Second Language Teaching, Learning and Bilingual Education*. Washington, D.C.: TESOL, 1975, 89–95.

Gary, Judith Olmstead. "Caution: Talking May Be Dangerous to Your Linguistic Health," *International Review of Applied Linguistics* 19 (1981), 1–14.

Gaskill, William H. "The Teaching of Intermediate Reading in the ESL Classroom," in Celce-Murcia and McIntosh, 1979, 144–154.

Gattegno, Caleb. *Teaching Foreign Languages in Schools: The Silent Way*. 2nd ed. New York: Educational Solutions, 1972.

Gattegno, Caleb. *The Common Sense of Teaching Foreign Languages*. New York: Educational Solutions, 1976.

Geddes, James. "The Old and the New," *French Review* 7:1 (1933), 26–38.

Genesee, Fred. "Acquisition of Reading Skills in Immersion Programs," *Foreign Language Annals* 12:1 (1979), 71–77.

Genesee, Fred. "Experimental Neuropsychological Research on Second Language Processing," *TESOL Quarterly* 16:3 (1982), 315–322.

Genesee, F., P. Rogers, and N. Holobow. "The Social Psychology of Second Language Learning: Another Point of View," *Language Learning* 33:2 (1983), 209–224.

Gilbert, Doris Wilcox. *Breaking the Reading Barrier*. Englewood Cliffs, NJ: Prentice-Hall, 1959.

Giroux, James A., and Glenn R. Williston. *Comprehension Skills Series* (with cassettes). Providence, RI: Jamestown, 1974.

Goble, Frank G. *The Third Force: The Psychology of Abraham Maslow*. New York: Grossman, 1970.

Goldstein, Kenneth M., and Sheldon Blackman. *Cognitive Style: Five Approaches and Relevant Research*. New York: Wiley, 1978.

Goodman, Kenneth S. "Reading: A Psycholinguistic Guessing Game," in Harry Singer and Robert B. Ruddell, eds. *Theoretical Models and Processes of Reading*. Newark, DE: International Reading Association, 1970.

Gorman, Thomas P. "Research on the Teaching of Writing," *UCLA Workpapers in English as a Second Language* 9 (1975), 75–82.

Gorman, Thomas P. "Teaching Reading at the Advanced Level," in Celce-Murcia and McIntosh, 1979, 154–161.

Gouin, François. *The Art of Teaching and Studying Languages*. Howard Swan and Victor Betis, trans. 5th ed. London: G. Philip & Son, 1896.

Graham, C. R. "Beyond Integrative Motivation: The Development and Influence of Assimilative Motivation," in P. Larson and E. Judd, eds. *On TESOL '84*. Washington, D.C.: TESOL, 1985.

Griffin, Suzanne, and John Dennis. *Reflections: An Intermediate Reader*. Rowley, MA: Newbury House, 1979.

Gwynn, Aubrey Osborn. *Roman Education from Cicero to Quintilian*. New York: Teachers College Press, Columbia University, 1966. (First published 1926)

Hall, Eugene J., and Sandra Costinett. *Orientation in American English*. Washington, D.C.: Institute of Modern Languages, 1970–71.

Halliday, M. A. K., and Ruqaiya Hasan. *Cohesion in English*. London: Longman, 1976.

Hammerly, Hector. *Synthesis in Second Language Teaching: An Introduction to Linguistics*. Blaine, WA: Second Language Publications, 1982.

Hanna, Paul R., and Richard E. Hodges. *Spelling: Structure and Strategies*. Boston: Houghton-Mifflin, 1971.

Harrison, Colin, and Terry Dolan. "Reading Comprehension: A Psychological Viewpoint," in Mackay, Barkman, and Jordan, 1979, 13–23.

Harrison, Grant Von. *Beginning English I*. Salt Lake City, UT: Interact, 1976.

Hatch, Evelyn. "A Lecture on Reading," *UCLA Workpapers in English as a Second Language* 5 (1971a), 27–46.

Hatch, Evelyn. "Composition: Control/Communication," *UCLA Workpapers in English as a Second Language* 5 (1971b), 47–53.

Hatch, Evelyn. "Reading a Second Language," in Celce-Murcia and McIntosh, 1979, 129–144.

Hatch, Evelyn. "Simplified Input and Second Language Acquisition," in Roger Anderson, ed. *Pidginization, Creolization and Language Acquisition*. Rowley, MA: Newbury House, 1979, 64–86.

Hatch, Evelyn, and Hossein Farhady. *Research Design and Statistics for Applied Linguistics*. Rowley, MA: Newbury House, 1982.

Henning, William A. "Adapting Reading Materials for Individualized Instruction," *Foreign Language Annals* 9 (1976), 542–547.

Henrichsen, Lynn E. "Distinctive Features of Written English," *TESL Reporter* 11:4 (Summer 1978), 1–3, 12–14.

Henrichsen, Lynn E. "Teacher Preparation in TESOL: The Results of an International Needs Assessment Survey." Presentation at TESOL Convention, Detroit (March, 1981).

Henrichsen, Lynn E. "Teacher Preparation Needs in TESOL: The Results of an International Survey," *RELC Journal* 14:1 (1983), 18–45.

Henzl, V. M. "Foreigner Talk in the Classroom," *International Review of Applied Linguistics* 17:2 (1979), 159–167.

Hilferty, Ann. "The Theoretical Foundations of GELC," *Zhongda English Studies* 3 (Forthcoming).

Holloway, Donna. "Teaching Advanced Reading and Writing Skills in Technical English." Presentation at the NAFSA Conference on the Use of Global Issues in the ESL Classroom, SUNY, Buffalo, NY (October, 1977).

Horn, Vivian. "Advanced Reading: Teaching Logical Relationships," in *The Art of TESOL: Selected Articles from the English Teaching Forum* Part 2. Washington, D.C.: English Teaching Forum, 1975, 216–218.

Hosenfeld, Carol. "A Preliminary Investigation of the Reading Strategies of Successful and Nonsuccessful Second Language Learners," *System* V (1977), 110–123.

Hosenfeld, Carol. "Cindy: A Learner in Today's Foreign Language Classroom," in W. Borne, ed. *The Foreign Language Learner in Today's Classroom Environment*. Montpelier, VT: New England Conference on the Teaching of Foreign Languages, 1979, 53–75.

Hosenfeld, Carol, Vicki Arnold, Jeanne Kirchofer, Judith Laciura, and Lucia Wilson. "Second Language Reading: A Curricular Sequence for Teaching Reading Strategies," *Foreign Language Annals* 14:5 (1981), 415–422.

Hymes, Dell. "Models of the Interaction of Language and Social Life," in John Gumperz and Dell Hymes, eds. *Directions in Sociolinguistics*. New York: Holt, Rinehart and Winston, 1972a, 35–71.

Hymes, Dell. "On Communicative Competence," in J. B. Pride and J. Holmes, eds. *Sociolinguistics*. Harmondsworth, England: Penguin Books, 1972b, 269–293.

Isaac, Stephen, and William B. Michael. *Handbook in Research and Evaluation*. San Diego, CA: EDITS Publishers, 1981.

Jones, Daniel. *An Outline of English Phonetics*. 6th ed. New York: Dutton, 1940.

Judson, Horace. *The Techniques of Reading*. New York: Harcourt, Brace, Jovanovich, 1972.

Kalivoda, Theodore B. "An Individual Study Course for Facilitating Advanced Oral Skills," *Modern Language Journal* 56:8 (1972), 492–495.

Kalnitz, Joanne, and Kathy R. Judd. "An Approach to Teaching E.S.L. Reading to Literate Adults," *TESOL Newsletter* 15:5 (1981), 15–19.

398   REFERENCES

Kameen, Patrick T. "Syntactic Skill and ESL Writing Quality," in Carlos A. Yorio, Kyle Perkins, and Jacquelyn Schachter, eds. *On TESOL '79*, Washington, D.C.: TESOL, 1979, 343–350.

Kearny, Mary Ann, and James Baker. *Life, Liberty and the Pursuit of Happiness*. Rowley, MA: Newbury House, 1978.

Keller, Eric, and Sylvia Taba Warner. *Gambits I–III*. Ottawa: Canadian Government Publishing Center, 1979.

Kelly, Louis G. *25 Centuries of Language Teaching*. Rowley, MA: Newbury House, 1969.

Krahnke, Karl J., and Mary Ann Christison. "Recent Language Research and Some Language Teaching Principles," *TESOL Quarterly* 17:4 (1983), 625–649.

Kramsch, Claire J. "Word Watching: Learning Vocabulary Becomes a Hobby," *Foreign Language Annals* 12:2 (1979), 153–158.

Krashen, Stephen D. "The Monitor Model for Adult Second Language Performance," in Marina Burt, Heidi Dulay, Mary Finocchiaro, eds. *Viewpoints on English as a Second Language*. New York: Regents, 1977, 152–161.

Krashen, Stephen D. "Theory Versus Practice in Language Training," in Blair, 1982a, 15–30.

Krashen, Stephen D. *Principles and Practice in Second Language Acquisition*. Oxford: Pergamon Press, 1982b.

Krashen, Stephen D., V. Sferlazza, L. Feldman, and Ann Fathman. "Adult Performance on the SLOPE Test: More Evidence for a Natural Sequence in Adult Second Language Acquisition," *Language Learning* 26 (1976), 145–152.

Krashen, Stephen D., and Tracy D. Terrell. *The Natural Approach: Language Acquisition in the Classroom*. Elmsford, NY: Pergamon Press, 1982.

Krashen, Stephen D., and Tracy D. Terrell. *The Natural Approach*. San Francisco, CA: Alemany, 1983.

Kroll, Barbara. "Sorting Out Writing Problems," in Charles H. Blatchford and Jacquelyn Schachter, eds., Washington, D.C.: TESOL, 1978, 176–182.

Kučera, Henry, and W. Nelson Francis. *Computational Analysis of Present-Day American English*. Providence, RI: Brown University Press, 1967.

Larsen-Freeman, Diane. "The Acquisition of Grammatical Morphemes by Adult ESL Students," *TESOL Quarterly* 9:4 (1975), 409–420.

Larsen-Freeman, Diane. "ESL Teacher Speech as Input to the ESL Learner," *UCLA Workpapers in English as a Second Language* 10 (1976), 45–49.

Larson, Jerry W., and Harold S. Madsen. "An Application of Computerized Adaptive Language Testing: Moving Beyond Computer Assisted Testing." Presentation at CALICO Symposium, Baltimore (February, 1985).

Larudee, Faze. "Language Teaching in Historical Perspective," Ph.D. dissertation, University of Michigan, Ann Arbor, MI, 1964.

Lawrence, Mary S. *Writing as a Thinking Process*. Ann Arbor, MI: The University of Michigan Press, 1972.

Leach, John N. "Bias in Standardized Testing: An Update." Presentation at TESOL Convention, Boston (March, 1979).

Leonard, Sterling Andrus. *The Doctrine of Correctness in English Usage, 1700–1800*. University of Wisconsin Studies in Language and Literature, No. 25. Madison, WI: University of Wisconsin, 1929.

Lezberg, Amy, and Ann Hilferty. "Discourse Analysis at the Intermediate and Advanced Levels of ESL: Language Control Through Reading Drills," in Richard L. Light and Alice H. Osman, eds. *Collected Papers in Teaching English as a Second Language and Bilingual Education: Themes, Practices, Viewpoints*. New York: NY State English for Speakers of Other Languages and Bilingual Education Association, 1978, 58–68.

Lipson, Alexander. "Some New Strategies for Teaching Oral Skills," in R. C. Lugton and J. Heinle, eds. *Toward a Cognitive Approach to Second Language Acquisition*. Philadelphia: The Center for Curriculum Development, 1971, 231–244.

Locke, John. *John Locke on Education*. Editing and Introduction by Peter Gay. New York: Bureau of Publications, Teachers College, Columbia University, 1964. (First published 1693)

Long, Michael H. "Inside the Black Box: Methodological Issues in Classroom Research on Language Learning," *Language Learning* 30:1 (1980), 1–42.

Long, Michael H. "Questions in Foreigner Talk Discourse," *Language Learning* 31:1 (1981), 135–157.

Long, Michael H. "Does Second Language Instruction Make a Difference? A Review of Research," *TESOL Quarterly* 17:3 (1983), 359–382.

Long, Michael H., and Charlene J. Sato. "Classroom Foreigner Talk Discourse: Forms and Functions of Teachers' Questions," in Seliger and Long, 1983, 268–285.

Lozanov, Georgi. *Suggestology and Suggestopedia: Theory and Practice*. Paris: United Nations Educational, Scientific and Cultural Organization, 1978.

Lozanov, Georgi. *Suggestology and Outlines of Suggestopedia*. New York: Gordon & Breach Science Publishers, 1979.

Lugton, Robert C. *American Topics*. Englewood Cliffs, NJ: Prentice-Hall, 1978.

Lukmani, Y. "Motivation to Learn and Language Proficiency," *Language Learning* 22 (1972), 261–273.

Mackay, Ronald. "Teaching the Information Gathering Skills," Singapore: *RELC Journal* 5:2 (1974), 56–68.

Mackay, Ronald, Bruce Barkman, and R. R. Jordan, eds. *Reading in a Second Language: Hypotheses, Organization and Practice*. Rowley, MA: Newbury House, 1979.

Mackay, Ronald, and Alan Mountford. "Reading for Information," in Mackay, Barkman, and Jordan, 1979, 106–141.

Mackay, Ronald, and Joe Palmer, eds. *Languages for Specific Purposes: Program Design and Evaluation*. Rowley, MA: Newbury House, 1981.

Mackey, William Francis. *Language Teaching Analysis*. London: Longmans, Green, 1965.

MacLeish, Andrew. "Adapting and Composing Reading Texts," *TESOL Quarterly* 2:1 (1968), 43–50.

Madsen, Harold S. "Innovative Methodologies Applicable to TESL," in Celce-Murcia and McIntosh, 1979, 26–38.

Madsen, Harold S. "A New Direction in Language Testing: Concern for the One," *BYU Studies* 21:2 (Spring 1981), 189–204.

Madsen, Harold S. "Determining the Debilitative Impact of Test Anxiety," *Language Learning* 32:1 (1982), 133–143.

Madsen, Harold S. *Techniques in Testing*. New York: Oxford University Press, 1983.

Madsen, Harold S., and J. Donald Bowen. *Adaptation in Language Teaching*. Rowley, MA: Newbury House, 1978.

Mahmoud, Amal Abdul Ghany. "A Study of the Stability of Alternative Deletion Patterns in Cloze Tests," MA thesis, American University in Cairo, 1977.

Mahmoud, Yousef. "On the Reform of the Arabic Writing System," *The Linguistic Reporter* 22:1 (1979), 4.

Marcel, Claude. *Rational Method, Following Nature Step by Step to Learn How to Read, Hear, Speak and Write French*. London: Hachette & Co., Booksellers, n.d.

Marcel, Claude. *The Study of Languages*. New York: Humboldt, 1980.

Martin, Anne V. "Proficiency of University-Level Advanced ESL Students in Processing General-to-Specific Information in Context." Presentation at TESOL Summer Meeting, Los Angeles (July, 1979).

Martin, Anne V. "Logical Relationships: Explanations by Native-Speaker and Advanced ESL Freshman." Presentation at TESOL Convention, San Francisco (March, 1980).

Maslow, Abraham H. *Motivation and Personality*. New York: Harper & Row, 1954.

Maslow, Abraham H. *Toward a Psychology of Being*. New York: Van Nostrand, 1962.

Maslow, Abraham H. *Eupsychian Management*. Homewood, IL: Irwin-Dorsey, 1965.

McChesney, Beverly. "Applications of the Computer Archive of Language Materials." Presentation at TESOL Summer Meeting, Los Angeles (July, 1979).

McConochie, Jean A. *20th Century American Short Stories*. New York: Collier-Macmillan International, 1975.

McKay, Sandra. "Semantic and Pragmatic Dimensions of Teaching Vocabulary." Presentation at TESOL Summer Meeting, Los Angeles (July, 1979).

McKitchan, Neil. *Focus on Reading*. Englewood Cliffs, NJ: Prentice-Hall, 1980.

Metz, Mary S. "An Audiolingual Methodology for Teaching Reading," *Foreign Language Annals* 6:3 (1973), 348–353.

Mercier, Louis J. A. "Is the Coleman Report Justified in Its Restatement of Objectives for Modern Language Study?" *The French Review* 3:6 (1930), 397–415.

Miller, George A. "The Magical Number Seven, Plus or Minus Two: Some Limits on Our Capacity for Processing Information," *The Psychological Review* 63:2 (1956), 81–97.

Montaigne, Michel de. "On the Education of Boys," in Michel de Montaigne, *The Essays of Montaigne*, E. J. Trechmann, trans. New York: The Modern Library (1946), 123–153.

Moskowitz, Gertrude. "Competency-based Teacher Education: Before We Proceed," *Modern Language Journal* 60:1–2 (1976), 18–23.

Moulton, William G. "Linguistics and Language Teaching in the United States: 1940–1960," *International Review of Applied Linguistics* 1:1 (1963), 21–41.

Munby, John. "Teaching Intensive Reading Skills," in Mackay, Barkman, and Jordan, 1979, 142–158.

Nakano, Patricia J. "Educational Implications of the Lau v. Nichols Decision," in Marina Burt, Heidi Dulay, and Mary Finocchiaro, eds. *Viewpoints on English as a Second Language.* New York: Regents, 1977, 219–234.

Nash, Ogden. *Custard and Company.* Boston: Little, Brown, 1980.

NCTE. "On the Need for Caution in the Use of Behavioral Objectives in the Teaching of English, a Resolution Passed by the National Council of Teachers of English at the 59th Annual Meeting, 1969," *The English Journal* 59:4 (1970), 501.

Neustadt, Bertha C. *Speaking of the U.S.A.* New York: Harper & Row, 1975.

Newmark, Maxim, ed. *Twentieth Century Modern Language Teaching: Sources and Readings.* New York: Philosophical Library, 1948.

Newmark, Peter. *Approaches to Translation.* Oxford: Pergamon Press, 1981.

Nilsen, Don L. F., and Alleen Pace Nilsen. *Pronunciation Contrasts in English.* New York: Regents (Simon & Schuster), 1971.

Norris, William. "Teaching Second Language Reading at the Advanced Level: Goals, Techniques and Procedures," *TESOL Quarterly* 4:1 (1970), 17–35.

Nystrom, Nancy Johnson. "Teacher-Student Interaction in Bilingual Classrooms: Four Approaches to Error Feedback," in Seliger and Long, 1983, 169–189.

Ochsner, Robert. "A Poetics of Second Language Acquisition," *Language Learning* 29:1 (1979), 53–80.

Ohashi, Yoshimasa. *English Style: Grammatical and Semantic Approach.* Rowley, MA: Newbury House, 1978.

Ollendorff, Heinrich Gottfried. *Ollendorff's New Method of Learning to Read, Write and Speak French.* J. L. Jewett, ed. New York: D. Appleton & Company, ca. 1849.

Ollendorff, Heinrich Gottfried. *Theoretical-Practical Method to Learn to Read, Write and Speak English in Six Months.* Chicago: Whadislaus Dyniewicz, n.d.

Oller, John W., Jr. "Dictation as a Device for Testing Foreign Language Proficiency," *English Language Teaching* 25:3 (1971), 254–259.

Oller, John W., Jr. "Cloze Tests of Second Language Proficiency and What They Measure," *Language Learning* 23:1 (1973), 105–118.

Oller, J. W., L. Baca, and L. Vigil. "Attitudes and Attained Proficiency in ESL: A Sociolinguistic Study of Mexican-Americans in the Southwest," *TESOL Quarterly* 11:2 (1977), 173–183.

Oller, John W., Jr. "Attitude Variables in Second Language Learning," in Marina Burt, Heidi Dulay, and Mary Finocchiaro, eds. *Viewpoints of English as a Second Language.* New York: Regents, 1977, 172–184.

Oller, John W., Jr. "Methods That Work." Plenary Address, Eighteenth Annual TESOL Convention, Houston, TX, March 9, 1984.

Oller, John W., Jr., and Patricia A. Richard-Amato, eds. *Methods That Work.* Rowley, MA: Newbury House, 1983.

Olshtain, Elite. "A Theoretical Model for Developing the Teaching of a Language of Wider Communication (LWC) on a National Scale." Los Angeles: UCLA Ph.D. dissertation, 1979.

Omaggio, Alice C. "Pictures and Second Language Composition: Do They Help?" *Foreign Language Annals* 12:2 (1979), 107–116.

O'Neil, Wayne. "The Spelling and Pronunciation of English," in *The American Heritage Dictionary of the English Language.* 1964, xxxv–xxxvii.

O'Neil, Wayne. "English Orthography," in Timothy Shopen and Joseph M. Williams, eds. *Standards and Dialects in English*. Cambridge, MA: Winthrop, 1980, 63–83.

Ornstein, R. E. "Right and Left Thinking," *Psychology Today* 6 (1973), 86–92.

Orthblad, Dennis. "Teaching Writing by an 'Anticipation Method,' " *English Teaching Forum* 16:2 (1978), 23–25.

Palmer, Adrian S., Peter J. M. Groot, and George A. Trosper, eds. *The Construct Validation of Tests of Communicative Competence*. Washington, D.C.: TESOL, 1981.

Palmer, Harold E. *The Principles of Language Study*. London: Oxford University Press, 1964.

Palmer, Harold E. *The Scientific Study and Teaching of Languages*. David Harper, ed. London: Oxford University Press, 1968. (First published 1917)

Palmer, Harold E., and H. Vere Redman. *This Language Learning Business*. London: Oxford University Press, 1969. (First published 1932)

Patterson, C. H. *Humanistic Education*. Englewood Cliffs, NJ: Prentice-Hall, 1973.

Patton, Michael Quinn. *Utilization—Focused Evaluation*. Beverly Hills, CA: Sage Publications, 1978.

Paulston, Christina Bratt. "Linguistic and Communicative Competence," *TESOL Quarterly* 8:4 (1974), 347–362.

Paulston, Christina Bratt, and Mary Newton Bruder. *Teaching English as a Second Language: Techniques and Procedures*. Cambridge, MA: Winthrop, 1976.

Pei, Mario. *The Story of the English Language*. New York: Simon & Schuster, 1972.

Perkins, Kyle. "Using Objective Methods of Advanced Writing Proficiency to Discriminate Among Holistic Evaluations," *TESOL Quarterly* 14:1 (1980), 61–69.

Pope, Lillie. *Guidelines to Teaching Remedial Reading* (revised). New York: Book-Lab, 1975.

Popham, W. James. *Educational Evaluation*. Englewood Cliffs, NJ: Prentice-Hall, 1975.

Postovosky, Valerian A. "The Effects of Delay in Oral Practice at the Beginning of Second Language Teaching," Ph.D. dissertation, University of California at Berkeley, CA, 1970.

Prator, Clifford H. "The Cornerstones of Method," in Celce-Murcia and McIntosh, 1979, 5–16.

Quintilianus, Marcus Fabius. *The Institutio Oratoria of Quintilian*. H. E. Butler, trans. Vol. 1. Cambridge, MA; Harvard University Press, 1920. (Reprinted 1958)

Quintilianus, Marcus Fabius. *Quintilian on Education*. Selected and translated with an introduction by William M. Smail. New York: Teachers College Press, Columbia University, 1966. (Originally published 1938)

Radford, John. "Reflections on Introspection," *American Psychologist* 29 (1974), 245–250.

Raimes, Ann. *Focus on Composition*. New York: Oxford University Press, 1978.

Rainsbury, Robert. "Who's He When He's at Home? or What Does What Does It Mean Mean?" in John F. Fanselow and Ruth H. Crymes, eds. *On TESOL '76*. Washington, D.C.: TESOL, 1976, 195–201.

Ramirez, M., and A. Castaneda. *Cultural Democracy, Bicognitive Development and Education*. New York: Academic Press, 1974.

Rand, Earl. "Analyses and Syntheses. Two Steps Toward Proficiency in Composition," *UCLA Workpapers in Teaching English as a Second Language* 2 (1967), 87–91.

Rappaport, D. A. *Emotions and Memory*. 5th ed. New York: International Universities Press, 1971.

Read, Donald A., and Sidney B. Simon, eds. *Humanistic Education Sourcebook*. Englewood Cliffs, NJ: Prentice-Hall, 1975.

Report of the Committee of Twelve of the Modern Language Association of America. Boston, Heath, 1900.

Richards, Jack C. "The Secret Life of Methods," *TESOL Quarterly* 18:1 (1984), 7–23.

Richterich, R. *Definition of Language Needs and Types of Adults*. Strasbourg: Council of Europe, 1973.

Rigg, Pat. "Reading in ESL," in John F. Fanselow and Ruth H. Crymes, eds. *On TESOL '76*. Washington, D.C.: TESOL, 1976, 203–210.

Riley, Pamela M. "Improving Reading Comprehension," *The Art of TESOL: Selected Articles from the English Teaching Forum* Part 2. Washington, D.C.: English Teaching Forum, 1975a, 198–200.

Riley, Pamela M. "The Dicto-Comp," *The Art of TESOL: Selected Articles from the English Teaching Forum* Part 2. Washington, D.C.: English Teaching Forum, 1975b, 238–240.

Rivers, Wilga M. *The Psychologist and the Foreign Language Teacher*. Chicago: University of Chicago Press, 1964.

Rivers, Wilga M. *Speaking in Many Tongues: Essays in Foreign-Language Teaching*. Rowley, MA: Newbury House, 1972a.

Rivers, Wilga M. "Talking Off the Tops of Their Heads," *TESOL Quarterly* 6:1 (1972b), 71–81.

Rivers, Wilga M. "From Linguistic Competence to Communicative Competence," *TESOL Quarterly* 7:1 (1973), 25–34.

Rivers, Wilga M., and Mary S. Temperley. *A Practical Guide to the Teaching of English as a Second or Foreign Language*. New York: Oxford University Press, 1978.

Robinett, Betty Wallace. *Teaching English to Speakers of Other Languages: Substance and Technique*. Minneapolis: University of Minnesota Press, and New York: McGraw-Hill, 1978.

Rousseau, Jean-Jacques. *Minor Educational Writings*. Williams Boyd, trans. New York: Bureau of Publications, Teachers College, Columbia University, 1962.

Rousseau, Jean-Jacques. *Emile, or On Education*. Translation and Introduction by Allan Bloom. New York: Basic Books, 1979.

Rubin, Joan. "What the 'Good Language Learner' Can Teach Us," *TESOL Quarterly* 9:1 (1975), 41–51.

Rutherford, William E. "Notional-Functional Syllabuses: 1978 Part Two," in Charles H. Blatchford and Jacquelyn Schachter, eds. *On TESOL '78: EFL Policies, Programs, Practices*. Washington, D.C.: TESOL, 1978, 20–23.

Sacks, Harvey, Emanuel Schegloff, and Gail Jefferson. "A Simplest Systematics for the Organization of Turn-taking for Conversation," *Language* 50:4 (1974), 696–735.

Savignon, Sandra J. *Communicative Competence: An Experiment in Foreign Language Teaching*. Philadelphia: The Center for Curriculum Development, 1972.

Schachter, Jacquelyn. "An Error in Error Analysis," *Language Learning* 24:2 (1974), 205–214.

Schegloff, Emanuel, Gail Jefferson, and Harvey Sacks. "The Preference for Self-Correction in the Organization of Repair in Conversation," *Language* 53:2 (1977), 361–382.

Scherer, George A. C., and Michael Wertheimer. *A Psycholinguistic Experiment in Foreign-Language Teaching*. New York: McGraw-Hill, 1964.

Schinke-Llano, Linda A. "Foreigner Talk in Content Classrooms," in Seliger and Long, 1983, 146–164.

Schultz, Renate A. "Many Learners—Many Styles: The 1977 Central States Conference," *Modern Language Journal* 61:5–6 (1977), 260.

Schumann, John. "Affective Factors and the Problem of Age in Second Language Acquisition," *Language Learning* 25:2 (1975), 209–235.

Schumann, John. "Social Distance as a Factor in Second Language Acquisition," *Language Learning* 26:1 (1976), 135–144.

Schumann, John. "The Acculturation Model for Second Language Acquisition," in R. C. Ginrus, ed. *Second Language Acquisition and Foreign Language Teaching*. Arlington, VA: Center for Applied Linguistics, 1978, 27–50.

Schumann, Francine M., and John M. Schumann. "Diary of a Language Learner: An Introspective Study of Second Language Learning," in H. Douglas Brown, Carlos Yorio, and Ruth Crymes, eds. *On TESOL '77*. Washington, D.C.: TESOL, 1977, 241–249.

Scovel, Thomas. "Review: Georgi Lozanov: Suggestology and Outlines of Suggestopedy," *TESOL Quarterly* 13:2 (1979), 255–266.

Scovel, Thomas. "Questions Concerning the Application of Neurolinguistic Research to Second Language Learning/Teaching," *TESOL Quarterly* 16:3 (1982), 323–331.

SEAMEO Regional Language Center. "Guidelines for Vocabulary Teaching," *RELC Journal Supplement No. 3* (1980). (RELC Building, 30 Orange Grove Road, Singapore)

Selekman, Howard R., and Howard H. Kleinmann. "Aiding Second Language Reading Comprehension," in Charles H. Blatchford and Jacquelyn Schachter, eds. *On TESOL '78*. Washington, D.C.: TESOL, 1978, 165–175.

Seliger, Herbert W. "On the Possible Role of the Right Hemisphere in Second Language Acquisition," *TESOL Quarterly* 16:3 (1982), 315–322.

Seliger, Herbert W. "Learner Interaction in the Classroom and Its Effect on Language Acquisition," in Seliger and Long, 1983, 246–267.

Seliger, Herbert W., and Michael H. Long, eds. *Classroom-Oriented Research in Second Language Acquisition*. Rowley, MA: Newbury House, 1983.

Seuss, Dr. *The Cat in the Hat*. New York: Beginner Books (Random House), 1974.

Seuss, Dr. *Horton Hatches the Egg*. New York: Random House, 1976.

Shopen, Timothy, and Joseph M. Williams, eds. *Standards and Dialects in English*. Cambridge, MA: Winthrop, 1980.

Singer, Harry. "I.Q. Is and Is Not Related to Reading," in Stanley Wanat, ed. *Linguistics and Reading Series I*. Washington, D.C.: Center for Applied Linguistics, 1977, 43–55.

Sledd, James. *A Short Introduction to English Grammar*. Chicago: Scott, Foresman, 1959.

Smith, E. Brooks, Kenneth Goodman, and Robert Meredith. *Language and Thinking in School*. New York: Holt, Rinehart and Winston, 1970.

Spache, George D., and Paul C. Berg. *The Art of Efficient Reading*. 3rd ed. New York: Macmillan, 1978.

Spargo, Edward, and G. R. Williston. *Timed Readings*, Levels 1–8. Providence, RI: Jamestown, 1975.

Spargo, Edward, and Raymond Harris. *Reading the Content Fields: Science* (Advanced and Middle Levels). Providence, RI: Jamestown, 1978.

Special English Word Book: A List of Words Used in the Voice of America Radio Broadcasts in Special English. Washington, D.C.: Voice of America, 1979. (First published in 1964)

Sperry, Len. *Learning Performances and Individual Differences: Essays and Readings*. Glenview, IL: Scott, Foresman, 1972.

Stansfield, Charles, and Jacqueline Hansen. "Field Dependence—Independence as a Variable in Second Language Cloze Test Performance," *TESOL Quarterly* 17:1 (1983), 29–38.

Steinberg, J. S. "Context Clues as Aids in Comprehension," *English Teaching Forum* 16:2 (1978), 6–9.

Stevick, Earl W. "The Riddle of the 'Right Method,' " *English Teaching Forum* 12:2 (1974), 1–5.

Stevick, Earl W. *Memory, Meaning and Method: Some Psychological Perspectives on Language Learning*. Rowley, MA: Newbury House, 1976.

Stevick, Earl W. *Teaching Languages: A Way and Ways*. Rowley, MA: Newbury House, 1980.

Stockwell, Robert P., and J. Donald Bowen. *The Sounds of English and Spanish*. Chicago: University of Chicago Press, 1965.

Stockwell, Robert P., J. Donald Bowen, and John W. Martin. *The Grammatical Structures of English and Spanish*. Chicago: The University of Chicago Press, 1965.

Sullivan Associates. *Sullivan Reading Program*. Palo Alto, CA: The Learning Line, 1980.

Sweet, Henry. *A New English Grammar Logical and Historical*. Part I. Oxford: Clarendon Press, 1955. (First edition 1891)

Sweet, Henry. *The Practical Study of Languages: A Guide for Teachers and Learners*. London: Oxford University Press, 1964. (Published originally in 1900 in New York by Henry Holt)

Syllabus in Modern Foreign Languages. Albany, NY: The University of the State of New York, 1937.

Syllabus of Minima in Modern Foreign Languages. New York: New York City Board of Education, 1931.

Taylor, C. V. *The English of High School Textbooks*. Canberra: Australian Government Publishing Service, 1979.

Taylor, Halsey P. *Reading for Meaning*. New York: Harcourt, Brace, Jovanovich, 1975.

Terrell, Tracy D. "A Natural Approach," in Blair, 1982, 160–173.

Thonis, Eleanor Wall. *Teaching Reading to Non-English Speakers*. New York: Collier-Macmillan, 1970.

Thorndike, Edward L., and Irving Lorge. *The Teacher's Word Book of 30,000 Words*. New York: Teachers College Press, Columbia University, 1944.

Ticknor, George. "Lecture on the Best Methods of Teaching the Living Languages," *Modern Language Journal* 22:1 (1937), 19–37.

Titone, Renzo. *Teaching Foreign Languages: An Historical Sketch*. Washington, D.C.: Georgetown University Press, 1968.

Toynbee, Arnold J. *A Study of History*. Abridgement of Vol. 1–6 by D. C. Somervell. London: Oxford University Press, 1946.

Tucker, G. Richard, and Marian Sarofim. "Investigating Linguistic Acceptability with Egyptian ESL Students," *TESOL Quarterly* 13:1 (1979), 29–39.

Tuckman, Bruce W. *Conducting Educational Research*. 2nd ed. New York: Harcourt, Brace, Jovanovich, 1978.

Twaddell, Freeman. "Vocabulary Expansion in the TESOL Classroom," *TESOL Quarterly* 7:1 (1973), 61–78.

Van Ek, J. A. *Systems Development in Adult Language Learning: The Threshold Level.* Strasbourg: Council of Europe, 1975.

Vann, Roberta J. "Oral and Written Syntactic Relationships in Second Language Learning," in *On TESOL '79.* Carlos A. Yorio, Kyle Perkins, and Jacquelyn Schachter, eds. Washington, D.C.: TESOL, 1979, 322–329.

Vasquez, J. A. "Locus of Control, Social Class and Learning," in *Bilingual Education Paper Series.* Northridge, CA: National Dissemination and Assessment Center, 1978.

Venezky, Richard L. "Orthography," in Ronald Wardhaugh and H. Douglas Brown, eds. *A Survey of Applied Linguistics.* Ann Arbor, MI: The University of Michigan Press, 1977, 69–91.

Villareal, Jesse J. "A Measure of Oral Output: A Test to Measure the Ability of Non-Native Speakers of English to Articulate English Speech." Austin, TX: University of Texas Center for Communication Research, 1969.

Wagner, Michael J., and Germaine Tilney. "The Effect of 'Superlearning Techniques' on the Vocabulary Acquisition and Alpha Brainwave Production of Language Learners," *TESOL Quarterly* 17:1 (1983), 5–17.

Wanat, Stanley F., ed. *Issues in Evaluating Reading.* Arlington, VA: Center for Applied Linguistics, 1977.

Wardhaugh, Ronald. "TESOL: Current Problems and Classroom Practices," *TESOL Quarterly* 3:2 (1969), 105–116.

Watts, Ron. "The Future of Science," in Barbara Fallis, Yinglong Wang, and Zengsheng Wu, eds. *LASER: Laboratory in Analysis and Synthesis for Efficient Reading.* Guangzhou, China: Guangzhou English Language Center. (Forthcoming)

Weber, Rose-Marie. "Reading," in Ronald Wardhaugh and Douglas Brown, eds. *A Survey of Applied Linguistics.* Ann Arbor, MI: The University of Michigan Press, 1977, 92–111.

Weissberg, Robert C. "Replication and Modification of an Indirect Measure of Oral Output," MA thesis, UCLA, Los Angeles, 1971.

Weissberg, Robert C. "Progressive Decontrol Through Deletion: A Guided Writing Technique for Advanced ESL Learners in Technical Fields," *TESL Reporter* 11:2 (Winter, 1978), 1–4, 14.

Weissberg, Robert, and Suzanne Buker. "Strategies for Teaching the Rhetoric of Written English for Science and Technology," *TESOL Quarterly* 12:3 (1978), 321–329.

West, Michael. *Useful Rhymes for Learners of English.* London: Longmans, 1966.

Widdowson, Henry G. "Notional-Functional Syllabuses: 1978 Part Four," in Charles H. Blatchford and Jacquelyn Schachter, eds. *On TESOL '78: EFL Policies, Programs, Practices.* Washington, D.C.: TESOL, 1978, 33–35.

Widdowson, Henry G. "The Relevance of Literature to Language Learning." Plenary address, TESOL Convention, Detroit, MI (March, 1981).

Wilkins, D. A. *Notional Syllabuses.* London: Oxford University Press, 1976.

Wilson, Robert D. "A Reading Program for ESL Primary Students," *UCLA Workpapers in Teaching English as a Second Language* 5 (1971), 151–156.

Winitz, Harris. *The Learnables.* Kansas City, MO: International Linguistics Corporation, 1978.

Winitz, Harris. *A Comprehension Approach to Foreign Language Teaching.* Rowley, MA: Newbury House, 1981.

Winitz, Harris, and James Reeds. "Rapid Acquisition of a Foreign Language (German) by the Avoidance of Speaking," *International Review of Applied Linguistics* 11 (1973), 295–315.

Winitz, Harris, and James Reeds. *Comprehension and Problem-Solving as Strategies for Language Training.* The Hague: Mouton, 1975.

Witkin, H. A., and D. R. Goodenough. *Cognitive Styles: Essence and Origins.* New York: International Universities Press, 1981.

Woodward, William Harrison. *Desiderius Erasmus Concerning the Aim and Method of Education.* New York: Bureau of Publications, Teachers College, Columbia University, 1964. (First published 1904)

Woodward, Williams H. *Studies in Education During the Age of the Renaissance, 1400–1600.* Cambridge, England: Cambridge University Press, 1906. (Also New York: Teachers College Press, Columbia University, 1967)

Wright, Benjamin D. "Solving Measurement Problems with the Rasch Model," *Journal of Educational Measurement* 14:2 (1977), 97–116.

Zamel, Vivian. "Re-evaluating Sentence-Combining Practice," *TESOL Quarterly* 14:1 (1980), 81–90.

INDEX